CAPITAL BUDGETING
Planning and Control of Capital Expenditures

CAPITAL BUDGETING
Planning and Control of Capital Expenditures

John J. Clark
Drexel University

Thomas J. Hindelang
Drexel University

Robert E. Pritchard
Glassboro State College

PRENTICE-HALL, INC., ENGLEWOOD CLIFFS, NEW JERSEY 07632

Library of Congress Cataloging in Publication Data

Clark, John J.
    Capital budgeting.

    Bibliography: p. 401
    Includes index.
    1.   Capital budget.   2.   Cash flow.   3.   Capital
assets pricing model.   I.   Hindelang, Thomas J., joint author.
II.   Pritchard, Robert E., joint author.
III.   Title.
HG4028.C4C6   658.1'54   79-10891
ISBN 0-13-113464-7

© 1979 by Prentice-Hall, Inc.
Englewood Cliffs, N.J. 07632

Printed in the United States of America

10   9   8   7   6   5

Cover design by Wanda Lubelska
Manufacturing buyer: R. Anthony Caruso

Prentice-Hall International, Inc., *London*
Prentice-Hall of Australia Pty. Limited, *Sydney*
Prentice-Hall of Canada, Ltd., *Toronto*
Prentice-Hall of India Private Limited, *New Delhi*
Prentice-Hall of Japan, Inc., *Tokyo*
Prentice-Hall of Southeast Asia Pte. Ltd., *Singapore*
Whitehall Books Limited, *Wellington, New Zealand*

CONTENTS

PREFACE

The field of capital budgeting is both comprehensive and challenging. It clearly plays a vital role in assisting most business firms to achieve their various goals (e.g., profitability, growth, stability, risk reduction, social goals, etc.). Recognizing the importance of capital budgeting and the diversity in backgrounds and interests among the readers, we developed various objectives with respect to content, organization, and teaching effectiveness.

The text includes all the traditional topics associated with capital budgeting. Based on this foundation we extend our discussion to include theoretical topics such as portfolio theory and the capital asset pricing model, and finally to the frontiers of long-range asset selection and management.

The text is organized to serve the needs of senior-level undergraduate students, graduate students doing advanced work toward their master's or doctoral degrees, and as a reference for business practitioners at all levels of the organization. Throughout the book, only a working knowledge of algebra and basic statistics is assumed. Many sections of the book (particularly in Chapters 8 and 12) begin with a review of statistical and programming tools that will later be applied to capital budgeting decision areas. In addition, one of the key features of the text is that each chapter includes a number of detailed examples that illustrate the application of theory and analytical methods to specific problem settings. Discussion questions and problems are found at the end of each chapter, with selected answers offered in Appendix E. To facilitate preparation of research papers and study for comprehensive examinations, we have included Appendix A, an extensive bibliography (classified by topic) which includes the most current journal articles as well as the classics.

The text is divided into four sections. Part I, consisting of Chapters 1 through 7, covers the fundamentals of capital budgeting. The impact of the depreciation method selected and taxation on project cash flows is treated extensively. Next, the mathematics of the discounting process is presented, followed by two chapters on traditional evaluative models for capital investment proposals. This entire section relies heavily on conventional wisdom, which has the advantage of wide usage by business firms. We allude frequently to business practice and alert the reader to the traps inherent in the application of such well-known techniques as payback, average rate of return, net present value, and internal rate of return. The section concludes with a chapter dealing with the resolution of conflicts that can arise in project ranking. In general, we provide evidence of the superiority of the net present value approach in selecting the set of projects that maximizes shareholders' wealth.

Part II, Chapters 8 through 11, treats the various types of risk encountered in long-term asset management when investors are free to place funds according to their risk–return preferences. This segment draws heavily upon the work of Dr. Harry M. Markowitz and Dr. William F. Sharpe, elaborated by a plethora of empirical articles. The theoretical discussion illustrates how the capital asset pricing model may be employed to calculate the cost of equity capital, evaluate capital projects, measure the impact of project selection on the firm's debt capacity, and value the firm.

Part III, Chapters 12 through 14, is devoted to mathematical programming and simulation, which offer a powerful set of tools to capture and manipulate the many decision variables and restrictions in the capital budgeting area. These techniques are applied to the capital budgeting problem under conditions of certainty and uncertainty in a multiperiod framework. These chapters provide the reader with an in-depth treatment of the work of Dr. H. Martin Weingartner in mathematical programming applied to the capital budgeting problem setting, and Dr. David B. Hertz in the application of Monte Carlo simulation to the capital expenditure decision. The importance of incorporating multiple goals and objectives in such problem settings is discussed and treated in several models. Much of the discussion centers on newly developed techniques and applications.

Part IV, Chapters 15 through 17, applies capital budgeting analysis to the multinational firm, leasing, and mergers and acquisitions. This section of the text also includes a discussion of reorganization of the firm's financial structure as a capital budgeting decision, thus tying together the questions of firm valuation, capital expenditure, and financing. Chapter 18 concludes the work with a discussion of forecasting, capital abandonment, and the necessity to make capital budgeting systems cost effective.

The text is designed to be adaptable to course objectives at various instructional levels. The flexible organization permits instructors to select topic areas and assign text problems and/or research consistent with audience background and interest.

The final text benefited significantly from the recommendations and discussions that were forthcoming from reviewers and our students at Drexel University, where the text was extensively class-tested at both the undergraduate and graduate levels. We would like to express special appreciation to the following reviewers:

Dennis E. Logue
The Amos Tuck School
Dartmouth College

Jonathan B. Welch
Northeastern University

John F. Muth
Graduate School of Business
Indiana University

Francis S. Yeager
University of Houston

George H. Hettenhouse
Graduate School of Business
Indiana University

Peter G. Goulet
University of Northern Iowa

In addition, several of our students at Drexel University deserve special acknowledgment for their contributions: Christine T. Kydd, Ronald J. Ridgway, Michael A. Bayuk, and Charles Schneider.

In addition to the reviewers and students, we appreciate the cooperation of Joseph L. Naar of The Conference Board, Inc., for timely inputs and advice on current business practices; Joseph F. Ward of The Institute for Business Planning, Inc., for use of their extensive depreciation tables; Arthur H. Rosenfeld of Warren, Gosham, and Lamont, Inc., for the use of their comprehensive annuity and discount tables; and to Dean Leo C. Beebe of Glassboro State College, for encouragement and financial grants and clerical support during the preparation of the book.

We would also like to express our thanks to Gertrude F. Kuck, who carefully and cheerfully typed and retyped the revised versions of the manuscript and the instructor's manual, and to Debora L. Pallante, who patiently coordinated the correspondence and reproduction necessary to the preparation of the manuscript. Numerous other individuals have improved the quality of the text and to them we say a collective thank you.

Comments from readers are welcomed and encouraged.

JOHN J. CLARK
THOMAS J. HINDELANG
ROBERT E. PRITCHARD

For Margaret, Chris, Jody

I

THE ESSENTIALS
OF CAPITAL BUDGETING

1 INTRODUCTION TO CAPITAL BUDGETING

Capital budgeting is the decision area in financial management which establishes goals and criteria for investing resources in long-term projects (two or more fiscal periods). Capital investment projects commonly include land, buildings, facilities, equipment, vehicles, and the like. These assets are extremely important to the firm because, in general, *nearly all of the firm's profit is derived from the use of its capital investments; these assets represent very large commitments of resources; and the funds will usually remain invested over a long period of time.* The future development of the firm hinges on the selection of capital investment projects, the decision to replace existing capital assets, and the decision to abandon previously accepted undertakings which turn out to be less attractive to the firm than was originally thought.

Generally, the subject matter of capital budgeting is concerned with projects that cover two or more periods, although obviously very short term projects do not pose the same degree of complexity found in projects of 10 to 20 years' duration.

The term *project* also requires some explanation. Too frequently, capital budgeting is believed to be synonomous with investment in new plant and equipment. The expansion or contraction of physical assets naturally is a major topic for the application of capital budgeting techniques. But these techniques apply equally to the valuation of advertising commitments, to the management of the company's financial structure (refunding of a bond issue, for example), to the decision of whether to own or lease an asset, to the valuation of *other* firms for purposes of combination, and to the management of research and development funds. Conversely, the decision to continue in business or to terminate a project is also a capital budgeting decision.

We should also note that capital budgeting offers a method of analysis and decision criteria that can be employed in government as well as in private enterprise and in the evaluation of both civilian and governmental projects. In the latter instance, the technique is generally referred to as *cost-effectiveness analysis* or, when placed in a broader context, as *systems analysis*. This has been applied mostly by the Department of Defense, but has since spread to other agencies of the federal government and is now filtering down to the state and local level.

The benefits of a capital project are received over some future period, and the *time element* lies at the core of capital budgeting. The firm must time the start of a project to take advantage of short-term business conditions (construction costs, for example, vary with the stage of the business cycle) and financing of the project to capitalize on trends in the money markets (such as the pattern of short-and long-term interest rates). In addition, the longevity of capital assets and the large outlays required for their acquisition suggest that the estimates of income and cost associated with the project be *discounted* for the time they are received or paid out. Moreover, investment decisions are always based upon incomplete information using *forecasts* of future revenues and costs. We know from experience that such forecasts will always err on one side or the other, and the *degree of error* may correlate (but not always) with the duration of the project. Short-term forecasts (1 year or less) generally display greater accuracy than long-term estimates (5 years or more). The future dimly seen entails *risk*, and any appraisal of a capital project, therefore, must necessarily comprehend some assessment of the *risk* accompanying the project. Finally, investment decisions must be matched against future outcomes to ascertain the accuracy of the forecasts and the viability of evaluative criteria. This is an aspect of capital budgeting too little examined in professional journals. A substantial body of literature exists on "how to forecast," but one sees few follow-up articles on the successes or inadequacies of the method recommended. *In summary, the components of capital budgeting analysis involve a forecast of the benefits and costs of the project, discounting the funds invested in the project at an appropriate rate, assessing the risk associated with the project, and following up to determine if the project is performing as expected.*

The applications of capital budgeting techniques are many and varied. In theory, a very large number of problems lend themselves to analysis by the methods described in the following pages. However, analysis absorbs time and money, especially the more sophisticated techniques of ranking and risk management. The cost of these approaches must be justified by the perceived benefits. Theory adapts to circumstances. Conceptually appealing but costly techniques of analysis do not merit across-the-board application. Accordingly, in establishing a capital budgeting program within the firm, the first rule involves establishing a cutoff by size of expenditure; that is, projects requiring an investment over a specified amount will be subject to searching scrutiny; below this amount, less costly criteria of acceptance will be applied.

The capital budget, thus, concentrates on the benefits and costs of projects, and the decisions made determine the composition of total assets and the business-risk complexion of the enterprise. The capital budget *shapes operating plans for several years into the future*—is future-oriented—in contrast to short-term budgets, which guide the current operations of the firm.

Nonetheless, it is not the project that is central to our planning but the firm —its continued existence and development. Hence, although the analysis may yield "reliable" estimates on the project's expected rate of return and risk, the question arises as to what impact these have on the firm's return on assets and risk posture. If the project enhances the rate of return on the firm's assets but makes the operation more risky or increases the possibility of insolvency, do we want the project? The answer may still be affirmative, but the question must be faced, nevertheless. Investors do not simply add new shares to their portfolios without regard to their current holdings; in like manner, financial managers do not (or at least, should not) simply add projects without regard to the firm's overall financial performances. *A high rate of return on a project is not enough to justify its acceptance. The key question is: Does the acceptance of the project increase the market value of the common shares?*

The analysis for long-term asset management is made on a cash-flow basis, as opposed to the determination of project accounting income. By the end of the project's life, of course, the cash and accounting basis will reconcile, but in any given fiscal period the net return calculated on a cash or accounting basis may diverge quite significantly. A project that appears favorable in the long run may show negative results in the early periods. This can create important political problems for management if the latter believes that accounting reports influence stock prices and investor decisions. As we shall see, the evidence on this point is not conclusive. In any event, the analyst must bear in mind the effects of the project on each period's accounting results.

Finally, every capital project has to be financed, and there are no free sources of capital. Most firms strive to maintain a capital structure (a combination of debt capital and equity capital) that will minimize their financing costs. Accordingly, we need to know not only whether the adoption of this or that project increases the market value of the common shares but also the related question of whether the acceptance of the project increases the debt-carrying capacity of the firm.

These and other questions constitute the subject matter of our text and we shall approach them from a dual aspect: using techniques generally accepted as conventional wisdom and employed in various guises by business managers; and also from the perspective of the Capital Asset Pricing Model (CAPM), which, for the first time, offers a comprehensive, integrated theory of the financial manager's decision-making process and the behavior of the investor, as well as many insights into the firm and security market behavior.

Also contributing to the uniqueness of the text is a set of chapters on such topics as mathematical programming techniques applied to the selection of preferred solutions to the questions raised above; the special problems of capital budgeting in multinational corporations; and the place of capital budgeting techniques in the decision to expand by means of combination with other firms. These represent a set of topics not normally found in a capital budgeting text, but given the setting of modern business, failure to deal with them would constitute a serious lapse of coverage on the subject matter.

DISCUSSION QUESTIONS

1. What are the basic components of capital budgeting analysis?
2. Explain what is meant by nondiscretionary capital budgeting projects and assess their significance.
3. What is the importance of a business establishing well-defined acceptance criteria for capital investment projects?

4. How can you, as financial manager, explain the possibility of inaccuracies in a forecasted cash flow for a given project?
5. The novice to capital budgeting may interpret the term "project" to mean only a new investment in plant and equipment. Evaluate this assumption as it relates to the overall theory of the firm.
6. What are the basic assumptions underlying capital budgeting theory?
7. If a project that enhances the rate of return on a firm's assets is rejected because it increases the possibility of insolvency, other goals of the firm have been brought into the decision process. What are some of the goals of a firm that should be considered in evaluating a capital investment project?

2 TAXATION AND DEPRECIATION

Proposed capital expenditures are evaluated by comparing the expected after-tax costs with the estimated after-tax revenues they are expected to generate. In order to compare costs with revenues, it is necessary to establish a systematic managerial process for collecting, summarizing, and analyzing pertinent financial and nonfinancial data. Commencing with this chapter, the authors will undertake a rigorous study of the data required in the decision-making process and indicate how the information may be used in the capital investment process.

Given the various types of requests for capital expenditures that management can anticipate, it is necessary to understand the depreciation and taxation procedures applicable in each instance, since depreciation and taxation impact profits and both cash inflows and outflows. Profits and (especially) cash flows are of particular importance to the process of evaluating capital expenditures.

In this chapter we shall discuss the methods used to determine depreciation and the effects of depreciation and taxation on profitability and cash flows. The reader must be aware of the constantly changing tax structure: altered by revision to statute, IRS rulings, and tax court decisions. The material presented herein forms only a base for analysis; the reader is cautioned to incorporate changes as they are forthcoming.

DEPRECIATION

When an asset is purchased, it is necessary to match the expense with revenues during the period in which it is used. Depreciation is a systematic recognition of such expenses in a historical framework in order to match the expense with revenues while the asset is being used. Depreciation recognizes the eventual wasting of the asset through wear, obsolescence, or the like, and provides for the recognition of the expense before or no later than its retirement.

The federal tax laws permit inclusion of depreciation as a tax-deductible expense. To be eligible for depreciation, an asset must have a useful life of 1 or more years and be used in a trade or business or held for production of income. Since depreciation does not require a cash outlay, it is categorized as an *implicit expense*; other expenses requiring payment are explicit costs.

To determine the depreciation for an asset, it is necessary to know three things:

1. *The depreciable value of the asset:*

$$\text{depreciable value} = \text{total capitalized cost} - \text{salvage value} \tag{1}$$

where the salvage value consists of the estimated resale value reduced by any costs of its removal or sale.

2. *The useful life of the asset.* The useful life is the period over which that asset may reasonably be expected to function in a business. The useful life may be estimated based on experience or by adopting one of the useful life standards formulated by the Internal Revenue Service. One method provided by the IRS is the "Class Life Asset Depreciation Range System." To employ this system, the useful life is selected from a range of years designated for that particular asset. Tables providing life ranges for numerous assets are contained in IRS Publication 534, "Tax Information on Depreciation."

3. *The method of depreciation to be used.* The method of depreciation selected depends on management objectives with respect to use of accelerated depreciation, and the method of depreciation allowable by law for the particular asset. The law allows any reasonable method for depreciation and explicitly recognizes the following methods as applicable to the types of property indicated:

> *Straight-line:* All new and used property.
> *Twice declining balance (double-declining):* New residential real estate and property other than real estate acquired new and having a life of 3 years or more.
> *One and one-half declining balance:* New real estate other than residential and property other than real estate acquired used and having a life of 3 or more years.
> *One and one-quarter declining balance:* Used residential real estate with a life of 20 years or more.
> *Sum-of-the-years' digits:* Same as twice declining balance.

Methods of Depreciation

1. *Straight-line depreciation* is computed by dividing the depreciable value by the number of years in the asset's life. This is expressed in equation form as follows[1]:

$$D = \frac{C - S}{n} \tag{2}$$

---

[1]For tax purposes, when S (salvage value) is less than 10% of the asset's cost, it may be ignored for computing depreciation.

where D = annual depreciation
C = cost of the asset
S = estimated salvage value
n = estimated number of years in the life of the asset

2. *Declining-balance depreciation* subtracts the cumulative total depreciation taken to date from the cost of the asset before computing the next year's depreciation; the same depreciation rate is applied to a smaller or a declining balance each year. Thus, a larger depreciation deduction is taken during the first year and gradually smaller deductions in succeeding years. The depreciation rate applied may be twice straight-line, $1\frac{1}{2}$, or $1\frac{1}{4}$, depending on the asset involved and managerial objectives.

When using declining balance, the salvage value is not deducted from the cost of the asset. That is, *the basis used to compute depreciation is the total cost, not the depreciable value*. However, property may not be depreciated beyond its depreciable value. In some instances, when an asset has either zero or a very low salvage value, the full depreciation will not be achieved during the useful life of the asset. In such cases, the law permits changing from a declining-balance method to straight-line or sum-of-the-years' digits. The switch allows for the full depreciation of the asset and is usually made about two-thirds of the way through the asset's life when double-declining-balance depreciation has been used.

$$D_t = \frac{X}{n}(C - DB_{t-1}) = \frac{X}{n}\left(C - \sum_{j=1}^{t-1} D_j\right) \qquad (3)$$

where D_t = depreciation in period t
C = cost of the asset
n = estimated number of years in the life of the asset
X = declining balance rate (i.e., 2, $1\frac{1}{2}$, or $1\frac{1}{4}$)
DB_{t-1} = accumulated depreciation at the end of year $t - 1$ (which, of course, is zero in year 1)
t = year of life of the asset (i.e., 1 in the first year, 2 in the second, etc.)

3. *Sum-of-the-years'-digits depreciation* applies a changing rate to a constant depreciable value (cost minus salvage value) to find the annual write-off. Each year a fraction is multiplied by the depreciable value to obtain the amount of yearly depreciation. The denominator of the fraction, which remains constant, is the total of the digits representing the useful life of the property. For example, if the useful life is 5 years, the denominator is 15, that is, the sum $1 + 2 + 3 + 4 + 5$. The numerator of the fraction changes each year to represent the years of useful life remaining at the beginning of the year for which the computation is made. For the first year of a 5-year estimated useful life, the numerator would be 5, for the second 4, and so on. Thus, the depreciation rate would decline over the life of the asset. Sum-of-the-years' digits may be expressed in equation form as follows:

$$D_t = \frac{n + 1 - t}{[n(1 + n)]/2}(C - S) \qquad (4)$$

where D_t = depreciation in period t
  C = cost of the asset
  S = estimated salvage value
  n = estimated number of years in the life of the asset
  t = year of life of the asset

4. *Units of production* ties depreciation directly to output so that the percentage of the depreciable value depreciated each year is the same as the percentage of the total estimated useful output utilized in that year. Thus, if a machine had a projected useful life of 1,000,000 units and 200,000 were produced in 1 year, 20% of the total depreciation would be deducted in that year. Depreciation based on use is expressed in equation form as follows:

$$D_t = \frac{(C - S)H_t}{H} \qquad (5)$$

where D_t = depreciation in period t
  C = cost of the asset
  S = estimated salvage value of the asset
  H_t = number of hours the asset was used or the number of units produced in period t
  H = estimated total number of hours the asset will be used or the total number of units it will produce over its life

● **EXAMPLE 1** *Declining-Balance Depreciation*
An asset costing $10,000 has a 10-year life and zero estimated salvage value. Determine the yearly depreciation using the double-declining rate.

Solution: Since the life is 10 years, the straight-line rate would be 10% per year. Therefore, the double-declining rate is 20%. The problem is solved in tabulation form as follows:

Year	Basis Less Cumulative Depreciation	Yearly Depreciation	Cumulative Depreciation
1.	0.20 × $10,000	= $2,000.00	$2,000.00
2.	0.20 × (10,000 − 2,000)	= 1,600.00	3,600.00
3.	0.20 × (10,000 − 3,600)	= 1,280.00	4,880.00
4.	0.20 × (10,000 − 4,880)	= 1,024.00	5,904.00
5.	0.20 × (10,000 − 5,904)	= 819.20	6,723.20
6.	0.20 × (10,000 − 6,723.20)	= 655.36	7,378.56
7.	0.20 × (10,000 − 7,378.56)	= 524.29	7,902.85
8.	0.20 × (10,000 − 7,902.85)	= 419.43	8,322.28
9.	0.20 × (10,000 − 8,322.28)	= 335.54	8,657.82
10.	0.20 × (10,000 − 8,657.82)	= 268.44	8,926.26

Note that using the double-declining method, we are not able to fully depreciate the asset during the useful life. Therefore, it is necessary to switch to straight-line. The switch may be made at any time, but to have the most rapid depreciation write-off, the switch to straight-line should be made after 6 years. After 6 years the cumulative depreciation is $7,378.56, leaving $2,621.44 to be depreciated in the last 4 years, or $655.36 per year. The reader may want to verify that the switch should be made in the seventh year.   •

Calculating depreciation, while a simple matter, is tedious. Therefore, Comparative Depreciation Tables, from the Institute for Business Planning's *Business and Financial Tables Desk Book*, are included as Appendix B.

Depreciation is included as an accounting expense but does not result in any outlay of cash. *The amount deducted for depreciation on the firm's income statement is added to any earnings after taxes to obtain the firm's cash flow from operations.* Profits are referred to as *return on investment* while the funds generated by means of depreciation, amortization, and the like are referred to as *return of investment. The total of profits plus depreciation and similar cash throw-offs is the cash flow from operations.* While depreciation does not require an out-of-pocket expenditure, it does impact tax liability, profits, and cash flow. The greater the depreciation, the lower the profits before taxes (and thus the taxes), and therefore the higher the cash flow.

The primary consideration in selecting an accelerated method of depreciation is that it tends to reduce earnings before taxes and, consequently, income taxes while increasing *cash flows* during the early years of the life of the asset. The reverse is true during the latter years. Since it is desirable to have both high profits and cash flows, firms frequently use two methods of depreciation: straight-line (which results in higher profits) for reporting income to shareholders, and an accelerated method (which results in lower taxable income and tax liability) for tax purposes. The difference in the results using the two methods is reconciled by establishing a deferred income tax liability account as a balance sheet line item.[2] *It should be noted that the total profitability and cash flows over the entire life of an asset are not affected by the choice of a method of depreciation. Only the timing of the profits and cash flows is changed.* Since it is generally considered desirable to receive cash flows from the use of an asset as early as possible in its life, accelerated depreciation methods are usually employed for tax computation.[3] But in some instances it may be desirable to have low depreciation in the early years of an asset's life and higher depreciation later. A new business, for example, might not have sufficient income to enjoy the advantages of accelerated depreciation and therefore elects to use reverse sum-of-the-years' digits. A television cable firm having high startup costs and few initial customers might find it useful to defer depreciation until it increased its market penetration.

[2]For a discussion of deferred income taxes, see Charles T. Horngren, *Introduction to Management Accounting*, 4th ed. (Englewood Cliffs, N.J.: Prentice-Hall, Inc., 1978), pp. 652–655.

[3]In addition to the depreciation described above, there is an additional first-year depreciation allowance deduction allowable equal to 20% of the cost of tangible personal property, up to a total cost basis of $10,000. If the additional 20% first-year depreciation is taken, then the normal basis is reduced by both the additional allowance and the salvage value. Since the additional first-year depreciation is so small, it will generally not impact cash flows significantly and therefore is not considered further in this text.

TAXATION AND CAPITAL EXPENDITURES

In order to estimate the cash flows involved in purchasing assets and to estimate the cash inflows resulting from their use, taxes must be computed. In this section we are primarily concerned with federal taxes on operating income, taxes on capital gains and losses, recapture of depreciation, investment tax credits, and state taxes on operating income.

Federal Taxation on Ordinary Income

The corporate taxable income (earnings before taxes) is that portion of the total income remaining after all the operating and administrative expenses and interest are paid and depreciation deducted. The calculation of tax payable is a simple matter once the taxable income has been determined.[4] All corporations bear federal income tax on ordinary income at the following rates:

> First $25,000 taxed at 20%
> Next $25,000 taxed at 22%
> Over $50,000 taxed at 48%

If the corporation incurs an operating loss for any year, the loss can be used to reopen the tax liability for previous years and/or carried forward and applied against income in future years. The firm has an election: it may carry the loss back 3 years and forward 7 or it may carry the loss forward 10 years. The former process, known as *loss carry-back and carry-forward*, operates as follows. The loss must first be applied against taxable income made 3 years prior to the loss, then 2 years prior working forward to the seventh year after the loss has occurred. Any unused loss remaining after the seventh year following the loss is no longer available to the corporation as a deduction. The latter process applies losses against future profits, commencing with the first year following the loss.

The selection of a process depends primarily on whether the firm has enjoyed profits in those years immediately prior to the loss and if those profits are still available to apply losses against. If this is the case, an advantage would result in carrying the loss back, as the refund of tax payments would be expedited.

State Taxation on Ordinary Income

There is little uniformity to the taxation of corporate income by states, but it should be noted that the state income tax is included as an income statement expense for computing federal income taxes. As such, its impact on earnings after taxes depends to a great extent on the rate of federal tax being paid. For example, in a state that imposes a 5% tax, if a firm has a 48% marginal federal tax rate, the effective state tax rate would be only 2.6%. The reader should be cognizant of state taxes, but because of the large variation among states and the detailed computations involved, we will not include them in our cash-flow calculations. Fed first state second

[4]The rates and methods indicated are current to 1977 Federal Income Tax Laws.

Capital Gains and Losses[5]

Capital gains and losses take place when a firm buys and subsequently sells assets or securities that are not ordinarily purchased and sold in the business of the firm. Capital gains and losses may be either long term or short term in nature. Short-term gains or losses occur when an asset is held for less than 1 year. In the evaluation of capital expenditures we will be primarily concerned with long-term capital gains and losses and recapture of depreciation (which is discussed below). Long-term capital gains are taxed at either the rate applied to ordinary income or 30%, whichever is lower:

1. Long-term capital gains are taxed as ordinary income at the 20% rate until the sum of the ordinary income plus capital gains exceeds $25,000.

2. When the sum of ordinary income plus capital gains exceeds $25,000, any excess up to $50,000 is taxed at 22%.

3. When the sum of ordinary income plus capital gains exceeds $50,000, capital gains are taxed at 30%.

● **EXAMPLE 2**   *Tax on a Long-Term Capital Gain*

A corporation had a taxable income of $30,000 and a long-term capital gain of $30,000. Determine its federal income tax liability.

Solution: The first $25,000 of ordinary income is taxed at 20%, the remaining $5,000 at 22%. Since $5,000 of ordinary income is to be taxed at 22%, only $20,000 of the capital gain may be taxed at 22%. The remaining $10,000 is taxed at 30%. The tax is summarized as follows:

Ordinary income	$25,000 × 0.20 =	$ 5,000
Ordinary income	5,000 × 0.22 =	1,100
Capital gain	20,000 × 0.22 =	4,400
Capital gain	10,000 × 0.30 =	3,000
Total tax		$13,500

●

Recapture of Depreciation

In some instances when property is depreciated and later sold for an amount in excess of its book value, recapture of depreciation will take place. Any recapture of depreciation on personal property (Section 1245) is taxed as

---

[5]In the study of capital gains and losses it is necessary to define capital assets and related property. A capital asset is any property except the following:

> Inventories.
> Property held primarily for sale to customers in the ordinary course of business.
> Depreciable property used in a trade or business.
> Real property used in a trade or business.
> Short-term non-interest-bearing government obligations issued at a discount basis.
> Copyrights, literary, musical, or artistic composition, letters, or similiar property.
> Accounts or notes receivable received in the ordinary course of business for services rendered or from the sale of property.

Land and depreciable property used in business are not capital assets, but if they are sold or exchanged, in most instances they are treated as capital assets with respect to capital gains and losses and recapture of depreciation.

ordinary income. Any time the book value is less than the sale price, the gain will be taxed as ordinary income up to the amount of the accumulated depreciation. If property is sold for an amount in excess of the purchase price, that excess is taxed as a capital gain. The tax on recapture of depreciation of real property (Section 1250) differs significantly from personal property. Since the portion of depreciation subject to recapture depends on date of asset acquisition, method of depreciation used, and type of property involved, the reader is referred to a tax service, such as that of the Commerce Clearing House or Prentice-Hall, for details in this area.

● **EXAMPLE 3**   *Determination of Recapture of Depreciation*
                 and Capital Gain

A corporation purchased personal (Section 1245) property 10 years ago for $1,000,000 and subsequently depreciated it to a book value of $600,000. If the corporation sells the property for $1,200,000 and has no other income this year, determine the recapture of depreciation, the long-term capital gain, and the tax liability.

Solution: The capital gain is the difference between the *sale price* and the *purchase price*.

Sale price	$1,200,000
Less purchase price	− 1,000,000
Capital gain	$ 200,000

The recapture of depreciation is the difference between the *purchase price* and the *book value* in this example, since the asset was sold for *more* than its original cost.

Purchase price	$1,000,000
Less book value	− 600,000
Recapture of depreciation	$ 400,000

The tax is calculated as follows:

Recapture	25,000 × 0.20 =	$ 5,000
	25,000 × 0.22 =	5,500
	350,000 × 0.48 =	168,000
Long-term capital gain	200,000 × 0.30 =	60,000
Total tax		$238,500

● **EXAMPLE 4**   *Determination of Recapture of Depreciation*
                 and Capital Gain

Same as Example 3 except that the sale price of property is $800,000.

Solution: Since the sale price did not exceed the purchase price, there is no capital gain. However, there is a recapture of depreciation. The recapture of depreciation in this case is the difference between the *sale price* and the *book value* since the asset was sold for *more* than the book value but *for less* than its original cost.

Sale price	$800,000
Less book value	− 600,000
Recapture of depreciation	$200,000

The recapture would be taxed as ordinary income as follows:

$$
\begin{aligned}
\$\ 25{,}000 \times 0.20 &= \$\ 5{,}000 \\
25{,}000 \times 0.22 &= 5{,}500 \\
150{,}000 \times 0.48 &= \underline{72{,}000} \\
\text{Total tax} &\quad\ \$82{,}500
\end{aligned}
$$

●

Section 1231 Assets

Section 1231 of the Internal Revenue Code provides that certain capital losses may be deducted from ordinary income. Several types of assets are included under the provisions of Section 1231. We are primarily concerned with the following:

1. Real property used in the taxpayer's business held for more than 1 year and not regularly for sale to customers:

2. Depreciable assets used in the taxpayer's business held for more than 1 year and not regularly for sale to customers.

Real and depreciable assets are those which are used in the business such as buildings, machinery, and the like. Land or precious metals purchased for speculative purposes and sold at a loss would not qualify for the liberal treatment offered under Section 1231.

The treatment of Section 1231 only applies when the total of all capital losses exceeds all capital gains. If there is a net capital loss, then the net losses occurring from sale of Section 1231 assets may be deducted from ordinary income.

The special provision for deducting net long-term capital losses on Section 1231 property from ordinary income is of particular importance to financial managers. The timing of the sale of assets becomes very significant. For example, suppose that a firm could sell two assets. The sale of the first would result in a $10,000 long-term capital gain, while the second would result in a $10,000 loss covered by Section 1231. If the firm sold both in the same year, the gain and loss would just offset each other, and there would not be any change in tax paid. However, if the gain were taken 1 year and the loss the next, a subsequential tax savings would be enjoyed. Assume that the firm's marginal tax rate is 48%. The tax savings on the Section 1231 loss would be $4,800. However, the additional tax payable on the gain would be only $3,000 since the tax rate is 30%. A net tax savings of $1,800 would be obtained. Section 1231 makes the timing of disposal of capital assets extremely important.

Capital Loss Carry-Back and Carry-Forward

If there is a net long-term capital loss in any year on the sale of assets not covered by Section 1231, *it may not be deducted from ordinary income of the same or any other year. It must be applied against long-term capital gains from the other years.* The loss must first be applied against long-term capital gains made 3 years prior to the loss, then 2 years prior, working forward to the fifth year after the loss has occurred. This permits the firm to apply a long-term capital loss in 1 year against gains in 8 years, starting 3 years prior to the loss and ending 5 years after the loss. Any loss remaining after the fifth year following the loss is no longer available to the corporation as a deduction.

Investment Tax Credit

Investment tax credit provides for the reduction of federal income tax liability by permitting part of the cost of certain types of assets to be deducted from the tax liability in the year the property is placed in service. Currently, investment tax credit is up to 10% of the purchase price of certain assets.

Investment credit does not affect depreciation calculations and represents a completely separate calculation. The purpose of the tax credit is to stimulate the purchase of certain types of property, meeting the following qualifications: the property must (1) be depreciable; (2) have a useful life of at least 3 years; (3) be tangible personal property or other tangible property[6] (except buildings and their structural components) used as an integral part of manufacturing, production, extraction, and so on; and (4) be placed in service in a trade or business or for the production of income during the year. Property is considered to be placed in service in the earlier of the following[7]:

1. The tax year in which, under your depreciation practice, the period for depreciation begins, or

2. The tax year in which the property is placed in condition or state of readiness and availability for service.

Tangible personal property includes depreciable tangible property except land and land improvements such as buildings. Machinery and equipment are the principal types of property that qualify as tangible personal property. Other types of property include accessories to a business, such as grocery counters and air conditioners, automobiles used for business, and livestock.

The amount of the investment tax credit allowed for qualifying property depends upon the property's useful life and whether it is new or used. Moreover, the amount of tax credit allowed in any one year is limited, but any excess may be carried back or forward in a manner similar to capital and operating losses. The process of carry-back and carry-forward is similar to that for losses but the period differs: credit may be carried back 3 years and forward 7 years.

For purpose of computing investment tax credit, the amount qualifying is the total purchase price less any deduction for old property traded in. This applies, in general, to the purchase of both new and used property. However, no more than $100,000 of the cost of qualifying used property may be counted toward investment tax credit.

The amount of investment tax credit that may be taken is based on the asset's depreciable life. For tax purposes, with guidelines as follows:

1. Property with a depreciable life of less than 3 years does not qualify for the credit.

---

[6]That is, Section 38 property.

[7]However, credits may be taken for expenditures, called *progress payments*, made in the building or acquiring of qualified investment property.

2. Only one-third of the investment in qualifying property with a depreciable life of at least 3 years but less than 5 years is subject to credit.

3. Two-thirds of the amount invested is subject to credit if the property has a depreciable life of at least 5 years but less than 7 years.

4. The full investment is subject to the credit if the property has a depreciable life of at least 7 years.

If property is disposed of before the end of its estimated useful life, the tax for the year of its disposal is increased by an amount equal to the difference between the credit originally allowed and the credit that would have been allowed if the computation had been based on a shorter useful life.

The amount of investment tax credit taken in any one year is limited to the income tax liability shown on the tax return, or $25,000 plus 50% of the tax liability in excess of $25,000, whichever is less. Reference should be made to IRS Publication 572, "Tax Information on Investment Credit," for further information on investment tax credit.

● **EXAMPLE 5** *Investment Tax Credit*

A corporation purchased new equipment with a life of 3 years, used machinery with a life of 4 years, used machinery with a life of 6 years, and new machinery with a life of 8 years. The prices paid were $10,000, $8,000, $12,000, and $16,000, respectively. The firm has tax liability of $60,000. Determine the reduction in taxes resulting from investment credit.

Solution: The tax credit may be calculated using the following tabular method:

Property	*Life*	*Basis*	*Part to Be Counted*	*Amount Subject to Credit*
New equipment	3	$10,000	$\frac{1}{3}$	$ 3,333
Used machinery	4	8,000	$\frac{1}{3}$	2,667
Used machinery	6	12,000	$\frac{2}{3}$	8,000
New machinery	8	16,000	All	16,000
Amount of investment subject to credit				$30,000

The investment tax credit would be $30,000 × 0.10 = $3,000. Hence, the corporation would save $3,000 in taxes. The new tax would be $57,000 rather than $60,000. ●

Special Consideration for Trade-ins

As noted above in the section on investment tax credit, if an asset is traded in, the basis for the investment tax credit is the price paid in excess of the trade-in value. Thus, if a qualifying asset (having a useful life of 7 or more years) costs $10,000 and an old asset is traded in for $2,000, the investment tax credit would be calculated based on the $8,000 cash payment. At the 10% rate, the credit would be $800. Instead, if the old asset was sold outright, the total price of the new asset would receive the full benefit of the investment tax credit, that is, 10% of $10,000, or $1,000. There appears to be an obvious advantage to selling the old asset rather than trading it in. The advantage depends, however, on the amount allowed for trade-in versus the amount that could be realized by means of an outright sale. Frequently, a vendor will allow a higher trade-in because being a dealer places him at an advantage in terms of reselling the old asset.

But there are other considerations. If an asset is sold, a capital gain, loss, or recapture of depreciation may take place. If an asset is traded in at a value other than the book value, such gains or losses are not incurred for tax purposes but, rather, the price of the newly acquired asset is adjusted for purposes of depreciation. Suppose that the old asset, described above as having a traded-in value of $2,000, had a book value of only $1,000. A capital gain would not be recognized for tax purposes if the asset were traded in. Rather, the cost of the new asset, for purposes of tax depreciation, would be $9,000 (i.e., $1,000 book value plus $8,000 cash). The $1,000 gain would be amortized over the life of the new asset by reducing its depreciation. If the new asset had a 10-year life with no expected salvage value and is depreciated straight-line, the depreciation would be $900 per year rather than $1,000. If the old machine had a book value of $3,000, the new machine would be depreciated using $11,000 as the cost (i.e., $3,000 book value plus $8,000 cash), for $1,100 annual depreciation. Again, a loss for tax purposes would not be recognized at the time of the transaction.

SUMMARY

This chapter provided the primary information pertaining to the calculation of depreciation and taxation as it relates to capital expenditure decision. Both depreciation as it affects profits, taxation, and cash flow, and corporate and state taxes as they affect profits and cash flows, are very important to the evaluation of capital investments.

PROBLEMS[8]

1. A corporation is considering the purchase of a new apartment building and land. The total cost of the new apartment and land will be $1,000,000. The building constitutes 40% of the purchase price with 25% of that amount as the salvage value. Determine the cumulative depreciation after the first 3 years of ownership, using double-declining balance depreciation with an estimated life of 20 years and no salvage value.

2. A corporation plans to sell machinery which it purchased 8 years ago. At that time it cost $90,000, had a 10-year projected life, and negligible salvage value. Depreciation was accomplished using double-declining balance with a switch to straight-line after the sixth year. If the machinery is sold for $20,000 at the end of the year, determine the recapture of depreciation and the additional tax liability if the corporation's marginal tax rate is 48%.

[8]Whenever possible, use Appendix B.

3. A corporation has decided to replace one of its coffee-processing machines with a newer model costing $65,000 and having a 10-year life. The old machine originally cost $25,000 and was estimated to have a 5-year life and $5,000 salvage value. It was depreciated using sum-of-the-years' digits. Four years later the corporation finds that the value of coffee has increased substantially and the market value of their machine has also increased, to $35,000. If the marginal tax rate is 48%, show the tax effects and the corporation's tax liability resulting from the transaction, assuming that the old machine is sold. Include a consideration of investment tax credits.

4. If in Problem 3 the old machine were traded in, indicate the tax effects and the corporation's tax liability resulting from the transaction.

5. A corporation purchased new equipment for $700,000 that had an estimated life of 6 years and qualified for investment tax credit. They traded in 10-year-old equipment for $100,000. Before considering investment tax credit, the corporation's taxable income was $50,000. Determine the amount of the corporation's investment tax credit and its tax liability for the year of the purchase.

6. A corporation has had operating incomes for the past 4 years as shown below. Assets bought and sold are also listed. Determine the federal tax liability for 1978. Include recapture of investment tax credits.

	1978	1979	1980	1981
Operating Income Pretax	$100,000	$50,000	$300,000	($200,000)

Assets	*Purchase Price 1/1/78*	*Sold 12/31/81*	*Depreciation*	*Asset Life*
Land	$10,000	$20,000	—	—
Building	50,000	30,000	SL	20 years
New machinery	20,000	20,000	SL	10 years

7. A corporation may replace older obsolete equipment with new equipment. The old equipment was purchased 6 years ago for $50,000. It was estimated to have a 10-year useful life with negligible salvage value but after 6 years has a market value of only $5,000. The new equipment costs $75,000, has an estimated life of 10 years, and has negligible salvage value. Straight-line depreciation is used. If the firm has an income of $70,000 during year 7 after deducting all expenses except depreciation on the equipment, determine the following:
   (a) The tax liability if the old machinery is not sold at the start of year 7 and new machinery not purchased.
   (b) The year-end tax liability if the old machine is sold and replaced with the new machine at the start of the year 7.

8. A corporation had taxable income from operations of $35,000. At the end of the year, they bought three new meat cutters, to replace old equipment, each costing $60,000 and having useful lives of 10 years. The old machines were purchased for $40,000 each and had book values of $25,000 when replaced. The first two machines were sold for $20,000 and $45,000, respectfully, and the third machine was traded in with an allowance of $35,000. Investment tax credit was not taken on the old machines but will be taken on the new machines. Determine the corporation's tax liability for the year.

9. A corporation purchased a machine 10 years ago for $1,500,000 and used double-declining depreciation on a useful expected life of 20 years. The corporation has a 48% marginal tax rate. If the machine can be sold today for $750,000, determine the

following:

(a) Long-term capital gains.

(b) The depreciation recapture.

(c) The tax liability.

10. A corporation has a 48% marginal tax rate and has two assets which it is planning to sell. The former will result in a $50,000 long-term capital gain, the latter in a $60,000 Section 1231 long-term capital loss. Determine the additional tax saving if the assets are sold in different years rather than in the same year.

11. The ABC Corporation, founded during 1972, operates on a fiscal year ending November 30 and has following financial history:

	1972	1973	1974	1975	1976
Ordinary income (loss)	$20,000	$20,000	$30,000	$15,000	($55,000)
Net long-term capital loss					(5,000)
Taxes paid	4,000	4,000	6,100	3,000	—

Compute the company's carry-back/carry-forward as of November 30, 1976, and the amount of the refund claim.

3 CASH FLOWS

The analysis of capital expenditures is predicated on knowledge of the cash outflows needed to acquire assets and the cash inflows that are expected to result from their use. It is the purpose of this chapter to indicate how these cash flows may be determined, based on sales and cost estimates combined with the relevant tax implications of the transactions that we are considering.

Our discussion of cash flows in this chapter will exclude any questions relating to economic and business forecasting. It will be assumed that appropriate forecasts have been made relating to sales, operating, and other costs, and tax rates. This is, of course, an oversimplification, and later in the book we will examine the problems of operating under conditions of risk and uncertainty.

COST OF ACQUISITION AND DISPOSAL OF ASSETS

The total funding requirements for the acquisition of new assets are summarized below.

Total fund requirements equal:
Land purchased.
Equipment and facilities purchased.
Patents and processes purchased.
All costs relating to purchases (transportation, legal fees, installation, etc.).
Additional working capital required.
Tax liability on the sale of replaced assets.
Interest on construction loans and the like.
Property taxes on land and buildings before they are placed in use.

less:

Funds realized from the sale of replaced assets.
Tax benefits arising from the sale of replaced assets.
Investment tax credits.
Tax benefits from payment of construction loan interest and property taxes.

All these items must be considered to obtain the *net cash outflow* required to acquire an asset.

The costs to purchase assets, whether they be equipment, land, or intangibles, are perhaps the easiest to estimate and, in general, may be estimated with the greatest degree of accuracy.

Tax law requires that all the costs relating to the acquisition of assets be capitalized and that the assets be depreciated over their useful lives, as described in Chapter 2. Thus, legal costs necessary to the purchase of real estate, for example, should be capitalized as a part of the total cost of acquisition. Also, costs such as shipping, receiving, and installing a machine would be capitalized. The question of capitalization actually varies appreciably according to the size of the firm making the acquisition. Consider the purchase of a new machine. The actual costs (in addition to the purchase price) could include the following: shipping, insurance during shipping, construction of a foundation, crane operation, plumbing, wiring, and final setup. If the firm had to pay outside contractors for each of these services, the costs would be capitalized. However, if the firm had a maintenance crew that did much of the work as a part of their normal duties, the costs would usually not be capitalized. Similarly, if a firm had its own legal staff, legal fees that would otherwise be capitalized would generally be included as a part of the ordinary expense of operating the business.

Working capital is the difference between current assets and current liabilities. In many instances when new assets are required, additional working capital is also needed. If a firm expanded its operations, it would likely need more cash and inventories. When the inventories are purchased, accounts payable will tend to increase. Similarly, when the product is sold, accounts receivable will be generated. Further, accruals for wages and taxes would tend to increase. In almost all instances, the increase in current assets exceeds the increase in current liabilities, and thus there is a requirement for added working capital. Additional working capital needed to support the operation of a fixed asset is expected to be recovered when the asset is removed from service. *Thus, if it is necessary to increase working capital to support additions to fixed assets, the increase represents a use of funds only during the life of those assets. It is expected that all of the additional working capital will be recovered when the asset is retired and is noted as a cash inflow at that time.*

The tax liability or benefit arising from the sale of an existing asset which is discontinued from service may be appreciable and must be considered as a part of the total cash flow involved in the acquisition of a new asset. The implications of sale versus trade-in on capital gains and losses and investment credits make this decision very important in capital expenditure analysis.

When new plant and facilities are acquired, there is often an appreciable time between the initial cash outlays to purchase land and the time when the facility is put into operation. Frequently, construction loans are required. For tax purposes, interest on such loans may be capitalized along with property taxes during the period prior to the asset being placed in operation. As a practical matter, such interest and taxes are usually not capitalized, *but*, for purposes of the economic analysis of a capital expenditure, they *must* be included as a part of the cost of acquisition, to the extent that they represent out-of-pocket expenses. Since it is likely that such costs will be included as

expenses for tax purposes in the year they are paid, the out-of-pocket cost
would be the actual cost less the tax savings.

Investment tax credits are provided when certain types of assets are
acquired. Since such credits are deducted directly from federal tax liability
(and generally within the same calendar quarter as the acquisition is made),
they represent a reduction in the cost of acquisition.

When an asset is retired from use, the firm may anticipate recovery of some
salvage value and working capital. The net portion of salvage and working
capital are noted as cash inflows at the time of asset retirement. Further, the
firm may have to pay taxes if capital gains or recovery of depreciation is
involved and may have to recapture some investment tax credit if the asset was
not held for as long a period as was originally anticipated. If capital losses are
involved, tax reductions may be enjoyed. It should be noted that while some
assets such as buildings are depreciated for tax purposes, their actual fair
market value may increase. If management anticipates an increase in value,
they should calculate the various taxes involved and project the amount, net of
taxes, which is likely to be received when the asset is sold. In some instances a
large portion of the profitability of an investment will be realized at the time of
its sale. This is especially true for residential real estate.

The process of determining the out-of-pocket cash flow for a major project
is demonstrated in the following examples.

● **EXAMPLE 1** *Funding Requirements*

A corporation is considering the construction of a new plant to replace its existing
facilities. Pertinent information relating to the current plant is listed below.

	Book Value	*Sale Price*
Land	$100,000	$2,500,000
Buildings	275,000	(60,000)[a]
Machinery	500,000	375,000

[a]Cost to demolish old buildings.

Cost factors for the new plant are as follows:

	Purchase Price	*Related Costs*
Land	$2,000,000	$200,000 real estate fees
		50,000 property taxes during construction
		80,000 interest during construction
Buildings	3,600,000	$ 60,000 property taxes during construction
		100,000 interest during construction
Machinery and equipment	1,600,000	$400,000 installation
Additional working capital	250,000	

All equipment and machinery has a life exceeding 7 years. The corporation is in the 48% marginal tax bracket. Determine the net out-of-pocket cost to purchase the new plant.

Solution: First calculate the gross amount to be received from the sale of the old property.

	Sale Price
Land	$2,500,000
Buildings	(60,000)
Machinery	375,000
Total	$2,815,000

The net amount received will be the sale price less capital gains taxes. The capital gains are determined as follows:

		Capital Gains (Losses)
Land		
(sale price −	book value)	
$2,500,000 −	$100,000	$2,400,000
Building		
(book value +	demolition costs)	
$275,000 +	$60,000	(335,000)
Machinery		
(book value −	sale price)	
$500,000 −	$375,000	(125,000)
Net capital gain		$1,940,000

The tax on the capital gain would be $1,940,000 × 0.30 = $582,000, so the net amount received from the sale is as follows:

Sale price	$2,815,000
Capital gains tax	− 582,000
Net sale price	$2,233,000

The total cost of the new plant plus working capital is listed below. Note that only 52% of the interest and property taxes is listed since these items would be included as expenses for tax purposes in the year they occurred and thus 48% absorbed as a tax reduction.

Land	$2,267,600
Buildings	3,683,200
Machinery and equipment	2,000,000
Added working capital	250,000
Total cost	$8,200,800

Investment tax credit of 10% of the cost of the new machinery and equipment will be enjoyed. The investment tax credit is $2,000,000 × 0.10 = $200,000. The net out-of-pocket cost equals the total purchase price of the new plant less the net sale price of the old, and less investment tax credits.

Total cost new plant	$8,200,800
Net sale price of old	− 2,233,000
Investment tax credits	− 200,000
Out-of-pocket cost	$5,767,800

The corporation would have to pay $5,767,800 to purchase the new plant. ●

● **EXAMPLE 2** *Funding Requirements with Trade-in*

Suppose that the corporation in Example 1 was able to trade in the machinery for $600,000 rather than sell it for $375,000. Assuming that the purchase price of the new machinery and equipment remains unchanged, determine the difference in funding requirements.

Solution: First, calculate the gross amount to be received from the sale and trade-in of the old property.

	Sale Price and Trade-in Allowance
Land	$2,500,000
Buildings	(60,000)
Machinery	600,000
Total	$3,040,000

The net amount received will be the sale price less capital gains taxes. The capital gains are determined as in Example 1, except that a gain is not recognized on the sale of the used machinery. Thus, the net capital gain would include the $2,400,000 gain on the land less the $335,000 loss on the buildings, or $2,065,000. The capital gain tax at the 30% rate is $619,500, so the net amount received is as follows:

Sales price and trade-in	$3,040,000
Capital gains tax	− 619,500
Net sales price	$2,420,500

The total cost of the new plant plus working capital remains unchanged at $8,200,800. The investment tax credit on the machinery and equipment would be reduced because the $600,000 trade-in value is subtracted from the $2,000,000 purchase price, leaving a $1,400,000 basis for the credit. The investment tax credit would be $140,000. The net out-of-pocket cost for the new plant is as shown.

Total cost of new plant	$8,200,800
Net sale price of old	− 2,420,500
Investment tax credits	− 140,000
Out-of-pocket cost	$5,640,300

●

Note that the reduction in the out-of-pocket cost resulting from the trade-in of $600,000 for the used machinery in Example 2 rather than the $375,000 sale price in Example 1 is only $127,500. The difference results from changes in the capital gains and investment tax credits. In the next section we will examine the differences in cash inflows resulting from the two types of transactions so that their bearing on capital expenditure decisions may be fully appreciated.

TIMING OF CASH OUTFLOWS

Examples 1 and 2 did not include a time analysis of expenditures, which is also an integral part of the economic analysis of capital expenditures. In the analysis of a large project such as the one outlined in Example 1, the development of a time-flow chart such as the one shown below is useful.

Time	Activity	Cash Flow	
0	Purchase land	−	$2,200,000
3 months	Start construction	−	900,000
6 months	Property taxes	−	5,200
1 year	Construction project	−	2,000,000
	Property taxes	−	11,400
	Loan interest	−	41,600
18 months	Complete construction	−	700,000
	Property taxes	−	15,600
	Purchase machinery	−	1,600,000
	Investment tax credit	+	200,000
21 months	Install machinery	−	400,000
24 months	Sell old plant	+	2,233,000
	Property taxes	−	25,000
	Interest	−	52,000
	Working capital		250,000
	Net cash flow		$5,767,800

CASH FLOWS FROM ASSET OPERATION

In order to evaluate proposed capital expenditures, it is necessary to estimate the after-tax cash flows which are likely to be received as a result of using the asset over its projected life. *After-tax cash flows* consist of the sum of the additional after-tax profits generated from the use of an asset plus the depreciation cash throw-offs. Determination of the cash flows is demonstrated in the following examples.

● **EXAMPLE 3** *Profitability and Cash Flow*

A machine costs $15,000. It has a life of 5 years and will be depreciated straight-line to zero salvage value. Use of the machine will result in an increase in income of $20,000 per year. Concurrently, operating expenses will rise by $16,000 per year. Assume that the firm considering the purchase of the machine has a 22% tax rate. Determine the profit and cash flow of the machine.

Solution: The profitability is calculated using the typical income statement method.

	Change in Income Statement	Change in Cash Flow
Income	$20,000	$20,000
Less operating expenses	− 16,000	− 16,000
Less depreciation	− 3,000	
Earnings before taxes	$ 1,000	
Less tax	− 220	− 220
Earnings after taxes	$ 780	
Increased cash flow		$ 3,780

The cash flow may also be determined by adding earnings after taxes to the depreciation. The depreciation expenses did not result in any outflow of cash, so at the end of the year, the firm would have $780 + $3,000 = $3,780 of increased cash inflow from operating the machine. ●

● **EXAMPLE 4** *Profitability and Cash Flows*

A machine purchased 5 years ago for $30,000 has been depreciated to a book value of $20,000. Its original projected life was 15 years with zero salvage value. Its current market value is $10,000 and, if sold, it would result in a Section 1231 long-term capital loss. A machine is available that has a purchase price of $45,000, including installation costs. The old machine could be sold for its market value. The new machine has a 20-year projected life, will be depreciated straight-line, has zero salvage value, and is expected to reduce operating costs by $7,000 per year. Compute the cash outflow needed to acquire the new machine and the inflows over its life. The firm has a 48% marginal tax rate.

Solution: The disposal of the old machine will result in a $10,000 capital loss under Section 1231. Since the marginal tax rate is 48%, the tax savings is $4,800. Thus, a total of $14,800 will be received. The cost of the new machine is $45,000, and the investment tax credit is therefore $4,500. The out-of-pocket cost for the new machine is as follows:

New machine purchase price	$45,000
Recapture investment tax credit, old machine	1,000
Investment tax credit	− 4,500
Sale of old machine	− 10,000
Section 1231 tax saving	− 4,800
	$26,700

The new machine cost $45,000, has a 20-year projected life, and zero salvage value. Depreciation on a straight-line basis is $2,250 per year. The existing machine was being depreciated at the rate of $2,000 per year, so $250 additional depreciation will result each year for the first 10 years of the new machine's life. The 10 years represents the remaining life of the old machine. The cash flows for the first 10 years are determined below.

Cost Reduction	Change in Income Statement	Change in Cash Flows
Cost reduction	$7,000	$7,000
Added depreciation	− 250	
Earnings before taxes	$6,750	
Less tax	− 3,240	− 3,240
Earnings after taxes	$3,510	
Increased cash flow		$3,760

During the last 10 years of the new machine's life the full amount of its depreciation is included in the cash-flow calculation, since the existing machine would be fully depreciated by that time.

.	Change in Income Statement	Change in Cash Flow
Cost reduction	$7,000	$7,000
Added depreciation	− 2,250	
Earnings before taxes	$4,750	
Less tax	− 2,280	− 2,280
Earnings after taxes	$2,470	
Increased cash flow		$4,720

The cash flows are summarized as follows:

Time	Cash Flow
Present	−$26,700
1–10	3,760
11–20	4,720

The examples used to develop cash flows are typical of the types of problems encountered in investment analysis. In the development of the examples, one important point should be underscored relative to sunk costs. *Sunk costs* represent cash outflows that were made in the past and are no longer recoverable. Thus, the economic significance of sunk costs within the context of capital investment decisions is limited to the impact which these costs may have on tax liabilities. For instance, in Example 4 the machine currently being used had a book value of $20,000 with a market value of only $10,000. The $10,000 difference represents a sunk cost, but part of it was recoverable so that the actual sunk cost was limited to only $5,200 since $4,800 was recoverable by means of tax reductions.

SALES VERSUS TRADE-IN: EFFECT ON CASH INFLOWS

Earlier in this chapter we demonstrated the impact on the cash outflows needed to acquire an asset resulting from the decision to trade in the asset versus selling it. Now we want to examine the impact of the same decision on the expected cash inflows. This will be accomplished in Example 5.

● **EXAMPLE 5** *Differential Cash Flows with Sale Versus Trade-in*

Refer to Examples 1 and 2 and assume a 10-year life for the new machinery and equipment, straight-line depreciation, zero salvage value, a 48% marginal tax rate, $1,500,000 earnings before depreciation and taxes, and $500,000 first-year depreciation on the buildings. Determine the difference in cash inflows in Examples 1 and 2.

Solution: Consider Example 1 first. The new machines and equipment had a total cost of $2,000,000, all of which would be subject to depreciation, or $200,000 per year. The financial statements for purposes of computing cash flows are as follows:

	Changes in Income Statement	Changes in Cash Flows
Earnings before taxes and depreciation	$1,500,000	$1,500,000
Less depreciation on buildings	− 500,000	
Less depreciation on machinery and equipment	− 200,000	
Earnings before taxes	$ 800,000	
Less tax	− 384,000	− 384,000
Earnings after taxes	$ 416,000	
Increased cash flow		$1,116,000

Next, consider Example 2. For purposes of depreciation, the cost of the machinery and equipment consists of the cash amount paid plus the book value of the old machinery. The amount paid equals the purchase price of $2,000,000 less trade-in of $600,000, or $1,400,000. The book value was $500,000, so the depreciable value is $1,900,000. The financial statements for purposes of computing cash flows are as follows:

	Changes in Income Statement	Changes in Cash Flows
Earnings before taxes and depreciation	$1,500,000	$1,500,000
Less depreciation on buildings	− 500,000	
Less depreciation on machinery and equipment	− 190,000	
Earnings before taxes	$ 810,000	
Less tax	− 388,800	− 388,800
Earnings after taxes	$ 421,200	
Increased cash flow		$1,111,200	●

The difference in cash flows between Examples 1 and 2 amounts to $4,800 per year in favor of Example 1 (sale rather than trade-in). Since the cash outflow of Example 1 exceeded that of Example 2 by $127,500, the increase in yearly cash flows of $4,800 would obviously not warrant the added expenditure. But the important point to recognize is that in many situations there are choices facing management which bear heavily on cash-flow projections, and each must be weighed. In Examples 1 and 2 the trade-in appears to be preferable.

FURTHER CONSIDERATIONS OF THE TIMING OF CASH FLOWS

Earlier in the chapter we included a time analysis showing the projected cash outflows for a two-year plant construction. In many instances cash flows must be adjusted to reflect the actual time of receipt or payment. Consider a firm opening a new plant with projected yearly sales, operating expenses, and related costs. During the first year the lags in accounts receivable and payable, inventory buildups, and accruals warrant special attention. The first year and subsequent yearly cash flows are developed in Example 6.

● **EXAMPLE 6**   *Operating Cash Flows*
A corporation anticipates additional sales of $1,000,000 per year resulting from its new plant. Cost and revenue projections are detailed below.

> *Revenues*:   All sales on credit with a 60-day average collection period.
> *Costs*:   Materials are 30% of sales with 2 months' safety stock; payment made 30 days after monthly deliveries. Labor costs are 25% of sales with payment two weeks after the end of salary period, which is monthly.
> Utilities and fuels are 15% of sales with bills received at end of month and paid 30 days after receipt.
> Administrative are 10% of sales and paid in month they occur.

Determine the pretax cash flows for the first and subsequent years, ignoring depreciation and taxes.

Solution: Consider the initial year first. Sales are projected at $1,000,000, but with a 60-day collection period, cash received can only be expected to be $833,333. Materials cost $25,000 per month and a 2-month safety stock is required. With payment in 30 days, the first year cost would be $50,000 plus $25,000 × 11 months, or $325,000. Monthly labor costs amount to $20,833. With a 2-week lag in payment, the first-year cost is $229,163, with the next salary payment due 2 weeks after the start of the second year of operation. Utilities and fuels cost $12,500 per month. A 30-day payment lag results in a first-year cost of $137,500. Administrative costs are paid in the month they occur, so the yearly cost is $100,000. The first year is summarized as follows:

Cash receipts	$833,333
Materials	− 325,000
Labor	− 229,163
Utilities and fuel	− 137,500
Administrative costs	− 100,000
Earnings before depreciation and taxes	$ 41,670

In subsequent years the cash flows would be as follows:

Cash receipts	$1,000,000
Materials	− 300,000
Labor	− 250,000
Utilities and fuel	− 150,000
Administrative costs	− 100,000
Earnings before depreciation and taxes	$ 200,000

Whenever a plant is expanded or a new operation undertaken, lower earnings and cash flow may result during the initial period of operation. In addition to the lags in collections and payments, start-up costs may also reduce profitability.

SUMMARY

Accurate estimates of cash flows, including all provisions for depreciation and taxation, are essential as inputs to the evaluation of proposed capital expenditures. In this chapter we have described how the cash flows are computed based on cost estimates. We further examined the implications of outright sale of used assets versus trade-ins and the lags in expenditures and receipts in new plant start-up.

Throughout the chapter we have emphasized that capital budgeting decisions are based upon evaluation of relevant benefits and costs which are incremental to the project under consideration. In each instance, we estimate the costs and anticipated revenues relating to the project under consideration, within the context of the firm as a whole. In later chapters we will apply decision criteria to the cash flows to determine if the proposed investments should be undertaken.

PROBLEMS[1]

1. A corporation is considering replacing an older truck with a newer model, which, owing to more efficient operation, will reduce operative costs from $20,000 to $16,000 per year. Sales are $30,000 per year. The old truck cost $30,000 when purchased nearly 5 years ago, had an estimated useful life of 15 years, zero salvage value, and is being depreciated straight-line. At present, its market value is estimated to be $20,000, if sold outright. The new truck costs $40,000 and would be depreciated straight-line to a zero salvage value over a 10-year life. The corporation has a 48% marginal tax rate. Determine the following:
   (a) The cash outflow required to acquire the new truck assuming the old truck is sold at the present time.
   (b) The yearly cash flows from operations resulting from the old truck and the new truck.

[1]Unless otherwise noted, be sure to consider the investment tax credit.

(c) Summarize the cash flows and calculate the differential cash flows over the 10-year period.

2. Consider Problem 1 with the following changes: the old truck cost $40,000 and had a $10,000 projected salvage value. Determine (a), (b), and (c) as in Problem 1.

3. Consider Problem 1 with the following changes: the old truck has useful life of 10 years, but with increased maintenance of $1,000 per year could be operated for another 5 years. Determine (a), (b), and (c) as in Problem 1.

4. Consider Problem 1 with the following changes: the old truck has useful life of 10 years and could be sold for a projected salvage value of $10,000 at the end of its useful life, or $20,000 at present. Determine (a), (b), and (c) as in Problem 1.

5. Consider Problem 1 with the following changes: the old truck cost $30,000 and had an expected 10-year life with negligible salvage value. The old truck could be rebuilt at the end of its 10-year life to operate at its current level of efficiency for another 5 years. This would cost $10,000, which would be depreciated straight-line to zero salvage. The old truck could be sold at present for $15,000. The salvage value of the truck when 15 years old is also expected to be negligible. Determine (a), (b), and (c) as in Problem 1.

6. A corporation has decided to purchase a new machine for their business. Following are the facts relating to the disposal of the old machine and purchase of the new:
   (a) The original cost of the old machinery was $2,000,000.
   (b) The book value of the old machinery is $400,000 and it can be traded in for $900,000. It is fully depreciated.
   (c) The cost to remove the old machinery is $30,000.
   (d) The cost of the new machine is $3,500,000.
   (e) Wiring by a contractor will cost $15,000.
   (f) The cost for installation by an outside contractor is $145,000.
   (g) The legal fees are $115,000.
   (h) The costs of wiring, installation, and legal fees will be capitalized.
   (i) The added working-capital requirements are $50,000.
   (j) The depreciation method used for financial and tax accounting is straight-line.
   (k) The marginal tax rate is 48%.
   (l) The expected useful life of the new machine is 20 years.
   Determine the out-of-pocket cost to purchase the new machine.

7. Suppose in Problem 6 that the old machine is sold for $750,000 rather than traded in. Determine the net cash outflow to purchase the new machine.

8. Referring to Problems 6 and 7, determine the depreciable base for the new machine, for tax purposes only, for both the trade-in and sale.

9. A corporation purchased new equipment costing $200,000 to support a new product line. The equipment has a 5-year life with negligible expected salvage value and will be depreciated double-declining balance. Additional first-year sales are expected to be $175,000 with fixed costs (not including depreciation) of $25,000 and variable costs of $35,000. General and administrative costs are estimated to be 15% of sales. Sales and variable and administrative costs are expected to increase at 10% per year. If the corporation's marginal tax rate is 48%, determine the after-tax profit and cash flow of each year and the cash outflow required to purchase the equipment.

10. A2Z Corporation is expanding its Hoboken, New Jersey, chemical cleaning-products plant in order to increase sales and market share. Construction will be completed in September and the plant will be in full operation October 1. A tabulation of projected incremental costs and revenue is shown below. Determine the incremental cash flows for the first 2 years (ignoring depreciation and taxes).

Item	$/Year	Notes
Sales	$2,520,000	[a]See collection experience.
Raw material *A*	408,000	3 months initial stock (includes permanent 2 months safety stock), required payment net 30 (end of month).
Raw material *B*	144,000	2 months initial stock required (includes permanent 1 month safety stock), payment net 30 (end of month).
Miscellaneous raw materials	180,000	Average 1 month stock required, net 25.
Electricity	9,600	Net 25 (first billing Nov. 1).
Fuel oil	12,000	Net 30 (first billing Nov. 1).
Water	6,000	Net 30 (first billing Nov. 1).
Labor hourly-paid	144,000	Paid weekly, 1-week lag.
Salaried supervision	60,000	Paid monthly on last working day.
Packages, containers, etc.	210,000	2 months initial supply required (includes permanent 1 month safety stock) net 30 (end of month).

[a]Collection experience on sales: 1st month 20%, 2nd month 70%, 3rd month 10%.

4 MATHEMATICS OF DISCOUNTED CASH FLOW

In order to be able to perform the numerous calculations associated with the analysis of capital expenditures, it is necessary to understand the procedures for computing interest as well as the reciprocal function of discounting funds expected to be received in the future to their present value. This chapter describes the types of calculations involved and presents detailed examples explaining their use.

SIMPLE AND COMPOUND INTEREST

Simple interest is computed on the principal outstanding at the time of the interest calculation. The time of calculation could be the end of a month, quarter, year, and so on. The compound sum after one period is calculated using Equation (1):

$$S = P(1 + i) \tag{1}$$

where S = compound sum
P = principal
i = rate of return (interest rate)

Funds may be compounded annually or more frequently. The easier case of annual compounding is considered first. If funds are invested with annual compounding, the compound sum after a period of n years is found using Equation (2):

$$S_n = P(1 + i)^n \tag{2}$$

where S_n = compound sum after n years
n = number of years

● **EXAMPLE 1** *Compound Interest*
A depositor puts \$3,000 in a bank at 5%, compounded annually, for 3 years. Determine the amount that will have accrued at the end of 3 years.

Solution: Use Equation (2), as follows:

$$S_n = \$3,000(1 + 0.05)^3$$
$$= \$3,000(1.157625)$$
$$= \$3,472.88$$

At the end of 3 years, the depositor would have $3,472.88. ●

The calculations involved in Example 1 are tedious. Use of the first column, "Amount of $1," in Appendix C, "Compound Interest and Annuity Table," greatly simplifies the problem. The factors are referred to as *single payment/compound amount factors*. For instance, in Example 1, reference to the 5% page, 3-year row, gives the interest factor 1.157625. This factor would be used rather than raising $(1 + 0.05)$ to the third power.

Frequently, interest is compounded semiannually, quarterly, daily, or continuously. Equation (3) may be used to determine the compound sum in such instances.

$$S_n = P\left(1 + \frac{i}{m}\right)^{mn} \tag{3}$$

where m is the number of times interest is compounded annually.

● **EXAMPLE 2** *Compound Interest*

A depositor placed $3,000 in a bank for 5 years, at 6%, with compounding quarterly. Determine the amount on deposit at the end of the 5-year period.

Solution:

$$S_n = \$3,000\left(1 + \frac{0.06}{4}\right)^{4 \times 5}$$
$$= \$3,000(1.015)^{20}$$
$$= \$3,000(1.347)$$
$$= \$4,041$$

At the end of 5 years the depositor would have $4,041. ●

Some financial institutions utilize continuous compounding. Equation (3) then becomes Equation (4):

$$S_n = P\left[\lim_{m \to \infty} \left(1 + \frac{i}{m}\right)^{mn}\right] \tag{4}$$

Equation (4) can be rearranged as follows:

$$S_n = P\left[\lim_{m \to \infty} \left[\left(1 + \frac{i}{m}\right)^{m/i}\right]^{in}\right]$$

The limit as m approaches infinity of $\left(1 + \dfrac{i}{m}\right)^{m/i}$ is e, the base of the natural or Naperian logarithm system. An irrational number, e has an approximate value of 2.7182.

Equation (4) can be rewritten as Equation (5):

$$S_n = Pe^{in} \tag{5}$$

Values of e^x are contained in Table 4-1.

TABLE 4-1   Values of e^x

x	e^x	x	e^x	x	e^x
0.01	1.0101	0.08	1.0833	0.35	1.4191
0.02	1.0202	0.09	1.0942	0.40	1.4918
0.03	1.0305	0.10	1.1052	0.45	1.5683
0.04	1.0408	0.15	1.1618	0.50	1.6487
0.05	1.0513	0.20	1.2214	0.55	1.7333
0.06	1.0618	0.25	1.2840	0.60	1.8221
0.07	1.0725	0.30	1.3499	0.65	1.9155

● **EXAMPLE 3**   Continuous Compounding
    A depositor placed $4,000 in a bank for 5 years, at 5%, with continuous compounding. How much did the depositor have at the end of the 5 years?

    Solution: Using Equation (5) and Table 4-1, we have

$$S_n = \$4,000e^{(0.05)5}$$
$$= \$4,000e^{0.25}$$
$$= \$4,000(1.2840)$$
$$= \$5,136$$

At the end of 5 years the depositor would have $5,136.   ●

COMPOUND SUM (FUTURE VALUE) OF AN ANNUITY

Frequently, it is necessary to save a certain sum each year in order to accumulate a required amount within a given time period. In general, savings are made at the end of the year and the annuity tables are constructed in that manner.

When a payment is made each year for a period of n years, at interest rate i, the future value is expressed as follows:

$$F = A_1(1 + i)^{n-1} + A_2(1 + i)^{n-2} + \cdots + A_n(1 + i)^0 \tag{6}$$

where
$$F = \text{future value of the annuity}$$
$$A_1, A_2, \ldots, A_n = \text{amounts paid into the annuity at the end of the year}$$
$$i = \text{rate of return}$$
$$n = \text{number of years}$$

If the payments are equal each period, then Equation (6) may be rewritten as Equation (7):

$$F = A(1 + i)^{n-1} + A(1 + i)^{n-2} + \cdots + A$$
$$= A\left[(1 + i)^{n-1} + (1 + i)^{n-2} + \cdots + (1 + i) + 1\right] \qquad (7)$$

Multiplying both sides of the equation by $(1 + i)$,

$$F(1 + i) = A\left[(1 + i)^{n} + (1 + i)^{n-1} + (1 + i)^{n-2}\right.$$
$$\left. + \cdots + (1 + i)\right] \qquad (8)$$

Subtracting Equation (7) from Equation (8),

$$Fi = A\left[(1 + i)^{n} - 1\right]$$

Dividing by i results in Equation (9),

$$F = A\left[\frac{(1 + i)^{n} - 1}{i}\right] \qquad (9)$$

Values of $\dfrac{(1 + i)^{n} - 1}{i}$, commonly referred to as *uniform series / compound amount factors*, symbolized by $S_{\overline{n}|}$ are provided in Appendix C, second column.

● **EXAMPLE 4**   *Future Value of an Annuity*

An investor plans to put $1,000 per year into an annuity at the *end* of each year for 10 years. If interest is compounded annually at 6%, how much will the investor have at the end of 10 years?

Solution: Use Equation (9) and Appendix C, 6% page, 10-year row:

$$F = \$1,000(13.180795)$$
$$= \$13,180.80$$

At the end of 10 years the investor will have $13,180.80.   ●

● **EXAMPLE 5**   *Future Value of an Annuity*

An investor plans to put $1,000 per year into an annuity at the *start* of each year for 10 years. If interest is compounded annually at 6%, how much will the investor have at the end of 10 years?

Solution: Use Equation (2) to find the value of the initial $1,000 after 10 years. Add this to the future value of an annuity for 10 years (per Example 4), and subtract $1,000. The $1,000 is equivalent to the last payment placed into a year-end annuity, which, of course, is not the case in this example, wherein payments are made at the start of each year. The first payment is denoted by the $1,000 compounded for 10 years.

$$\begin{array}{rl}
\$1,000(1.790848) = & \$\ \ 1,790.85 \\
\$1,000(13.180795) = & \ \ 13,180.80 \\
- & \underline{\ \ \ 1,000.00} \\
& \$13,971.65
\end{array}$$

At the end of 10 years the investor would have $13,971.65. Notice that the accumulated value is $13,971.65 when payments are made at the start of each year, while the value is $13,180.80 with payments made at year's end. The entire $790.85 difference is attributable to the interest earned on the initial $1,000 payment.   ●

SINKING-FUND PAYMENTS

A *sinking fund* is a fund created to provide for payment of a debt or other obligation by setting aside a certain amount at stated intervals, usually at the end of each year. Sinking-fund payments may be determined using *sinking-fund factors*, which are the reciprocals of the uniform series/compound amount factors. Sinking-fund factors are found in Appendix C, third column.

sinking-fund payment = fund obligation

$\times$ sinking-fund factor

$$A = F \left[\frac{i}{(1 + i)^n - 1} \right] \tag{10}$$

where the sinking-fund factor is expressed as

$$\frac{1}{S_{\overline{n}|}} = \frac{i}{(1 + i)^n - 1} \tag{11}$$

● **EXAMPLE 6** Sinking Fund

A corporation needs $15,000,000 in 15 years to pay off a bond issue. The bond indenture requires the establishment of a sinking fund with annual year-end payments. If the corporation can earn 6% on its sinking fund, how much must it put into the fund for 15 years to accumulate the full $15,000,000?

Solution: Use Equation (10) and the sinking-fund factor from Appendix C, third column.

sinking-fund payment = $15,000,000 \times 0.04296276$

= $644,441.40

The corporation must put $644,441.40 into the fund each year for 15 years to accumulate $15,000,000.   ●

PRESENT VALUE

When using the discounted-cash-flow procedures for capital investment evaluation, it is necessary to know the present value of a sum to be received at a future time. The present value of a sum to be received in the future may be obtained using Equation (2), reproduced here as Equation (12):

$$S = P(1 + i)^n \tag{12}$$

Solving Equation (12) for P results in Equation (13), which is the present value (PV) of the sum S to be received in n years.

$$\bullet \qquad PV = \frac{S}{(1 + i)^n} \quad \text{or} \quad PV = S\left(\frac{1}{1 + i}\right)^n \quad \text{or} \quad PV = SV^n \qquad (13)$$

Values for the factor $\left(\dfrac{1}{1 + i}\right)^n$, symbolized by V^n, and termed *single payment/present value factors*, are found in Appendix C, fourth column.

● **EXAMPLE 7**   *Present Value*

A corporation expects to receive $10,000 in 3 years as payment for a note from a customer. The corporation needs cash now and has decided to sell the note to a bank. If the bank discounts the note at 10%, how much will the corporation receive?

Solution: Utilize Equation (13) and Appendix C, fourth column, at 10% as follows:

$$PV = S(\text{present value factor})$$
$$= \$10,000(0.751315)$$
$$= \$7,513.15$$

The corporation will receive $7,513.15 from the bank. Stated another way, the present value of $10,000 to be received in 3 years, discounted at 10%, is $7,513.15.   ●

Present Value of an Annuity

In many capital budgeting problems, funds are expected to be received at the end of each year for a period of years. The present value of a series of payments is the sum of the individual payments to be received each year. The sum is expressed in Equation (14):

$$PV = \frac{S_1}{1 + i} + \frac{S_2}{(1 + i)^2} + \cdots + \frac{S_n}{(1 + i)^n} \qquad (14)$$

where PV is the present value of the funds to be received.

If the payments are equal and the discount rate (i) is held constant, Equation (14) can be reduced to Equation (15):

$$PV = \sum_{t=1}^{n} \frac{S}{(1 + i)^t} \qquad (15)$$

where PV is the present value of a stream of funds to be received in equal amounts at year end, discounted at rate i.

In order to obtain the *uniform series/present worth factors*, symbolized by $A_{\overline{n}|}$, located in Appendix C, fifth column, start with Equation (9):

$$F = A\left[\frac{(1 + i)^n - 1}{i}\right] \qquad (9)$$

where F = future amount of an annuity
A = equal yearly payment

Recall from Equation (13) that

$$PV = S\left[\frac{1}{(1 + i)^n}\right] \qquad (13)$$

Since we are concerned with the present value of an annuity, substitute Equation (9) for S in Equation (13):

$$PV = A\left[\frac{(1 + i)^n - 1}{i}\right]\left[\frac{1}{(1 + i)^n}\right]$$

$$= A\left[\frac{(1 + i)^n - 1}{i(1 + i)^n}\right] \qquad (16)$$

Then

$$A_{\overline{n}|} = \frac{(1 + i)^n - 1}{i(1 + i)^n} = \frac{1 - V^n}{i} \qquad (17)$$

where $A_{\overline{n}|}$ is the present worth of $1 per period. $A_{\overline{n}|}$ is found in Appendix C, fifth column, commonly referred to as uniform series/present worth factors.

● **EXAMPLE 8**   *Present Value of an Annuity*

A corporation expects to receive cash inflows of $3,000 each year for 10 years as the result of implementing a new project. Determine the present value of the sum discounted at 8%.

Solution: Utilize Equation (16) and Appendix C, fifth column, 8% for 10 years, as follows:

$$P = \$3,000(6.710081)$$
$$= \$20,130.24$$

The present value of $3,000 to be received each year for 10 years, discounted at 8%, is $20,130.24. ●

Present Value of an Increasing Annuity

To obtain Equation (15) it was assumed that the annual payments were constant. In some instances payments increase at a constant annual rate. If the rate of increase is g, then Equation (14) may be rewritten as Equation (18):

$$PV = \frac{S}{(1 + i)^1} + \frac{S(1 + g)^1}{(1 + i)^2} + \cdots + \frac{S(1 + g)^{n-1}}{(1 + i)^n} \qquad (18)$$

For example, if we are considering a stream of dividends, and if D_0 is the dividend at time zero, then the present value of the stream of dividends, growing annually at rate g may be expressed as shown in Equation (19).

$$PV = \frac{D_0(1 + g)}{1 + i} + \frac{D_0(1 + g)^2}{(1 + i)^2} + \cdots + \frac{D_0(1 + g)^\infty}{(1 + i)^\infty} \tag{19}$$

$$PV = D_0 \sum_{t=1}^{\infty} \frac{(1 + g)^t}{(1 + i)^t} \tag{20}$$

Equation (20) represents a dividend valuation model for common stock. It assumes that growth in the dividend will continue at rate g forever. If this is the case, then the present value of the stock is expressed in Equation (20). Frequently, the value of the stock is noted as P_0 and the rate of discount as r rather than i, so Equation (20) may be rewritten as Equation (21):

$$P_0 = D_0 \sum_{t=1}^{\infty} \frac{(1 + g)^t}{(1 + r)^t} \tag{21}$$

Equation (21) may be expanded as shown in Equation (22):

$$P_0 = \frac{D_0(1 + g)}{1 + r} + \frac{D_0(1 + g)^2}{(1 + r)^2} + \cdots + \frac{D_0(1 + g)^\infty}{(1 + r)^\infty} \tag{22}$$

Multiplying both sides of Equation (22) by $(1 + r)/(1 + g)$ results in Equation (23):

$$P_0 \left[\frac{1 + r}{1 + g} \right] = D_0 + \frac{D_0(1 + g)}{1 + r} + \frac{D_0(1 + g)^2}{(1 + r)^2} + \cdots \tag{23}$$

Subtracting Equation (22) from Equation (23) yields Equation (24):

$$P_0 \left[\frac{1 + r}{1 + g} \right] - P_0 = D_0 + \frac{D_0(1 + g)^\infty}{(1 + r)^\infty} \tag{24}$$

If g were greater than r, the value of the stock would be infinite. If r is greater than g, then the second term on the right of Equation (24) is zero and Equation (24) reduces to Equation (25):

$$P_0 \left[\frac{1 + r}{1 + g} - 1 \right] = D_0 \tag{25}$$

$$P_0 \left[\frac{(1 + r) - (1 + g)}{1 + g} \right] = D_0$$

$$P_0(r - g) = D_0(1 + g)$$

$$P_0 = \frac{D_0(1 + g)}{r - g}$$

Since $D_1 = D_0(1 + g)$, then

$$P_0 = \frac{D_1}{r - g} \tag{26}$$

where D_1 is the dividend to be received at the end of the year. Rearranging,

$$r = \frac{D_1}{P_0} + g \qquad (27)$$

where r is the value placed on the outstanding common stock, using the dividend valuation model. Later we will refer to this value as K_e.

Equation (27) is the critical equation for obtaining the cost of equity in the *dividend valuation model*, which will be used as a part of the cost of capital in Chapter 11.

During the life of a firm it is not unusual for the rate of growth of the dividend to change. If the growth rate changes, the value of the firm may be expressed as Equation (28):

$$P_0 = D_0 \sum_{t=1}^{k} \frac{(1 + g_1)^t}{(1 + r)^t} + D_1 \sum_{t=k+1}^{\infty} \frac{(1 + g_2)^{t-k}}{(1 + r)^t} \qquad (28)$$

where g_1 = dividend growth rate for periods 1 through k
g_2 = growth rate for periods $k + 1$ through infinity
$D_1 = D_0(1 + g_1)^k$

For computational purposes, Equation (28) may be rewritten as Equation (29):

$$P_0 = D_0 \sum_{t=1}^{k} \frac{(1 + g_1)^t}{(1 + r)^t} + D_0 \left(\frac{1 + g_1}{1 + r} \right)^k \sum_{t=1}^{\infty} \frac{(1 + g_2)^t}{(1 + r)^t} \qquad (29)$$

In addition to a changing rate of growth for the dividends, the rate of discount may change from period to period. The more general case is described in Equation (30):

$$P_0 = D_0 \sum_{t=1}^{k_1} \frac{(1 + g_1)^t}{(1 + r_1)^t} + D_1 \sum_{t=1}^{k_2} \frac{(1 + g_2)^t}{(1 + r_2)^t} + \cdots$$

$$+ D_n \sum_{t=1}^{k_n} \frac{(1 + g_n)^t}{(1 + r_n)^t} \qquad (30)$$

where n = number of intervals, an interval consists of one or more periods
$g_1, g_2, \ldots g_n$ = dividend growth rate in intervals 1, 2, . . . , n
$r_1, r_2, \ldots r_n$ = discount rate in intervals 1, 2, . . . , n
k_n = number of periods in interval n
D_0 = initial dividend
D_n = dividend at the beginning of each interval calculated using Equation (31):

$$D_n = D_{n-1} \frac{(1 + g_{n-1})^{k_{n-1}}}{(1 + r_{n-1})^{k_{n-1}}} \qquad (31)$$

● **EXAMPLE 9**   *Present Value of an Increasing Annuity*

A corporation's dividend is presently $3 and is expected to grow at an annual rate of 5% for 10 years and at an annual rate of 10% thereafter. A shareholder, in valuing the corporation's stock, plans to use an 8% discount rate for the first 5 years and 12% thereafter, for a total of 25-year valuation period.

Solution: Using Equation (30), the solution is shown below in tabular form.

Interval, n	1 (*years 1–5*)	2 (*years 6–10*)	3 (*years 11–25*)
Number of Periods, k	5	5	15
Growth Rate, g	5%	5%	10%
Discount Rate, r	8%	12%	12%
Dividend Value at Beginning of Interval, D_n	$3.00	$3.00 $\dfrac{(1.05)^5}{(1.08)^5}$ =$2.605848	$2.605848 $\dfrac{(1.05)^5}{(1.12)^5}$ =$1.88715
$\displaystyle\sum_{t=1}^{k}\dfrac{(1+g_n)^t}{(1+r_n)^t}$ (*B*)	$\displaystyle\sum_{t=1}^{5}\dfrac{(1.05)^t}{(1.08)^t}$ =4.598447	$\displaystyle\sum_{t=1}^{5}\dfrac{(1.05)^t}{(1.12)^t}$ =4.137053	$\displaystyle\sum_{t=1}^{15}\dfrac{(1.10)^t}{(1.12)^t}$ =13.025780
$(D_n) \times (B)$	$13.795342	$10.780532	$24.581602

The summation of $(D_n) \times (B)$ is $49.16. The shareholder would value the corporation's stock at $49.16.   ●

PERPETUITIES

A *perpetuity* is a series of periodic payments that are to run indefinitely. A perpetuity is, therefore, a special form of an annuity, differing from the annuities previously discussed in terms of duration. Perpetuities frequently result from the establishment of an endowment, although bonds lacking any maturity also qualify.

The value of a perpetuity is determined simply by dividing the yearly payment by the rate of return being received on the principal as shown in Equation (32):

$$\text{PV} = \frac{P}{i} \qquad (32)$$

where PV = present value of the perpetuity
    P = annual payment
    i = rate of return

● **EXAMPLE 10**   *Present Value of Perpetuity*

If a perpetuity yields $1,000 per year, determine the present value based on a 6% required return.

Solution: Use Equation (32) as shown:

$$PV = \frac{\$1,000}{0.06}$$
$$= \$16,666.67$$

An investor requiring a 6% return would be willing to pay $16,666.67 for a perpetuity yielding $1,000 per year. Put another way, if someone wanted to establish a perpetual endowment of $1,000 per year, $16,666.67 would be required if the funds could be invested at 6%.   ●

CAPITAL RECOVERY

In financial problems it is frequently necessary to find the yearly payment needed to repay a debt such as a mortgage. The *capital recovery factor*, which is the reciprocal of the uniform series/present worth factor, may be used for this purpose. These factors are found in Appendix C, sixth column.

$$\text{capital recovery factor} = \frac{1}{A_{\overline{n}|}} = \frac{i(1 + i)^n}{(1 + i)^n - 1} \tag{33}$$

$$A = PV\left[\frac{i(1 + i)^n}{(1 + i)^n - 1}\right] = PV\left[\frac{1}{A_{\overline{n}|}}\right] \tag{34}$$

● **EXAMPLE 11**   *Capital Recovery*

A borrower needs $20,000. A bank will provide a mortgage at 8% for 25 years with equal annual year-end payments. Determine the amount of the year-end payment.

Solution: Use Equation (34) and Appendix C, sixth column, 8% for 25 years.

$$\text{mortgage payment} = \$20,000(0.09367878)$$
$$= \$1,873.58$$

A borrower would pay $1,873.58 each year for 25 years to repay the $20,000 mortgage.
                                                                              ●

SUMMARY

This chapter provides the background mathematical methods required for the various discounted-cash-flow computations which are an integral part of the economic evaluation of capital expenditures. The several tables for compound interest, present value, and the like are cross-referenced within the chapter to Appendix C at the back of the book.

1. Sharpe is 40 years old, anticipates retirement at age 65, and may invest up to $1,500 per year in an individual retirement account (IRA). He expects to live to age 80. If he can invest the funds at year's end at an annual rate of 8% and receive a return of 6% after retirement, determine the lump-sum value of his IRA at 65 and the annual pretax payment after retirement.

2. Referring to Problem 1, if Sharpe wants to receive $15,000 per year, how large an initial payment must he make into a retirement fund in addition to the $1,500 yearly payments?

3. How much must be paid at the end of each year to repay a $10,000 mortgage in 10 years at 8% annual interest?

4. An investor placed $1,000 in an 8% investment trust for 20 years, compounded continuously. How much did the investor have at the end of that period?

5. What amount must be deposited today so that $10,000 may be withdrawn at years 12, 13, 14, and 15, if the funds are invested at 8%?

6. A newly formed corporation is offering stock with projected dividends of $2 for the first 3 years and a yearly increase in dividend of 5% per year thereafter. At what current price can the stock be valued assuming a 10% discount rate and dividend payments at the end of each year?

7. An investor bids on a 3-year annuity paying $25 per year. He wishes to compensate for inflation, which is currently 8%, but which he feels will increase by 1% each year. Determine the present value of the annuity if an investor requires a 10% return.

8. An investor plans to value a stock over a 10-year period. The current dividend is $2. He expects dividend growth rates as follows: years 1 through 3, 8%; years 4 through 7, 9%; years 8 through 10, 7%. Determine the dividend valuation for the stock for the 10-year period if the investor's discount rate is 8%.

9. A sinking fund is needed to pay off $10,000,000 in 20 years. If payments are made at the end of each year, determine the amount of each payment for the last 5 years assuming that $250,000 is placed in the fund each year for the first 15 years and all funds receive 7% interest compounded annually.

10. A bond pays interest in the amount of $40 each 6 months. The bond will mature in 10 years paying $1,000 (the principal) at that time. Determine the present values assuming the following interest rates:
    (a) 8%
    (b) 10%
    (c) 6%

11. An individual has $2,000, which he can invest in one of two ways. One investment will pay 10% for the next 15 years. As an alternative the individual can expect to put his investment in an initial 8% savings certificate over 5 years. The expectation is that savings certificate rates will increase 2% every 5 years. Which alternative should he choose? Ignore income taxes.

12. You have just won the "Millionaire" state lottery first prize of $50,000 per year for 20 years. You receive your first prize installment immediately. Assuming you can invest funds at 7%, determine the amount that you would accept now in lieu of $50,000 per year for 20 years. (Ignore tax effects.)

13. You have just won the top prize in a state lottery of $1,000 per week for life. Assuming an investment rate of 7%, how much of the current lottery proceeds must be invested to fund your prize? (Assume a perpetuity.)

45

5 EVALUATION OF ALTERNATIVE INVESTMENT OPPORTUNITIES

Once the firm's management has established its goals and priorities for capital expenditures, it must address the question of evaluating proposed expenditures in some systematic manner. Since in all organizations the amount of funds available for capital expenditures is limited, *management is faced with the dual problem of establishing some basic criteria for the acceptance, rejection, or postponement of proposed investments, and then ranking the projects that meet the criteria for acceptance in order of their value to the firm.* Our studies indicate that at least 35 methods have been devised to guide management in the acceptance or rejection of proposed investments. Some of the methods are general in nature and readily applicable to many firms. Others are designed for particular industries such as utilities. Some are special applications of more general procedures and have been developed to deal, for example, with the question of variability of risk among proposals.

Two recent surveys by The Conference Board[1] and Petry[2] of 136 and 284 firms, respectively, indicate that payback and internal rate of return (IRR) are used by the largest percentage of firms, while net present value (NPV) and return on investment are used to a lesser degree. Results of the studies are referred to throughout this chapter and the next. On the average, capital-intensive firms tend to use 2.25 or more measures, while labor-intensive firms use fewer measures. Frequently, large firms use several methods of evaluation.

It is important to note that the various measures can be helpful to management, as Pflomm[3] notes, provided that:

1. The measure that is used is applied consistently and uniformly to all projects.

2. The measure is used as a guide rather than the sole basis for approval or disapproval of capital projects.

3. Management understands how the computations are made and what the answers really mean.

[1]Patrick J. Davey, *Capital Investments: Appraisals and Limits* (New York: The Conference Board, 1974).
[2]Glenn H. Petry, "Effective Use of Capital Budgeting Tools," *Business Horizons*, October 1975.
[3]N. E. Pflomm, *Managing Capital Expenditures* (New York: The Conference Board, 1963).

In the course of our study of the methods used to evaluate capital investments, we shall explore six alternatives: payback, return on investment, annual capital charge (also called equivalent annual cash flow), net present value, profitability index, and internal rate of return. Each of the methods is defined below. The latter four are termed *discounted cash-flow procedures*, since they consider the time value of money by discounting expected cash flows to their present value.

1. Payback. The payback period is defined as the number of years required to recover the original investment in a project by its net cash inflows.

2. Return on investment. This name has been given to a variety of methods that divide yearly cash inflows or net income (either before or after taxes) by the project's cost or book value.

3. Annual capital charge. This method involves discounting all the expected after-tax cash inflows to present value and then determining their equivalent annual charge over the project's life.

4. Net present value. This method requires discounting all expected after-tax cash flows to present value, and taking the difference between the sum of the discounted cash inflows and outflows.

5. Profitability index. This method divides the present value of cash inflows by present value of cash outflows. The quotient provides an index for measuring return per dollar of investment.

6. Internal rate of return. This method is similar to net present value but rather than compare the discounted values of the cash flows, the goal is to determine the discount rate that exactly equates the inflows and outflows. That discount rate is termed the *project's internal rate of return.*

In this chapter we shall commence our study with payback and return on investment. The other methods will be examined in Chapter 6.

BASIC ASSUMPTIONS

In our initial study of capital evaluation procedures we shall assume that the investment decisions made will not alter the firm's existing risk complexion. This does not mean that we are operating in a risk-free atmosphere. *Rather, it means that projects accepted have the same average risk as characterized by the firm.*

All firms operate under some degree of business and financial risk. The unique combination of risk elements determines the firm's risk complexion. The risk complexion is integrated by the securities markets and results in the rate at which the market discounts the price of the firm's securities. Types of investments that generally will not affect the risk complexion or market discount rate include replacements for equipment currently in use, where the market and economic structure surrounding the use of the equipment are expected to maintain stable. In Chapters 8 through 11 we shall examine decision-making techniques that will permit us to evaluate the impact of risk on the capital investment decision.

The second assumption needed at this juncture is that management has established benchmarks for evaluating capital investments. The benchmark for payback is the maximum number of years required by the firm for the complete recovery of the investment in a project. For rate of return the benchmark is the minimum rate of return required by management, which may vary appreciably, depending on the method used to compute the rate of return. Several methods are in common use, as noted below.

For the discounted cash-flow methods, the criteria for evaluation will initially be assumed to be the firm's marginal cost of capital, commonly referred to as the cost of capital. This represents the cost of funds used to acquire the firm's total assets and is found by averaging the rate of return expected to be received by all parties contributing to the firm's financial structure. Actual computation of the firm's cost of capital is discussed in Chapter 11. At this point in our study, we assume the firm's cost of capital as our benchmark; in our study of capital asset pricing theory and risk analysis, we will find that other benchmarks may be more appropriate under certain circumstances. Application of the evaluative criteria to the discounted cash-flow procedures is discussed in the following chapter.

Given these two assumptions, we are prepared to start our study of the capital budgeting evaluation procedures, examining payback first.

PAYBACK

Payback is actually a measure of a project's liquidity and capital recovery rate rather than its profitability. The payback period is defined as the number of years required to recover the investment in a project. If the anticipated after-tax cash inflows are *equal each year*, then the payback period may be obtained by dividing the after-tax cash inflows expected to be derived from the project into the after-tax outflows relating to the cost of the project. If the cash inflows are uneven, the payback period may be found as shown in Example 1.

When payback is used, projects may be accepted or rejected based on the number of years required to recover their cost. Projects may also be ranked using payback; the shorter the payback period, the higher the ranking. However, payback is more commonly used as a constraint rather than as a method for deciding among or ranking projects.

● *EXAMPLE 1* Payback

Corporation plans to invest funds to purchase a new machine. The projected cash inflows and outflows are shown below. Determine the payback period.

Time	Expected Cash Flows
Present	$-\$10,000$
1	$-$ 4,000
2–6	$+$ 3,000
7–15	$+$ 6,000
15[a]	$+$ 2,000

[a]Recovery of working capital.

Solution: Since the cash flows are not constant over the life of the project, the payback period may be found using the tabular form as follows:

Time	Expected Cash Flow	Net Cash Outflow
Present	− $10,000	− $10,000
1	− 4,000	− 14,000
2	+ 3,000	− 11,000
3	+ 3,000	− 8,000
4	+ 3,000	− 5,000
5	+ 3,000	− 2,000
6	+ 3,000	+ 1,000

The total investment is recovered during the sixth year. Since $2,000 remains outstanding at the start of the sixth year, and $3,000 is expected to be received during the sixth year, the total investment will be recovered two-thirds of the way through the sixth year. The payback period is thus 5 years and 8 months.   ●

When payback is used as demonstrated in Example 1, cash flows are only considered up to the time that the initial investment is recovered. As a result, the only question answered is the length of time needed to recover the initial investment. Weingartner[4] notes: "Generally, the break-even point is a point of indifference—with qualifications—beyond which an accounting profit is expected to be generated by the operation under analysis, and below which loss is expected." If the net revenues are constant, the aggregate profit will be proportional to project's life after the payback period has elapsed. "Thus, a longer anticipated life yields a higher initial profit, other things remaining equal, because depreciation expense will be lower. Indeed, the life of the project may be overestimated by the proposer not only to enhance its total profitability, but also to reduce the payback period on the accounting profit basis. A bias countering this one may arise in the selection of the shortest project or asset life which the tax authorities permit to improve the actual after-tax cash flow profitability. Cash flow payback, the usual concept, is less affected since depreciation enters only as a tax shield."[5]

The use of payback, then, depends on the importance to management of knowing the capital recovery period. Merritt and Sykes[6] note that: "It (payback) causes assessors to concentrate on unimportant and often irrelevant characteristics of an investment project to the detriment of its significant characteristics. It has harshly, but not unfairly, been described as the 'fish bait' test, since effectively it concentrates on the recovery of the bait (the capital outlay) paying no attention to the size of the fish (the ultimate profitability), if any."

The payback method has been further discredited for at least five reasons:

1. It fails to consider the expected revenues beyond the payback period established by the firm. Frequently, such payback periods are set from 2 to 5 years. The time period established generally is not based on an economic measure that would attach a cost to the use of funds and to the application of managerial effort, but rather may depend to a great extent on the firm's risk

[4]H. Martin Weingartner, "Some New Views on the Payback Period and Capital Budgeting Decisions," *Management Science*, Vol. 15, No. 12, August 1969, p. B-599.
[5]Ibid., p. B-601.
[6]A. J. Merritt and A. Sykes, *The Finance and Analysis of Capital Projects* (London: Longmans Green and Co. Ltd., 1963).

preferences for liquidity. Thus, for example, if a firm established a 3-year payback period requirement, revenues generated after the third year would not be considered when applying this method.

2. It fails to consider the time value of money.

3. It does not differentiate between projects requiring different cash investments.

4. While it does measure a project's rate of capital recovery or liquidity, it does not consider the firm's liquidity position as a whole, which is a much more important question. As Weingartner[7] points out: "The usually designated speculative and/or precautionary motive of firms to hold liquid or near liquid funds in order to seize upon unexpected opportunities is a different motive from that which requires each new investment separately to recover its original cost within a short time."

5. It ignores the cost of funds used to support the investment, even during the payback period. By ignoring the cost of funds, a very important cost is overlooked. Reconciliation of this problem is considered below.

A somewhat different approach to the application of payback, which takes into consideration the cost of funds necessary to support an investment, is demonstrated in Example 2[8]. This process not only overcomes the fifth shortcoming described above but is also useful in dealing with certain classes of potential *cataclysmic risk* (which is defined and discussed below).

● **EXAMPLE 2** Payback

A corporation requires a rate of return of 10%. Using the project having cash flows shown in Example 1, determine the period necessary to recover both the capital expenditures and the cost of funds required to support those expenditures. Assume that all cash flows are year-end.

Solution: Construct a table showing cash flows and costs of capital to support those funds as follows:

Time	Expected Cash Flow	Dollar Cost of Funds at 10%	Cumulative Net Cash Flow
Present	− $10,000	0	− $10,000
1	− 4,000	− $1,000	− 15,000
2	+ 3,000	− 1,500	− 13,500
3	+ 3,000	− 1,350	− 11,850
4	+ 3,000	− 1,185	− 10,035
5	+ 3,000	− 1,004	− 8,039
6	+ 3,000	− 804	− 5,843
7	+ 6,000	− 584	− 427
8	+ 6,000	− 43	+ 5,530

[7]H. Martin Weingartner, "Some New Views on the Payback Period and Capital Budgeting Decisions," *Management Science*, Vol. 15, No. 12, August 1969, p. B-599.

[8]W. G. Lewellen, H. P. Lanser, and J. McConnell, "Payback Substitutes for Discounted Cash Flow," *Financial Management*, Vol. II, No. 2, Summer 1973, present a procedure for establishing a one-to-one conversion of zero-net-present value conditions into counterpart payback maxima. This approach renders the two approaches of discounted cash flow and payback operationally equivalent.

The total investment plus the funds necessary to support the investment are recovered in just over 7 years.   ●

When the payback is used as shown in Example 2, it provides the period of time for the project to just provide a return equal to the cost of capital. The reader may verify this by discounting the expected cash flows to their present value at 10% for the 7-year payback period. We can conclude that the project must remain in use just over 7 years in order for the firm to cover its cost of capital and recover the funds invested in the project.

Since payback, when employed as demonstrated in Example 2, indicates the period for both capital recovery and for recovery of the associated cost of funds, it can be used to advantage for analysis of cataclysmic risk. Such risks would include a major technological change which renders an ongoing process valueless, a sudden plant takeover by a foreign government, and the like. These are risks associated with the possibility of a business going on for a period and then collapsing entirely. Payback then is an all-or-nothing risk indicator and may be used to advantage in assessing risks relative to the time period during which an investment is expected to remain in use. For example, suppose that a firm were considering a project in a foreign country having cash flows in Example 2. Payback shows that if the project remains in use and delivers the expected cash flows for just over 7 years, the firm will not suffer, because it will have met its cost of capital. If the project operates more than 7 years, it will yield a return in excess of the firm's cost of capital. If management could estimate the possibility of the project's expropriation in terms of time from implementation, then payback, as used in Example 2, would provide an excellent cutoff time for risk analysis.

Although payback suffers from some severe limitations, The Conference Board's report indicates that three out of four participants in their study, including all but one company with an annual capital expenditure budget exceeding $500 million, use it typically, as shown in Example 1. Various reasons are attributed to its frequent use.

1. It is very simple.

2. Many managers have severe reservations about the estimates of expected cash flows to be received beyond the next 2 to 5 years and feel from past experience that if they can recover their investment in, say, 3 years, they will make a profit.

3. Many firms have liquidity problems and are very concerned as to how rapidly invested funds will be recovered.

4. Some firms have high costs of external financing and must look to internally generated funds to support their future ventures. Hence, they are especially interested in the rate at which their investment will be recovered.

5. It is a simple matter to compensate for the differences in risk associated with alternative proposed projects: projects having higher degrees of risk are evaluated using shorter payback periods.

6. Some firms are involved in areas where the risk of obsolescence as a result of technical changes and severe competition is great. Therefore, they are anxious to recover funds rapidly.

7. Some firms manufacture products that are subject to model period changes and therefore must recover their investment within the model life.

Automobile manufacturers exemplify such firms. While payback does have severe limitations and is not a measure of profitability, it has been widely accepted for the reasons just described.

We recommend that payback be used as a supplemental evaluation tool, in conjunction with a discounted-cash-flow procedure. When payback is employed as in Example 2, we recommend its use in the following situations:

1. As a measure of a project's liquidity if such liquidity is of particular importance to the firm. Project liquidity should not be confused with profitability or with the firm's overall liquidity preference, as discussed above.

2. For projects involving very uncertain returns, especially when those returns become increasingly more uncertain in future time periods.

3. During periods of very high external financing costs, making capital recovery very important.

4. For projects involving a high degree of cataclysmic risk.

5. For projects subject to model-year changes.

RETURN ON INVESTMENT

The return-on-investment method compares the yearly after-tax (or pre-tax) income with the investment in the asset. The underlying idea is to compare the return expected to be received from a project with some preestablished requirement. Pflomm[9] notes four methods in common use (see Exhibit 5-1). The simplest is to divide the average annual income by the total investment, as shown. The three other methods noted by Pflomm are also shown in the figure.

In each calculation, the income figure refers to additional after-tax profits and may include depreciation cash throw-offs or may be net of those throw-offs. It is important for management to be aware of the differences in the potential results based on the procedure used. The investment refers to the actual after-tax out-of-pocket cash flow and may or may not include the required additional working capital.

The primary shortcoming of all the rate of return procedures is that they do not consider the timing of the expected cash inflows. Thus, a project having low initial inflows and high future inflows would have the same average return as a project having the inflows in the reverse order. The former project would have much less value to the firm than the latter. The difference between the average rate of return and the project's internal rate of return becomes increasingly significant for projects having relatively large inflows in the latter years of their lives.

A second fault is much more insidious and warrants special attention, as it demonstrates some very important aspects of capital expenditure management. The real value of any asset to a firm is a function of management's ability to employ the asset in a productive manner. The firm's balance sheet (which indicates the book value of assets) is only a listing of the investments that the firm has made and the sources of capital used to obtain and maintain those

[9]N. E. Pflomm, *Managing Capital Expenditures* (New York: Conference Board, 1963).

EXHIBIT 5-1 Return on Investment Computed by Four Different Methods

Proposal—Bench Lathe

Investment	$1,000.00
Estimated useful life	5 years
Income: Year 1	300.00
" 2	300.00
" 3	300.00
" 4	300.00
" 5	300.00
Total	$1,500.00

Return-on-Investment Computations

Method 1: Annual Return on Investment:

$$\frac{\text{annual income}}{\text{original investment}} \times 100 = \frac{300}{1{,}000} \times 100 = 30\%$$

Method 2: Annual Return on Average Investment:

$$\frac{\text{annual income}}{\dfrac{\text{original investment}}{2}} \times 100 = \frac{300}{500} \times 100 = 60\%$$

Method 3: Average Return on Average Investment:

$$\frac{\text{total income} - \text{original investment}}{\dfrac{\text{original investment}}{2} \times \text{years}} \times 100 = \frac{500}{\dfrac{1{,}000}{2} \times 5 \text{ years}} \times 100 = 20\%$$

Method 4: Average Book Return on Investment:

$$\frac{\text{total income} - \text{original investment}}{\text{weighted average investment}^{a}}$$

$$= \frac{500}{\dfrac{1{,}000 + 800 + 600 + 400 + 200}{5} \times 5 \text{ years}} \times 100 = 16\tfrac{2}{3}\%$$

[a] Sum of book values of asset each year, straight-line depreciation over life of the project.
Source: N. E. Pflomm, *Managing Capital Expenditures* (New York: The Conference Board, 1963).

investments. The amounts listed on the balance sheet reflect accounting values, which may differ substantially from both market values and productive values. *Since the balance-sheet book values neither reflect the value of assets in terms of their earning ability nor their market value, the return-on-investment method may be extremely misleading.* Consider, for example, an apartment house having an original cost of $1 million 10 years ago, currently producing cash inflows (after-tax profits plus depreciation cash throw-offs) of $250,000 per year, and having a book value of $500,000. Based on the book value, the rate of return would be 50%. However, experience indicates that apartment house values, in general, have doubled over the last 10 years, so that the fair market value is probably close to $2 million. A $250,000 return on a $2 million investment is only 12.5%. This simple example clearly demonstrates two important facts: the rate-of-return method may give very misleading results and, in any capital investment problem, it is the fair market value or the productive value of the asset to the firm, not the book value, which must be considered. The book value is not relevant because it just represents sunk costs and only comes into play when computing the tax impact of investments.

The Conference Board's survey indicates that about one-fourth of the firms surveyed use the method, but generally only as a supplemental tool. While rate of return is still used by some firms, we do not recommend it. The results frequently are erroneous, as the rate of return seldom, if ever, indicates the real value or earning power of a project.

SUMMARY

This chapter commenced our study of procedures used to evaluate alternative capital investments. Payback, it was noted, has found a high level of acceptance, primarily as a result of its simplicity, even though in its usual form it suffers from many shortcomings. An alternative form of payback was introduced which does consider the time value of money, thereby overcoming a chief objection to payback. Rate of return is found in many variations. Its use is not recommended since the results frequently differ substantially from an investment's internal rate of return. In the next chapters, discounted-cash-flow procedures will be examined and compared.

PROBLEMS

1. A corporation plans to invest funds in a new machine. The initial after-tax cash outflow amounts to $10,000 and yearly cash inflows over its 6-year life are $2,200. Determine the payback period for the machine.

2. A certain project has yearly after-tax cash outflows and inflows as follows:

Year	Outflow	Inflow
Present	−$10,000	0
1	− 5,000	$3,000
2	0	4,000
3–6	0	5,000

Determine the payback period.

3 A corporation has a policy of rejecting any investment that does not result in recovery of cost within 4 years. They are considering three projects

Time	Project A	Project B	Project C
Present	−$10,000	−$12,000	−$3,000
1	4,000	0	500
2	4,000	5,000	500
3	2,000	4,000	500
4	2,000	3,000	2,000
5	2,000	3,000	2,000
6	2,000	3,000	2,000
7	2,000	3,000	2,000

Determine the acceptable projects and rank them by payback period.

4. If a corporation requires a 10% after-tax return on its investments, determine the payback period for each investment listed in Problem 3.
5. The Johnson Company is considering the acquisition of a small company that will fit nicely into their present distribution system and complement present operations. Senior management requires a maximum 9-year payback period. The acquisition cost of the company is $8 million and the company yielded after-tax cash flows of $750,000 in the past year. A 5% after-tax growth rate has been projected. Additionally, the Johnson Company can save $50,000 per year by combining the two distribution systems. Should the acquisition be made assuming that the Johnson Company has a cost of capital of 9%?
6. Obel International Corporation is considering manufacturing a new product line in one of its three plants. The plants are located in the United States, Canada, and Mexico and the cost of capital at each location is 8%, 9%, and 14%, respectively. Expected cash flows at each location are as follows:

Time	United States	Canada	Mexico
Present	− $25,000	− $28,000	− $32,000
1	− 9,000	− 12,000	− 16,000
2	− 6,000	+ 2,000	+ 1,000
3	+ 1,000	+ 8,000	+ 13,000
4	+ 8,000	+ 16,000	+ 18,000
5–10	+ 18,000	+ 18,000	+ 18,000

Provide for management a payback-period chart based on net cash flow from each country and indicate your choice of location.
7. The Green Thumb Sod Company has a required rate of return of 12%. Pete Moss, the company's financial wizard, must decide between two different heavy-duty sod-cutting machines. Sod Cutter A will cost $8,000 to purchase this year, plus an additional $2,000 next year for testing and tuning. After this period, Pete estimates cash inflow generated by the machine will be $3,000 for the next 4 years, $2,000 the next 3 years, and $1,000 per year to the end of its 12-year useful life. Sod Cutter B will cost $15,000, with no additional costs, and is expected to generate an income of $4,000 for the first 3 years, $3,000 the next 6 years, and $900 per year to the end of its 10-year useful life. Which machine should Pete recommend purchasing, assuming that he wants to recover both the capital expenditures and the cost of funds required to support these funds as soon as possible? All cash flows are year-end.
8. A project will provide cash inflows of $1,000 for 10 years. What is the maximum amount that could be invested in the project if capital recovery can take no more than 5 years? The cost of capital is 12%.

6 DISCOUNTED-CASH-FLOW EVALUATION METHODS

The methods of discounted cash flow are based on the concept of discounting cash outflows and inflows to their present value, thus fully considering the time value of money. In this chapter we describe four methods: net present value (NPV), profitability index (PI), internal rate of return (IRR), and annual capital charge.

NET PRESENT VALUE AND PROFITABILITY INDEX

The *present value criterion* for evaluating proposed capital investments involves algebraically summing the present values of the cash outflows required to support an investment with the present value of the cash inflows resulting from operations of the project. The inflows and outflows are discounted to present value using the appropriate discount rate, which may be the firm's cost of capital or another rate developed using capital asset pricing. The *net present value* (NPV) is the difference in the present value of the inflows and outflows:

$$\text{NPV} = \sum_{t=0}^{n} \frac{S_t}{(1 + k)^t} - A_0 \tag{1}$$

where A_0 = present value of the after-tax cost of the project
S_t = cash inflow to be received each period
k = appropriate discount rate (hurdle rate)
t = time period
n = use life of asset

If the project cost is incurred over a period of time, then A_0 represents the present value of those cash outflows and may be expressed as shown in Equation (2):

$$A_0 = \sum_{t=0}^{n} \frac{A_t}{(1 + k)^t} \tag{2}$$

where A_t is the cash outflow in each period.

If the NPV is positive, it means the project is expected to yield a return in excess of the required rate; if the NPV is zero, the yield is expected to exactly equal the required rate; if the NPV is negative, the yield is expected to be less than the required rate. Hence, only those projects that have positive or zero NPVs meet the NPV criterion for acceptance.

The primary difficulty encountered with NPV is in deciding the appropriate rate of return (the hurdle rate) to use in discounting the cash flows. While the firm's cost of capital may be used as the discount rate, there exist questions as to how the cost of capital should be calculated. These are examined in Chapter 11. Also, there may be difficulty involved in obtaining the data needed to perform the calculations, even after the procedural questions are resolved.

The *profitability index* (PI) is the ratio of the present value of the after-tax cash inflows to the outflows. A ratio of 1 or greater indicates that the project in question has an expected yield equal to or greater than the discount rate. The profitability index is a measure of a project's profitability per dollar of investment. As a result, it may be used to rank projects of varying costs and expected economic lives in order of their profitability. But a word of caution is in order. If projects are ranked just by profitability index, the investment in a typewriter might appear better than one in a steel mill. The size of projects is ignored. And, as previously noted, the group of projects having the greatest combined net present value should be selected within the constraints of budget limitations, projects interdependency, mutual exclusivity, and the like.

$$\text{PI} = \frac{\text{present value of cash inflows}}{\text{present value of cash outflows}} \tag{3}$$

$$\text{PI} = \frac{\displaystyle\sum_{t=0}^{n} \frac{S_t}{(1 + k)^t}}{A_0} \tag{4}$$

The relationship among net present value, profitability index, and the required rate of return is as follows:

Net Present Value	Profitability Index	Expected Returns
Negative	Less than 1	Less than required return
Zero	1	Exactly equal to required return
Positive	Greater than 1	Greater than required return

● **EXAMPLE 1** *Net Present Value Calculation*

A corporation owns a machine that has been fully depreciated to $2,000, but has a market value and can be sold for $5,000. A new machine costing $20,000 is available to replace the old machine. It is expected to reduce costs by $3,200 annually while being depreciated to $3,000 salvage value over its 10-year life. If a corporation has a 22% marginal tax rate, a 14% required rate of return, and uses straight-line depreciation, decide if the new machine should be purchased.

Solution: First, calculate the cash outflow required to acquire the new machine.

Purchase price of new machine	$20,000
Less sale price of old machine	− 5,000
Less investment tax credit	− 2,000
Plus tax on sale of used equipment	660
Cash outflow to purchase	$13,660

Next, calculate the increase in annual cash inflows.

	Change in Income Statement	Change in Cash Flows
Reduction in costs	$3,200	$3,200
Increase in depreciation	− 1,700	
Increase in earnings before taxes	1,500	
Increase in tax	− 330	− 330
Increase in earnings after taxes	$1,170	
Increase in cash flow		$2,870

The yearly cash inflows will increase by $2,870. The solution table is shown below, with discount factors from Appendix C.

Solution Table for NPV Using 14% Discount Rate

Time	Amount		Discount Factor	Present Value
Present	− $13,660	×	1.	− $13,660
1–10	2,870	×	5.216116	14,970
10	3,000[a]	×	0.269744	809
			NPV	$ 2,119

[a]Salvage value.

Since the NPV is positive, the machine represents an eligible candidate for purchase. ●

● **EXAMPLE 2** *Present Value with Accelerated Depreciation*

Solve Example 1 using sum-of-the-years'-digits depreciation. The cash outflows are not changed, but the inflows will be. Refer to Appendix B for depreciation factors and determine the annual depreciation.

Solution: Each year's depreciation is computed first.

Year	Depreciable Value	Depreciation Factor (%)	Depreciation
1	$17,000	18.18	$3,091
2		16.37	2,783
3		14.56	2,475
4		12.73	2,164
5		10.91	1,855
6		9.09	1,545
7		7.27	1,236
8		5.46	928
9		3.63	617
10		1.82	309

The cash flows may be found using the following tabular form.

	(1)	(2)	(3) = (1) − (2)	(4) = (3) × 0.22	(5) = (3) − (4)	(6) = (2) + (5)
Year	Reduction in Expenses	Depreci- ation	Net Reduction in Expenses	Increase in Taxes	Increase in Earnings Af- ter Taxes	Increase in Cash Flow
1	$3,200	$3,091	$ 109	$ 24	$ 85	$3,176
2		2,783	417	92	325	3,108
3		2,475	725	160	565	3,040
4		2,164	1,036	228	808	2,972
5		1,855	1,345	296	1,049	2,904
6		1,545	1,655	364	1,291	2,836
7		1,236	1,964	432	1,532	2,768
8		928	2,272	500	1,772	2,700
9		617	2,583	568	2,015	2,632
10		309	2,891	636	2,255	2,564
						$28,700

Note that the total of the yearly cash flows over the life of the project is $28,700, which is exactly the same as using straight-line depreciation in Example 1. However, notice also that the timing of the cash inflows has changed since during the first 5 years of the project's life the inflows exceed the $2,870 annual inflow using straight-line depreciation.

Solution Table for NPV Using 14% Discount Rate

Time	Cash Flow		Discount Factor		Present Value
Present	− $13,600		1	=	− $13,600
1	3,176	×	0.877193	=	2,786
2	3,108	×	0.769468	=	2,392
3	3,040	×	0.674972	=	2,052
4	2,972	×	0.592080	=	1,760
5	2,904	×	0.519369	=	1,508
6	2,836	×	0.455587	=	1,292
7	2,768	×	0.399637	=	1,106
8	2,700	×	0.350559	=	947
9	2,632	×	0.307508	=	809
10	5,564[a]	×	0.269744	=	1,501
			NPV		$2,553

[a]This amount represents the $2,564 from year 10 in the table plus $3,000 salvage value.

The NPV has increased from $2,119, using straight-line depreciation, to $2,553 using sum-of-the-year's-digits depreciation, owing to the favorable changes in the timing of the cash flows. ●

● **EXAMPLE 3** *Ranking Projects Using the Profitability Index*

Three projects have been suggested to a corporation. The after-tax cash flows for each are tabulated below. If the corporation's cost of capital is 12%, rank them in order of profitability.

After-Tax Cash Flows

Time	Project A	Project B	Project C
Present	− $10,000	− $30,000	− $18,000
1	2,800	6,000	6,500
2	3,000	10,000	6,500
3	4,000	12,000	6,500
4	4,000	16,000	6,500

Solution: Each project must be evaluated to obtain the present value of the cash inflows and outflows. The present values of the inflows and outflows are as follows:

	Project A	Project B	Project C
PV of outflows	− $10,000	− $30,000	− $18,000
PV of inflows	10,281	32,040	19,743

The profitability indexes are calculated as follows:

$$PI_A = \frac{\$10,281}{\$10,000} = 1.0281$$

$$PI_B = \frac{\$32,040}{\$30,000} = 1.068$$

$$PI_C = \frac{\$19,743}{\$18,000} = 1.0968$$

The projects would be ranked as follows: *C*, *B*, and *A*. ●

Note that the ranking using profitability indexes measures return per dollar of investment. Thus, although project *B* in Example 3 has the highest NPV, it is not the most profitable per dollar of investment. Rather, project *C* is the most profitable per dollar of investment. Note further that all the projects have positive net present values, and hence all meet the 12% required rate of return.

INTERNAL RATE OF RETURN

By definition, the internal rate of return is that rate which exactly equates the present value of the expected after-tax cash inflows with the present value of the after-tax cash outflows. This is expressed in Equation (5):

$$\sum_{t=0}^{n} \frac{S_t}{(1 + r)^t} = \sum_{t=0}^{n} \frac{A_t}{(1 + r)^t} \tag{5}$$

Where r is the internal rate of return. Thus, at the internal rate of return, the net present value is zero.

Internal rate of return recognizes the time value of money and considers the anticipated revenues over the entire economic (useful) life of an investment, thereby overcoming the two most severe criticisms of payback. Also, it may be easily adjusted so as to compare projects having different degrees of risk: projects having greater risk are required to have greater internal rates of return. However, emphasis is not placed on the liquidity of an investment and, like net present value, it depends greatly on the accuracy of the estimate of future cash inflows.

A 1968 study by Lerner and Rappaport[1] of 163 firms selected from the Fortune 500 indicated that, at that time, less than half used internal rate of return. Their article indicates a trade-off between "orderly and sustained earnings growth, and high rates of growth (profitability) subject to the risk of erratic earnings and stock prices." Some managers felt that adoption of the method could lead to erratic earnings patterns. The Conference Board's[2] 1974 study found that two out of three respondents were using internal rate of return. In explaining why his firm, a motor vehicle manufacturer, uses internal rate of return as one of five methods to evaluate projects, one manager stated:

> Use of discounted cash flow as primary criteria vis-à-vis others recognizes the time value of money and income beyond the payoff period and emphasizes long-term profitability more than liquidity. Also, it is an excellent device for the comparison of alternative investment.

The use of internal rate of return is on the increase, especially by larger firms.

● **EXAMPLE 4**   *Internal Rate of Return*

A new project has an after-tax cost of $10,000 and will result in after-tax cash inflows of $3,000 in year 1, $5,000 in year 2, and $6,000 in year 3. Determine the internal rate of return.

Solution: First, set up a solution table.

Time	Amount		Discount Factor	Present Value
Present	− $10,000	×	1	− $10,000
1	3,000	×	Unknown	Unknown
2	5,000	×	Unknown	Unknown
3	6,000	×	Unknown	Unknown
			NPV	$ 0.00

Since only the sum of the present values of the three cash inflows is known to be $10,000, there is no direct way of obtaining the answer. Therefore, it must be estimated and then checked. In order to make a first estimate of the answer, *it is possible to reconstruct the problem using an average cash inflow each year rather than the exact amounts given.* The average of $3,000, $5,000, and $6,000 is $4,666 per year. Based on the amount of $4,666, we can reconstruct a solution table.

---

[1] E. M. Lerner and A. Rappaport, "Limit DCF in Capital Budgeting," *Harvard Business Review*, September–October 1968.

[2] Patrick J. Davey, *Capital Investments: Appraisals and Limits* (New York: The Conference Board, 1974).

Time	Amount		Discount Factor	Present Value
Present	−$10,000	×	1	−$10,000
1−3	4,666	×	Unknown	10,000
			NPV	$ 0.00

Now there is only one unknown, and this may be found as follows:

$$\$4,666 \times \text{d.f.} = \$10,000$$

$$\text{d.f.} = \frac{\$10,000}{\$ 4,666} = 2.1431$$

The discount factor is 2.1431. To determine the corresponding internal rate of return, refer to Appendix C, fifth column. The closest factor is 2.139917, which corresponds to 19%. Thus, 19% is the estimate to be used in solving the problem. Refer back to the original solution table, and replace the unknown discount factors with the discount factors corresponding to 19%. Then multiply these by the cash inflows to determine the present values. The table is as follows:

Solution Table for NPV Using 19% Discount Rate

Time	Amount		Discount Factor	Present Value
Present	−$10,000	×	1	−$10,000
1	3,000	×	0.840336	2,521
2	5,000	×	0.706165	3,531
3	6,000	×	0.593416	3,560
			NPV	−$ 388

The NPV is negative. This means that the discount factors applied to the inflows are too small. Larger discount factors are obtained by using *lower* rates of return. The solution table for 17% is as follows:

Solution Table for NPV Using 17% Discount Rate

Time	Amount		Discount Factor	Present Value
Present	−$10,000	×	1	−$10,000
1	3,000	×	0.854701	2,564
2	5,000	×	0.730514	3,652
3	6,000	×	0.624371	3,746
			NPV	−$ 38

The NPV is much closer to zero, but still negative. Therefore, the rate of return must be lower than 17%. The solution table for 16% is as follows:

Solution Table for NPV Using 16% Discount Rate

Time	Amount		Discount Factor	Present Value
Present	−$10,000	×	1	−$10,000
1	3,000	×	0.862069	2,586
2	5,000	×	0.743163	3,716
3	6,000	×	0.640658	3,844
			NPV	$ 146

The NPV for 16% is positive. Therefore, we can conclude that the actual internal rate of return is between 16% and 17% and may be found using linear interpolation, as demonstrated in Example 5.   ●

● **EXAMPLE 5**   *Linear Interpolation*

Refer to Example 4 and determine the internal rate of return. The answer lies between 16% and 17%. The NPV's corresponding to those rates are as follows:

Rate of Return	NPV
16%	$146
17%	−$ 38

Solution: The actual rate of return corresponds to NPV = 0. The situation is shown on the graph. The width of the lower scale is $146.00 + $38.00 = $184.00, as shown. The zero value is

$$\frac{\$38}{\$184} = 0.2$$

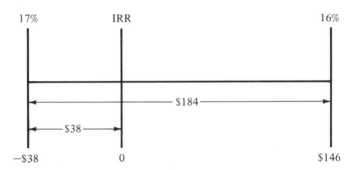

or 0.2 of the way below the 17% point. Therefore, the internal rate of return is 17% − 0.2% = 16.8%.   ●

Once the IRR of a project has been determined, it is a simple matter to compare it with the required rate of return to decide whether or not the project is acceptable. If the IRR equals or exceeds the required rate, the project is acceptable. Ranking the projects is also a simple matter. Projects are ranked according to their IRRs: the project with the highest IRR is ranked first, and so on.

In most instances, the use of either the present value or internal-rate-of-return methods will lead to the same ranking of projects. Differences in ranking are due to the basic differences in the underlying assumptions of the two methods and characteristics of the projects. *The present value method assumes that the cash inflows will be reinvested at the required rate of return. The internal-rate-of-return method assumes that the cash inflows will be reinvested at the calculated internal rate of return.* The discounted-cash-flow methods are extensively examined in Chapter 7 in terms of conflicts in project ranking which may arise owing to differences in projects' sizes and expected lives, as well as timing of cash inflows. Further, multiple internal rates of return are examined.

ANNUAL CAPITAL CHARGE

The annual-capital-charge method involves discounting all the cash in-flows and outflows to present value and determining the equivalent annual charge over the life of the project. The method is of particular importance in the areas of public price regulation such as for utilities. A utility may, for example, construct a power-generating station at great cost. The life and annual operating costs may also be projected. The annual-capital-charge method is used to find the equivalent annual charge that should be made to customers to cover the construction and operating costs, while also providing a required rate of return. The required rate of return may be the firm's cost of capital or another appropriate rate. The process is demonstrated in Example 6.

● **EXAMPLE 6**   *Equivalent Annual Charge*
A utility has spent $10,000,000 on a new facility. Operating costs are expected to be $800,000 per year over its 30-year life. If the utility requires a 9% return, determine the equivalent annual charge.

Solution: The equivalent annual charge consists of two parts: the $800,000 per year and the periodic payment needed to amortize $10,000,000 over 30 years at 9%. For the latter, refer to Appendix C, sixth column.

$$\text{annual charge} = 0.09733635 \times \$10,000,000$$
$$= \$973,363.50$$

The total equivalent annual charge is $973,363.50 plus $800,000 = $1,773,363.50.   ●

In many problems a salvage value or recovery of working capital will be involved. This may be handled easily by multiplying salvage value by the appropriate sinking-fund factor (Appendix C, third column). The product is then subtracted from the annual equivalent charge for the entire cost. The process is demonstrated in Example 7.

● **EXAMPLE 7**   *Equivalent Annual Charge with Salvage Value*
Suppose in Example 6 that the facility had a $1,000,000 salvage value. Recompute the equivalent annual charge.

Solution: First, find the present value of the salvage value:

$$PV = 0.075371 \times \$1,000,000 = \$75,371$$

Second, subtract the present value of the salvage value from the original cost:

$$\$10,000,000 - \$75,371 = \$9,924,629$$

Third, determine the equivalent annual charge:

$$\text{annual charge} = 0.09733635 \times \$9,924,629 = \$966,027.16$$

Last, add the equivalent annual charge to the $800,000 yearly operating cost to obtain the total annual charge:

$$\$800,000 + \$966,027.16 = \$1,766,027.16$$ ●

The equivalent-annual-charge method is also useful for comparing alternatives, which have unequal lives, as demonstrated in Example 8.

● **EXAMPLE 8** *Equivalent Annual Charge*
Two projects which are mutually exclusive have projected cash flows as shown.

Time	Project A	Project B
Present	− $10,000	− $ 8,000
1	− 2,000	− 2,500
2	− 2,000	− 2,500
3	− 2,000	− 2,500
4	− 2,500	− 3,800
5	− 2,500	− 3,800
6	− 2,500	− 3,800
7	− 3,000	
8	− 3,000	
9	− 3,000	
10	− 3,000	

In addition, project A will recover salvage value of $1,500 in year 10 while project B will recover $1,000 in year 6. Determine the equivalent annual charge for each project at 10% required rate of return.

Solution: Consider project A. The equivalent annual charge of the initial cost and salvage value are determined as in Examples 6 and 7.

$$\text{annual charge} = 0.16274539 \times \$10,000$$
$$= \$1,627.45$$
$$\text{equivalent payment} = 0.06274539 \times \$1,500$$
$$= \$94.12$$

The equivalent annual charge of the initial cost less salvage value is $1,533.33.
Next, find the present value of the outflows over the 10-year operating life:

$$\text{present value} = 2.48685 \times \$2,000 + 1.868409$$
$$\times \$2,500 + 1.789306 \times \$3,000$$
$$= \$4,973.70 + \$4,671.02 + \$5,367.92$$
$$= \$15,012.64$$

The present value of the outflows is $15,012.64. The equivalent annual charge is found in the same manner as that used for the initial investment:

$$\text{annual charge} = 0.16274539 \times \$15,012.64$$
$$= \$2,443.24$$

The total equivalent annual charge is, therefore, $1,533.33 + $2,443.24 = $3,976.57.
Consider project B. The equivalent annual charge of the initial cost and salvage value are determined in the same manner as for project A.

$$\text{annual charge} = 0.22960738 \times \$8,000$$
$$= \$1,836.86$$
$$\text{equivalent payment} = 0.12960738 \times \$1,000$$
$$= \$129.61$$

The equivalent annual.charge of the initial cost less the salvage value is $1,707.25. The present value of the outflows is determined as follows:

$$\text{present value} = 2.486852 \times \$2,500 + 1.868409 \times \$3,800$$
$$= \$6,217.13 + \$7,099.95$$
$$= \$13,317.08$$

The present value of the outflows is $13,317.08. The equivalent annual charge is determined below.

$$\text{annual charge} = 0.22960738 \times \$13,317.08$$
$$= \$3,057.70$$

The total equivalent annual charge is therefore $1,707.25 + $3,057.70 = $4,764.95. Project A is clearly superior to project B, as its equivalent annual cost is lower.   ●

The annual-capital-charge method described above is a valuable managerial tool in that it does consider the time value of money and the flows over the entire asset life. Further, it is especially useful in serving as a baseline for setting rate structures as previously indicated, for evaluating nondiscretionary expenditure alternatives that are not profit producing, and for comparing projects having unequal lives. For example, to meet clean water requirements, a firm may have to install pollution control equipment, but there may be choices as to the particular equipment to be installed and its associated operating costs. The annual-capital-charge method is ideal for comparing the costs of alternatives of this type.

SUMMARY

In this chapter we examined the four discounted-cash-flow methods used to evaluate proposed capital expenditures. It was noted that the annual-capital-charge method is especially useful for public utilities, where rate structures are usually based on the annual equivalent of operating and capitalized costs. This procedure is also very useful for examining the costs involved in nondiscretionary expenditures in order to minimize costs.

Net present value, profitability index, and internal rate of return are all useful in evaluating proposed projects in that they fully consider the time value of money. Net present value and profitability index have the shortcoming of necessitating the establishment of a required rate of return to be used as an input in the computations, whereas internal rate of return does not. All methods may be used to rank projects.

The following chapter examines the conditions under which conflicts in project ranking can occur among the methods and how such conflicts should be resolved in order to maximize shareholder wealth.

PROBLEMS

1. The Fisher Beer Company is evaluating two brewing projects. The after-tax cash flows for the alternative proposals are summarized in the table.

Time	Project A	Project B
Present	−$20,000	−$28,000
1	5,000	8,000
2	5,000	8,000
3	6,000	8,000
4	6,000	8,000
5	6,000	8,000

Using a 10% rate, determine the NPV and PI for both projects.

2. Leisure Incorporated is evaluating two investment opportunities and will pick one. Project Fun requires an investment of $10,000, while Project Lazy requires an investment of $19,000. The after-tax cash flows are as follows:

	Cash Flows	
Year	Fun	Lazy
1	$2,000	$4,000
2	3,000	5,000
3	4,000	6,000
4	3,000	4,000
5	3,000	3,000

Determine the NPV of each project at 10% and the profitability index.

3. A new computer can be purchased for $42,000. It is expected to have a useful life of 6 years and zero salvage value. Cash revenues before depreciation and taxes are expected to increase by $9,000 over the life of the computer. Assuming straight-line depreciation, a 12% required return, and 48% marginal tax rate, determine the NPV and IRR.

4. A corporation wants to replace old machinery which originally cost $70,000 and has a $20,000 book value. The new machinery is available for $100,000 and will reduce the operating cost by $19,000 annually. The old machine is fully depreciated and it can be sold for $50,000. The new machine will be depreciated on a straight-line basis over 5 years with a salvage value of $10,000. The corporation has a 48% marginal tax rate and requires at least an 8% return on its investments. Determine the NPV of the new machine. Assume that the old machine is in good working condition and could be kept another 5 years, at which time its salvage value would equal its book value of $20,000.

5. A project costs $75 and will yield after-tax cash flows of $5 in years 1 and 2, $20 in years 3 and 4, and $25 in years 5 to 10. Find the IRR of the project.

6. Referring to Problem 5, determine the equivalent annual inflows which, when discounted at the IRR, will give a NPV of zero.

7. A utility company is considering building a new generating facility for $50,000,000 with inflation-adjusted operating expenses of $1,000,000 annually for 30 years, the life of the installation after completion of construction. The salvage value is estimated at $1,500,000, and construction will take 2 years before the new facility can be brought on line. Consider the cost of construction to represent outflows of $25,000,000 each at the end of the first 2 years. Alternatively, the company can rebuild the present facility for $10,000,000 and reduce annual operating expenses from $2,000,000 to $1,500,000. If this alternative is chosen, power will have to be bought from a network grid for a year at a cost of $30,000,000 until the work is finished. Consider the costs of construction and purchase of power to be paid in

equal installments at the start and end of the current year. This rebuilding project has an expected life of 15 years after rebuilding with no salvage value. Ignore investment tax credits and depreciation and determine the equivalent annual cost of each project based on a 7% return.

8. A firm has to choose from among three weaving machines, which will replace an existing machine. The new machines, *A*, *B*, and *C*, cost $5,000, $7,000, and $10,000, respectively, and each has a 10-year life. The old machine, which will be sold, has a market value of $2,000, a book value of $1,000, and has been fully depreciated. The firm uses straight-line depreciation. Each new machine has different features and different expected after-tax cash flows. Machine *A* is expected to produce additional revenues of $1,5000 per year; machine *B*, $2,000; and machine *C*, $3,500. Finally, the salvage value of each machine is $1,000, zero, and $1,500, respectively. The firm's marginal tax rate is 48% and the discount rate is 10%. Determine the NPV for each machine and the associated profitability index.

9. Inner City Memorial Hospital has been plagued with continuous operating deficits. Based on a study made by an outside consulting firm, it is decided that the deficits are due to the outdated structure of the current facility. The hospital's consultants have made the following recommendation. They indicated that they can update the current facility for $10,000,000. With these renovations the hospital's annual budget will be $8,000,000. They also state that they can build an entirely new facility for $15,000,000. This new facility would have an annual operating budget of $7,000,000. A state health care planner has been called in to decide which project would be less costly to the consumer. The planner has accumulated the following facts:

   (1) Both projects would have a useful life of 25 years with no salvage value.
   (2) Expenses are expected to increase equally over the years for both projects due to inflation.
   (3) A 10% discount rate is assumed.
   Prepare an analysis that would indicate the least costly alternative.

10. An investor paid $65,000 for a duplex that he intends to keep 5 years and then sell. The first year he knows that he will have to spend a considerable amount for repairs. If he desires a 9% after-tax return and the cash flows are as tabulated below, will he achieve this return? Determine the net present value and profitability index.

Year	Cash Flows
1	$-\$\ \ \ 100$
2	4,900
3	5,300
4	4,800
5	74,500

7 CONFLICTS IN PROJECT RANKING AND THEIR RESOLUTION

The methods of ranking capital proposals illustrated in Chapter 6 rest upon certain assumptions which also describe the limitations of each model. Therefore, unless the analyst comprehends the assumptions supporting the conclusions, he may be entrapped by the model. With the same data base, different ranking methods can produce disparate orders of preference when evaluating mutually exclusive projects. *The resolution of such conflicts is simple: ascertain which model's assumptions are most consistent with the facts of the project as well as the goals and circumstances of the business and follow the recommendations of this model.*

Since the different methods of ranking can produce contrary recommendations and since the future cash flows will in some degree vary from the forecasted amounts, the prudent financial manager evaluates his projects using two or more techniques of ranking. Each method highlights something significant about the financial dimensions of the project. This procedure gives a more complete picture of the projects under consideration than could be obtained by using a single approach, and conflicts in rankings point to the need for further investigation. Conflicts in ranking mutually exclusive projects may result from a difference in the original investment required by the projects, disparate cash-flow patterns, or a lack of comparability due to unequal useful lives. Examination of these aspects provides additional insight into the intricacies of the evaluation techniques as well as the suitability of the various projects under consideration.

In this chapter we shall examine the sources of possible conflicts in ranking, their resolution, and the general question of project comparability. Our analyses commence with a classification of projects. Next, we review the assumptions made by the methods treated in Chapter 6. Then, we examine projects having size disparities, time disparities, and unequal useful lives. Last, as a preview of the treatment in later chapters, we examine the necessity of considering portfolios of projects and the impact of multiple goals on the capital budgeting decision process; that is, we show that it may be desirable to select a set of projects that does not provide maximum net present value because of the importance of reported earnings stability and growth, financial statement presentation, and other objectives. As an appendix we examine the problems of multiple internal rates of return.

CLASSIFICATION OF PROJECTS

The construction of a capital budget must take note of interrelationships among proposed projects. If the acceptance or rejection of one project does not affect the cash flows of another project, the two are said to be *independent*. On the other hand, dependency effects occur whenever the cash flows of one project influence or are influenced by the cash flows of another. Three situations involving dependency warrant examination:

1. *Mutually exclusive projects.* If the acceptance of one project precludes the acceptance of another project, the two are mutually exclusive. An airline pondering the future of its fleet may have to choose between the slower 747, which has a larger seating capacity, and the SST, which has a lower passenger capacity but supersonic speed.

2. *Complementary projects.* If the acceptance of one project enhances the cash flows of another project, the two are complementary. Thus, the cash flows from an automobile service station on a superhighway might be increased by the construction of restaurant facilities.

3. *Prerequisite or contingent projects.* If the acceptance of one project depends upon the prior acceptance of another project, the acceptance of the former is prerequisite to the acceptance of the latter. The construction of an oil refinery at a given location may depend upon the prior commitment to construct port facilities.

Obviously, dependent projects must be presented together if the manager is to consider the full range of alternatives. In this respect, one of the major problems in capital budgeting lies in the identification of all viable alternatives. *The ranking process is relative and any capital project may appear attractive when compared against a sufficiently poor alternative.* Throughout this chapter as well as in several subsequent chapters, we will see that the various types of project dependencies play an important role.

Some projects are mandatory; they must be accepted if the firm wishes to remain in business. Others are discretionary, acceptable if financially attractive. Utilities, for example, are required by law to make investments needed to provide service on demand, even though more rewarding projects may be available. For the telephone company, switching equipment would fall into the mandatory category while the installation of new, lower-cost generating equipment would constitute a discretionary investment. On the other hand, *the evaluation of mandatory investments does not exclude the possibility of abandonment, based on a discounted cash-flow analysis. One has the option of going out of business.*

THE ASSUMPTIONS REVIEWED

At this point in our discussion, it is beneficial to review and formally state the underlying assumptions to the capital budgeting techniques which were illustrated in Chapters 5 and 6. The most important assumptions include the following:

1. *Projects being evaluated have the same risk posture as the firm overall.*

2. *The firm's cost of capital is constant over time and is not affected by the amount of funds that is invested in capital projects.*

3. Investment opportunities are independent of each other. There are no interrelationships among projects under consideration (mutually exclusive, contingent, and complementary projects do not exist), *and there is no correlation between the cash flows of any pair of projects under consideration by the firm* or between the cash flows of any project and the on-going operations of the firm.

4. Borrowing and lending rates are equal, which means that the rate that must be paid by the firm to obtain capital from the capital markets (borrowing) is equal to the rate the firm can earn if it purchases securities in the capital markets (lending).

5. Perfect capital markets exist, which means that (a) no lender or borrower in the markets possesses sufficient power to influence prices; (b) any participant in the markets can lend or borrow as much as desired without affecting security prices (i.e., there is not an upward-sloping supply curve for capital); (c) bankruptcy and transaction costs do not exist; (d) all participants in the markets have access to the same cost-free information, this information is interpreted in exactly the same way by all participants, and such information is immediately incorporated into all security prices; and (e) capital rationing does not exist.

6. Investment decisions are independent of consumption decisions over time. Of course, several of these assumptions differ from the reality faced by decision makers. Our discussion in this and a number of subsequent chapters will relax most of these assumptions. For example, in the present Chapter we will explore the relaxation of assumptions 2 and 3. Assumptions 1 and 3 will be relaxed in Chapters 8, 9, 10, and 14, and assumptions 2, 4, and 5 will be relaxed in Chapters 11, 13, and 14. Assumptions 4 and 5 relate primarily to the capital asset pricing model, which will be examined in depth in Chapter 10.

In addition to the assumptions listed above, recall from Chapter 6 that *the internal rate of return (IRR) implicitly assumes that intermediate cash flows over the life of the project can be reinvested at the IRR for the project under consideration while the net present value (NPV) and the profitability index (PI) techniques implicitly assume that the intermediate cash flows can be reinvested at the required rate of return or the cost of capital.* Further, the PI measures the discounted cash inflow per dollar of discounted cash outflow while the NPV measures the magnitude of the difference between discounted cash inflows and outflows.

Given the six assumptions cited above, conflicts can arise among IRR, NPV, and PI in the way which the three approaches rank mutually exclusive investment opportunities *due to the reinvestment assumption and due to differences between the absolute dollar value measured by NPV vs. the relative profitability per dollar of discounted cash outflow measured by PI.* Specifically, *conflicts could arise* among IRR, NPV, and PI when:

1. A size disparity exists between (or among) the cash outflows required by the mutually exclusive projects under consideration.

2. A time disparity exists between (or among) the cash inflows generated by the mutually exclusive projects under consideration.

3. A disparity exists in the useful lives of the mutually exclusive projects under consideration.

Two important points should be further stressed. *First, notice that it was mentioned that two or more mutually exclusive projects are required in order to have even the chance of a conflict among NPV, PI, and IRR.* This is the case because if we had only one investment project under consideration (wherein the cash flows are "conventional," i.e., one or more cash outflows followed by an uninterrupted series of cash inflows until the end of the project's useful life), all three of the methods would consistently signal to either accept or reject the project. Notice the NPV profile for a conventional investment project shown in Exhibit 7-1, where the net present value has been computed at several discount rates. Assuming that the firm's cost of capital (i.e., required rate of return) is 15%, we see that NPV equals $427.49, which signals that the project is attractive. This necessarily means that PI must exceed 1, since $PI = \dfrac{\text{discounted cash inflows}}{\text{discounted cash outflows}}$ and NPV = discounted cash inflows − discounted cash outflows. For project A, NPV = $427.49 ($1,427.49 in discounted cash inflows less $1,000 in discounted cash outflows) and PI = 1.42749 = $1,427.49/$1,000.00. Furthermore, since NPV at the cost of capital is positive, we know that the IRR must exceed the cost of capital because the only way that NPV can be equated to zero (which is the internal rate of return by definition) is to use a larger discount rate. For project A, the IRR is slightly less than 35% (where the NPV profile crosses the horizontal axis), which certainly exceeds the 15% cost of capital. Therefore, for a single conventional investment project, all three of the discounted-cash-flow

EXHIBIT 7-1   NPV Profile For Project *A*

Year	Cash Flows	Discount Rate (%)	NPV
0	− $1,000	0	$1,000.00
1	+ 500	5	772.98
2	+ 500	10	584.93
3	+ 500	15	427.49
4	+ 500	20	294.37
		25	180.80
		30	83.12
		35	− 1.53
		40	− 75.39

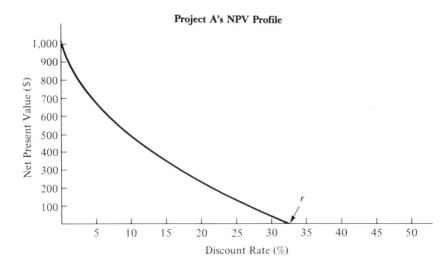

Project A's NPV Profile

techniques (NPV, IRR, PI) will give consistent accept or reject decisions. Furthermore multiple independent conventional investment projects can be considered and evaluated one at a time, and again all three of the techniques will render the same "go" or "no go" signals.

The second point is that even if we have two or more mutually exclusive projects and even if one of the three disparities (size, time, or useful life) exists, there may or may not be a conflict between the rankings given the projects by NPV, PI, and IRR. Consider Figure 7-1. Notice that figure (a) shows that project B dominates project C, in that the former's NPV profile is everywhere above the NPV profile of the latter; thus, project B will have a greater NPV and PI than project C, regardless of what the cost of capital is and project B also has a higher IRR than project C. In figure (b), the NPV profiles of projects D and E are tangent only at one point, but project D's profile is everywhere else above project E and project D has a higher IRR; thus, again there will be no conflict between the rankings given D and E by the three techniques. In figure (c), we see that (1) the profiles for projects F and G have a single point of

FIGURE 7-1 Examples of NPV Profiles for Three Sets of Two Mutually Exclusive Projects

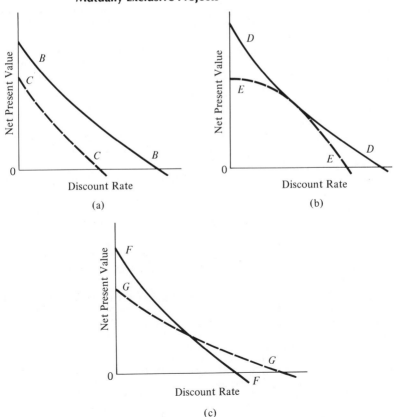

TABLE 7-1 Possible Conflicts Among NPV, PI, And IRR

Possible Conflict / Type of Disparity	NPV vs. PI	PI vs. IRR			NPV vs. IRR		
		Intersection[a]		No Intersection[b]	Intersection[a]		No Intersection[b]
		$k < r'$	$k \geqslant r'$		$k < r'$	$k \geqslant r'$	
Size	Could be a conflict	Could be	Could be	Could be	Yes	No	No
Time	Never could be a conflict	Yes	No	No	Yes	No	No
Useful life							
(a) and size disparity	Could be a conflict	Could be	Could be	Could be	Yes	No	No
(b) and no size disparity	Never could be a conflict	Yes	No	No	Yes	No	No

[a] "Intersection" means that there is a unique point r' where the two NPV profiles cross in the first quadrant, as shown in Figure 7-1 (c). r' is the discount rate at which the unique intersection of NPV profiles occurs; k is the firm's cost of capital (assumed to remain constant over the life of the projects under consideration).

[b] "No intersection" means that the two NPV profiles do not cross in the first quadrant, as shown in Figure 7-1 (a), or that there is a single tangency point, as shown in Figure 7-1 (b);

intersection, (2) the NPV for project F at a zero discount rate is greater than the NPV at a zero discount rate for project G, and (3) the IRR for project G is greater than the IRR for project F.[1] Under these conditions, *there will be a conflict between NPV and IRR if the firm's cost of capital is less than the discount rate at which the intersection in NPV profiles occurs.* Under these conditions, *there may be a conflict between NPV and PI only if there is a size disparity between projects F and G, and there will be a conflict between PI and IRR only if NPV and PI agree in their rankings of the projects.* Table 7-1 summarizes our discussion thus far in terms of when conflicts could arise between the three techniques.

Several authors have addressed the problem of the existence and uniqueness of the Fisherian intersection.[2] There could be zero, one, or multiple intersections between two NPV profiles. However, we shall limit our attention to cases wherein there are zero or one intersection, since these are the more usual cases.

We now turn to a discussion of the three major types of disparities and how conflicts caused thereby among NPV, PI, and IRR can be resolved.

[1] It should be noted that the point of intersection has been called the "rate of return over cost" or the "Fisherian intersection," since many of the conflicts among NPV, PI, and IRR were first pointed out by Irving Fisher in his *The Rate of Interest* (New York: Macmillan Publishing Co., Inc., 1907); and *The Theory of Interest* (New York: Macmillan Publishing Co., Inc., 1930).

[2] See J. C. T. Mao, "The Internal Rate of Return as a Ranking Criterion," *The Engineering Economist*, Summer 1966, pp. 1–13; J. C. T. Mao, *Quantitative Analysis of Financial Decisions* (New York: Macmillan Publishing Co., Inc., 1969), Chap. 7; W. H. Jean, *The Analytical Theory of Finance* (New York: Holt, Rinehart and Winston, Inc., 1970), Chap. 2; and E. F. Fama and M. H. Miller, *The Theory of Finance* (New York: Holt, Rinehart and Winston, Inc., 1972), Chap. 3.

SIZE DISPARITY BETWEEN PROJECTS

Frequently, management must analyze mutually exclusive projects that require differing magnitudes of discounted cash outflows (i.e., a size disparity exists between or among the projects). Under such conditions there *could be* conflicts in the rankings assigned the various projects by NPV, PI, and IRR. The major reason that such conflicts exist is that NPV measures the absolute magnitude of the excess of discounted cash inflows over discounted cash outflows (which could favor larger investments), whereas PI measures relative profitability of the discounted cash inflows per dollar of discounted cash outflow, and IRR measures the compounded rate of return earned on the original investment or the discount rate, which equates discounted cash inflows to discounted cash outflows (both of the latter techniques usually favor smaller investments). Consider Example 1, which illustrates a size disparity.

● **EXAMPLE 1** *A Size Disparity Between Two Projects*
A firm that has a 12% cost of capital is evaluating two mutually exclusive projects, X and Y, which have the following characteristics:

	Project X	Project Y
Original investment	$500,000	$100,000
Cash inflows each year	$150,000	$ 40,000
Useful life	10 yr	10 yr

Compute the NPV, PI, and IRR for these two projects and sketch their NPV profiles on the same graph.

Solution:

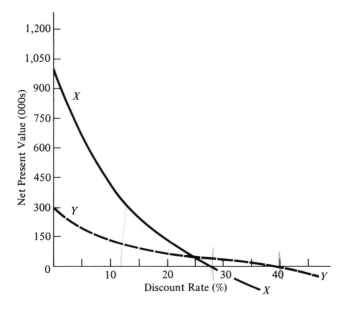

	Project X	Project Y
Cash inflows discounted at 12%	$847,533.45	$226,008.92
Cash outflow	$500,000.00	$100,000.00
NPV	$347,533.45	$126,008.92
Rank by NPV	1	2
P.I.	1.695	2.26
Rank by P.I.	2	1
IRR	27.32%	38.45%
Rank by IRR	2	1

As can be seen, NPV prefers project X, while both PI and IRR prefer project Y. Sketching the two NPV profiles would yield the accompanying graph. We know that project X passes through the NPV values of $1,000,000 at 0%, $347,533.45 at 12%, and $0 at 27.32%. Project Y, on the other hand, passes through the NPV values of $300,000 at 0%, $126,008.92 at 12%, and $0 at 38.45%. The Fisher's intersection occurs between 24% and 25% with an NPV of $45,454. (Check these values; more will be said momentarily about how they were determined.)   ●

In Example 1, the question would naturally arise: How is the conflict between NPV and PI and IRR resolved? The resolution depends upon what conditions are faced by the firm in making its capital expenditure decisions. *If all six of the assumptions cited in the previous section are present, then the conflict should be resolved in favor of the preferred project using NPV since (as will be demonstrated later in the chapter) the set of projects that maximizes NPV will also maximize shareholders' wealth, that is, the market price of the common stock.*

Under the more likely case that some of the assumptions are not met, we must modify this general rule. *If capital rationing exists (which violates the perfect capital market assumption), we must evaluate the returns on the incremental investment in the larger project. If the incremental investment required by the larger project is available and if it offers a positive NPV at the appropriate hurdle rate, the larger project should be considered for acceptance. The larger project should be accepted if the incremental investment in the larger project cannot be placed into another project or projects which offers a greater aggregate NPV at the appropriate hurdle rate.* This process is illustrated in Example 2.

● **EXAMPLE 2**   *Resolution of Conflicts in Size Disparity*

Consider again the two mutually exclusive projects from Example 1. For the incremental investment in project X, compute the NPV, PI, and IRR.

Solution:

	Project X	Project Y	Incremental Flows, $X - Y$
Original investment	$500,000	$100,000	$400,000
Cash inflows each year	$150,000	$ 40,000	$110,000
NPV at 12%			$221,524.53
PI			1.554
IRR			24.4%

Notice that all three of the techniques would rate the incremental investment as being justified; NPV is positive ($221,524.53); PI is 1.554, which exceeds 1.0; and IRR is

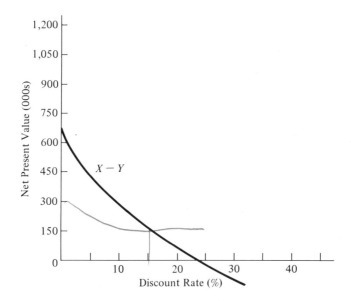

24.4%, which exceeds the 12% hurdle rate. Thus, all three of the techniques would consistently argue that the incremental investment of $400,000 in project X is justified by the incremental returns generated. Finally, project X would be accepted if alternatives available for the commitment of the incremental $400,000 would not generate an aggregate NPV of more than $221,524.53. This is equivalent to saying that if all the firm can invest is $500,000, then project X should be accepted unless some other feasible combination of projects generates an NPV in excess of $347,533.45 (the NPV for project X).

In concluding this example, consider the NPV profile of the incremental investment $X - Y$. As might be expected, this profile is merely the geometric difference between the profiles for project X and project Y. Notice that the IRR (24.4%) for the incremental project is precisely equal to rate of return over cost (Fisher's intersection). It is often much easier to find the IRR for the incremental project than it is to solve for the rate of return over cost (designated r') directly. The former strategy was used in Example 1 to determine (r'). To solve for r' directly for projects X and Y would require solution of the following equation for r':

$$\text{NPV of project } X \text{ at } r' = \text{NPV of project } Y \text{ at } r'$$

$$-\$500,000 + \sum_{t=1}^{10} \frac{\$150,000}{(1 + r')^t} = -\$100,000 + \sum_{t=1}^{10} \frac{\$40,000}{(1 + r')^t}$$

The solution of this equation is simplified by the equal annual cash inflows, which enables the use of the present value of an annuity factor. Notice that upon simplification the preceding expression becomes

$$\sum_{t=1}^{10} \frac{\$150,000 - \$40,000}{(1 + r')t} = \$400,000$$

This is exactly the IRR of the incremental investment in project X.   ●

We next turn to difficulties encountered in the time-disparity problem.

NPV & PI always the same w/
Time disparity.

TIME DISPARITY BETWEEN PROJECTS

In addition to projects that vary as to size of original investment, firms often have to evaluate mutually exclusive projects wherein differences exist with respect to the sequence of the time of cash inflows. These time disparities, coupled with differing implicit assumptions about the rate of return that can be earned on intermediate cash inflows, can lead to conflicts in ranking between NPV (or PI) and IRR (recall that under time disparities, NPV and PI will always produce consistent project rankings, since the two methods make the same reinvestment assumption). Example 3 illustrates a time disparity between two projects.

● **EXAMPLE 3** *A Time Disparity Between Two Projects*

A firm whose cost of capital is 10% is considering two mutually exclusive projects, A and B, whose characteristics are as follows:

	Project A	Project B
Investment	$ 70,000	$ 70,000
Cash flows		
Period 1	10,000	50,000
Period 2	20,000	40,000
Period 3	30,000	20,000
Period 4	45,000	10,000
Period 5	60,000	10,000
Total cash flows	$165,000	$130,000

Compute the NPV, PI, and IRR for the two projects and sketch their NPV profiles.

Solution:

	Project A	Project B
Discounted cash inflows at 10%	$116,150.16	$106,578.03
NPV	$ 46,150.16	$ 36,578.03
PI	1.659	1.523
IRR	27.2%	37.55%

Notice that project B has a significantly higher IRR than project A, but at the firm's cost of capital, project B has a significantly lower NPV than project A. *The IRR technique favors projects that have high cash inflows early in the life of the project (i.e., such cash flows significantly increase the internal rate of return because it is assumed that they can be reinvested at this higher rate). The NPV method, on the other hand, assumes reinvestment at a lower rate (i.e., the firm's cost of capital) and hence assesses a smaller penalty for cash inflows received later in the project's life compared to the IRR technique.* Project A has greater cash inflows ($165,000) over its life than project B ($130,000), and at lower reinvestment rates (such as the cost of capital) this difference more than compensates for the bulk of the cash inflows occurring in the last 2 years of its useful life. Thus, the NPV profiles for the two projects demonstrate that project A is preferred to B at all discount rates less than 16.1%. Fisher's intersection occurs at approximately 16.1%, which, as we shall see, will play an important role in resolving the conflict between NPV and IRR. ●

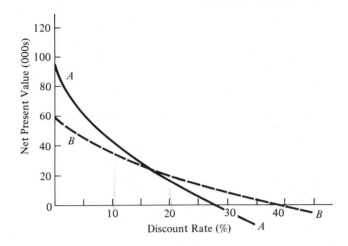

Net Present Value (000s)

Discount Rate (%)

The compound interest process of the internal rate and present value methods assumes that at the end of each period the cash inflow (including both recovery of principal and return on investment) is reinvested from period to period at a relevant rate. In particular, NPV assumes that the funds are reinvested at the discount rate applied to the project (usually a weighted cost of capital). By contrast, the IRR approach assumes that the funds are reinvested at the project's internal rate of return. If cash inflows can be reinvested at a rate that exceeds the firm's cost of capital, the NPV method understates the value of the investment. Conversely, if the cash flows can only be reinvested at a rate below the internal rate of return, the IRR model overstates the true rate of return on the project.

The conflict between NPV and IRR demonstrated in Example 3 (which can occur when a time disparity exists between mutually exclusive projects) can be resolved by explicitly incorporating a reinvestment rate into both the NPV and IRR approaches. This is accomplished by calculating the terminal value of the project, given that intermediate cash inflows can be reinvested at a specified rate. Then, the terminal value can be discounted to the present value using the NPV method; similarly, the true internal rate of return can be found by ascertaining the discount rate that equates the terminal value to the discounted cash outflows. The *terminal value* (TV) for a given project is determined using Equation (1):

$$TV = \sum_{t=1}^{n} S_t(1 + i)^{n-t} \qquad (1)$$

where S_t = cash inflow from the project that occurs at the end of period t
 i = reinvestment rate
 n = useful life of the project

Of course, the terminal value is merely the sum of the cash inflows compounded out to the end of the life of the project at the reinvestment rate i.

The *modified NPV method* (NPV*) would employ Equation (2):

$$NPV^* = \frac{TV}{(1 + k)^n} - A_0 \qquad (2)$$

where k = firm's cost of capital

A_0 = discounted cash outflow associated with the project

It should be pointed out that NPV* relaxes assumption 4 cited earlier in the chapter wherein equal borrowing and lending rates were posited (i.e., the reinvestment rate i no longer is implicitly assumed to be equal to the firm's cost of capital k).

The *modified IRR method* (IRR*) would be implemented using Equation (3):

$$\frac{TV}{(1 + r^*)^n} - A_0 = 0 \tag{3}$$

where r^* is the true rate of return on the project given that the cash inflows from the project can be reinvested at the rate i used in determining TV.

Given these modifications to the NPV and IRR models, conflicts in project rankings that could arise when a time disparity exists will be eliminated. This is demonstrated in Example 4.

● **EXAMPLE 4**   Resolution of Conflict in Time Disparities

For projects A and B shown in Example 3, determine TV, NPV*, IRR*, and the preferred project assuming the following reinvestment rates: (a) 14% and (b) 20%.

Solution: (a) Assuming a reinvestment rate of 14%, the terminal value for projects A and B are:

$$TV_A = 10,000(1.14)^4 + 20,000(1.14)^3 + 30,000(1.14)^2$$
$$+ 45,000(1.14)^1 + 60,000(1.14)^0$$

Using the compound interest factors from the first column on the 14% page in Appendix D:

$$TV_A = \$10,000(1.688960) + \$20,000(1.481544) + \$30,000(1.299600)$$
$$+ \$45,000(1.14) + \$60,000$$
$$= \$196,808.48$$

$$TV_B = \$50,000(1.688960) + \$40,000(1.481544) + \$20,000(1.299600)$$
$$+ \$10,000(1.14) + \$10,000$$
$$= \$191,101.76$$

Given that these two projects have equal costs of $70,000, we can see that project A is clearly superior at a reinvestment rate of 14%, since its terminal value exceeds that of project B by more than $5,700. Proceeding with our calculations:

$$NPV_A^* = \frac{\$196,808.48}{(1.10)^5} - \$70,000$$
$$= \$196,808.48(0.620921) - \$70,000$$
$$= \$52,202.58$$

$$NPV_B^* = \frac{\$191,101.76}{(1.10)^5} - \$70,000$$

$$= \$191,101.76(0.620921) - \$70,000$$

$$= \$48,659.16$$

$$IRR_A^* \Rightarrow \frac{\$196,808.48}{(1 + r_A^*)^5} - \$70,000 = 0$$

$$\$196,808.48 = \$70,000(1 + r_A^*)^5$$

Therefore,

$$(1 + r_A^*)^5 = 2.8155$$

Look for a factor of 2.81155 in the first column on year 5 in Appendix C. Therefore,

$$r_A^* \doteq 23\%$$

$$IRR_B^* \Rightarrow \frac{\$191,101.76}{(1 + r_B^*)^5} - \$70,000 = 0$$

$$\$191,101.76 = \$70,000(1 + r_B^*)^5$$

Therefore,

$$(1 + r_A^*)^5 = 2,811.55$$

Look for a factor of 2.73003 in the first column on year 5 in Appendix C. Therefore,

$$r_B^* \doteq 22\%$$

Notice the dramatic drop in the true rate of return on project B—from—37.55%, its internal rate, which assumed reinvestment of cash flows at that rate, to about 22% when the reinvestment rate is assumed to be 14%.

We now see that $NPV_A^* > NPV_B^*$ and $IRR_A^* > IRR_B^*$, so project A is clearly the more desirable project if intermediate cash inflows can be reinvested at 14%.

(b) Under the assumption that cash flows can be reinvested at 20% [quite a different case than that handled in part (a)], we obtain the following results:

$$TV_A = \$10,000(2.0736) + \$20,000(1.7280) + \$30,000(1.44)$$

$$+ \$45,000(1.20) + \$60,000$$

$$= \$212,496.00$$

$$TV_B = \$50,000(2.0736) + \$40,000(1.7280) + \$20,000(1.44)$$

$$+ \$10,000(1.20) + \$10,000$$

$$= \$223,600.00$$

As in part (a), these terminal values are sufficient for us to conclude that project B is clearly superior at a reinvestment rate of 20%, since its terminal value exceeds that of project A by over \$11,100 and the original costs of the two projects are equal. This will be reflected in both NPV* and IRR*:

$$NPV_A^* = \frac{\$212,496.00}{(1.10)^5} - \$70,000$$

$$= \$61,943.30$$

$$\text{NPV}_B^* = \frac{\$223,600.00}{(1.10)^5} - \$70,000$$

$$= \$68,838.00$$

$$\text{IRR}_A^* \Rightarrow \frac{\$212,496}{(1 + r_A^*)^5} - \$70,000 = 0$$

Therefore,

$$r_A^* \doteq 24.87\%$$

$$\text{IRR}_B^* \Rightarrow \frac{\$223,600.00}{(1 + r_B^*)^5} - \$70,000 = 0$$

Therefore,

$$r_B^* \doteq 26.2\%$$

In this case we see that $\text{NPV}_A^* < \text{NPV}_B^*$ and $\text{IRR}_A^* < \text{IRR}_B^*$, so project B is clearly the more desirable project if intermediate cash flows can be reinvested at 20%.   •

An important generalization can be made based on the results of Example 4. *Given the NPV profiles of two projects, the preferred project will be the one having the greater NPV at the discount rate corresponding to the rate at which cash inflows can be reinvested; hence, Fisher's intersection plays a key role in that it is the point at which project preference changes. This provides important information in doing sensitivity analysis on reinvestment rates.* In Examples 3 and 4, we can conclude that as long as the reinvestment rate on cash inflows throughout the life of either project does not exceed 16.1% (Fisher's intersection), project A is preferred; if the reinvestment rate exceeds 16.1%, project B is preferred. These conclusions are consistent with the rankings using the terminal values that can be computed for the projects as well as NPV* and IRR*.

Our discussion up to this point has assumed that the reinvestment rate, i, and the firm's cost of capital k, remain constant throughout all future periods. However, it could very well be that both of these rates will change in the future. If this occurs, the equations presented above for NPV, TV, and NPV* must be modified.

If the cost of capital is expected to change in the future, the method of finding the net present value for a project is shown in Equation (4):

$$\text{NPV} = \sum_{t=1}^{n} \frac{S_t}{\prod_{j=1}^{t} (1 + k_j)} - A_0 \tag{4}$$

where S_t = cash inflow that occurs at the end of period t
A_0 = discounted cash outflow associated with the project
$\prod$ = symbol for a geometric sum (i.e., product of the terms that follow)
k_j = firm's cost of capital (or required rate of return) in period j

Equation (4) merely states that the net present value of a project is the sum of the discounted cash inflows minus the discounted cash outflows; the appropriate discount rate can be different each period and in order to find the present value of the cash inflow S_t, we divide it by the product of the quantities one plus the discount rate $(1 + k_j)$ for each period from the first period up to time period t.

Along similar lines, the terminal value of a project can easily be expressed as a function of a changing reinvestment rate over time using Equation (5):

$$TV = \sum_{t=1}^{n} S_t \left[\prod_{j=t+1}^{n} (1 + i_j) \right] \tag{5}$$

where i_j is the reinvestment rate that can be earned during period j. Notice here that the compounding process begins in period $t + 1$ because it is assumed that cash inflows, S_t, occur at the end of period t and hence can be reinvested starting in period $t + 1$.

Finally, the *modified NPV method* (NPV*) can also be rewritten to incorporate a changing cost of capital:

$$NPV^* = \frac{TV}{\prod_{t=1}^{n} (1 + k_t)} - A_0 \tag{6}$$

Note that Equation (6) provides substantial flexibility in project evaluation, since the terminal value calculation allows reinvestment rates to change each period, and the discounting process allows the cost of capital to change each period.

The IRR* calculated in Equation (3) does not require modification because of the factors discussed above. However, since IRR* utilizes the terminal value in its calculation, the impact of changing reinvestment rates has been taken into account.

Example 5 demonstrates how Equations (4), (5), and (6) are utilized in resolving the conflict between NPV and IRR where a time disparity exists.

● **EXAMPLE 5** *Time Disparity with Changing Cost of Capital and Reinvestment Rates*

The XYZ Company is evaluating the two mutually exclusive projects shown below:

t	X	Y	k_t	i_t
0	− $1,000	− $1,000	10%	
1	+ 300	+ 600	12%	15%
2	+ 700	+ 700	13%	18%
3	+ 1,500	+ 1,000	14%	20%

For both projects:
(a) Compute IRR and NPV [using Equation (4)].
(b) Compute TV using Equation (5), NPV* using Equation (6), and IRR* using Equation (3).

Solution:
(a)

$$IRR_X \doteq 47.02\% \qquad IRR_Y \doteq 50.59\%$$

$$NPV_X = -\$1,000.00 + \frac{\$300.00}{1.12} + \frac{\$700.00}{(1.12)(1.13)} + \frac{\$1,500.00}{(1.12)(1.13)(1.14)}$$

$$= -\$1,000.00 + \$267.86 + \$553.10 + \$1,039.66$$

$$= \$860.62$$

$$\text{NPV}_Y = -\$1,000.00 + \frac{\$600.00}{1.12} + \frac{\$700.00}{(1.12)(1.13)} + \frac{\$1,000.00}{(1.12)(1.13)(1.14)}$$

$$= -\$1,000.00 + \$535.71 + \$553.10 + \$693.10$$

$$= \$781.91$$

Hence, a conflict exists between the rankings assigned these two projects by IRR and NPV.

(b)

$$\text{TV}_X = \$300(1.18)(1.20) + \$700(1.20) + \$1,500$$

$$= \$424.80 + \$840.00 + \$1,500$$

$$= \$2,764.80$$

$$\text{TV}_Y = \$600(1.18)(1.20) + \$700(1.20) + \$1,000$$

$$= \$849.60 + \$840.00 + \$1,000$$

$$= \$2,689.60$$

$$\text{NPV}_X^* = \frac{\$2,764.80}{(1.12)(1.13)(1.14)} - \$1,000.00$$

$$= \$1,916.30 - \$1,000.00$$

$$= \$916.30$$

$$\text{NPV}_Y^* = \frac{\$2,689.60}{(1.12)(1.13)(1.14)} - \$1,000.00$$

$$= \$1,864.17 - \$1,000.00$$

$$= \$864.17$$

$$\text{IRR}_X^* \Rightarrow \frac{\$2,764.80}{(1 + r_X^*)^3} - \$1,000.00 = 0$$

$$r_X^* \doteq 40.3\%$$

$$\text{IRR}_Y^* \Rightarrow \frac{\$2,689.60}{(1 + r_Y^*)^3} - \$1,000.00 = 0$$

$$r_Y^* \doteq 39\%$$

Using the estimated reinvestment rates, we see that project X is superior to project Y, as shown by TV, NPV*, and IRR*, and the true NPV and IRR values for the two projects are much closer than it originally appeared in part (a) of the solution.   ●

To conclude this section, we caution the reader that the general rule stated above concerning a comparison of the reinvestment rate and Fisher's intersection to select the preferred project breaks down when either the reinvestment rate or the cost of capital is allowed to vary over time. In fact, the NPV profiles cannot be drawn for the projects, since such profiles assume a constant discount rate over the life of the project. *Therefore, to determine the preferred project, the procedure illustrated in Example 5 should be carried out. Namely, the terminal value of each project should be computed using the appropriate reinvestment rates for each period; next, the NPV* and IRR* values should be computed using (for the former) the appropriate cost of capital for each period; last, the preferred project is that which maximizes TV, IRR*, and NPV*.* We now turn to a consideration of mutually exclusive projects with unequal lives.

PROJECTS HAVING UNEQUAL USEFUL LIVES

Many capital budgeting problems involve decisions between mutually exclusive projects having unequal useful lives. Such projects are not directly comparable, because they usually suffer from both a size disparity (since the original investments often differ) and a time disparity [since the cash inflows of one project fall to zero before the other(s)]. Hence, under this combination of the two disparities, conflicts in ranking *could occur* among NPV, PI, and IRR (as pointed out earlier, if a size disparity does not exist, NPV and PI will agree in their rankings). The critical question here is what will take place at the end of the shorter-lived project: Will it be replaced by another asset of similar profitability, or will the funds be reinvested elsewhere in the firm at a relevant rate?

One common situation wherein mutually exclusive projects exhibit both a time and size disparity as well as have unequal useful lives involves the decision between replacing equipment versus rebuilding equipment. In general, replacement will provide a longer life than rebuilding; and, in general, replacement will have a higher NPV, owing to its longer life, even though the initial cost is greater. On the other hand, rebuilding could very well have a higher IRR and PI, because of its smaller cost. One way of resolving the conflict is to utilize the equivalent annual charge (EAC) method, described in Chapter 6. However, as will be seen in Example 6, the equivalent annual charge approach carries with it an assumption that may or may not be valid in a given problem setting. Namely, *EAC assumes that each investment will be replaced at the end of its respective useful life with another asset having the same profitability*. Example 6 utilizes a comparison between two assets originally cited by Solomon.[3]

● **EXAMPLE 6** *Mutually Exclusive Projects with Unequal Useful Lives*

Consider a firm (whose cost of capital is 10%) which is evaluating the following two projects:

t	X	Y
0	− $100	− $100
1	+ 120	0
2	0	0
3	0	0
4	0	+ 174.90

The NPVs, PIs, and IRRs are as follows:

	X	Y
IRR	20%	15%
NPV at 10%	$9.09	$19.46
PI at 10%	1.0909	1.1946

[3]See Ezra Solomon, "The Arithmetic of Capital Budgeting Decisions," *The Journal of Business*, Vol. 29, No. 2, April 1956, pp. 124–129.

Compute the EAC for each project and demonstrate the assumption that project X will be replaced by assets having the same profitability until the end of the life of project Y.

Solution: As shown in Chapter 6, the EAC approach finds an annualized figure for savings by multiplying the total savings (i.e., NPV) over the life of the project by the "capital recovery factor" (i.e., the reciprocal of the PV of an annuity factor or the factor found directly in the sixth column of Appendix C) for the appropriate hurdle rate (or cost of capital) and life of the project. Hence, for project X we use the capital recovery factor for 1 year in the 10% table, or 1.10, while for project Y we use the factor 0.3154708 from the year 4 line of the 10% table.

$$\text{EAC}_X = \$9.09 \times 1.10 = \$10.00$$
$$\text{EAC}_Y = \$19.46 \times 0.3154708 = \$6.14$$

Thus, on the basis of the equivalent annual charge method, project X is preferred to project Y even though project Y had a higher net present value. The reason for the conflict is again a result of the assumptions made about what happens at the end of the useful life of the shorter-lived project. *The EAC method assumes that each project is replaced at the end of its useful life by a project of like profitability (technically this process is assumed to continue out to infinity); on the other hand, the NPV and PI models assume that the cash inflows of both projects are reinvested at the cost of capital or the required rate of return used in the discounting process.*

Thus, the EAC method would assume that project X would be a series of four replacements throughout the useful life of project Y, as follows:

Time	Project X 1	2	3	4	Net Cash Flows	Discount Factors at 10%	Discounted Cash Flows
0	−$100				−$100	1.00000	−$100.00
1	+ 120	−$100			+ 20	0.909091	18.18
2		+ 120	−$100		+ 20	0.826446	16.53
3			+ 120	−$100	+ 20	0.751315	15.03
4				+ 120	+ 120	0.683013	81.96
						NPV at 10% = $31.70	
						PI at 10% = 1.3170	
						IRR = 20%	

As can be seen, when the implicit assumption of the EAC approach is made explicit, all four of the techniques (NPV, PI, IRR, and EAC) consistently prefer project X to project Y. Thus, project X is more attractive as long as it can be replaced by a similar asset over the 4-year life of project Y.

Note that the internal rate of return for the series of four replacements shown above is exactly the same as the original IRR for project X. This is what is meant by the EAC assumption that at the end of its useful life, *a project is replaced by one of like profitability.* Another interesting point is that there is a relationship between the EAC value for project X and the NPV found for the series of four replacements found over the 4-year life of project Y. Namely, if the EAC for project X ($10.00) is multiplied by the present value of an annuity factor for 10% and 4 years (the useful life of the longer project), which is 3.169865, we arrive at the NPV (using a 10% discount rate) of the series of four replacements, which is $31.70. This provides a shortcut for finding the NPV (over the life of the longer project) of a series of replacements of like profitability of the shorter-lived project.   ●

The EAC approach as illustrated in Example 6 provides an appropriate methodology for ranking projects with unequal lives as long as the assumption that each project will be replaced by one of similar profitability until a common horizon date is valid. If this is not the case, we need to know the best estimate for the rate at which cash flows from each project can be reinvested up to a common horizon date (usually the end of the useful life of the longer-lived project). Given this estimate (which could vary from year to year), we can call upon the techniques of the previous section and find the terminal value (TV), NPV*, and IRR*. The latter approach should be implemented any time that projects having unequal lives are analyzed and the reinvestment rate differs from the cost of capital. This should be done even though there may not be a conflict among NPV, PI, and IRR originally because, given the relevant reinvestment rate, the preferred project may be different. Example 7 illustrates the approach.

● **EXAMPLE 7** *Unequal Useful Lives with Differing Reinvestment Rates*

A firm with a present cost of capital of 14% is evaluating the following two mutually exclusive projects, which have different useful lives:

Time	*C*	*D*
0	− $10,000.	− $12,000.
1	+ 5,506.27	+ 4,991.11
2	+ 5,506.27	+ 4,991.11
3	+ 5,506.27	+ 4,991.11
4		+ 4,991.11
IRR	30%	24%
NPV at 14%	$ 2,783.53	$ 2,542.66
PI at 14%	1.278	1.212

Given the reinvestment assumptions of the models above, project C dominates project D. However, management feels that during the next 4 years there will be a business slowdown and the reinvestment rates will be 6%, 8%, 9%, and 10%, respectively. Determine the preferred project assuming that the firm's cost of capital will be 14% during year 1 and 10% thereafter.

Solution: We begin by computing the terminal values for the two projects at the end of year 4 (the useful life of the longer-lived project):

$$TV_C = \$5,506.27[(1.08)(1.09)(1.10)] + \$5,506.27[(1.09)(1.10)]$$
$$+ \$5,506.27(1.10)$$
$$= \$7,130.18 + \$6,602.02 + \$6,056.92$$
$$= \$19,789.10$$

$$TV_D = \$4,991.11[(1.08)(1.09)(1.10)] + \$4,991.11[(1.09)(1.10)]$$
$$+ \$4,991.11(1.10) + \$4,991.11$$
$$= \$6,463.09 + \$5,984.34 + \$5,490.22 + \$4,991.11$$
$$= \$22,928.76$$

Next, we find NPV* and IRR* for each project:

$$NPV_C^* = \frac{\$19,789.10}{(1.14)(1.10)(1.10)(1.10)} - \$10,000$$

$$= \$3,041.97$$

$$NPV_D^* = \frac{\$22,928.76}{(1.14)(1.10)(1.10)(1.10)} - \$12,000$$

$$= \$3,111.16$$

$$IRR_C^* \Rightarrow \frac{\$19,789.10}{(1 + r_C^*)^4} - \$10,000 = 0$$

$$r_C^* \doteq 18.605\%$$

$$IRR_D^* \Rightarrow \frac{\$22,928.76}{(1 + r_D^*)^4} - \$12,000 = 0$$

$$r_D^* \doteq 17.57\%$$

Notice above that $NPV_C^* < NPV_D^*$, but $IRR_C^* > IRR_D^*$ which is a problem that did not occur when only a time disparity existed between the projects. There can be a conflict in the ranking assigned NPV* and IRR* if a size disparity exists between the projects.

Thus, we would select project D if capital rationing does not exist since it has the greater NPV*. If capital rationing does exist, we have to evaluate other projects to see whether either C or D will be included in the portfolio that maximizes NPV* while not violating the budget limitation.   ●

We can now summarize our recommendations for handling mutually exclusive projects with unequal useful lives. *If it can realistically be assumed that at the end of the life of each project it will be replaced by another of like profitability, the EAC approach will rank the projects correctly. On the other hand, if cash flows from the shorter-lived project can be assumed to be reinvested at a relevant rate, we should compute TV and NPV*. If capital rationing does not exist, then the project with the greater NPV* should be accepted (as long as this value is positive). If capital rationing does exist, we have to evaluate various sets of feasible (satisfying both budget requirements and mutually exclusive conditions) assets so that the set that maximizes NPV* can be selected.*

Throughout the text we have advocated the use of NPV and NPV* criteria as being superior to IRR, PI, and others. Our reason was that given the six assumptions cited above, the maximization of NPV or NPV* leads to a maximization of shareholders' wealth or utility. The next section demonstrates the superiority of the NPV criterion in striving to maximize shareholders' wealth.

NPV VS. IRR VS. PI

Surveys of practitioners have shown that among the firms using discounted-cash-flow techniques, a significantly greater number use IRR than either NPV or PI. This is probably due to the ease of interpreting a discounted rate of return (IRR) as opposed to the apparent difficulty that managers have understanding the meaning of the "net present value of an investment project."

However, there is widespread confusion about what the internal rate of return really shows and whether it is an appropriate criterion to use as a surrogate for maximizing shareholders' wealth. *This section provides added insight to the true meaning of IRR and demonstrates that it is not a particularly relevant criterion to use in order to attempt to maximize shareholders' wealth. In fact, it leads to wrong decisions when it conflicts with the NPV criterion in evaluating mutually exclusive projects.* The internal rate of return has an additional problem in that multiple rates of return can be found where there are changes in the signs of cash flows (from positive to negative) over the life of the project. This difficulty is examined in Appendix 7A.

To begin, consider the two projects shown in Exhibit 7-2. Notice that the two projects have equal IRRs of 20%, and equal original investments of

EXHIBIT 7-2   Two Projects Under Evaluation

Time	Cash Flows I	II
0	$-$10,000.	$-$10,000.
1	+ 3,862.89	0
2	+ 3,862.89	0
3	+ 3,862.89	0
4	+ 3,862.89	+ 20,736
IRR	20%	20%

$10,000, but that the timing of the cash inflows differs over their 4-year useful lives. According to the IRR criterion, these two projects are equivalent; hence, given the reinvestment assumption of the IRR model, the two projects should have equivalent terminal values. The first question to be addressed is: what is the amount assumed to be reinvested at the IRR return? The answer is, the *entire cash inflow*, as shown by the following calculation of terminal value for project I using Equation (1), where $i = 20\%$:

$$TV_I = \$3,862.89(1.20)^3 + \$3,862.89(1.20)^2 + \$3,862.89(1.20)$$
$$+ \$3,862.89$$
$$= \$6,675.07 + \$5,562.56 + \$4,635.47 + \$3,862.89$$
$$= \$20,736$$

Of course, this terminal value equals that for project II.

A second question also requires discussion. What does the "internal" of internal rate of return mean or imply? To answer this question, refer to Exhibit 7-3, which utilizes the data for project I given in Exhibit 7-2. *Exhibit 7-3 emphasizes the fact that to say that a project has an internal rate of return of 20% means that the cash inflows less a 20% return on the value of investment will reduce the original investment to zero at the end of the life of the project. Thus, the word "internal" means that the IRR shows the return on the funds that remain internally invested in the project.*

Hence, for project I, as shown in Exhibit 7-3, 20% is earned on $10,000 for one year, 20% is earned on $8,137.11 during year 2, 20% is earned on $5,901.64

EXHIBIT 7-3 Value of Funds Remaining Invested in Project I[a]

t	(1) Beginning Value of Investment	(2) Cash Inflow	(3) 20% Return on Value of Investment	(4) Cash Throwoff	(5) Ending Value of Investment
1	$10,000.00	$3,862.89	$2,000.00	$1,862.89	$8,137.11
2	8,137.11	3,862.89	1,627.42	2,235.47	5,901.64
3	5,901.64	3,862.89	1,180.33	2,682.56	3,219.08
4	3,219.08	3,862.89	643.81	3,219.08	0

[a]Column (2), as well as the initial $10,000 figure in column (1), were given for project I in Exhibit 7-2; column (3) equals 20% of the value shown in column (1); column (4) equals column (2) less column (3); column (5) equals column (1) less column (4); and the value from column (5) for period t is carried down to column (1) in period $t + 1$.

during year 3, and 20% is earned on $3,219.08 during year 4. Project I does not earn a 20% rate of return on $10,000 for the entire 4-year useful life; the return of 20% is only earned on funds that remain internally invested in the project (i.e., the value of the investment in each of the 4 years). *This is why the IRR criterion makes the assumption that cash inflows are reinvested at the same rate so that it can claim a true compounded rate of return on the entire original investment for the entire useful life of the project.* However, it can be said that project I will generate a true compounded rate of return on $10,000 for 4 years if and only if the cash inflows of $3862.89 each year can be reinvested at a 20% return for the rest of the project's useful life. This is demonstrated in the computation of the terminal value for project I and comparing its value with the terminal value for project II. Furthermore, as illustrated in the previous sections, if the reinvestment rate on cash inflows is less than the IRR, the true compounded rate of return over the project's life (IRR*) will be less than the computed IRR; the converse is also true.

The next question that arises is whether selecting the project or projects that maximizes IRR will lead to a maximization of shareholders' wealth. The answer is an emphatic *no*. In fact, following the IRR criterion can often act against the best interest of the shareholders. As a demonstration of how this can occur, consider the two mutually exclusive projects shown in Example 8, which is adapted from an example originally presented by Hirshleifer.[4]

EXAMPLE 8 *Inability of IRR to Maximize Shareholders' Wealth*

A firm is evaluating two mutually exclusive but rather profitable projects:

t	I	II
0	−$ 10,000	−$ 10,000
1	0	+ 20,000
2	+ 40,000	+ 10,000

[4]J. Hirshleifer, "On the Theory of Optimal Investment Decisions," *Journal of Political Economy*, August 1958, pp. 329–352.

90

Using the general guidelines described in previous sections, we would anticipate that at low or moderate discount rates, the NPV criterion would favor project I, because it has the greater amount of undiscounted total cash inflows over the life of the project; on the other hand, we would anticipate that the IRR criterion would favor project II, because it has more rapid cash inflows and a shorter payback period than those of project I. For the two projects above:

(a) Compute the two IRRs, for both projects.

(b) Sketch the NPV profiles and determine the Fisher's intersection.

(c) Show that for any discount rate less than Fisher's intersection (say 10%), the firm would be sacrificing wealth by following the IRR criterion rather than the NPV criterion.

Solution:

(a)

$$\text{IRR}_I \Rightarrow \frac{-\$10,000}{(1 + r_I)^0} + \frac{0}{(1 + r_I)^1} + \frac{\$40,000}{(1 + r_I)^2} = 0$$

Therefore,

$$r_I = 100\%$$

$$\text{IRR}_{II} \Rightarrow \frac{-\$10,000}{(1 + r_{II})^0} + \frac{\$20,000}{(1 + r_{II})^1} + \frac{\$10,000}{(1 + r_{II})^2} = 0$$

Therefore,

$$r_{II} = 141.4\%$$

(b) Of course, Fisher's intersection would be the discount rate (r'), where the NPV of the two projects equaled each other.

$$\text{NPV}_I = \text{NPV}_{II}$$

$$\frac{-\$10,000}{(1 + r')^0} + \frac{0}{(1 + r')^1} + \frac{\$40,000}{(1 + r')^2} = \frac{-\$10,000}{(1 + r')^0} + \frac{\$20,000}{(1 + r')^1} + \frac{\$10,000}{(1 + r')^2}$$

$$\frac{-\$20,000}{(1 + r')^1} + \frac{\$30,000}{(1 + r')^2} = 0$$

Therefore,

$$r' = 50\%$$

Given this information, we can now sketch the two NPV profiles.

(c) Based on the information above, we see that project II has the higher IRR but that project I would be the preferred project using the NPV criterion at any cost of capital less than 50% (Fisher's intersection). We will now show that if the firm's cost of capital is 10% (and the same would be true if it were any rate $< 50\%$), project I dominates project II and that the firm would be acting contrary to the best interests of the shareholders if it followed the IRR criterion.

In order to show that project I dominates project II (since the original investments were the same), we would just have to modify the cash flows (through the discounting process) so that the cash flows are equal in all years except for one, and greater for project I in that last year. Looking at the cash-flow patterns for project I, we would

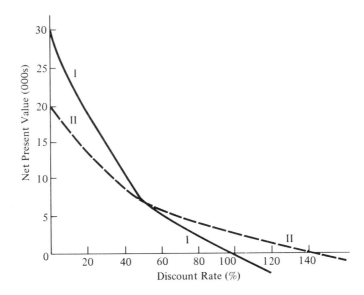

leave $10,000 of the $40,000 cash inflow in year 2 there and discount the remaining $30,000 back one year to year 1. The resulting equivalent year 2 cash flow is $27,272.73 ($30,000 × 0.909091), and thus the modified (but equivalent) cash inflow patterns for the two projects are as follows:

t	I	II
0	−$10,000.00	−$10,000.00
1	+ 27,272.73	+ 20,000.00
2	+ 10,000.00	+ 10,000.00

Thus, we can see that project I dominates project II and that any rational decision maker would prefer project I to II. The project preferred by the NPV criterion (project I) would leave the firm with greater wealth than the project preferred by the IRR criterion (project II). In fact, by examining the modified cash-flow series above, we can see that the firm would be throwing away $7,272.73 of wealth if it followed the IRR criterion rather than the NPV criterion.

Consider again the original cash-flow series:

t	I	II
0	−$10,000	−$10,000
1	0	+ 20,000
2	+ 40,000	+ 10,000

Some IRR proponents might argue that project II is preferred because it gives the $20,000 cash inflow in period 1 which can be used for reinvestment in attractive opportunities. However, if such attractive opportunities exist, the firm would still be better off by accepting project I and borrowing $20,000 in period 1 at the cost of capital of 10% and repaying the loan in period 2 with part of the $40,000 cash inflow. The comparison is as follows:

	I			
t	*Original*	*Loan*	*Revised*	*II*
0	−$10,000	0	−$10,000	−$10,000
1	0	+$20,000	+ 20,000	+ 20,000
2	+ 40,000	− 22,000[a]	+ 18,000	+ 10,000

[a]This value includes $2,000 in interest plus the $20,000 principal.

We can see that the revised project I again clearly dominates project II. ●

As noted in Example 8, IRR can have a detrimental impact on shareholders' wealth. This fact can also be demonstrated by showing how much shareholders' wealth would increase at the end of the life of the project as a result of accepting that project. This is done for two mutually exclusive projects in Example 9.

● **EXAMPLE 9** *Inability of IRR to Maximize Shareholder's Wealth, Revisited*

A firm with a 10% cost of capital is evaluating projects *A* and *B* as follows:

t	*A*	*B*
0	−$200,000	−$200,000
1	+ 50,000	+ 102,500
2	+ 50,000	+ 102,500
3	+ 235,000	+ 102,500
$NPV_{10\%}$	$63,335.84	$54,902.33
$PI_{10\%}$	1.31668	1.2745
IRR	23.0%	25.03%

NPV and PI rank project *A* higher while IRR prefers project *B*. Somewhat artificially, assume that the firm will obtain the $200,000 required at their cost of capital and that any amount can be repaid each year. Show the impact on shareholders' wealth at the end of the life of each project, where cash inflows over the life are used to pay interest and principal on the $200,000 required.

Solution: The analysis would proceed by preparing the following tables for each project:

Project A

Year	*Beginning Balance*	*Interest at 10%*	*Cash Inflow*	*Retirement of Principal*	*Ending Balance*	*Increase in Shareholders' Wealth*[a]
1	$200,000	$20,000	$50,000	$30,000	$170,000	
2	170,000	17,000	50,000	33,000	137,000	
3	137,000	13,700	235,000	137,000	0	$84,300

[a]Cash inflow in year 3 less the interest in year 3 less the beginning balance for year 3.

Project B

Year	Beginning Balance	Interest at 10%	Cash Inflow	Retirement of Principal	Ending Balance	Increase in Shareholders' Wealth[a]
1	$200,000	$20,000	$102,500	$82,500	$117,500	
2	117,500	11,750	102,500	90,750	26,750	
3	26,750	2,675	102,500	26,750	0	$73,075

[a]Equals cash inflow in year 3 minus the interest in year 3 minus the beginning balance for year 3.

Project *A* increases shareholders' wealth by $84,300 compared to $73,075 for Project *B*. So again, if the firm followed the IRR criterion and accepted project *B*, it would lead to a sacrifice of $11,225 in the shareholders' wealth position at the end of the 3-year life of both projects. IRR is clearly an inferior criterion compared to NPV in maximizing shareholders' wealth.

If it is argued that there are attractive reinvestment opportunities in years 1 and 2 for the $102,500 cash inflows of project *B*, it can again easily be shown that project *A* is still superior when an additional loan is obtained (at the cost of capital) to have this amount of funds available in each year. The comparison would be as follows:

Project A

Time	Original	Loan	Revised	Project B
0	− $200,000		− $200,000	− $200,000
1	+ 50,000	+$ 52,500	+ 102,500	+ 102,500
2	+ 50,000	+ 52,500	+ 102,500	+ 102,500
3	+ 235,000	− 120,750[a]	+ 114,250	+ 102,500

[a]The loan repayment is $105,000 in principal, $5,250 in interest for the loan outstanding in period 2, and $10,500 in interest for the loan outstanding in period 3.

Again, project *A* clearly dominates project *B*, and any rational decision maker would select *A* rather than *B*.

At this juncture one might question why such difficulties are experienced in the use of IRR. It could be said that IRR does a good job of measuring the *compounded rate of return over time on the funds that remain invested in an asset, but the problem is that this figure has nothing at all to do with maximizing shareholders' wealth.* A firm that attempted to *maximize IRR* could very well find that the highest IRR project had an original cost of $100 and a return next year of $150, leading to a 50% IRR; shareholders would be pleased over the $50 return, but would raise more questions about how the remaining portion of the capital budget was invested. If management replied that they did not want to invest any more than $100 because to do so would deteriorate the IRR below the very attractive 50% level achieved, they would be looking for new jobs. *The NPV criterion shows clearly and unambiguously the impact of projects on shareholders' wealth or the present value of the firm. However, the same is obviously not true for IRR.*

If three projects have NPVs of $10,000, $14,000, and $16,000, these figures show the magnitudes of the increase in shareholders' wealth if the respective investments are accepted. On the other hand, if these same projects have IRRs of 40%, 30%, and 25% and PIs of 1.68, 1.22, and 1.53, respectively, we have no idea which of the three will lead to the greatest increase in shareholders' wealth by looking at their IRRs and PIs. In fact, as has been illustrated in many examples in this chapter, the increase in shareholders' wealth can be the opposite of the rankings indicated by either the IRR or PI criterion. In an informative and hard-hitting article, Keane points out:

> The internal rate of return, therefore, is invalid not because of any implicit reinvestment assumption or because of the possibility of producing multiple yields, but simply because a rate of return expressed in percentage terms is inappropriate for discriminating between projects of different sizes. All but *identical* projects have different sizes whatever their initial outlays or expected lives may suggest, and although the rate of return method might appear at times to give correct investment advice, it is *never* in fact correct in principle.[5]

Weingartner[6] also has a number of uncomplimentary things to say about the profitability index. He demonstrates that given a size disparity between two mutually exclusive projects, there will be a conflict between NPV and PI whenever

$$\frac{b_1}{b_2} < \frac{c_1}{c_2}$$

where b_j = net present value of project j
c_j = cost of project j

Assume that $b_1 > b_2$, which means that the NPV criterion prefers project 1. Under the condition specified above, the PI will rank project 2 higher than 1, which is in conflict with NPV. This can be seen by noting that since all the b's and c's are positive, the following inequality exists.

$$\frac{b_1}{c_1} < \frac{b_2}{c_2}$$

The relationship between the PIs is as follows:

$$PI_1 = \frac{b_1 + c_1}{c_1} < \frac{b_2 + c_2}{c_2} = PI_2$$

To obtain this expression, we simply added unity to both sides of the inequality. In such circumstances, as Weingartner[7] points out, the PI criterion "would lead to selection of the project with the *lower net present value which would make a lower contribution to the wealth of the owners of the firm*" [emphasis added]. Finally, Weingartner concludes his article by stating:

> Our examples of mutually exclusive alternatives reinforce the conclusion that PI does not provide aid in the choice among such alternatives. In two

[5]S. M. Keene, "Let's Scrap IRR Once and For All!," *Accountancy*, February 1974, pp. 78–82.
[6]H. Martin Weingartner, "The Excess Present Value Index—A Theoretical Basis and Critique," *Journal of Accounting Research*, Autumn 1963, pp. 213–224.
[7]Ibid., p. 220.

examples, ranking by means of PI and by IRR led to the same *incorrect choice.* In the third example, these rankings were different, and the PI criterion resulted in the wrong choice. In all these instances, *the NPV criterion and Fisher's rate of return yield similar answers which are correct* in the absence of capital rationing or more complex interrelationships between investments [emphasis added].[8]

To conclude this section, the next example demonstrates in another way that utilizing the NPV criterion will lead to wealth maximization even when NPV conflicts with IRR and PI in the ranking of mutually exclusive projects. Irving Fisher was probably the first to rigorously use the type of analysis called upon in the demonstration.

● **EXAMPLE 10**   *Inability of IRR and PI to Maximize Shareholders'*
                   Wealth (Second Revisit)

A firm with a cost of capital of 10% has a current wealth position of $250,000. The accompanying graph shows combinations of consumption this year and consumption next year that can be obtained given the firm's current wealth position, the cost of capital (or market rate of interest), and the six assumptions cited earlier in the chapter, including the equality of borrowing and lending rates. Notice that one possible consumption pattern would be $250,000 this year and $0 next year; another would be $0 this year and $275,000 next year [$275,000 would be available for consumption next year since the $250,000 could be invested at the market rate of interest, 10%—$275,000 = $250,000(1.10)]. Consider that the firm has determined its desired consumption pattern and that is to consume $150,000 this year and $110,000 next year. Notice, of

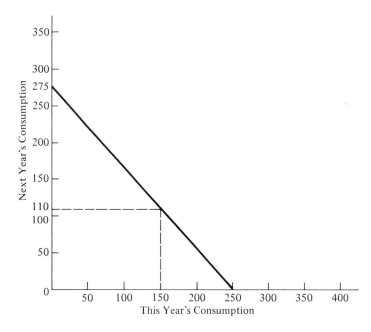

[8]Ibid., p. 224.

course, that this consumption pattern, as is true for all others on the line, has a present value of $250,000 (using the market discount rate of 10%) and a future value next year of $275,000. The firm is evaluating two mutually exclusive projects:

Year	I	II
0	−$40,000	−$ 80,000
1	+ 80,000	+ 150,000
$NPV_{10\%}$	$32,727	$ 56,364
$PI_{10\%}$	1.82	1.70
IRR	100%	87.5%

Both PI and IRR rank project I above project II, whereas NPV reverses this order.

Using a graph similar to the one shown above, demonstrate that project II, if accepted by the firm, will place the firm in a superior wealth position than if project I were accepted (i.e., demonstrate that following the NPV criterion maximizes shareholders' wealth, whereas PI and IRR fail to).

Solution: The graph showing the original wealth position, that achieved by accepting project I (labeled I) and that achieved by accepting project II (labeled II), is as shown. Note in the figure that the lines for projects I and II are determined geometrically by two points: (1) the point found by first moving horizontally to the left along the line $110,000 of consumption next year in the amount of the investment for each project, and then moving vertically upward in the amount of the cash inflow in period

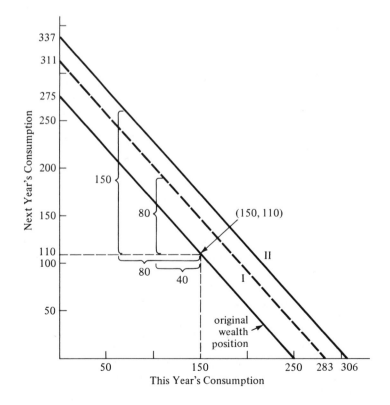

1; and (2) the point on the horizontal axis at $250,000 (the original wealth position) plus the NPV of the project.

As can clearly be seen, the wealth position of the firm after accepting project II dominates that of the firm after accepting project I. The present wealth position of the former exceeds that of the latter by the difference in the NPVs of the two projects— $29,630 ($56,360 for II less $32,730 for project I). It should also be noted that the present wealth position of the firm with either project is merely its wealth position currently ($250,000) plus the NPV of the accepted project. Thus, the direct link between the NPV criterion and wealth maximization has been established—the selection of the project or projects that maximize NPV will lead to shareholder wealth maximization. This is obviously *not* the case for either the PI or IRR criterion.

The Fisherian analysis depicted here points to the reason for the inferiority of both PI and IRR. Namely, *both of these criteria measure the rate of change in the firm's wealth position due to the acceptance of a new project while totally ignoring the absolute wealth position that results.* Geometrically, this is equivalent to saying that the slope of the vector from point (150, 110), showing the desired consumption pattern given the current wealth of $250,000, is steeper to project I's wealth line than the corresponding vector to project II's wealth line. Of course, the slope of the vectors has nothing to do with the excellence of the wealth position arrived at by the acceptance of either project.　　　●

The several examples included in our analysis should convince even the skeptical reader that the NPV criterion is clearly superior in maximizing shareholders' wealth than either the IRR or PI criterion. We turn now to an introductory discussion of the special problems imposed by constraints on the capital budgeting process.

CONSTRAINTS ON THE CAPITAL BUDGET

The financial manager will devise the capital budget so as to maximize the present value of the firm; this suggests the acceptance of new capital projects as long as the project shows a positive NPV. The preferred capital budget is that combination of projects which maximizes total NPV. The admonition holds even if the firm must resort to new financing to absorb all viable projects. In reality, new financing may not be feasible for several reasons, such as the delay entailed in marketing new securities, problems of corporate control created by new stockholders, restrictive provisions in bond indentures, and the like.

More important perhaps than the limits imposed by financing arrangements is the ability of the firm to digest new projects due to manpower bottlenecks and scarce management talent. Capital budgets are not simply an exercise in applied finance but comprise a host of technological and managerial problems. Consequently, for a variety of reasons, the firm may be pragmatically estopped from accepting more than a restricted number of projects in a given time period or over a longer span. What principle should guide the preparation of a capital budget in the presence of such constraints?

Within the limits imposed by the constraints, the firm should select that combination of projects which maximizes the NPV of the budget. To accomplish the objective, management might have to look beyond the present fiscal period to a longer planning horizon. These problems—the need to allocate resources to projects over several fiscal periods, limited financial and managerial resources, and technological uncertainties—become critically important in constructing a capital budget and modify the strict adherence to the NPV criterion. The problem of maximizing NPV subject to such stated constraints is best described and resolved by mathematical programming techniques discussed in Chapters 12, 13, and 14.

MANAGERIAL GUIDELINES

Preceding sections focused on the complications frequently encountered in practice when the financial manager grapples with formulation of the firm's capital budget. The issues presented really represent a set of alert signals suggesting further investigation. The financial manager should show caution whenever the following situations arise:

1. The projects analyzed are different in size.

2. The projects have different life spans.

3. The cash-flow patterns (increasing, decreasing, or uniform) vary from one project to the next.

4. The company's future reinvestment opportunities are expected to change significantly from the present set of investment options.

5. The firm's marginal cost of capital is expected to rise significantly over time.

6. There exists capital and/or manpower constraints on the budget. In these circumstances, the mechanical application of ranking techniques without regard to the underlying assumptions can trap the financial manager into manifestly wrong decisions.

THE IMPACT OF CAPITAL INVESTMENTS ON ACCOUNTING STATEMENTS

The ranking of capital projects by discounted-cash-flow (DCF) techniques does not allow for the impact of capital investments on the firm's reported earnings. In fact, DCF can favor projects which, although attractive in the long run, produce erratic net income figures from year to year. Yet management frequently places great emphasis on the stability of earnings growth from year to year. One survey of 163 companies in the Fortune 500 showed that the most frequently cited financial objective of management was the steady and regular growth rate of earnings per share (EPS).

Lerner and Rappaport[9] focused on the problem and attempted a solution that would make DCF sensitive to requirements in reporting earnings. They incorporated three assumptions:

1. The financial objective is to maximize the price of company shares and that management has decided to use reported growth in EPS to advance the objective.

[9]Eugene M. Lerner and Alfred Rappaport, "Limit DCF Capital Budgeting," *Harvard Business Review*, September–October 1968, pp. 133–138.

TABLE 7-2   Year Project Number

Project Number	1	2	3	4	5	6	7	8	9	10	11	12	13	14	15	16
1	$(239)	$45	$59	$64	$71	$70	$59									
2	(25)	(40)	(30)	(10)	20	70	100	$150	$150	$150	$100	$60				
3	(10)	(10)	(10)	20	30	50	40	20								
4		(120)	25	25	30	35	30	25	20	15	10	5				
5		(100)	(60)	(60)	80	74	66	56	44	30	14					
6		(20)	80	100	(10)	50	(100)	50	400	200						
7		(200)	(100)	0	50	200	300	200	50	50						
8		50	100	(200)	100	150										
9		(10)	50	100	(200)	(100)	100	300								
10			(80)	20	20	15	15	15	10	10	10					
11			(300)	(50)	200	300	400	200	0	100	100	$100				
12			(50)	200	150	(100)	(100)	100	200	150	100					
13				(300)	(50)	(100)	100	200	200	200	200	100				
14				(200)	10	80	100	300	500	300	200	(50)	100	$100	$100	
15				(100)	(50)	(50)	80	70	100	200	(50)	100	200	100	50	

Estimated Earnings After Taxes for Years
1 Through 5 (hundreds of dollars)

Project Number	NPV[a] at 20%	Year 1	2	3	4	5
0[b]		$100	$95	$90	$90	$80
1	$(35.75)	(20)	5	15	30	50
2	96.89	(25)	(40)	(30)	10	20
3	33.20	(40)	(30)	(20)	100	120
4	(10.67)		(50)	5	20	25
5	(29.82)		(100)	(60)	(60)	80
6	187.41		(20)	80	100	(10)
7	31.95			(50)	(30)	(20)
8	72.14			(80)	100	200
9	45.07			(10)	50	100
10	(9.21)				(80)	50
11	151.76				(100)	(200)
12	138.42				(50)	200
13	(12.19)					(10)
14	185.45					(200)
15	32.84					(100)
	$975.13					
Earnings to be reported[a]		$35	$5	$(20)	$270	$190

Total earnings:
$48,000

[a]Based on accepting projects having positive net present values.
[b]Earnings after taxes if no additional investments are made.
Source: Eugene M. Lerner and Alfred Rappaport, "Limit DCF in Capital Budgeting," *Harvard Business Review*, September–October 1968, pp. 133–138. Copyright © 1968 by the President and Fellows of Harvard College; all rights reserved.

TABLE 7-3 Calculation of Cash Flows and Earnings After Taxes for Project I (hundreds of dollars)

Project description:	expansion of machine capacity
Estimated investment cost:	$280
Estimated economic life:	7 years
Depreciation method:	sum-of-the-years' digits

	Year						
	1	2	3	4	5	6	7
Sales	$30	$90	$110	$130	$160	$160	$130
Depreciation	$70	$60	$50	$40	$30	$20	$10
Other operating expenses	0	20	30	30	30	40	40
Total expenses	$70	$80	$80	$70	$60	$60	$50
Net income before tax	$(40)	$10	$30	$60	$100	$100	$80
Federal income tax							
(50% of income)	(20)	5	15	30	50	50	40
Earnings after taxes	$(20)	$ 5	$15	$30	$50	$50	$40
Cash receipts (70% of sales)	$21	$72	$104	$124	$151	$160	$139
Cash disbursements	280	20	30	30	30	40	40
	$(259)	$52	$74	$94	$121	$120	$99
Federal income tax							
(50% of income)	(20)	5	15	30	50	50	40
Net cash flow	$(239)	$47	$59	$64	$71	$70	$59

2. All projects are evaluated by DCF, cash flows are certain, and the projects are independent.

3. The firm has the opportunity to invest in 15 projects over the next 5 years.

The upper portion of Table 7-2 lists the estimated cash flows for the 15 projects over their expected lives, while the lower portion for the first 5 years and the NPV of each project are discounted at 20%. The earnings to be reported shown for each year include only the earnings from those projects having positive net present values. Thus, for year 1, the earnings from projects 2 and 3, which have positive net present values, are included. The earnings from both of these are negative, so the total earnings for year 1 is $3,500.

If all projects with positive NPVs are accepted, the company will accept 10 projects and reject 5. The total NPV of the capital budget will be $97,513 and the total earnings are $48,000.

Table 7-3 shows how the cash flows and earnings after taxes are computed for the projects, using project 1 as an example. Note that for computing cash flows, 70% of the revenues are collected in the year of the sale and 30% the following year. Earnings after taxes are, however, calculated on an accrual basis: sales are recorded as revenues in the year they are made.

The subsequent discussion of capital budgeting under conditions of uncertainty will stress that the present value of a firm is the product of two variables: the size of the cash-flow stream over time and the variability (riskiness) of this stream. If erratic behavior in reported earnings suggests greater risk to investors, this could result in a lower price–earnings (P/E) ratio and reduced market values on company shares. To the security markets this might evidence poor planning by management. Investors might respond by placing a lower P/E multiple on reported earnings, and in turn the share prices would be lower than would result from a more stable pattern of earnings growth.

But the issue is complex. Security market prices register opinions about information, not the information per se, and this, too, in light of investor objectives. Do investors rely primarily on accounting information? There is evidence that investors are not fooled by accounting numbers (i.e., the security markets see through the accounting numbers to the underlying cash flows). If this be so and assuming the capital projects accepted are properly discounted for risk, the market value of the shares would not be adversely affected by the erratic quality of the accounting earnings. On the other hand, some research does indicate that investors respond to accounting earnings, in which case the Lerner–Rappaport hypothesis has merit.

Assume now that the objective of the firm was restated to maximize net present value subject to the constraint that earnings of the company must grow at a stipulated 5%. Table 7-4 lists the projects that would be accepted on the basis of the revised criterion. Some of the projects have been split on the assumption that the scope of the project can be reduced or that spending can proceed at a slower rate during the 5-year period. If this not be feasible, the project can be dropped or adopted *in toto*, with an adjustment made either in another investment or in earnings target. As will be demonstrated later, the problem is readily solved by mathematical programming techniques with the aid of computerized solution algorithms.

The new total NPV of $71,892 compares unfavorably with the total NPV of $97,513 using the unconstrained model, but the consistency of earnings has improved substantially, as shown in Table 7-4. The total reported earnings have increased to $51,414 from $48,000.

Note that projects 1 and 10 were selected, although they have negative NPVs at the chosen discount factor. The justification is that these projects permit the company to report relatively large earnings during the 5-year planning period. Conversely, projects 11, 14, and 15 have negative earnings during the planning period, but their large cash flows beyond the planning period increase the present values of the accepted projects.

SUMMARY

This chapter concludes our initial analysis of the allocation of funds for capital investment. We examined the problems in ranking projects caused by size disparities, differences in project lives, and time disparities of cash flows. In each instance we recommended a viable solution technique to aid the financial planner in decision making.

TABLE 7-4 Projects Adopted to Assure Growth Rate of 5% or More per Year

Project Number	Proportion Adopted (%)	NPV[a] ($000)	Weighted NPV
1	100.00	($35.75)	($35.75)
2	—		—
3	16.25	33.20	5.40
4	—	—	—
5	—	—	—
6	76.50	187.41	143.37
7	—	—	—
8	83.90	72.14	60.53
9	100.00	45.07	45.07
10	88.75	(9.21)	(8.17)
11	100.00	151.76	151.76
12	100.00	138.42	138.42
13	—	—	—
14	100.00	185.45	185.45
15	100.00	32.84	32.84
			$718.92

[a]The NPV under conditions of constraint is $71,892.

Earnings After Taxes to Be Reported

Year	Unconstrained Model	Constrained Model
1	$ 3,500	$ 7,350
2	500	7,717
3	(2,000)	8,379
4	27,000	12,565
5	19,000	15,403
	$48,000	$51,414

Source: Eugene M. Lerner and Alfred Rappaport, "Limit DCF in Capital Budgeting," *Harvard Business Review*, September–October 1968, pp. 133–138. Copyright © 1968 by the President and Fellows of Harvard College; all rights reserved.

In general, we have argued in favor of the NPV technique because of its uniquely consistent superiority in maximizing shareholders' wealth given the assumptions enumerated in an early section of the chapter. One of these assumptions was that perfect capital markets exist, which rules out the possibility of capital rationing. Our initial recommendations for resolving conflicts among NPV, PI, and IRR were made under this set of assumptions. Thus, to resolve possible conflicts in the ranking of mutually exclusive projects that exhibit a size disparity, we recommend computing the NPV, PI, and IRR on the incremental investment in the larger project. If these computed values meet the decision rules for the three criteria (e.g., the NPV on the incremental project is positive, etc.), the larger investment should be accepted (which would have been the originally higher ranked project using the NPV criterion);

otherwise, the smaller project should be accepted (in this situation, the smaller project would again have the larger NPV).

To resolve possible conflicts in ranking mutually exclusive projects which have a time disparity, we recommend computing the terminal value of the projects given a relevant reinvestment rate and then selecting the project with the higher NPV* and IRR* (these two criteria will always agree given that there is no size disparity between the projects).

Last, when mutually exclusive projects have unequal useful lives, there are two methods of resolving potential conflicts among NPV, PI, and IRR. If the projects will all be replaced at the end of their useful lives by another of similar profitability, selection of the one with the highest equivalent charge will be the correct decision. On the other hand, if the cash inflows from each project will merely be reinvested at a relevant rate in other projects, then the terminal value should be computed for both projects at the end of the longer-lived project using the relevant reinvestment rate. From this terminal value, NPV* should be computed and the project with the larger NPV* accepted.

When capital rationing exists, the appropriate method of maximizing shareholders' wealth is not immediately obvious. First, questions have been raised about the appropriate objective(s) to strive for, given the constraints and imperfections in the capital markets. Second, the focus shifts away from that of evaluating individual sets of mutually exclusive projects to that of evaluating all possible portfolios of projects that do not exceed the budget limitations and which satisfy the project interrelationship constraints. Mathematical programming has been suggested as an effective tool in capturing the relevant dimensions of this more-complex problem setting and as an efficient way of evaluating feasible portfolios of projects. Thus, the final topic covered was a constrained optimization problem wherein NPV was maximized subject to a constraint on earnings growth over a 5-year period. We noted how project selection under this constraint resulted in the selection of different projects than would have been accepted using the criterion of maximizing NPV without an earnings constraint. We address this issue later in the text, where mathematical programming is examined in depth. Mathematical programming allows simultaneous consideration of multiple goals and multiple constraints or restrictions, which is a critically important requirement, in order to handle the complex capital budgeting problem setting.

APPENDIX 7A: MULTIPLE INTERNAL RATES OF RETURN

When a project has a sequence of changes in the signs of cash flows, it may have more than one internal rate of return. By Descartes' rule, a project could have as many IRRs as there are changes in signs of the cash flows. Consider a project with the following cash flows:

Time	Cash Flow
Present	−$234,030
1	552,250
2	− 324,300

This project has two internal rates of return: 10% and approximately 26%. This is demonstrated as follows:

Time	Cash Flow	Discount Factor at 10%	PV at 10%	Discount Factor at 26%	PV at 26%
Present	− $234,030	1.00000	− $234,030	1.00000	− $234,030
1	552,250	0.909091	502,046	0.793651	438,294
2	− 324,300	0.826446	− 268,016	0.629882	− 204,271
		NPV	$ 0	NPV	$ 7

In the sequence of cash flows the signs of the cash flow (minus to plus to minus) changed twice. In this particular instance it is possible to have two rates of return. In general, there can be one rate of return for each change in sign. Thus, if there were three changes in sign, there could be up to three internal rates of return.

Positive and negative cash flows result from a *mix* of two basic income streams:

1. Borrowing stream: A series of cash inflows (+) followed by outflows (−). In this condition, the financial manager opts for the lowest rate that discounts the cash flows to zero.

2. Investment stream: A negative outflow (−), followed by a series of inflows (+). Here the preferred option represents the highest rate discounting the cash flows to zero (i.e., the highest IRR). The combination results in project cash flows on a pattern of −, +, − or +, −, +. Sequences of this type (common in the extractive industries and in replacement decisions) complicate the use of computer routines. Unless the analyst is alert to the problem of multiple rates of return, the single rate provided by the computer may be accepted without recognizing the existence of other possibly preferred solution, or if the computer routine does indeed produce multiple solutions, the analyst may not know how to select the optimum solution.

Auxiliary Discount Rates and Multiple Internal Rates of Return[10]

One approach to selecting the appropriate internal rate of return is to use an auxiliary discount rate. This should represent the firm's cost of funds (i.e., the firm's marginal cost of capital projected for the time frame of the analysis). For example, assume the following cash flows:

Period (t)	1	2	3	4	5	6	7	8	9	10	11
Cash Flow	+120	+90	+60	+30	−1,810	+600	+500	+400	+300	+200	+100

[10]The following examples are modifications of the discussion by Eugene L. Grant, W. Grant Ireson, and Richard S. Leavenworth, *Principles of Engineering Economy*, 6th ed. (New York: The Ronald Press Company, 1976).

Periods 1 to 5 typify the cash flows in a borrowing sequence; 5 to 11, the cash flows typical of an investment. However, in terms of magnitude, the project is primarily an investment undertaking. The cash flows may be divided into borrowing and investment sequences, as follows:

Period	Borrowing Flows	Investment Flows
1	+ $120	
2	+ 90	
3	+ 60	
4	+ 30	
5	− x	− $1,810 + x
6		+ 600
7		+ 500
8		+ 400
9		+ 300
10		+ 200
11		+ 100

Note the amount designated by x in year 5. This represents the terminal value of the borrowing sequence, discounted at the assumed auxiliary rate.

If we assume three auxiliary rates, (0, 5%, and 10%) and find the terminal value of the borrowing stream at each rate, three internal rates of return will result:

Assumed Auxiliary Rate	Terminal Value	Terminal Value Less $1,810	IRR (%)
0	$300	− $1,510	14
5%	348	− 1,462	15.5
10%	401	− 1,409	17.4

If the appropriate cost of financing is 10%, the IRR for the project is 17.4%.

As another illustration, consider a project having the following sequence of cash flows:

Time	Cash Flow
Present	− $ 700
1–10	+ 200
11–20	+ 100
21	− 3,000

The two IRRs associated with the project are 2.8% and 26.3%. With the exception of the initial cash outflow of $700, the distribution and magnitude of the cash flows indicate a borrowing sequence. The initial $700 outflow merely detracts from the desirability of the project as a financing venture. Treating the project from a financing perspective, two features should be noted:

1. The positive cash flows in the first few years are taken to "recapture" the $700 investment at some stipulated rate of return.

2. The auxiliary rate computed for the investment project is the opportunity cost of assigning the $700 as a financing project rather than considering the project as a typical investment.[11]

The investment and financing flows may be divided into the following sequence, where y represents the number of years required to recover the $700 outflow at a stipulated auxiliary rate, and x is the *future value* of the investment flows for y periods at the stipulated rate.

Time	Investment Flows	Financing Flows
0	− $700	
1 to $(y - 1)$	+ 200	
y	x	+ $ 200
$(y + 1)$ to 10		+ 200
11 to 20		+ 100
21		− 3,000

The results of discounting the investment flows at various discount rates are as follows:

Assumed Auxiliary Rate (%)	y	x	$200 - x$	Cost of Financing (%)
0	4	$100.00	$100.00	2.6
5	4	188.80	11.20	3.0
10	5	106.30	93.70	3.7
15	6	68.40	131.60	4.8
20	7	125.00	75.00	6.9

The value of x is obtained by finding the future value of $200 for 5 years and subtracting the future value of $700 for the same period using the same auxiliary rate. At the 5% auxiliary rate, the computation is as follows:

$$\$200 \times 4.310125 = \$862.03$$
$$-700 \times 1.215506 = \underline{850.85}$$
$$\underline{\underline{\$11.20}}$$

Continuing with the 5% auxiliary, the cost of financing (IRR) is found by discounting the cash flow using year 4 as the base year.

Year	Period	Amount	Discount Factor 3%	PV
4	Present	$11.20	1	$ 11.20
5–10	1–6	200.00	5.417191	1,083.44
11–20	7–16	100.00	7.14391	714.39
21	17	− 3,000.00	.605016	− 1,815.05
			NPV	$ 6.02

Therefore, we may conclude that if the firm's cost of capital is 5%, an

[11]Note that if the firm's marginal cost of capital is computed, it would be the opportunity cost applied to the investment flows.

investment at that rate for a period of just under 4 years will permit the firm to borrow the funds described at an annual after-tax cost of almost exactly 3%. Similarly, if the firm's cost of capital is 15%, the after-tax cost of borrowing the funds would be 4.8%. Should the firm undertake the borrowing? The question depends on two factors:

1. The alternative use of the initial $700 investment for the period involved.

2. The after-tax cost of debt from other debt sources available to the firm.

PERPETUITIES AND MULTIPLE INTERNAL RATES OF RETURN

In some instances when there exists a continual and regular sequence of sign reversals, it is possible to consider the problem as one of a perpetuity. A mix of such positive and negative cash flows occurs frequently in *replacement decisions*. For example, a taxicab firm or an auto rental service may adopt a policy of replacing its fleet, say, every third year. The investment is mandatory if the firm is to remain in business. However, as to the selection of a car model, the firm has discretion and can choose a manufacturer on an NPV criterion. The analysis has two interesting features:

1. Since replacement is continuous as long as the firm remains in business, the life of the project is indefinite. This suggests the use of perpetuities.

2. A major investment is made at stated intervals so that cash flows are alternatively positive and negative. This suggests multiple rates of return.

Suppose that an auto rental firm, seeking to replace its fleet, can choose between two models. Model *A* has a 4-year life, costs $30,000, and will result in yearly cash inflows of $12,000. Model *B* has a 3-year life, costs $25,000, and will result in yearly cash inflows of $11,000. Salvage values are expected to be negligible. The cash-flow sequence is as follows:

Year	Model A	Model B
Present	− $30,000	−$25,000
1	12,000	11,000
2	12,000	11,000
3	12,000	− 14,000
4	− 18,000	11,000
5	12,000	11,000
6	12,000	− 14,000
7	12,000	11,000
8	− 18,000	11,000
etc.	etc.	etc.

If the firm's cost of capital is given as 10%, the net present value of each may be determined using a perpetuity model and annualizing the costs and inflows as shown below for model *A*.

First, the operating cash flows are put on a perpetuity basis: $12,000/0.10 = $120,000. The present value of $12,000 to be received indefinitely at the 10% rate is $120,000.

Next, annualize the $30,000 cash outflows. Utilize Appendix C, sixth column. $30,000 × 0.31547080 = $9,464.12. The present value of this annual cost, on a perpetual basis, is $9,464.12/0.10 = $94,641.20. Last, determine the NPV: $120,000 − $94,641.20 = $25,358.80. In a similar manner, the NPV of model *B* may be found to be $9,471.30.

This method avoids the problem of multiple internal rates of return by assuming that the firm has selected the appropriate reinvestment rate and annualizes costs using the perpetuity model.

PROBLEMS AND QUESTIONS

1. Why would you, as financial manager, use more than one ranking technique in evaluating capital projects?

2. Indicate various causes for conflicts in ranking among projects.

3. List those characteristics of capital projects and the firm that warrant special attention when making capital investment decisions.

4. A corporation is faced with two mutually exclusive projects, *A* and *B*. The required return is 10%. The expected cash flows are as follows:

Year	Project A	Project B
Present	−$25,000	−$25,000
1	10,000	0
2	10,000	5,000
3	10,000	10,000
4	10,000	30,000

(a) Determine the NPV of projects *A* and *B*.

(b) Determine the IRR of projects *A* and *B*.

(c) Determine the reinvestment rate assumed under IRR.

(d) How can the internal rate-of-return method be modified to make a valid comparison when both proposals have an IRR greater than the required return? Which proposal would you select?

5. A firm is faced with deciding between the following two investment alternatives. Assume a cost of capital of 10%.

Year	Project A	Project B
Present	−$20,000	−$20,000
1	5,000	17,000
2	9,000	5,000
3	16,000	5,000

(a) Determine the NPV and IRR for both projects.

(b) In this situation, which is the better selection criterion? Why?

(c) Determine the IRR for the differential cash flows. What is the significance of this IRR?

(d) What is the discount rate, which when applied to both projects, will result in no conflict in ranking between them?

6. The Rinky Dink Rickshaw Transport Company has a capital budget of $15,000. There are two alternative projects in which the entire sum may be invested: Graffiti

Remover and a Roach Zapper. Each project has an initial cost of $15,000 and an estimated life of 4 years. The Roach Zapper will produce greater returns later in the project life, owing to the tenacious quality of Rickshaw roaches and the difficulty in extermination. The graffiti Remover will produce greater returns at the beginning of the project, because the machine will become less efficient as it gets older.

Roach Zapper		*Graffiti Remover*	
Year	*Cash Flows*	*Year*	*Cash Flows*
0	$(15,000)	0	$(15,000)
1	3,500	1	8,000
2	5,000	2	6,500
3	6,000	3	4,000
4	8,000	4	2,000
Total cash inflows	$ 22,500	Total cash inflows	$ 20,500

Rinky Dink's cost of capital is 10% and the reinvestment rate is 15%. Determine the following.

(a) Rinky Dink management suspects that the NPV and IRR of the two projects conflict. Is this the case?

(b) Using the terminal value method, determine which investment is preferable.

7. Mr. Surekill, the administrator of Savelife Hospital, a small general-care hospital in the Appalachian Mountains, is in a quandary. He has alleviated all his capital budgeting problems for the coming fiscal year except for the electrocardiology and stress-testing departments.

EKG is an established department which preferred to buy a new electrocardiograph machine every 4 years. They presently have two machines. The newest machine has been the primary machine for the past 4 years with the older machine used as backup. Most of the income from a new machine, if purchased, would be in the first 4 years.

Stress Testing, on the other hand, is a new department which wants a treadmill device used to measure stress on the cardiovascular system. Since it is a new department, not yet in operation, it is estimated that initially its income would be low but would increase as the availability of the new test became known to the house staff and was accepted by them.

The following table illustrates the expected after-tax cash flows by year for the two machines, each of which would cost $10,000:

Year	*EKG*	*Stress Test*
Present	− $10,000	− $10,000
1	4,000	1,000
2	4,000	1,000
3	4,000	1,000
4	4,000	3,000
5	1,000	3,000
6	1,000	3,000
7	1,000	7,000
8	1,000	7,000

Assume a required return of 10% and a reinvestment rate of 15%.

(a) Determine the NPV and IRR for each project.

(b) Using the terminal value method, determine which project is preferable.

8. Two of the most widely used methods of evaluating capital investment projects are the net present value (NPV) technique and the internal rate of return (IRR) method. When two or more mutually exclusive investments are being evaluated, conflicts can arise between the rankings given the projects by NPV and IRR. The questions below point to potential difficulties that can arise.

Consider the following two mutually exclusive investment proposals,[12] which are graphed below:

Project A

Year	Net Cash Flows	Discounted at: 6%	15.5%	28.5%
0	−$100			
1	+ 30	$28.29	$25.95	$23.34
2	+ 30	26.70	22.50	18.18
3	+ 70	58.80	45.36	32.97
4	+ 70	55.44	39.34	25.69
		$169.23	$133.15	$100.18

Project B

Year	Net Cash Flows	Discounted at: 6%	15.5%	34%
0	−$100			
1	+ 60	$56.58	$51.90	$44.82
2	+ 60	53.40	45.00	33.42
3	+ 30	25.20	19.44	12.48
4	+ 30	23.76	16.86	9.30
		$158.94	$133.20	$100.02

(a) The project whose discounted-cash-flow pattern is shown by the curve intersecting the axes at points 1 and 5 is:
  A. Project *A*
  B. Project *B*
(b) The dollar value that point 1 on the graph equals is:
  A. $169.23
  B. $158.94
  C. $200.00
  D. $100.00
  E. $69.23
(c) The dollar value that point 2 on the graph equals is:
  A. $158.94
  B. $169.23
  C. $58.94
  D. $180.00
  E. $80.00

[12]The two projects used in this problem originally appeared in example from R. Conrad Doenges, "The 'Reinvestment Problem' in A Practical Perspective," *Financial Management*, Spring 1972, pp. 85–91.

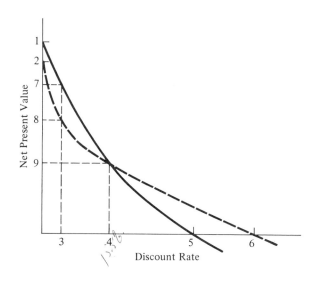

(d) The discount rate that point 5 on the graph equals is:
   A. 0%
   B. 6%
   C. 15.5%
   D. 28.5%
   E. 34%
(e) The dollar amounts that points 7 and 8 equal, respectively, are:
   A. $200 and $180
   B. $169.23 and $158.94
   C. $100 and $80
   D. $69.23 and $58.94
   E. None of the above
(f) Using the NPV criterion, project *B* would be preferred to project *A* for all discount rates:
   A. Greater than 0%
   B. Less than 6%
   C. Less than 15.5%
   D. Greater than 15.5%
   E. Less than 28.5%
(g) Using the NPV criterion, *only one* project would be *acceptable* at the following discount rate:
   A. 6%
   B. 15.5%
   C. 28.5%
   D. 32%
   E. 40%
(h) Using the IRR criterion, project *A* would be preferable to project *B* when the discount rate is:
   A. Greater than 0%
   B. Greater than 15.5%
   C. Less than 15.5%
   D. Greater than 28.5%
   E. None of the above

(i) There would be a conflict between the rankings of the two projects using NPV vs. IRR when the discount rate is:
  A. Greater than 0%
  B. Greater than 6%
  C. Less than 15.5%
  D. Greater than 15.5%
  E. None of the above

(j) Using the IRR criterion, project B would be preferable to project A when the discount rate is:
  A. Greater than 0%
  B. Greater than 6%
  C. Less than 15.5%
  D. Greater than 15.5%
  E. Greater than 28.5%

(k) At a discount rate of 32%, there would be a conflict between the preferred investment using NPV vs. IRR:
  A. True
  B. False

(l) At a discount rate of 40%, there would be a conflict between the preferred investment using NPV vs. IRR:
  A. True
  B. False

(m) The value for point 9 on the graph would equal
  A. $\dfrac{-100}{(1+r)^0} + \dfrac{30}{(1+r)^1} + \dfrac{30}{(1+r)^2} + \dfrac{70}{(1+r)^3} + \dfrac{70}{(1+r)^4}$, where $r = 4$
  B. $\dfrac{-100}{(1+r)^0} + \dfrac{60}{(1+r)^1} + \dfrac{60}{(1+r)^2} + \dfrac{30}{(1+r)^3} + \dfrac{30}{(1+r)^4}$, where $r = 4$
  C. Expression A, where r will equate it to zero
  D. Expression B, where r will equate it to zero
  E. Both A and B
  F. None of the above

(n) Referring to question (m), the value for point 4 on the graph will be
  A. The value of r that will equate expression A with that of B
  B. The value of r that will equate expression A to zero
  C. The value of r that will equate expression B to zero
  D. Both B and C
  E. None of the above

9. The Philly Bus Service is seeking to add to its fleet to improve its service. It has a choice of three models of bus:
   Model O: 3-year life, cost of $26,000, and cash inflow of $12,000 per year.
   Model P: 4-year life, cost of $38,000, and cash inflows of $19,000 per year.
   Model Q: 7-year life, cost of $52,000 and cash inflows of $26,000 per year.
   The firm has a cost of capital of 12% and the buses have no salvage value. Using the perpetuity method, determine the net present value of each model.

10. Generous Electric Corporation has a contractual agreement with Faultydelphia Electric Company, a utility, to repair or replace existing generating equipment. Project Repair involves the rebuilding of a 10-year-old, 500,000-kW-capacity steam turbine. The rebuilt turbine will be operable for another 8 years. The net present value of future cash flows is $3,600,000. Project Replace involves the installation of a 6,000,000-kW-capacity steam turbine. The new turbine will have an operating life of 25 years and a net present value of $6,501,500. Assuming Faultydelphia Electric's hurdle rate is 8% for capital projects of this magnitude, determine which project is desirable.

11. Referring to Problem 10, what other factors should be considered before making the replace-versus-repair decision?

12. If Faultydelphia Electric's cost of capital was 11%, what would you do under these circumstances with respect to choosing one of the proposed projects?

13. A company is considering the purchase of machine A, which has an initial cost of $2k and an estimated operating life of 8 years. Annual operating costs (including maintenance) are $1k. Machine A will have zero salvage value in 8 years. Machine B cost $5,000 and is being considered as an alternative. It has an estimated life of 12 years and an estimated salvage value of $1,000. Annual operating costs are $500. Compare the annual costs for the two machines, assuming a required rate of 10%.

14. An amusement park has just purchased an additional piece of property adjacent to its park. It is trying to choose between two rides in which to invest, to be situated on this recently acquired property. Ride A costs $76,000 and has an expected life of 5 years. Ride B costs $90,000 and has an expected life of 7 years. Both are forecast to generate total annual cash inflows of $47,000. Ride B requires $8,000 higher annual power costs than ride A. Ride A requires an annual painting amounting to $5,000. All other cash outflows are equal at $20,000 per year.

    Using the perpetuity model, determine the preferred investment, if the firm's cost of capital is 10%.

II

INTRODUCTION
TO RISK ANALYSIS
IN CAPITAL BUDGETING

8 INTRODUCTION TO RISK ANALYSIS

During the first part of our study of capital investments, we assumed that any decisions involving investments would not alter the risk complexion of the firm. This is not to say that we were operating under conditions of certainty but rather that we held risk constant. However, it is a truism that it is frequently difficult to make either short-or long-term estimates of the cash flows for capital investments with a high degree of accuracy. As a consequence, in this and the following chapters, we will examine capital investment decisions under conditions of risk and uncertainty. Initially, we will direct our attention to individual projects and then to portfolios of projects during one time period. Later, in the section on programming, we will examine multiperiod analysis under conditions of certainty and risk.

CERTAINTY, RISK, AND UNCERTAINTY

Up to this point we have assumed that projects being considered have a risk posture consistent with that of the firm overall. This meant that the acceptance of projects would not change the firm's risk complexion (i.e., the risk has been held constant). A decision maker may be faced with conditions of certainty, risk, and uncertainty. These are differentiated below:

Certainty postulates that the decision maker knows in advance the precise values that all the parameters that may affect the decision will take on.

Risk postulates that the decision maker (1) is aware of all possible future states of the economy, business, and so on, which may occur and thereby affect relevant decision parameters and (2) is able to place a probability on the value of the occurrence of each of these states.

Uncertainty postulates that the decision maker (1) may or may not be aware of all the possible states that affect the decision and (2) may or may not be able to place a probability distribution on the occurrence of each.

We shall deal with conditions of certainty and risk, assuming for the present that it is possible to reduce problems under conditions of uncertainty to those of risk by collecting additional data (at some cost). We recognize that techniques such as adaptive and optimal control processes, heuristic programming, and artificial intelligence methods are currently being developed to deal with capital investment evaluation under conditions of uncertainty. Although we shall not deal with any of these, we expect, as they are more fully developed, that they will become an integral part of the risk analysis methodology.

At this juncture it is useful to review the general kinds of risk faced by financial managers. Although the types of risk tend to be interrelated, it is helpful in financial planning, decision making, and control to identify various categories. We shall refer to these in this and the following chapters as we examine the capital investment decision under conditions of risk.

1. Business risk is the variability in earnings which is a function of the firm's normal operations (as impacted by the changing economic environment) and management's decisions with respect to capital intensification. The use of more capital equipment (increasing operating leverage) generally results in higher fixed costs and thereby increases the variability of EBIT with output (as measured by the degree of operating leverage). It should be noted that business risk considers only the variability in EBIT, and does not consider the effect of debt or other financing on the firm's risk posture. Although business risk encompasses the variability in earnings due to economic changes and management investment policies, it is instructive to view these as investment and portfolio risk.

2. Investment risk is the variability in earnings due to variations in the cash inflows and outflows of capital investment projects undertaken. This risk is associated with forecasting errors made in market acceptance of products, future technological changes, degree of intertemporal relationship of cash flows, changes in costs related to projects, and other environmental risks discussed below.

3. Portfolio risk is the variability in the earnings due to the degree of efficient diversification that the firm has achieved in its operations and its overall portfolio of assets. The risk is reduced by the firm seeking out capital projects and merger candidates that have a low or negative correlation with their present operations. The full impact of portfolio effects is discussed in Chapter 9.

4. Cataclysmic risk is the variability in earnings which is a function of events beyond managerial control and anticipation. Such events would include expropriation, erratic changes in consumer preferences, severe energy shortages, and the like.

5. Financial risk is the variability in earnings which is a function of the financial structure and the necessity of meeting obligations on fixed-income securities. The use of more debt or preferred stock (increasing financial leverage) results in greater obligatory payments and thereby increases the variability of EAT and EPS (as measured by the degree of financial leverage).

Business and financial risk and the effects of operating and financial leverage will be discussed further in Chapter 11. Our next objective is to discuss methods of measuring expected return and the possible dispersion of return resulting from the various risks facing the firm.

RISK AND RETURN

Since risk is an inherent part of almost all capital investment decisions, it is necessary to consider it as well as the expected return associated with various decision alternatives. The probability distribution, which describes possible outcomes, must be defined along with the mean or expected value of cash flows in order to evaluate alternative courses of action. The expected value of a probability distribution is defined in Equation (1):

$$\bar{R} = \sum_{i=1}^{N} (R_i P_i) \qquad (1)$$

where $\bar{R}$ = expected value
R_i = return associated with the ith outcome
P_i = probability of occurrence of the ith outcome
N = number of possible outcomes

Calculation of the expected return for an investment is demonstrated in Example 1.

● EXAMPLE 1   Expected Return

A financial manager faces conditions of risk in terms of economic strength in the coming year. Three different states may occur: strong economy with probability 0.3; moderately strong economy, 0.5; and weak economy, 0.2. Three alternative 1-year investments are under consideration offering returns as follows:

| | | *Expected Investment Outcomes* | | |
State of Economy	Probability	*A*	*B*	*C*
Strong	0.3	$1,800	$1,600	$2,000
Moderately strong	0.5	1,500	1,200	1,600
Weak	0.2	800	1,000	900

Determine the expected return for project A.

Solution: For investment A:

$$\bar{R} = (0.3)(\$1,800) + (0.5)(\$1,500) + (0.2)(\$800)$$
$$= \$540 + \$750 + \$160$$
$$= \underline{\underline{\$1,450}}$$

The mean return for investment A is $1,450. This return is determined by weighting the return for each state of the economy by its respective probability of occurrence. The expected return for investment B is $1,280 and for investment C is $1,580.   ●

The amount of variability or dispersion that is present in the probability distribution of returns associated with a decision alternative is referred to as the risk of that decision alternative. There are several measures of risk that have been advocated for use by financial managers. Statisticians speak of both *absolute* and *relative measures of risk* (variability or dispersion). *Absolute measures of dispersion* include the range, mean absolute deviation, variance, standard deviation, and semivariance. The *relative measure of dispersion is the coefficient of variation.* Each of these measures is defined in equation form below:

$$R_g = R_h - R_l \tag{2}$$

where R_g = range of the distribution
R_h = highest value in the distribution
R_l = lowest value in the distribution

$$\text{MAD} = \sum_{i=1}^{N} P_i\left(|R_i - \bar{R}|\right) \tag{3}$$

where MAD is the mean absolute deviation

$$\sigma^2 = \sum_{i=1}^{N} P_i\left(R_i - \bar{R}\right)^2 \tag{4}$$

where σ^2 is the variance of the distribution

$$\sigma = \sqrt{\sum_{i=1}^{N} P_i\left(R_i - \bar{R}\right)^2} \tag{5}$$

where σ is the standard deviation

$$\text{SV} = \sum_{j=1}^{K} P_j\left(R_j - \bar{R}\right)^2 \tag{6}$$

where SV = semivariance
j = index set which includes all values of the random variable which are less than the expected value
K = number of outcomes which are less than the expected value

$$\nu = \frac{\sigma}{\bar{R}} \tag{7}$$

where ν is the coefficient of variation.

The calculation of the various measures of risk or dispersion is demonstrated in Example 2.

● **EXAMPLE 2** *Measurement of Risk*

Using the information in Example 1, determine the value for each measure of risk defined above for investment A.

Solution: R_g = range = $1,800 - $800 = $1,000

This value simply means that there is a $1,000 difference between the lowest return that could be earned with investment A and the highest possible return. The range for investment B is $600 and for investment C is $1,100.

$$\begin{aligned}
\text{MAD} &= (0.3)(|\$1,800 - \$1,450|) + (0.5)(|\$1,500 - \$1,450|) + (0.2)(|\$800 - \$1,450|) \\
&= (0.3)(\$350) + (0.5)(\$50) + (0.2)(\$650) \\
&= \$260
\end{aligned}$$

The MADs for investment B and C are \$192 and \$272, respectively. MAD shows that average variability of the values of the distribution from the mean without regard to the sign of the deviation.

$$\sigma^2 = (0.2)(\$800 - \$1{,}450)^2 + (0.5)(\$1{,}500 - \$1{,}450)^2 + (0.3)(\$1{,}800 - \$1{,}450)^2$$
$$= (0.2)(\$650)^2 + (0.5)(\$50)^2 + (0.3)(\$350)^2$$
$$= 122{,}500$$
$$\sigma = \sqrt{\sigma^2} = \$350$$

The standard deviation is a measure of how representative the expected return is of the entire distribution. The larger the standard deviation, the less representative the mean is because of the greater scatter around the mean. The variance and standard deviation for investment B are, respectively, 49,600 and \$222.71 and for investment C are 145,600 and \$381.58.

The final absolute measure of dispersion is the semivariance, which is similar to the variance but only looks at deviations below the mean, since these are the unfavorable deviations that quantify the "downside risk."

$$SV = (0.2)(\$800 - \$1{,}450)^2 = (0.2)(422{,}500)$$
$$= 84{,}500$$

Note that the downside risk as measured by the semivariance is about 70% of the total variability as measured by the variance for investment A (84,500 as compared to 122,500). The semivariance for investments B and C are 18,880 and 92,480, respectively. Finally,

$$\nu = \frac{\$350}{\$1{,}450} = 0.2414$$

The coefficient of variation is 0.2414 for investment A and 0.1742 and 0.2418 for investments B and C, respectively. The coefficient of variation shows the amount of risk (as measured by the standard deviation) per dollar of expected return. That is, the lower the coefficient of variation, the smaller is the amount of relative risk. When evaluating alternatives that have different expected returns, a relative measure of variability such as the coefficient of variation is required to accurately compare the riskiness of the alternatives. ●

The expected value of return and measures of risk for all three investments are as follows:

**Comparison of Expected Return and Risk
for Three Investment Alternatives**

	Investment A	*Investment B*	*Investment C*
Expected return	\$1,450	\$1,280	\$1,580
Range	\$1,000	\$600	\$1,100
Mean absolute deviation	\$260	\$192	\$272
Variance	122,500	49,600	145,600
Standard deviation	\$350	\$223	\$382
Semivariance	84,500	18,880	92,480
Coefficient of variation	0.2414	0.1742	0.2418

Given the expected value and various measures of risk surrounding each investment we will now interpret the measures within the context of Example 2. The range simply measures the total variability in possible returns for each investment. It establishes the upper and lower limits of possible outcomes. It is rarely used in practice because it (1) considers only the extremal values (and, by default, ignores all the others) and (2) ignores the probabilities attached to any of the values within the distribution.

The variance, its counterpart the standard deviation, and the mean absolute deviation (MAD) all measure dispersion in terms of the probabilities associated with each possible outcome. The variance and standard deviation are preferred in decision making under conditions of risk, since the value provided by MAD is distorted by disregard for the signs of the deviations of each value from the mean. As a practical matter, *the standard deviation is used most commonly as it has the same units as the original variable and is the measure of dispersion used with the expected value to characterize several distributions, including the normal distribution.* The semivariance is a special case of the variance, used to measure downside risk. Advocates of the semivariance say that deviations above the mean add to an investment's attractiveness, but since investors frequently tend to avoid downside risk, only deviations below the mean need be quantified. Risk aversion will be further addressed in the following sections.

Thus far, our discussion has been limited to measures of absolute dispersion. While these are statistically valid, their use in financial decision making requires evaluation of risk within the framework of the expected return. Therefore, it is necessary to simultaneously consider both risk and return by means of the measure of relative dispersion, the coefficient of variation. Refer to the preceding table and note that investments A and C have equal coefficients of variation, indicating equal risk per dollar of expected return, whereas investment B has a significantly lower coefficient of variation, indicating a lower risk per dollar of expected return.

Given all of the above, which of the three alternatives should the financial manager select? In this problem setting, as in most under conditions of risk, the statistics provide additional information about the alternatives, but they do not specify which should be selected by all decision makers. *None of the alternatives is dominant, which would mean that it simultaneously has a higher expected value and a lower level of risk.* The final decision would have to be made in terms of the decision maker's utility function, that is, his specification of preferences considering all relevant aspects of the problem setting. We turn now to a formal discussion of utility theory.

UTILITY THEORY

As discussed above, the relaxation of the certainty assumption necessitates consideration of both the expected return and risk criteria for evaluating decision alternatives. However, decision makers will view varying degrees of risk and return differently, hence will select divergent decision alternatives. Utility theory is an attempt to formalize rational decision making, wherein preferences among alternatives are specified by a given decision maker. The utility value attached to various alternatives represents an integration of all aspects relevant to the decision.

In this section we provide an introduction to the theory of utility analysis. Our particular interest lies in its application to the trade-off between risk and return, which is developed further in the section on certainty equivalents, which follows. The treatment of utility theory contained herein is very brief. The reader should refer to Appendix A for a list of additional readings on this subject.

When faced with a decision, the decision maker must consider the following within the framework of personal preferences.

1. The opportunity set of all relevant goals and objectives.

2. The hierarchy of goals and acceptable trade-offs of goals within the hierarchy.

3. The perceptions of risk per se and risk–return preference (i.e., the incremental expected return required to justify acceptance of an additional unit of risk).

4. The preferences for current versus future consumption as affected by present wealth position, liquidity requirements, and so on.

In order to be able to specify and differentiate among various classes of risk preference (or aversion), it is useful to define the decision maker's utility function with respect to required return and risk. This necessitates acceptance of the *axioms of coherence*.[1]

1. Given any two payoffs (which may involve nonmonetary, as well as monetary values), a decision maker can specify preference of one over the other or indifference between the two.

2. If a given decision maker prefers payoff P_1 to P_2 and P_2 to P_3, then necessarily P_1 is preferred to P_3 (*transitivity or consistency of preferences*).

3. If a decision maker prefers P_1 to P_2 and P_2 to P_3, there is some mixture of P_1 and P_3 which is preferred to P_2, some other mixture of P_1 and P_3 which is inferior to P_2, and a third mixture of P_1 and P_3 which will leave the decision maker indifferent relative to P_2.

4. If a decision maker prefers P_1 to P_2 and P_3 is some other payoff, a mixture of P_1 and P_3 will be preferred to the same mixture of P_2 and P_3.

5. If a decision maker is indifferent between payoffs P_4 and P_5, they may be substituted for each other in any decision setting.

6. If a decision maker prefers P_1 to P_2, two mixtures of P_1 and P_2 will find the former preferred if, and only if, the former has a larger proportion of P_1.

If the decision maker accepts the axioms of coherence, it is reasonable to assume that he or she will act so as to maximize utility. This means selection of those available decision alternatives that will lead to the greatest level of satisfaction. Since preferences are necessarily subjective, the exact specification of a decision maker's utility function is fraught with operational difficulties. Further, individual utility preferences are likely to change over time. However, we can specify three general categories of decision makers based on their risk preferences: risk-averse, risk-indifferent, and risk-taking. The utility functions for each category of decision maker are shown in Figure 8-1.

---

[1]Robert L. Winkler, *Introduction to Bayesian Inference and Decision* (New York: Holt, Rinehart, and Winston, Inc., 1972), pp. 260–264.

FIGURE 8-1   Relationship Between Income or Wealth and Utility

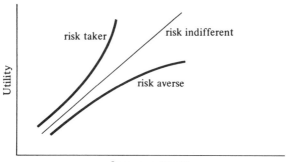

Income or Wealth

With respect to risk, decision makers may be classified as follows:

1. Risk-averse decision makers have decreasing marginal utilities for increases in wealth. For the risk-averse decision maker, the chances to enjoy additional wealth are less attractive than the possibility of the pain associated with a decrease in wealth or income.

2. Risk-indifferent decision makers have constant marginal utilities; hence, their utility curves are linear.

3. Risk-taking decision makers have increasing marginal utilities for larger potential increases in wealth.

Within each of the three categories, decision makers demonstrate varying degrees of preference or aversion to risk. Thus, we can anticipate a different utility function for each individual decision maker. Further, each decision maker has a whole family of nonintersecting utility curves, showing successively higher levels of satisfaction. To maximize expected utility, the decision maker will strive to achieve the highest feasible curve within the available alternatives and constraints.

Within the arena of capital investment decision making, experience indicates that the great majority of managers are risk averters, but again the specific degree of aversion varies over a wide spectrum. Figure 8-2 shows risk–return utility functions (indifference curves) for two managers. Manager *A*

FIGURE 8-2   Risk–Return Indifference Curves

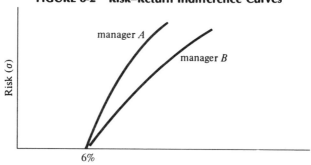

Expected Rate of Return

FIGURE 8-3   **Family of Indifference Curves for One Manager**

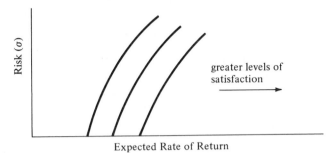

is less risk-adverse than manager *B*. Both managers are willing to accept a 6% risk-free rate of return, but manager *B* requires increasingly greater returns as risk increases than does manager *A*. Thus, Figure 8-2 shows the risk–return preferences for two managers at one point in time.

As described above, each manager has a whole set of indifference curves, indicating successively higher levels of satisfaction. Such a family of indifference curves is shown in Figure 8-3. As we move to the right, each curve indicates a higher level of satisfaction.

Given the risk–return preferences, we are now in the position to discuss methods used to compensate for risk in the capital investment process. *There are three formal approaches which are commonly used to incorporate risk into the analysis: the risk-adjusted discount rate technique, the certainty equivalent method, and the capital asset pricing model.* The first two approaches are discussed in this chapter and the third is treated in Chapter 10.

CERTAINTY EQUIVALENT METHOD FOR RISK ADJUSTMENT

The certainty equivalent method permits adjustment for risk by incorporating the manager's utility preference for risk versus return directly into the capital investment process. The method is especially useful when management perceives different levels of risk associated with the estimated annual cash flows over the life of a project. Given the limitations of economic forecasting, it is reasonable to assume that the estimates of cash flows during the early periods in a project's life are likely to be more accurate than those corresponding to the latter years. It is just this reasoning that motivates many firms to rely on payback as a surrogate measure of risk to supplement the discounted-cash-flow methods. However, the formal methods discussed in this and the following sections overcome all the drawbacks associated with payback while permitting management to impute its risk preference directly into the capital budgeting decision.

When the certainty equivalent method is used, the estimated annual cash flows (which represent the expected value of a probabilistic distribution of returns) are multiplied by a certainty equivalent coefficient (CEC), designated in equation form as α.

The CEC reflects management's perception of the degree of risk associated with the estimated cash-flow distribution as well as management's degree of aversion to perceived risk, as evidenced by their utility function. The product of the expected cash flow and the CEC represents the amount that management would be willing to accept for certain in each year of the project's life as opposed to accepting the cash-flow distribution and its associated risk. Hence, the name "certainty equivalent method."

The CEC's range in value from zero to 1. The higher values indicate a lower penalty assigned by management to that cash-flow distribution. A value of 1 indicates that management does not associate any risk with the estimated cash flow and therefore is willing to accept the expected value of the cash-flow estimate as certain. *Since the certainty equivalent method compensates for risk in its entirety, it is therefore appropriate to discount all certainty equivalent adjusted cash flows at the risk-free rate of return* as opposed to the firm's cost of capital. The risk-free rate of return is that return normally associated with the return available from Treasury Bills, since these are short-term and have guaranteed return and principal repayment at maturity. The risk-free rate of return is an accurate representation of the time value of money given that the cash flows are not subject to variability.

In our discussion of the NPV technique, we employed a cost of capital as the discount rate. *The cost of capital reflected the normal risk posture of the firm and included the risk-free rate of return plus additional return requirements to compensate for the business and financial risk as defined above. The certainty equivalent method is designed to compensate for risk in its entirety (including the normal business and financial risks), and therefore the risk-free rate of return is the appropriate discount rate when this method is used.*

The certainty equivalent value is defined in Equation (8):

$$\overline{CE} = \sum_{t=0}^{n} \frac{\alpha_t \overline{R}_t}{(1 + i)^t} \tag{8}$$

where $\overline{CE}$ = expected certainty equivalent value over the life of the project

$\overline{R}_t$ = expected cash inflow in period t

α_t = certainty equivalent factor which converts the expected risky cash flow $\overline{R}_t$ into its perceived certainty equivalent value

i = risk-free rate which is assumed to remain constant over the life of the project

n = number of years in the project's life

The value of the certainty equivalent coefficient is one only for risk-free investments, such as Treasury Bills. The values for the certainty equivalent coefficients corresponding to projects falling within the firm's normal risk posture are less than 1. One method for developing certainty coefficient values (corresponding to projects having the same risk complexion as that normally associated with the firm) is demonstrated in Example 3.

● **EXAMPLE 3** *Certainty Equivalent Coefficient Values*

A corporation has a cost of capital of 10% and the risk-free rate of return is 5%. A project falling within the firm's normal risk posture is being evaluated. It has a 1-year life and an expected cash flow of $1,000 to be received in 1 year. Determine the certainty coefficient value for this project.

Solution: Using the net-present-value method, we would first determine the present value of the project's cash flow, as follows:

$$PV = \frac{\$1,000}{1 + 0.10} = \$909.09$$

The value of the corresponding certainty equivalent coefficient may be found using this present value.

$$\frac{\alpha_1 \cdot \$1,000}{1 + 0.05} = \$909.09$$

$$\alpha_1 = \frac{(\$909.09)(1.05)}{\$1,000}$$

$$= 0.95454 \qquad \bullet$$

Note that the NPV approach lumps together the discounting for time and the adjustment for risk, whereas the certainty equivalent method disaggregates the two by adjusting for risk with the α factor and discounting for the time value of money at the risk-free rate. The value for the certainty equivalent coefficient in the single period case was found easily, as shown in Example 3. However, since most projects have lives that extend over several periods, it is necessary to incorporate managers' risk preferences on a multiperiod basis. One procedure for ascertaining CEC values for different time periods is to undertake a historical review of project performance. Projects are first divided into general categories, such as normal replacement, expansion, and R & D. Then within each category, on a year-by-year basis, the measures of risk and return are determined. The result is a probability distribution of cash flows by year of project life, from which the coefficient of variation may be obtained. The CEC for each year and each category of project would then be assigned according to the magnitude of the coefficient of variation weighted by managers' preference for risk aversion. An example of the result of dividing projects into categories, determining coefficients of variation based on historical preference, and assigning CECs is shown in Table 8-1 for the 4-year period, based on *the utility preferences for one firm at a point in time*. It should be noted that the logical choice for categories of investments is predicated on the historical values of the coefficient of variation. Thus, in Table 8-1, "Replacement investment—category I" groups all projects that *normally* have coefficient of variation in year 1 of less than 0.10. However, it may be that a new machine, which by verbal definition falls into category I, has a coefficient of variation for year 1 between 0.10 and 0.25. Thus, this project would fall into "Replacement—category II." Further, from year to year over a project's life it is possible for the project to change categories. That is, its projected riskiness may not fall into the historical norm for a given category of projects each year. The CEC factor is determined based on the expected coefficient of variation for each year of the project's life. Further, the factors are for a point in time with given risk-free rate of return and cost of capital. A change in the risk-free rate, cost of capital, or management's utility preferences will result in a revision of the CEC values. The results of evaluating a project having the same risk complexion as the firm should be consistent when using the firm's cost of capital and the risk-free rate with certainty equivalent adjustment.

TABLE 8-1 Certainty Equivalent Factors for Different Investment Groups

	Coefficient of Variation, v	Certainty Equivalent Coefficient			
		Year 1	Year 2	Year 3	Year 4
Replacement investments—category I (new machines or equipment, vehicles, etc., that will perform essentially the same function as older equipment which is to be replaced)	$v \leqslant 0.10$	0.95	0.92	0.89	0.85
Replacement investments—category II (new machines or equipment that replace older equipment but are more technologically advanced, require different operator skills, require different manufacturing approaches, or the like; examples include implementation of electronic data processing equipment to replace manual accounting and payroll systems)	$0.10 < v \leqslant 0.25$	0.9	0.86	0.82	0.77
Replacement investments—category III (new facilities such as buildings and warehouses that will replace older facilities; the new plants may be in the same or a different location)	$v > 0.25$	0.84	0.79	0.74	0.68
New investment—category I (new facilities and associated equipment that will produce or sell the same products as are already being produced)	$v \leqslant 0.10$	0.92	0.88	0.85	0.80
New investment—category II (new facilities or machinery to produce or sell a product line that is closely related to the existing product line)	$0.10 \leqslant v \leqslant 0.25$	0.86	0.82	0.78	0.73
New investment—category III (new facilities or machinery or acquisition of another firm to produce or sell a product line that is unrelated to the company's primary business)	$v > 0.25$	0.80	0.75	0.70	0.64
Research and development—category I (research and development which is directed toward specific goals such as developing new computer circuitry with which the firm's engineers are already very familiar)	$v \leqslant 0.20$	0.82	0.76	0.70	0.60
Research and development—category II (research in basic areas where goals have not been precisely defined and the outcome may be unknown)	$v > 0.20$	0.70	0.60	0.50	0

The change in a project's expected coefficient of variation from year to year depends on the intertemporal correlation of expected cash flows. This leads to multiperiod and portfolio analyses, which are discussed in subsequent chapters. As a final note, the CEC value assigned to year 4 for "Research and development—category II" in our sample firm is zero. This implies that management is completely disregarding the cash flows for year 4, and the analysis thereby approaches the payback method, wherein *all* cash flows are ignored after a stated period.

The procedure for using certainty equivalent coefficients is demonstrated in Example 4.

● **EXAMPLE 4** *Certainty Equivalent Coefficient*

A new investment project has expected returns and standard deviations during its 4-year life as follows:

Year	Expected Return	Standard Deviation	Coefficient of Variation
1	$1,000	$200	0.20
2	1,200	216	0.18
3	1,200	168	0.14
4	1,800	144	0.08

The cash outflow is $3,000 and the risk-free rate of return is 6%. Find the certainty equivalent factors corresponding to the coefficient of variation listed above (see Table 8-1). Then, determine the expected certainty equivalent value, $\overline{CE}$.

Solution: The following table is helpful in computing $\overline{CE}$:

Time	$\overline{R}_t$	α_t	$\alpha_t \overline{R}_t$	Discount Factor at 6%	Discounted $\alpha_t \overline{R}_t$
Present	− $3,000	1.0	− $3,000	1.00	− $3,000
1	+ 1,000	0.86	860	0.943	811
2	+ 1,200	0.82	984	0.890	876
3	+ 1,200	0.78	936	0.840	786
4	+ 1,800	0.80	1,440	0.792	1,140
					$\overline{CE}$ = $ 613

The meaning of $\overline{CE}$ is discussed below. ●

The certainty equivalent value is analogous to the net present value in that the decision rule for both methods is to reject projects that have negative CEs or NPVs. In Example 4, since the project in question had a positive CE (i.e., $613), it represents a candidate for acceptance.

In our earlier discussions, we pointed out that to maximize shareholders' wealth, the set of projects that maximized NPV should be accepted. If we limit our examination of certainty equivalents to $\overline{CE}$, we would select that set of projects having the largest total $\overline{CE}$. However, another powerful evaluation tool is available to us: *we may ascertain the probability distribution for the certainty equivalent of each project and then develop acceptance criteria in keeping with both risk aversion and maximization of shareholder wealth.* For example, we might select a decision rule requiring rejection of any project that has a probability less than 90% of achieving a positive CE value. Then, from the remaining group, select the set of projects having the largest total $\overline{CE}$. We will treat the probability distribution of certainty equivalents later in the chapter.

Thus far in our discussion, we have assumed that the risk-free rate remains constant over time. If this assumption is relaxed, Equation (8) may be rewritten in its more general form as Equation (9).

$$\overline{CE} = \sum_{t=0}^{n} \frac{\alpha_t \overline{R}_t}{\prod_{k=1}^{t} (1 + i_k)} \tag{9}$$

where i_k = risk-free rate in year k

$\prod$ = geometric sum

The application of Equation (9) is demonstrated in Example 5.

● **EXAMPLE 5** *Certainty Equivalent Value for a Change in Risk-Free Rates*

Suppose that the estimated cash flows for a project, the risk-free rates of return, and the certainty equivalent coefficients are as follows:

Time	α_t	$\overline{R}_t$	Risk-Free Return
Present	1	−$3,000	—
1	0.95	1,000	0.05
2	0.92	1,500	0.06
3	0.89	1,700	0.07

Determine $\overline{CE}$.

Solution:

$$\overline{CE} = -\$3,000 + \frac{0.95(\$1,000)}{1 + 0.05} + \frac{0.92(\$1,500)}{(1 + 0.05)(1 + 0.06)}$$

$$+ \frac{0.89(\$1,700)}{(1 + 0.05)(1 + 0.06)(1 + 0.07)}$$

$$= -\$3,000 + \$905 + \$1,240 + \$1,270$$

$$= \$415$$

RISK-ADJUSTED DISCOUNT RATE

The rationale underlying the use of the risk-adjusted discount rate (RADR) technique is that projects which have greater variability in the probability distributions of their returns should have these returns discounted at a higher rate than projects having less variability or risk. A project that had no risk associated with it would be discounted at the risk-free rate, since this is the appropriate rate just to account for the time value of money. Any project that has risk associated with it has to be discounted at a

rate in excess of the risk-free rate in order to discount both for futurity (the time value of money) and for the risk associated with the project (a risk premium). Projects that are of average riskiness vis-à-vis the firm's normal operations should be discounted at the firm's cost of capital, since this figure reflects the normal risk faced by the firm. Those projects having greater-than-normal risk should be discounted at a rate in excess of the cost of capital; conversely, projects that exhibit less risk than that associated with a firm's normal operations should be discounted at a rate between the risk-free rate and the cost of capital. The risk-adjusted rate is found by Equation (10):

$$r' = i + u + a \qquad (10)$$

where r' = risk-adjusted discount rate
$\quad i$ = risk-free rate
$\quad u$ = adjustment for the firm's normal risk
$\quad a$ = adjustment for above (or below) the firm's normal risk

It should be noted that the sum of i and u is the firm's cost of capital, since that discount rate is appropriate for projects having average or "normal" risk. Notice that the term for the abnormal risk adjustment could either be positive or negative, based on whether the project has more or less risk associated with it than the average project for the firm in question.

It should be pointed out that the amount of risk adjustment is based on management's utility preference for risk aversion so that this adjustment reflects the management's perception of the risk associated with the project per se, its risk-return preferences, the firm's wealth position, and the impact of the project on the firm's other goals. Table 8-2 provides risk adjustments for the categories of investments defined in Table 8-1, reflecting the utility preferences for a firm at a particular time. Although all the project types shown in Table 8-2 are required to achieve the firm's cost of capital as a minimum return, there may be some categories of projects that have a risk sufficiently low to warrant their implementation, even though their projected return is below the firm's cost of capital.

Reference to Table 8-2 indicates that a firm having a cost of capital of 10% would apply a 16% hurdle rate to a project falling into "Replacement investment—category III." *It should also be noted that unlike the certainty equivalent method, the RADR technique as it is generally used in practice applies the same discount rate to the project throughout its useful life.*

Equation (11) may be used to determine the expected present value when employing a risk-adjusted discount rate:

$$\overline{\text{RAR}} = \sum_{t=0}^{n} \frac{\overline{R}_t}{(1 + r')^t} \qquad (11)$$

where $\overline{\text{RAR}}$ = expected value of the distribution of discounted cash flows over the life of the project (risk-adjusted net present value)
$\quad \overline{R}_t$ = expected value of the distribution of cash flows in year t
$\quad r'$ = risk-adjusted discount rate based on the perceived riskiness of the project under consideration
$\quad n$ = number of years in the project's life

The application of Equation (11) is demonstrated in Example 6.

TABLE 8-2   Return Requirements for Various Investment Groups

Investment Grouping	Required Return
Replacement investments— category I	Cost of capital
Replacement investments— category II	Cost of capital plus 3%
Replacement investments— category III	Cost of capital plus 6%
New investment— category I	Cost of capital plus 5%
New investment— category II	Cost of capital plus 8%
New investment— category III	Cost of capital plus 15%
Research and development— category I	Cost of capital plus 10%
Research and development— category II	Cost of capital plus 20%

● **EXAMPLE 6**   Calculation of $\overline{RAR}$

A firm is considering the adoption of a "Replacement investment—category II" project which has the cash flows as shown by the following distribution:

Original Cost		Cash Inflows Years 1–5		Years 6–10	
Probability	Amount	Probability	Amount	Probability	Amount
0.3	$13,000	0.2	$2,000	0.2	$2,600
0.4	14,000	0.4	2,400	0.6	3,200
0.3	15,000	0.3	2,800	0.1	3,400
		0.1	3,400	0.1	3,600

The firm's cost of capital is 11%. Determine the risk-adjusted net present value.

Solution: First, determine the mean value for each cash flow and incorporate into Equation (11) as follows:

$$\overline{RAR} = -\$14,000 + \sum_{t=1}^{5} \frac{\$2,540}{(1.14)^t} + \sum_{t=6}^{10} \frac{\$3,140}{(1.14)^t}$$

$$= -\$14,000 + \$8,720 + \$5,599$$

$$= \$319$$

Since the $\overline{RAR}$ is positive, this project represents a candidate for acceptance.   ●

In addition to the expected value of the return, we may also examine the probability distribution in a manner similar to that discussed above for the certainty equivalent method. This task will be addressed later in this chapter.

The following section compares the certainty equivalent and risk-adjusted methods and describes some conflicts that may arise when using the two methods.

COMPARING CERTAINTY EQUIVALENT AND ADJUSTMENT OF THE DISCOUNT RATE

Risk adjustment using the risk-adjusted discount rate method has been criticized primarily for two reasons.

1. The method does not examine the riskiness associated with each project or the changes in riskiness over its life, but rather groups projects into general risk categories. It applies the same discount-rate risk premium over the entire life of the project. Certainty equivalent requires individual examination of projects in each time period since riskiness associated with a given project may change over its life. In fact, investment uncertainty may be concentrated in only a few years of the project's life, and once this uncertainty is resolved, all future years have a much more moderate risk posture.

2. Risk adjustment combines the two parts of the discounting process: the risk-free return for time and the risk premium. The use of a high constant discount rate over a project's entire useful life implies that its riskiness is increasing over time. The implication results from the fact that discounting equates to an exponential decay of the value of cash as a function of time. The difference between the present value of cash flows discounted at the risk-free rate and the present value of those same cash flows when discounted at a risk-adjusted hurdle rate increases exponentially with the passage of time. The process is illustrated in Example 7.

● **EXAMPLE 7** *Risk-Adjusted Discount Rate and Certainty Equivalent*

A project costing $10,000 has a 12-year life and expected cash inflows of $1,800 each year. The risk-free rate of return is 7%, the firm's cost of capital is 10%, and the hurdle rate to be applied for this project is 15%. (The project is a "New investment —category I," as previously defined in Tables 8-1 and 8-2.) Management anticipates that the dispersion of earnings after the fifth year will be relatively constant given that all start-up problems will be resolved by that time. Therefore, they will apply the CEC's from Table 8-1 for the first four periods and 0.75 thereafter. Determine the project's NPV using the risk-adjusted discount rate and the certainty equivalent, and compare the two.

Solution: First consider the risk-adjusted discount method.

Time	$\bar{R}_t$	Discount Factor at 15%	Present Values
Present	−$10,000	1	−$10,000
1–12	1,800	5.420619	9,757
		RAR	= −$ 243

Next consider the certainty equivalent method.

Time	$\bar{R}$	α_t	$\alpha_t\bar{R}_t$	Discount Factor at 7%	Discounted $\alpha_t R_t$
Present	−$10,000	1	−$10,000	1	−$10,000
1	1,800	0.92	1,656	0.934579	1,548
2	1,800	0.88	1,584	0.873439	1,384
3	1,800	0.85	1,530	0.816298	1,249
4	1,800	0.80	1,440	0.762895	1,099
5–12	1,800	0.75	1,350	4.555475	6,150
				$CE =$	$ 1,430

The two solutions demonstrate the contrasting results of using the two methods. The project would be rejected using the risk-adjusted method, but accepted using certainty equivalent. The difference can be highlighted by looking at the table below, which compares the discounted cash flows using the certainty equivalent method, the risk-adjusted discount rate (15%), and the cost of capital (10%).

	(1) Discounted $\alpha_t R_t$	(2) $\bar{R}_t$ Discounted at 15%	(3) $\bar{R}_t$ Discounted at 10%
Year			
1	$1,548	$1,565	$1,636
2	1,384	1,361	1,488
3	1,249	1,184	1,352
4	1,099	1,029	1,229
5	963	895	1,118
6	900	778	1,016
7	841	677	924
8	786	588	840
9	734	512	763
10	686	445	694
11	641	387	631
12	599	336	574
	$CE =$ $1,430	$RAR = -$ 243	$NPV =$ $2,265

The table shows the value of the cash flows using each of the three approaches. If the certainty equivalent factors are an accurate risk adjustment for this project, it can be seen that the use of a constant risk-adjusted rate of 15% overcompensates for the risk of the project in every year except the first (since the present value using a discount rate of 15% is less than the present values of the $\alpha_t\bar{R}_t$ values). Notice that the difference between these present values is as small as $23 in year 2 and as large as $263 in year 12. It should be stressed that RAR method, with a constant discount rate, assumes that the risk of the project grows over time; in fact, that it grows at an exponential rate over time, owing to the compounding process associated with the discount factors (since the discount factors are the reciprocals of the compound interest factors). However, if the certainty equivalent factors are an accurate risk adjustment for this project, then risk is constant in years 5–12 (evidenced by the constant α_t factor of 0.75) rather than growing exponentially, as implicitly assumed by the RAR method. Finally, it should be noted by comparing columns (1) and (3) that for the first 10 years of the project's life, the project is more risky than the firm in general (since the present values using the cost of capital are higher than the discounted $\alpha_t\bar{R}_t$ values), but for the last 2 years the project is less risky than the firm overall (since in years 11 and 12 the discounted $\alpha_t\bar{R}_t$ values are higher than the present values using the cost of capital). However, considering the entire life of the project, it is more risky than the firm overall, since $\overline{CE}$ is less than the NPV value found using the appropriate discount rate for projects of average riskiness to the firm (i.e., the 10% cost of capital).   ●

The concepts of correlation and covariance will be used in the next section as well as in the next two chapters. As will be seen, the variance of any portfolio or sum of random variables is dependent upon the covariance of all possible pairs of the components. The covariance, in turn, is a function of the correlation coefficient, which expresses the nature and strength of the relationship between components.

VARIABILITY IN THE RISK-ADJUSTED DISCOUNT RATE AND CERTAINTY EQUIVALENT PROBABILITY DISTRIBUTIONS

In previous sections we have discussed the necessity for expressing cash inflows as probability distributions having both a mean and a standard deviation. Because each year's cash inflow is known only by means of a probability distribution, the composite picture of a project's attractiveness over its entire life will also be described by a probability distribution having these two statistics: a mean, $\overline{RAR}$ or $\overline{CE}$, and a standard deviation, σ_{RAR} or σ_{CE}. We have shown how the expected RAR and CE values are determined. It remains for us to show how the standard deviation is arrived at and how this measure is used to assess the project's attractiveness.

The standard deviation of the RAR or the CE distribution uses as data inputs the standard deviations of each year's cash-inflow distribution *and* the degree of correlation between the cash-flow distributions over the life of the project. This latter aspect (i.e., the intertemporal correlations between cash-flow distributions) plays an important part in determining the magnitude of σ_{RAR} and σ_{CE}, since the interrelationships can either intensify or reduce risk.

To begin our discussion of how to find σ_{RAR} or σ_{CE}, consider the general formula for finding the variance of the sum of three random variables ($\tilde{X}$, $\tilde{Y}$, $\tilde{Z}$), where each is multiplied by a constant (a, b, and c, respectively).

$$\text{Var}\,(a\tilde{X} + b\tilde{Y} + c\tilde{Z}) = a^2\sigma_{\tilde{X}}^2 + b^2\sigma_{\tilde{Y}}^2 + c^2\sigma_{\tilde{Z}}^2$$
$$+ 2ab\rho_{\tilde{X},\tilde{Y}}\sigma_{\tilde{X}},\sigma_{\tilde{Y}} + 2ac\rho_{\tilde{X},\tilde{Z}}\sigma_{\tilde{X}},\sigma_{\tilde{Z}}$$
$$+ 2bc\rho_{\tilde{Y},\tilde{Z}}\sigma_{\tilde{Y}},\sigma_{\tilde{Z}} \qquad (12)$$

where $\sigma_{\tilde{X}}^2$ and $\sigma_{\tilde{X}}$ = the variance and the standard deviation of the random variable $\tilde{X}$, respectively

$\rho_{\tilde{X},\tilde{Y}}$ = correlation coefficient between the random variables $\tilde{X}$ and $\tilde{Y}$

Notice that the first three terms show the contribution of the three variances, and the last three terms show the contribution of the covariances between all pairs of the three random variables.

To derive the expressions for σ_{RAR} and σ_{CE}, consider that Equation (12) refers to a capital investment project that has a 3-year useful life. Thus, the random variables $\tilde{X}$, $\tilde{Y}$, and $\tilde{Z}$ are the cash-inflow distributions of years 1, 2, and 3, respectively; similarly, the constants a, b, and c refer to the discount factors in years 1, 2, and 3, which reflect the time value of money for a given risk-free rate. [These discount factors are, of course,

$$\frac{1}{1+i}, \quad \frac{1}{(1+i)^2}, \quad \text{and} \quad \frac{1}{(1+i)^3}$$

respectively, for the risk-free rate i.] At this point we will consider only two types of cash-flow interdependencies: case I, independent cash flows; and case II, perfectly correlated cash flows.

Case I: Independent Cash Flows

Under this assumption, the cash flows over the life of the project are independent, meaning that successive years' cash flows are not related in any systematic way (i.e., there is a random relationship among cash flows). This condition probably occurs in highly competitive markets devoid of trade names, advertising, and so on, where exogenous forces shape the market demand. Thus, variability in cash flows over the life of the project will be reduced, owing to a canceling out of the cash flows above and below the expected values. If independence is assumed, the correlation coefficient ρ_{xy} for all pairs of years in Equation (12) are equal to zero. Hence, the last three covariance terms will drop out and we have

$$\text{Var}\left(a\tilde{X} + b\tilde{Y} + c\tilde{Z}\right) = a^2\sigma_{\tilde{X}}^2 + b^2\sigma_{\tilde{Y}}^2 + c^2\sigma_{\tilde{Z}}^2$$

Recall that $\tilde{X}$, $\tilde{Y}$, and $\tilde{Z}$ refer to the cash-inflow distributions of years 1, 2, and 3 of a project and that a, b, and c are the discount factors in those three respective years. Hence, calling $\text{Var}\left(a\tilde{X} + b\tilde{Y} + c\tilde{Z}\right)$, σ_{RAR}^2 or σ_{CE}^2, we arrive at the desired general expression for case I:

$$\sigma_{\text{RAR}}^2 \text{ or } \sigma_{\text{CE}}^2 = \sum_{t=0}^{n} \frac{\sigma_t^2}{(1+i)^{2t}} \tag{13}$$

It should be noted that the discount factor is raised to the $2t$ power because of the fact that the values of a, b, and c, which equaled the discount factors

$$\frac{1}{1+i}, \quad \frac{1}{(1+i)^2}, \quad \text{or} \quad \frac{1}{(1+i)^3}$$

were all squared in Equation (12); hence, each factor is raised to the $2t$ power. Of course, if the standard deviation σ_{RAR} or σ_{CE} were desired, we will simply take the square root of Equation (13).

Case II: Perfectly Correlated Cash Flows

Under the assumption that cash flows are perfectly correlated, we are positing that given the outcome of year 1's cash inflow, all subsequent cash inflows are predetermined, since they will be as many standard deviations above or below their respective means as year 1's cash inflow was. Such a relationship among cash inflows would exist in monopolistically competitive markets, replete with brand names, high-pressure advertising, limited entry, and so on. The variability here will be greater than that found in case I. This is due to the risk-intensification tendencies of positive correlation, which results from the lack of counteracting variations above and below the means over the life of the project found in the independent cash-flow case.

If perfect correlation is assumed, the correlation coefficients $\rho_{\tilde{X}\tilde{Y}}$ for all pairs of years in Equation (12) are equal to $+1$. Hence, Equation (12) becomes

$$\text{Var}\,(a\tilde{X} + b\tilde{Y} + c\tilde{Z}) = a^2\sigma_{\tilde{X}}^2 + b^2\sigma_{\tilde{Y}}^2 + c^2\sigma_{\tilde{Z}}^2$$
$$+ 2ab\sigma_{\tilde{X}}\sigma_{\tilde{Y}} + 2ac\sigma_{\tilde{X}}\sigma_{\tilde{Z}}$$
$$+ 2bc\sigma_{\tilde{Y}}\sigma_{\tilde{Z}}$$

where the right side can be factored as follows:

$$\text{Var}\,(a\tilde{X} + b\tilde{Y} + c\tilde{Z}) = (a\sigma_{\tilde{X}} + b\sigma_{\tilde{Y}} + c\sigma_{\tilde{Z}})^2$$

Hence, again calling the left-hand side of this expression σ_{RAR}^2 or σ_{CE}^2 and substituting the usual values for the constants and standard deviations, we arrive at

$$\sigma_{\text{RAR}}^2 \text{ or } \sigma_{\text{CE}}^2 = \left[\frac{\sigma_1}{1+i} + \frac{\sigma_2}{(1+i)^2} + \frac{\sigma_3}{(1+i)^3} \right]^2$$

For the general project with a useful life of n years, the expression above would become

$$\sigma_{\text{RAR}}^2 \text{ or } \sigma_{\text{CE}}^2 = \left[\sum_{t=0}^{n} \frac{\sigma_t}{(1+i)^t} \right]^2 \tag{14}$$

The use of the two formulas for σ_{CE}^2 (i.e., both for independent cash flows and for perfectly correlated cash flows) will be illustrated in Example 8.

● **EXAMPLE 8** *Variance for Perfectly Correlated and Independent Cash Flows*

Consider project Alpha, which has an original cost of $200, a 3-year useful life, and cash-inflow distributions as follows:

Outcome	Period 1 R_{A1}	P_{A1}	Period 2 R_{A2}	P_{A2}	Period 3 R_{A3}	P_{A3}
1	$100	0.10	$ 40	0.10	$ 10	0.10
2	120	0.20	80	0.25	60	0.30
3	140	0.40	120	0.30	100	0.30
4	160	0.20	160	0.25	160	0.20
5	180	0.10	200	0.10	270	0.10

The risk-free rate is 6%.

Compute σ_{CE}^2 under the assumption that (a) cash inflows are independent over Alpha's useful life; and (b) cash inflows are perfectly correlated over Alpha's useful life.

Solution: Computing the standard deviations for each of the 3 years above, we would find:

$$\sigma_1 = 21.91, \qquad \sigma_2 = 45.61, \qquad \sigma_3 = 69.54$$

These three standard deviations are now used to compute σ_{CE}^2.
(a) Assuming independent cash inflows,

$$\sigma_{CE}^2 = \sum_{t=0}^{n} \frac{\sigma_t^2}{(1 + i)^{2t}}$$

$$= \frac{(21.91)^2}{(1.06)^2} + \frac{(45.61)^2}{(1.06)^4} + \frac{(69.54)^2}{(1.06)^6}$$

$$= \underline{\underline{5,484.07}}$$

or

$$\sigma_{CE} = \underline{\underline{\$74.05}}$$

(b) Assuming perfectly correlated cash inflows,

$$\sigma_{CE}^2 = \left[\sum_{t=0}^{n} \frac{\sigma_t}{(1 + i)^t} \right]^2$$

$$= \left[\frac{21.91}{1.06} + \frac{45.61}{(1.06)^2} + \frac{69.54}{(1.06)^3} \right]^2$$

$$= (20.67 + 40.59 + 58.39)^2$$

$$= (119.65)^2 = \underline{\underline{14,316.1225}}$$

or

$$\sigma_{CE} = \underline{\underline{\$119.65}}$$

Of course, it can be seen that σ_{CE} assuming perfectly correlated cash inflows is significantly greater than σ_{CE} where cash inflows are assumed to be independent. This is due to the risk-intensifying result produced by high positive correlation among the cash flows over the life of the project rather than the canceling-out effect of independent (zero-correlation) cash inflows over the project's life.   ●

The natural reactions of the financial manager to the computation of σ_{CE} under various assumptions might be:
1. How can the degree of intertemporal correlation among the cash flows be accurately determined?
2. How can σ_{CE} be used to help evaluate capital projects?
These questions will be examined in turn.

We admit that the degree of intertemporal correlation among the cash-inflow distributions over the life of the project is indeed difficult to estimate. However, some comfort can be taken in the fact that σ_{CE} *will take on its maximum value when perfect correlation exists among cash-inflow distributions. Further, a somewhat moderate value of* σ_{CE} *is arrived at when it is assumed that cash inflows are independent. It should be noted that* σ_{CE} *would get smaller as the degree of correlation were allowed to take on negative values and that* σ_{CE} *would equal zero if it were assumed that the cash inflows were perfectly negatively correlated over the life of the project.* Hence, it is suggested that σ_{CE} be used to evaluate capital projects along the lines of sensitivity analysis, following three steps:

1. σ_{CE} should be computed under the two assumptions of independence and perfect correlation, as demonstrated in the Example 8.

2. The risk–return characteristics of the project should be evaluated under the extreme assumption of perfect correlation and the more moderate assumption of independence.

3. The firm, based on its utility curve and its best estimate of the intertemporal correlation, should either reject the proposal or let it stand as a candidate for possible adoption.

The latter two steps in the approach above point to the answer to the second question posed: How can σ_{CE} be used to help evaluate capital projects? The argument would proceed as follows: If it can be reasonably assumed that each year's cash-inflow distribution is normal or approximately normal, the central limit theorem would tell us that the certainty equivalent distribution will be normal or approximately normal with mean $\overline{CE}$ and standard deviation σ_{CE}. The latter distribution can then be used to make probability statements about the certainty equivalent value, taking on any value of interest using the familiar standardized Z value and tables of the normal distribution (see Appendix D): $Z = (X - \overline{X})/\sigma$. Such probability values are helpful for the firm to evaluate a single project in isolation or to compare several projects. The ultimate decision about project acceptance is determined by the firm's utility function ranking of the project attractiveness based on the relevant risk–return information given above. An illustration of this situation follows.

● **EXAMPLE 9** *Comparison of Two Projects Using the Certainty Equivalent Method*

The firm in Example 8 is also evaluating project Delta, which costs $300 and whose cash-inflow distributions are as follows:

	Period 1		Period 2		Period 3	
Outcome	R_{D1}	P_{D1}	R_{D2}	P_{D2}	R_{D3}	P_{D3}
1	$ 80	0.10	$ 80	0.05	$ 80	0.01
2	100	0.20	100	0.10	100	0.04
3	120	0.40	120	0.15	120	0.10
4	140	0.20	140	0.60	140	0.70
5	160	0.10	160	0.10	160	0.15

The firm assigns the following certainty equivalent factors for the two projects based on their variability in cash flows over their useful lives:

Project Alpha	Project Delta
$\alpha_1 = 0.92$	$\alpha_1 = 0.95$
$\alpha_2 = 0.80$	$\alpha_2 = 0.92$
$\alpha_3 = 0.65$	$\alpha_3 = 0.90$

(a) Compute $\overline{CE}$ for both projects.
(b) Compute σ_{CE} for project Delta based on the following assumptions:
   (1) Cash inflows are independent.
   (2) Cash inflows are perfectly correlated.
(c) Compute and explain the coefficient of variation for the certainty equivalent distributions for both projects under both correlation assumptions.
(d) Compute the probability that both projects will have positive certainty equivalent values, where σ_{CE} is computed under both assumptions of independence and perfect correlation, where the CE distributions are normal.

Solution: (a) To compute $\overline{CE}$ for each project, we need the expected cash inflow for each of the 3 years.
Project Alpha:

$$\bar{R}_1 = \$100(0.1) + \$120(0.2) + \$140(0.4) + \$160(0.2) + \$180(0.1)$$
$$= \$10 + \$24 + \$56 + \$32 + \$18 = \underline{\underline{\$140}}$$

$$\bar{R}_2 = \$40(0.1) + \$80(0.25) + \$120(0.3) + \$160(0.25) + \$200(0.1)$$
$$= \$4 + \$20 + \$36 + \$40 + \$20 = \underline{\underline{\$120}}$$

$$\bar{R}_3 = \$10(0.1) + \$60(0.3) + \$100(0.3) + \$160(0.2) + \$270(0.1)$$
$$= \$1 + \$18 + \$30 + \$32 + \$27 = \underline{\underline{\$108}}$$

Now, to determine $\overline{CE}$, we multiply the expected cash inflows by their respective certainty equivalent factors and discount at the risk-free rate. Finally, the original cost of projects A and D of $200 and $300, respectively, were substituted.

$$\overline{CE}_A = \frac{(0.92)(\$140)}{1.06} + \frac{(0.80)(\$120)}{(1.06)^2} + \frac{(0.65)(\$108)}{(1.06)^3} - \$200$$
$$= \$265.89 - \$200.00 = \underline{\underline{\$65.89}}$$

Project Delta:

$$\bar{R}_1 = \$80(0.1) + \$100(0.2) + \$120(0.4) + \$140(0.2) + \$160(0.1)$$
$$= \$8 + \$20 + \$48 + \$28 + \$16 = \underline{\underline{\$120}}$$

$$\bar{R}_2 = \$80(0.05) + \$100(0.1) + \$120(0.15) + \$140(0.6) + \$160(0.1)$$
$$= \$4 + \$10 + \$18 + \$84 + \$16 = \underline{\underline{\$132}}$$

$$\bar{R}_3 = \$80(0.01) + \$100(0.04) + \$120(0.10) + \$140(0.7) + \$160(0.15)$$
$$= \$0.80 + \$4 + \$12 + \$98 + \$24 = \underline{\underline{\$138.80}}$$

$$\overline{CE}_D = \frac{(0.95)(\$120)}{1.06} + \frac{(0.92)(\$132)}{(1.06)^2} + \frac{(0.90)(\$138.80)}{(1.06)^3} - \$300$$

$$= \$107.55 + \$108.08 + \$104.89 - \$300$$

$$= \$320.52 - \$300.00 = \$20.52$$

(b) Computing σ_{CE} for project Delta:

    (1) For independent cash flows:

$$\sigma_1 = 21.90, \qquad \sigma_2 = 19.39, \qquad \sigma_3 = 14.09$$

The reader should verify these values.

$$\sigma_{CE}^2 = \frac{(21.90)^2}{(1.06)^2} + \frac{(19.39)^2}{(1.06)^4} + \frac{(14.09)^2}{(1.06)^6}$$

$$= 864.61$$

or

$$\sigma_{CE} = \$29.40$$

    (2) For perfectly correlated cash flows:

$$\sigma_{CE}^2 = \left[\frac{21.90}{(1.06)^1} + \frac{19.39}{(1.06)^2} + \frac{14.09}{(1.06)^3} \right]^2$$

$$= (20.66 + 17.26 + 11.83)^2$$

$$= 2475.06$$

or

$$\sigma_{CE} = \$49.75$$

    (c) The coefficient of variation can now be computed for the two projects, which is a relevant method of comparison because of the size disparity between the two projects:

    (1) For independent cash flows:

Project Alpha	Project Delta
$v = \dfrac{\sigma_{CE}}{CE}$	$v = \dfrac{\sigma_{CE}}{CE}$
$= \dfrac{\$74.05}{\$65.89}$	$= \dfrac{\$29.40}{\$20.52}$
$= 1.12$	$= 1.43$

This means that for project Alpha there is 1.12 times as much risk as there is expected return, *or* that for every dollar of expected return there is $1.12 of risk, as measured by the standard deviation. For project Delta, the standard deviation is 143% of the expected certainty equivalent return, *or* there is $1.43 of risk for each dollar of expected return. Further, because the two coefficients of variation can be directly compared, project Delta has about 1.3 times as much risk per dollar of expected return as project Alpha.

(2) For perfectly correlated cash flows:

Project Alpha	*Project Delta*
$\nu = \dfrac{\sigma_{CE}}{CE}$	$\nu = \dfrac{\sigma_{CE}}{CE}$
$= \dfrac{\$119.65}{\$65.89}$	$= \dfrac{\$49.75}{\$20.52}$
$= 1.82$	$= 2.42$

Similar interpretations can be attached to these values, as was given above. Notice that the relative variability of the two projects has increased proportionately compared with independent cash flows; project Delta's coefficient of variation is still about 1.3 times as great as project Alpha's.

(d) Finally, the probability that each project achieves a positive certainty equivalent factor is determined as follows:

(1) For independent cash flows:

Project Alpha:

$$Z = \frac{0 - \$65.89}{\$74.05} = -0.89 \Rightarrow 0.3133$$

This means that 31.33% of the area under the curve falls between a CE value of 0 and $\overline{CE} = 65.89$. Thus, the probability that project Alpha achieves a positive certainty

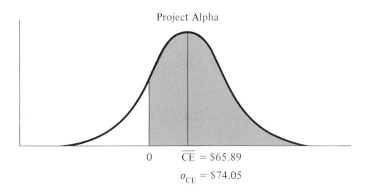

Project Alpha

$$0 \qquad \overline{CE} = \$65.89$$
$$\sigma_{CE} = \$74.05$$

equivalent value is 0.8133 (0.5000 + 0.3133). It should be noted that the above probability exceeded 0.5000 because $\overline{CE}$ was positive; if $\overline{CE}$ was negative, the probability that the CE value would take on a value greater than zero would be less than 0.5000 and is quantified by the area in the upper tail of the distribution.

Project Delta:

$$Z = \frac{0 - \$20.52}{\$29.40} = -0.698 \Rightarrow 0.2574$$

Thus, the probability that project Delta achieves a positive CE value is 0.7574. Project Delta has almost a 75% chance of achieving a positive CE value, whereas project Alpha has about an 80% chance of doing this *under the assumption that cash flows of the two projects are independent over time.*

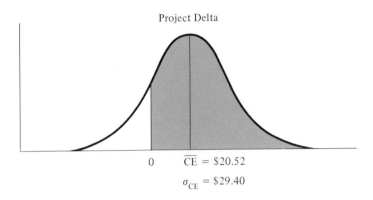

Project Delta

$$0 \qquad \overline{CE} = \$20.52$$
$$\sigma_{CE} = \$29.40$$

(2) For perfectly correlated cash flows:
Project Alpha:

$$Z = \frac{0 - \$65.89}{\$119.65} = -0.551 \Rightarrow 0.2092$$

$$P\{CE \geqslant 0 \text{ for project Alpha}\} = \underline{0.7092}$$

Project Delta:

$$Z = \frac{0 - \$20.52}{\$49.75} = -0.412 \Rightarrow 0.1598$$

$$P\{CE \geqslant 0 \text{ for project Delta}\} = \underline{0.6598}$$

Under the assumption of perfectly correlated cash flows, the probability of the two projects achieving positive CE values is rather close: 0.7092 for Alpha vs. 0.6598 for Delta. Which of these two projects (if either) would meet the firm's criteria for acceptance and what ranking would be assigned to each depends upon the firm's utility function, which quantifies its hierarchy of goals, risk preferences, and attitudes toward risk-return trade-offs. Neither project dominates the other by simultaneously offering a higher expected CE value and a lower σ_{CE}. The measures computed in part (c) of this example plus the probabilities computed in part (d) under the two intertemporal correlation assumptions provide data inputs that help the financial manager rank the two projects and decide which, if either, should be accepted. The ultimate decision depends upon the firm's utility function.

SUMMARY

This chapter discussed the important area of risk analysis in capital budgeting. We saw that when the certainty assumption was relaxed, the need arose to examine both a measure of central tendency (i.e., expected return) and a measure of the variability in the distribution of returns (e.g., the standard deviation, coefficient of variation, etc.) Further, because of the importance of other goals, trade-offs between them, and risk preferences of decision makers, the "maximize expected utility criterion" was suggested as being appropriate for decision making under conditions of risk.

The two conventional models to evaluate single projects under conditions of risk—the risk-adjusted discount rate technique and the certainty equivalent method—were introduced and examined in some depth. Both the expected values for these two models and their standard deviations (computed under different assumptions about intertemporal correlations among cash-inflow distributions) were computed. Finally, under the assumption that the component cash-flow distributions were normal, it was demonstrated how probability statements could be made concerning the likelihood that various values were taken on by the random variable measuring certainty equivalent values.

This chapter concentrated on the evaluation of a single project. Chapter 9 looks at the area of portfolio effects wherein the risk of a combination of projects can be reduced by careful selection to minimize the covariance among all pairs of projects. After that, capital asset pricing theory is examined as a way of integrating this chapter and the following one, which deals with portfolio effects.

PROBLEMS

1. A petrochemical company had two investment proposals under the following states of the economy: normal, deep recession, mild recession, minor boom, and major boom. The probabilities of various states of the economy are as follows:

| | Proposal A | | Proposal B | |
State	Probability	Cash Flow	Probability	Cash Flow
Deep recession	0.10	$3,000	0.10	$2,000
Mild recession	0.20	3,500	0.20	3,000
Normal	0.40	4,000	0.40	4,000
Minor boom	0.20	4,500	0.20	5,000
Major boom	0.10	5,000	0.10	6,000

Determine the following:
(a) Expected return.
(b) Mean absolute deviation.
(c) Variance.
(d) Standard deviation.
(e) Semivariance.
(f) Coefficient of variation.
Interpret the measures.

2. A hospital administrator is faced with the problem of having a limited amount of funds available for capital projects. He has narrowed his choice down to two pieces of x-ray equipment, since the radiology department is his greatest producer of revenue. The first piece of equipment (project A) is a fairly standard piece of equipment which has gained wide acceptance and should provide a steady flow of income. The other piece of equipment (project B), although more risky, may provide a higher return. After deliberation with his radiologist and director of finance, the administrator has developed the following table:

| | Expected Cash Inflow per Year | | |
Probability	Project A	Probability	Project B
0.6	$2,000	0.2	$4,000
0.3	1,800	0.5	1,200
0.1	1,000	0.3	900

Discovering that the Budget Director of the hospital is taking graduate courses in business, the hospital administrator has asked him to analyze the two projects and make his recommendations. Prepare an analysis that will aid the Budget Director in making his recommendation.

3. Determine the certainty coefficient value for a proposed project whose expected risky cash flow is $2,300, to be received in 1 year. The corporation's cost of capital is 15% and the risk-free rate of return is 8%.

4. A company has a cost of capital of 12% and the anticipated risk-free interest rate is 7% for the coming 5 years. A proposed project which is of average riskiness to the firm under evaluation has an expected after-tax cash flow of $6,500 per year. Determine the certainty equivalent coefficient value for this project for each of the 5 years.

5. A machine with a 4-year life is being replaced with a modern, more efficient piece of equipment with a longer expected life. The equipment will require a payment of $55,000 in the first 30 days of its operation. The expected returns and standard deviation are as follows:

Year	Expected Returns	Standard Deviation
1	$14,000	$1,200
2	16,000	1,800
3	18,000	2,000
4	20,000	1,950
5	22,000	3,000

The risk-free rate of return is 5%. The CEC values and the coefficient of variation are as follows for the 5-year period:

Coefficient of Variation	Certainty Equivalent Coefficient				
	Year 1	Year 2	Year 3	Year 4	Year 5
$v \leqslant 0.10$	0.92	0.88	0.85	0.80	0.74
$0.10 \leqslant v \leqslant 0.25$	0.86	0.82	0.78	0.73	0.69

Determine the expected certainty equivalent value.

6. A boiler manufacturing company uses a certainty equivalent approach in its evaluation of risky investments. Currently, the company is faced with two alternative projects. Project A is Replacement investment—category II, project B is New investment—category II, according to Table 8-1. The expected values of net cash flows for each project and risk-free returns are as follows:

Year	A	B	Risk-Free Return
Present	−$40,000	−$50,000	—
1	20,000	20,000	0.05
2	20,000	25,000	0.06
3	20,000	30,000	0.07

Which of the alternatives should be selected?

7. A corporation is considering two projects and will choose one or the other based upon their RAR. The corporation's cost of capital is 14%. Project A is a Replacement investment—category II. Project B is a New investment—category II. Project

A's projected cash-flow distribution is as follows:

Original Cost		Cash Flows for Years 1–6	
Probability	Amount	Probability	Amount
0.3	$100,000	0.15	$20,000
0.3	110,000	0.25	25,000
0.4	120,000	0.25	30,000
		0.15	35,000
		0.10	45,000
		0.10	45,000

Project B's projected cash-flow distribution is as follows:

Original Cost		Cash Flows for Years 1–6	
Probability	Amount	Probability	Amount
0.5	$225,000	0.25	$50,000
0.2	210,000	0.25	60,000
0.3	200,000	0.15	70,000
		0.15	75,000
		0.10	80,000
		0.10	85,000

Determine the RAR for each project using Table 8-2 for return requirements for investment groups.

8. A company is considering an investment costing $8,000. The investment is such that the size of the inflows will be correlated with the state of the economy. Economists can reliably estimate the following probabilities for the next 3 years.

State	Probabilities for Years 1–3
Recession	0.3
Normal	0.6
Boom	0.1

Company officials can reliably predict the inflows associated with each state of the economy.

State	Net Cash Inflows
Recession	$2,000
Normal	$5,000
Boom	$8,000

Assume a cost of capital of 11% and a risk premium of 9%. Compute the risk of adjusted NPV.

9. A corporation has a cost of capital of 12%, a risk-free rate of return of 6%, and is considering project replacement, which has an 8-year expected life. The project will cost approximately $50,000 and will generate cash inflows of $10,000 each year.

This project is a category II investment (Table 8-1) and the corporation has a hurdle rate of 15%. The corporation also expects that the dispersion of cash flows after year 4 will be relatively constant and that the CECs from the table will be used during the initial period and 0.77 thereafter. Determine the project's NPV using the risk-adjusted discount rate and the certainty equivalent and evaluate the results.

10. The Hothouse Corporation is considering project "Woody," the construction of a wood-pruning machine that has the ability to turn entire forests into bundled cords of firewood ready to be delivered to customers.

The project is anticipated to have an initial cost of $30,000,000, a 3-year useful life, and cash-inflow distributions as follows:

	Cash Inflow per Year		
Probability	RW_1	RW_2	RW_3
0.2	$15	$ 8	$20
0.3	20	25	25
0.4	30	40	30
0.1	40	50	35
1.0			

Compute σ_{CE} under the assumption that cash inflows are independent over Woody's useful life and under the assumption that cash inflows are perfectly correlated over Woody's useful life. Assume that the risk-free rate of return is 6%.

11. A manufacturing company is evaluating two alternative projects. Project A consists of an expansion of the same business by building a new facility at the same location. The total project cost is estimated to be $30,000. Project B consists of an acquisition of another firm selling products unrelated to the company's primary business. The total cost of the project is $40,000. The following table shows the cash-inflows distribution.

Project A (cash flow, $000)						Project B (cash flow, $000)					
Outcome	RA_1	PA_1	RA_2	PA_2	RA_3	PA_3	Outcome	RA_1	PA_1	RA_2	PA_2	RA_3	PA_3
1	10	0.3	15	0.2	10	0.3	1	15	0.2	20	0.3	15	0.2
2	15	0.5	20	0.6	25	0.6	2	20	0.6	25	0.5	30	0.6
3	20	0.2	25	0.2	30	0.1	3	25	0.2	30	0.2	40	0.2

(a) Compute $\overline{CE}$ for both projects.
(b) Compute σ_{CE} for both projects based on the assumption that cash flows are independent and cash flows are perfectly correlated.
(c) Compute and explain the coefficient of variation of the certainty equivalent distributions for both correlation assumptions.
Assume that the risk-free rate is 6%, constant over the life of projects, and that the company considers cash flows for the first 3-year period.

12. The Energystics Corporation is evaluating two projects. One is the installation of a load shedder, which costs $5,000, including peripheral sensing equipment, and the other, the installation of a 5-ton high-efficiency air conditioning unit at a cost of $8,000 installed. The energy savings from these two projects are listed below. Distributions are based on the probabilities of future rate increases as set by a local electric company. The risk-free rate in this area is 6%.

Load Shedder

Rate Inc. (%)	Period 1		Period 2		Period 3	
	R_{ls}	P_{ls}	R_{ls}	P_{ls}	R_{ls}	P_{ls}
4%	$2,000	0.50	$3,000	0.25	$4,000	.25
8%	4,000	0.25	5,000	0.50	6,000	.25
12%	6,000	0.25	7,000	0.25	8,000	.50

Air Conditioner

Rate Inc. (%)	Period 1		Period 2		Period 3	
	R_{ac}	P_{ac}	R_{ac}	P_{ac}	R_{ac}	P_{ac}
4%	$3,000	0.50	$ 4,000	0.25	$ 5,000	0.25
8%	6,000	0.25	7,000	0.50	8,000	0.25
12%	9,000	0.25	10,000	0.25	11,000	0.50

Energystics assigns the following certainty equivalent factors for the two projects under consideration based on their variability over the three time periods.

Load Shedder	Air Conditioner
$\alpha = 0.95$	$\alpha = 0.95$
$\alpha = 0.85$	$\alpha = 0.75$
$\alpha = 0.75$	$\alpha = 0.60$

(a) Compute $\overline{CE}$ for both projects.
(b) Compute σ_{CE} based on independent and perfectly correlated cash flows.
(c) Compute the coefficient of variation for the CE distributions for both projects under both correlation assumptions.
(d) Compute the probability that both projects will have positive certainty equivalent values when σ_{CE} is computed under both assumptions of independence and perfect correlation.

9 PORTFOLIO EFFECTS

In this chapter we view the firm and the capital budget as a portfolio of projects, each project having an expected return and standard deviation. Projects that may not be acceptable when considered individually might merit acceptance when analyzed *in combination* with other projects. The risk–return characteristics of a project examined in isolation may indicate that it does not warrant investment, but the way the project interacts with other projects (the covariance or portfolio effects) could result in its acceptance. Hence, this chapter shifts the focus of evaluation from individual projects to combinations of projects.[1] The business firm, after all, is merely an amalgam of previously accepted projects.

PORTFOLIO EFFECTS

Suppose that we consider combinations of projects as possible investment portfolios or capital budgets. Each project in the combination has an expected return and risk, the latter measured by its standard deviation. To evaluate different combinations (or budgets) we need an expected return and standard deviation on *each combination*. The expected return, $E(R_p)$, on the combination may be computed using Equation (1):

$$E(R_p) = \sum_{j=1}^{N} X_j E(R_j) \tag{1}$$

---

[1] This chapter draws heavily on the work of Harry Markowitz, who has been called the father of modern portfolio theory. See H. Markowitz, "Portfolio Selection," *Journal of Finance*, March 1952, and *Portfolio Selection: Efficient Diversification of Investment* (New York: John Wiley & Sons, Inc., 1959).

where X_j = proportion of the total budget allocated to the jth project

$E(R_j)$ = expected rate of return on the jth project[2]

The standard deviation of the budget (σ_p), however, is not simply a weighted average of the project sigmas (σ_j), although these represent one component. Rather, the risk of the budget (σ_p), in addition, reflects the covariances among projects in combination. *Covariance measures the impact that a pair of securities will have on the portfolio variance due to their interactive effects* (*i.e., correlation*) *and their respective standard deviations*. The covariance between two projects (or securities) is the product of three terms: the correlation coefficient and the standard deviations of the two projects, as expressed in Equation (2):

$$\text{Cov}_{ij} = \rho_{ij}\sigma_i\sigma_j \tag{2}$$

Note that the covariance will take on the sign of the correlation coefficient (ρ_{ij}) since both standard deviations must be greater than or equal to zero. Thus, the covariance can be positive, negative, or zero, depending on whether the correlation coefficient is positive, negative, or zero, respectively. (The covariance could also be zero if either standard deviation were zero, which would be the case for a risk–free asset.)

The three cases are discussed below:

1. Positive covariance implies that if the cash flows of one project exceed its expected value, the cash flows of the other project in turn will exceed its expected value, and vice versa. Positive covariance intensifies the risk of the combination of assets.

2. Negative covariance, by contrast, suggests that if the cash flows of one project exceed its expected value, the cash flows of the other will tend to fall below its expected value, and vice versa. Negative covariance, accordingly, tends to significantly reduce risk in the budget combination.

3. Zero covariance (when it results from $\rho_{ij} = 0$) means that the cash flows of the two projects move independently of each other, whereby if the cash flows of one project exceed its expected value, the other project's cash flows are just as likely to exceed as to fall below its expected value. Zero covariance reduces risk in the portfolio.

The standard deviation of the combination is expressed in Equation (3):

$$\sigma_p = \sqrt{\sum_{j=1}^{N} X_j^2\sigma_j^2 + 2\sum_{j=1}^{N-1}\sum_{i=j+1}^{N} X_iX_j\,\text{Cov}_{ij}} \tag{3}$$

---

[2]Equation (1) applies if $E(R_j)$ and σ_j are expressed as a rate and portions of projects may be accepted. This would denote a partial interest in a project as opposed to total ownership. (i.e., the project is divisible). Further, Equation (1) is useful when evaluating security portfolios. In Chapter 13 we introduce linear and integer programming techniques, which are applied to the evaluation of portfolios of divisible and nondivisible projects, respectively. However, if the $E(R_j)$ represents a dollar value and projects are not divisible, the NPV of the combination is expressed as follows:

$$E(R_p) = \sum_{j=1}^{N} X_jE(R_j)$$

where $X_j = \{0, 1\}$. Note that this expression does not include any weighting, since the projects are not divisible. The budget combines the whole project (if $X_j = 1$) or none of it (if $X_j = 0$); that is, the firm must take the whole project or nothing.

where i and j represent all projects in the budget, *paired off* for purposes of computing covariance.

The covariance term may be plus (positive covariance), minus (negative covariance), or zero. Obviously, in constructing a portfolio, one would strive *in theory* for a negative covariance sufficient to offset the first term and produce $\sigma_p = 0$. In practice, the returns on capital projects and securities tend to move with the general economy so that negative covariance is seldom obtainable. Generally, the crux of portfolio construction lies in minimizing the degree of positive covariance.

CALCULATING THE COVARIANCE

One approach to computing the covariance considers pairs of observations for the returns on two projects. Deviations of these returns from the respective expected values are multiplied by each other, and then by the joint probability that this pair of returns will occur as shown in Equation (4):

$$\text{Cov}_{ij} = \sum_{t=1}^{N} \left[R_{it} - E(R_i) \right] \left[R_{jt} - E(R_j) \right] P_t \qquad (4)$$

where Cov_{ij} = covariance between the ith and jth projects
  P_t = joint probability of the paired cash flows for project i and project j
  R_{it} = return on the ith project in period t (an element in the probability distribution of returns in project i)
  R_{jt} = return on the jth project in period t (an element in the probability distribution of returns in project j)

It should be pointed out that the joint probability, P_t, in Equation (4) can be based on historical experience, an informed subjective estimation, or a simulation of possible outcomes for the two projects under evaluation. Example 1 illustrates the computation of the covariance using Equation (4).

● **EXAMPLE 1** *Expected Value, Standard Deviation, and Portfolio Covariance*

Assume that a corporation is evaluating two projects, X and Y. After performing 400 simulation runs showing the interaction of the cash flows generated by the two projects, the following table was prepared to summarize the results:

Table of Cash Flows Generated in 400 Simulation Runs

Project X	Project Y			Total
	$100,000	$250,000	$400,000	
$100,000	50	20	5	75
$200,000	72	155	3	230
$300,000	28	25	42	95
Total	150	200	50	400

Compute the following:

(*a*) The expected value and the standard deviation of the cash-flow distribution for each of the two projects.

(*b*) The covariance between the cash flows of projects X and Y using Equation (4) and a contingency-table format.

Solution: To facilitate the computations, the contingency table of the number of observations is first converted into joint and marginal probabilities:

		Project Y		
Project X	$100,000	$250,000	$400,000	Total
$100,000	0.125	0.05	0.0125	0.1875
$200,000	0.180	0.3875	0.0075	0.5750
$300,000	0.070	0.0625	0.1050	0.2375
Total	0.375	0.5000	0.1250	1.0000

To compute the expected cash inflow and the standard deviation for each project, we use the marginal probabilities of each of the three possible outcomes:

Project X:

$$E(R_x) = \$100,000(0.1875) + \$200,000(0.5750) + \$300,000(0.2375)$$
$$= \$18,750 + \$115,000 + \$71,250$$
$$= \$205,000$$
$$\sigma_x = \sqrt{(100,000 - 205,000)^2(0.1875) + (200,000 - 205,000)^2(0.5750)}$$
$$+ (300,000 - 205,000)^2(0.2375)$$
$$= \sqrt{2,067,187,500 + 14,375,000 + 2,143,437,500}$$
$$= \$65,000$$

Project Y:

$$E(R_y) = \$100,000(0.375) + \$250,000(0.500) + \$400,000(0.125)$$
$$= \$37,500 + \$125,000 + \$50,000$$
$$= \$212,500$$
$$\sigma_y = \sqrt{(100,000 - 212,500)^2(0.375) + (250,000 - 212,500)^2(0.5)}$$
$$+ (400,000 - 212,500)^2(0.125)$$
$$= \sqrt{4,746,093,750 + 703,125,000 + 4,394,531,250}$$
$$= \$99,216$$

Next, compute the covariance between projects X and Y. Use the joint probabilities in the body of the table and restate the table in a form consistent with Equation (4) by showing each cash flow as a deviation from its respective mean (i.e., subtract $205,000 from each cash flow for project X and $212,500 from each of project Y's cash flows):

		Project Y		
Project X	− $112,500	+ $ 37,500	+ $ 187,500
− $105,000	0.1250	0.0500	0.0125
− $ 5,000	0.1800	0.3875	0.0075
+ $ 95,000	0.0700	0.0625	0.1050

The covariance is computed by multiplying the respective values for each row and column by the corresponding joint probability, with due regard to the signs.

$$\begin{aligned}
\text{Cov}_{xy} &= (-105,000)(-112,500)(0.1250) + (-5,000)(-112,500)(0.18) \\
&\quad + (+95,000)(-112,500)(0.07) + (+37,500)(-105,000)(0.05) \\
&\quad + (+37,500)(-5,000)(0.3875) + (+37,500)(+95,000)(0.0625) \\
&\quad + (+187,500)(-105,000)(0.0125) + (+187,500)(-5,000)(0.0075) \\
&\quad + (+187,500)(+95,000)(0.1050) \\
&= +(1,476,562,500) + (101,250,000) + (-748,125,000) \\
&\quad + (-196,875,000) + (-72,656,250) + (222,656,250) \\
&\quad + (-246,093,750) + (-7,031,250) + (1,870,312,500) \\
&= 3,670,781,250 - 1,270,781,250 \\
&= +2,400,000,000 \qquad\qquad \bullet
\end{aligned}$$

A more convenient method of calculating the covariance between two projects makes use of Equation (2):

$$\text{Cov}_{ij} = \rho_{ij}\sigma_i\sigma_j \tag{2}$$

This requires that the correlation coefficient ρ_{ij} be computed directly by regressing the paired cash flows of the two projects under consideration. Since the covariance can be computed using Equation (2), Equation (2) can be substituted directly into Equation (3) as shown in Equation (5):

$$\sigma_p = \sqrt{\sum_{j=1}^{N} X_j^2 \sigma_j^2 + 2 \sum_{j=1}^{N-1} \sum_{i=j+1}^{N} X_i X_j \rho_{ij} \sigma_i \sigma_j} \tag{5}$$

Note in Equation (5) that the standard deviation on a portfolio or combination of assets is the square root of the sum of the weighted variances plus twice the sum of the weighted covariances between all possible pairs of securities or projects. Thus, the covariance plays a critical role in determining the size of the portfolio standard deviation.

To see this computational approach for both Cov_{ij} and σ_p, consider Example 2.

● **EXAMPLE 2** *Portfolio Expected Value and Standard Deviation*

A firm desires to evaluate the combination of two projects having the following characteristics as a portfolio.

	R_1	R_2
$E(R_j)$	32%	35%
σ_j	7%	0.7%
X_j	0.5	0.5
ρ_{ij}		-0.32

Compute $E(R_p)$ and σ_p.

Solution:

$$E(R_p) = \sum_{j=1}^{N} X_j E(R_j)$$

$$= (0.5)(0.32) + (0.5)(0.35)$$

$$= 0.335 \quad \text{or} \quad 33.5\%$$

and

$$\sigma_p = \sqrt{\sum_{j=1}^{N-} X_j^2 \sigma_j^2 + 2 \sum_{j=1}^{N-1} \sum_{i=j+1}^{N} (X_i)(X_j)(\rho_{ij})(\sigma_j)(\sigma_i)}$$

$$= \sqrt{(0.5)^2(0.07)^2 + (0.5)^2(0.007)^2 + 2(0.5)(0.5)(-0.32)(0.07)(0.007)}$$

$$= \sqrt{0.001225 + 0.00001225 - 0.0000784}$$

$$= \sqrt{0.00115885}$$

$$= 0.0340 \quad \text{or} \quad 3.4\%$$ ●

It should be noted that the slightly negative correlation between projects R_1 and R_2 in Example 2 substantially reduces the risk on R_1 through pooling. Hence, while R_1 considered in isolation might be rejected, the combination of R_1 with R_2 could become a more attractive alternative than other combinations.

To summarize the key points in terms of building a portfolio of assets, the crux of the problem lies in balancing σ_j, X_j, and Cov_{ij} to minimize risk for a desired level of return. Since σ_i, σ_j, and ρ_{ij} are fixed for a given pair of projects i and j, finding X_i and X_j to minimize risk becomes of interest to the financial manager building a portfolio of assets.

Considering two projects i and j, σ_p is minimized if the proportion invested in project i is determined as shown in Equation (6):

$$X_i = \frac{\sigma_j^2 - \text{Cov}_{ij}}{\sigma_i^2 + \sigma_j^2 - 2\,\text{Cov}_{ij}} \tag{6}$$

Equation (6) was derived by differentiating Equation (5) with respect to X_i, setting the deviative equal to zero, and solving for X_i.

Based on our discussion, the following observations (decision rules) should provide the financial manager with insight and strategies for diversification in building a portfolio or capital budget. We consider two assets, i and j, but the results can be generalized for a large number of projects.

1. If $\rho_{ij} = 0$, the covariance term in Equation (5) for σ_p drops out and the portfolio's standard deviation is the square root of the weighted sum of the project variances:

$$\sigma_p = \sqrt{\sum_{j=1}^{N} X_j^2 \sigma_j^2}$$

Further, the proportion of project i that should be selected to minimize risk under these conditions (i.e., $\rho_{ij} = 0$) is found using Equation (6), modified as follows:

$$X_i = \frac{\sigma_j^2}{\sigma_i^2 + \sigma_j^2}$$

That is, to minimize risk in the combination, X_i should equal the ratio of the variance of j to the sum of the variances of i and j.

2. If $0 < \rho_{ij} < \sigma_i/\sigma_j$ (where σ_i is the smaller of the two standard deviations), the portfolio standard deviation will be determined using Equation (5), where both the sum of the weighted variances and the weighted positive covariance plays a part. However, diversification is still attractive, since σ_p will be smaller than either σ_i or σ_j individually if the proportion invested in X_i is determined using Equation (6).

3. If $\rho_{ij} > \sigma_i/\sigma_j$, diversification will not be attractive, since the positive correlation and covariance are too great to reduce σ_p below the smaller standard deviation, σ_i. Hence, to minimize risk, X_i should equal 1.

4. If $\rho_{ij} < 0$, σ_p will be less than the square root of the sum of the weighted variances, owing to the negative weighted covariance. σ_p and X_i are then determined using Equations (5) and (6), respectively.

5. If $\rho_{ij} = -1$, σ_p can be driven to zero by selecting the proper proportions of the two securities or projects whereby the weighted covariance in Equation (5) is equal to the sum of the weighted variances. This proper proportion is found by simplifying Equation (6) for the $\rho_{ij} = -1$ case, as follows:

$$X_i = \frac{\sigma_j}{\sigma_i + \sigma_j}$$

The observations are illustrated in Example 3.

● **EXAMPLE 3** *Portfolio Expected Return and Standard Deviation*
    Two projects have the following risk–return characteristics:

	P_1	P_2
$E(R_j)$	15%	20%
σ_j	12%	16%

Determine E_p and σ_p for the minimum risk portfolio, where the correlation coefficient between the two projects is: (a) zero, (b) 0.20, (c) 0.90, and (d) -1.

Solution:
(a) Given that $\rho_{ij} = 0$, the optimal proportion is determined as follows:

$$X_i = \frac{\sigma_j^2}{\sigma_i^2 + \sigma_j^2}$$

$$X_1 = \frac{(0.16)^2}{(0.12)^2 + (0.16)^2}$$

$$= \frac{0.0256}{0.0144 + 0.0256}$$

$$= 0.64$$

Thus, the minimum–risk combination is to invest 0.64 of the portfolio in P_1 and 0.36 in P_2.

Now the expected value and standard deviation of the portfolio may be computed.

$$E_p = 0.64(0.15) + 0.36(0.20)$$
$$= 0.96 + 0.072$$
$$= 0.168 \quad \text{or} \quad 16.8\%$$

$$\sigma_p = \sqrt{(0.64)^2(0.12)^2 + (0.36)^2(0.16)^2}$$
$$= \sqrt{0.00589824 + 0.00331776}$$
$$= 0.9600 \quad \text{or} \quad 9.60\%$$

Notice that σ_p is significantly lower than either σ_{p_1} or σ_{p_2}.

(b) Given that $\rho_{ij} = +0.20$, the optimal proportion is determined as follows:

$$X_i = \frac{\sigma_j^2 - \text{Cov}_{ij}}{\sigma_i^2 + \sigma_j^2 - 2\,\text{Cov}_{ij}}$$

$$X_1 = \frac{(0.16)^2 - (0.2)(0.12)(0.16)}{(0.12)^2 + (0.16)^2 - 2(+0.2)(0.12)(0.16)}$$

$$= \frac{0.02176}{0.03232}$$

$$= 0.673$$

$$E_p = (0.673)(0.15) + (0.327)(0.20)$$
$$= 0.10095 + 0.0654$$
$$= 0.16635 \quad \text{or} \quad 16.6$$

$$\sigma_p = \sqrt{(0.673)^2(0.12)^2 + (0.327)^2(0.16)^2 + 2(0.673)(0.327)(0.2)(0.12)(0.16)}$$

$$= \sqrt{0.0065221776 + 0.0027373824 + 0.0016901452}$$
$$= 0.10464 \quad \text{or} \quad 10.5$$

Notice that σ_p is still lower than the smaller standard deviation but that we are investing a greater percent of funds (0.673 vs. 0.64) in P_1 than when $\rho_{ij} = 0$. In general, as the correlation becomes more highly positive, more of the funds will be invested in the less risky project. This continues until $\rho_{ij} = \sigma_1/\sigma_2$ (where $\sigma_1 < \sigma_2$), at which point 100% of the available funds are invested in the less-risky project.

(c) Given that $\rho_{ij} = +0.90$, by rule 3 we see that $\rho_{ij} = +0.90 > 12\%/16\% = +0.75$, diversification will not be beneficial, and 100% of the funds should be invested in P_1. Given this degree of correlation, we can demonstrate that even a high percentage invested in P_1 (say 85% in P_1 and 15% in P_2) will not reduce σ_p below $\sigma_{p_1} = 12\%$:

$$\sigma_p = \sqrt{(0.85)^2(0.12)^2 + (0.15)^2(0.16)^2 + 2(0.85)(0.15)(0.90)(0.12)(0.16)}$$

$$= \sqrt{0.010404 + 0.000576 + 0.004464}$$

$$= 0.12404 \quad \text{or} \quad 12.4\%$$

As X_1 increases from 0.85 to 1.00, the σ_p value would continually get smaller, decreasing from 12.404% to 12%.

(d) Given that $\rho_{ij} = -1.0$, we see by rule 5 that the proportion to invest in P_1 is just over 57%:

$$X_1 = \frac{\sigma_2}{\sigma_1 + \sigma_2} = \frac{0.16}{0.12 + 0.16} = 0.571429$$

Having this percent invested in P_1 should drive σ_p to zero.

$$E_p = (0.571429)(0.15) + (0.428571)(0.20)$$

$$= 0.08571435 + 0.0857142$$

$$= 0.17142855 \text{ or } 17.1\%$$

$$\sigma_p = \sqrt{ (0.571429)^2(0.12)^2 + (0.428571)^2(0.16)^2 } $$
$$\overline{+ 2(-1)(0.12)(0.16)(0.571429)(0.428571)}$$

$$= \sqrt{0.0047020478 + 0.0047020314 - 0.0094040792}$$

$$= 0 \qquad\qquad \bullet$$

Based on the results of Example 3, we may draw the following conclusions:

1. As ρ_{ij} decreases from $+1.0$ through σ_1/σ_2 ($\sigma_1 < \sigma_2$), 100% of the funds will be invested in the less-risky project.

2. As ρ_{ij} gets smaller, eventually decreasing to -1.0, a smaller and smaller percentage will be invested in the less-risky security, since the interaction between ρ_{ij}, σ_i, σ_j, X_i, and X_j causes σ_p to be minimized as X_i is decreased and X_j increased to capitalize on the favorable covariance effects between the two projects or securities. Figure 9-1 illustrates these facts. As shown in Figure 9-1, the minimum-risk percentages invested in P_1 go from 0.673 (point 1 in Figure 9-1) when $\rho_{12} = +0.20$, to 0.64 (point 2 in Figure 9-1) when $\rho_{12} = 0$, to 0.571 (point 3 in Figure 9-1) when $\rho_{12} = -1.0$.

FIGURE 9-1 **Portfolio Standard Deviations (σ_p) as the Correlation Coefficient (ρ_{ij}) Varies from $+1$ to -1**

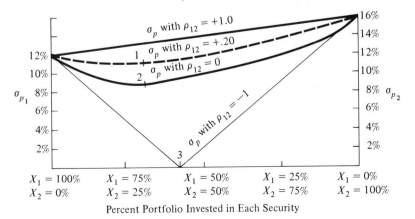

EFFICIENT PORTFOLIOS OR BUDGETS

In earlier chapters, individual projects were ranked by net present value. Since the objective of capital budgeting is to increase the present value of the firm, "rational" management accepted all projects with a positive NPV, within the constraints of available capital, and the like. However, this decision rule for individual projects suggests that there does not exist a combination of projects that would be superior to a single investment meeting the criterion. The single project standard ignored the advantage of diversification to improve the quality of earnings through reduction of risk.

When the firm must choose among several capital proposals, a wiser decision rule seeks the combination of projects that maximizes expected present value and minimizes the variance or standard deviation. But experience attests that expected present value and standard deviation generally vary directly, and management can trade off additional risk against additional income. The better decision rule, therefore, stresses the concept of efficient portfolios: those combinations that for any given expected value have a minimum standard deviation (risk); or for any chosen level of risk (standard deviation), the highest expected return.

Assume that management has a fixed sum to invest and can choose from a number of possible combinations as illustrated in Figure 9-2. Out of all the combinations obtainable, only some will be efficient. *A combination is inefficient if there exists another portfolio with a higher expected value and a lower standard deviation, a higher expected return and the same standard deviation, or the same expected return and a lower standard deviation.* Eliminating the inefficient portfolios from the set of all possible combinations, the array of efficient portfolios may be plotted as line *AF* in Figure 9-3. Combinations to the left of this *efficient frontier* are inefficient: a better return or lower risk or both can always be secured by moving to the frontier. To the right of *AF*, the portfolios are unobtainable with the funds available for investment.

FIGURE 9-2   Attainable Portfolios   **FIGURE 9-3   Efficient Frontier**

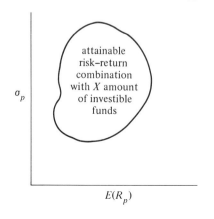

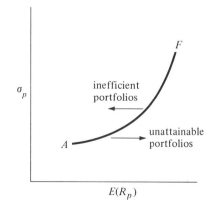

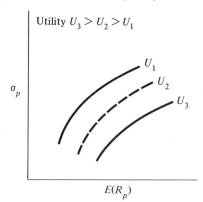

FIGURE 9-4   Utility Isoquants

Utility $U_3 > U_2 > U_1$

σ_p

U_1

U_2

U_3

$E(R_p)$

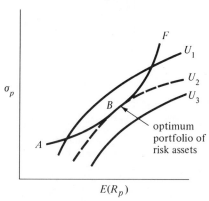

FIGURE 9-5   Optimal Portfolio

F

U_1

U_2

U_3

σ_p

B

A

optimum
portfolio of
risk assets

$E(R_p)$

Among the efficient set we want to select that combination representing the optimum portfolio (i.e., the combination of risk and return preferred by the investor). The solution lies in the application of utility theory. Figure 9-4 depicts a set of utility isoquants (1, 2, and 3) for a risk-averse decision maker. *Each isoquant plots a series of combinations with different risks and returns which have the same total utility for the investor. As the curves move to the right, total utility increases, so total utility 3 > 2 > 1.* All combinations of risk and return on curve 2 have the same total utility, but this quantum is larger than the total utility of the combinations on curve 1. *Accordingly, the optimal portfolio for a given investor is found at the tangency point between the efficient frontier and utility isoquant.* This tangency point (B), as shown in Figure 9-5, marks the highest level of satisfaction the investor can attain with the funds available for investment. Other decision makers with unique utility functions would locate their maximum satisfaction at other points of tangency. Each decision maker has his or her own preferred combinations of risk assets (projects or securities).

Let income connote utility and risk, disutility. At the point of equilibrium (B),

$$\frac{\Delta_{\text{utility}}}{\Delta_{\text{disutility}}} = \frac{\Delta E(R)}{\Delta \sigma}$$

The equilibrium point is important to the subsequent discussion. Since all portfolios in the efficient set comprise risk assets, the equilibrium defines the decision maker's preferred combination of risk assets—that combination which dominates all other risk-asset packages.

Managers and investors also have the opportunity to purchase risk-free assets. Continuing with the assumption that funds may be borrowed or loaned at the risk-free rate, management has several choices:

1. To continue to invest all funds in the optimum risk portfolio denoted by point B.

2. To lend all or a portion of the funds at the risk-free rate, thereby developing a portfolio of assets consisting of risk-free assets (Figure 9-6, point

FIGURE 9-6   Efficient Frontier: Risk and Risk-Free Assets

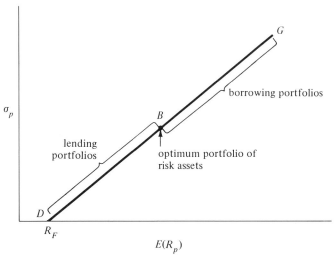

D) and assets consisting of the established portfolio of risk assets (Figure 9-6, point B).

3. To borrow funds at the risk-free rate and invest in portfolio B.

This permits the decision maker to develop portfolios anywhere along the line DBG rather than being limited solely to point B. Line DBG is the new efficient frontier, referred to later as the capital market line. The new frontier commences at point D (the risk-free portfolio); continues from point D through B (portfolios composed of varying proportions of risk and risk-free assets), to point B (the 100% risk asset portfolio). Beyond B, the decision maker borrows at the risk-free rate and invests these additional funds in portfolio B, the preferred package of risk assets.

Most decision makers could increase their utility by electing to take advantage of the lending and borrowing opportunity at the risk-free rate. Along the frontier DBG, the decision maker increases yield by changing the portfolio weights: the proportions committed to risk and risk-free assets. *But within the risk portion of the portfolio, the "rational" decision maker always acquires the same package of risk assets described by point B, since this point represents the decision maker's optimum portfolio of risk assets, as shown in Figure 9-5.* With the return on the risk portfolio established and similarly for the risk-free portfolio, the line DBG is linear. The yields on all combinations vary directly with the weights assigned to the risk and risk-free packages.

Portfolios on the line segment DB are lending portfolios. The decision maker buys package B and lends the balance of his funds (buys risk-free securities) at the risk-free rate (R_F). Portfolios on the line segment B through G are borrowing portfolios. The decision maker borrows at the risk-free rate and adds these funds to the original sum to invest all in package B. Thus, portfolios on the line segment BG are leveraged. The returns remain linear in the net worth invested in package *B*. Each investment in package *B* brings the same $E(R)$ and σ, but leveraging [deducting R_F from the portfolio return $E(R)$] improves the yield on the net worth invested in the portfolio and increases the variability of the combination.

PORTFOLIO THEORY AND CAPITAL BUDGETING

Application of the portfolio model to capital budgeting is not without some difficulty. An investment in common stocks is *divisible*; the purchaser acquires units (or shares) each with the same expected return and standard deviation. The efficient frontier is thus a continuous line and the weighting system reflects the percentage of the total investment allocated to one asset or to the amounts of risk and risk-free assets.

Few capital projects divide into homogenous units with the same expected return and standard deviation. Most projects are lumpy or *indivisible*. Acceptance means taking the entire project: the whole return and whole standard deviation. The firm cannot buy fractions. It cannot acquire 60% of the return and standard deviation of a project. The continuity of the line between portfolios in Figure 9-3 is due to variations in fractional holdings in a group of divisible projects. For *indivisible projects*, it would not be realistic to join the efficient sets with a continuous line, since fractional changes are not permitted. In constructing portfolios of indivisible projects, therefore, the weighting system is either 0 or 1. The solution in terms of optimum expected return and standard deviation for a portfolio of indivisible projects is most easily reached using integer programming.

Lower-Confidence-Limit Criterion

If the number of projects considered is large, the efficient set might involve a substantial number of combinations from which to choose. The use of the lower confidence limit model can reduce the problem to a manageable size. The approach assumes that the investor can state his preference in terms of a minimum acceptable return (the lower confidence limit) as opposed to minimizing risk for a given specified return. The lower confidence limit (L) is found using Equation (7):

$$L = E(R_p) - K\sigma_p \tag{7}$$

where K is a constant chosen by the investor and refers to the number of standard deviations in the normal distribution. Thus, the investor (or manager) establishes a floor below which the return on the budget should not fall. Depending on the minimum return stipulated, K may represent 1, 1.5, 2, . . . standard deviations below the expected return. In other words, the investor, by putting a value on K, establishes a minimum acceptable return on the budget and/or the amount of downside risk she or he willingly bears. If $K=2$, this means that the manager is willing to accept only a 2.5% probability of the return falling below the minimum acceptable amount.

As the minimum acceptable return (L) increases for a given budget, there will be fewer efficient combinations to choose from. The efficient frontier shrinks as previously efficient portfolios are now considered inefficient. To illustrate the concept, consider Example 4.

● **EXAMPLE 4**   *Application of Lower-Confidence-Limit Criterion*

An investor is evaluating the following three portfolios:

Portfolio	$E(R_p)$	σ_p
A	0.22	0.10
B	0.28	0.12
C	0.38	0.14

All three of these portfolios are efficient. Depending upon his or her utility function, the investor might choose any one of the three portfolios. Assume that she or he is only willing to accept a 0.025 chance of the return falling below L. Determine the value of K that would be assigned and the minimum acceptable returns on the portfolios.

Solution: Assuming a normal distribution, a value of $K = 2$ would include about 95% of the cases. Hence, a K equaling 2 would find only 2.5% of the cases falling below L. (More risk-adverse investors would increase the value of K since they would require fewer cases falling below L.) The minimum acceptable returns on the portfolios now become:

Portfolio	$E(R_p)$	$-$	$K(\sigma_p)$	$=$	L
A	0.22	$-$	2(0.10)	$=$	0.02
B	0.28	$-$	2(0.12)	$=$	0.04
C	0.38	$-$	2(0.14)	$=$	0.10

Portfolio C now dominates based on the following rule: Specify the value of K and choose the portfolio with the highest minimum return, L.   ●

Risk Premium of Single Projects

Once management views the firm as a portfolio, it will assess the risk potential of an additional project in terms of the expected covariance with the operational projects making up the firm. What is the required premium (θ_j) for the incremental risk associated with the acceptance of the next project? The response follows directly from the preceding discussion:

$$\theta_j = \frac{E(R_p) - R_F}{\sigma_p^2}(\rho_{jp}\sigma_j\sigma_p) \tag{8}$$

where $E(R_p)$ = expected return on the portfolio (i.e., the firm)
  R_F = risk-free rate
  σ_p^2 = variance of the portfolio
  ρ_{jp} = coefficient of correlation between jth project and portfolio
  σ_j = standard deviation of the jth project

The greater the covariance between the jth project and the portfolio, the greater the risk premium embodied in the discount rate for that project; or, given the risk-free rate, the larger the discount rate that should be applied against the project's cash flows. However, a word of caution in using the analysis: the order in which projects are reviewed affects the risk premium, since the incremental risk depends upon the package of projects accepted to which the latest candidate is compared.

SUMMARY

This chapter explored the important area of portfolio effects in which the focus of the capital investment process shifts from the individual project to that of combinations of projects. The discussion centered around the concept of covariance between pairs of candidate projects which might be included in the capital budget. The computation of the covariance was considered as well as the determination of the expected return and standard deviation on the portfolio of assets. The area of efficient portfolios was introduced, as was that of selecting the optimal efficient portfolio when either exclusively risk assets or a combination of risk and risk-free assets are available for the investor. This chapter serves as a bridge to introduce Chapter 10, which deals with capital asset pricing theory. In addition, concepts introduced here will be called upon again in Chapters 14 and 18.

PROBLEMS

1. Empirical studies have derived the following probabilities of the specific outcomes for two projects.

	Project B			
Project A	*$250,000*	*$300,000*	*$400,000*	*Total*
$50,000	0.1254	0.1073	0.0764	0.3091
$75,000	0.0909	0.0673	0.1691	0.3273
$90,000	0.1654	0.0618	0.1364	0.3636
Total	0.3817	0.2364	0.3819	

Compute the mean and standard deviation of each project as well as the covariance between the two projects, using the contingency-table format.

2. Consider the returns for these four securities:

OBS	Sec 1	Sec 2	Sec 3	Sec 4
1	$ 9	$25	$30	$5
2	10	23	31	6
3	12	22	31	5
4	15	20	32	4
5	16	19	30	2

The correlation coefficients for all combinations of securities are shown below, along with the standard deviations of each security:

$$
\begin{array}{ll}
\rho_{12} = -0.98 & \sigma_1 = 3.05 \\
\rho_{13} = 0.24 & \sigma_2 = 2.39 \\
\rho_{14} = -0.85 & \sigma_3 = .84 \\
\rho_{23} = -0.28 & \sigma_4 = 1.52 \\
\rho_{24} = 0.79 & \\
\rho_{34} = 0.28 &
\end{array}
$$

(a) Compute the covariances for all possible pairs of securities.
(b) Compute the variance of the six two-security portfolios assuming a 50%–50% allocation.

3. Given $\rho_{xy} = 0$ and the incomplete joint and marginal probability table below, calculate the variance of the portfolio of the two securities X and Y in equal proportions. Use the completed table to show that the covariance of the two securities is equal to 0.

Joint and Marginal Probabilities of Cash Flow Generated in 500 Simulation Runs

Project X	Project Y $100	Project Y $200	Project Y $300	Total
$150	0.20			
$200			0.05	0.20
$250				
Total	0.50			1.00

Hint: Recall that if two events A and B are independent of each other, $P(A \cap B) = P(A) \cdot P(B)$. Use this hint to fill in all the joint probabilities in the table and then proceed with the solution.

4. RCA is evaluating two securities, which have the following means and standard deviations:

$$
\begin{array}{ll}
E(R_A) = 20\% & E(R_B) = 28\% \\
\sigma_A = 10\% & \sigma_B = 14\%
\end{array}
$$

RCA feels that the following correlation coefficients could exist between the two securities: (a) +0.85, (b) +0.40, (c) zero, and (d) −1.0. Determine the minimum-risk portfolios for each of these correlation coefficients as well as the portfolio return and standard deviation. Selling short is not permitted.

5. For securities A and B and each of the correlation coefficients shown in Problem 4, compute the expected portfolio return and the portfolio standard deviation for the following mixtures:

% in A	% in B
100	0
75	25
50	50
25	75
0	100

Also, sketch the four efficient frontiers that are generated on the same graph.

6. Consider Problems 4 and 5 and that RCA might also include a risk-free security yielding 7% in its portfolio with securities A and B. Further, the efficient frontier, as shown in Figure 9-6, is tangent to the efficient frontier that you drew for a correlation coefficient of zero in Problem 5 at the point where 50% is invested in each security. The firm has $1,000 to invest but wants to limit its portfolio risk as measured by σ_P to 7%. Find the optimal portfolio in terms of the mixture between securities A and B (in the proportion one-half each of the amount invested in risky securities) and the risk-free security so as to limit the portfolio risk to 7%.

7. A firm is evaluating the following four efficient portfolios:

Portfolio	$E(R_p)$	σ_p
1	0.12	0.04
2	0.24	0.06
3	0.30	0.10
4	0.32	0.12

Determine the optimal portfolio if the firm is willing to accept only a 5% chance that the portfolio return falls below the lower confidence level (L).

8. The Hansen Company has the following risk posture:

$$E(R_H) = 12\%, \qquad \sigma_H = 4\%$$

The firm is considering the acquisition of company B, which has the following characteristics:

$$E(R_B) = 10\%, \qquad \sigma_B = 3\%, \qquad \rho_{HB} = +0.75$$

where ρ_{HB} is the correlation between Hansen Company and firm B and the risk-free rate is 6%. Determine the risk premium (θ_B) over and above the risk-free rate that would be required by Hansen in order to make it worthwhile to acquire firm B. Should firm B be acquired, given its expected return, R_F and the computed value of θ_B?

10 CAPITAL ASSET PRICING

In our discussion of portfolio effects, we measured portfolio risk by determining the covariance of each project (or security) with all other projects (or securities) in the combination. The calculations (variances and covariances) for even a small number of projects quickly become voluminous. The number of inputs for a portfolio of N projects equals $N(N + 3)/2$, since we need to consider the expected return and standard deviation for each security and the covariance between all possible pairs of securities. If management were evaluating 12 projects, this approach entails 90 calculations. As N increases in size, the input requirements grow geometrically; witness, that 100 projects would require 5,150 inputs and 200 projects would require 20,300 inputs! In addition, the problem of estimating probabilities and joint probabilities of the cash flows further complicates the application of the portfolio model to capital budgeting. Theoreticians can point to conceptual devices for estimating probabilities, but at this stage of their development, they do not enjoy wide currency among managers.

An alternative approach, employing techniques familiar to financial managers and corporate economists, uses the Capital Asset Pricing Model (CAPM). This relates the return and standard deviation of a project (or security) to a broad-based economic indicator of risk asset[1] returns, such as Standard & Poor's 500 Index of Stocks, industry profitability ratios, and so on. The model posits a linear correlation between the returns on the risk asset and the index.

In contrast to the number of calculations demanded by the full variance–covariance portfolio model, the new input requirement is simply $3N + 2$ when using Sharpe's single-index model, expressed as Equation (1). For 12 projects, this totals 38 inputs, a reduction of 52; for 100 projects, 302 inputs are required; for 200 projects, 602, which are reductions of 94% and 97%, respectively, compared to the full variance–covariance model. Moreover, simple

---

[1]For purposes of study of capital asset pricing, we define capital asset as one with a life of more than 1 year, expected to earn an income sufficient to cover the amortization of its acquisition cost and operational expenses plus a net yield commensurate to the time value of money and risk. The term includes long-lived physical assets (plant and equipment) plus claims on such assets (common stocks, bonds, and other securities).

linear correlation is a rudimentary technique in statistical analysis and sales forecasting. Thus, business managers and staff specialists have at least a nodding acquaintance with the idea involved. In sum, we shall pursue the same objective—constructing and evaluating portfolios by their expected return and standard deviation—but use market-based data rather than direct comparison of project cash flows. This has the added advantage of stressing the link between the financial manager and the investor. How the latter values the decisions of the former determines the present worth of the enterprise.

CAPM has a growing significance in capital budgeting:

1. It provides a method of determining the expected or required return of a capital project or security, if they can be related to a broad-based economic indicator.

2. It provides an alternative calculation for the cost of equity capital, one component of the marginal cost of capital used as a hurdle rate in evaluating capital projects.

3. It can be used in the valuation of the firm and to determine the firm's incremental debt capacity if a project is accepted. Thus, it ties together the investment and financing decisions as well as the valuation process. This application of CAPM is illustrated in Chapter 11.

CAPITAL ASSET PRICING MODEL

To start the study of CAPM, consider the single-index model developed by Sharpe[2]:

$$\tilde{R}_{jt} = \alpha_j + B_j(\tilde{R}_{mt}) + \tilde{e}_{jt} \tag{1}$$

where $\tilde{R}_{jt}$ = random variable showing the return on asset j (a project or security) in period t

$\tilde{R}_{mt}$ = random variable showing the return on a broad-based market index in period t

α_j, B_j = parameters for asset j (which are developed by regression analysis) which best describe the *average relationship* between the returns $\tilde{R}_{jt}$ and $\tilde{R}_{mt}$

$\tilde{e}_{jt}$ = random-error term for asset j in period t

This simple linear regression model determines the parameters α_j and B_j so that returns on individual projects (or securities) can be estimated using the equation plus an estimate for the value of the market index. It should be pointed out that because $\tilde{R}_{jt}$ and $\tilde{R}_{mt}$ are both random variables, the simple linear relationship will not be 100% accurate; thus, the random-error term $\tilde{e}_{jt}$ measures the difference between the actual returns on project j in period t and

[2]William F. Sharpe, "A Simplified Model for Portfolio Analysis," *Management Science*, January 1963, pp. 277–293.

those predicted using the regression equation. In regression analysis, the parameters α_j and B_j are determined by the method of least squares, which necessitates that the random-error term $\tilde{e}_{jt}$ will have an expected value of zero and a variance that is a positive, finite constant, Q_j^2, for all values of t (the time variable). In addition to the assumptions above, the following three assumptions are also made in order to arrive at the significant simplications discussed above:

1. The random-error term is uncorrelated with the market index: Cov $(\tilde{e}_{jt}, \tilde{R}_{mt}) = 0$.

2. The random-error terms are nòt serially correlated over time: Cov($\tilde{e}_{jt}$, $\tilde{e}_{j, t+n}$) = 0 for any value of n.

3. The random-error term for project j is not correlated with any other project's random-error term: Cov $(\tilde{e}_{jt}, \tilde{e}_{it}) = 0$.

Given the assumptions above, we can determine the expected value and the variance of Equation (1):

$$E(\tilde{R}_{jt}) = E(\alpha_j + B_j(\tilde{R}_{mt}) + \tilde{e}_{jt})$$

$$= \alpha_j + B_j(E(\tilde{R}_{mt})) + E(\tilde{e}_{jt})$$

$$= \alpha_j + B_j(E(\tilde{R}_{mt})) \qquad (2)$$

where $E(\tilde{R}_j)$ and $E(\tilde{R}_m)$ are, respectively, the expected value of the return on project j and the expected value of the return on the market index.

$$\text{Var}(\tilde{R}_{jt}) = \text{Var}(\alpha_j + B_j(\tilde{R}_{mt}) + \tilde{e}_{jt})$$

$$= \text{Var}(\alpha_j) + \text{Var}(B_j(\tilde{R}_{mt})) + \text{Var}(\tilde{e}_{jt})$$

$$= B_j^2\sigma_m^2 + Q_j^2 \qquad (3)$$

where σ_m^2 and Q_j^2 are, respectively, the variance on the market index and the variance on the random-error term $\tilde{e}_{jt}$.

Equation (3) will be discussed in greater detail later.

Examining Equation (2) we see that the expected return on project j can be divided into two independent components:

α_j = return on project j due exclusively to its own merits

$B_j(E(\tilde{R}_{mt}))$ = return on project j due to the response of project j to changes in the broad-based index of economic activity $\tilde{R}_{mt}$.

In ordinary regression analysis, these two components are respectively the y intercept and the slope of the regression line. Both values (α_j, B_j) can be determined using the usual least-squares equations. Figure 10-1 shows the relationships. Equations (4) and (5) are the least-squares equations for α_j and B_j:

FIGURE 10-1   Simple Linear Regression Equation Relating $\tilde{R}_j$ to $\tilde{R}_m$

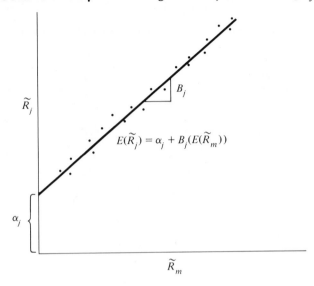

$$B_j = \frac{n \sum\limits_{t=1}^{n} \tilde{R}_{mt}\tilde{R}_{jt} - \left(\sum\limits_{t=1}^{n} \tilde{R}_{mt} \right)\left(\sum\limits_{t=1}^{n} \tilde{R}_{jt} \right)}{n \sum\limits_{t=1}^{n} \tilde{R}_{mt}^2 - \left(\sum\limits_{t=1}^{n} \tilde{R}_{mt} \right)^2} \qquad (4)$$

$$\alpha_j = E(\tilde{R}_j) - B_j(E(\tilde{R}_m)) \qquad (5)$$

Example 1 demonstrates the use of Equations (4) and (5).

● **EXAMPLE 1** *Regression Model*

A new project is under consideration. This project is very similar to the project whose precentage returns over a 10-period horizon are shown below. The returns on a market index (also in percentage terms) are also shown.

Period (t)	Similar Project $\tilde{R}_{jt}$	Market Index $\tilde{R}_{mt}$
1	9	7
2	10	9
3	10	10
4	11	12
5	10	11
6	11	10
7	11	10
8	10	9
9	9	8
10	7	7

(a) Compute the values for α_j and B_j.
(b) Write and explain the regression equation.

Solution: The following table will be helpful in computing α_j and B_j:

t	$\tilde{R}_{jt}$	$\tilde{R}_{mt}$	$\tilde{R}_{jt}\tilde{R}_{mt}$	$\tilde{R}_{mt}^2$
1	0.09	0.07	0.0063	0.0049
2	0.10	0.09	0.0090	0.0081
3	0.10	0.10	0.0100	0.0100
4	0.11	0.12	0.0132	0.0144
5	0.10	0.11	0.0110	0.0121
6	0.11	0.10	0.0110	0.0100
7	0.11	0.10	0.0110	0.0100
8	0.10	0.09	0.0090	0.0081
9	0.09	0.08	0.0072	0.0064
10	0.07	0.07	0.0049	0.0049

Total $\quad \Sigma \tilde{R}_{jt} = 0.98 \quad \Sigma \tilde{R}_{mt} = 0.93 \quad \Sigma \tilde{R}_{jt}\tilde{R}_{mt} = 0.0926 \quad \Sigma \tilde{R}_{mt}^2 = 0.0889$

$$
\begin{aligned}
B_j &= \frac{n \Sigma \tilde{R}_{mt}\tilde{R}_{jt} - (\Sigma \tilde{R}_{mt})(\Sigma \tilde{R}_{jt})}{n \Sigma \tilde{R}_{mt}^2 - (\Sigma \tilde{R}_{mt})^2} \\
&= \frac{10(0.0926) - (0.98)(0.93)}{10(0.0889) - (0.93)^2} \\
&= \frac{0.9260 - 0.9114}{0.8890 - 0.8649} \\
&= 0.6058 \\
\alpha_j &= E(\tilde{R}_j) - B_j(E(\tilde{R}_m)) \\
&= 0.098 - (0.6058)(0.093) \\
&= 0.0417
\end{aligned}
$$

Thus, the regression equation is

$$
\begin{aligned}
E(\tilde{R}_j) &= \alpha_j + B_j(E(\tilde{R}_m)) \\
&= 0.0417 + 0.6058(E(\tilde{R}_m))
\end{aligned}
$$

The meaning of the regression equation is that the project on its own merits earns a return of 4.17% and, in addition, it will earn 60.58% of the expected return on the market index $E(\tilde{R}_m)$.   ●

To complete our discussion of the single-index model, we now return to Equation (3), which indicates that the variance of the returns on project j can be attributed to two distinct types of risk:

1. The risk associated with project j's response to the market index multiplied by the variability in the market index itself: $B_j^2\sigma_m^2$.

2. The risk associated with the random-error term of project j (i.e., due to unexplained causes other than the market index), Q_j^2.

The first of these has come to be known as *systematic risk*. This risk cannot be diversified away since it is the result of variability in the market of risky assets. The latter is known as *unsystematic risk*. It can be diversified away through the selection of other risky assets which are lowly or negatively correlated with the asset in question. Thus, we can speak of partitioning the total risk associated with the returns on project *j* into its two components:

$$\text{Total risk} = \underset{\substack{\text{on project } j \\ \text{(non-diversifiable)}}}{\text{systematic risk}} + \underset{\substack{\text{(diversifiable)}}}{\text{unsystematic risk}}$$

$$\sigma_{R_j}^2 = B_j^2 \sigma_m^2 \qquad\qquad + Q_j^2$$

Several interrelationships are worthy of note. The unsystematic risk on a given project, Q_j^2, is the square of a familiar measure in regression analysis, the standard error of estimate. The *standard error of estimate* is the average amount of error that is made in predicting returns on project *j* using the regression equation.

$$Q_j = \sqrt{\frac{\text{variation due to error}}{n-2}}$$

To more fully explain the numerator of this expression, we will partition the variance in returns on project *j* in a slightly different way than we did above. In regression analysis, the partitioning is as follows:

$$\underset{\substack{\text{in returns of} \\ \text{project } j}}{\text{total variation}} = \underset{\substack{\text{explained by} \\ \text{the regression} \\ \text{equation}}}{\text{variation}} + \underset{\substack{\text{due to error} \\ \text{(unexplained} \\ \text{variation)}}}{\text{variation}}$$

$$\sum_{t=1}^{n} (\tilde{R}_{jt} - \bar{R}_j)^2 = \sum_{t=1}^{n} (E(\tilde{R}_{jt}) - \bar{R}_j)^2 + \sum_{t=1}^{n} (\tilde{R}_{jt} - E(\tilde{R}_{jt}))^2 \qquad (6)$$

It should be noted the $\tilde{R}_{jt}$ refers to the actual return on project *j*; $E(\tilde{R}_{jt})$ is the expected value of the return on project *j* in period *t* using the regression equation. R_j is the expected value for the return on project *j*. The standard error of estimate is stated more formally as

$$Q_j = \sqrt{\frac{\Sigma (\tilde{R}_{jt} - E(\tilde{R}_{jt}))^2}{n-2}} \qquad (7)$$

Further, there are two final regression statistics of interest. The *coefficient of determination* shows the percentage of the total variation in the dependent variable that is explained by variations in the independent variable. The *coefficient of nondetermination* shows the percentage of the total variation that is left unexplained by the independent variable being used. Of course, the sum of these two coefficients must be 100%. By examining Equation (6) we see that these two statistics may be expressed as shown in Equations (8) and (9):

$$\underset{\substack{\text{of determination}}}{\text{coefficient}} = \rho^2 = \frac{\Sigma (E(\tilde{R}_{jt}) - \bar{R}_j)^2}{\Sigma (\tilde{R}_{jt} - \bar{R}_j)^2} \qquad (8)$$

$$\underset{\substack{\text{coefficient of} \\ \text{nondetermination}}}{} = K^2 = \frac{\Sigma (\tilde{R}_{jt} - E(\tilde{R}_{jt}))^2}{\Sigma (\tilde{R}_{jt} - \bar{R}_j)^2} \qquad (9)$$

It should be pointed out that the coefficient of determination is the square of the correlation coefficient. Thus, this value is also related to the amount of covariance between the project returns and the returns on the market index. The computation of these statistics and their precise interpretation in the terms of our problem are illustrated in Example 2.

● **EXAMPLE 2**   *Calculation of Relevant Statistics*

For the data shown in Example 1, compute the following:
(a) The standard error of estimate.
(b) The coefficient of determination.
(c) The coefficient of nondetermination.
(d) The variance in the market index.
(e) The variance of the returns on project j.
(f) The correlation coefficient and the covariance between $\tilde{R}_{jt}$ and $\tilde{R}_{mt}$.

Solution: The following table will be helpful in computing the desired statistics above:

	(1) $\tilde{R}_{jt}$	(2) $\tilde{R}_{mt}$	(3) $E(\tilde{R}_{jt})$	(4) $(\tilde{R}_{jt} - \bar{R}_j)^2$	(5) $(\tilde{R}_{jt} - E(\tilde{R}_{jt}))^2$	(6) $(E(\tilde{R}_{jt}) - \bar{R}_j)^2$	(7) $(\tilde{R}_{mt} - \bar{R}_m)^2$
t							
1	0.09	0.07	0.0841	0.000064	0.00003481	0.00019321	0.000529
2	0.10	0.09	0.0962	0.000004	0.00001444	0.00000324	0.000009
3	0.10	0.10	0.1023	0.000004	0.00000529	0.00001849	0.000049
4	0.11	0.12	0.1144	0.000144	0.00001936	0.00026896	0.000729
5	0.10	0.11	0.1083	0.000004	0.00006889	0.00010609	0.000289
6	0.11	0.10	0.1023	0.000144	0.00005929	0.00001849	0.000049
7	0.11	0.10	0.1023	0.000144	0.00005929	0.00001849	0.000049
8	0.10	0.09	0.0962	0.000004	0.00001444	0.00000324	0.000009
9	0.09	0.08	0.0902	0.000064	0.00000004	0.00006084	0.000169
10	0.07	0.07	0.0841	0.000784	0.00019881	0.00019321	0.000529
	$\Sigma \tilde{R}_{jt}$	$\Sigma \tilde{R}_{mt}$	$\Sigma E(\tilde{R}_{jt})$	$\Sigma (\tilde{R}_{jt} - \bar{R}_j)^2$	$\Sigma (\tilde{R}_{jt} - E(\tilde{R}_{jt}))^2$	$\Sigma (E(\tilde{R}_{jt}) - \bar{R}_j)^2$	$\Sigma (\tilde{R}_{mt} - \bar{R}_m)^2$
Total	0.98	0.93	0.9804	0.001360	0.00047466	0.00088426	0.00241

Columns (1) and (2) in the table are the historical observations of $\tilde{R}_{jt}$ and $\tilde{R}_{mt}$, respectively, for the last 10 periods, as shown in Example 1. Column (3) shows the values computed using the regression equation and substituting the values of $\tilde{R}_{mt}$. Column (4) shows the values for the square of the quantity of the actual $\tilde{R}_{jt}$ $\bar{R}_j = \Sigma \tilde{R}_{jt}/10 = 0.098$. Column (5) is the square of the difference between the actual $\tilde{R}_{jt}$ [column (1)] and the predicted value using the regression equation $E(\tilde{R}_{jt})$ [column (3)]. Column (6) is the square of the difference between column (3) and $\bar{R}_j = 0.098$. Column (7) is the square of the difference between column (2) and $\bar{R}_m = \Sigma \tilde{R}_{mt}/10 = 0.093$. Thus, we see that the

$$\text{total variation or total sum of squares} = 0.00136$$
$$\text{variation explained by the regression equation} = 0.00088426$$
$$\text{variation unexplained by the regression equation} = 0.00047466$$
$$\text{total variation} = \text{explained variation} + \text{unexplained variation}$$
$$0.00136 = 0.00088426 + 0.00047466$$
$$0.00136 \cong 0.00135892$$

(a) Standard error of estimate:

$$Q_j = \sqrt{\frac{0.00047466}{10-2}} = \sqrt{0.0000593325}$$

$$= 0.007703 \quad \text{or} \quad 0.7703\%$$

This measure shows that the average amount of error made in predicting the return on project j using the return on the market index and our regression equation $E(\tilde{R}_j) = 0.0417 + 0.6058(E(\tilde{R}_m))$ is 0.7703%. Further, assuming that the variability around the regression line approximates a normal distribution, ± 2 standard errors would include approximately 95% of the variations. Thus, we could say that we could be 95% sure that the true return on project j will be within 1.5406% ($2 \times 0.7703\%$) of the value predicted for the return on project j using the regression equation.

(b) and (c) Coefficients of determination and nondetermination:

$$\rho^2 = \frac{0.00088426}{0.001360} = 65\%$$

$$K^2 = \frac{0.00047466}{0.001360} = 35\%$$

These two measures show that 65% of the variation in the returns on project j is explained by the variation in the market index, while 35% of the variation in returns on project j is due to factors other than the variation in the market index used in the regression equation.

(d) Variance in the market index: This measure is computed using the usual formula for variance:

$$\sigma_m^2 = \frac{\Sigma \left(\tilde{R}_{mt} - \bar{R}_m\right)^2}{n-1} = \frac{0.00241}{10-1}$$

$$= 0.0002677 \quad \text{or} \quad 0.02677\%$$

The variance in the market index is the average variability in the return on the market index around the mean return.

(e) Variance in returns on project j: This measure can be computed using either the general formula for the variance shown in part (d) or Equation (3):

$$\sigma_{R_j}^2 = \frac{\Sigma \left(\tilde{R}_{jt} - \bar{R}_j\right)^2}{n-1} = \frac{0.001360}{10-1}$$

$$= 0.0001511 \quad \text{or} \quad 0.01511\%$$

Using Equation (3), we have the following:

$$\text{Var}\left(\tilde{R}_j\right) = \sigma_{R_j}^2 = B_j^2 \sigma_m^2 + Q_j^2$$

$$= (0.6058)^2 (0.0002677) + 0.0000593325$$

$$\sigma_{R_j}^2 = 0.0000982441 + 0.0000593325$$

$$= 0.0001576 \quad \text{or} \quad 0.01576\%$$

The difference between these two figures is due to rounding.

(f) Finally, the correlation coefficient and the covariance between the returns on project j and the market are of interest.

$$\rho = \sqrt{\rho^2} = \text{coefficient of determination} = \sqrt{0.6501911765}$$

$$\rho_{\tilde{R}_j, \tilde{R}_m} = +0.806$$

The covariance is found in the usual manner:

$$\text{Cov} \left(\tilde{R}_j, \tilde{R}_m \right) = (\rho_{\tilde{R}_j, \tilde{R}_m})(\sigma_{\tilde{R}_j})(\sigma_m)$$

$$= (+0.806)(0.0126)(0.0164) = 0.0001666$$

Last, it can be shown that B_j has an alternative definition of interest:

$$B_j = \frac{\text{Cov} \left(\tilde{R}_j, \tilde{R}_m \right)}{\sigma_m^2}$$

$$= \frac{0.0001666}{0.0002677}$$

$$= 0.622 \approx 0.6058 \qquad \text{as computed in Example 1}$$

This definition underscores the nature of B_j; it monitors the sensitivity of the project returns to changes in the market index.   ●

To conclude this section it should be noted that the capital asset pricing model, subject to qualification, produces the same information on the project, an expected return, $E(R_j)$, and sigma, σ_j, as that developed from the probability distributions of period cash flows. However, by contrast, the $E(R_j)$ and σ_j from the CAPM model uses market data (i.e., the relationship of project returns to a broad-based index). In this regard, the illustrations in Examples 1 and 2 assume that the relationship between the risk asset returns and the index described by the beta value will hold for the future or at least the life of the asset. Hence, if the analyst has the expected return on the index over the relevant period, he or she can forecast the expected return on the project, $E(R_j)$, from the regression equation. The expected return, $E(R_j)$, based upon the regression equation should also be thought of as a required return given the relationship with the market index of risk asset returns. In the capital budgeting situation, this required return can be compared to an expected return calculated by conventional means (i.e., the expected internal rate of return) and a decision made on the acceptability of the project. Our discussion of the cost of capital in Chapter 11 picks up this theme.

PORTFOLIO PARAMETERS

An important application of CAPM is its use to calculate the risk–return characteristics of portfolios. The portfolio return $E(R_p)$ offers no special problems: a simple weighted average of the expected returns on the individual projects (or securities), as shown in Equation (10):

$$E(R_p) = \sum X_j E(R_j) \tag{10}$$

where X_j denotes the proportion of the total budget or portfolio invested in the jth project (or security).

In the same manner, the beta value of the portfolio[3] (B_p) is given by Equation (11):

$$B_p = \Sigma \, X_j \, B_j \tag{11}$$

However, the measurement of portfolio risk by the CAPM approach provides interesting insights into the construction of portfolios. Recall from Chapter 9 that the Markowitz formulation described portfolio risk as the weighted variance of the individual projects plus twice the sum of the weighted covariances:

$$\sigma_p = \sqrt{\sum_{j=1}^{N} X_j^2 \sigma_j^2 + 2 \sum_{j=1}^{N-1} \sum_{i=j+1}^{N} X_i X_j (\rho_{ij})(\sigma_i)(\sigma_j)}$$

Under CAPM, σ_p, based upon market data, becomes

$$\sigma_p = \sqrt{B_p^2 \sigma_m^2 + \sum_{j=1}^{N} X_j^2 Q_j^2} \tag{12}$$

Equation (12) recognizes two kinds of risk in a similar vein to that for individual securities discussed above:

1. Systematic risk ($B_p^2 \sigma_m^2$) is that portion of total risk (σ_p) based upon the relationship with the market index (R_m). Since all risk assets in the portfolio correlate to some degree with the index of risk assets, the systematic risk is nondiversifiable. No combination of risk assets can eliminate the market risk.

2. Unsystematic risk ($\Sigma \, X_j^2 Q_j^2$) is that element of total risk (σ_p) responding to forces beyond the market index. If the market discounts all that is known about the risk asset's values, the unsystematic risk measures the variability in the returns due to unanticipated, or random factors. For example, the market may discount all that is known about the production, marketing, and financial strategies of General Motors, yet the price and yield on GM stock will still vary because of new, unforeseen, randomly occurring events (the energy crisis, technological innovation, political turns, etc.). This is diversifiable risk and in a properly diversified portfolio, $\Sigma_{j=1}^{N} \, X_j^2 Q_j^2$ will *tend to zero*. The reason is as follows: Q_j^2 is the square of the standard error of the estimate or the unexplained variance. As N is increased in the summation above, the X_j^2 values become proportionately smaller, so that in the limit the summation approaches zero. Since the limit is never actually reached, the diversifiable risk will only approach zero.

Figure 10-2 shows how the two risks change as randomly selected securities are added to a portfolio. Empirical studies[4] have shown that with as few as 10 to 15 securities in a portfolio, total risk can be reduced to almost the systematic level.

Example 3 illustrates the calculation of portfolio parameters under CAPM.

---

[3]The reader should note that the portfolio beta value is also the beta for the firm as a whole, since the firm is an aggregate of all existing projects.

[4]See J. Evans and S. H. Archer, "Diversification and the Reduction of Dispersion: An Empirical Analysis," *Journal of Finance*, December 1968, pp. 761–767; and K. H. Johnson and D. S. Shannon, "A Note on Diversification and the Reduction of Dispersion," *Journal of Financial Economics*, December 1974, pp. 365–372.

FIGURE 10-2 Effects of Diversification on Systematic, Unsystematic, and Total Risk

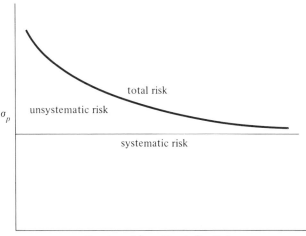

Number of Securities in Portfolio

● **EXAMPLE 3** *Calculation of Portfolio Parameters Using CAPM*

Consider a firm desiring to combine projects Alpha and Delta into a portfolio in the proportions shown in the table below. The procedures described in the previous section have already been applied and the regression equations developed with the market index also shown:

	Project Alpha	*Project Delta*
α_j	0.05	0.02
B_j	0.5	1.5
X_j	0.6	0.4
Q_j	0.0088	0.007

Market index statistics:

$$E(\tilde{R}_m) = 0.093, \qquad \sigma_{Rm} = 0.016$$

Compute $E(R_p)$, B_p, and σ_p.

Solution: To compute $E(R_p)$, we must first compute the expected return on each project, using Equation (2).

Project Alpha:

$$\begin{aligned} E(R_A) &= \alpha_A + B_A(E(\tilde{R}_m)) \\ &= 0.05 + 0.5(0.093) \\ &= 0.097 \end{aligned}$$

Project Delta:

$$\begin{aligned} E(R_D) &= \alpha_D + B_D(E(\tilde{R}_m)) \\ &= 0.02 + 1.5(0.093) \\ &= 0.159 \end{aligned}$$

Portfolio expected return:

$$E(R_p) = \Sigma \; X_j \; E(R_j)$$
$$= 0.6(0.097) + 0.4(0.159)$$
$$= 0.1218$$

Portfolio beta:

$$B_p = \Sigma \; X_j \; B_j$$
$$= 0.6(0.5) + 0.4(1.5)$$
$$= 0.9$$

Portfolio standard deviation:

$$\sigma_p = \sqrt{(B_p)^2(\sigma_{Rm})^2 + \Sigma \; X_j^2 Q_j^2}$$
$$= \sqrt{(0.9)^2(0.016)^2 + (0.6)^2(0.0088)^2 + (0.4)^2(0.007)^2}$$
$$= \sqrt{0.00020736 + 0.0000278 + 0.00000784}$$
$$= \sqrt{0.000243}$$
$$= 0.0156 \qquad \bullet$$

EFFICIENT FRONTIER UNDER CAPM

CAPM assumes a linear relationship between project returns and the market index. The random-error term, Q_j, is assumed to be independent of the index and independent of the random terms for all other projects. As a result, some part of the true variability of $E(R_j)$ is lost. Hence, portfolios constructed by CAPM are less efficient compared to those constructed using the more elaborate covariance technique. Figure 10-3 compares the approximate character of index frontier to the true efficient frontier.

The proximity of the index frontier to the true efficient set derived from the covariances of the cash flows depends on two related considerations:

1. Whether a linear function best describes the dependence of the projects (or securities) on the index. This advises experimentation with higher degree polynomials and transformations.

2. Whether the index selected is the best predictor of changes in the dependent variable *j*. In turn, this recommends the selection of an index after experimentation with a number of possible choices or the use of multi-index models.

Capital Market Line

Granted risk aversion, each investor holds a portfolio along the efficient frontier. For a given investor, the optimum portfolio locates at the tangency between his indifference map and the efficient frontier (Figure 9-5) common to all investors. But investors are a diverse group, their utility maps differ, and each might prefer a different point (optimum portfolio) along the common

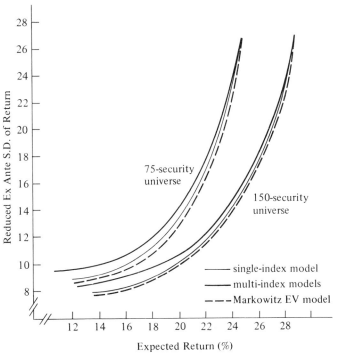

FIGURE 10-3   Comparison of Efficient Frontiers CAPM
vs. Covariance Technique

Source: Kalman J. Cohen and Jerry A. Pogue, "An Emperical Evaluation of Alternative Portfolio-Selection Models," *The Journal of Business*, Vol. 40, No. 2, April 1967, p. 179.

efficient frontier. *The aggregate of these individual investor preferences is represented by the capital market line, as shown in Figure 10-4. For the market to be in equilibrium, the portfolio at M must contain every risk asset in the exact proportion to that asset's fraction of the total market value of all risk assets.* That is, if all investors are holding a part of the same portfolio as their risk asset commitment, this portfolio would have to consist of all risk assets available in the marketplace. The portfolio at M, therefore, with each risk asset weighted by its market value relative to the total market value of all risk assets is termed the *market portfolio*. The formula for the capital market line (CML) is given by Equation (13):

$$E(R_p) \; = \; R_F \; + \; \frac{R_m - R_F}{\sigma_m} \sigma_p \qquad (13)$$

where $E(R_p)$ = expected return on an efficient portfolio
$\quad\quad \sigma_p$ = standard deviation of returns on portfolio p
$\quad\quad R_F$ = risk-free rate
$\quad\quad R_m$ = return on the market portfolio of risk assets
$\quad\quad \sigma_m$ = standard deviation of the market portfolio

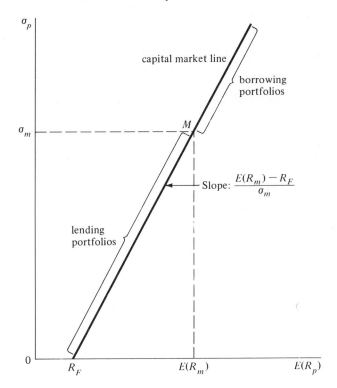

FIGURE 10-4 Capital Market Line

capital market line

borrowing
portfolios

σ_m

M

Slope: $\dfrac{E(R_m) - R_F}{\sigma_m}$

lending
portfolios

σ_p

0

R_F $E(R_m)$ $E(R_p)$

Several conclusions follow:

1. The expected return on an efficient portfolio is a linear function of its risk.

2. All efficient portfolios would have to be on the capital market line.

3. The slope of the line, $[E(R_m) - R_F]/\sigma_m$, is called the *market price of risk* or the *price of risk reduction.*

4. The intercept of the line, R_F, is the *market price of time.*

5. The relationship does not apply to individual securities or portfolios that are imperfectly diversified. This implies that there is no reward for assuming risk that could be eliminated by proper diversification.

6. All investors *with the market in equilibrium* elect to hold the same portfolio of risk assets (the market portfolio), and individual risk preferences only affect the allocation of funds within individual portfolios between risky and riskless assets. If, for example, General Motors stock comprised 3% of the total value of all publicly traded stocks, the risk segment of each investor's portfolio should allocate 3% to GM. The dollar size of an investor's portfolio depends on his wealth, but the profile of risk assets will be proportionately the same for each investor.

7. Since all rational investors share in the market portfolio, each will perceive the riskiness of any given security in terms of its contribution to the riskiness of a fully diversified portfolio (i.e., the market portfolio). Hence, the financial manager needs to define risk in terms of the market portfolio if he or she is to be consistent with the criteria used by investors in valuing securities.

8. Investors increase their returns by changing the proportions of their portfolio (X_j) invested in risk and risk-free securities. Higher risk and return result from increasing the proportion invested in risk assets.

Security Market Line

The capital market line dealt with required return on a portfolio. The security market line (SML) shows the required return on each security in relation to risk. Termed the *market-price-of-risk line*, every security in the market portfolio of risk assets will be priced so that its expected return may be calculated using Equation (14):

$$E(R_j) = R_F + [E(R_m) - R_F] \frac{\text{Cov}(R_j, R_m)}{\sigma_m^2} \qquad (14)$$

where $E(R_j)$ designates the required return on a given security.

The required return demanded by investors on a security, therefore, depends on the following three factors:

1. The risk-free rate.
2. The expected return and variance on the market portfolio.
3. The covariance of the security's returns with the market portfolio.

The equation for the security market line is graphed in Figure 10-5.

The SML differs from the CML in two major respects:

1. For the individual security, the risk measure is the covariance instead of the standard deviation. The substitution underscores that the risk of an individual security or firm depends upon its contribution to the risk of the portfolio in which it is placed.
2. The risk of the market portfolio is measured by its variance, not the standard deviation.

If a security had a beta value of 2 [recall that $B_j = \text{Cov}(R_j, R_m)/\sigma_m^2$] and $R_F = 0.06$ and $E(R_m) = 0.10$, then

$$E(R_j) = 0.06 + 2(0.10 - 0.06)$$
$$= 0.14 \quad \text{or} \quad 14\%$$

A rational, risk-averse investor would not acquire the risk asset unless it promised a return at least equal to 14%. In Figure 10-5, therefore, security X earns a return in excess of the market portfolio $(E(R_m))$ but is not a desirable investment, owing to its strong covariance with market returns; Y has a lower expected return but may be a worthwhile investment, owing to its low correlation with the market portfolio; Z, a risky asset, correlates negatively with the market portfolio and hence $E(R_Z)$ is less than the risk-free rate and therefore may also be worthy of consideration. *Generally, with the SML drawn as shown in*

FIGURE 10-5   Security Market Line

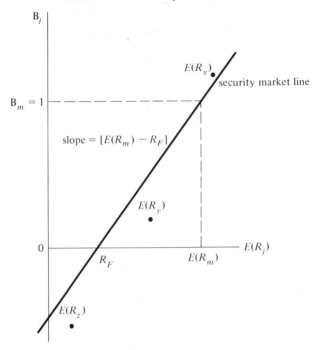

Figue 10-5, returns below the SML are acceptable (i.e., securities Y and Z); above the SML, the amount of risk assumed is not justified by the expected return (i.e., security X). An extensive example of CAPM applied to the selection of capital budgeting projects is included in Chapter 11.

ASSUMPTIONS OF CAPM

Portfolio theory and CAPM are powerful analytical tools which for the first time provide a comprehensive conceptual framework linking financial management and investor behavior. However, like the neoclassical economic theory from which they are derived, portfolio theory and CAPM rest upon assumptions that at first glance appear to severely limit possible application in managerial situations. These include the following:

1. *Assumptions about investor behavior*:
    (a) Investors are risk-averse. They expect to be rewarded for assuming risk.
    (b) Acting rationally, they choose only efficient portfolios: the largest return, $E(R_p)$, for a given level of risk, σ_p; or the lowest risk, σ_p, for a specified return, $E(R_p)$.
    (c) As a corollary, they optimize their portfolio combinations by efficient diversification.

(d) They have the same time horizon regarding the risk–return payoff on risk assets. They strive to maximize the single period expected utility of terminal wealth.

(e) All investors have the same subjective estimates of the expected return and risk, $E(R_p)$, σ_p, and Cov (R_p, R_m) for all risk assets traded.

2. *Assumptions about the market*:

(a) All investors can borrow or lend in unlimited amounts at the risk-free rate (R_F).

(b) There are no taxes or transaction costs.

(c) Information is freely available to all investors.

(d) All assets are perfectly divisible and perfectly liquid (i.e., marketable at the going price).

(e) The quantities of all assets are given.

By extension, portfolio theory and CAPM assume that the market is efficient: that it quickly discounts all publicly available information. Some go further and affirm that the market has discounted all information, public and otherwise, on a security. This, in turn, leads to the *Random-Walk Hypothesis*, stating that changes in stock prices cannot be predicted on the basis of past price movements. Hence, historical data on market price changes will not enable the trader to earn above-normal risk-adjusted returns. The best strategy then lies in buying into the market portfolio and sitting tight. The strategy assures that the investor always does as well as the market and he cannot beat the market in any event.

Such an array of assumptions would seem to abort practical application. If the market is not in truth efficient, if investors in fact have different borrowing/lending rates and different expectations with various time horizons, they will not be subject to one capital market line. There will not be one best market portfolio. Yet the CAPM construction has not come to naught. In the professional literature, statistical studies that relax some of the preceding assumptions nevertheless obtained results consistent with the suppositions of theory. In short, the models successfully describe tendencies that apparently hold up even when the assumptions are not fully met. As in scientific investigation, it is sometimes possible to predict results without fully knowing all the causes.

STABILITY OF BETA

Alpha (α_j) and beta (B_j) describe an average relationship between the behavior of the security and market index existing in some prior period and assumed to hold for the future. Although the parameter values can be updated annually or quarterly, the model fundamentally relies on past performances, capturing the influences on the market at the time of calculation. Is the beta computed from historical data a good surrogate for the true beta reflecting investors' estimates of the stock's *future* volatility? If so, the financial manager has a significant new tool to assist his or her deliberations aimed at maximizing shareholder wealth or the present value of the enterprise.

Some recent surveys indicate that the historically computed beta closely approximates the true, contemporary beta. Blume,[5] for example, showed that the beta of a firm:

1. Is fairly stable over time.

2. Can be forecasted accurately from historical data.

3. Generally tends over a long time span, 1926 to 1968, to unity, the beta of the market as a whole.

Logue and Merville[6] found that beta values bear a significant correlation to the firm's financial policies expressed in liquidity ratios, leverage measures, dividend payout, and profitability.

Not all the evidence is affirmative. In another investigation, Levy[7] examined the weekly returns for over 500 NYSE stocks over the period December 30, 1960, through December 18, 1970 (520 weeks) to establish stationary data for betas over 52-week, 26-week, and 13-week forecast periods for stock portfolios ranging from 1, 5, 10, 25, and 50 stocks per portfolio. Levy concluded:

1. Average betas are reasonably predictable for large portfolios, less predictable for smaller portfolios, quite unpredictable for individual securities.

2. Forecasts are clearly better over longer periods than over shorter periods.

3. Although predictability improves as the forecast period lengthens, the relative improvement tends to be less for larger portfolios.

4. For portfolios of 25 stocks and larger over forecast intervals of 26 weeks and longer, historical betas seem to be fairly good and stable indicators of future risk.

Levitz's[8] study supported Levy's conclusions. He showed that for individual stocks the correlation of historical and actual betas was extremely poor (i.e., 0.55 for the test period). For portfolios, however, even with as few as 10 stocks, statistically significant correlations were obtained, in some instances up to 0.90. He states:

> For individual stocks the historical beta coefficient is not an accurate predictor
> of future relative volatility, although it may provide a "best-guess" estimate.

There is doubt, too, over the interpretation of alpha. Alpha, the *y* intercept of the regression line, Figure 10-1, indicates the rate of return produced, on the average, by the investment independent of the market. Stocks with high alphas tend to have lower betas, and vice versa. Welles[9] notes that one means of obtaining above-average performance lies in selecting a stock with a positive alpha. When one stock has a higher or lower return than another stock with

[5]Marshall E. Blume, "On the Assessment of Risk," *Journal of Finance*, Vol. 26, March 1971, pp. 1–10.

[6]Dennis E. Logue and Larry J. Merville, "Financial Policy and Market Expectations," *Financial Management*, Summer 1972, pp. 37–44.

[7]R. A. Levy, "On the Short-term Stationarity of Beta Coefficients," *Financial Analysts Journal*, November–December, 1971, pp. 55–62.

[8]G. D. Levitz, *A Study of the Usefulness of Beta Analysis in the Management of Common Stock Portfolios* (New York: Brown Brothers, Harriman & Co., 1972).

[9]C. Welles, "The Beta Revolution: Learning to Live with Risk," *Institutional Investor*, September 1971, pp. 21–64.

the same beta, when it does better or worse against the market than its beta would have predicted, this is said to be due to its alpha factor or the residual, nonmarket influences unique to each stock. Alpha reflects influences from the industry, technological breakthroughs, management shifts, merger prospects, and so on. However, more research is needed to assess the full significance of alpha.

SUMMARY

This chapter examined the capital asset pricing model, which is a powerful new approach that can be beneficially applied to the valuation of risk assets, whether they be securities or capital projects. Accordingly, this chapter called upon several concepts and statistics developed in previous chapters on risk analysis and portfolio effects. Examples were used to illustrate the calculations of important new CAPM parameters. The chapter concluded by citing several empirical studies which demonstrate that capital asset pricing theory still holds as several of its somewhat restrictive assumptions are relaxed. Our discussion of CAPM is continued in Chapter 11 as we study applications to the firm's cost of capital.

PROBLEMS

1. For the data given below for project j and the market index, compute the values for α_j, B_j, and write the regression equation:

Period, t	Project, R_{jt} (%)	Market Index, R_{mt} (%)
1	9	10
2	8	9
3	8	8
4	10	8
5	11	10

2. For the data given in Problem 1, compute the following:
   (a) The $E(R_{jt})$ value for each R_{mt}.
   (b) The covariance between $\tilde{R}_{jt}$ and $\tilde{R}_{mt}$.
   (c) The correlation coefficient between $\tilde{R}_{jt}$ and $\tilde{R}_{mt}$ and explain its meaning.
   (d) The standard error of estimate.
   (e) The coefficient of determination.
   (f) The coefficient of nondetermination.
3. For the data given in Problem 1, compute the following:
   (a) The variance of the returns on the market index.
   (b) The variance of the returns on project j.
   (c) The systematic risk on project j.
   (d) The unsystematic risk on project j.

4. The Notos Company is analyzing a project shown below. To facilitate the computation of relevant statistics, the firm has prepared the following tables:

Year	$\tilde{R}_{jt}$	$\tilde{R}_{mt}$	$\tilde{R}_{jt}\tilde{R}_{mt}$	$\tilde{R}_{mt}^2$	$E(\tilde{R}_{jt})$
1	0.11	0.10	0.0110	0.0100	0.1086
2	0.12	0.11	0.0132	0.0121	0.1179
3	0.12	0.12	0.0144	0.0144	0.1271
4	0.13	0.11	0.0143	0.0121	0.1179
5	0.10	0.10	0.0100	0.0100	0.1086
Total	0.58	0.54	0.0629	0.0586	0.5801

Year	$\tilde{R}_{jt} - \bar{R}_j$	$(\tilde{R}_{jt} - \bar{R}_j)^2$	$\tilde{R}_{jt} - E(\tilde{R}_{jt})$
1	$0.11 - 0.116 = -0.006$	0.000036	$0.11 - 0.1086 = 0.0014$
2	$0.12 - 0.116 = 0.004$	0.000016	$0.12 - 0.1179 = 0.0021$
3	$0.12 - 0.116 = 0.004$	0.000016	$0.12 - 0.1271 = -0.0071$
4	$0.13 - 0.116 = 0.014$	0.000196	$0.13 - 0.1179 = 0.0121$
5	$0.10 - 0.116 = -0.016$	0.000256	$0.10 - 0.1086 = -0.0086$
Total		0.000520	

Year	$[\tilde{R}_{jt} - E(\tilde{R}_{jt})]^2$	$E(\tilde{R}_{jt}) - \bar{R}_j$	$[E(\tilde{R}_{jt}) - \bar{R}_j]^2$
1	0.0000062	$0.1086 - 0.116 = -0.0074$	0.00005476
2	0.0000028	$0.1179 - 0.116 = 0.0019$	0.00000361
3	0.0000176	$0.1271 - 0.116 = 0.0111$	0.00012320
4	0.0001368	$0.1179 - 0.116 = 0.0019$	0.00000361
5	0.0001562	$0.1086 - 0.116 = -0.0074$	0.00005476
Total	0.0003196		0.00023994

Compute the following:
(a) α, B.
(b) The covariance between $\tilde{R}_{jt}$ and $\tilde{R}_{mt}$.
(c) The correlation coefficient.
(d) The total risk on $\tilde{R}_{jt}$.
(e) The systematic risk.
(f) The unsystematic risk.
(g) The standard error of estimate.
(h) The coefficient of determination.
5. In 1967, a security of the Dru-White Corporation yielded a return of 4%. For the next 6 years it returned a steady 2% above the prime rate, which was 5% in 1968, 1969, and 1970, and 6% in 1971, 1972, and 1973. In the past 3 years, the stock returned 11%, 12%, and 13%. Our analysts have charted a regression line using the single index model. They tell us that their line explains three-fourths of the total variation in returns of the Dru-White security. If we want 90% certainty, within what limits of the predicted value will the true value lie?
6. Random Investments Corporation is planning to combine these two projects into a portfolio. The various statistics are listed for each security and the market index.

Compute the expected return on the portfolio, the beta of the portfolio, and the portfolio standard deviation.

	Security A	Security B
α_j	-0.03	0.04
B_j	$+0.75$	$+0.95$
X_j	0.33	0.67
Q_j	0.0075	0.0025

$E(\tilde{R}_m) = 0.095$

$\sigma R_m = 0.012$

7. Consider the following four portfolios and market parameters:

Year	$E(R_p)$	σ_p	$R_f = 0.06$
1	0.12	0.04	
2	0.13	0.06	$E(R_m) = 0.12$
3	0.16	0.10	$\sigma_m = 0.05$
4	0.22	0.12	

Using the capital asset pricing model, determine which of these portfolios have expected rates of return that exceed the required rates of return and thus are underpriced, and those which are overpriced.

8. Starting with the equation for the security market line:

$$E(R_j) = R_f + \left[E(R_m) - R_f\right]\frac{\text{Cov}_{jm}}{\sigma_m^2}$$

Derive the equation for the capital market line by recalling that in equilibrium, an efficient portfolio is perfectly correlated with the market (i.e., $\rho_{jm} = +1.0$).

9. A firm is evaluating the following three securities.

j	$E(R_j)$	ρ_{jm}	σ_j
1	0.075	$+0.3$	0.04
2	0.14	$+0.9$	0.09
3	0.12	$+0.2$	0.14

The market parameters are: $R_f = 0.07$, $E(R_m) = 0.13$, and $\sigma_m = 0.05$.

(a) Compute the beta coefficients for each of these three securities and explain both the absolute risk of each security and the relative riskiness or volatility of each of the securities compared to the market.

(b) Using the equation for the security market line, determine whether each of these securities falls above or below the security market line (i.e., whether each is overpriced or underpriced).

(c) Briefly discuss why each security is over- or underpriced (be precise) and various ways that each could become priced appropriately.

11 COST OF CAPITAL

The four discounted-cash-flow procedures used to evaluate alternative investments (internal rate of return, net present value, profitability index, and annual capital charge) all measure cash flows in terms of a required rate of return (hurdle rate) to determine their acceptability. This hurdle rate was referred to earlier as the firm's cost of capital, and as noted in our discussion of risk analysis, the actual hurdle rate applied may be the cost of capital adjusted to compensate for project risk differing from that of the normal risk complexion of the firm. But what exactly is the cost of capital and how do we go about determining it? These are the questions that will be addressed in this chapter. This will necessitate an examination of the general problem of managing the financial structure and the valuation of the firm.

We shall confront the problem initially utilizing traditional methodology. Later in the chapter, we will apply CAPM and use it to determine the following:

1. The cost of equity capital based upon systematic risk.
2. The value of a project to the firm based on the market price of risk.
3. The value of the firm after acceptance of a project.
4. The firm's average cost of capital after acceptance of a project.

CONVENTIONAL WISDOM

The *cost of capital* refers to the rates of return expected by those parties contributing to the financial structure: creditors and preferred and common shareholders. It represents the cost of funds used to acquire the total assets of the firm. Thus, it is generally calculated as a weighted average of the costs associated with each type of capital included in the financial structure of the enterprise. Several factors merit additional comment and examination.

1. The cost of capital, considered as a rate of return, disaggregates into a risk-free rate plus a premium for risk. The risk premium covers the business and financial risk of the firm relative to available, alternative investments. Since the risk-free rate is common to all firms, differences in cost of capital among firms originate in their riskiness. *The cost of capital embodies the average risk posture of the firm, that is, the composite risk of the firm as a portfolio of operational projects which makes up its risk complexion.*

2. Since one man's cost is another's income, *the cost of capital represents a rate of return that will maintain the market value of the outstanding securities within the context of overall market movements.* Investors have available to them a wide range of investment options, from risk-free government securities to common stocks of varying quality. Hence, in arranging their portfolio, they expect to receive a risk premium appropriate to the quality of a given investment. If the security concerned does not appear to promise such a yield at its current price, the price will drop until the yield equates with investor expectations.

3. *The cost of capital is that rate which will enable the firm to sell new securities at current price levels.* The firm must have the potential of using the new funds in ways that generate yields sufficient to cover the risk-free rate and the required premium for risk.

The reader will note that we have expressed the concept of the cost of capital in three different ways. But there is an underlying commonality: the firm must manage its assets and select capital projects with the goal of obtaining a yield at least sufficient to cover its cost of capital. If it fails in this objective, the market price of its outstanding securities will decline. If it achieves yields greater than the cost of capital, it is likely that the price of securities, especially the common stock, will be bid upward. Consequently, *the cost of capital is seen as an opportunity cost.* As an opportunity cost, it has dual aspects: from the investment standpoint, the firm competes against a variety of alternative uses of funds to attract investor capital, while internally the firm must select business projects with estimated yields that maintain the market value of its securities by promising returns commensurate with investor expectations (i.e., which cover the required risk premium).

As a final note, a firm does not calculate the cost of capital and post it on the company bulletin board. Nor does one calculate it by picking up the annual report. Rather, it is a *dynamic concept: a synthesis of the costs of new equity and debt.* It conforms to the *marginal cost* of each; a weighted average cost for the next dollar of capital apportioned between debt and equity securities. Capital budgeting deals with future cash flows and calculates yields (or internal rates of return) on the next dollar of invested capital. The cost of capital stresses the cost of that dollar based upon market expectations. The theory of marginal cost pricing dictates, therefore, the acceptance of projects to the point of equality between the internal rate and the hurdle rate based upon the cost of capital.

The discussion of the cost of capital thus far has assumed some optimum balance of the financial mix, but the question is yet to be addressed. The following section examines those factors which affect the financial structure and indicates how we may go about selecting a financial structure. But again it is important to note that the firm's optimum financial structure is not fixed, but dynamic.

FINANCIAL STRUCTURE

The firm manages assets and selects capital projects to secure the maximum return appropriate to the level of acceptable risk. Conversely, it manages the financial structure to minimize the cost of capital (i.e., to obtain the lowest

EXHIBIT 11-1 Cost of Capital

(1) Percentage Debt	(2) Percentage Equity	(3)[a] Interest × (1 − t) where t = 50%	(4)[b] Required Return on Equity (%)	(5)[c] Weighted-Average Cost [(1) × (3) + (2) × (4) = (5)]	(6)[d] Value of Business EAT = $100,000 ÷ (5)
0	100	—	10.0	10.0	$1,000,000
10	90	4.0	10.1	9.5	1,052,631
20	80	4.0	10.2	9.0	1,111,111
30	70	4.0	10.3	8.4	1,190,476
40	60	4.5	10.5	8.1	1,234,567
50	50	5.0	11.0	→8.0	1,250,000
60	40	6.0	11.5	8.2	1,219,512
70	30	7.0	12.5	8.7	1,149,425
80	20	7.5	16.0	9.2	1,086,956

[a] t is the firm's marginal tax rate, 50%.

[b] The required return on common stock equity can be expected to increase as a function of risk. The greater the proportion of debt, the greater the financial risk.

[c] Optimum capital structure comprises 50% debt and equity with a weighted-average cost of capital (K) of 8%. At this point, the pretax, explicit cost of debt (10%) plus the implicit cost of debt represented by the rise in the cost of equity (1%), for the first time in the series exceeds the basic cost of all equity financing, which is 10%. In a continuous distribution, the lowest value of K coincides with the point at which the *total* cost of debt (K_D) equates to the cost of equity (K_s).

[d] The value of the business is the earnings after taxes, which is assumed to be constant at $100,000 divided by the cost of capital. Notice that the value is maximized at the point of optimum financial structure for this method of valuation. This is but one method of valuation.

weighted average cost of capital). Assuming that both business risk and financial risk influence the weighted-average cost of capital, the introduction of debt into the financial structure up to some point lowers the weighted-average cost. Debt capital has cost advantages:

1. Owing to higher priority in the order of payment, the interest of debt is *normally* lower than the other types of capital.

2. Unlike payments to equity, interest qualifies as a tax deduction so that some portion of these charges is borne by Uncle Sam. Tax deductibility reduces the effective cost of debt capital.

3. Given a long-term upward trend in the price level, inflation makes debt cheaper in real terms if the rate of increase in the price level exceeds the anticipated inflation rate at the time of floatation.

Therefore, in managing the financial structure, the firm strives to achieve that combination of debt and equity that results in the lowest weighted-average cost of capital. This is the optimum financial structure. For any given level of earnings after taxes, it will also maximize the value of the firm. Thus, cost of capital is inextricably linked to the valuation of the firm and of capital projects.

To determine the optimum capital structure (i.e., debt/equity ratio) it is necessary to know investor preferences for risk, that is, their utility functions for risk versus return. This subject has been discussed at some length in previous chapters. Assume that we know the investor risk preferences in terms of both the interest rates charged and the return on equity required for different financial mixes. Given this information, we may find the optimum financial mix by determining the weighted-average cost of capital for each possible mix and selecting that mix with the lowest cost. This procedure is demonstrated in Exhibit 11-1.

In this exhibit the optimum financial structure is shown to consist of equal portions of debt and equity. In reality, the proportions vary from industry to industry based upon debt capacity and the variability of net-operating income (EBIT). Therefore, in accepting a capital project, the manager should assess not only the NPV of the project but how it affects the variability of net operating income and whether it enhances or detracts from the debt capacity of the firm.

Before we enter into the discussion of those calculations required to compute the firm's cost of capital, we will briefly discuss the impact of debt on the variability of earnings.

Debt and Variability of Earnings

Two kinds of risk influence the variability of earnings after taxes: business and financial. These were discussed in Chapter 8 and now warrant further attention in terms of operating and financial leverage.

Business risk relates to the variability of net operating income or *earnings before interest and taxes* (EBIT). It is measured by the *degree of operating leverage* (DOL). Operating leverage arises from the mix of fixed and variable costs in the manufacturing and administrative design of the firm. All things equal, the degree of operating leverage typically increases with the relative importance of fixed costs in total costs. Bear in mind: net operating income constitutes the funds available for distribution to creditors, stockholders, and tax collectors. After this point, the income statement describes the division among the shareholders. The degree of operating leverage at an output Q may be determined using Equation (1):

$$\text{DOL} = \frac{Q(P - \text{vc})}{Q(P - \text{vc}) - \text{FC}} = \frac{\%\text{ change in EBIT}}{\%\text{ change in output and sales}} \quad (1)$$

where P = unit price
    vc = variable cost per unit
    FC = total fixed costs

Financial risk relates the variability of *earnings after taxes* (EAT) to the way the firm is financed, the *debt–equity ratio*. Variability tends to increase as the proportion of fixed interest charges rises. The *degree of financial leverage* (DFL) measures financial risk and may be found using Equation (2):

$$\text{DFL} = \frac{\text{EBIT}}{\text{EBIT} - F} = \frac{\%\text{ change in EPS or EAT}}{\%\text{ change in EBIT}} \quad (2)$$

where F is the cost of interest.

How do we interpret the leverage measures? DOL and DFL are multipliers describing the effects of a percentage change in sales or operating income on the bottom line. For example, assuming a linear relationship between sales and variable costs and a constant tax rate, if the DOL were 5, a 10% change in sales would generate a 50% change in operating income. Or if the DFL were 3, a 10% change in operating income (EBIT) would cause a 30% change in earnings after taxes (EAT). It follows that combined leverage (the product of DOL and DFL) measures the effect of a percentage change in sales on EAT. For example, in financial structure A of Exhibit 11-2, a 10% increase in sales (from $100,000 to $110,000) creates a 43.3% increase (rounded) in both EBIT ($15,000 to $21,500) and EAT ($7,500 to $10,750). In financial structure E, the same 10% increase in sales generates a 43.3% increment in EBIT ($15,000 − $21,500), a 67.1% increase in both EBT ($9,600 to $16,100) and EAT ($4,800 to $8,050). In short, adding debt to the capital structure raises the variability of earnings before and after taxes. Financial structure E shows how financial risk adds to the firm's business risk (represented by operating leverage).

Yet the common shareholders may applaud leveraging. The reason is not far to seek. In Exhibit 11-2, leveraging the financial structure has increased earnings per share from $0.75 to $4.80. As long as EPS increases in greater proportion than risk, the market price of the shares will rise. How far the process goes depends upon the risk–return trade-offs of investors in assessing the prospects of the firm.

A Modifying Position

To this point, the discussion has assumed that both operating and financial risk influence the cost of capital. Thus, the way the company is financed, the debt/equity ratio, can raise or lower the cost of capital and, in turn, the market value of the common shares. Not everyone shares these views.

EXHIBIT 11-2 Leverage Effects: Total Variability

Basic data:
Selling price (P) $1.00
Fixed operating costs (FC) $50,000
Variable costs (vc) $0.35/unit
Number of units (Q) 100,000 units

	Financial Structure A *All Equity: 10,000 Shares*	Financial Structure B *Equity: 7,000 shares* *Debt: $30,000 at 6%*	Financial Structure C *Equity: 5,000 shares* *Debt: $50,000 at 6%*	Financial Structure D *Equity: 3,000 shares* *Debt: $70,000 at 6%*	Financial Structure E *Equity: 1,000 shares* *Debt: $90,000 at 6%*
Net sales	$100,000	$100,000	$100,000	$100,000	$100,000
Less					
Cost of sales:					
Opening inventory	$ 5,000	$ 5,000	$ 5,000	$ 5,000	$ 5,000
Net purchases	40,000	40,000	40,000	40,000	40,000
Total	$45,000	$45,000	$45,000	$45,000	$45,000
Closing inventory	15,000 30,000	15,000 30,000	15,000 30,000	15,000 30,000	15,000 30,000
Gross operating income	$ 70,000	$ 70,000	$ 70,000	$ 70,000	$ 70,000

	(1)	(2)	(3)	(4)	(5)
Less					
Selling expenses	$25,000	$25,000	$25,000	$25,000	$25,000
Administrative expenses	30,000	30,000	30,000	30,000	30,000
	55,000	55,000	55,000	55,000	55,000
Net operating income (EBIT)	$15,000	$15,000	$15,000	$15,000	$15,000
Financial charges	—	1,800	3,000	4,200	5,400
Net income (EBT)	$15,000	$13,200	$12,000	$10,800	$9,600
Taxes (rate = 50%)	7,500	6,600	6,000	5,400	4,800
Net income (EAT)	$7,500	$6,600	$6,000	$5,400	$4,800
Earnings per share (EPS)	$0.75	$0.94	$1.20	$1.80	$4.80

Operating leverage (DOL)

$$\frac{Q(P - \text{vc})}{Q(P - \text{vc}) - \text{FC}}$$

$$\frac{100,000(1.00 - 0.35)}{100,000(1.00 - 0.35) - 50,000} =$$

$\underline{4.3}$	$\underline{4.3}$	$\underline{4.3}$	$\underline{4.3}$	$\underline{4.3}$

Financial leverage (DFL)

$$\frac{\text{EBIT}}{\text{EBIT} - F}$$

$\dfrac{15,000}{15,000} = \underline{1}$	$\dfrac{15,000}{13,200} = \underline{1.14}$	$\dfrac{15,000}{12,000} = \underline{1.25}$	$\dfrac{15,000}{10,800} = \underline{1.39}$	$\dfrac{15,000}{9,600} = \underline{1.56}$

Combined leverage

DOL × DFL

$4.3 \times 1 = \underline{4.3}$	$4.3 \times 1.14 = \underline{4.9}$	$4.3 \times 1.25 = \underline{5.38}$	$4.3 \times 1.39 = \underline{5.98}$	$4.3 \times 1.56 = \underline{6.71}$

Some authorities look to business risk as the basic risk of the business which determines the cost of capital. All things equal, the cost of capital responds only to a change in business risk (i.e., the variability of net operating income). The segment of the income statement after net operating income deals simply with "financial packaging"; it cannot alter the amount of funds available or their variability. The position does not deny the reality of financial risk, but instead holds that it is discounted solely against the common stock and does not affect the valuation of the firm.

Both the modifying proposition and the conventional wisdom recognize that financial leverage affects the required yield on the common shares. The issue is whether a firm can lower its cost of capital by manipulating the financial structure; whether it can raise the market value (within limits) of the common shares by additions of debt to the financial structure. Probably the weight of practitioner opinion would answer "yes," but the available research does not give a definitive response. The issue is of major importance in the evaluation of projects that involve revision of the financial structure (refunding projects or conglomerate mergers).

CALCULATING THE MARGINAL COST OF CAPITAL

The marginal cost of capital is determined by taking a weighted average of the marginal costs of each of the components in the firm's financial structure. Initially, we will examine how the marginal costs of each of the components may be determined. Then we will discuss the averaging process.

Throughout our discussion of the cost of capital, we will use current market values as opposed to historical book values to represent the amounts of each component in the financial structure. Our choice is based on the fact that the book values represent only historical amounts. For example, the dollar amount of common stock reflected on the firm's balance sheet is not indicative of its current market value. Similarly, the market values of preferred stock and many forms of debt may change appreciably from their book values as market interest rates and money supplies fluctuate.

Common Stock Equity

In Chapter 4 we developed Equation (3), which relates the firm's cost of equity to the price of the common stock and its dividend, where it is assumed that the dividend will grow at a given rate, g, for the foreseeable future.

$$K_e = \frac{D_1}{P_0} + g \tag{3}$$

where K_e = cost of common stock equity
D_1 = expected dividend in the next period
P_0 = current market price
g = annual growth rate of the dividend

Since the marginal cost of capital represents the amount that the firm must earn on the net proceeds derived from new issues, it is necessary to consider floatation costs. Therefore, for new issues equation (3) is rewritten as equation (4):

$$_nK_e = \frac{D_1}{P_0(1 - F)} + g \tag{4}$$

where $_nK_e$ = cost of new equity capital
   F = floatation cost expressed as a percentage of the market price

$_nK_e$ discounts the anticipated return on new common to equal the net proceeds of the issue. However, once new common is issued, there is no distinction on the security markets between the cost of new and old common. The earnings on the funds raised by the sale of additional shares must be sufficient to cover floatation costs and reward risk or the price of the common shares will decline.

An an alternative to Equation (4), the cost of common stock equity capital may be thought to consist of the return on a risk-free investment such as that available from Treasury Notes, plus premiums to compensate for the business and financial risks associated with the particular investment.

Retained Earnings

The market value of the common stock reflects the residual value of the firm as perceived by the investors. As such it encompasses the total common equity portion and therefore includes the firm's retained earnings. Thus, we argue that retained earnings are not relevant to the calculation of the cost of capital since when using market weights, the value of the common stock includes the retained earnings. We are not interested in book values and rather argue that the market discounts retained earnings as a part of the value of common stock. Others take a differing view.

After-tax profits may either be retained in the firm or distributed as cash dividends. Retention of profits presumes the availability of sufficient investment opportunities (either internal or external) to make it more attractive to shareholders for the firm to retain rather than distribute the earnings. As a practical matter, there is generally an upper limit to the amount of earnings a firm may retain. This limit is predicated on the need for the firm to maintain a stable cash dividend policy.

If there are sufficient internal investment opportunities to use all the retained earnings, the question must be resolved as to how much return is required from the retained earnings. The opportunity cost from the shareholder's viewpoint is the dividend foregone. If the opportunity cost to investors is the dividend, we will want to determine how much that opportunity cost will be. Assuming that shareholders must pay taxes on the dividends (albeit at varying rates) and that they desire a return on funds available for reinvestment at the same rate they are obtaining from existing investments (namely, K_e), then Equation (5) provides the cost of retained earnings:

$$R = K_e(1 - t_p)(1 - B) \tag{5}$$

where R = cost of retained earnings
K_e = cost of equity capital
t_p = average of all the shareholders' marginal tax rates
B = average brokerage fee

It is necessary to introduce brokerage costs into Equation (5), since it is almost never possible to achieve a return of K_e without the use of a broker.

The cost of retained earnings is also a meaningful factor in determining the firm's optimal capital structure. Its computation is principally significant for internal planning: choosing the proportion of new debt, new common, and retained earnings that will minimize the marginal cost of capital. Internally, the cost of *new* common will be greater than the cost of financing by retained earnings, since the funds raised from the new common must earn an amount sufficient to cover the floatation costs plus the yield required to maintain the market value of the common shares.

Cost of Preferred Stock

Most preferred stocks are perpetual in nature, and therefore their explicit cost may be viewed in the same terms as a perpetuity. However, in the same manner as debt, preferred affects financial risk. Accordingly, the true cost of preferred from the perspective of the common shareholders is the rate that must be earned on the assets acquired through preferred financing to cover the yield on the preferred plus the increased yield on the common. The cost of the firm's outstanding preferred is simply its dividend divided by its current market price.

$$K_p = \frac{D_p}{P_p} \qquad (6)$$

where K_p = cost of preferred stock
D_p = preferred dividend
P_p = price of the preferred

As was the case for common stock, we must consider floatation costs for new issues of preferred. Thus, Equation (6) is modified as Equation (7):

$$_nK_p = \frac{_nD_p}{_nP_p(1 - F)} \qquad (7)$$

where $_nK_p$ = cost of new preferred equity capital
$_nD_p$ = dividend on the new issue
F = floatation cost expressed as a percentage of the market price
$_nP_p$ = sale price of the new preferred issue

Cost of Debt

Firms have both short- and long-term debts, and it is therefore necessary to consider all forms of debt financing as input to the cost of capital. Some authorities argue that certain short-term obligations are "free" (non-interest-bearing) and also that capital budgeting relates only to long-term commitments of invested capital. We reject the position. First, accounts payable and some accruals are only superficially "free" if the debts are discharged within a defined penalty period. At times, firms make regular use of trade credit and choose not to accept the discount for prompt payment. Second, some firms consistently resort to commercial credit to finance current assets, and these finance charges must be covered by earnings just as interest on long-term debt. Third, many capital projects drain working capital and require additional short-term financing. Fourth, the financial structure has interchangeable components. The amount and cost of one type of capital depends upon the proportions raised from other sources. The combination, in turn, shapes the firm's financial risk and the cost of capital. Fifth, the accounts payable and accruals, while short-term in terms of payments, tend to roll over and thereby are a part of the firm's permanent financing.

The cost of debt represents an estimate of the yield required to raise designated amounts of short- and/or long-term financing. The firm's commercial banker or investment banker would provide the estimates based on market conditions. The projected yield is placed on an after-tax basis. *However, the total cost of debt involves two elements: the nominal yield based on the face amount of the securities issued when sold at par and the implicit cost or the yield increment on the common needed to maintain its market value in view of the added financial risk.* Note in Exhibit 11-1 the increased return required of the common as debt is added to the capital structure. The required return on the common increases from 10% to 16% with implicit cost of debt, 6%. *Thus, from the viewpoint of the equity holders, the cost of debt is the rate that must be earned on debt-financed assets to cover the net cost of borrowed funds and the incremental yield on the common stock.*

Since we have already dealt with the question of optimum structure with respect to amounts of debt and equity, it is necessary to examine the overall debt structure to ascertain at a given point in time the marginal cost of debt. We will assume that the firm has attempted to achieve an optimum debt structure consisting of varying amounts and types of long- and short-term obligations. The optimum structure will, of course, vary over time. The calculation of the explicit marginal cost of debt is demonstrated in Example 1.

● **EXAMPLE 1** *Cost of Debt*

A corporation has a debt structure shown on its balance sheet as follows:

Accounts payable	$ 3,000,000
Short-term debt	
(12% revolving credit)	2,000,000
Accrued expenses	3,000,000
Bonds Series A	
(5%, due in 12 years)	5,000,000
Bonds Series B	
(8%, due in 26 years)	7,000,000
Total	$20,000,000

The Series A bonds are selling at $750, while the Series B bonds are selling at $900. The corporation takes any available discounts for prompt payment and there is, therefore, no explicit cost to either the accounts payable or accrued expenses. Determine the marginal cost of debt.

Solution: First, determine the market financial structure using market amounts for the bonds. The market structure is as follows:

Accounts payable	$ 3,000,000
Short-term debt	
(12% revolving credit)	2,000,000
Accrued expenses	3,000,000
Bonds, Series A	
(5%, due in 12 years)	3,750,000
Bonds, Series B	
(8%, due in 26 years)	6,300,000
Total	$18,050,000

The sum disaggregates into short- and long-term debts amounting to $8,000,000 and $10,050,000, or 44.3% and 55.7%, respectively.

The explicit cost of the short-term debt amounts to only $240,000, or 3% based on the total $8,000,000 short-term debt. This represents the marginal cost of the short-term component. This conclusion is based on the fact that as the firm expands in terms of acquiring more fixed assets, the relative amounts of accounts payable and accruals will remain fixed, and that since the firm is currently paying 12% on its revolving credit, 12% is the marginal pretax rate for revolving credit.

The explicit cost of the long-term debt is, of course, the interest paid. But what we need to know is the marginal cost of the next dollar of long-term debt. This requires a consideration of the preference for capital gains versus ordinary income. For a person in the 40% marginal tax bracket (a reasonable position for a bondholder), we find that Series A has a 5.63% after-tax yield to maturity while Series B has only 5.18%.[1] To obtain the marginal explicit cost of long-term debt, we must find the yield to maturity the composite group of current bondholders would require for new bonds sold at par (i.e., the coupon rate). Put another way, what yield would investors require on new bonds amounting to $10,050,000 (the market value of the outstanding issues) to be indifferent as to keeping their existing portfolio or trading it for the new?

The current portfolio has a weighted yield determined as follows:

Debt	Amount	Proportion	Yield	Weighted Yield
Series A	$ 3,750,000	0.373	0.0563	0.0210
Series B	6,300,000	0.627	0.0518	0.0325
	$10,050,000			0.0535

Since all the income from the new bonds will be ordinary income, 5.35% is 60% of the total required yield (assuming the 40% investor marginal tax rate). The required yield is therefore 8.9%. The marginal explicit pretax cost of the outstanding bonds is 8.9%.

The marginal explicit cost of debt is the weighted-average cost of the short- and long-term debt and is calculated to be 6.3%.

Debt	Amount	Proportion	Cost	Weighted Cost
Short-term	$ 8,000,000	0.443	0.030	0.0133
Bonds	$10,050,000	0.557	0.089	0.0496
	$18,050,000			0.0629

[1] Use the after-tax cash inflows (i.e., 60% of the yearly interest) and adjust for capital gains appropriately.

The marginal *pretax* cost of debt is 0.0629. If the firm had a 50% marginal tax rate, the after-tax cost would be 3.15%. ●

When floatation costs are involved, the marginal costs of the various components of debt are determined using Equation (8):

$$K_i = \frac{I(1 - t)}{P(1 - F)} \tag{8}$$

where K_i = after-tax cost of the specific component of debt
 I = dollar amount of interest
 t = firm's marginal tax rate
 P = sale price of the debt
 F = floatation cost as a percentage of the sale price

Cost of Depreciation

Depreciation provides a source of funds if the firm generates sufficient sales to cover the costs of production and interest. This is usually the case, and in most instances depreciation is an important source of funds. Depreciation may be used as a source of funds to replace plant and equipment, improve liquidity, or returned to stockholders by means of the mechanism of stock repurchase or, if law permits, through dividends. Since there are a variety of uses for the funds generated through depreciation, they are certainly not free, but rather have an opportunity cost.

Central to the argument of the cost of funds generated through depreciation is the question of how the funds will be used. If the funds are not going to be used to replace assets but rather to repay debts or distributed to shareholders, the whole process of determining the firm's cost of capital comes into question. The reason for determining the cost of capital is to use it as a benchmark in the evaluation of proposed capital investments. If the firm is not making capital investments, which includes external expansion, the important question is not how to obtain the cost of capital but rather how to otherwise use the funds to best increase shareholder wealth. This might be accomplished by means of reduction of debt (with concurrent reduction of interest expense and financial risk), improving liquidity balances (which also reduces financial risk), distributing funds as dividends (which automatically increases shareholder wealth), or repurchasing stock (which should result in an increase in the market price). All the choices enumerated above should increase shareholder wealth. With respect to utilization of funds generated by means of depreciation, the question to be addressed is which use or combination of uses will result in the greatest increases to shareholder wealth. The question may be further expanded to deal with that portion of funds generated through profits but which is not normally distributed as dividends. In general, management who cannot find appropriate uses for funds as investment in capital equipment and the like must then develop plans for using the funds in some other manner to increase shareholder wealth. Since this text deals with capital investment, the subject of alternative uses for funds will not be discussed except as a part of the topic of capital abandonment.

Assuming that funds generated through depreciation are to be utilized as a part of the capital expenditure process, what is their cost? *Since the funds generated through depreciation are a return of investment, and since the investment was composed of funds obtained from equity and debt, it is therefore reasonable to use the cost of capital as the cost of depreciation. If this line of reasoning is followed, it is not necessary to include depreciation in the calculation of the cost of capital.* With respect to obtaining the cost of capital, funds generated through depreciation may be ignored, but in making capital expenditures, we should require the same return on investments made using funds generated by means of depreciation as we do for all other funds.

The Marginal Cost of Capital

The marginal cost of capital is calculated by taking a weighted average of the marginal costs of each component in proportion to the respective amounts of each that the firm will raise. The process is demonstrated in Example 2.

● **EXAMPLE 2**   Marginal Cost of Capital

A corporation plans to raise $400,000 of new capital as follows:

Current liabilities: $20,000 at 11% (assume no floatation or service charge)

Long-term debt: $50,000 at 9% (floatation costs, $\frac{1}{2}$ of 1%)

Preferred stock B: $30,000, floatation cost (F) estimated at 2%; sold at $42 per share with a stated dividend of $2.50

Common stock: $300,000, floatation cost (F) estimated at 10%, dividend $1 per share; market price $50 per share, anticipated growth rate of dividend, 10%

The firm's marginal tax rate is 50%. Determine the cost of each component and the marginal cost of capital.

Solution: *Cost of long-term debt:*

$$K_i = \frac{I(1-t)}{P(1-F)} = \frac{\$4,500(1-0.5)}{\$50,000(1-0.005)} = \frac{\$2,250}{\$49,750} = 0.0452$$

Cost of preferred:

$$_nK_p = \frac{_nD_p}{_nP_p(1-F)} = \frac{\$2.50}{\$42(1-0.02)} = \frac{\$2.50}{\$41.16} = 0.0607$$

Cost of new common:

$$_nK_e = \frac{D_1}{P_0(1-F)} + g = \frac{\$1.00}{\$50(1-0.10)} + 0.10 = \frac{\$1.00}{\$45} + 0.10 = 0.1222$$

Marginal Cost of Capital (K_{mc})

	Market Values	Market Weights	After-Tax Cost	Weighted After Tax
Current liabilities	$ 20,000	0.050	0.055	0.00275
Long-term debt	50,000	0.125	0.0452	0.00565
Preferred stock B	30,000	0.075	0.0607	0.00455
New common	300,000	0.75	0.1222	0.09165
	$400,000	Marginal cost of capital =		0.1046

The marginal cost of capital is approximately 10.5%.   ●

ALTERNATIVE APPROACH: THE CAPITAL ASSET PRICING MODEL IN CAPITAL BUDGETING

The marginal cost of capital captures the risk position of the firm in its entirety. However, when used as a hurdle rate in the selection of capital projects, it does not reflect the risk of the particular project or projects under consideration. Thus, in Chapter 8 we noted the necessity to adjust for the particular risk inherent in each project under consideration. We discussed several methods for risk adjustment and indicated another method was available through the application of the Capital Asset Pricing Model (CAPM). It is the purpose of this section to demonstrate how CAPM can be employed in project evaluation.

One potential difficulty that may be encountered with the application of conventional methods for risk adjustment is increasing, or racheting upward, the firm's cost of capital. This could come about by accepting projects having risk postures in excess of the firm's risk complexion and thereby increasing the firm's risk posture. If this were to happen, the firm's marginal cost of capital would increase to reflect the firm's new risk structure. If, however, the conventional methods are correctly applied, the firm will also accept projects having a lower risk complexion than the firm overall, and the racheting effect should not take place. Put another way, the average cost of capital represents a strategic rate that management strives to earn on the totality of the operation; management accepts some projects with higher and others with lower risk–return levels, but the average risk–return posture approximates that embodied in the marginal cost of capital.

The capital asset pricing model can also be used to calculate a market-based hurdle rate, risk-adjusted to the project under evaluation. The methodology relates a project's expected returns to an index representing a broad-based measure of economic activity. In Exhibit 11-3, a project's expected return, $E(R_j)$, and the expected return on the index, $E(R_m)$, are computed based upon different states of the economy and their respective probability of occurrence.

In Table A of Exhibit 11-3, the returns from the index, R_m, and four projects (a, b, c, and d) are shown for four possible states of the economy. The probability of each state of the economy is denoted by P_s. All of the forecasted

EXHIBIT 11-3 Illustration of Project Evaluation Using CAPM

Table A

State of the Economy	P_s	R_m	R_a	R_b	R_c	R_d
Revival (S_1)	0.20	20%	15%	40%	15%	10%
Prosperity (S_2)	0.50	30%	20%	30%	40%	15%
Recession (S_3)	0.20	6%	13%	00%	00%	−6%
Depression (S_4)	0.10	0%	3%	−30%	00%	−3%
	1.00					

Table B

State of the Economy	P_s	R_m	$P_s \times R_m$	$[R_m - E(R_m)]$	$[R_m - E(R_m)]^2$	$[R_m - E(R_m)]^2 P_s$
S_1	0.20	0.20	0.040	−0.002	0.000004	0.0000008
S_2	0.50	0.30	0.150	+0.098	0.009604	0.004802
S_3	0.20	0.06	0.012	−0.142	0.020164	0.0040328
S_4	0.10	0.00	0.000	−0.202	0.040804	0.0040804
		$E(R_m) =$	0.202		$\sigma_m^2 =$	0.0129160
					$\sigma_m =$	0.1136485

Table C

State of the Economy	P_s	R_a	$P_s \times R_a$	$\dfrac{d_a}{R_a - E(R_a)}$	$\dfrac{d_m}{R_m - E(R_m)}$	$d_a d_m$	$d_a d_m P_s$
S_1	0.20	0.15	0.030	−0.009	−0.002	+0.000018	+0.0000036
S_2	0.50	0.20	0.100	+0.041	+0.098	+0.004018	+0.0020090
S_3	0.20	0.13	0.026	−0.029	−0.142	+0.004118	+0.0008236
S_4	0.10	0.03	0.003	−0.129	−0.202	+0.026058	+0.0026058
		$E(R_a) =$	0.159			$\text{Cov}(R_a, R_m) =$	+0.005442

$$B_a = \frac{\text{Cov}(R_a, R_m)}{\sigma_m^2} = \frac{+0.005442}{0.012916} = 0.421$$

Table D

$E(R_a) = 0.159$	$\text{Cov}(R_a, R_m) = +0.005442$	$B_a = 0.421$
$E(R_b) = 0.20$	$\text{Cov}(R_b, R_m) = +0.02062$	$B_b = 1.596$
$E(R_c) = 0.23$	$\text{Cov}(R_c, R_m) = +0.019543$	$B_c = 1.513$
$E(R_d) = 0.08$	$\text{Cov}(R_d, R_m) = +0.00962$	$B_d = 0.745$

returns (R_m, R_a, R_b, R_c, and R_d) and probabilities in Table A represent estimates for single periods for each of the projects and the market index. Estimates may be the result of projections from historical data or simulation. The data in Table A are the results of economic forecasts.

Table B is a summary of the calculations needed to obtain the expected return, variance, and standard deviation for the market index. Note that the estimated returns for the market index, R_m, are expressed in decimal form in Table B rather than as percentages as in Table A. The results show that the expected return on the market index is 20.2%, with a standard deviation of 11.36%.

Table C derives the necessary inputs to determine the required return from investment a, consistent with its risk characteristics. The results for all four projects are shown in Table D. The required return as determined using Equation (9) is compared with the project's expected return. The project's expected return is the weighted average of the estimated returns of each of the possible states of the economy. If the expected return equals or exceeds the required return, the project is accepted; otherwise, it is rejected.

$$R_j^0 = R_F + [E(R_m) - R_F]B_j \qquad (9)$$

where R_j^0 = required return from project j
R_F = risk-free rate of return
$E(R_m)$ = expected return on the market index
B_j = Beta factor for project j, which is defined in Equation (10)

$$B_j = \frac{\text{Cov}(R_j, R_m)}{\sigma_m^2} \qquad (10)$$

where $\text{Cov}(R_j, R_m)$ = covariance between the returns on project j and the returns on the market index
σ_m^2 = variance of the market index

Based on the inputs of Table D, it is possible to compute the required return for each project, R_j^0, employing Equation (9). In our computation we will assume that the risk-free rate of return, R_F, is 8%:

		R_j^0	$E(R_j)$
$R_a^0 =$	$0.08 + (0.202 - 0.08)0.421$	$= 13.14\%$	15.9%
$R_b^0 =$	$0.08 + (0.202 - 0.08)1.596$	$= 27.47\%$	20%
$R_c^0 =$	$0.08 + (0.202 - 0.08)1.513$	$= 26.46\%$	23%
$R_d^0 =$	$0.08 + (0.202 - 0.08)0.745$	$= 17.09\%$	8%

Using the CAPM approach, only project A would be accepted, since its expected return exceeds its required return.

Figure 11-1 shows where each project falls relative to the market price of risk line [i.e., the security market line (SML)]. Only project A falls below the SML, indicating that it offers a rate of return sufficient to compensate for its risk. The other three projects fall above the SML, since their returns are not sufficient to cover the market-related risk.

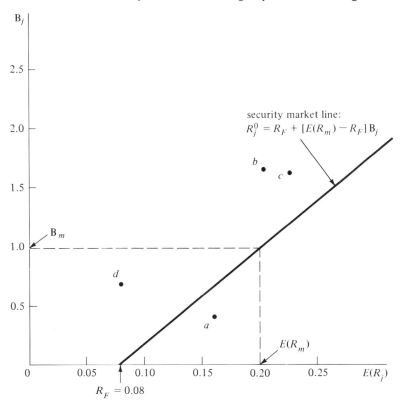

FIGURE 11-1   Project Selection Using Capital Asset Pricing

security market line:
$$R_j^0 = R_F + [E(R_m) - R_F] B_j$$

B_j

B_m

$E(R_m)$

$E(R_j)$

$R_F = 0.08$

Several aspects of the capital asset pricing approach illustrated above warrant attention.

1. The possible states of the economy over the life span of the projects must be forecasted. It should be noted that intermediate and long-term forecasting as commonly practiced by business firms have larger variances than do short-term projections.

2. The probabilities related to different states of the economy can be derived from historical data on cyclical behavior and/or by simulation.

3. Based upon these variables, the forecaster can project returns on the broad-based market index. It will suffice that the market index consists of assets comparable or meaningfully related to the projects studied. Alternatively, the analysis could have employed historical data on the relationship between similar projects and the market index to calculate Beta.

4. The forecasted returns of the index and the projects are correlated to derive the Beta on each project. Managers seek projects such as project *A*, with returns in excess of the levels required by the risk–return market relation illustrated in Figure 11-1. When such projects are added to the firm's portfolio, the expected returns on the firm's common stock (at its previous existing price) will be higher than those required by the market line.

5. In practical implementation, the success of the method hinges on the stability of Beta. Empirical evidence here points to instability when a few time periods are utilized in the calculation, but the variance in Beta tends to decrease as the number of time periods increases. The reader is also referred to a number of cautions cited by Myers and Turnbull[2] in the use of CAPM in capital budgeting decisions.

6. CAPM provides an alternative approach for estimating the firm's cost of equity capital. If we know the Beta of the firm, B_p, then the cost of common stock equity capital can be defined using Equation (11):

$$K_e = R_F + [E(R_m) - R_F]B_p \tag{11}$$

Equation (11) may be used to determine the firm's cost of equity capital in place of the dividend valuation model derived in Chapter 4 and discussed earlier in this chapter.

7. The project's acceptance or rejection is a function of the investment's own systematic risk. Thus, since the contribution of the project to the firm's variance of equity rate does not affect the accept or reject decision given by the security market line, diversification can be ignored in capital budgeting decisions. Each project is evaluated on its own merits without reference to the firm's existing investments.

DEBT CAPACITY AND VALUE OF THE FIRM AFTER ACCEPTANCE OF THE PROJECT

The CAPM, in a capital budgeting context, provides the decision maker with a risk-adjusted hurdle rate peculiar to the project evaluated and an alternative methodology to compute the cost of equity capital. It follows that CAPM relates immediately to the valuation process discussed earlier in this chapter. Hence, in looking at a project, it is pertinent to assess the value of the project based upon systematic risk and with that knowledge to estimate the debt-carrying capacity of the proposed acquisition. Martin and Scott[3] make a valuable contribution to the analysis of these questions.

Based upon the work of Modigliani and Miller,[4] Martin and Scott define the value of the firm as well as any asset to comprise the present value of an uncertain income stream (EBIT) plus the present value of a certain stream of

[2]S. C. Myers and S. M. Turnbull, "Capital Budgeting and the Capital Asset Pricing Model: Good News and Bad News," *The Journal of Finance*, May 1977, pp. 321–333. Also see comments on this article by R. S. Hamada, "Discussion," *The Journal of Finance*, May 1977, pp. 333–336.
[3]See John D. Martin and David F. Scott, Jr., "Debt Capacity and the Capital Budgeting Decision," *Financial Management*, Summer 1976, pp. 7–14.
[4]Franco Modigliani and Merton Miller, "Corporate Income Taxes and the Cost of Capital: A Correction," *The American Economic Review*, June 1963, pp. 433–443.

tax savings generated by debt as shown in Equation (12):

$$V = \frac{\text{EBIT}(1 - t)}{K_e} + \frac{D(K_d)(t)}{K_d} \tag{12}$$

where t = marginal tax rate on the firm or the project
 D = market value of debt in firm's capital structure
 K_d = rate at which the market capitalizes a certain stream of tax savings generated by debt
 K_e = rate at which the market capitalizes the expected after-tax returns of an unlevered (debt-free) company with the same EBIT and risk posture
 V = value of the firm (V_F) or value of the project (V_P), depending on the purpose of the analysis

Equation (12) facilitates the incorporation of added information bearing on the acceptance of the project.

K_e is calculated using Equation (11) as modified by substituting B_0 for B_p in Equation (13):

$$K_e = R_F + \left[E(R_m) - R_F \right] B_0 \tag{13}$$

B_0 represents the Beta coefficient of an unlevered stream of income (EBIT) of the same size and risk level. It is *approximated* using Equation (14):

$$B_0 = B_p \frac{S}{S_0 - \text{MTS}} \tag{14}$$

where B_p = Beta of the firm's common stock assuming its current levered position
 S = market value of the firm's equity shares in period $t - 1$
 S_0 = market value of the firm's equity, debt and preferred
 MTS = market value of the tax shelter on the outstanding debt for the preceding period as defined in Equation (15)

For example,[5] assume the following information relative to a firm before the acceptance of a capital project:

$$\begin{array}{lll} \text{EBIT} = \$95,000 & K_d = 0.10 & S = \$23,800 \\ D = \$17,000 & t = 0.5 & S_0 = \$40,800 \\ E(R_m) = 0.15 & R_F = 0.06 & B_p = 2.41 \end{array}$$

Then we may determine the following:
 1. Market value of tax shelter:

$$\text{MTS} = \frac{D(K_d)(t)}{K_d} \tag{15}$$

---

[5]The following example is adapted from Martin and Scott, "Debt Capacity."

where D = current amount of outstanding debt
K_d = pretax average cost of outstanding debt

$$\text{MTS} = \frac{\$17,000(0.10)(0.5)}{0.10} = \$8,500$$

2. *Beta value of the unencumbered cash flow:*

$$B_0 = B_p \frac{S}{S_0 - \text{MTS}}$$

$$= 2.41 \frac{\$23,800}{\$40,800 - \$8,500} = 2.41 \frac{\$23,800}{\$32,300} = 1.78$$

3. *Unlevered cost of equity:*

$$K_e = R_F + [E(R_m) - R_F]B_0$$
$$= 0.06 + (0.15 - 0.06)1.78$$
$$= 0.22 \quad \text{or} \quad 22\%$$

4. *Value of firm before acceptance of the project* (V_F):

$$V_F = \frac{\text{EBIT}(1 - t)}{K_e} + \frac{D(K_d)(t)}{K_d}$$

$$= \frac{\$95,000(1 - 0.5)}{0.22} + \frac{17,000(0.10)(0.5)}{0.10}$$

$$= \$215,909.09 + \$8,500$$
$$= \$224,409.09$$

5. *Firm's average cost of capital before acceptance of the project:*

$$K = \frac{\text{EBIT}(1 - t)}{V_F} \tag{16}$$

where K = firm's average cost of capital before acceptance of the project
t = firm's marginal tax rate
V_F = value of the firm before acceptance of the project

Applying Equation (16), we have the following:

$$K = \frac{\$95,000(1 - 0.5)}{\$224,409.09} = 0.21 \quad \text{or} \quad 21\%$$

Debt capacity is here defined as the risk of insolvency resulting from the use of financial leverage, that is, the risk that the unencumbered cash flows will be less than or equal to zero. The unencumbered cash flows may be found using Equation (17):

$$C = \text{EBIT} + \text{depreciation} - [I + \text{SF}(1 - t)] \tag{17}$$

where C = unencumbered cash flow prior to the acceptance of the project
I = annual interest expense prior to the acceptance of the project
SF = sinking-fund payments or principal payments required under existing debt agreements

If C is assumed to be normally distributed with an expected value of $E(C)$ and standard deviation σ_C, the risk of insolvency is defined by the probability statement, Equation (18):

$$P(C \leqslant 0) = P[E(C) - Z\sigma_C \leqslant 0] \qquad (18)$$

where Z is the ratio of $E(C)/\sigma_C$ corresponding to the number of standard deviations that the firm's expected unencumbered cash flow $E(C)$ lies away from zero. In short, we have a probability distribution of unencumbered cash flows. Assume for the firm in our illustration that $E(C) = \$100,000$ and $\sigma_C = \$78,125$; then the Z value is determined as follows:

$$Z = \frac{\$100,000}{\$78,125} = 1.28$$

Reading from the normal table, Appendix D, 1.28 corresponds to approximately a 10% risk of insolvency.

Shifting the focus to the capital project that the firm is considering, assume that the project has an unencumbered cash flow $E(P)$ of \$10,000 and a σ_P of \$7,800. The coefficient of correlation between the cash flows of the firm and the project is 0.80. What does acceptance of the project add to the debt capacity of the firm? Using the Markowitz portfolio model described in Chapter 9, the standard deviation of the firm's unencumbered cash flows after acceptance of the project is determined using Equation (19):

$$\sigma_{FC} = \left[\sigma_C^2 + \sigma_P^2 + 2(\rho)(\sigma_C)(\sigma_P)\right]^{1/2} \qquad (19)$$

where σ_{FC} = standard deviation of the firm's unencumbered cash flows after the acceptance of the project

σ_C^2 = variance of the firm's unencumbered cash flows prior to acceptance of the project

σ_P^2 = variance of project's unencumbered cash flows

ρ = correlation coefficient between the firm's unencumbered cash flows and those of the new project

Using the information for the firm and project discussed above and applying Equation (19) results in the following:

$$\sigma_{FC} = \left[(78,125)^2 + (7,800)^2 + 2(0.80)(78,125)(7,800)\right]^{1/2}$$

$$= \$84,495$$

The expected unencumbered cash flows of the firm now total \$110,000 (\$100,000 originally plus \$10,000 on the new project). To find the risk of insolvency we again employ the normal distribution.

$$Z = \frac{\$110,000}{\$84,495} = 1.3$$

A Z value of 1.3 corresponds to a probability of 0.0968; that is, acceptance of the project has reduced the risk of insolvency from 10% to 9.68%.

6. *Computation of additional debt capacity:* The acceptance of a new project may affect the capacity of the firm to utilize additional debt while retaining its

original risk of insolvency. To determine the *debt service* that may be added, we employ Equation (20):

$$Z = \frac{E(C') - d}{\sigma_{FC}} \qquad (20)$$

where $E(C')$ = expected unencumbered cash flow after acceptance of the project
d = added debt service that can be carried at the 10% risk level

Applying Equation (20) to our example, where $Z = 1.28$, yields the following:

$$1.28 = \frac{\$110,000 - d}{\$84,495}$$

$$d = \$1,846$$

Since $K_d = 10\%$, $1,846 of added *debt service* translates to an $18,460 increment in debt capacity ($1,846/0.10).

7. *Value of firm after acceptance of the project* (V_{FC}): To compute the value of the firm after acceptance of the project, we use Equation (12), where the EBIT value is the new $E(C')$ value less depreciation on the new project, and the value of D is the original debt plus the incremental debt capacity determined in step 6. For our example, the calculations are as follows, assuming a new value for EBIT of $105,000 after acceptance of the project.

$$V_{FC} = \frac{EBIT(1 - t)}{K_e} + \frac{D(K_d)(t)}{K_d} \qquad (12)$$

$$= \frac{\$105,000(1 - 0.5)}{0.22} + \frac{\$35,460(0.10)(0.5)}{0.10}$$

$$= \$238,636.36 + \$17,730$$

$$= \$256,366.36$$

The increase in the value of the firm is $31,957.27 ($256,366.36 less the value of the firm before acceptance, $224,409.09).

8. *Average cost of capital after acceptance of the project:*

$$K_{FC} = \frac{EBIT(1 - t)}{V_{FC}} \qquad (21)$$

where K_{FC} = firm's average cost of capital after acceptance of the project
V_{FC} = value of the firm after acceptance of the project

Applying Equation (21) results in the following:

$$K_{FC} = \frac{\$105,000(1 - 0.5)}{\$256,366.36}$$

$$= 0.20$$

We have now come full cycle with CAPM, using it as follows:
1. As an alternative in the computation of the cost of equity.
2. As a hurdle rate in the selection of capital projects.

3. In combination with the Modigliani–Miller tax model, as a technique for valuing the firm and determining its debt capacity.

4. To determine the firm's average cost of capital.

SUMMARY

We have examined the problem of determining the firm's cost of capital, starting with the study of capital structure. The optimum capital structure is defined as that structure which will result in the minimum cost of capital. Our argument incorporated the concepts of both operating and financial leverage as affecting earnings after taxes, and both explicit and implicit cost of debt.

Throughout we stressed the importance of using market values and market costs (yields to maturity) as the inputs in the cost of capital calculation. Using these inputs provides us with the marginal cost of capital as a consequence of the mechanisms of arbitrage. With the methodology established, we examined the cost of the various sources of funds. We concluded that there need be only three sources of funds considered: common stock, preferred stock, and debt. The market cost of common stock already embodies retained earnings. Depreciation as a source of funds has the same cost as the cost of capital. The methodology of CAPM was introduced as an alternative procedure to determine the acceptability of projects, thus providing the reader with two approaches to the evaluative process.

PROBLEMS

---

1. McLaughlin Industries has a debt structure shown on its balance sheet as follows:

Accounts payable	$ 7,200,000
Short-term debt	4,800,000
(12% revolving credit)	
Accrued expenses	7,200,000
Bonds Series A	12,000,000
(5%, due in 12 years)	
Bonds Series B	16,800,000
(8%, due in 26 years)	

The Series A bonds are selling at $80, while the Series B bonds are selling at $120. The firm takes advantage of prompt-payment discounts, so there is no explicit cost to either the accounts payable or accrued expenses. Determine the marginal cost of capital, assuming that the firm's tax rate is 48% and that the tax rate for the average investor is 40%.

2. The Trebelhorn Growth Corporation has the following debt structure:

Trade accounts payable	$5,000,000
Short-term debt (8%)	4,000,000
Accrued expenses	3,000,000
Series A Bonds	7,000,000
(7%, due in 15 years)	

Series B Bonds   7,000,000

(8%, due in 26 years)

Series A bonds are presently selling for $800 and Series B bonds are presently selling for $900. Assume that the average tax bracket of the shareholders is 40%. Further assume that the corporation's marginal tax rate is 50%.

In a stepwise sequence, calculate the following:
(a) The market financial structure using the market amounts for the bond.
(b) The explicit cost of short-term debt (assume payments made within the discount period).
(c) The marginal pretax cost of outstanding bonds.
(d) The marginal after-tax cost of debt.

3. The Kay Manufacturing Corporation plans to raise $2,000,000 of new capital for a plant expansion. The debt structure it plans is as follows:

Current liabilities	$100,000 at 12%
Long-term debt	$550,000 at 9.25%, floata-tion costs 0.75%
Preferred stock	$350,000, floatation cost 2.5%; sold at $35 per share with $1.75 dividend
Common stock	$1,000,000, floatation cost estimated at 10%, divi-dend $1.25 per share, market price $47, anti-cipated growth in divi-dend, 8%

The firm's marginal tax rate is 48% and the average tax rate of its shareholders is 35%. Determine the cost of each component and the after-tax marginal cost of capital.

4. The Lemanski Corporation intends to raise $6,000,000 of new capital by the following methods:

Current liabilities	Increase by $600,000 at 13.46% financing
Long-term debt	$1,800,000 at 7.78% finan-cing with a floatation cost of 9%
Preferred stock	$600,000 with a floatation cost of 15%; stock will be sold at $50 per share with a stated dividend of $4
Common stock	$3,000,000 with a floatation cost of 12%; stock will be sold at $50 per share; the expected EPS is $2.50, with a dividend growth rate of 12%

The corporation tax rate is 48%.
(a) Determine the cost of each component and calculate the marginal cost of capital.
(b) What is the marginal cost of capital if all floatation costs are reduced by one-third?

5. The Capital Asset Pricing Corporation is evaluating the three projects shown below, which have various returns based on the states of nature shown:

State of Nature	Probability	Market Returns	Project Returns		
			P_1	P_2	P_3
1	0.1	−0.10	−0.30	−0.15	0.00
2	0.2	0	−0.10	−0.05	0.04
3	0.3	0.05	0.15	0.04	0.08
4	0.2	0.09	0.25	0.10	0.09
5	0.2	0.12	0.35	0.15	0.10

(a) Compute the expected returns for each project as well as the expected return and standard deviation for the market, based on the probability distributions above.

(b) Compute the covariance between each project and the market.

(c) Compute the Beta for each project.

(d) Compute the required rate of return for each project based on the capital asset pricing model, assuming that the risk-free rate is 6%.

(e) Discuss which of the projects are candidates for acceptance, and why.

MATHEMATICAL PROGRAMMING
AND MULTIPERIOD ANALYSIS

12 INTRODUCTION TO MATHEMATICAL PROGRAMMING

Throughout the text we have examined various types of financial decisions, all of which have the following characteristics:

1. Scarce resources had to be allocated among competing decision alternatives.

2. The decision maker was striving to achieve an overriding goal or objective.

3. Various restrictions and requirements were imposed on the decision maker.

The decision-making process becomes more complex as the number of alternatives increases, as these alternatives become interdependent, and as the number of constraints on the decision maker increases. Given the decision-making setting described above, a natural and powerful set of tools referred to as *mathematical programming models* can be utilized to facilitate the evaluation of decision alternatives. This chapter surveys the area of mathematical programming as an introduction to the following two chapters, where these models are applied to the capital budgeting problem setting, first under conditions of certainty and then under conditions of risk.

MATHEMATICAL PROGRAMMING MODELS

Mathematical programming (MP) models are a set of techniques in the broader fields of operations research or management science. These fields utilize quantitative models to describe various business, industrial, or governmental problem settings to gather information, obtain greater insight, or evaluate various decision alternatives. In our definition of mathematical programming, we used the term "quantitative models," which deserves further elaboration. Quantitative models are descriptive representations of a real problem setting using mathematical equations. Such models are constructed to obtain information and insight about a problem setting more quickly and in a less costly and less disruptive way than by experimenting directly on the actual system. These models are, therefore, "abstractions" of the real system; that is, they try to capture only the most critical elements and relationships that exist in the real system; otherwise, it would be as difficult, time-consuming, and costly to analyze the model as the real system. Because quantitative models can be rather involved, a "solution algorithm" must generally be used to solve the model. A solution algorithm is merely a step-by-step process that guarantees reaching the correct solution to the model formulation.

The complexity of real systems, as well as hidden interrelationships among system components, makes it advantageous for the analyst to perform "sensitivity analysis" on the solution obtained. Sensitivity analysis is a process whereby the analyst determines how significantly the solution to the problem will change if various assumptions about the system are modified in the model. This process points to the characteristics of the system that are most critical and that require most attention in the management control area. Sensitivity analysis generally leads to changes in the model representation that may require re-solving the model to obtain information on the new solution. The results of the sensitivity analysis become inputs to the decision-making process wherein additional quantitative and qualitative factors (not reflected in the original model) which differentiate the various alternatives are taken into account before the "best" alternative is selected for implementation into the real system. Periodically after this implementation, feedback is obtained to determine how

FIGURE 12-1   Model-Building and Decision-Making Process

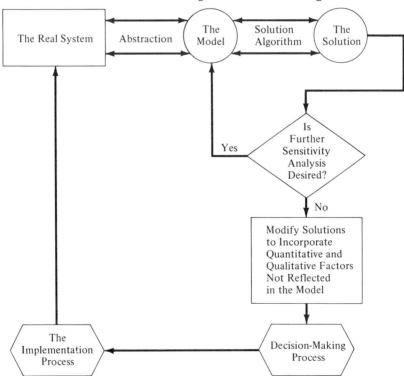

well the system is functioning, so that timely corrective action can be taken, if necessary. This model-building and decision-making process is summarized in Figure 12-1.

To begin our discussion of MP models, we must define a number of terms. There are two major categories of equations that are used in MP models:

1. The objective function describes the goal or objective the decision maker desires to achieve.

2. Constraint equations describe any limitations on resources, restrictions imposed by the environment within which the system functions, or managerial policies that the firm desires to observe.

The basic approach of MP models is to optimize the objective function while simultaneously satisfying all the constraint equations that limit the activities of the decision maker. In formulating both the objective function and the constraint equations used in MP models, two types of variables are used:

1. Input parameters are values specified by the decision maker to describe characteristics of the system.

2. Decision variables will be determined by the model as a part of achieving the optimal solution.

As a brief illustration of these definitions, consider a firm manufacturing and selling two products (X and Y) and desiring to determine that product mix which will maximize total dollar profit. The firm estimates that the unit profit figures are $6 and $18, respectively. The objective function to maximize profit for this firm would therefore be expressed as follows:

$$\text{maximize profit} = \$6X + \$18Y$$

In this objective function the two values $6 and $18 are the "input parameters," since management had to specify these values pertaining to their two products. The variables X and Y, which designate the number of units of product X and the number of units of product Y that should be produced, are "decision variables," since the model will determine their values to maximize profits.

CATEGORIES OF MATHEMATICAL PROGRAMMING MODELS

Within the general class of models referred to as *mathematical programming,* there are several that find specific application, depending on the assumptions made about the operation of the system being analyzed and the interrelationships among system components. Several categories of mathematical programming models are shown in Table 12-1. Each utilizes different types of equations in the objective function or constraint equations and/or permits different assumptions about the input parameters: either these values are assumed to be known with certainty or they are assumed to be known only by means of a probability distribution (i.e., conditions of risk exist). *Herein lie the major strengths of mathematical programming models: they are optimization models (i.e., they find the best possible solution for a given problem representation), and they can accurately describe virtually any real-world system assuming that either conditions of certainty or risk exist.* Hence, MP models provide a powerful tool for the decision maker.

TABLE 12-1 Categories of Mathematical Programming Models

Conditions of Certainty	*Conditions of Risk*[a]
1. Linear programming (LP)	1. Stochastic LP (SLP) LP under uncertainty (LPUU) Chance-constrained programming (CCP)
2. Integer programming (IP)	2. IP under uncertainty (IPUU)
3. Goal programming (GP)	3. Stochastic GP (SGP)
4. Nonlinear programming (NLP) Quadratic programming (QP)	4. NLP under uncertainty (NLPUU) QP under uncertainty (QPUU)
5. Dynamic programming (DP)	5. DP under uncertainty (DPUU)

[a]Based on our definitions of risk and uncertainty in Chapter 8, the models listed below technically assume conditions of risk while in the literature they are frequently referred to in terms of "uncertainty."

The use of the basic *linear programming* (LP) model, which we will discuss in more detail in the following section, requires three assumptions:

1. The input parameters are known with certainty.

2. Both the objective function and the constraint equations can be accurately described using linear equations.

3. The decision variables are continuous (i.e., they can take on any value).

Linear programming is the most widely known and used MP model because it represents problems with reasonable accuracy utilizing linear equations that may be solved easily with computerized solution algorithms.

If the assumption of certainty is relaxed, the decision maker may select among three alternative models available for handling conditions of risk in a linear programming setting:

1. Stochastic LP is a two-stage decision process wherein stage 1 decisions are fixed, random events generated, and then the stage 2 decisions are determined in order to optimize the objective function given the stage 1 decisions and the random events.

2. LP under uncertainty is also a two-stage decision process wherein stage 1 decisions are fixed, random events generated, and then stage 2 decisions are determined to minimize the penalty assessed for violation of any of the constraints caused by the random events that were encountered.

3. Chance-constrained programming attempts to maximize the expected return or minimize the variance of returns, where, owing to the stochastic nature of the input parameters, the constraint equations are required to hold only with some probability less than 1.

Integer programming (IP) relaxes the third assumption required by the LP model, namely, that the decision variables must be continuous. IP allows the decision variables to take on integer values. This seemingly small change in the LP model greatly increases solution time as compared to the corresponding LP problem but permits the solution of large classes of problems wherein the decision variables must take on integer values. IP under uncertainty is analogous to LP under uncertainty.

Goal programming (GP) is a powerful and interesting extension cf LP wherein a hierarchy of multiple objectives is incorporated into the model; thus, the objective function becomes multidimensional. GP provides an effective operational methodology to maximize expected utility as discussed in Chapter 8. Stochastic GP is analogous to stochastic LP and is treated in a similar manner.

Nonlinear programming (NLP) is an MP model wherein either the objective function or the constraint equations must be described using nonlinear equations or both the objective function and the constraint equations must be described using nonlinear equations. NLP is frequently used to solve problems involving curvilinear cost functions.

Quadratic programming is a special type of nonlinear programming model wherein the only nonlinearity is in the objective function. QP models are significantly easier to solve than NLP models because there is no general way to solve the latter type of problem. Again, the "risk" setting merely necessitates incorporating the probability distributions of the input parameters, which may also be incorporated into the QP model.

Dynamic programming (DP) is a useful method of optimizing a system over time. In addition, DP may be used to divide large decision problems into a sequence of smaller, interrelated decision problems wherein recursive equations are used to describe the flow of decisions and the state of the system. Recursive equations relate adjacently indexed variables of a set so that if we know the value of one variable, we can determine the value of the next one; and so on. DP under uncertainty assumes that new information is acquired as the decision maker moves through time and that this information is used to update system parameters and to aid in the sequential decision process.

This brief introduction to the various MP models is designed to give an overview rather than specific details of each model. Several of the models will be examined in more depth in this and the following chapters. Extensive research has been undertaken in the area of mathematical programming applied to various problem areas in finance, as evidenced by the entries cited in the selected bibliography. The interested reader is encouraged to seek out such references.

LINEAR PROGRAMMING

Because of the widespread use and importance of linear programming (LP), it is examined in greater detail in this section. In our initial discussion of LP, three major assumptions underlying its use were cited. These assumptions imply various other aspects of LP models, which are delineated in Exhibit 12-1. In our discussion of other MP models, we noted that several of the assumptions required for LP can be relaxed in order to establish models that more closely describe the real-world decision settings faced by the analyst. For example, the LP assumption of certainty can be relaxed by utilizing SLP, LPUU, or CCP; the limitation of a single objective function can be overcome by using GP; and the need for continuous rather than discrete variables may be relaxed by using

EXHIBIT 12-1 Assumptions of Linear Programming Models

The major assumptions of linear programming models are as follows:

1. The objective of the system under analysis and all its relevant resource limitations, restrictions, and requirements can be accurately described using *linear equations*. That is, the objective function and all constraint equations must be linear.

2. Conditions of *certainty* exist. All the model's parameters (i.e., the objective function coefficients, the technical coefficients in the constraints, and the right-hand-side values in the constraints) are known precisely and are not subject to variation.

3. All decision variables are restricted to *nonnegative* values.

4. Only a *single objective* is optimized.

5. The decision variables are considered to be continuous rather than discrete. This is known as the *divisibility* assumption.

6. Resources available are *homogenous*. Example: if 10 hours of direct labor are available, each of these hours is just as productive as any other and can be used equally well on any activity that requires direct labor.

7. Proportionality exists. This means that if it is desired to increase the activity level of any decision variable, proportionately greater amounts of each resource are required. The linearity assumption implies proportionality.

8. All parameters of the model are *unaffected* by changes in methods used, level of utilization, economics of scale, and so on. Again, the linearity assumption implies this.

9. The system is *additive* in nature: the whole is equal to the sum of the parts. The effectiveness of the system equals the sum of each system component's effectiveness. The total resources utilized equal the sum of the resources used on each activity variable.

10. Independence exists throughout the system. This means there is no interaction among decision variables, resources available, or different operations performed.

IP. Of course, each of these enrichments to the basic LP model necessitates greater input requirements, as well as more computer time and memory to solve the model. It should be stressed that the LP model, although it has shortcomings, is a reasonable starting point for many practical decision problems. Thus, the methodology of LP problem-solving deserves study.

The basic approach to LP problem-solving proceeds through the following stages:

1. Formulate the problem in the LP framework. This requires specification of input parameters and decision variables, the objective function, and all relevant constraint equations. The latter two sets of equations must all be linear in nature.

2. Solve the problem using either a graphical approach, the simplex method, or a computer-based solution algorithm.

3. Interpret the optimal solution which is expressed in terms of an alternative decision point within the feasible solution domain.

4. Perform a detailed sensitivity analysis on the optimal solution to determine ranges for each of the input parameters wherein the optimal solution remains valid.

In order to illustrate stages 1 and 2, consider the graphical LP solution demonstrated in Example 1.

• *EXAMPLE 1*   *Graphical Solution to LP Problem*

A firm manufactures and sells two grades of leather wallets, standard and deluxe. Two resources are constrained for the coming week: production time (80 hours are available) and process and shipping time (1,000 wallets can be shipped during the coming week regardless of which of the two types of wallets make up the order). The firm has sufficient raw materials, working capital, and so on, to support any desired product mix. Further, the firm can sell any number of units of either type of wallet at the going market price. However, the firm wants to produce a minimum of 400 units of its deluxe wallet in order to satisfy the demands of its prime customers for this type of wallet. Management has been provided with the following financial and production data:

Model	Production Time (hr)	Sale Price
Standard	0.05	$ 7.00
Deluxe	0.1	$10.00

Production time is estimated to cost the firm $40/hr. Shipping and processing costs are estimated to be $3/unit. Management desires to select the product mix that will maximize the total dollar contribution needed to cover fixed costs and generate profits. Formulate this problem using the LP model and solve it graphically.

Solution: To formulate this problem using the LP model, the following decision variables must be defined:

$$X_1 = \text{number of units of the } standard \text{ wallet to be produced}$$

$$X_2 = \text{number of units of the } deluxe \text{ wallet to be produced}$$

To specify the objective function, variable cost per unit must be determined for each product so that this amount can be subtracted from selling price per unit to determine the contribution margin per unit:

	Standard	Deluxe
Sale price/unit	$ 7.00	$ 10.00
Variable production cost/unit	− 2.00	− 4.00
Variable shipping cost/unit	− 3.00	− 3.00
Contribution margin/unit	$ 2.00	$ 3.00

The LP formulation is as follows:

$$\text{Maximize total dollar contribution} = \$2X_1 + \$3X_2$$

subject to

Production capacity:	$0.05X_1 + 0.10X_2 \leqslant 80$ hr
Shipping capacity:	$1X_1 + 1X_2 \leqslant 1000$ units
Minimum requirements:	$X_2 \geqslant 400$ units
Nonnegativity condition:	$X_1, X_2 \geqslant 0$

The graphical solution is shown in Figure 12-2 and the method of arriving at the optimal solution is described below.

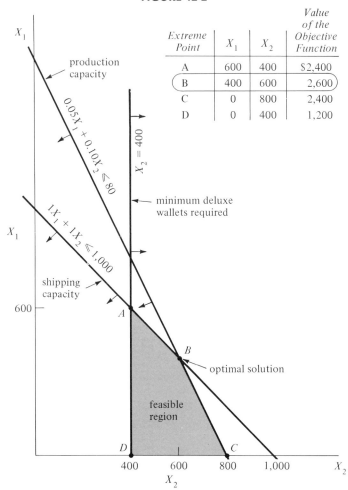

FIGURE 12-2

Extreme Point	X_1	X_2	Value of the Objective Function
A	600	400	$2,400
B	400	600	2,600
C	0	800	2,400
D	0	400	1,200

As shown in Figure 12-2, the area that is labeled "feasible region" consists of all possible X_1 and X_2 values which simultaneously satisfy all the constraint equations. Not all of these possible combinations must be evaluated to determine the optimal solution, since we have a helpful theorem in LP which states that the optimal solution can only occur at an "extreme point" to the feasible region (i.e., at the intersection of two or more constraints or a constraint and either axis) or possibly along a boundary between two extreme points. There are two methods of determining the optimal solution in the graphical approach:

   1. The objective function could be graphed at successively higher values moving farther away from the origin; the optimal solution is reached when the objective function line is as far away from the origin but still touching the feasible region—the point or boundary where the objective function is tangent is the optimal solution.

   2. The coordinates for each extreme point are determined either graphically or algebraically and these values are substituted into the objective function, with the results being tabulated as shown in the insert to Figure 12-2; the extreme point with the largest value of the objective function is the optimal solution.

As shown in Figure 12-2, the objective function is maximized at point B (400 standard and 600 deluxe wallets), where it equals $2,600. Since the objective function decreases as we move toward either point A or C, the optimal solution is only at point B rather than along either boundary. If the value of the objective function at *either* point A or C had also been $2,600, then any combination of X_1 and X_2 along the relevant boundary AB or BC would represent an optimal solution to the problem. ●

Whenever there are more than two decision variables, or if there are numerous constraint equations, the graphical LP method is of limited value. Hence, it becomes necessary to resort to an algebraic technique to arrive at the optimal solution. One of the most widely used techniques of solving LP problems is the *simplex method*, developed by George B. Dantzig[1] in the 1940s.

Several new definitions are necessary in order to understand the simplex method. First, the approach requires that all the constraint equations be converted to strict equalities if they are "less than or equal to" ($\leqslant$) or "greater than or equal to" ($\geqslant$) constraints in the original formulation of the problem. This requires that a unique "slack variable" be added to each "less than or equal constraint" to convert it into a strict equality. Similarly, a unique "surplus variable" must be subtracted from each "greater than or equal to constraint" to convert it into a strict equality.

As mentioned, packaged computer algorithms can be used to perform all the LP problem calculations. An LP package available to users of IBM computers is referred to as LINPROG, which is part of their MATHPROG software package. Similar LP packages are available to users of other computers. Such packaged programs facilitate the analyst's capitalization on the speed and accuracy of the computer to handle the tedious calculations required by the simplex method. The reader can obtain documentation detailing the use and interpretation of any such software package.

INTERPRETATION OF THE OPTIMAL LP SOLUTION

At this juncture, we assume readers are able to solve LP problems (the first two stages in the solution problem listed above are complete). The last two stages will be illustrated using computer printouts from the LINPROG packaged LP program. Stage 3 entails a complete interpretation of the optimal solution, including the *shadow prices*. *Shadow prices show how much the decision maker would be willing to pay to acquire 1 unit of each resource that is constrained in the problem.* Stage 4 is the sensitivity analysis of the optimal solution, which determines by how much each input parameter could change and leave the basis in the optimal solution unchanged.

Interpretation of the optimal solution and the discussion of shadow prices is demonstrated in Example 2.

[1]George B. Dantzig, *Linear Programming and Extensions* (Princeton, N.J.: Princeton University Press, 1963).

● **EXAMPLE 2** *Interpretation of the Optimal Solution: Shadow Prices*

Using the information provided in Example 1 and the optimal solution given below, completely interpret the optimal solution.

Solution: Given the following optimal solution:

Basic Variables	X_1	X_2	S_1	S_2	R_1	RHS
X_1	1	0	−20	2	0	400
X_2	0	1	20	−1	0	600
R_1	0	0	20	−1	1	200
Objective function	0	0	20	1	0	$2,600

As can be seen, the basic variables are X_1, X_2, and R_1. These variables have a value of 1 in one of the rows and zeros everywhere else in the column for that variable. These variables are basic in the row where the 1 appears, which means that they take on the value shown on the right-hand side (RHS) in the table. Thus, $X_1 = 400$, $X_2 = 600$, and $R_1 = 200$. The value of the objective function is shown in the objective function row on the right-hand side ($2,600).

The two variables whose columns do not have a 1 in one row and zeros everywhere else in the column (i.e., S_1 and S_2) are nonbasic variables and hence take on values of zero in the optimal solution.

It is easy to demonstrate that these values satisfy the original constraints by substituting the values into the constraint equations.

Production capacity	$\begin{cases} 0.05X_1 \\ 0.05(400) \\ 20 \end{cases}$	$\begin{matrix} +0.10X_2 \\ +0.10(600) \\ +60 \end{matrix}$	$\begin{matrix} +S_1=80 \\ +0 =80 \\ +0 =80 \end{matrix}$
Shipping capacity	$\begin{cases} 1X_1 \\ 400 \end{cases}$	$\begin{matrix} +1X_2 \\ +600 \end{matrix}$	$\begin{matrix} +S_2=1,000 \\ +0 =1,000 \end{matrix}$
Minimum requirement for X_2	$\begin{cases} X_2 - R_1 \\ 600 - 200 \end{cases}$		$\begin{matrix} =400 \\ =400 \end{matrix}$

The values shown in the objective function row under the slack and surplus variables have special significance. They are the *shadow prices* and *for slack variables, show the amount by which the value of the objective function would increase* (in a maximization problem) *if the original right-hand-side value associated with the slack variable were increased by 1 unit. For surplus variables, the shadow prices show the amount by which the objective function would increase if the original right-hand side associated with the surplus variable were decreased by 1 unit.* Thus, the shadow prices show the maximum amount that the decision maker would be willing to pay to acquire 1 additional unit of a resource (for slack variables) or to have a requirement relaxed by 1 unit (for surplus variables). In this example, the shadow price for $S_1 = \$20.00$, for $S_2 = \$1.00$, while it is $0 for R_1. This means that the firm would be willing to pay up to a maximum of $20.00 (in addition to the current variable production cost of $40.00 per hour) to acquire 1 hour of added production time and $1.00 (in addition to the variable shipping cost of $3/unit) to acquire 1 unit of added shipping capacity. To verify that these shadow prices are correct, consider a customer's order for 10 additional deluxe wallets. If the shadow prices are paid in addition to the current variables costs, the marginal revenue will just equal the marginal cost and the marginal profit will be zero. If the variable inputs can be obtained at a cost less than the shadow prices, profit will increase.

Incremental contribution margin from the new order		Incremental cost of filling new order if maximum shadow prices are paid to acquire additional resources
		Production capacity:
		10 units × 0.10 hr/unit × $20/hr = $20
10 units at $3 = $30		Shipping capacity:
		10 units × $1/unit = $10
$30	=	$30

It should be stressed that shadow prices are incremental in nature—that is, they indicate the maximum additional amount that the firm would be willing to pay over and above the current prices paid for needed resources. To demonstrate this for this example, refer back to Example 1 to get the selling price per unit of the deluxe wallet and the variable cost per hour of production capacity as well as the variable cost per unit of shipping capacity. These values are respectively $10/unit, $40/hour, and $3/unit. It is now shown that marginal revenue equals marginal cost for the new order of 10 wallets:

Marginal revenue	= marginal cost of filling new order if maximum shadow prices are paid (in addition to current cost) to acquire additional resources	
	Production capacity: 10 units × 0.10 hr/unit × $60/hr	= $60.00
10 units at $10	Shipping capacity: 10 units × $4/unit	= $40.00
$100.00	=	$100.00

Notice that the variable costs of $60/hour and $4 per unit for production capacity and shipping capacity, respectively, are the sum of current costs (i.e., $40/hour and $3 per unit, respectively) and the incremental shadow prices (i.e., $20 per hour and $1 per unit, respectively).

The shadow price for R_1 is zero because R_1 is a basic variable in the optimal solution which means that this constraint was not binding. That is, we exceeded the 400-unit minimum requirement for deluxe wallets by 200 units, so we would not be willing to pay anything to get this minimum requirement reduced. A similar interpretation would be given to a slack variable that was basic in the optimal solution. That is, since the constraint was not binding, not all of the amount of the resource originally available was utilized in the optimal solution. Thus, the firm would not be willing to pay anything to obtain additional units of the resource, because these units would just add to the already existing excess in the optimal solution.   •

The shadow prices discussed in Example 2 remain valid only within the specific range of additional units that the firm could acquire. In addition, questions often arise concerning the impact of changes in original values of input parameters on the optimal solution. Both of these areas may be addressed using the important tool referred to as *sensitivity analysis*.

Sensitivity Analysis

Sensitivity analysis can be performed either on the original right-hand-side values for each of the constraint equations or on the objective function coefficients for each decision variable. *In sensitivity analysis, on the right-hand side, Δ^+ and Δ^- are the amounts by which the original right-hand-side value could increase or decrease, respectively, without changing the basic variables in the optimal solution. In sensitivity analysis, on the objective function coefficients, Δ^+ and Δ^- are the amounts by which the objective function coefficient could increase or decrease, respectively, without changing the optimal solution.* Notice the difference in the statements made concerning the two types of sensitivity analysis. With respect to the right-hand-side values, we talked about leaving the same basic variables in the optimal solution but that the optimal values for each basic variable would change with any change of a right-hand-side value of a binding constraint. For objective function coefficients, we talked about the range within which the *optimal solution* (both the basic variables and their specific values) would remain unchanged. For all these input parameters, a range can be determined as specified in Equations (1) and (2):

$$\text{upper limit} = \text{original value plus } \Delta^+ \tag{1}$$

$$\text{lower limit} = \text{original value less } \Delta^- \tag{2}$$

We will first undertake a sensitivity analysis of the right-hand-side values. *For slack variables that are basic variables in the optimal solution:*

$$\Delta_{S_j}^+ = \infty \tag{3}$$

and

$$\Delta_{S_j}^- = \text{amount of this resource that is still available in the optimal solution} \tag{4}$$

These two values are consistent with the discussion presented above. If there is some quantity of a resource still available in the optimal solution (i.e., the definition of slack variable being basic in the optimal solution), then if we had more of it originally, we would merely have more of it left over in the optimal solution. This would be true for any increase in the original amount available; hence, the value of Δ^+ is infinite. On the other hand, we could only decrease the original amount available by the amount left over in the optimal solution, since to decrease it by an amount greater than this would lead to a different optimal solution.

For surplus variables that are basic variables in the optimal solution:

$$\Delta_{R_j}^+ = \text{value of this basic variable in the optimal solution} \tag{5}$$

$$\Delta_{R_j}^- = \infty \tag{6}$$

These values should be clear based on the discussion presented above relating to the complements of surplus variables (i.e., slack variables).

The same values for nonbasic variables in the optimal solution require computations based on the tableau from the optimal solution. *Thus, for slack or surplus variables that are nonbasic in the optimal solution:*

$$\Delta_{R_j}^+ \quad \text{or} \quad \Delta_{S_j}^+ = \min\left|\frac{b_i}{a_{ij} < 0}\right| \tag{7}$$

$$\Delta_{R_j}^- \quad \text{or} \quad \Delta_{S_j}^- = \min\left\{\frac{b_i}{a_{ij} > 0}\right\} \tag{8}$$

where b_i = right-hand-side value in row i of the optimal solution

a_{ij} = coefficient in column j (i.e., the column of slack or surplus variable j) and row i

S_j = slack variable in column j which is associated with the original resource that we are interested in changing

R_j = surplus variable in column j which is associated with the original resource that we are interested in changing

To perform sensitivity analysis on, say, slack variable S_1, which is nonbasic in the optimal solution, we look up and down in S_1 column for values that are negative. For each that is found, divide its corresponding right-hand-side value by the a_{ij} value and take the absolute value. Among the resulting values, select the smallest: this value is Δ^+. Repeat the process looking for positive values in the S_1 column in order to compute Δ^-.

Finally, we look at sensitivity analysis on the objective function coefficients for a maximization problem. Of course, we perform this analysis on decision variables in the problem which again can either be basic or nonbasic in the optimal solution.

For decision variables that are nonbasic in the optimal solution:

$$\Delta^+_{X_k} = \text{value of the shadow price for this decision variable in the optimal solution} \tag{9}$$

$$\Delta^-_{X_k} = \infty \tag{10}$$

If a decision variable is nonbasic in the optimal solution, the values found using Equations (9) and (10) should indicate that the decision variable was not attractive enough to enter the solution. Hence, it will remain unattractive if its objective function coefficient is decreased by any amount (i.e., $\Delta^- = \infty$). Furthermore, as pointed out above, the shadow price in the optimal solution shows the amount by which the objective function would decrease if a nonbasic variable were forced into solution; thus, the objective function coefficient would have to increase by more than its shadow price in order to make the nonbasic variable in question attractive (i.e., Δ^+ = shadow price in the optimal solution).

For decision variables that are basic in the optimal solution:

$$\Delta^+_{X_k} = \min \left| \frac{C_j}{a_{ij} < 0} \right| \tag{11}$$

$$\Delta^-_{X_k} = \min \left\{ \frac{C_j}{a_{ij} > 0} \right\} \tag{12}$$

where C_j = value in the objective row of the optimal tableau in column j

a_{ij} = coefficient in row i (i.e., the row in the optimal tableau where X_k is basic) and column j

X_k = decision variable k of interest which is basic in row i of the optimal tableau

To perform sensitivity analysis on, say, decision variable X_2, which is basic in row 4 of the optimal tableau, we would look across row 4 for negative a_{ij} values.

For each one that is found, divide the C_j value (i.e., the value in the objective function row of the tableau) for that column by the a_{ij} value and take the absolute value. Among the resulting values, select the smallest: this is $\Delta_{X_2}^+$. The process would then be repeated looking for positive a_{ij} values in row 4 in order to compute $\Delta_{X_2}^-$.

All the computations above were for *maximization problems*. In order to compute the Δ^+ and Δ^- values for a *minimization problem*, the identities of the two values are interchanged; that is, Equations (9) and (11) became the appropriate formulas for Δ^- and Equations (10) and (12) are used to compute Δ^+.

Example 3 illustrates the computation of Δ^+ and Δ^- values.

● **EXAMPLE 3** *Sensitivity Analysis*

Perform a complete sensitivity analysis on the following optimal solution:

Basic Variables	X_1	X_2	S_1	S_2	R_1	RHS
X_1	1	0	-20	2	0	400
X_2	0	1	20	-1	0	600
R_1	0	0	20	-1	1	200
Objective function	0	0	20	1	0	$2,600

Solution: Sensitivity analysis will first be performed on the original right-hand-side values. Recall that in the original problem we had the following resources available and minimum requirements:

> Production capacity ⩽ 80 hours
> Shipping and processing capacity ⩽ 1,000 units
> Minimum requirement for deluxe wallets ⩾ 400 units

Slack variables S_1 and S_2 correspond to the production and shipping capacity constraints, respectively; surplus variable R_1 corresponds to the minimum requirement for deluxe wallets. Thus, these columns in the tableau are relevant for sensitivity analysis on the original right-hand-side values for rows 1, 2, and 3, respectively.

Since R_1 is a basic variable in the optimal solution, we will examine it first. R_1 is a surplus variable that is basic in the optimal solution, so its Δ^+ and Δ^- values are found using Equations (5) and (6).

$$\Delta^+ = 200, \text{ the value of } R_1 \text{ in the optimal solution}$$

$$\Delta^- = \infty$$

The range of possible values that the minimum requirement for deluxe wallets could take on using Equations (1) and (2) is as follows:

$$\text{Range} \begin{cases} \text{upper limit} = \text{original amount plus } \Delta^+ & = 400 + 200 & = 600 \\ \text{lower limit} = \text{original amount minus } \Delta^- & = 400 - \infty & = -\infty \end{cases}$$

Hence, if our minimum requirement were any value less than 600 units of the deluxe wallet, we would have the same optimal basis that we presently have.

The two capacity constraints have slack variables that are nonbasic. Therefore, performance of a sensitivity analysis using Equations (7) and (8) yields the following results:

$$\Delta_{S_1}^+ = \min \left| \frac{400}{-20} \right| = 20 \text{ hours}$$

$$\Delta_{S_1}^- = \min \left\{ \frac{600}{20}, \frac{200}{20} \right\} = \min (30, 10) = 10 \text{ hours}$$

Thus, if the actual production capacity falls anywhere in the range of 70 hours (80 − 10 hours) to 100 hours (80 + 20 hours), we would have the same optimal basis as currently (X_1, X_2, R_1), and their new optimal values could be determined by performing calculations on the optimal tableau.

In addition, the shadow price of $20/hour of production capacity would remain valid as long as the firm did not attempt to purchase more than 20 additional hours $(\Delta_{S_1}^+)$ of production capacity or to sell more than 10 hours $(\Delta_{S_1}^-)$ at that price. Outside this range there would be a new shadow price, indicating the value of each production hour to the firm. Thus, there is a close and important relationship between shadow prices and the Δ^+ and Δ^- values determined in sensitivity analysis.

For S_2, the sensitivity analysis yields the following results:

$$\Delta_{S_2}^+ = \min \left| \frac{600}{-1}, \frac{200}{-1} \right| = 200 \text{ units}$$

$$\Delta_{S_2}^- = \min \left\{ \frac{400}{2} \right\} = 200 \text{ units}$$

Thus, if the actual shipping capacity falls anywhere in the range 800 units (1,000 − 200) to 1,200 units (1,000 + 200), we would again have the same optimal basis and would not have to re-solve the problem in order to determine the optimal solution. The same comments as above hold true for the shadow price of $1 for each unit of shipping capacity remaining valid only within the range 800 to 1,200 units of shipping capacity.

To perform sensitivity analysis on the original objective function coefficients for the two decision variables, which are both basic in the optimal solution, we use Equations (11) and (12):

$$\Delta_{X_1}^+ = \min \left| \frac{20}{-20} \right| = \$1.00$$

$$\Delta_{X_1}^- = \min \left\{ \frac{1}{2} \right\} = \$.50$$

Thus, if the profit coefficient for standard wallets falls anywhere between $3.00 ($2.00 + $1.00) and $1.50 ($2.00 − $.50), we would have the same optimal solution. Similarly, for deluxe wallets:

$$\Delta_{X_2}^+ = \min \left| \frac{1}{-1} \right| = \$1.00$$

$$\Delta_{X_2}^- = \min \left\{ \frac{20}{20} \right\} = \$1.00$$

Thus, if the profit coefficient for deluxe wallets falls anywhere between $4.00 ($3.00 + $1.00) and $2.00 ($3.00 − $1.00), we would have the same optimal solution as before. ●

Up to this point we have been saying that within the ranges for right-hand-side values which are determined by means of sensitivity analysis, the optimal basis would remain unchanged. Further, it was mentioned that the new optimal values for each of the basic variables could be determined by looking at the optimal tableau rather than having to re-solve the complete problem. We now explore how this is done.

Whenever a specific right-hand-side value in the original problem is changed to take on some other value within its sensitivity-range limits, the column of its slack variable becomes the relevant column to use in the optimal tableau in order to determine the new optimal value for each basic variable. The new optimal values are computed using Equation (13):

$$\begin{pmatrix} \text{new optimal value} \\ \text{of basic variable } i \end{pmatrix} = \begin{pmatrix} \text{current optimal} \\ \text{value of basic} \\ \text{variable } i \end{pmatrix} + (a_{ij})\begin{pmatrix} \text{change in original} \\ \text{right-hand-side value} \end{pmatrix} \quad (13)$$

where a_{ij} is the value in the current optimal tableau in row i and in column j which is the column of the slack or surplus variable associated with the right-hand-side value that is being changed. Note that the "change in original right-hand-side value" shown in Equation (13) has *both* a magnitude (numerical value) and a direction (sign) which must be incorporated in the calculations.

Example 4 illustrates the use of Equation (13).

● **EXAMPLE 4**   *Optimal Solution Using Sensitivity Range Limits*

Find the new optimal solution in our example problem if the number of *production hours* were actually:
(a) 105 hours
(b)   72 hours

Solution: (a) If the actual number of production hours were 105 hours, the problem would have to be re-solved to obtain the new optimal solution, because the value 105 hours falls outside the range 70 to 100 hours determined by sensitivity analysis in Example 3.

It should be noted that if we attempted to use Equation (13) to find the value of X_1 for the change up to 105 hours, the result would be

$$X_1 = 400 \text{ units} + (-20)(+25 \text{ hr}) = -100 \text{ units}$$

which is of course *infeasible* since the nonnegativity constraint would be violated.

(b) Since 72 hours does fall within the range 70 to 100 hours, we can proceed with calculations as follows:

$$\begin{pmatrix} \text{new optimal} \\ \text{value of basic variable} \end{pmatrix} = \begin{pmatrix} \text{current} \\ \text{optimal value} \end{pmatrix} + \begin{pmatrix} a_{ij} \\ \text{value} \end{pmatrix}\begin{pmatrix} \text{change in} \\ \text{production capacity} \end{pmatrix}$$

$$X_1 = 400 \text{ units} + (-20)(-8 \text{ hr}) = 560 \text{ units}$$
$$X_2 = 600 \text{ units} + (+20)(-8 \text{ hr}) = 440 \text{ units}$$
$$R_1 = 200 \text{ units} + (+20)(-8 \text{ hr}) = 40 \text{ units}$$

new profit = original profit + (shadow price)(change in production capacity)
$$= \$2,600 + (+\$20)(-8 \text{ hr})$$
$$= \$2,440$$

The new profit can also be computed by multiplying the number of units of each product by its respective contribution margin and totaling.   ●

DUALITY THEORY

Another important area related to linear programming problem formulation and solution is referred to as *duality theory*. Corresponding to every maximization LP problem, usually called the *primal problem*, there is a closely related minimization problem called the *dual problem*. From our point of view, the major attractiveness of duality theory lies in the interesting economic interpretation of the dual problem and the insight that the dual problem provides for extensions of LP, mainly to integer linear programming.

The following properties of duality are the most important:

1. The primal problem is generally a maximization problem which has "less than or equal to" constraint equations.

2. The dual problem is generally a minimization problem which has "greater than or equal to" constraint equations.

3. The dual of the dual is the primal.

4. The decision variables in the dual correspond to constraint equations in the primal, and vice versa. Thus, if there are n decision variables and m constraint equations in the primal problem, there will be m decision variables and n constraint equations in the dual.

5. An optimal solution to the dual exists only when the primal has an optimal solution, and vice versa. Further, the optimal value of the objective function must be the same for the primal and the dual.

6. By examining the optimal tableau of the primal problem we can also determine the optimal values for the dual variables, since they are the shadow prices associated with each of the slack and surplus variables.

SUMMARY

This chapter has surveyed the rather broad field of mathematical programming with an eye toward the use of this powerful class of management science models in the capital budgeting area. Model building was discussed in general as well as in the specific area of mathematical programming. Various mathematical programming models were introduced to handle problems under the assumption that either conditions of certainty or risk were present in the decision setting.

Linear programming (LP) was treated in depth because of the importance of this technique, its widespread use, and reliance of more advanced techniques on the LP formulation and solution. Problem formulation, graphical and computerized solution approaches, and sensitivity analysis were all discussed and illustrated with examples. Finally, the important area of duality was examined to show the interesting interrelationships and important economic interpretations of the primal–dual LP problems.

The material in this chapter forms a basis for the following two chapters. The strengths of mathematical programming techniques are examined as tools to assist the financial manager in evaluating capital investment alternatives and to integrate investment decisions with financing and dividend decisions.

1. The Datamax Company has recently become enthralled with linear programming and wants to utilize it in determining the optimal product mix for its two product lines.
   The revelant information about its products is as follows:

	Product X	Product Y
Selling price	$16.00	$23.00
Standard material cost	$ 1.50	$ 2.25
Standard labor cost	6.00	8.00
Standard machine time cost	4.50	5.25
Standard shipping cost	1.00	1.00
Maximum demand	None	500 units
Minimum requirements	100 units	None

   In addition, Datamax has several resource constraints that cannot be violated:

Raw-material constraint	1,000 units at 1.50 standard cost
Labor hours constraint	1,200 hours at 4.00 standard cost
Machine-hours constraint	2,800 hours at 1.50 standard cost
Shipping-capacity constraint	650 units at 1.00 standard cost

   Formulate this linear programming problem and solve it using the graphical technique.
2. Find the optimal solution to Problem 1 using the simplex method or a packaged LP algorithm.
3. Perform a sensitivity analysis on the right-hand-side values for the solution arrived at in Problem 2.
4. Perform a sensitivity analysis on the objective function coefficients for the solution arrived at in Problem 2.
5. Formulate the dual LP problem for Problem 1. Solve it using the simplex method or a packaged LP algorithm.
6. A sophisticated farmer uses LP to determine the amount of various crops to plant. He has 1,000 acres of land on which he can grow corn, wheat, or soybeans. Each acre of corn costs $100 for preparation, requires 7 man-days of labor, and yields a profit of $30. Each acre of wheat costs $120 for preparation, requires 10 man-days of labor, and yields $40 in profit. Finally, soybeans cost $70 to prepare the land, require 8 man-days, and yields a $20 profit. If the farmer has $100,000 available for preparation expenses, has 8,000 man-days of labor available, and wants to maximize profit, his LP formulation would be:

$$\text{Maximize } 30X_1 + 40X_2 + 20X_3$$

subject to

$$100X_1 + 120X_2 + 70X_3 + S_1 = 100,000$$
$$7X_1 + 10X_2 + 8X_3 + S_2 = 8,000$$
$$X_1 + X_2 + X_3 + S_3 = 1,000$$

$$X_i, S_i \geqslant 0 \qquad i = 1, 2, 3$$

Solve this problem using the simplex method or a packaged LP algorithm.

7. The optimal LP solution to Problem 6 is as follows:

	X_1	X_2	X_3	S_1	S_2	S_3	RHS
	0	1	1.9375	−0.04375	0.625	0	625
	1	0	−1.625	0.0625	−0.75	0	250
	0	0	0.6875	−0.01875	0.125	1	125
Z	0	0	8.75	0.1250	2.50	0	32,500

Answer the following questions about the optimal solution:
   (a) What is the optimal amount of each of the three crops that should be planted?
   (b) What is the dollar profit generated by the optimal planting? Show a proof that this figure is correct.
   (c) Are there any excess resources given the optimal planting? Demonstrate that this is correct by plugging the optimal values for X_1, X_2, and X_3 into the constraint equations.
   (d) How much would the farmer be willing to pay for an additional dollar of capital? An additional man-day of labor? An additional acre of land?
   (e) Demonstrate that the answers given for part (d) are correct assuming that the farmer wanted to plant 10 more acres of wheat.
   (f) What is the meaning of the value in the Z row and the X_3 column?
   (g) Demonstrate that the value mentioned in part (f) is correct by computing the cost of planting an acre of X_3 using the shadow prices shown in the optimal tableau.

8. For the optimal solution given in Problem 7, perform a sensitivity analysis on the right-hand-side values.

9. For the optimal solution given in Problem 7, perform a sensitivity analysis on the objective function coefficients.

10. For the optimal solution given in Problem 7, find the new optimal solution if the original labor availability was 8,100 man-days (i.e., what would be the new values for each of the basic variables if there were originally 8,100 man-days of labor available?).

11. For the optimal solution shown in Problem 7, find the new optimal solution if the original amount of capital available was $104,000.

13 MULTIPERIOD ANALYSIS UNDER CONDITIONS OF CERTAINTY

Throughout the first seven chapters of the book, several assumptions were made that are at variance from the practical problem setting faced by decision makers relative to capital investment decisions. Namely, it was assumed that capital investment projects were independent of each other and that the firm could obtain as much capital as is desired at the market rate of interest. These two assumptions, plus the assumption that conditions of certainty existed (the last of which was relaxed in Chapter 8), enabled the decision maker to consider each project individually to determine whether it should be accepted or rejected. However, when the former two assumptions are relaxed, a number of complexities arise in the decision setting. This chapter explores the important tools of mathematical programming that are available to financial managers as they endeavor to handle these new complexities.

HISTORICAL PERSPECTIVE

In 1955, Lorie and Savage[1] discussed the shortcomings of various methods of analysis, especially the internal-rate-of-return method, when capital was rationed. They presented examples demonstrating:

1. Problems that develop because multiple projects under consideration are not independent.

2. Problems that develop when capital is rationed in more than a single time period.

3. Problems that develop when analyzing projects that have both cash inflows and outflows dispersed over their lives.

They overcame problems 1 and 3 by utilizing the net present value approach rather than the internal rate of return. They *attempted* to overcome problem 2 by means of "generalized Lagrange multipliers." However, the

---

[1] J. H. Lorie and L. J. Savage, "Three Problems in Capital Rationing," *The Journal of Business*, October 1955, pp. 229–239.

breakdown of their approach opened the way for the subsequent research that applied mathematical programming to the capital rationing problem area.

Charnes, Cooper, and Miller,[2] and Weingartner,[3] were the pioneers who concentrated on Lorie and Savage's second problem of capital rationing and how to resolve it. These authors demonstrated that Lorie and Savage's generalized multipliers do not exist for all types of capital rationing problems, that an optimal solution is not guaranteed using the multipliers, and that the transformed problem using the approach may not be equivalent to the original problem. Charnes, Cooper, and Miller formulated a linear programming (LP) model to assist the firm in allocating funds among competing uses considering both operating decisions and financial planning. Weingartner's outstanding work formulates the capital rationing problem first as an LP then as an integer programming (IP) model. His work also provided valuable insights concerning the shadow prices and dual variables for the integer programming formulation.

Since these pioneering works, there have been many advances in the area of mathematical programming applied to the capital budgeting problem. The major extensions have either sought to integrate other financial decision areas with the capital budgeting decision, relaxed the single goal assumption of LP and IP, or have attempted to handle the capital rationing problem under conditions of risk. The focus of this chapter will be to survey the important areas of linear, integer, and goal programming as they apply to the capital rationing problem. Example problems will be formulated in the necessary framework and the optimal solutions interpreted for the reader.

MOTIVATION FOR THE USE OF MATHEMATICAL PROGRAMMING

As we have pointed out above, it can be demonstrated that (under the assumptions enumerated in Chapter 7) the selection of that set of projects which maximizes the net present value will simultaneously maximize shareholders' wealth or shareholders' utility. However, as argued in Chapter 7, when capital is rationed in one or more periods, no longer should we merely rank projects according to their net present values (or profitability indexes) and just continue to select them in order until the budget(s) are exhausted. This is true due to disparities in the original costs of projects under consideration, which may find that several projects with smaller original costs have a greater combined net present value than one larger project. Hence, what must be done is to find the combination of *projects that will maximize net present value while not violating any budget constraint.* As the number of projects and/or the number of years in the planning horizon increase, the number of feasible combinations of projects grows exponentially. Thus, it becomes advantageous to call upon a set

[2] A. Charnes, W. W. Cooper, and M. H. Miller, "An Application of Linear Programming to Financial Budgeting and the Cost of Funds," *The Journal of Business* (January 1959), pp. 20–46.
[3] H. Martin Weingartner, *Mathematical Programming and the Analysis of Capital Budgeting Problems* (Englewood Cliffs, N. J.: Prentice-Hall, Inc., 1963).

of models such as mathematical programming which does not require the explicit evaluation of each feasible combination and which can be solved within modest computer time and memory requirements (even for rather large problems). Mathematical programming models are powerful in that they are optimization techniques (i.e., they find the best possible solution to a given problem representation) and they can be used to accurately describe virtually any real-world problem setting. Numerous computerized solution algorithms are available through every computer manufacturer; thus, even small firms can afford to call upon mathematical programming techniques to facilitate the decision-making process in the capital budgeting area as well as other problem areas.

LINEAR PROGRAMMING REPRESENTATION

Based on the introduction to linear programming provided by Chapter 12, we can proceed directly to the formulation of the capital rationing problem using the LP model:

$$\text{Maximize NPV} = \sum_{j=1}^{N} b_j X_j \tag{1}$$

subject to

$$\sum_{j=1}^{N} C_{jt} X_j \leqslant K_t \qquad t = 1, 2, \ldots, T \tag{2}$$

$$0 \leqslant X_j \leqslant 1 \tag{3}$$

where X_j = percent of project j that is accepted
   b_j = net present value of project j over its useful life
   C_{jt} = cash outflow required by project j in year t
   K_t = budget availability in year t

The following aspects should be noted about the problem formulation above:
   1. The X_j decision variables are assumed to be continuous—that is, partial projects are allowed in the LP formulation.
   2. The usual nonnegativety constraint of LP is modified as shown in Equation (3) to also show an upper limit for each project—that is, it is required that each project have a maximum value of 1.00 or that it is accepted 100% (there is only one project of each type available).
   3. It is assumed that all the input parameters—b_j, C_{jt}, K_t—are known with certainty.
   4. The b_j parameter shows the net present value of project j over its useful life, where all cash flows are discounted at the cost of capital, which is known with certainty.
   To illustrate the general approach, consider the following classic example.

● **EXAMPLE 1** *Lorie–Savage Nine-Project Problem*

The following nine-project, two-period problem was originally considered by Lorie and Savage. Later, it was used by Weingartner to illustrate the use of LP to represent the capital rationing problem:

Project	NPV_j	C_{1j} = Cash Outflow in Period 1	C_{2j} = Cash Outflow in Period 2
1	$14	$12	$ 3
2	17	54	7
3	17	6	6
4	15	6	2
5	40	30	35
6	12	6	6
7	14	48	4
8	10	36	3
9	12	18	3

Budget available: $\Sigma C_{1j} X_j \leqslant \$50$; $\qquad \Sigma C_{2j} X_j \leqslant \$20$

Formulate this problem as an LP and solve it using a packaged solution algorithm.

Solution: The LP formulation is as follows:

$$\text{Maximize NPV} = 14X_1 + 17X_2 + 17X_3 + 15X_4 + 40X_5$$

$$+ 12X_6 + 14X_7 + 10X_8 + 12X_9$$

subject to

$$12X_1 + 54X_2 + 6X_3 + 6X_4 + 30X_5 + 6X_6 + 48X_7$$

$$+ 36X_8 + 18X_9 + S_1 = 50 \qquad \text{budget constraint year 1}$$

$$3X_1 + 7X_2 + 6X_3 + 2X_4 + 35X_5 + 6X_6 + 4X_7$$

$$+ 3X_8 + 3X_9 + S_2 = 20 \qquad \text{budget constraint year 2}$$

$$\left. \begin{array}{lll} X_1 + S_3 = 1 & X_4 + S_6 = 1 & X_7 + S_9 = 1 \\ X_2 + S_4 = 1 & X_5 + S_7 = 1 & X_8 + S_{10} = 1 \\ X_3 + S_5 = 1 & X_6 + S_8 = 1 & X_9 + S_{11} = 1 \end{array} \right\} \begin{array}{l} \text{upper limits on} \\ \text{project acceptance} \end{array}$$

$$X_j, S_i \geqslant 0 \qquad i = 1, 2, \ldots, 11; \qquad j = 1, 2, \ldots, 9 \qquad \text{nonnegativity constraint}$$

The following aspects should be pointed out concerning this formulation.

The general approach taken in this example is similar to that shown in Equations (1) through (3). However, "slack variables" have been added to each less-than constraint so that a fuller interpretation can be given to the optimal solution. Slack variables S_1 and S_2 represent, respectively, the number of budget dollars in years 1 and 2 that remain unallocated to any of the nine projects under evaluation. Slack variables S_3 through S_{11} represent the percent of projects 1 through 9, respectively, which are not accepted by the firm—the sum of X_j and its corresponding slack variable S_{j+2} must equal 1.00 or 100%, since the entire project must be either accepted or not accepted.

The optimal LP solution obtained from IBM's LINPROG package is shown on the facing page.

Interpreting the optimal solution, we see that the basic variables, that is, the variables that are equal to a positive value in the optimal solution, are X_1, X_3, X_4, X_6, X_7, X_9, S_4, S_7, S_8, S_9, S_{10}, which are equal to their corresponding values on the right-hand side of the optimal tableau (i.e., $X_1 = 1.0$, $X_3 = 1.0$, $X_4 = 1.0$, $X_6 = 0.969697$, etc.). Any of the variables in the problem that are not listed as basic variables are, in fact, nonbasic variables in the optimal solution, which means that they are equal to zero. Thus, $X_2 = X_5 = X_8 = 0$, which shows that these three projects should be completely rejected; in addition, $S_1 = S_2 = 0$, shows that the entire budget allotment of $50 in year 1 and $20 in year 2 has been spent on the six projects that have been designated for acceptance; further, $S_3 = S_5 = S_6 = S_{11} = 0$, since the projects corresponding to these slack variables (i.e., X_1, X_3, X_4, X_9) have been 100% accepted. To summarize, projects 1, 3, 4, and 9 have been fully accepted; 97% of project 6 is accepted; and only 4.5% of project 7 is accepted. These projects require the use of the entire budget in both years and generate the maximum objective function value of $70.273, which is the net present value of the accepted projects.   ●

Of course, it could be asked: Do the partial projects in our LP solution to Example 1 really make sense? The answer is, maybe. The LP solution above, which was arrived at using only tenths of a second of computer time, does provide considerable insight about the nine projects under evaluation. The fully accepted projects (1, 3, 4, and 9) are clearly very attractive to the firm. Project 6, which is recommended to be 97% accepted, should probably be accepted in total. Project 7 is rather marginal primarily because of its high cash outlay in period 1. The firm would probably reject project 7 or at least delay it until the following year; with the funds freed up in each of the 2 years, the firm would be able to fully accept project 6 with $2 of excess funds in year 1. Thus, partial projects do provide insight to the decision maker:

1. If the value of the decision variable equaled 0.80 or more, the firm would probably seek additional funds in order to be able to fully accept the project.

2. If the X_j is in the range 0.30 to 0.80, the firm may be able to find a partner to enter into the project with it as a joint venture.

3. If the X_j value is less than 0.30, the firm will probably want to reject the project or at least delay it for a year, when more information would be available about it as well as other new alternatives.

It should be mentioned that the LP formulation of the capital rationing problem above is significantly easier to solve than the integer programming formulation (which is discussed below), wherein no partial projects are allowed. Integer programming problems can take up to 100 times longer to solve on the computer than the equivalent LP formulation. Furthermore, Weingartner points out that the *number of partial projects accepted in an LP cannot exceed the number of years in which there is a budget constraint.* Thus, if a firm were evaluating 100 projects over a 3-year planning horizon using LP, it is assured that there will be no more than three projects that are accepted only partially. This fact, plus the much more rapid solution time, makes it definitely advantageous to utilize the LP formulation.

Optimal Tableau for LP Formulation of Lorie–Savage Nine-Project Problem

Basic Variables	X_1	X_2	X_3	X_4	X_5	X_6	X_7	X_8	X_9	S_1	S_2	S_3	S_4	S_5	S_6	S_7	S_8	S_9	S_{10}	S_{11}	RHS
X_1	1.0																				1.00
X_3			1.0																		1.00
X_4				1.0								1.0									1.00
X_6		0.455			5.91	1.0				-0.015	0.1818	-0.364		-1.0	-0.273					-0.273	0.969697
X_7		1.068			-0.114		1.0			+0.023	-0.023	-0.205			-0.091					-0.341	0.045455
X_9								0.75	1.0											1.0	1.00
S_4		1.0			1.0								1.0	1.0	1.0						1.00
S_7														1.0		1.0					1.00
S_8		-0.455			-5.91			-0.75		0.015	-0.1818	0.364			0.273		1.0			0.273	0.030303
S_9		-1.068			0.114					-0.023	0.023	0.205			0.091			1.0		0.341	0.954545
S_{10}								1.0											1.0		1.00
Z	0	3.41	0	0	29.32	0	0	0.50	0	0.1364	1.864	6.77	0	-5.0	10.45	0	0	0	0	-3.95	70.273

[handwritten marginal note: "w/ my tar / Opt. solution"]

239

OTHER CONSTRAINED RESOURCES

Example 1 included as "less than" constraints only the budget limitation in 2 years and the upper limit on the acceptance of any project. Linear programming models can incorporate numerous other constraints which show other constrained resources, legal requirements, managerial policies, and requirements imposed by the environment. Example 2 illustrates several of these constraints.

● EXAMPLE 2 Modified Lorie-Savage Problem

Consider a firm that is evaluating the same nine projects as in Example 1 but that there are limitations imposed on working-capital requirements for all projects ($25) over their useful lives, managerial supervision of the projects (120 hours), and a legal requirement for water purity control. (The firm feels that EPA will not bother it if it achieves at least 10 water purity control points in the projects it accepts.)

Project	NPV_j	$C_{1j} = $ Cash Outflow in Period 1	$C_{2j} = $ Cash Outflow in Period 2
1	$14	$12	$ 3
2	17	54	7
3	17	6	6
4	15	6	2
5	40	30	35
6	12	6	6
7	14	48	4
8	10	36	3
9	12	18	3
Budget available:		$\Sigma C_{1j}X_j \leqslant \$50;$	$\Sigma C_{2j}X_j \leqslant \$20$

$W_j = $ Working-Capital Requirement	$M_j = $ Managerial Supervision in Man-Hours	$P_j = $ Water Purity Control in Points
$ 5	20	1.2
11	80	6.3
7	18	2.7
4	14	2.2
8	88	8.8
5	16	2.0
12	74	5.7
9	60	5.9
6	28	3.2

Other constraints: $\Sigma X_j W_j \leqslant \$25;$ $\Sigma X_j M_j \leqslant 120;$ $\Sigma X_j P_j \geqslant 10$

Formulate and solve this problem as an LP and interpret the optimal solution.

Solution: The formulation is as follows:

$$\text{Maximize} \quad \text{NPV} = 14X_1 + 17X_2 + 17X_3 + 15X_4 + 40X_5 + 12X_6$$
$$+ 14X_7 + 10X_8 + 12X_9$$

subject to

$$12X_1 + 54X_2 + 6X_3 + 6X_4 + 30X_5 + 6X_6$$
$$+ 48X_7 + 36X_8 + 18X_9 + S_1 = 50 \qquad \text{Budget year 1}$$

$$3X_1 + 7X_2 + 6X_3 + 2X_4 + 35X_5 + 6X_6$$
$$+ 4X_7 + 3X_8 + 3X_9 + S_2 = 20 \qquad \text{Budget year 2}$$

$$
\left.
\begin{array}{lll}
X_1 + S_3 = 1 & X_4 + S_6 = 1 & X_7 + S_9 = 1 \\
X_2 + S_4 = 1 & X_5 + S_7 = 1 & X_8 + S_{10} = 1 \\
X_3 + S_5 = 1 & X_6 + S_8 = 1 & X_9 + S_{11} = 1
\end{array}
\right\}
\begin{array}{l}
\text{Upper limits} \\
\text{on project} \\
\text{acceptance}
\end{array}
$$

$$5X_1 + 11X_2 + 7X_3 + 4X_4 + 8X_5 + 5X_6$$
$$+ 12X_7 + 9X_8 + 6X_9 + S_{12} = 25 \qquad \text{Working capital}$$

$$20X_1 + 80X_2 + 18X_3 + 14X_4 + 88X_5 + 16X_6$$
$$+ 74X_7 + 60X_8 + 28X_9 + S_{13} = 120 \qquad \text{Management supervision}$$

$$1.2X_1 + 6.3X_2 + 2.7X_3 + 2.2X_4 + 8.8X_5 + 2.0X_6$$
$$+ 5.7X_7 + 5.9X_8 + 3.2X_9 - \boxed{R_1} = 10 \qquad \text{Water purity control}$$

$$X_j, S_i, R_1 \geqslant 0 \qquad j = 1, \ldots, 9; \, i = 1, 2, \ldots, 13$$

Surplus variable

Notice that this formulation is exactly the same as the formulation in Example 1 except for the last three constraints, which show the new limited resources (working capital and management supervision) and a restriction imposed by legal authorities outside the firm (water pollution control). The new slack variables S_{12} and S_{13} show, respectively, the number of unused working capital dollars of the 25 originally available and the number of unallocated hours of management supervision among the 120 hours originally available. There is another new variable (R_1) in the last constraint, which is a "surplus variable," showing the number of water purity control points that accepted projects score above the minimum level of 10 specified by management. The optimal solution to this formulation is shown on the next page.

The optimal solution shows a number of changes resulting from the additional constraints. As can be noticed from the tableau, projects 1, 3, 4, and 9 are still fully accepted. The two partial projects in this example are projects 5 and 6, which are accepted 9.45% and 44.88%, respectively. There are excess budget dollars in year 1 (slack variable S_1) in the amount of \$2.472, as well as excess hours of management supervision (slack variable S_{13}) in the amount of 24.5 hours. The accepted projects used the entire budget in year 2 and the entire working capital availability (slack variables S_2 and S_{12} are not among the basic variables and hence are equal to zero), while they generated an excess number of water purity points (1.029) over the minimum level of 10 as shown by the surplus variable R_1 being basic in the optimal solution. The new value of the objective function is \$67.165, which is down from \$70.273 in Example 1 because the current problem has additional constraints that must be met. ●

Optimal Solution to Modified Lorie–Savage Nine-Project Problem

Basic Variables	X_1	X_2	X_3	X_4	X_5	X_6	X_7	X_8	X_9	S_1	S_2	S_3	S_4	S_5	S_6	S_7	S_8	S_9	S_{10}	S_{11}	S_{12}	S_{13}	R_1	RHS
X_1	1.0																							1.00
X_3			1.0																					1.00
X_4				1.0																				1.00
X_5		-0.244			1.0		-0.409	-0.307			0.0394	0.118		0.0945	0.110					0.165	-0.0472			0.094488
X_6		2.59				1.0	3.055	2.291			-0.063	-1.19		-1.55	-0.976					-1.46	0.276			0.448819
X_9									1.0											1.0				1.00
S_1		45.78					41.95	31.46		1.0	-0.803	-8.41		0.472	-3.45					-14.17	-0.236			2.472441
S_4													1.0											1.00
S_7		0.244					0.409	0.307			-0.039	-0.118		-0.0945	-0.110	1.0				-0.165	0.047			0.905512
S_8		-2.59					-3.055	-2.29			0.063	1.189		1.55	0.976		1.0			1.46	-0.276			0.551181
S_9							1.0											1.0						1.00
S_{10}								1.0											1.0					1.00
S_{13}		63.03					61.15	50.36			-2.46	-11.37		-1.496	-8.08					-19.12	-0.252	1.0		24.50394
R_1		-3.27					-3.19	-4.02			0.220	-0.139		0.429	1.22					1.73	0.135		1.0	1.029134
Z		4.323					6.283	5.213			0.819	4.46		2.165	7.693					1.039	1.417			67.165

242

SHADOW PRICES AND SENSITIVITY ANALYSIS

As pointed out in Chapter 12, sensitivity analysis is a critically important aspect of problem solving using mathematical programming models. Recall that *sensitivity analysis allows an interpretation of the shadow prices associated with each constraint equation, as well as determining the range of possible values that each of the model's input parameters could take on without changing the basic variables in the optimal solution to the problem.* Sensitivity analysis is important from the viewpoint of marginal analysis. Furthermore, it provides valuable insight to the decision maker concerning the impact that LP's assumption that each input parameter is known precisely and with certainty has on the flexibility of the optimal solution. Of course, precious few factors in the capital budgeting problem setting are known precisely and with certainty. Hence, the decision maker should be aware of how sensitive the optimal solution is to changes in each of the input parameters (i.e., objective function coefficients, right-hand-side values for the constraints, and coefficients of each decision variable in the constraints). The more critical parameters should receive more attention from management to make sure that control measures keep these parameters within acceptable limits.

In the LP formulation of the capital budgeting problem, *there are shadow prices associated with both accepted and rejected projects. These values enable the decision maker to rank all projects according to their relative attractiveness.* For accepted projects, the shadow prices are found under the slack variables (S_k) for the following constraints:

$$X_j + S_k = 1$$

The shadow prices are computed using the following expression:

$$\gamma_j = b_j - \sum_{t=1}^{T} \rho_t^* C_{jt} \tag{4}$$

where γ_j = shadow price associated with accepted project j (shown under the slack variable associated with project j)

b_j = net present value for project j shown in the objective function

ρ_t^* = shadow price in the optimal solution associated with each resource t which is required to accept a project (shown under the slack variable associated with the corresponding resource)

C_{jt} = quantity of resource of type t required by project j

The shadow prices γ_j may very well give a ranking for the projects which differs from that given by any of the simple models as payback, NPV, IRR, or the profitability index. Such differences in ranking will exist because the latter models look at the projects independently, whereas *the shadow prices show interrelationships among projects by means of the budget constraints; they evaluate the projects at the cost of capital (ρ_t^*) that is implied by the optimal use of resources of type t.*

In addition to the shadow prices for accepted projects discussed above, the rejected projects have shadow prices that are computed in an analogous way:

$$\mu_j = \sum_{t=1}^{T} \rho_t^* C_{jt} - b_j \tag{5}$$

where μ_j is the shadow price associated with rejected project j (shown in the objective function row in the column for X_j). *The μ_j value shows the amount by which the objective function would decrease if the firm were forced to accept the unattractive project j.* If such projects were accepted, this would mean that the scarce capital budget dollars would be used in a suboptimal way, since the opportunity cost associated with the cash outflows ($\Sigma \rho_t^* C_{jt}$) exceeds the present value of the benefits generated by the project. It should be mentioned that the μj values must be zero *for all projects that are accepted (including partially accepted projects) because the benefits of these projects must justify the cash outlays in the various periods of the planning horizon (C_{jt}) when they are evaluated at the implied cost of capital (ρ_t^*) when the budgets each year are used in an optimal way.*

The next example illustrates the computation of these shadow prices and explains their significance.

● **EXAMPLE 3** *Interpretation of Shadow Prices*

For Example 2, interpret all shadow prices.

Solution: Let's start with the shadow prices for the slack and surplus variables S_1, S_2, S_{12}, S_{13}, and R_1, which are the slack and surplus variables associated with the resources that were originally available for our capital investment program—namely, the budget for years 1 and 2 (S_1 and S_2), working-capital funds (S_{12}), managerial supervision (S_{13}), and minimum requirement for water purity control (R_1). As the reader will notice, slack variables S_1, S_{13}, and surplus variable R_1 are basic variables in the optimal solution, since there are \$2.472 of the first year's capital budget (S_1) still remaining, 24.5 hours of management supervision time (S_{13}) available, and the desired level of 10 water purity control points established by management has been exceeded by 1.029 points (R_1). Hence, the shadow prices for all of these variables are zero, since the firm would be unwilling to purchase any additional units of these resources (first year's capital budget or hours for supervision of projects by management) or to pay anything to reduce the original 10-unit lower limit for the desired level of water purity control points of accepted projects. If any of these corresponding right-hand-side values were changed (resources increased or minimum requirements decreased), the objective function would not increase, since the other constraints are binding on the optimal solution. They are the ones that would have to be altered. Since the objective function would not increase, the firm would not be willing to pay anything for any of these changes because the end result would only be that more of these resources would be left over in the optimal solution. On the other hand, variables S_2 and S_{12} are nonbasic variables in the optimal solution, which means that their corresponding resources (budget dollars in year 2 and working capital funds, respectively) are completely exhausted in the optimal solution. The shadow price for S_2 is 0.819, which means that we would be willing to pay up to a maximum of 81.9% interest on new capital that we could raise in year 2 (a somewhat significant cost of capital) because the objective function would increase by this amount (0.819) for each dollar of additional budget that we could obtain. Naturally, we would not borrow unlimited amounts at 81.9%, but rather would limit the amount to a sum consistent with the other constraints within the problem. The exact amount is determined by the Δ^+ and Δ^- values. We now demonstrate that the 81.9% is correct. The two projects that would be affected are partial projects X_5 and X_6; if we had additional funds in year 2, we could purchase additional portions of one or both of these projects. Currently, the contribution of these two projects to the objective function is the percent accepted of each multiplied by the objective function coefficients for the respective project:

	% Accepted		NPV Objective Function Coefficient		Contribution to Value of Objective Function
Project 5	(0.094488)	×	$40	=	$3.77952
Project 6	(0.448819)	×	$12	=	5.385828
					$9.165348

Consider now that we could obtain $2 of additional budget in year 2. The way that we determine the impact that this would have on each basic variable in the optimal solution is by looking up the column for S_2 in the optimal tableau. Notice that the coefficients in the row for X_5 and X_6 are 0.0394 and -0.063, respectively. This means that additional dollars in year 2 would *increase the percentage purchased of project 5* (by 3.94% for each dollar) and *decrease the percentage of project 6 purchased* (by 6.3% for each dollar). Thus, the new percentage of each project accepted if we had $2 additional in year 2 would be:

	Current Percent Accepted		Change per Dollar		Change in Dollars		New Percent Accepted		NPV Objective Function Coefficient		Contribution to Value of Objective Function
Project 5	0.094488	+	(0.0394)	×	(+$2)	=	0.173288	×	$40	=	$ 6.93152
Project 6	0.448819	+	(−0.063)	×	(+$2)	=	0.322819	×	12	=	3.873828
											$10.805348

Less current contribution to value of objective function	9.165348
Increase in value of objective function	$ 1.640000
Divided by change in $ in year 2	÷ 2
Increase in objective function value per dollar change	= $0.82 ≈ $0.819 shadow price

In a similar fashion we can demonstrate that the shadow price for additional working capital dollars of $1.417 means that the objective function would increase by this amount for each dollar of such funds that could be raised over the original amount of $25. *Shadow prices are valid only within given ranges of change for each original resource*, as demonstrated in the next example.

As was pointed out above, each rejected project also has a shadow price which can be interpreted and verified. The shadow prices under X_2, X_7, and X_8 (the three rejected projects) show the amount by which the objective function would decrease if we were forced to accept one of these three projects. Thus, these values give a ranking of the rejected projects; the smaller the shadow price, the less objectionable it would be to be forced to accept the project.

	Shadow
Project	Price
2	$4.323
8	$5.213
7	$6.283

Using Equation (5), we can show how each of these shadow prices was determined. The shadow price for project 8 is verified as follows:

$$\mu_8 = \sum_{t=1}^{T} \rho_t^* C_{8t} - b_8$$

$$= \underbrace{(0)(36)}_{\text{budget 1}} + \underbrace{(0.819)(3)}_{\text{budget 2}} + \underbrace{(1.417)(9)}_{\substack{\text{working} \\ \text{capital}}} + \underbrace{(0)(60)}_{\substack{\text{management} \\ \text{supervision}}} + \underbrace{(0)(5.9)}_{\substack{\text{water purity} \\ \text{control}}} - \underset{b_8}{10}$$

$$= 0 + 2.457 + 12.753 + 0 + 0 - 10 = \$5.21$$

Similarly, using expression (4), we can verify any or all of the following shadow prices, which show the rank order of accepted projects:

$$\gamma_4 = 7.693$$
$$\gamma_1 = 4.46$$
$$\gamma_3 = 2.165$$
$$\gamma_9 = 1.039$$
$$\left. \begin{array}{l} \gamma_5 = 0 \\ \gamma_6 = 0 \end{array} \right\} \text{ partially accepted—marginal projects}$$

The shadow price for project 1 is verified as follows:

$$\gamma_1 = b_1 - \sum_{t=1}^{T} \rho_t^* C_{1t}$$

$$= 14 - [\underbrace{(0)(12)}_{\text{budget 1}} + \underbrace{(0.819)(3)}_{\text{budget 2}} + \underbrace{(1.417)(5)}_{\substack{\text{working} \\ \text{capital}}} + \underbrace{(0)(20)}_{\substack{\text{management} \\ \text{supervision}}} + \underbrace{(0)(1.2)]}_{\substack{\text{water purity} \\ \text{control}}}$$

$$= 14 - (2.457 + 7.085) = 4.458 \qquad \bullet$$

The shadow prices determined from the optimal solution are valid only within a given relevant range that each of the input parameters can take on. This area was discussed in Chapter 12, wherein we computed Δ^+ and Δ^- for each original right-hand-side value and each objective function coefficient. For instance, in Example 3 it was mentioned that the shadow price for budget dollars in year 2 was 0.819 or that we would be willing to pay a rate of interest of 81.9% to obtain additional budget dollars in year 2. However, we would not be willing to pay this rate indefinitely. In fact, we would only be willing to pay such a high rate until:

1. One of the other resources still available (i.e., budget dollars in year 1, or managerial supervision time) became exhausted because of the acquisition of an additional portion of a partial project enabled by the new budget dollars obtained for year 2.

2. A partially accepted project became completely accepted through the new budget dollars obtained for year 2.

3. A partially accepted project became completely rejected since funds were removed from it as new budget dollars were obtained for year 2.

Notice that the occurrence of any of these conditions would change the basis of the optimal solution or make it infeasible. Thus, the values of Δ^+ and Δ^- for each input parameter will be the smallest of 1, 2, or 3. Sensitivity analysis is now completed in Example 4 by means of the computation of all Δ^+ and Δ^- values.

● **EXAMPLE 4** *Sensitivity Analysis*

Compute and interpret all Δ^+ and Δ^- values for the optimal solution shown in Example 2.

Solution: Start with the right-hand-side values. Again, we notice that slack variables S_1 and S_{13}, as well as surplus variable R_1, are basic variables in the optimal solution. Hence, using the approach shown in Chapter 12, we would find that

$$\Delta_{S_1}^+ = \infty \qquad \Delta_{S_{13}}^+ = \infty \qquad \Delta_{R_1}^+ = 1.029$$
$$\Delta_{S_1}^- = 2.472 \qquad \Delta_{S_{13}}^- = 24.504 \qquad \Delta_{R_1}^- = \infty$$

The values above imply that we would have the same basis in the optimal solution (i.e., the same set of optimal projects will be accepted and the same resources will still be available) as long as each of the following resources takes on values within the respective ranges:

$$\text{Budget in year 1} \begin{cases} \text{upper limit} = \infty = 50 + \infty \\ \text{lower limit} = \$47.528 = 50 - 2.472 \end{cases}$$

$$\text{Management supervision} \begin{cases} \text{upper limit} = \infty = 120 + \infty \\ \text{lower limit} = 95.496 \text{ hr} = 120 - 24.504 \end{cases}$$

$$\text{Water purity control} \begin{cases} \text{upper limit} = 11.029 = 10 + 1.029 \\ \text{lower limit} = -\infty = 10 - \infty \end{cases}$$

The other two slack variables of interest are the nonbasic variables associated with the budget dollars in year 2 (S_2) and working capital (S_{12}). Using the approach shown in Chapter 12 to compute Δ^+ and Δ^- for nonbasic variables:

$$\Delta^+ = \min \left| \frac{b_i}{a_{ij} < 0} \right| \qquad \Delta^- = \min \left\{ \frac{b_i}{a_{ij} > 0} \right\}$$

we would find

$$\Delta_{S_2}^+ = \min\left\{\left|\frac{0.44819}{-0.063}\right|, \left|\frac{2.472441}{-0.803}\right|, \left|\frac{0.905512}{-0.039}\right|, \left|\frac{24.50394}{-2.46}\right|\right\}$$
$$= \min\{7.114, 3.079, 23.218, 9.96\}$$
$$= \underline{\underline{3.079}}$$

$$\Delta_{S_2}^- = \min\left\{\frac{0.094488}{0.0394}, \frac{0.551181}{0.063}, \frac{1.029134}{0.220}\right\}$$
$$= \min\{2.398, 8.749, 4.678\}$$
$$= \underline{\underline{2.398}}$$

$$\Delta_{S_{12}}^+ = \min\left\{\left|\frac{0.094488}{-0.0472}\right|, \left|\frac{2.472441}{-0.236}\right|, \left|\frac{0.551181}{-0.276}\right|, \left|\frac{24.50394}{-0.252}\right|\right\}$$
$$= \underline{\underline{1.997}}$$

$$\Delta_{S_{12}}^- = \min\left\{\frac{0.448819}{0.276}, \frac{0.905512}{0.047}, \frac{1.029134}{0.135}\right\}$$
$$= \underline{\underline{1.626}}$$

Thus, the ranges wherein the optimal basis will remain unchanged are:

$$\text{Budget in}\begin{cases} \text{upper limit} = \$23.079 = \$20 + 3.079 \\ \text{lower limit} = \$17.602 = \$20 - 2.398 \end{cases}$$
$$\text{year 2}$$

$$\text{Working}\begin{cases} \text{upper limit} = \$26.997 = \$25 + 1.997 \\ \text{lower limit} = \$23.374 = \$25 - 1.626 \end{cases}$$
$$\text{capital}$$

Again, the ranges above show the possible changes wherein the shadow prices would remain valid. For example, we would only be willing to pay the interest cost of 81.9% for additional budget dollars in year 2 until we acquired $3.079. Beyond that level the problem would have to be completely re-solved, because we would get a new optimal set of projects. A similar interpretation can be put on each of the other shadow prices and ranges.

Finally, we will compute Δ^+ and Δ^- for each of the objective function coefficients (i.e., for the nine projects under consideration). For the rejected projects (i.e., nonbasic variables in the optimal solution), the determination is immediate:

$$\Delta_{X_2}^+ = 4.323 \quad \Delta_{X_7}^+ = 6.283 \quad \Delta_{X_8}^+ = 5.213$$
$$\Delta_{X_2}^- = \infty \quad \Delta_{X_7}^- = \infty \quad \Delta_{X_8}^- = \infty$$

These values show that if the objective function coefficient for any rejected project were reduced by any amount, the project would still be rejected. Further, the objective function coefficients would have to be increased by the amount of their shadow prices to make the rejected projects start to become attractive.

For any of the completely accepted projects (i.e., $X_j = 1.00$), the computations for Δ^+ and Δ^- are again straightforward:

	X_1	X_3	X_4	X_9
$\Delta_{X_j}^+$	∞	∞	∞	∞
$\Delta_{X_j}^-$	4.46	2.165	7.693	1.039

This table shows that the objective function coefficient for any completely accepted project j could be increased by any amount or decreased up to the value of the shadow price γ_j and the project would still be attractive enough to accept.

The partially accepted projects require computations covered in Chapter 12 to arrive at Δ^+ and Δ^-:

$$\Delta^+ = \min \left| \frac{C_j}{a_{ij} < 0} \right|$$

$$\Delta^- = \min \left\{ \frac{C_j}{a_{ij} > 0} \right\}$$

$$\Delta_{X_5}^+ = \min \left\{ \left| \frac{4.323}{-0.244} \right|, \left| \frac{6.283}{-0.409} \right|, \left| \frac{5.213}{-0.307} \right|, \left| \frac{1.417}{-0.0472} \right| \right\}$$

$$= \min\{17.717, 15.362, 16.980, 30.02\}$$

$$= \underline{\underline{15.362}}$$

$$\Delta_{X_5}^- = \min \left\{ \frac{0.819}{0.0394}, \frac{4.46}{0.118}, \frac{2.165}{0.0945}, \frac{7.693}{0.110}, \frac{1.039}{0.165} \right\}$$

$$= \min\{20.787, 37.797, 22.91, 69.936, 6.297\}$$

$$= \underline{\underline{6.297}}$$

$$\Delta_{X_6}^+ = \min \left\{ \left| \frac{0.819}{-0.063} \right|, \left| \frac{4.46}{-1.19} \right|, \left| \frac{2.165}{-1.55} \right|, \left| \frac{7.693}{-0.976} \right|, \left| \frac{1.039}{-1.46} \right| \right\}$$

$$= \min\{13.000, 3.748, 1.397, 7.882, 0.712\}$$

$$= \underline{\underline{0.712}}$$

$$\Delta_{X_6}^- = \min \left\{ \frac{4.323}{2.59}, \frac{6.283}{3.055}, \frac{5.213}{2.291}, \frac{1.417}{0.276} \right\}$$

$$= \min\{1.669, 2.057, 2.275, 5.134\}$$

$$= \underline{\underline{1.669}}$$

Management can now see how sensitive the acceptance of each project is to its objective function coefficient. As can be seen, projects 3, 6, and 9 are rather sensitive to downside changes in their objective function coefficients. Management may very well take a close look at the estimates for cash flows associated with these projects to make sure they are realistic in that minor changes could make these projects unattractive. ●

In concluding this section on sensitivity analysis, it should be stressed that the Δ^+ and Δ^- values for the objective function coefficients are critically important in that these coefficients may have significant biases because of the assumptions of LP and the capital budgeting problem setting. That is, the objective function coefficients are arrived at by discounting both cash inflows and outflows that are assumed to be known with certainty where the discounting is done at a rate that is assumed to be known with certainty. Thus, even small percentage changes in these inputs can cause large changes in the objective function coefficients, which could easily throw them outside the range wherein the optimal set of projects would remain unaffected. These facts have noteworthy managerial implications for accuracy in forecasting cash flows, accuracy in estimating future costs of capital, optimal project selection, and managerial control activities.

THE DUAL LP FORMULATION FOR THE
CAPITAL BUDGETING PROBLEM

As discussed in Chapter 12, the dual linear programming formulation has important implications for the financial manager. Namely, the dual formulation and its optimal solution provide valuable information for both planning and control functions in the capital budgeting decision process; the solution contributes to both coordination of activities and motivation of decision makers in decentralized organizations.

The dual formulation of the capital budgeting problem is constructed in the same manner, as discussed in Chapter 12. That is, there will be a dual decision variable associated with each constraint in the primal problem and there will be a constraint equation associated with each project in the primal problem. Further, these dual variables will be found in exactly the way that the shadow prices in the primal problem were computed (as illustrated in the previous section).

The general dual formulation that corresponds to the primal formulation in Equations (1), (2), and (3) is:

$$\text{Minimize} \quad \sum_{t=1}^{T} \rho_t K_t + \sum_{j=1}^{N} \gamma_j \tag{6}$$

subject to

$$\sum_{t=1}^{T} \rho_t C_{jt} + \mu_j \geqslant b_j \qquad j = 1, 2, \ldots, N \tag{7}$$

$$\rho_t, \mu_j \geqslant 0 \qquad t = 1, 2, \ldots, T; \qquad j = 1, 2, \ldots, N \tag{8}$$

where ρ_t = dual decision variable which represents the cost associated with each resource of type t

γ_j = dual decision variable associated with project j which shows the excess of its net present value (b_j) over its required use of resources (C_{jt}) when the latter are "costed out" at the appropriate rate ρ_t for each resource t

It should be noted that constraint equation (7) was used in rearranged fashion to compute the values of the shadow prices γ_j and μ_j in the optimal primal solution as shown by Equations (4) and (5). Of course, this is another illustration of our discussion in Chapter 12 concerning the close relationship between the primal and dual LP problems and their optimal solutions.

It is only necessary to solve *either* the primal or the dual problem because the optimal solution for either contains all the information that is in the other. The only difference is the economic interpretation that is given the optimal values of the variables. The correspondence is interesting and helpful in arriving at a complete interpretation and can lend assistance in solving problems more efficiently.

PROGRAMMING AND THE COST OF CAPITAL: A CONTROVERSY

Look we

Before we leave the area of linear programming to look at two interesting and powerful extensions (integer programming and goal programming), a noteworthy controversy relative to the appropriate LP formulation should be mentioned. Weingartner's[4] pioneering work, which saw him formulate the primal and the dual LP capital budgeting problem along the lines that we have illustrated above, was not without its detractors. Baumol and Quandt[5] contend that the primal problem as formulated by Weingartner runs afoul due to the "Hirschleifer paradox."[6] A simple statement of the paradox is: under capital rationing, *the appropriate discount* rate to use in determining the net present values of projects under consideration cannot be determined until the optimal set of projects is determined, so that the size of the capital budget is ascertained as well as the sources of the subsequent financing and hence the cost of capital (or the appropriate discount rate to use in calculating NPVs). However, the authors of the text contend that this is *not* a paradox at all, but rather a simultaneous problem wherein the firm should concurrently determine through an iterative mathematical programming process *both the optimal set of capital projects and the optimal financing package, with its associated marginal cost of capital to be used in the discounting process.*

Nevertheless, Baumol and Quandt suggest a formulation that maximizes the utility of the dollars withdrawn from the firm by the owners for their consumption over the planning horizon. Weingartner[7] counters that this is not an operational approach; it assumes that all shareholders have the same linear utility preferences for consumption, it requires the assignment of utility values in advance of information about withdrawal possibilities, and it makes the period-by-period utilities independent of one another. He then proposes a more operational model, which maximizes the dividends to be paid in a terminal year, where throughout the planning horizon dividends are nondecreasing and can be required to achieve a specified annual growth rate. Over the past decade, several other authors have jumped into the controversy, each suggesting his own reformulation. The interested reader should consult the appropriate references in Appendix A.

We now turn to the area of integer linear programming, wherein one of the LP assumptions—that decision variables can take on any value (i.e., that partial projects can be accepted in the capital budgeting problem setting)—is relaxed.

---

[4]Weingartner, *Mathematical Programming.*

[5]W. J. Baumol and R. E. Quandt, "Investment and Discount Rates Under Capital Rationing—A Programming Approach," *The Economic Journal*, June 1965, pp. 317–329.

[6]J. Hirshleifer, "On the Theory of Optimal Investment Decisions," *The Journal of Political Economy*, August 1958, pp. 329–352.

[7]H. Martin Weingartner, "Criteria for Programming Investment Project Selection," *Journal of Industrial Economics*, November 1966, pp. 65–76.

INTEGER PROGRAMMING APPLIED TO THE CAPITAL BUDGETING PROBLEM

In his pioneering work, Weingartner also suggested an integer programming approach to the capital budgeting problem in addition to the LP models discussed above. The main motivations for the use of integer programming (ILP) in the capital budgeting setting are as follows:

1. Difficulties imposed by the acceptance of partial projects in LP are eliminated, since ILP requires that projects either be completely accepted or rejected.

2. All the project interdependencies discussed in Chapter 7 can be formally included in the constraints of the ILP, while the same is not true for LP due to the possibility of accepting partial projects.

The general ILP formulation for the capital budgeting problem is shown in Equations (9) through (11):

$$\text{Maximize NPV} = \sum_{j=1}^{N} b_j X_j \tag{9}$$

subject to

$$\sum_{j=1}^{N} C_{jt} X_j \leqslant K_t \quad t = 1, 2, \ldots, T \tag{10}$$

$$X_j = \{0, 1\} \quad j = 1, 2, \ldots, N \tag{11}$$

Notice that the only change in the formulation above compared to the primal LP formulation shown in Equations (1), (2), and (3) on page 236 is that Equation (11) replaces Equation (3). Equation (11), which is the zero–one condition of ILP, guarantees that each project is either completely accepted ($X_j = 1$) or that it is rejected ($X_j = 0$).

The second attractive feature of ILP mentioned above deserves elaboration. In using the simple capital budgeting models (NPV, IRR, PI, etc.), it is assumed that all the investment projects are independent of each other (i.e., that project cash flows are not related to each other and do not influence or change one another if various projects are accepted). In using ILP, virtually any project dependencies can be incorporated on the model by means of the special constraints discussed below. The three types of project dependencies defined in Chapter 7—mutually exclusive, prerequisite, and complementary projects—can be handled in a straightforward manner. Each will be discussed in turn.

Recall that *mutually exclusive* projects are defined as a set of projects wherein the acceptance of one project in the set precludes the simultaneous acceptance of any other project in the set. The existence of such a set of projects is incorporated in an ILP model by the following constraint:

$$\sum_{j \in J} X_j \leqslant 1 \tag{12}$$

where J = set of mutually exclusive projects under consideration

$j \in J$ = that project j is an element of the set of mutually exclusive projects J

Note that the constraint states that *at most* one project from set J can be accepted; this means that the firm could choose not to accept any project from set *J*. On the other hand, if it was necessary to select one project from the set, constraint (12) would appear as a strict equality:

$$\sum_{j \in J} X_j = 1 \tag{13}$$

Another important application of this constraint is the situation wherein a firm is considering the possibility of delaying a project for one or more years. For example, consider project *X*, which has the following characteristics:

Time	Cash Flows Project X
0	−$100
1	+ 75
2	+ 75
3	+ 75

The NPV of this project at 10% is $86.53. If the firm wants to determine whether it would be desirable to delay project *X* either 1 or 2 years, the following two new projects, *X'* and *X''*, respectively, can be defined:

Time	Cash Flows Project X'	Project X''
0	$ 0	$ 0
1	− 100	0
2	+ 75	− 100
3	+ 75	+ 75
4	+ 75	+ 75
5		+ 75

The NPVs (with a cost of capital of 10%) that would be included in the objective function for project *X'* and *X''*, respectively, are $78.66 and $71.47. These values differ from the NPV of project *X* because of the 1- and 2-year delays, respectively, in the cash flows, which necessitate multiplying project *X*'s NPV by 1/1.10 to arrive at the NPV for *X'* and by $1/(1.10)^2$ to arrive at the NPV for *X''*. Of course, the $100 cash outflow would be shown in the budget constraint for year 0 for project *X*, year 1 for project *X'*, and year 2 for project *X''*. Finally, to show that at most one of these three versions of project *X* could be accepted, the following constraint would be included in the ILP formulation:

$$X + X' + X'' \leqslant 1$$

Prerequisite (or contingent) projects are two or more projects wherein the acceptance of one project necessitates the prior acceptance of some other project(s). For example, if project *A* cannot be accepted unless project *Z* is accepted, we would say that project *Z* is a prerequisite project for acceptance of project *A*; alternatively, we could also say that acceptance of project *A* is contingent upon the acceptance of project *Z*. Again, the representation of the above project interrelationships in ILP is immediate:

$$X_A \leqslant X_Z \tag{14}$$

where X_A and X_Z are decision variables denoting projects A and Z. Note in Equation (14) that if project A is accepted (i.e., $X_A = 1$), then necessarily, project Z must be accepted also. However, project Z can be accepted on its own and project A rejected. Of course, there are many possible variations to constraints (12), (13), and (14), as shown in Example 5.

● **EXAMPLE 5**   *Project Interrelationship Constraints in ILP*

Formulate the appropriate ILP constraints for each of the following cases:

(a) Two projects (6 and 8) are mutually exclusive and a third project (16) is contingent upon the acceptance of *either* project 6 or 8.

(b) Project 10 cannot be accepted unless both project 7 and project 9 are accepted.

(c) In the set of projects 1, 2, 3, 4, and 5, at most three can be accepted; furthermore, for project 11 to be accepted, at least two projects from the set above must be accepted, and for project 14 to be accepted, three projects from the set above must be undertaken.

Solution:

(a) Two constraints are required to capture the conditions specified; one for the mutually exclusive relationship between projects 6 and 8 and the second for the contingency relationship between 16 and the two projects above:

$$X_6 + X_8 \leqslant 1$$
$$X_{16} \leqslant X_6 + X_8$$

(b) Only one constraint similar to Equation (14) is required to express this contingency:

$$2X_{10} \leqslant X_7 + X_9$$

We see that the only way project 10 can be accepted is for the constraint above to hold as an equality, which means that both sides will equal 2, which necessitates the acceptance of both $X_7 + X_9$.

(c) Three constraints are necessary to relate these conditions: one for the acceptance of at most three projects from the first set, and one each for the contingency between projects 11 and 14 and the first set:

$$X_1 + X_2 + X_3 + X_4 + X_5 \leqslant 3$$
$$2X_{11} \leqslant X_1 + X_2 + X_3 + X_4 + X_5$$
$$3X_{14} \leqslant X_1 + X_2 + X_3 + X_4 + X_5$$ ●

The final type of project interrelationship is that of *complementary projects* wherein the acceptance of one project enhances the cash flows of one or more other projects. This synergistic effect is reflected in an ILP formulation by using the strategy outlined below.

Consider that we have two complementary projects, 7 and 8. Either of these projects can be accepted in isolation. However, if both are accepted simultaneously:

1. The cost will be reduced by say 10%.

2. The net cash inflow will be increased by, say, 15%. To handle the problem, a new project (call it 78) would be constructed having a cost equal to 90% of the cost of project 7 plus project 8 and net cash inflows equal to 115% of those of project 7 plus project 8. In addition, we would need the following constraint to preclude acceptance of both projects 7 and 8 as well as 78, because the latter is the composite project consisting of the two former projects:

$$X_7 + X_8 + X_{78} \leqslant 1$$

Before this section is concluded with a comprehensive example illustrating the formulation of an ILP model for the capital budgeting problem, two significant shortcomings of the ILP methodology should be discussed.

Clearly, the ability to include the various types of constraints for project interrelationships adds to the realism of the problem representation using ILP as compared to LP (which encounters difficulty handling such constraints). Furthermore, the existence of partial projects in the optimal LP solution raises questions about how realistic the problem representation is. However, the question arises whether the price that has to be paid in moving to ILP is worth the benefits gained, considering the difference in solution time and the lack of meaningful shadow prices in ILP compared to LP.

As mentioned earlier, the seemingly innocent change in the ILP formulation has a significant impact on the time it takes to solve the problem. For example, Pettway[8] reported in his 1972 study on an ILP formulation which had 15 budget constraints and 28 projects that four of the six solution algorithms he tested failed to arrive at the optimal solution in 5 minutes of CPU time on an IBM 360-65; the two algorithms that did locate the optimal solution took 118 seconds and 181 seconds. The solution time on the same problem formulated as an LP would be on the order of 1 to 2 seconds. Furthermore, the solution time for ILP problems grows exponentially with the number of projects, owing to the combinatorial nature of the problem. One baffling aspect of ILP solution times is their variability. Often, smaller problems (in terms of number of constraints and number of decision variables) can take longer to solve than larger problems. Further, very minor changes in the problem (even with the same number of constraints and decision variables) can significantly increase solution times. No single solution approach works best on all types of ILP problems. However, given this somewhat bleak picture, Geoffrion and Nauss[9] cite progress that is being made on several fronts in developing more efficient solution algorithms. Currently, ILP is probably only feasible for small to medium-size capital budgeting problems (25 constraints and 100 projects).

The second shortcoming of ILP formulations and solutions is perhaps more devastating: meaningful shadow prices (which show the marginal change in the value of the objective function for an incremental change in the right-hand sides of various constraints) are not available in ILP. That is, many of the constraints on ILP problems which are not binding on the optimal integer solution will be assigned shadow prices of zero, which indicates that these resources are "free goods." In reality, this is not true since the objective function would clearly decrease if the availability of such resources were decreased. Furthermore Baumol, who was one of the pioneers in the area of dual variables

[8]Richard H. Pettway, "Integer Programming in Capital Budgeting: A Note on Computational Experience," *Journal of Financial and Quantitative Analysis*, September 1973, pp. 665–672.
[9]A. M. Geoffrion and R. Nauss, "Parametric and Post-Optimality Analysis in Integer Linear Programming," *Management Science*, January 1977, pp. 453–466.

in ILP (see his article with Gomory[10]), summarizes the problem of shadow prices in ILP quite well:

> However, we must be careful here—the preceding interpretation amounts to our thinking of these dual prices as the marginal revenue of these inputs. In the integer programming case, this concept runs into difficulties. In integer programming, inputs clearly must be thought of as coming in *indivisible units*. For that reason we cannot speak, e.g., of the marginal profit contribution of a small change in input, i.e., we must deal with $\Delta R/\Delta X$ rather than dR/dX (as we do in LP) where ΔX is an indivisible unit of input X and R is total profit. But a dual price represents dR/dX, which may change over the range of a *unit change in X*, and hence it may well give an *incorrect evaluation* of the marginal revenue of input X [emphasis added].[11]

Thus, the ILP model, in trying to handle the problem of indivisibilities, runs into problems itself because the feasible region consists only of points that have integer values for all decision variables. This same problem of "gaps in the feasible region" is the culprit in creating both of the problems cited above: computer time required to solve ILP problems and difficulties in interpreting the shadow prices in ILP. On the brighter side of things, Geoffrion and Nauss[12] cite progress also on this latter problem area in their exceptional paper on parametric and postoptimality analysis in ILP.

To conclude this section on ILP, we turn to a comprehensive example of the flexibility of ILP in representing the capital budgeting problem.

● **EXAMPLE 6**   *Complete ILP Formulation*

Consider the following 15 projects:

Cash Outflows

Project	C_{1j}	C_{2j}	C_{3j}	NPV
1	40	80	0	24
2	50	65	5	38
3	45	55	10	40
4	60	48	8	44
5	68	42	0	20
6	75	52	20	64
7	38	90	14	27
8	24	40	70	48
9	12	66	20	18
10	6	88	17	29
11	0	72	60	32
12	0	50	80	38
13	0	34	56	25
14	0	22	76	18
15	0	12	104	28

Budget
constraints: $\Sigma C_{1j} X_j \leq \$300;\ \Sigma C_{2j} X_j \leq \$540;\ \Sigma C_{3j} X_j \leq \$380$

[10]R. E. Gomory and W. J. Baumol, "Integer Programming and Pricing," *Econometrica*, September 1960, pp. 521–550.

[11]W. J. Baumol, *Economic Theory and Operations Analysis*, 2nd ed. (Englewood Cliffs, N. J.: Prentice-Hall, Inc., 1965), pp. 165–166.

[12]Geoffrion and Nauss, "Parametric and Post-Optimality Analysis."

The following project interrelationships exist:

1. Of the set of projects 3, 4, and 8, at most two can be accepted.

2. Projects 5 and 9 are mutually exclusive, but one of the two must be accepted.

3. Project 6 cannot be accepted unless both projects 1 and 14 are accepted.

4. Project 1 can be delayed 1 year—the same cash outflows will be required, but the NPV will drop to $22.

5. Projects 2 and 3 and projects 10 and 13 can be combined into complementary or composite projects wherein total cash outflows will be reduced by 10% and NPV increased by 12% compared to the total of the separate projects.

6. At least one of the two composite projects above must be accepted.

(a) Define the new decision variables which are needed for the problem above.

(b) Formulate the problem as an ILP.

Solution:

(a) The required new decision variables, in addition to X_1 through X_{15} for the original 15 projects described above, are as follows:

X_{16} is a decision variable to denote the delay of project 1 for 1 year

X_{17} is a decision variable to denote the acceptance of the composite of projects 2 and 3

X_{18} is a decision variable to denote the acceptance of the composite of projects 10 and 13

(b) The ILP formulation for this problem is as follows:

Maximize NPV =

$$24X_1 + 38X_2 + 40X_3 + 44X_4 + 20X_5 \qquad\qquad\qquad (a)$$
$$+64X_6 + 27X_7 + 48X_8 + 18X_9 + 29X_{10}$$
$$+32X_{11} + 38X_{12} + 25X_{13} + 18X_{14} + 28X_{15}$$
$$+22X_{16} + 87.36X_{17} + 60.48X_{18}$$

subject to

$$40X_1 + 50X_2 + 45X_3 + 60X_4 + 68X_5$$
$$+75X_6 + 38X_7 + 24X_8 + 12X_9 + 6X_{10}$$
$$+85.5X_{17} + 5.4X_{18} \qquad\qquad\qquad \leqslant 300 \qquad (b)$$

$$80X_1 + 65X_2 + 55X_3 + 48X_4 + 42X_5$$
$$+52X_6 + 90X_7 + 40X_8 + 66X_9 + 88X_{10}$$
$$+72X_{11} + 50X_{12} + 34X_{13} + 22X_{14} + 12X_{15}$$
$$+40X_{16} + 108X_{17} + 109.8X_{18} \qquad \leqslant 540 \qquad (c)$$

$$5X_2 + 10X_3 + 8X_4 + 20X_6 + 14X_7$$
$$+70X_8 + 20X_9 + 17X_{10} + 60X_{11} + 80X_{12}$$
$$+56X_{13} + 76X_{14} + 104X_{15} + 80X_{16} + 13.5X_{17}$$
$$+65.7X_{18} \qquad\qquad\qquad \leqslant 380 \qquad (d)$$

$$X_3 + X_4 + X_8 \leqslant 2 \qquad\qquad (e)$$
$$X_5 + X_9 = 1 \qquad\qquad (f)$$
$$\left. \begin{array}{l} 2X_6 \leqslant X_1 + X_{14} \\ 2X_6 \leqslant X_{16} + X_{14} \end{array} \right\} \begin{array}{l} \text{either constraint (g) or} \\ \text{(h) must be satisfied} \end{array} \qquad \begin{array}{l} (g) \\ (h) \end{array}$$

$$X_1 + X_{16} \leqslant 1 \tag{i}$$

$$X_2 + X_3 + X_{17} \leqslant 1 \tag{j}$$

$$X_{10} + X_{13} + X_{18} \leqslant 1 \tag{k}$$

$$X_{17} + X_{18} \geqslant 1 \tag{l}$$

$$X_i = \{0, 1\} \quad i = 1, 2, \ldots, 18 \tag{m}$$

A few comments should be made concerning this formulation. In expression (a), the objective function, the coefficients for $X_1 - X_{16}$ were given in the problem description, the coefficient for X_{17} equals 1.12 times (38 + 40), or 87.36, in order to show the 12% increase in NPV over the benefits generated by projects 2 and 3 separately. The coefficient for X_{18} is arrived at in a similar fashion. Equations (b), (c), and (d) are the budget constraints for years 1, 2, and 3, respectively. The coefficients for projects 1–15 are straightforward; the coefficients for X_{16} are those of X_1 delayed by 1 year; for X_{17} and X_{18} the coefficients are 90% of the sum of the coefficients for the respective pairs of projects. Equation (e) shows that no more than two of projects 3, 4, and 8 can be accepted. Equation (f) shows that either project 5 or project 9 must be accepted but that both cannot be accepted, because they are mutually exclusive; the strict equality sign conveys that one of the two must be accepted (i.e., either $X_5 = 1$ or $X_9 = 1$). Equations (g) and (h) show that for project 6 to be accepted, *either* project 1 and project 14 must be accepted [Equation (g)] or project 1 delayed by 1 year (i.e., project 16) and project 14 must be accepted [Equation (h)]; it is assumed here that project 1 delayed by 1 year still satisfies the requirement that both project 1 and project 14 are accepted. Notice also that even if one of these combinations of projects 1 and 14 is accepted, project 6 can either be accepted or rejected because of the $\leqslant$ inequality. Further, if desired, equations (g) and (h) can be combined to arrive at a single constraint which must be satisfied: $2X_6 \leqslant X_1 + X_{14} + X_{16}$. Equation (i) shows that *only one* of the two projects 1 or 16 (i.e., project 1 delayed by 1 year) *can be accepted*; if we wanted to force acceptance of one of these two, a strict equality would replace the $\leqslant$ sign. Equations (j) and (k) convey that with the two composite projects, at most one of the individual projects or the composite project can be accepted. Equation (1) indicates that either one or both of the composite projects must be accepted.   ●

This concludes our discussion of ILP. We now turn to goal programming, which is another powerful extension of LP in handling the capital budgeting problem.

GOAL PROGRAMMING APPLIED TO THE
CAPITAL BUDGETING PROBLEM[13]

Throughout the text, we have pointed out that the primary goal of financial management is the maximization of shareholders' wealth. Given the ever-present complexities, this is a rather tall order, since it is not always

---

[13]This section draws on the paper by A. Fourcans and T. J. Hindelang, "The Incorporation of Multiple Goals in the Selection of Capital Investments," presented at the 1973 Financial Management Association Convention, Atlanta, Ga., October 1973.

obvious how to maximize shareholders' wealth in an operational manner. Thus, it seems logical that progress toward this global goal will be facilitated if it is disaggregated into various subgoals; the rationale being that as the subgoals are achieved, definite strides will be made in the direction of shareholder wealth maximization. It was demonstrated in Chapter 7 that under conditions of certainty and perfect capital markets, the selection of the set of capital projects that maximizes NPV will guarantee maximization of shareholders' wealth or utility.[14]

However, if capital market imperfections exist (such as capital rationing, differences in lending and borrowing rates, etc.), then the maximization of NPV *may very well not* lead to the maximization of shareholders' wealth. In addition, observation plus empirical studies have demonstrated that investors and managers are interested in and motivated by several objectives. The following are representative of the more significant: growth and stability of earnings and dividends per share; growth in sales, market share and total assets; growth and stability of reported earnings or accounting profit (as argued by the Lerner and Rappaport[15] article); favorable use of financial leverage; diversification to reduce variability in earnings; and return on sales, equity, and operating assets. Thus, only a model that incorporates multiple criteria or objectives can be a robust, yet operational, representation of the pluralistic decision environment found in real-world capital budgeting problem setting. Goal programming (GP) is such a multi criteria model, in that it allows the establishment of a hierarchy of multiple objectives with diverse penalties associated with deviations from different goals. A brief survey of GP is presented prior to its application to the capital budgeting problem.

Goal programming (GP) was originally proposed in 1961 by Charnes and Cooper.[16] The technique has been expanded and popularized by the more recent works of Ijiri,[17] Lee,[18] and Ignizio.[19] The approach is an extension of linear programming (LP) wherein the usual "unidimensional" objective function (i.e., the optimization of a single measure of effectiveness) is transformed into a "multidimensional" criterion (i.e., the deviations from several goals are minimized according to a priority ranking scheme). The priority structure specifies a hierarchy of multiple goals wherein the highest-order goals are strived for first. Only after the optimal level of priority 1 goals has been achieved will priority 2 goals be considered, and so on. In addition, the relative importance of two or more goals at any priority level is shown by the weights assigned to each. The model is flexible enough to handle conflicting objectives, situations wherein only underachievement or overachievement of a goal is

---

[14]See also I. Fisher, *The Theory of Interest* (New York: Macmillan Publishing Co., Inc., 1930), and Hirshleifer, "On the Theory of Optimal Investment Decisions."

[15]E. M. Lerner and A. Rappaport, "Limit DCF in Capital Budgeting," *Harvard Business Review*, September–October 1968, pp. 133–138. See also Chapter 7, pp. 99–103.

[16]A. Charnes and W. W. Cooper, *Management Models and Industrial Applications of Linear Programming*, Vols. I and II (New York: John Wiley & Sons, Inc., 1961).

[17]Y. Ijiri, *Management Goals and Accounting for Control* (Amsterdam: North-Holland Publishing Co., 1965).

[18]S. M. Lee, *Goal Programming for Decision Analysis* (Philadelphia: Auerbach Publishing Co., 1972).

[19]J. P. Ignizio, *Goal Programming and Extensions* (Lexington, Mass.: Lexington Books, 1976).

penalized, and conditions where the decision maker seeks to come as close as possible to a desired target. Thus, GP offers an operational method of approximating a decision maker's utility curve which does not require the derivation of a family of utility functions in a multidimensional space. GP requires the assignment of ordinal priorities to the respective goals with relative weights required by any goals placed on the same priority level. The optimal trade-off among goals on the same or different priority levels can be established through various interactive approaches[20] or through sensitivity analysis, which is discussed below.

In formulating decision problems using the goal programming format, three major components are required:

1. The usual *economic constraints* of LP, which are also called "hard constraints," in that they cannot be violated since they represent resource limitations or restrictions imposed by the decision environment.

2. The *goal constraints,* which are also called "soft constraints" because they represent managerial policies and desired levels of various objectives which are being sought after by the decision maker.

3. The *objective function,* which minimizes the weighted deviations from the desired levels of the various objectives according to a specified priority ranking.

Each of these components deserves elaboration. The economic constraints in GP are exactly like the constraints in LP problems. Thus, such constraints still require the usual slack or surplus variables. On the other hand, goal constraints are most conveniently specified as strict equalities which contain *two* "deviational variables," represented as d_i^+ and d_i^-, which indicate that the desired level of goal i was either overachieved or underachieved, respectively. Of course, one of the two deviational variables will always be zero and the other will equal the magnitude of the deviation from the desired goal level; if the desired goal level was exactly met, both deviational variables will equal zero. The deviational variables are the mechanism that is used to tie the goal constraints into the objective function. That is, for each goal the appropriate deviational variable(s) is(are) placed in the objective function, depending upon the desired action for that goal. For example, if it was desired to achieve a minimum level of net income, the only deviational variable required in the objective function would be d^-; on the other hand, if the decision maker did not want to exceed a cost goal, the only deviational variable required in the objective function would be d^+, since only exceeding the cost goal should be penalized.

More complex actions relative to goals require the use of both deviational variables. If the decision maker wanted to "come as close as possible" to some

[20]See J. S. Dyer, "Interactive Goal Programming," *Management Science*, Vol. 19, No. 1, September 1972, pp. 62–70; J. S. Dyer, "A Time-Sharing Computer Program for the Solution of the Multiple Criteria Problem," *Management Science*, Vol. 19, No. 12, August 1973, pp. 1379–1383; and A. Geoffrion, J. S. Dyer, and A. Feinberg, "An Interactive Approach for Multi- Criterion Optimization with an Application to the Operation of an Academic Department," *Management Science*, Vol. 19, No. 3, November 1972, pp. 357–368.

TABLE 13-1   Appropriate Objective Function Terms in Goal Programming

Desired Action	*Objective Function Term*
Achieve a minimum level of some goal	minimize d^-
Do not exceed a specified level of some goal	minimize d^+
Come as close as possible to a specified goal level	minimize $(d^+ + d^-)$
Maximize the value achieved relative to a given goal level	minimize $(d^- - d^+)$
Minimize the value achieved relative to a given goal level	minimize $(d^+ - d^-)$

goal level, then both overachieving and undershooting the goal would be penalized; hence, the objective function term would be minimize $(d^+ + d^-)$. If the decision maker desires to "maximize net income" and has established an achievable minimum level of net income as referred to above, the maximization would be carried out in two steps—first achieving the minimum level and then overshooting the minimum by the greatest possible amount; hence, the objective function term would be minimize $(d^- - d^+)$; it should be noted that we want to maximize d^+ but recall that the overall objective function is being minimized, which means that we minimize $-d^+$ to obtain the same result. Finally, if the decision maker wanted to "minimize the cost" referred to above and has established a maximum level, the appropriate objective function term would be minimize $(d^+ - d^-)$ using the same logic traced out for the maximization case. The discussion above is summarized in Table 13-1 for convenient reference.

To formally represent the objective function in a GP problem, the following three aspects must be specified:

1. The *priority level* that the goal is placed on, which indicates the ordinal ranking scheme whereby the goals will be optimized.

2. The *relative weight* assigned to each goal where there are two or more goals on the same priority level, which shows the relative importance of the goals.

3. The *relevant deviational variable(s)*, which should be penalized with respect to each goal and is dependent upon the desired action as just discussed.

The priority level is shown by P_i, where the subscript i designates the level —the smaller the value of i, the more important is the goal. Further, it should be noted that there is an absolute dominance among the priority levels; that is, priority 2 will be considered only after all the goals on priority 1 are optimized and nothing on priority 2 can act to the detriment of the goals on priority 1, and similarly for all lower-priority levels. The relative weights are shown as coefficients of the various goals, with the higher weights representing the more important goals.

Goal programming formulations can be used to optimize over a planning horizon consisting of many time periods. Goals can be established for the entire horizon or for various subperiods within the horizon. GP can handle deterministic or stochastic problem settings. The GP model discussed in this chapter is a multiperiod goal program where conditions of certainty are assumed.

It should be mentioned that GP models in their fullest context should be viewed as an iterative process. A set of priorities and relative weights are assigned to the various goals and the optimal solution is obtained. Next, based on the degree of consensus of the original priorities and weights as well as to gain insight into trade-offs among goals, a sensitivity analysis should be performed to see the impact that varying priorities and weights has on the optimal values of decision variables. The less significant the impact on the decision variables, the less effort management has to expend in arriving at a consensus to specify the precise priority structure. Using the sensitivity information, the trade-off question can also be addressed based on management perceptions, risk posture, and preferences.

GP models are solved in the same fashion as LP models. Very simple problems with only two decision variables can be solved by a graphical procedure. More complex problems can be solved using the simplex method of GP[21] or, more preferably, using computerized algorithms.[22] The solution of GP problems can be visualized as follows. The original feasible region of the problem is bounded by the economic (hard) constraints, which cannot be violated. The highest-priority goal(s) is(are) examined first; we try to drive the appropriate deviational variables for all priority 1 goals to zero.

This results in a reduction in the size of the feasible region as we move on to priority 2 goals. Thus, each lower-priority level will have a successively smaller feasible region where any portion of the region previously eliminated cannot be reexamined, owing to the absolute dominance relationship of higher over all successively lower priority levels. As we move from one priority level to the next lower one, the relevant feasible region could be a region, a plane, a line, or a single point in n-dimensional space, where n is the number of decision variables in the problem. Of course, the priority structure assigned to the goals will determine the order in which various regions will be "cut off from" the feasible region, and hence the optimal solution can differ significantly as different priority structures are utilized (including relative weights) for any given problem. This is why we stressed the importance of the iterative approach to GP problems through sensitivity analysis. Of course, once the feasible solution consists of only a single point, there is no way that we can move from that point on any lower priority level; thus, it must be the optimal solution. For this reason it is recommended that high-priority goals be stated as "achieving minimum levels" of various goals or "not exceeding a maximum level" rather than to maximize or minimize, because the latter alternatives will drive the decision maker to a single point in the feasible region. Maximization or minimization operations can be carried out on low priority levels once all other relevant goals have been achieved.

We now illustrate the formulation and graphical solution of a simple two-project capital budgeting problem using a GP model.

[21]See Lee, *Goal Programming*, Chap. 5; S. M. Lee, *Linear Optimization for Management* (New York: Petrocelli/Charter Publishers, Inc., 1976), Chap. 7; and Ignizio, *Goal Programming*, Chap. 4.

[22]See Ignizio, *Goal Programming*, Chaps. 3, 5, and 6, where FORTRAN programs are presented for integer GP and nonlinear GP problems.

• **EXAMPLE 7** Two-Project GP Formulation

Consider that a firm is evaluating two projects with the following characteristics:

	Economic Constraints			Managerial Goals			
Project	Cash Outflow Year 1	Cash Outflow Year 2	Management Supervision	NPV	Net Income Year 1	Net Income Year 2	Net Income Year 3
1	25	20	5	14	10	11	12
2	40	15	16	60	4	7	11
Amount available	30	20	10 units				
Desired goals levels				Maximum	6	8	10

This firm has a strict limitation on the funds that can be utilized for capital expenditures in years 1 and 2 as well as the amount of time available for the management supervision of new projects (the amount of each of these resources available is shown above); hence, there are three economic or hard constraints. Furthermore, partial projects can be accepted, but only one complete project of each type is available; cash outflows occur at the beginning of the period, while the subsequent cash inflows that generate net income cannot be used to finance the current year's or any later year's cash outflows. Four managerial goals have also been established: to achieve minimum levels of net income in the first 3 years of the asset's life and to maximize NPV over the entire useful life of the asset. Management has assigned the net income goals in years 1, 2 , and 3 to priority levels 1, 2, and 3, respectively, and the NPV goal to priority 4.

Formulate this problem as a GP and solve it using the graphical method.

Solution: First, the problem is formulated as a GP. The objective function shown below will be optimized subject to the economic and goal constraints shown first:

Economic constraints:

$$25X_1 + 40X_2 \leqslant 30 \qquad \text{Budget in year 1}$$
$$20X_1 + 15X_2 \leqslant 20 \qquad \text{Budget in year 2}$$
$$5X_1 + 16X_2 \leqslant 10 \qquad \text{Management supervision}$$
$$X_1 \qquad\quad \leqslant 1 \qquad \text{Upper limits on}$$
$$X_2 \leqslant 1 \qquad \text{project acceptance}$$
$$X_i, d_j^+, d_j^- \geqslant 0 \qquad i = 1, 2; j = 1, 2, 3, 4 \qquad \text{Nonnegativity}$$
$$P_k \gg P_{k+1} \qquad \text{for all } k \qquad \text{Absolute dominance between priority levels}$$

Goal constraints:

$$10X_1 + 4X_2 + d_1^- - d_1^+ = 6 \qquad \text{Net income year 1}$$
$$11X_1 + 7X_2 + d_2^- - d_2^+ = 8 \qquad \text{Net income year 2}$$
$$12X_1 + 11X_2 + d_3^- - d_3^+ = 10 \qquad \text{Net income year 3}$$
$$14X_1 + 60X_2 + d_4^- - d_4^+ = 10 \qquad \text{NPV}$$

Objective function:

$$\text{Minimum weighted deviations} = P_1 d_1^- + P_2 d_2^- + P_3 d_3^- + P_4(d_4^- - d_4^+)$$

263

Note in this formulation that the goal level for the NPV goal (i.e., 10) was selected simply because it is an achievable value for the NPV of accepted projects given the economic constraints.

The problem above is solved using the graphical method by drawing the lines representing all the economic constraints; these boundaries form the initial feasible region shown below:

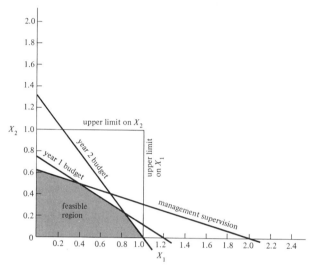

In (a) through (d), the four goal constraints are plotted and the region representing the deviation to be penalized has been eliminated as we move to the next lower priority level.

(a) Priority 1:

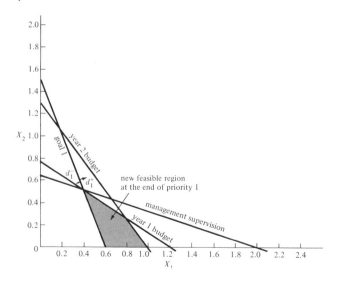

(b) Priority 2:

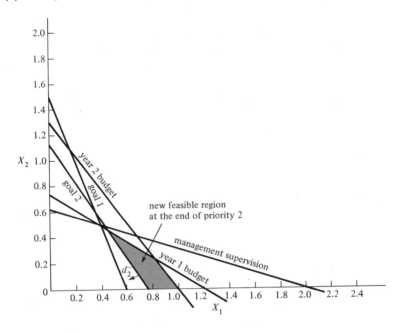

(c) Priority 3:

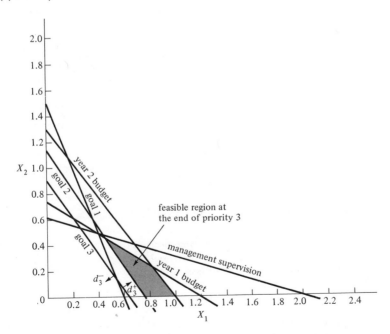

Notice that we have the same feasible region at the end of priority 3 as we had at the end of priority 2, since goal 3 is dominated by goal 2.

(d) Priority 4:   Here we maximize NPV by first graphing goal 4, which has an NPV value of $10 and then moving as far above the line for the NPV goal as possible, which leads to the optimal solution of $X_1 = 0.415$ and $X_2 = 0.49$.

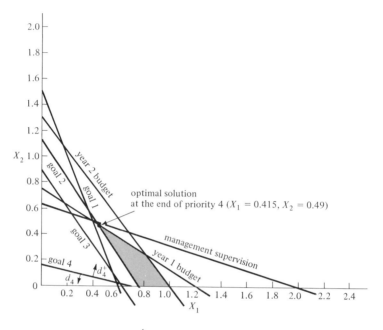

This optimal solution is quite different from the optimal solution if we just maximized NPV, which would have been to accept 0.625 of project 2 and nothing of project 1. This concludes our straightforward example of the use of GP in the capital budgeting area.

        ●

Our next illustration of the use of GP in the capital budgeting setting will show how sensitivity analysis provides valuable information for management in addressing issues about trade-offs among their goals. In order to also be able to compare the results obtained here with the LP solution, we refer back to the Lorie–Savage problem shown in Example 1.

● **EXAMPLE 8**   *GP Formulation and Solution of the Lorie–Savage Problem*

The same firm that was evaluating the nine projects under the conditions described in Example 1 now feels that the NPV objective should be supplemented with four other goals which reflect the short-run attractiveness of the projects. Specifically, the firm feels that stability and growth in sales as well as net income are very important vehicles to assist the firm in maximizing shareholders' wealth.[23]

---

[23]A similar type of analysis was performed by C.A. Hawkins and R.A. Adams, "A Goal Programming Model for Capital Budgeting," *Financial Management*, Spring 1974, pp. 52–57.

The following table shows the contribution that each of the projects will make to net income and sales growth in the next 2 years.

Project	Net Income Year 1	Net Income Year 2	Sales Growth Year 1	Sales Growth Year 2
1	2.0	4	0.02	0.03
2	2.0	4.2	0.01	0.03
3	1.6	2.5	0.02	0.02
4	1.2	2.8	0.01	0.02
5	3.0	5.0	0.03	0.04
6	1.1	1.4	0.01	0.01
7	1.5	3.0	0.01	0.02
8	1.2	1.8	0.01	0.015
9	1.3	2.4	0.01	0.018

The firm wants to achieve net income levels of 8 and 16, respectively, in years 1 and 2, and sales growth of 0.08 in each year, as well as to maximize NPV.

(a) Besides the information just presented, use the basic data on the nine projects from Example 1 to formulate all the economic and goal constraints for this problem.

(b) The firm is interested in evaluating two objective functions in order to determine the impact on the optimal set of projects:

1. Placing the net income goals on priority 1, the sales goals on priority 2, and the NPV goal on priority 3; on the first two priority levels the year 1 goals should be weighted twice as importantly as the year 2 goals.

2. All five goals placed on priority level 1 but with relative weights of 10 for net income in year 1, 2 for net income in year 2, 5 for sales growth in year 1, and 2 for sales growth in year 2, and 1 for NPV.

Formulate these two objective functions.

(c) After setting the target levels for net income and sales growth mentioned above, the firm feels it may be over optimistic. Thus, the levels are revised to 7 and 12 in years 1 and 2, respectively, for net income and 0.07 in each year for sales growth. How will this affect the formulation in part (a)?

(d) If a computerized GP algorithm is available, obtain the optimal solutions for the two objective functions in part (b) and for the changes in the target levels mentioned in part (c). Briefly discuss differences in the optimal sets of projects. If a computerized algorithm is not available using the optimal solutions shown, briefly discuss the differences in the optimal sets of projects.

Solution:
(a) The GP formulation is as follows:
Economic constraints:

$$12X_1 + 54X_2 + 6X_3 + 6X_4 + 30X_5$$
$$+6X_6 + 48X_7 + 36X_8 + 18X_9 + S_1 \quad = 50 \qquad \text{Budget constraint year 1}$$
$$3X_1 + 7X_2 + 6X_3 + 2X_4 + 35X_5$$
$$+6X_6 + 4X_7 + 3X_8 + 3X_9 + S_2 \quad = 20 \qquad \text{Budget constraint year 2}$$

$$\left.\begin{array}{lll} X_1 + S_3 = 1 & X_4 + S_6 = 1 & X_7 + S_9 = 1 \\ X_2 + S_4 = 1 & X_5 + S_7 = 1 & X_8 + S_{10} = 1 \\ X_3 + S_5 = 1 & X_6 + S_8 = 1 & X_9 + S_{11} = 1 \end{array}\right\} \quad \begin{array}{l}\text{Upper limits on}\\ \text{project acceptance}\end{array}$$

$$\left.X_j, S_i \geqslant 0 \quad \begin{array}{l} j = 1, 2, \ldots, 9 \\ i = 1, 2, \ldots, 11 \end{array}\right\} \quad \text{Nonnegativity constraint}$$

Goal constraints:

$$
\begin{aligned}
2X_1 + 2X_2 + 1.6X_3 + 1.2X_4 + 3X_5 + 1.1X_6 & \\
+ 1.5X_7 + 1.2X_8 + 1.3X_9 + d_1^- - d_1^+ &= 8 \quad\text{Net income year 1} \\
4X_1 + 4.2X_2 + 2.5X_3 + 2.8X_4 + 5X_5 + 1.4X_6 & \\
+ 3X_7 + 1.8X_8 + 2.4X_9 + d_2^- - d_2^+ &= 16 \quad\text{Net income year 2} \\
0.02X_1 + 0.01X_2 + 0.02X_3 + 0.01X_4 + 0.03X_5 + 0.01X_6 & \\
+ 0.01X_7 + 0.01X_8 + 0.01X_9 + d_3^- - d_3^+ &= 0.08 \quad\text{Sales growth year 1} \\
0.03X_1 + 0.03X_2 + 0.02X_3 + 0.02X_4 + 0.04X_5 + 0.01X_6 & \\
+ 0.02X_7 + 0.015X_8 + 0.018X_9 + d_4^- - d_4^+ &= 0.08 \quad\text{Sales growth year 2} \\
14X_1 + 17X_2 + 17X_3 + 15X_4 + 40X_5 + 12X_6 & \\
+ 14X_7 + 10X_8 + 12X_9 + d_5^- - d_5^+ &= 40 \quad\text{NPV}
\end{aligned}
$$

Notice again that the goal level for the NPV goal is an arbitrary achievable value.

(b) The two objective functions are as follows:

1. Minimize weighted deviations $= P_1(2d_1^- + d_2^-) + P_2(2d_3^- + d_4^-) + P_3(d_5^- - d_5^+)$

2. Minimize weighted deviations $= P_1(10d_1^- + 2d_2^- + 5d_3^- + 2d_4^- + d_5^- - d_5^+)$

(c) The only changes that will be necessitated by the desired changes in the target goal levels is that the right-hand sides of goals one through four become 7, 12, 0.07, and 0.07, respectively.

(d) The optimal solutions for the two objective functions and the two different sets of goal levels are shown below:

Objective function 1 and goal values of 8, 16, 0.08, and 0.08:

Project Acceptance	Goal Levels Achieved	
$X_1 = 1.0000$	7.231	Net income year 1
$X_2 = 0.0426$		
$X_3 = 1.0000$	13.209	Net income year 2
$X_4 = 1.0000$		
$X_5 = 0$	0.0699	Sales growth year 1
$X_6 = 0.9504$		
$X_7 = 0.0000$	0.0988	Sales growth year 2
$X_8 = 0.0000$		
$X_9 = 1.0000$	70.129	NPV

Objective function 2 and goal values 8, 16, 0.08, and 0.08:

Project Acceptance	Goal Levels Achieved	
$X_1 = 1.0000$	7.235	Net income year 1
$X_2 = 0$		
$X_3 = 1.0000$	13.194	Net income year 2
$X_4 = 1.0000$		
$X_5 = 0$	0.0702	Sales growth year 1
$X_6 = 0.9697$		
$X_7 = 0.0455$	0.0986	Sales growth year 2
$X_8 = 0.0000$		
$X_9 = 1.0000$	70.273	NPV

Objective function 1 and goal values 7, 12, 0.07, and 0.07:

Project Acceptance	Goal Levels Achieved	
$X_1 = 1.0000$	7.252	Net income year 1
$X_2 = 0.0000$		
$X_3 = 1.0000$	13.215	Net income year 2
$X_4 = 1.0000$		
$X_5 = 0$	0.0703	Sales growth year 1
$X_6 = 0.9858$		
$X_7 = 0.0451$	0.0988	Sales growth year 2
$X_8 = 0.0000$		
$X_9 = 1.0000$	70.273	NPV

Objective function 2 and goal values 7, 12, 0.07, and 0.07:

Project Acceptance	Goal Levels Achieved	
$X_1 = 1.0$	7.252	Net income year 1
$X_2 = 0$		
$X_3 = 1.0$	13.215	Net income year 2
$X_4 = 1.0$		
$X_5 = 0$	0.0703	Sales growth year 1
$X_6 = 0.9858$		
$X_7 = 0.0451$	0.0988	Sales growth year 2
$X_8 = 0$		
$X_9 = 1.0$	70.273	NPV

The optimal solutions above were obtained using the GP algorithm from Ignizio.[24] As will be recalled, the optimal LP solution showed 100% acceptance of projects 1, 3, 4, and 9 as well as 97% acceptance of project 6 and 4.5% acceptance of project 7, which generated an NPV level of 70.273. All of the GP solutions above also accept 100% of projects 1, 3, 4, and 9. The only difference among the solutions is in the area of the partially accepted projects. With the original goal levels and priority structure, we find that projects 2 and 6 were partially accepted. Project 2 enters into the solution because of its contribution to the achievement of the new goals in the GP formulation. The other three GP solutions are virtually the same as the LP optimal solution. Greater variation in the optimal solutions would probably have been found if more projects were under evaluation and/or a greater diversity of goals were included in the formulation.   ●

Our final illustration will be a GP model that is a global capital investment model which considers both replacement alternatives and new investment projects wherein multiple goals are sought after and conditions of capital rationing exist. The model is comprehensive in that it integrates the capital investment, financing, and dividend decisions of firms into a single optimization approach. New financing for the firm, which can take the form of either debt or equity, is incorporated into the model. In addition, cash inflows generated during the planning horizon by projects that are accepted as well as replacements that are made are taken into consideration.

[24]Ignizio, *Goal Programming*.

The Goals

The GP model recommends six goals which are of significant importance to firms in evaluating the selection of new capital projects, the optimal timing of equipment replacements, and the best way to finance such capital commitments:

1. Attainment of a minimum yearly level of net income generated by the new investments (both new projects and replacements).

2. Achievement of a minimum desired growth in productivity of operating assets (both for new projects and equipment replacement decisions).

3. Achievement of a minimum desired level of earnings per dollar of stockholders' equity each year (a surrogate goal for earnings per share).

4. Minimization of the deviation from a financial or operating leverage goal at the end of the planning horizon.

5. Attainment of a minimum desired growth rate in total assets over the planning horizon.

6. Maximization of the net present value of accepted projects given the budget constraints and that the goals above are satisfied as far as possible.

Other goals could be added to the list, but it is felt that these six represent the most important criteria that firms use in evaluating new capital investment and replacement decisions.

Exhibit 13-1 gives the mathematical representation of the six goals mentioned above using the symbols defined in Exhibit 13-2. A brief rationale will now be presented for the inclusion of each of the goals in the model.

EXHIBIT 13-1   Goal Constraints of the Model

Net income:
$$e_j + \sum_{i \in n_1} a_{ij}X_{ij} + \sum_{i \in n_2} \bar{a}_{ij}Y_{ij} - (1 - t)I_j - d_{1j}^+ + d_{1j}^- = P_j$$
$$j = 1, 2, \ldots, T$$

Productivity:
$$\sum_{j=1}^{T}\sum_{i \in n_1} r_{ij}X_{ij} + \sum_{j=1}^{T}\sum_{i \in n_2} \bar{r}_{ij}Y_{ij} - d_2^+ + d_2^- = U$$

Earnings / dollar equity:
$$e_j + \sum_{i \in n_1} a_{ij}X_{ij} + \sum_{i \in n_2} \bar{a}_{ij}Y_{ij} - (1 - t)I_j - q_j\left(E_0 + \sum_{k=1}^{j-1} E_k\right)$$
$$- d_{3j}^+ + d_{3j}^- = 0 \qquad j = 1, 2, \ldots, T$$

Leverage:
$$E_0 + \sum_{j=1}^{T} E_j + \sum_{j=1}^{T} e_j + \sum_{j=1}^{T}\sum_{i \in n_1} a_{ij}X_{ij} + \sum_{j=1}^{T}\sum_{i \in n_2} \bar{a}_{ij}Y_{ij} - \sum_{j=1}^{T} (1 - t)I_j$$
$$- \sum_{j=1}^{T} V_j\left(E_0 + \sum_{k=1}^{j-1} E_k\right) - S\left(D_0 + \sum_{j=1}^{T} D_j\right) - d_4^+ + d_4^- = 0$$

Growth rate in assets:
$$\sum_{j=1}^{T}\sum_{i \in n_1} BV_{ij}^T X_{ij} + \sum_{j=1}^{T}\sum_{i \in n_2} \overline{BV}_{ij}^T Y_{ij} - gA_0 - d_5^+ + d_5^- = 0$$

Net present value:
$$\sum_{j=0}^{T}\sum_{i \in n_1} \frac{1}{(1 + k)^j}(b_{ij}X_{ij} - C_{ij}X_{ij} + W_T) +$$
$$\sum_{j=0}^{T}\sum_{i \in n_2} \frac{1}{(1 + k)^j}(\bar{b}_{ij}Y_{ij} - \bar{C}_{ij}Y_{ij} + \overline{W}_T) - d_6^+ + d_6^- = 0$$

EXHIBIT 13-2 Glossary of Symbols in Alphabetical Order

$A_0 =$ book value of total operating assets at time zero

$a_{ij} =$ net income generated by project i in year j

$\bar{a}_{ij} =$ net income generated by the replacement of machine i in period j

$b_{ij} =$ net cash inflow generated by project i in year j

$\bar{b}_{ij} =$ net cash inflow generated by replacement of machine i in period j

$BV_{ij}^T =$ book value in year T of project i acquired in year j

$\overline{BV}_{ij}^T =$ book value in year T of replacement of machine i in period j

$C_{ij} =$ cash outflow required for project i in year j

$\bar{C}_{ij} =$ cash outflow required to replace machine i in period j

$D_0 =$ dollar amount of long-term debt outstanding at time zero

$D_j =$ dollar amount of long-term debt acquired during year j

$D_j^* =$ upper limit of the dollar amount of debt funds that can be acquired in year j

$E_0 =$ dollar amount of equity outstanding at time zero

$E_j =$ dollar amount of equity acquired during year j

$E_j^* =$ upper limit of the dollar amount of equity funds that can be acquired in year j

$e_j =$ dollar amount of net income generated by ongoing operations in year j

$g =$ desired growth rate in assets over the planning horizon

$I_0 =$ dollar amount of interest paid on long-term debt outstanding in year zero

$I_j =$ dollar amount of interest paid on long-term debt outstanding in year j

$i_j =$ percent interest rate paid on long-term debt in year j

$k =$ firm's cost of capital to be used in discounting cash flows

$n_1 =$ class of accepted projects in year j

$n_2 =$ class of machine replacements undertaken in year j

$n_1^* =$ class of accepted projects that have cash flows beyond the end of the planning horizon T

$n_2^* =$ class of machine replacements that have cash flows beyond the end of the planning horizon T

$P_j =$ net income goal in year j

$q_j =$ earnings per dollar of equity goal in year j

$r_{ij} =$ productivity growth per dollar invested achieved by accepting project i in year j

$\bar{r}_{ij} =$ productivity growth per dollar invested achieved by replacing machine i in year j

$S =$ leverage goal to be achieved by the end of the planning horizon

$t =$ corporate tax rate

$U =$ productivity growth goal to be achieved by the end of the planning horizon

$V_j =$ percent of dividends per dollar of equity to be paid in year j

$X_{ij} =$ decision variable representing project i in period j

$Y_{ij} =$ decision variable representing the replacement of machine i in period j

The net income goal was included in the model because both investors and managers have an objective of stable and steadily rising earnings. Such earnings are achieved only through judicious capital investments and equipment-replacement decisions over time. Thus, this goal for each year of the planning horizon is arrived at by adding the net income generated by ongoing operations plus the net income generated by new investments plus the net income generated by replacements less the after-tax cost of interest expense.

Productivity increases over the planning horizon are another relevant area of concern in making new capital commitments, especially equipment-replacement decisions. Hence, how attractive a particular capital investment is can be measured in part by how much it increases productivity compared with current operations. The goal of achieving the minimum productivity increase established by management merely adds together the productivity growth per dollar invested in equipment replacements and new capital projects.

Earnings per share is one of the most closely watched statistics by investors and managers. Of course, this figure is based directly upon the level of net income (discussed in the first goal above) but also implicitly reflects the way that new capital investments (both new projects and equipment replacements) are financed (debt vs. equity) and the dividend policy utilized by the firm. Thus, the next two goals—earnings per dollar of equity and leverage—incorporate two important dimensions used to judge how well a firm is doing in its profitability endeavors and its search for an optimal capital structure. The earnings per dollar of equity goal (which is a surrogate for earnings per share) adds net income of ongoing operations to the net income generated by new capital investments (after deducting interest charges on debt). This result is compared to management's target return per dollar of stockholders' equity to determine the quality of capital investment alternatives undertaken. The financial leverage goal can be expressed as follows:

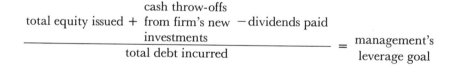

$$\frac{\text{total equity issued} + \begin{array}{c}\text{cash throw-offs}\\\text{from firm's new}\\\text{investments}\end{array} - \text{dividends paid}}{\text{total debt incurred}} = \begin{array}{c}\text{management's}\\\text{leverage goal}\end{array}$$

Therefore, through these two goals the model integrates the important investment, financing, and dividend policy dimensions of the capital budgeting and equipment-replacement decisions.

Growth rate in assets is a natural consideration in allocating capital among competing alternatives, because such growth contributes to the intrinsic value of the firm and its potential for stable and rising earnings. This goal is simply:

$$\frac{\begin{array}{c}\text{book value of}\\\text{new capital investments}\\\text{at end of planning horizon}\end{array} + \begin{array}{c}\text{book value of}\\\text{equipment replacements}\\\text{at end of planning horizon}\end{array}}{\begin{array}{c}\text{book value of initial assets at the}\\\text{beginning of the planning horizon}\end{array}} = \begin{array}{c}\text{management's}\\\text{desired growth}\\\text{rate in assets}\\\text{over the plan-}\\\text{ning horizon}\end{array}$$

Finally, the introduction of capital-market imperfections weakens the validity of NPV as a *unique* criterion of investment evaluation. However, in conjunction with the goals above, definite strides are taken toward the maximization of shareholder's wealth. Hence, new investments and replacement decisions will be evaluated in terms of the first five goals. Then the feasible set of capital commitments that maximizes NPV will be undertaken. This goal adds the NPV of new investment projects to the NPV of equipment-replacement alternatives.

The Economic Constraints

Exhibit 13-3 shows the economic constraints of the model. The interest expense constraint states that the dollar interest will be the amount of interest on debt outstanding at the beginning of the planning horizon plus the interest

EXHIBIT 13-3   Economic Constraints of the Model

Interest expense:
$$I_j = I_0 + \sum_{k=1}^{j-1} i_k D_k \qquad j = 1, 2, \ldots, T$$

Budget:
$$\sum_{i \in n_1} C_{ij} X_{ij} + \sum_{i \in n_2} \bar{C}_{ij} Y_{ij} \leqslant D_j + E_j + e_j + \sum_{k=1}^{j-1} \sum_{i \in n_1} a_{ik} X_{ik}$$
$$+ \sum_{k=1}^{j-1} \sum_{i \in n_2} \bar{a}_{ik} Y_{ik} - (1 - t) I_j - V_j (E_o + \sum_{k=1}^{j-1} E_k) \qquad j = 1, 2, \ldots, T$$

Horizon value:
$$W_T = \sum_{j=T+1}^{J} \sum_{i \in n_1^*} \frac{1}{(1 - k)^{j-T}} (b_{ij} X_{ij} - C_{ij} X_{ij});$$

$$\overline{W}_T = \sum_{j=T+1}^{J} \sum_{i \in n_2^*} \frac{1}{(1 + k)^{j-T}} (\bar{b}_{ij} Y_{ij} - \bar{C}_{ij} Y_{ij})$$

Upper limits: $\quad D_j \leqslant D_j^* \qquad E_j \leqslant E_j^* \qquad j = 1, 2, \ldots, T$

Mutually exclusive replacements:
$$\sum_{j=1}^{T} Y_{ij} \leqslant 1 \qquad i = 1, 2, \ldots, N$$

Mutually exclusive projects: $\quad \sum_{i \in C} X_{ij} \leqslant 1 \qquad$ where C is a class of mutually exclusive projects in any year j

Decision variables: $\quad X_{ij} = \begin{cases} 1 & \text{if project } i \text{ is accepted in year } j \\ 0 & \text{otherwise} \end{cases}$

$$Y_{ij} = \begin{cases} 1 & \text{if machine } i \text{ is replaced in year } j \\ 0 & \text{otherwise} \end{cases}$$

Nonnegativity: $\quad d_{ij}^+, d_{ij}^-, D_j, E_j \geqslant 0 \qquad j = 1, 2, \ldots, T \qquad i = 1, 2, \ldots, 6$

on new debt issued. It is assumed that no long-term debt matures or is retired during the planning horizon. The next constraint is the all-important budget constraint, which states that new funds committed to projects in any year cannot exceed the amount of new debt issued plus the amount of new equity issued plus the internally generated funds (i.e., ongoing operations of the firm plus cash inflows generated by new projects and replacements undertaken to date) less interest and dividend payments. These first two economic constraints are tied into the net income, leverage, and earnings per dollar of equity goals. Such interrelationships are needed to achieve the following important aspects: (1) the integration of the investment, financing, and dividend policy aspects of the capital budgeting and equipment-replacement decision areas; and (2) the optimal timing of changes in the firm's capital structure based on the cost and availability of funds in the capital markets, the firm's leverage goal, the attractiveness of new projects and replacements, and the portfolio of assets accepted to date in the planning horizon.

The next two constraints show the values of the discounted cash inflows less outflows for all accepted projects and replacements, respectively, which occur beyond the end of the planning horizon. These two values are used in the net present value goal. Upper limits are shown for the amount of new debt and new equity that can be issued each year to reflect market or self-imposed limits on the amount of external financing that the firm can undertake.

Finally, two constraints are shown which incorporate the fact that replacements of existing assets are mutually exclusive (i.e., if a given asset is replaced in year 1, the same original asset cannot be replaced in any other year of the planning horizon) and that new capital projects can be mutually exclusive (i.e., if one project is accepted, then any other project in the mutually exclusive set may not be accepted). Other project interdependencies discussed in the section on integer programming could also be incorporated in the model. The usual zero–one conditions are imposed both on the decision variables for new projects and for replacements. The nonnegativity requirement is placed on deviational variables and the debt and equity decision variables.

The Objective Function

The model's objective function consists of minimizing the appropriate deviations (d^+, d^-, or both) from the multiple goals according to the priority scheme established by the firm. Thus, for the first three goals and goal 5, only the d^- deviation will be penalized, since a minimum level of these goals is sought; for goal 4, both the d^+ and d^- deviations are important, because we seek to come as close as possible to the leverage goal that is established; and finally, we penalize ($d^- - d^+$) for goal 6 because we are seeking to maximize the NPV of accepted investments. For each of the six goals a priority level must be specified which shows its ordinal importance in the firm's hierarchy of objectives.

Owing to the flexibility of goal programming discussed above, a firm can tailor the model to its own hierarchy of goals and its own circumstances. For illustrative purposes, suppose that a corporation under consideration is concerned about the market price of its stock, since it finds equity issues a favorable way to obtain new financing for capital acquisitions. It also sees maintaining its image as a growth firm rather important. Given these conditions, the firm may find the following priority structure appropriate:

Priority 1 (P_1)—the achievement of a minimum earnings per dollar of equity and the achievement of a minimum level of annual net income.

Priority 2 (P_2)—the attainment of a specified growth in productivity of operating assets and a desired growth rate in assets over the planning horizon.

Priority 3 (P_3)—coming as close as possible to the firm's desired leverage goal at the end of the planning horizon.

Priority 4 (P_4)—the maximization of the NPV of all accepted projects and replacements.

In addition, the firm may decide that on the first priority level the earnings per dollar of equity goal is three times as important as the net income goal; on the second priority level, the growth rate in assets may be thought to be twice as important as the productivity growth goal.

The hierarchy above would be expressed mathematically by the following objective function:

$$\text{min. dev.} = 3P_1 \sum_{j=1}^{T} d_{3j}^- + P_1 \sum_{j=1}^{T} d_{1j}^- + 2P_2 d_5^- + P_2 d_2^- + P_3(d_4^+ + d_4^-)$$

$$+ P_4(d_6^- - d_6^+)$$

We now illustrate this comprehensive formulation with an example.

● **EXAMPLE 9** *Comprehensive Twenty-Eight-Project Example*

The table below presents cash flow data for 28 investment proposals. The data are adapted from test problems originally presented by Weingartner.[25] The projects have varying initial investments, cash flow patterns, and useful lives from 7 to 26 years. The planning horizon of interest was 10 years. To slightly simplify matters, the productivity goal will not be considered nor will the integer requirements on project acceptance or project interrelationship constraints. The desired levels of the various goals are also given at the bottom of the table, together with other input parameters for the model.

[25]Weingartner, *Mathematical Programming*, pp. 180–181.

Years

Project Number	1	2	3	4	5	6	7	8	9	10
			Cash Flows (dollars)							
1	−100	20	20	20	19	19	18	16	14	11
2	−100	20	18	18	18	18	14	14	14	14
3	−100	15	15	15	15	15	13	13	13	13
4	−100	20	6	11	7	16	5	14	18	3
5	−100	−60	−60	80	74	66	56	44	30	14
6	−200	25	25	25	25	25	25	25	25	25
7	−150	20	20	20	20	20	20	20	20	20
8	−100	20	18	16	14	12	10	4	−20	20
9	−150	−75	−75	60	60	55	50	44	38	36
10	−50	−100	−175	50	55	60	65	60	50	40
11	−100	−150	−100	10	20	30	40	60	60	60
12	−250	45	45	40	30	25	20	15	10	−40
13	−75	−75	−40	40	40	40	35	35	30	25
14	−180	20	12	16	13	11	19	17	12	15
15	−275	40	45	45	40	35	30	25	20	15
16	−140	20	20	18	16	14	11	8	−25	18
17		−100	18	17	15	12	8	−10	18	17
18		−85	20	20	16	15	13	10	7	3
19		−270	−100	125	115	105	80	60	35	25
20		−200	60	40	30	15	−25	−25	50	40
21		−355	60	70	80	70	55	40	25	15
22			−150	25	25	30	35	30	25	20
23							−80	20	20	20
24								−95	−60	47
25								−50	10	10
26									−60	−30
27										−175
28										−40

	1	2	3	4	5	6	7	8	9	10
Cash throw-off of existing assets (e_j)	$400	360	320	280	240	200	160	120	80	40
Profit targets (p_j) (3% increase per year)		$404	416	428	441	454	468	482	496	511
Earnings per dollar of equity goal (q_j)		3%	3%	3%	4%	4%	4%	5%	5%	5%

Growth rate in assets goal (G)   90% over the planning horizon

Leverage goal (S) $\dfrac{\text{Equity}}{\text{Debt}} = 250\%$ over the planning horizon

Upper bound on borrowing $200 every year

Upper bound on equity issue $500 every year

Cost of borrowing   5% every year

Depreciation method   Straight line over the life of each project

Existing assets $2000

Existing debt $300

Existing equity $800

Tax rate   50% every year

								Years								
11	12	13	14	15	16	17	18	19	20	21	22	23	24	25	26	NPV of Projects at k = 6%
								Cash Flows (dollars)								
6	−8															19.31
14	10	10	10	10	10	6	6	6	6	6						52.68
13	11	11	11	11	11	9	9	9	9	9						43.21
20	2	22	8	10	18	6	9	14	24							32.29
																57.50
25	25	25	25	25	25	25	25	25	25	25	25	25	25	25	25	112.82
20	20															7.30
18	16	14	12	10	4											13.71
35	34	33	30	25	17	9										47.90
30	20	10	−25	50	41	35	25	15	5							57.35
60	60	60	60	60	60	60	60	60	60	60	60	60	60	60	60	204.06
40	32	25	19	14	10	7	5									−8.77
15	5															6.02
19	13	14	17	20	14	11	15	17	12							−9.90
−75	35	30	25	20	15	10	5									−17.27
18	16	13	10	6	−25	16	16	14		11	8	5	2			−9.33
15	12	8	−10	18	17	15	12	8								18.26
																0.25
15	10															73.10
30	20	10														−12.90
5																−13.52
15	10	5														42.16
19	17	14	10	6	2											15.08
42	37	31	24	18	13	9	6	4	3							17.12
9	7	4	−14	9	9	8	6	3	−16	8	8	4				−1.97
−10	45	34	25	16	12	8	−20	21	16	12	9	7	5	3		20.92
50	45	35	25	10	−60	45	35	25	10							−0.64
15	13	9	7	5	2											2.22

The optimal solution and goal achievements are presented and discussed below.

Solution: The following table shows the optimal solution and goal achievements.

Model Solution

Goal Attainment

Year	Earnings per Dollar of Equity	Profit p			Amount Borrowed	Amount of Stock Issued
1					$200.00	$500.00
2	Achieved	Achieved,	$p =$	$404		500.00
3	Achieved	Not achieved,	$p =$	333.75		183.18
4	Achieved	Achieved,	$p =$	572.27		
5	Achieved	Achieved,	$p =$	513.33		
6	Achieved	Achieved,	$p =$	454		
7	Achieved	Not achieved,	$p =$	336.71		
8	Achieved	Not achieved,	$p =$	248.60		
9	Achieved	Not achieved,	$p =$	206.33		
10	Achieved	Not achieved,	$p =$	106.66	200.0	

Leverage at the end of the planning horizon	Growth rate in assets	Net present value of accepted projects (at 6%)
$\dfrac{\text{Common stock}}{\text{Debt}} = 283\%$	111%	$381.30

Accepted Projects

Project	Proportion Accepted	Project	Proportion Accepted
1	1.00	17	1.00
2	1.00	18	1.00
3	1.00	19	1.00
´4	1.00	20	1.00
5	0.092	21	1.00
6	1.00	22	1.00
7	0.948	23	1.00
13	0.559	25	1.00
15	1.00	28	1.00

It is interesting to analyze the achievement of the various goals. The earnings per dollar of equity goal is achieved each year in the planning horizon, while the profit targets exhibit a more erratic behavior. These goals are generally attained in the first 6 years (except in year 3), but the low magnitude of the cash throw-offs generated by existing operations prevents their achievement in the final years of the planning horizon.

Borrowing occurs in the very first and the last year of the planning period. Of course, the large outlays at the beginning of the horizon triggers the $200 borrowing in year 1. The bond issue of the last year, however, takes place so as to bring the leverage ratio closer to the desired target. In spite of this final borrowing, the leverage goal is overshot by a nonnegligible amount (283% for equity/debt).

The limit on the new stock issued is operative for the first 2 years, whereas only $183.18 is raised in the third year. Again, the firm would enter the stock market in order to meet the charges associated with the capital outlays of the first periods.

The accepted projects allow the firm to maintain a very comfortable growth in assets (111%), somewhat over the 90% desired level. Finally, the net present value of the portfolio of accepted projects is equal to $381.30.

It is also instructive to analyze the values of the slack variables—d^+ and d^-—for each goal. Since the earnings per dollar of equity goal was achieved in each year, d_{2j}^- was equal to zero for each year, and d_{2j}^+ would equal the excess of the percent returns over the goals shown in the table of input values and goals. Similarly, for each year that the net income goal was achieved, the d_{1j}^- term would equal zero, which means that there would be no penalty in the objective function and that d_{1j}^+ would equal the excess of actual profits over the goal established. For example, in year 4, the net income goal was 428 and the actual level was 572.27; thus, the goal was achieved, $d_{14}^- = 0$, and $d_{14}^+ = 144.27$ (572.27 − 428.00). An analogous interpretation can be provided for the deviational variables for the other three goals. As in the previous example, sensitivity analysis could be performed to determine the impact on the optimal projects and goal achievement as the priority structure is changed.   ●

SUMMARY

This chapter has explored in depth the extensive area of mathematical programming applied to the capital budgeting problem under conditions of certainty. We examined the areas of linear programming, integer linear programming, and goal programming. Each approach provides a powerful methodology to determine the optimal set of projects under various conditions and considers several types of constraints or restrictions. Chapter 14 explores mathematical programming models under conditions of risk.

PROBLEMS

1. The LP Company is considering the adoption of 10 projects that require varied budget commitments over the next 3 years. In addition, the projects have different manpower, managerial supervision, and machine-hour requirements. The table shows the relevant data:

Projects	NPV	Manpower Requirements	Management Supervision	Machine Hours	Budget Year 1	Budget Year 2	Budget Year 3
X_1	$10	5	1	50	$2	$1	$3
X_2	20	2	1	20	3	2	4
X_3	35	20	1	10	5	4	2
X_4	45	25	3	30	1	3	2
X_5	60	10	1	15	6	2	5
X_6	75	7	2	16	3	1	2
X_7	15	12	1	18	4	5	1
X_8	50	15	1	22	5	3	3
X_9	90	30	4	35	7	4	2
X_{10}	55	3	1	45	2	1	1

Constraints: $K_1 \leqslant 70$ $K_2 \leqslant 8$ $K_3 \leqslant 150$ $K_4 \leqslant 20$ $K_5 \leqslant 15$ $K_6 \leqslant 20$

Formulate this as an LP problem and solve it using the simplex method or a package LP algorithm.

2. The Hyperspace Company is evaluating 12 projects which have cash outflow requirements and NPVs as shown in the following table:

Projects	NPV	Year 1	Year 2	Year 3
		Cash Outflows		
X_1	$19.31	$100	$ 0	$ 0
X_2	52.68	100	0	0
X_3	43.21	100	0	0
X_4	32.29	100	0	0
X_5	57.50	100	60	60
X_6	112.82	200	0	0
X_7	7.30	150	0	0
X_8	13.71	100	0	0
X_9	47.90	150	75	75
X_{10}	57.35	50	100	175
X_{11}	204.06	100	150	100
X_{12}	18.26	0	100	0
Constraints:		$K_1 \leqslant 1000$	$K_2 \leqslant 400$	$K_3 \leqslant 308$

Formulate this as an LP problem to maximize NPV and solve it using the simplex method or a packaged LP algorithm.

3. Formulate the Hyperspace Company problem (Problem 2) as an LP to maximize the present value of the cash inflows and solve it using the simplex method or a packaged LP algorithm. Hyperspace's cost of capital is 6%.

Optimal Solution

Basic Variables	X_1	X_2	X_3	X_4	X_5	X_6	X_7	X_8	X_9	X_{10}	X_{11}	X_{12}	S_1	S_2	S_3
X_1	1.0														
X_2		1.0													
X_3			1.0												
X_4				1.0											
X_6						1.0									
X_7							1.0		0.857					0.0067	−0.0019
X_8								1.0							
X_{10}									0.429	1.0					0.0057
X_{11}											1.0				
X_{12}												1.0			
X_5					1.0										
S_2									32.14					1.0	−0.571
S_{10}									−0.857					−0.0067	0.0019
S_{12}									1.0						
S_{13}									−0.429						−0.0057
Objective function									92.625					1.0467	1.7467

4. For the optimal solution to Problem 1:
   (a) Completely interpret the optimal solution by enumerating projects to be accepted and rejected, ranking of all projects, and the shadow prices.
   (b) Perform a complete sensitivity analysis.
5. For the optimal solution to Problem 2:
   (a) Completely interpret the optimal solution by enumerating projects to be accepted and rejected, ranking of all projects, and the shadow prices for budget constraints.
   (b) Is the ranking of the accepted projects the same as a simple ranking of the projects by their NPVs? If these rankings differ, why do they, and which ranking is more relevant?
   (c) Perform a complete sensitivity analysis.
6. The optimal solution to Problem 3 is shown at the bottom of this and the facing page. For this optimal solution:
   (a) Completely interpret the optimal solution by enumerating projects to be accepted and rejected, ranking of all projects, and the shadow prices for budget constraints. (*Caution:* Be careful in interpreting the shadow prices.)
   (b) Is the ranking of the accepted projects the same as a simple ranking by their present value of cash inflows or by their NPVs? If these rankings differ, why do they, and which ranking is more relevant to the Hyperspace Company?
   (c) Perform a complete sensitivity analysis.
7. Firm XYZ has 10 projects with the following characteristics. Projects 1, 3, and 5 are mutually exclusive. For project 6 to be accepted, project 3 must also be accepted. Of projects 2, 4, 7, and 10, at least two must be accepted; however, project 7 cannot be accepted unless projects 8 and 9 are also accepted. If projects 5 and 9 are accepted together, their cost in combination is only 90% of the cost of the two individual projects. Finally, the firm feels that it must undertake at least 5 of the 10 proposed projects to maintain stable employment levels.
   Formulate the appropriate ILP constraints for Firm XYZ.

for Problem 6

S_4	S_5	S_6	S_7	S_8	S_9	S_{10}	S_{11}	S_{12}	S_{13}	S_{14}	S_{15}	RHS
1.0												1.0000
	1.0											1.0000
		1.0										1.0000
			1.0									1.0000
					1.0							1.0000
−0.667	−0.667	−0.667	−0.667	−0.552	−1.33		−0.667			−0.476		0.4000
							1.0					1.0000
				−0.343						−0.571		0.8000
										1.0		1.0000
											1.0	1.0000
												1.0000
				1.0								1.0000
				−25.71						−92.86	−100.	10.0000
0.667	0.667	0.667	0.667	0.552	1.33	1.0	0.667			0.476		0.6000
								1.0				1.0000
				0.343					1.0	0.571		0.2000
14.44	47.81	38.34	27.42	58.35	103.09		8.843			255.38	112.56	2237.71

8. Firm TUB is evaluating the following 10 projects:

<table>
<tr><th></th><th colspan="3">Cash Outflows</th><th></th></tr>
<tr><th>Project</th><th>Year 1</th><th>Year 2</th><th>Year 3</th><th>NPV</th></tr>
<tr><td>X_1</td><td>250</td><td>200</td><td>100</td><td>60</td></tr>
<tr><td>X_2</td><td>300</td><td>250</td><td>150</td><td>80</td></tr>
<tr><td>X_3</td><td>275</td><td>250</td><td>175</td><td>55</td></tr>
<tr><td>X_4</td><td>225</td><td>225</td><td>50</td><td>50</td></tr>
<tr><td>X_5</td><td>150</td><td>250</td><td>150</td><td>25</td></tr>
<tr><td>X_6</td><td>400</td><td>150</td><td>0</td><td>100</td></tr>
<tr><td>X_7</td><td>200</td><td>150</td><td>100</td><td>90</td></tr>
<tr><td>X_8</td><td>350</td><td>50</td><td>25</td><td>40</td></tr>
<tr><td>X_9</td><td>250</td><td>100</td><td>150</td><td>75</td></tr>
<tr><td>X_{10}</td><td>175</td><td>175</td><td>175</td><td>75</td></tr>
</table>

Constraints: $K_1 \leqslant 2,000$ $K_2 \leqslant 1,500$ $K_3 \leqslant 1,000$

The following interrelationships exist between the projects:
(1) Only X_6 or X_7 can be accepted; not both.
(2) If X_6 is accepted, X_2 cannot be accepted.
(3) If X_7 is accepted, X_8 must be accepted.
(4) X_9 and X_{10} are mutually exclusive, but one must be accepted.
(5) If projects 2 and 4 are accepted in combination, 120% of the NPV will be generated and the cost will only be 85% of the combined cash outflows for the two projects separately.
Completely formulate this problem as an integer LP.

9. Acme Market is considering five new supermarkets, which have the following characteristics:

<table>
<tr><th>Project
Characteristics</th><th>1</th><th>2</th><th>3</th><th>4</th><th>5</th></tr>
<tr><td>Cash outflow year 1</td><td>$10,000</td><td>0</td><td>$14,000</td><td>$30,000</td><td>$12,000</td></tr>
<tr><td>Cash outflow year 2</td><td>20,000</td><td>$18,000</td><td>10,000</td><td>15,000</td><td>0</td></tr>
<tr><td>Cash inflow year 1</td><td>8,000</td><td>0</td><td>5,000</td><td>3,000</td><td>4,000</td></tr>
<tr><td>Cash inflow year 2</td><td>12,000</td><td>8,000</td><td>6,000</td><td>18,000</td><td>20,000</td></tr>
<tr><td>Net income year 1</td><td>5,000</td><td>12,000</td><td>3,000</td><td>2,500</td><td>−2,000</td></tr>
<tr><td>Net income year 2</td><td>10,000</td><td>6,000</td><td>5,000</td><td>14,000</td><td>16,000</td></tr>
<tr><td>Profitability
index</td><td>1.4</td><td>1.8</td><td>0.6</td><td>1.2</td><td>0.9</td></tr>
<tr><td>Salvage value year 10</td><td>4,000</td><td>0</td><td>3,000</td><td>2,000</td><td>1,000</td></tr>
</table>

Acme has a budget constraint of $50,000 in year 1 and $40,000 in year 2. Any unused funds in year 1 can be invested in Treasury Bills at 6% and carried over into year 2. In addition, of the benefits received from accepted projects, 60% will be required for operating expenses or dividends; the remainder can be used for reinvestment in other projects. Acme's cost of capital is 10%. The projects noted above require cash outflows only in year 1 or 2 or both.

Among the five supermarkets, several interrelationships must be taken into account:
(1) Either project 1 or project 4 *must* be accepted.
(2) If project 2 is accepted, project 3 must also be accepted.
(3) Project 1 cannot be accepted unless project 5 is also accepted.
(4) Of the set of projects 1, 2, and 4, at most two may be accepted.

The firm has established the following goals:

Priority 1:   Achieve a *minimum* net income of $15,000 in year 1.

Priority 2:   Weight 2—maximize NPV of accepted projects,

   Weight 1—come *as close as possible* to a net income goal of $20,000 in year 2

Formulate this problem as an integer GP problem showing the economic constraints, goal constraints, and the objective function.

14 MULTIPERIOD ANALYSIS UNDER CONDITIONS OF UNCERTAINTY

In Chapter 13 we explored the important models in the area of mathematical programming under conditions of certainty. Such models enable the decision maker to select the set of projects that maximize net present value or (in the case of goal programming) which endeavor to simultaneously achieve a hierarchy of multiple goals. Such models also enable the decision maker to consider more realistic and complex problem settings than those handled by the simple models covered in Chapters 5 to 7. This chapter parallels Chapter 13 in that it introduces sophisticated approaches for handling conditions of risk in the capital budgeting problem. The new models surveyed here will enrich the simple risk models handled in Chapters 8, 9, and 10 will determine the set of projects that will maximize expected shareholder utility under the complex conditions of multiperiod uncertainty. The chapter begins with a discussion of decision trees and how they can be used in the capital budgeting problem under conditions of risk. Next, the important area of Monte Carlo simulation is surveyed and then applied to the problem area. Finally, the most helpful mathematical programming models under conditions of risk are discussed and illustrated.

DECISION TREES

A technique that has been recommended to handle complex, sequential decisions over time is the use of decision trees. A *decision tree* is a formal representation of available decision alternatives at various points through time which are followed by chance events that may occur with some probability. A ranking of the available decision alternatives is usually achieved by finding the expected returns of the alternatives, which merely requires multiplying the returns earned by each alternative for various chance events by the probability that the event will occur and summing over all possible events. To illustrate the use of decision trees in a very simple problem setting, consider Example 1.

● **EXAMPLE 1**   Decision Tree Example

A firm is considering three alternative single-period investments, A, B, and C, whose returns are dependent upon the state of the economy in the coming period. The state of the economy is known only by a probability distribution:

State of the Economy	Probability
Fair	0.25
Good	0.40
Very good	0.30
Super	0.05
	1.00

The returns for each alternative under each possible state of the economy are as follows:

	State of the Economy			
Alternative	Fair	Good	Very Good	Super
A	$10	$40	$ 70	$ 90
B	− 20	50	100	140
C	− 75	60	120	200

Use a decision tree to evaluate the three alternatives.

Solution: The decision tree for this problem is shown below. Notice that we have followed the somewhat standard convention of using a square node to represent decision alternatives and round nodes to show chance events. On the far right side of the tree, the returns for each state of the economy have been weighted by the probability that the

Decision Alternative	State of the Economy	Probability of State of Economy	Return Earned	Weighted Return
	fair	0.25	$10	$ 2.50
	good	0.40	40	16.00
	very good	0.30	70	21.00
	super	0.05	90	4.50
A			$E(R_A)$ =	$44.00
	fair	0.25	−$20	−$ 5.00
	good	0.40	50	20.00
	very good	0.30	100	30.00
B	super	0.05	140	7.00
			$E(R_B)$ =	$52.00
C	fair	0.25	−$75	−$18.75
	good	0.40	60	24.00
	very good	0.30	120	36.00
	super	0.05	200	10.00
			$E(R_C)$ =	$51.25

state will occur. The sum of these values for all possible states of the economy is the expected return associated with each of the three decision alternatives. Thus, once the decision tree has been "folded back," the selection of the alternative that maximizes expected return is immediate.

Decision Alternative	Expected Return
A	$44.00
B	$52.00
C	$51.25

Alternative *B* maximizes the expected return, alternative *C* is a close second, and alternative *A* is a rather distant third.   ●

Of course, even in this simple example, it would be imprudent for the firm to immediately implement the alternative with the highest expected return. This "optimal" action with the unidimensional criterion cries out for further analysis. Namely, we should investigate the following:

1. The degree to which the estimated *probabilities* of the various states of the economy would have to change for the "optimal" solution to no longer be "optimal."

2. The extent to which the estimated *returns* associated with the alternatives and states of the economy would have to change in order to shift the "optimal" decision.

3. The degree of risk associated with each of the alternatives.

4. The *utility* that the firm attaches to each of the returns for each of the states of the economy based on the firm's goals, risk posture, risk–return preferences, and so on.

Thus, decision tree analysis is advocated as an initial step which requires further analysis rather than the final word in the firm's efforts to maximize shareholders' expected utility. Given the caveats listed above, we illustrate the use of decision trees in the multiperiod capital budgeting setting.

Recall that our discussion in Chapter 8 looked at the calculation of the expected certainty equivalent value and the standard deviation of the certainty equivalent under the two extremes of perfect correlation and independence of the cash flows over the life of the project. However, most business and financial cash flows generally fall somewhere between the two extremes (i.e., moderate correlation exists between successive years' cash flows). To some extent, the events in one period influence the outcomes in the following period, which implies that *conditional probabilities* are required. In addition to the expressions describing these two extremes, Hillier[1] also derived an equation for the standard deviation of the certainty equivalent value, where moderate intertemporal correlation exists between successive years' cash flows. Since the expression for this standard deviation is quite complex, decision trees (for two or more projects) or tree diagrams (for a single project) have been recommended as a

---

[1]F. S. Hillier, "The Derivation of Probabilistic Information for the Evaluation of Risky Investments," *Management Science*, April 1963, pp. 443–451.

way to handle the problem.[2] Tree diagrams are used to evaluate a single project and show chance events which can occur over successive periods with various probabilities conditioned on prior outcomes. Using either tree diagrams or decision trees enables the analyst to compute the mean and standard deviation of the discounted cash flows with formulas similar to those shown in Chapter 8. Namely, the expected discounted cash inflow $(\overline{A})$ for a project is determined using Equation (1):

$$\overline{A} = \sum_{s=1}^{M} A_s P_s \tag{1}$$

The standard deviation of the discounted cash inflows is determined using Equation (2):

$$\sigma_A = \sqrt{\sum_{s=1}^{M} \left(A_s - \overline{A} \right)^2 P_s} \tag{2}$$

where A_s = discounted cash inflow associated with series s in the distribution $\sum_{t=1}^{N} A_t^s$

A_t^s = discounted cash inflow which occurs in series s during period t

P_s = joint probability of a single-line series s =

$$P\{A_1^s\}\left[\prod_{t=2}^{N} P\{A_t^s | A_{t-1}^s\} \right]$$

s = given series in the distribution
t = given period in the life of the project
M = number of line series in the distribution
N = number of periods in the life of the project

It should be noticed that P_s is a joint probability which is found by multiplying several conditional probabilities for successive chance events. Computation of the parameters above is illustrated in Example 2.

● **EXAMPLE 2**   *Tree Diagram for Three-Period Project*

Consider project P, which has a three-period useful life. Owing to the moderate correlation between cash flows over successive periods which changes between pairs of periods, the analyst feels that a tree diagram and Equations (1) and (2) are the most efficient and accurate ways to evaluate the project.

The possible cash inflows for each period (which are already discounted back to the present) and their associated probabilities are as follows:

---

[2]See J. F. Magee, "How to Use Decision Trees in Capital Investments," *Harvard Business Review*, September–October 1964, pp. 79–96; and R. D. Hespos and P. A. Strassmann, "Stochastic Decision Trees for the Analysis of Investment Decisions," *Management Science*, August 1965, pp. 244–259.

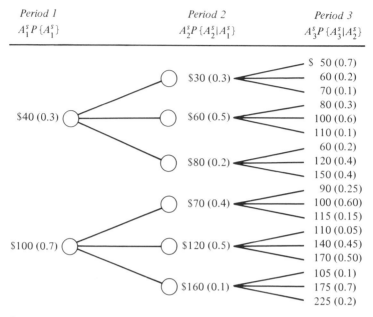

	Period 1 $A_1^s P\{A_1^s\}$	Period 2 $A_2^s P\{A_2^s|A_1^s\}$	Period 3 $A_3^s P\{A_3^s|A_2^s\}$

Using these data, determine the expected discounted cash inflow and its standard deviation.

Solution:

	Period 1		Period 2		Period 3				
Series	A_1^s	$P\{A_1^s\}$	A_2^s	$P\{A_2^s|A_1^s\}$	A_3^s	$P\{A_3^s|A_2^s\}$	$A_s = \sum\limits_{t=1}^{3} A_t^s$	P_s	$(A_s \times P_s)$
1	\$ 40	0.3	\$ 30	0.3	\$ 50	0.7	\$120	0.063	\$ 7.56
2	40	0.3	30	0.3	60	0.2	130	0.018	2.34
3	40	0.3	30	0.3	70	0.1	140	0.009	1.26
4	40	0.3	60	0.5	80	0.3	180	0.045	8.10
5	40	0.3	60	0.5	100	0.6	200	0.090	18.00
6	40	0.3	60	0.5	110	0.1	210	0.015	3.15
7	40	0.3	80	0.2	60	0.2	180	0.012	2.16
8	40	0.3	80	0.2	120	0.4	240	0.024	5.76
9	40	0.3	80	0.2	150	0.4	270	0.024	6.48
10	100	0.7	70	0.4	90	0.25	260	0.070	18.20
11	100	0.7	70	0.4	100	0.60	270	0.168	45.36
12	100	0.7	70	0.4	115	0.15	285	0.042	11.97
13	100	0.7	120	0.5	110	0.05	330	0.0175	5.775
14	100	0.7	120	0.5	140	0.45	360	0.1575	56.70
15	100	0.7	120	0.5	170	0.50	390	0.175	68.25
16	100	0.7	160	0.1	105	0.1	365	0.007	2.555
17	100	0.7	160	0.1	175	0.7	435	0.049	21.315
18	100	0.7	160	0.1	225	0.2	485	0.014	6.79
								1.000	\$291.725

$$\bar{A} = \sum_{s=1}^{18} A_s P_s = \$291.725$$

It should be pointed out that in the table above, the A_s column is the sum of the three columns A_1^s, A_2^s, and A_3^s; furthermore, the P_s column is the product of the three probabilities $(P\{A_1^s\})(P\{A_2^s|A_1^s\})(P\{A_3^s|A_2^s\})$ and that the latter two probabilities are conditional on prior period outcomes.

The following table is helpful in computing σ_A:

Series	A_s	$A_s - \bar{A}$	$(A_s - \bar{A})^2$	P_s	$(A_s - \bar{A})^2 P_s$
1	$120	− $171.725	29,489.476	0.063	$1,857.837
2	130	− 161.725	26,154.976	0.018	470.790
3	140	− 151.725	23,020.476	0.009	207.184
4	180	− 111.725	12,482.476	0.045	561.711
5	200	− 91.725	8,413.476	0.090	757.213
6	210	− 81.725	6,678.976	0.015	100.185
7	180	− 111.725	12,482.476	0.012	149.790
8	240	− 51.725	2,675.476	0.024	64.211
9	270	− 21.725	471.976	0.024	11.327
10	260	− 31.725	1,006.476	0.070	70.453
11	270	− 21.725	471.976	0.168	79.292
12	285	− 6.725	45.226	0.042	1.899
13	330	38.275	1,464.976	0.0175	25.637
14	360	68.275	4,661.476	0.1575	734.182
15	390	98.275	9,657.976	0.175	1,690.146
16	365	73.275	5,369.226	0.007	37.585
17	435	143.275	20,527.726	0.049	1,005.859
18	485	193.275	37,355.226	0.014	522.973
				1.000	$8,348.274

Now,

$$\sigma_A = \sqrt{8{,}348.274}$$
$$= \$91.77$$

Thus, the expected discounted cash inflow for project P is $291.73, and the standard deviation of the cash inflows is $91.77. ●

Of course, even a casual view of Example 2 would prompt the question: How practical is the decision tree (or tree diagram) approach as the useful life of the project and/or the number of feasible states that the cash flows can take on grows? Growth in either of these areas or, for that matter, in the number of projects under evaluation would hasten the need for calling on the computer to assist in the analysis. Furthermore, it can be argued that a more accurate picture of a project's attractiveness is better evaluated by analyzing the underlying random variables which contribute to the size of the annual cash flows rather than just looking at the aggregate figure (i.e., the annual cash flow itself). For these reasons (as well as others), Monte Carlo simulation has been found to be a useful technique in evaluating capital investments under conditions of risk.

FIGURE 14-1   Schematic of a Simulation Model

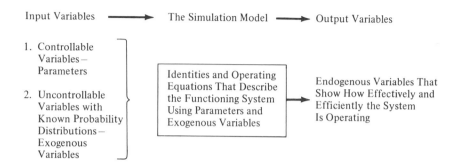

Input Variables   ⟶   The Simulation Model   ⟶   Output Variables

1. Controllable
   Variables –
   Parameters

2. Uncontrollable
   Variables with
   Known Probability
   Distributions –
   Exogenous
   Variables

Identities and Operating
Equations That Describe
the Functioning System
Using Parameters and
Exogenous Variables

Endogenous Variables That
Show How Effectively and
Efficiently the System
Is Operating

MONTE CARLO SIMULATION

Monte Carlo simulation is a flexible and useful operations research technique that can handle any finite problem whose structure and logic can be specified. *Simulation* is the imitation of a real-world system by using a mathematical model which captures the critical operating characteristics of the system as it moves through time encountering random events. Groff and Muth[3] identify three major uses for simulation models:

1. To determine improved operating conditions (i.e., systems design).

2. To demonstrate how a proposed change in policy will work and/or how the new policy compares with existing policies (i.e., systems analysis or sensitivity analysis).

3. To train operating personnel to make better decisions, to react to emergencies in a more efficient and effective manner, and to utilize different kinds of information (i.e., simulation games and heuristic programming).

Figure 14-1 shows a schematic of a simulation model composed of the following four major elements:

1. Parameters, which are input variables specified by the decision maker which will be held constant over all simulation runs.

2. Exogenous variables, which are input variables outside the control of the decision maker which are subject to random variation—hence, the decision maker must specify a probability distribution which describes possible events that may occur and their associated likelihood of occurrence.

3. Endogenous variables, which are output or performance variables describing the operations of the system and how effectively the system achieved various goals as it encountered the random events mentioned above.

4. Identities and operating equations, which are mathematical expressions making up the heart of the simulation model by showing how the endogenous variables are functionally related to the parameters and exogenous variables.

A flowchart for a general simulation model is shown in Figure 14-2. The focus of the simulation is to develop empirical distributions for each endogenous

[3]G. K. Groff and J. F. Muth, *Operations Management: Analysis for Decisions* (Homewood, Ill.: Richard D. Irwin, Inc., 1972), pp. 369–370.

FIGURE 14-2 General Flowchart of a Simulation

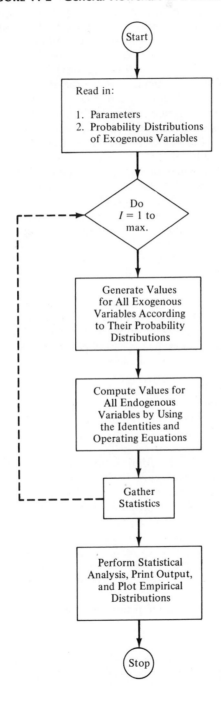

variable in order to describe how efficiently and effectively the system operated during the 500 or 1,000 sampling trials that represent various combinations of random events encountered. As shown in Figure 14-2, the simulation progresses as follows. The parameters of the model are initialized and the probability distributions for each exogenous variable are read in; the simulation itself consists of the DO-LOOP, which will be executed the number of times the user specified (i.e., MAX is a parameter set by the decision maker to show how many trials are desired wherein system behavior will be studied); on each simulation run, a value is generated for each exogenous variable by randomly selecting from its input probability distribution; based on these randomly generated values and the values of the parameters, a value is computed for each endogenous variable using the appropriate identity or operating equation; each simulation run provides one sampling observation for each endogenous variable, and when these observations are aggregated for all simulation runs, the analyst has an empirical distribution from which the usual statistics can be computed and probability statements made about the likelihood of the endogenous variable taking on a value within any given range; based on the empirical distributions and their statistics which are printed out after the completion of all simulation runs (as well as other such distributions arrived at through prior simulations performed using other values for the parameters, etc.), decisions are made.

A very good survey of the simulation technique appears in Groff and Muth.[4] In addition, Naylor et al. and Shannon[5] provide an extensive treatment of simulation studies, as well as an in-depth discussion of several applications.

Monte Carlo simulation has a number of significant advantages over comparable analytic techniques for handling conditions of risk. First, simulation can handle problems that may have the following characteristics:

1. Numerous exogenous random variables that are described by any kind of a probability distribution.

2. Any number of system interrelationships among variables.

3. Identities or operating equations taking on nonlinear, differential, or integral equation forms.

Virtually any analytic or optimization technique would have severe difficulties in handling such problems, if they could be handled at all. Second, sensitivity analysis can be performed in a straightforward manner so that the impact on the system can be pinpointed as parameters or the probability distribution for any combination of exogenous variables is varied. Third, even though simulation models are powerful and flexible, the cost of carrying out simulation runs is relatively small and simulation programs can be modified easily to reflect new structure and relationships in the system under study. However, simulation models (like any decision facilitating model) have their limitations:

1. Input requirements can often put great demands on the decision maker.

[4]Ibid., Chap. 12.
[5]T. H. Naylor, J. L. Balintfy, D. S. Burdick, and K. Chu, *Computer Simulation Techniques* (New York: John Wiley & Sons, Inc., 1966); and R. E. Shannon, *System Simulation: The Art and Science* (Englewood Cliffs, N.J.: Prentice-Hall, Inc., 1975).

2. Valid specification of system variables and interrelationships in the simulation model require a rather extensive understanding of the logical and mathematical properties (many of which can be hidden or nonobvious) of the real system under analysis.

3. Experimental design requires careful attention by the analyst so that the simulation model can be verified and so that it provides output that is as free of error and as informative as possible.

SIMULATION APPLIED TO CAPITAL BUDGETING

One of the first authors to recommend that simulation be used in evaluating capital expenditures was David B. Hertz[6] in his famous 1964 *Harvard Business Review* article. Hertz, a consultant with McKinsey and Co., Inc., described the approach that his firm utilized to assist an industrial chemical producer who was evaluating a $10 million expansion of its processing plant which would have a 10-year service life. The simulation approach that was used had nine input variables:

Variables for investment cost analysis:
1. Original investment required.
2. Useful life of the facility.
3. Residual value of the investment.
Variables related to revenue generated by the investment:
4. Selling price of the product.
5. Size of the market.
6. Annual growth rate in the size of the market.
7. Share of the market captured by the firm.
Variables related to the operating costs associated with the investment:
8. Variable operating costs per unit of output.
9. Fixed operating costs per year.

The flowchart used by Hertz is shown in Figure 14-3. As can be seen, simulation encounters no difficulties in handling exogenous variables with any desired shape or moments (i.e., mean, variance, skewness, or kurtosis—the first four moments of the probability distribution). It is important to note that the probability distributions must be assessed by management so that they reflect the statistical dependence that exists between various combinations of variables: selling price and size of the market, size of the market and market growth rate, the trade-off between fixed and variable operating costs, and so on. Hertz does not discuss the exact methodology he used to accomplish the task but, as indicated, building interrelationships between variables into the model is one of the rather important aspects of simulation and requires careful attention by management and staff experts involved in building the simulation model.

Interpretation of the information about endogenous variables which is printed out and/or plotted by the computer at the end of the desired number

---

[6]David B. Hertz, "Risk Analysis in Capital Investment," *Harvard Business Review*, January–February 1964, pp. 95–106.

FIGURE 14-3

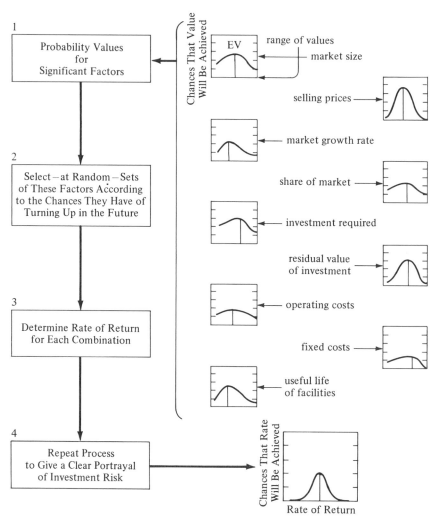

Simulation for investment planning. EV = expected value =average, or the "one best estimate."

of simulation runs is another essential phase of the overall simulation process. Of course, this output information usually provides valuable data that management uses to compare the risk–return characteristics of investment alternatives under consideration and then to select the alternative that offers the maximum expected utility. To illustrate the ideas described above, consider Figure 14-4, again from the Hertz article. The figure shows the rate of return on two hypothetical alternatives (*A* vs. *B*) that could be competing designs for the new plant addition in the chemical firm mentioned earlier. The differences are based on the degree of automation. The latter alternative has a higher intensity of capital equipment. The former requires the same dollar investment because more and better facilities to accommodate greater numbers of workers are necessitated by the nature of the less-automated plant. As can be seen, alternative *B* has both a higher expected return and a greater risk, owing to the increased variability in its returns as compared with alternative *A*. Management should use this information as well as similar results on other endogenous variables, in order to select the alternative that is preferred given the firm's utility function.

To summarize our discussion and illustrate the components of a simulation model, introduced in the previous section, we will now formally define the parameters, exogenous variables, endogenous variables, and the identities and operating equations for the capital budgeting problem setting using Example 3.

● **EXAMPLE 3** *Formulation of Simulation Model for Capital Budgeting Problem*

For the general capital budgeting problem discussed in this section, formulate a simulation model by specifying the parameters, exogenous variables, endogenous variables, identities, and operating equations. A flowchart should also be drawn. It can be assumed that the selling price of the product is controlled by the firm and thus is not subject to uncertainty and that the risk-free rate will remain constant over the life of the project. Further, the firm will evaluate any projects under consideration by determining its net income after taxes each year, net cash flows each year, net present value over the life of the project, internal rate of return, and payback period.

Solution: The simulation model with the required components is presented in the table below:

General Capital Budgeting Simulation Model

Parameters:

SP_t = unit selling price in year t

DR_t = depreciation rate for year t

i = risk-free rate

MAX = total number of simulation runs to be performed

Exogenous variables:

Stochastic variables with known probability distributions:

MG_t = market growth rate during year t

MS_i = initial market size in number of units

SM_t = share of the market in year t

FIGURE 14-4 Comparison of Two Investment Opportunities

Selected Statistics

	Investment A	Investment B
Amount of investment	$10,000,000	$10,000,000
Life of investment (years)	10	10
Expected annual net cash inflow	$1,300,000	$1,400,000
Variability of cash inflow		
1 chance in 50 of		
being *greater* than	$1,700,000	$3,400,000
1 chance in 50 of		
being *less*[a] than	$900,000	($600,000)
Expected return on investment	5.0%	6.8%
Variability of return		
on investment		
1 chance in 50 of		
being *greater* than	7.0%	5.5%
1 chance in 50 of		
being *less*[a] than	3.0%	(4.0%)
Risk of investment		
Chances of a loss	Negligible	1 in 10
Expected size of loss		$200,000

[a] In the case of negative figures (indicated by parentheses), "less than" means "worse than."

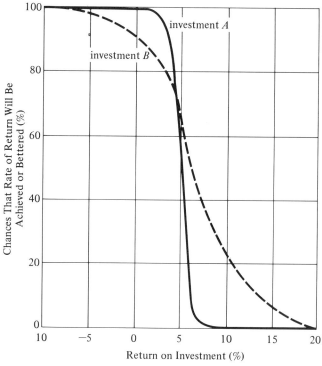

Source: David B. Hertz, "Risk Analyiss in Capital Investment," *Harvard Business Review,* January–February 1964, p. 105. Copyright © 1963 by the President and Fellows of Harvard College; all rights reserved.

INV = initial investment required by the project

N = useful life of the investment

FC_t = total operating fixed costs in year t

VC_t = variable operating costs per unit in year t

OC_t = other project related costs in year t

TR_t = tax rate in year t

Endogenous variables:

Performance variables computed by using identities and operating equations:

$USAL_t$ = unit sales generated by the project in year t

REV_t = total revenue generated by the project in year t

DEP_t = depreciation on the project in period t

TVC_t = total variable costs associated with the project in year t

TC_t = total costs associated with the project in year t

$NIAT_t$ = net income after tax generated by the project in year t

NCI_t = net cash inflow generated by the project in year t

BV_t = book value of the project at the end of year t

NPV_m = net present value for the investment on the mth simulation run

IRR_m = internal rate of return for the investment on the mth simulation run

$PAYB_m$ = payback period for the investment on the mth simulation run

Identities and operating equations:

$$BV_0 = INV$$

$$DEP_t = (DR_t)(BV_{t-1})$$

$$BV_t = BV_{t-1} - DEP_t$$

$$MS_t = (MS_{t-1})(1 + MG_{t-1})$$

$$USAL_t = (MS_t)(SM_t)$$

$$REV_t = (USAL_t)(SP_t)$$

$$TVC_t = (VC_t)(USAL_t)$$

$$TC_t = TVC_t + FC_t + OC_t + DEP_t$$

$$TAX_t = TR_t(REV_t - TC_t)$$

$$NIAT_t = REV_t - TC_t - TAX_t$$

$$NCI_t = NIAT_t + DEP_t$$

$$NPV_m = \sum_{t=1}^{N} \frac{NCI_t}{(1 + i)^t} + \frac{BV_n}{(1 + i)^n} - INV$$

IRR_m = rate r such that

$$\sum_{t=1}^{N} \frac{NCI_t}{(1 + r)^t} + \frac{BV_n}{(1 + r)^n} - INV = 0$$

$PAYB_m$ = payback period is the value K such that

$$\sum_{t=1}^{K} NCI_t = INV$$

A flowchart showing how the foregoing model would operate is as follows:

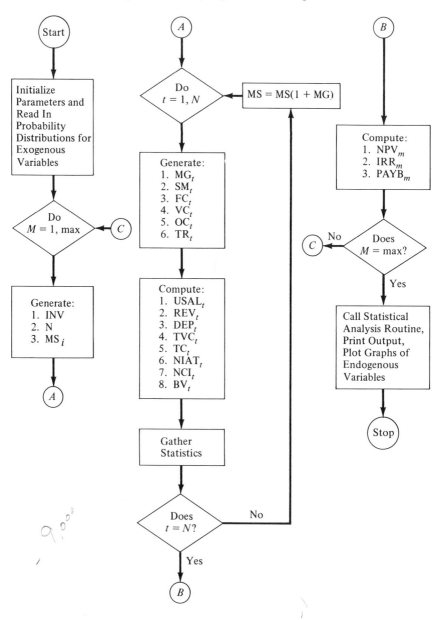

The general model can be enriched or reduced in terms of the number of variables based on the firm's needs. The approach used in Example 3 is straightforward and conventional except for the computation of NPV on each simulation run. It should be noticed that the risk-free rate (rather than the cost of capital or a risk-adjusted discount rate) is used to compute NPV, since the discounting process within a simulation model must only reflect discounting for futurity or the time value of money and not for the specific riskiness of the project under consideration. The degree of risk of the investment project is ascertained in the simulation runs themselves and will be reflected in all the empirical distributions of the endogenous variables. To discount the cash flows of the project at a rate in excess of the risk-free rate would burden the project with an improper double adjustment for uncertainty.[7] Thus, all that is required is to discount the cash flows at the risk-free rate in order to arrive at an empirical NPV distribution that contains valuable information regarding both the expected value and the risk associated with the project under consideration.

Any large-scale simulation would, of course, be performed on a computer since a minimum of 500 to 1,000 simulation runs are required to achieve stability in the results, and because there are usually many factors to monitor, as can be seen in Example 3. However, to provide insight concerning the operation of the simulation technique, the next example demonstrates a very simple hand simulation.

● **EXAMPLE 4**   *Capital Budgeting Simulation Experiment*
The Monte Carlo Company is evaluating an investment proposal which has uncertainty associated with the three important aspects: the original cost, the useful life, and the annual net cash inflows. The three probability distributions for these variables are shown below:

Original Cost		Useful Life		Annual Net Cash Inflows	
Value	*Probability*	*Value*	*Probability*	*Value*	*Probability*
$60,000	0.3	5 yr	0.4	$10,000	0.1
70,000	0.6	6 yr	0.4	15,000	0.3
90,000	0.1	7 yr	0.2	20,000	0.4
				25,000	0.2

The firm wants to perform five simulation runs of this project's life. The firm's cost of capital is 15% and the risk-free rate is 6%; for simplicity it is assumed that these two values are known for certain and will remain constant over the life of the project.
Determine the NPV, IRR, and payback period for each of the five simulation runs.

Solution: In order to perform the desired simulation runs by hand, a random-number table would be required. An excerpt from the RAND table which shows random numbers uniformly distributed between zero and 1 is shown below. From this table we can randomly generate values from each of the three discrete probability distributions shown above.

---

[7]See W. G. Lewellen and M. S. Long, "Simulation vs. Single-Value Estimates in Capital Expenditure Analysis," *Decision Sciences*, Vol. 3, No. 4, October 1972, pp. 22ff.

Table of Random Digits

09656	96657	64842	49222	49506	10145	48455	23505	90430	04180
24712	55799	60857	73479	33581	17360	30406	05842	72044	90764
07202	96341	23699	76171	79126	04512	15426	15980	88898	09658
84575	46820	54083	43918	46989	05379	70682	43081	66171	38942
38144	87037	46626	70529	27918	34191	98668	33482	43998	75733
48048	56349	01986	29814	69800	91609	65374	22928	09704	59343
41936	58566	31276	19952	01352	18834	99596	09302	20087	19063
73391	94006	03822	81845	76158	41352	40596	14325	27020	17546
57580	08954	73554	28698	29022	11568	35668	59906	39557	27217
92646	41113	91411	56215	69302	86419	61224	41936	56939	27816
07118	12707	35622	81485	73354	49800	60805	05648	28898	60933
57842	57831	24130	75408	83784	64307	91620	40810	06539	70387
65078	44981	81009	33697	98324	46928	34198	96032	98426	77488
04294	96120	67629	55265	26248	40602	25566	12520	89785	93932
48381	06807	43775	09708	73199	53406	02910	83292	59249	18597
00459	62045	19249	67095	22752	24636	16965	91836	00582	46721
38824	81681	33323	64086	55970	04849	24819	20749	51711	86173
91465	22232	02907	01050	07121	53536	71070	26916	47620	01619
50874	00807	77751	73952	03073	69063	16894	85570	81746	07568
26644	75871	15618	50310	72610	66205	82640	86205	73453	90232

The simulation process is now undertaken. In order to generate random numbers from the table, we would just start anywhere at random in the table, reading any pair of adjacent columns, since we need a two-digit random number and read either down the column or across the row. For this example we will simply use the first two columns in the table and start at the top with the number "09" and then read down the column. In addition, the above three probability distributions should be cumulated to facilitate running the simulation.

Original Cost			Useful Life			Annual Net Cash Inflows		
Value	Prob.	Cum. Prob.	Value	Prob.	Cum. Prob.	Value	Prob.	Cum. Prob.
$60,000	0.3	0.30	5 yr	0.4	0.40	$10,000	0.1	0.10
70,000	0.6	0.90	6 yr	0.4	0.80	15,000	0.3	0.40
90,000	0.1	1.00	7 yr	0.2	1.00	20,000	0.4	0.80
						25,000	0.2	1.00

Thus, we can immediately see that the original cost of the project will be $60,000 if the two-digit random number generated is between 00 but less than 30; the cost will be $70,000 if the random number generated is between 30 but less than 90; the cost will be $90,000 if the random number generated is between 90 and 99. This methodolgy carries over to the other two distributions.

The five simulations are now performed and the results tabulated below:

Simulation Results

Run	Original Cost R.N.	Value	Useful Life R.N	Value	Annual Cash Flows R.N.	Value	NPV	IRR	Payback
1	09	$60,000	24	5 yr	07	$10,000	−$17,876.36	Negative	None
2	84	70,000	38	5 yr	48	20,000	14,247.28	13.12%	3.5 yr
3	41	70,000	73	6 yr	57	20,000	28,346.48	18.00%	3.5 yr
4	92	90,000	07	5 yr	57	20,000	5,752.72	3.55%	4.5 yr
5	65	70,000	04	5 yr	48	20,000	14,247.28	13.12%	3.5 yr

Recall that the NPV is computed using the risk-free rate of 6%. Of course, this simulation is greatly simplified, but it should provide the general flavor of the approach. Notice that there is substantial variability in the results due to the small number of exogenous variables, their discrete distributions, and the small number of simulation runs performed.   ●

The basic simulation approach has been extended in several directions. Some of the more interesting are now discussed briefly with references given so that the interested reader can explore them further.

Kryzanowski, Lusztig, and Schwab[8] discuss the application of a Hertz-type simulation model to a plant-expansion decision by a natural-resource firm. Thuesen[9] described the use of simulation by the Georgia Power Company in performing risk analysis in the evaluation of nucelar vs. fossil-fuel power plants. Philippatos and Mastai[10] designed a model to assist a wholesaler of nondurable goods in evaluating a proposed computer-controlled automated warehouse. Chambers and Mullick[11] present a simulation model that they designed and used at Corning Glass Works to evaluate five alternative manufacturing facilities in various foreign countries for one of their major product lines. Fourcans and Hindelang[12] formulated a general two-stage simulation model wherein both the subsidiary and the parent company of a multinational firm can evaluate and rank investment opportunities considering both project-related and critical international variables as well as various interrelationships among these variables.

---

[8]L. Kryzanowski, P. Lusztig, and B. Schwab, "Monte Carlo Simulation and Capital Expenditure Decisions—A Case Study," *The Engineering Economist*, Vol. 18, Fall 1972, pp. 31–48.

[9]G. J. Thuesen, "Nuclear vs. Fossil Power Plants: Evolution of Economic Evaluation Techniques," *The Engineering Economist*, Vol. 21, Fall 1975, pp 21–38.

[10]G. C. Philippatos, and A. J. Mastai, "Investment in an Automated Warehouse: A Monte Carlo Simulation and Post-Optimality Analysis," *Proceedings of the 1971 Conference on Systems, Networks and Computers*, January 1971, Mexico City; also see G. C. Philippatos, *Financial Management: Theory and Techniques* (San Francisco: Holden-Day, Inc., 1973), Chap. 21.

[11]J. C. Chambers and S. K. Mullick, "Investment Decision Making in a Multinational Enterprise," *Management Accounting*, August 1971.

[12]A. Fourcans and T. J. Hindelang, "A Simulation Approach to Capital Budgeting for the Multinational Firm," presented to the *1976 Financial Management Association Conference*, October 1976, Montreal, Canada; also see Appendix 15A of this text.

Cohen and Elton[13] suggested simulation as an efficient way of determining the elements of the variance–covariance matrix required to evaluate joint returns on a portfolio of capital budgeting projects under evaluation. Salazar and Sen[14] developed a simulation model which they combined with Weingartner's linear programming model; their simulation incorporated two types of uncertainty: environmental uncertainty based on what future economic, social, and competitive conditions may be; and cash flow uncertainty, wherein only the shape and parameters of a probability distribution are specified. Their approach generates efficient portfolios of projects which are ranked as a function of differing environmental conditions and/or managerial preferences toward risk and return. Finally, Carter[15] has suggested an interactive simulation model wherein all projects under consideration are simulated jointly in order to derive covariances among the projects. Based on this simulation, the expected return and variance of various portfolios are computed and managers can obtain further information on any desired portfolio in order to make the final selection.

Our overview of the simulation methodology, plus the survey of the direction of simulation research, will be helpful in the following section, which introduces the complex area of mathematical programming under conditions of risk.

MATHEMATICAL PROGRAMMING UNDER RISK

This section surveys the application of mathematical programming models under conditions of risk to the capital budgeting problem. Table 12-1 identified the five categories of mathematical programming models under conditions of risk:

1. Stochastic linear programming (SLP)
   Linear programming under uncertainty (LPUU)
   Chance-constrained programming (CCP)
2. Integer programming under uncertainty (IPUU)
3. Stochastic goal programming (SGP)
4. Nonlinear programming under uncertainty (NLPUU)
   Quadratic programming under uncertainty (QPUU)
5. Dynamic programming under uncertainty (DPUU)

Among these approaches, the major applications in the capital budgeting area have been in stochastic LP, chance-constrained programming, and quadratic programming under uncertainty. A brief overview will be presented for each of these models as well as the significance of their application within the field of capital investment.

[13]K. J. Cohen and E. J. Elton, "Intertemporal Portfolio Analysis Based on Simulation of Joint Returns," *Management Science*, Vol. 14, September, 1967, pp. 5–18.

[14]R. C. Salazar and S. K. Sen, "A Simulation Model of Capital Budgeting Under Uncertainty," *Management Science*, Vol. 15, December 1968, pp. 161–179.

[15]E. E. Carter, *Portfolio Aspects of Corporate Capital Budgeting* (Lexington, Mass.: Lexington Books, 1974).

Stochastic Linear Programming

Stochastic LP (SLP) is a method of handling conditions of risk which is similar to Monte Carlo simulation already discussed. In SLP, a linear programming model replaces the identities and operating equations of the simulation model and the two-stage process proceeds as follows. In stage 1, we first set a number of decision variables and consider that they will be fixed (just like "parameters" in a simulation model) for all subsequent observations of random events. In stage 2, random events are generated and these values plus the parameters from stage 1 are substituted into the LP model. The LP is solved which provides one empirical observation of the optimal value of the LP objective function and the optimal values of the decision variables. Next, we go back and repeat the process of generating random events and solving LP problems some desired number of times, thereby deriving a complete empirical distribution for the LP objective function. Finally, we compare this empirical distribution with other empirical distributions arrived at using different stage 1 decisions in order to ascertain that set of stage 1 decisions which optimizes the decision maker's utility function.

The major SLP approach to capital budgeting is due to Salazar and Sen.[16] To provide greater insight concerning their approach and to further describe SLP, several figures from their article are presented. Recall that Salazar and Sen incorporate two kinds of uncertainty into their model: uncertainty related to significant economic and competitive variables which are likely to affect project cash flows and uncertainty related to the cash flows of the projects under consideration based on these variables. Salazar and Sen handle the first type of uncertainty by a tree diagram similar to those introduced in the preceding section, shown in Figure 14-5. Notice that there are 12 branches in the tree diagram with their respective joint probabilities of occurrence shown on the far right of the tree; the derivation of those probabilities is based on the table below the tree. In the SLP frameowrk, the 12 branches in this tree diagram will be considered as stage 1 decisions that will be fixed; for each branch in the tree, cash flows for each project under consideration will be randomly generated and then plugged into the LP model To elaborate, consider the flowchart used by Salazar and Sen, which is shown in Figure 14-6. The first processing box in the flowchart randomly selects a branch from the tree shown in Figure 14-5. Next, the time counter, t, is set to 1 and then the project counter, j, is also set to 1. The two Do-Loops randomly generate the cash flows for all projects (up to $j = 15$—all 15 projects under consideration) over all time periods (up to $t = 21$—the planning horizon of the model). These random cash flows are plugged into the model's LP algorithm (which would be similar to the models discussed in Chapter 13) and the optimal set of projects, and the optimal objective function value is obtained. We then check to see if we have performed the desired number of simulations (S^*). If not, we got back and randomly select another branch from the tree diagram in Figure 14-5 and repeat the simulation and LP solution again. When all simulation runs have been performed, the empirical LP objective function results would be plotted

---

[16]Salazar and Sen, "A Simulation Model."

FIGURE 14-5 Tree Diagram Used by Salazar and Sen

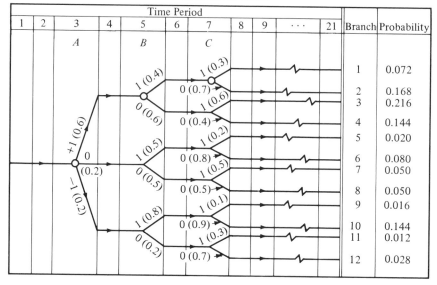

Structure of the Model

Time Period											Branch	Probability
1	2	3	4	5	6	7	8	9	⋯	21		
		A		*B*		*C*					1	0.072
											2	0.168
											3	0.216
											4	0.144
											5	0.020
											6	0.080
											7	0.050
											8	0.050
											9	0.016
											10	0.144
											11	0.012
											12	0.028

Interpretation of Chance Nodes

Variable			Environmental State		Probability of
Name	Symbol	Time Period	Name	Symbol	Occurrence
GNP	*A*	3	Rises	+1	0.6
			No change	0	0.2
			Falls	−1	0.2
(Competitor's price − our price)	*B*	5	(0 or +)	1	0.4
			(−)	0	0.6
Introduction of new product by competitor	*C*	7	Yes	1	0.3
			No	0	0.7

Structure of the Model
Interpretation of Chance Nodes

Variable			Environmental State		
Name	Symbol	Time Period	Name	Symbol	Probability of Occurrence
GNP	A	3	Rises	+1	0.6
			No change	0	0.2
			Falls	−1	0.2
(Competitor's price— our price)	B	5	(0 or +)	1	0.4
			(−)	0	0.6
Introduction of new product by competitor	C	7	Yes	1	0.3
			No	0	0.7

Source: R. C. Salazar and S. K. Sen, "A Simulation Model of Capital Budgeting Under Uncertainty," *Management Science*, Vol. 15, December 1968, p. 165.

FIGURE 14-6   Macro Flowchart of System Program

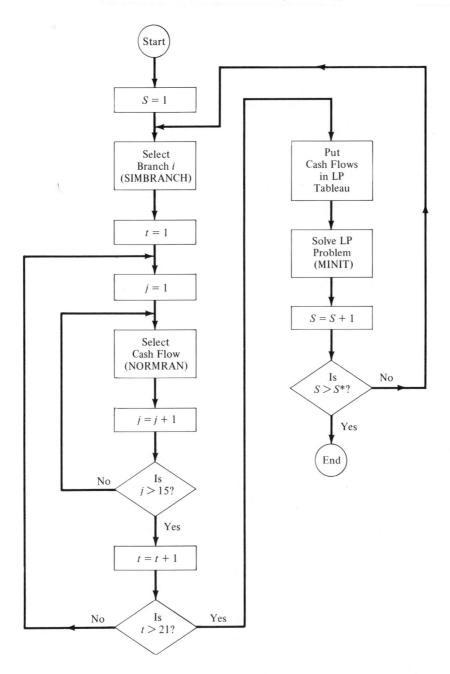

Source: R. C. Salazar and S. K. Sen, "A Simulation Model of Capital Budgeting Under Uncertainty," *Management Science*, Vol. 15, December 1968, p. 169.

on the risk–return axes.[17] Given this summary of the results, management would have to decide which portfolio of assets optimized its utility function. This approach is a flexible and powerful combination of mathematical programming and the simulation technique.

Chance-Constrained Programming

The next major category which has seen capital budgeting applications is that of *chance-constrained programming* (CCP). The approach of CCP is to maximize the expected value of the objective function subject to constraints that are allowed to be violated some given percentage of the time due to random variations in the system. Chance constraints are arrived at as follows. Consider the usual constraints of LP:

$$\sum_{j=1}^{N} a_{ij} X_j \leqslant b_i$$

Owing to randomness in either the a_{ij} coefficients or the b_i right-hand-side values, we show that the constraints do not have to be satisfied all the time by associating a probability statement with the following constraint:

$$P\left\{ \sum_{j=1}^{N} a_{ij} X_j \leqslant b_i \right\} \geqslant \alpha_i \tag{3}$$

where P = probability
   α_i = minimum probability that the decision maker is willing to accept that a given constraint is satisfied

In such constraints, if $\alpha_i = 0.90$, for example, this would mean that the decision maker requires that the constraint be satisfied at least 90% of the time and that he is willing to allow $\Sigma a_{ij} X_j$ to exceed b_i up to 10% of the time.

The solution methodology for CCP problems requires that the "deterministic equivalent" be derived for all chance constraints by taking into account the shape and parameters of the probability distributions for all random variables, as well as the degree of correlation between all pairs of random variables. This derivation usually results in nonlinear equations, which greatly threatens the feasibility of solving all but the smallest problems. Difficulties in problem solution escalate rapidly as the size of the problem grows or as the distributions of random variables describing the system depart from normality. The finding of these "deterministic equivalents" is beyond our scope, but the interested reader is referred to Charnes and Cooper[18] or Taha.[19]

[17]Ibid, p. 173.
[18]A. Charnes, and W. W. Cooper, "Deterministic Equivalents for Optimizing and Satisficing Under Chance Constraints," *Operations Research*, Vol. 11, January 1963, pp. 18–39.
[19]H. A. Taha, *Operations Research: An Introduction* (New York: Macmillan Publishing Co., Inc., 1971), pp. 649–653.

Three significant contributions have been made in the area of CCP applied to capital budgeting. The earliest work was due to Naslund.[20] The expected horizon value of the firm was maximized subject to probabilistic constraints on financing alternatives that could be violated some fraction of the time. He considered both perfect and imperfect capital markets. Naslund's work extended Weingartner's (covered extensively in Chapter 13) to the risk area.

The second contribution was an article in 1967 by Byrne, Charnes, Cooper, and Kortenek.[21] Their model incorporates probabilistic payback and liquidity constraints as well as requirements for the firm's posture at the end of the planning horizon. Using the deterministic equivalents, the authors are able to derive a numerical solution for a small three-period, four-project example. They also present strategies for doing sensitivity analysis on the results. Because of the unresolved difficulty of solving large CCP problems, the same four authors recommended two alternative solution techniques based on assumptions that project cash flows could be closely approximated by discrete probability distributions.[22] The second article of the pair develops an integer LP model to approximate the nonlinear CCP model (for which no efficient solution technique exists).

The final major model was formulated by Hillier[23] when he maximized the expected utility of the shareholders at the end of the planning horizon subject to probabilistic constraints on the net cash flows in each period, as well as cumulative net cash flows in each period over the planning horizon. The author suggests two solution techniques:

1. An approximate LP model based on the deterministic equivalents for the chance constraints.

2. An exact branch-and-bound algorithm that he developed for handling continuous zero–one chance-constrained programming problems.[24]

To illustrate the CCP formulations and the results of finding the deterministic equivalent for chance constraints, consider the model suggested by Naslund.[25] His model consisted of the objective function plus the chance constraints shown below:

$$\text{Maximize } E\left(\sum_{j=1}^{N} A_j X_j + V_T - W_T \right)$$

[20]B. Naslund, "A Model for Capital Budgeting Under Risk," *Journal of Business*, Vol. 39, April 1966, pp. 257–271.

[21]R. Byrne, A. Charnes, W. W. Cooper, and K. Kortenek, "A Chance-Constrained Programming Approach to Capital Budgeting," *Journal of Financial and Quantitative Analysis*, Vol. 2, December 1967, pp. 339–364.

[22]R. Byrne, A. Charnes, W. W. Cooper, and K. Kortenek, "A Discrete Probability Chance Constrained Capital Budgeting Model—I and II," *Opsearch*, Vol. 6, December 1969, pp. 171–198, 226–261.

[23]F. S. Hillier, *The Evaluation of Risky Interrelated Investments* (Amsterdam: North-Holland Publishing Co., 1969); also F. S. Hillier, "A Basic Model for Capital Budgeting of Risky Interrelated Investments," *The Engineering Economist*, Vol. 17, No. 1, pp. 1–30.

[24]F. S. Hillier, "Chance-Constrained Programming with Zero–One or Bounded Continuous Decision Variables," *Management Science*, Vol. 14, September 1967, pp. 34–57.

[25]Naslund, "A Model for Capital Budgeting," pp. 258–261.

subject to

$$P\left(\sum_{j=1}^{N} a_{i\,j}X_j + V_1 - W_1 \leqslant D_1 \right) \geqslant \alpha_1$$

$$P\left(\sum_{i=1}^{t} \sum_{j=1}^{N} a_{i\,j}X_j - \sum_{i=1}^{t-1} V_i r + \sum_{i=1}^{t-1} W_i r + V_t - W_t \leqslant \sum_{i=1}^{t} D_i \right) \geqslant \alpha_t$$

$$t = 2, 3, \ldots, T$$

$$0 \leqslant X_j \leqslant 1 \qquad V_t, W_t \geqslant 0$$

where E = expected value operator

P = probability of the expression within the parentheses

A_j = horizon value at time T of all cash flows subsequent to the horizon associated with project j

X_j = fraction of project j accepted

V_t = amount of money lent in period t at interest rate r

W_t = amount of money borrowed in period t at interest rate r

a_{ij} = cash flows associated with project j in time period t—positive signs for this variable are associated with cash outflows while negative signs are associated with cash inflows

D_t = cash flow generated by other activities than the investment projects that we are going to consider

α_t = probability with which we require that the constraint within the parentheses hold

In the formulation, the following variables can be considered random: a_{ij}, A_j, D_i. Owing to this randomness, the constraints within the parentheses may not always be satisfied, but the decision maker requires that they be satisfied at least α_t percent of the time. Thus, the formulation maximizes the expected value of the horizon value of all accepted projects plus money lent, minus money borrowed at the horizon date, T. This maximization is carried out subject to a budget limitation expressed as a chance constraint in each period over the planning horizon. The constraint for period 1 states that the amount spent on new projects ($\Sigma a_{i\,j}X_j$) plus the amount of funds lent (V_1) less the amount of funds borrowed (W_1) cannot exceed the cash flows generated by operations (D_1). The probabilistic constraint in each subsequent period considers cumulative cash inflows and outflows on all projects ($\Sigma\Sigma a_{ij}X_j$), the cumulative amount of interest received on funds lent to the present period ($\Sigma V_i r$). The cumulative amount of interest paid on borrowed funds up to the present period ($\Sigma W_i r$), and the cumulative cash inflow from operations (ΣD_i). The constraint states that cumulative net cash outflows for all projects up to the period minus cumulative interest earned plus cumulative interest paid plus amount lent less amount borrowed cannot exceed cumulative cash inflow from operations; finally, we have the nonnegativity constraint and the upper limit on project acceptance. As indicated, to solve this problem the deterministic equivalent must be taken considering the random variables that are present. Naslund[26] assumed that the only random variables were the a_{ij}, which he

[26]Ibid., p. 261.

further assumed were normally distributed with means U_{ij} and variances σ_{ij}^2 and further that all these variables were independent of one another. Given these assumptions, the deterministic equivalent that Naslund derived is shown below:

$$\text{maximize} \sum_{j=1}^{N} A_j X_j + V_T - W_T$$

subject to

$$\sum_{j=1}^{N} U_{1j} X_j + V_1 - W_1 + \sqrt{\sum_{j=1}^{N} \sigma_{1j}^2 X_j^2} \; F^{-1}(\alpha_1) \leqslant D_1$$

$$\sum_{i=1}^{t} \sum_{j=1}^{N} U_{ij} X_j - \sum_{i=1}^{t-1} V_i r + \sum_{i=1}^{t-1} W_i r + V_t - W_t$$

$$+ \sqrt{\sum_{j=1}^{N} \sigma_{ij}^2 X_j^2} \; F^{-1}(\alpha_t) \leqslant \sum_{i=1}^{t} D_i \qquad t = 2, 3, \ldots, T$$

$$0 \leqslant X_j \leqslant 1 \qquad V_t, W_t \geqslant 0$$

where F^{-1} is the inverse cumulative density function associated with the random variables a_{ij}. As can be seen, all the constraints are nonlinear in the decision variables X_j because of the square root of the sum of the variances times X_j squared. Of course, these nonlinearities in the constraints cause significant problems in solving the formulation, since there is no general way of solving nonlinear programming problems. The approximation methods discussed above provide assistance in solving CCP problems. We now turn to a discussion of the final mathematical programming model under risk.

Quadratic Programming

Quadratic programming (QP) is the math programming model wherein a nonlinear objective function is optimized subject to linear constraints. This model is far easier to solve than the nonlinear programming model, because the feasible region is convex. The convexity assures that a local optimal solution is also the global optimal solution. This greatly facilitates the optimization process, since the feasible region for a nonlinear model is not necessarily convex.

The earliest QP model in the capital budgeting area was due to Farrar,[27] who in 1962 extended the work of Markowitz (who used QP in portfolio selection) and Weingartner (who did pioneering work in the capital budgeting area) by reflecting both the project's expected net present value (NPV) and the variance of the NPVs in the objective function. The general QP formulation recommended by Farrar is as follows:

$$\text{maximize } Z = \sum_{j=1}^{N} X_j U_j - A \sum_{i=1}^{N} \sum_{j=1}^{N} X_i X_j \sigma_{ij}$$

[27] D. F. Farrar, *The Investment Decision Under Uncertainty* (Englewood Cliffs, N.J.: Prentice-Hall, Inc., 1962).

subject to

$$\sum_{j=1}^{N} X_j = 1$$

$$X_j \geqslant 0$$

where X_j = proportion of the total budget invested in project j
  U_j = expected NPV of project j
  A = stockholders' average coefficient of risk aversion
  σ_{ij} = covariance between the NPV of project i and project j—when $i = j$ this is the variance of project j

It should be noticed that the objective function seeks to maximize shareholders' expected utility, since it reflects both the mean and variance of all possible protfolios of projects plus the average coefficient of risk aversion. Thus, the trade-offs between risk and return are incorporated, as are the interactions between all possible pairs of investments projects.

One problem with this formulation is that the decision variables are continuous (i.e., $X_j \geqslant 0$) and that the decision variables are stated in the portfolio convention of percent of the budget availability (in a single period) to be invested in each project. To overcome these difficulties it would be necessary to arrive at an integer quadratic programming algorithm that could efficiently handle realistic-size problems. Such a development was forthcoming when Mao and Wallingford[28] extended a previous integer LP "branch-and-bound" algorithm developed by Lawler and Bell.[29] They reported promising computational results showing that problems with 15 projects and 15 constraints were solved in less than 1 second of computer time. Of course, the variance–covariance matrix grows exponentially with the number of projects under evaluation.

The most recent quadratic programming capital budgeting model was developed by Thompson[30] in a capital asset pricing context. He formulates a single-period model which handles competitive and complementary projects where the market value is determined by the capital asset pricing model. However, he concludes his article with a word of caution[31]:

> The programming approach has been shown to deal effectively with multi-period problems. Its credentials are strong. The capital asset pricing model, however, deals with a single period. Developing a multiperiod approach to capital budgeting using a multiperiod capital asset pricing model appears more formidable.

[28]J. C. T. Mao and B. A. Wallingford, "An Extension of Lawler and Bell's Method of Discrete Optimization," *Management Science*, October 1968, pp. 51–61.
[29]E. E. Lawler and M. D. Bell, "A Method for Solving Discrete Optimization Problems," *Operations Research*, November–December 1966, pp. 1098–1112.
[30]H. E. Thompson, "Mathematical Programming, The Capital Asset Pricing Model, and Capital Budgeting of Interrelated Projects," *The Journal of Finance*, Vol. 31, No. 1, March 1976, pp. 125–131.
[31]Ibid. p. 130.

This concludes the discussion of QP, which provides the decision maker with assistance in capturing the covariance between projects and between projects and the ongoing operations of the firm.

SUMMARY

This chapter presented an overview of sophisticated approaches for handling conditions of risk in a multiperiod setting. The initial approaches introduced were those of tree diagrams and decision trees. The next section presented Monte Carlo simulation as a powerful and flexible approach to handling the capital budgeting problem. Finally, the mathematical programming models under risk of stochastic LP, chance-constrained programming, and quadratic programming were surveyed and illustrated.

DISCUSSION QUESTIONS AND PROBLEMS

1. Discuss the difference between the types of problems handled by decision trees and those handled by tree diagrams.

2. Discuss the strengths and weaknesses of Monte Carlo simulation in decision making under conditions of risk.

3. Discuss the major components of a Monte Carlo simulation model and illustrate these in the capital budgeting problem setting.

4. Discuss the strengths and weaknesses of stocastic LP, chance-constrained programming, and quadratic programming for handling the capital budgeting problem under conditions of risk.

5. The Hatchet Company is evaluating four alternative single-period investment opportunities whose returns are based on the state of the economy. The possible states of the economy and the associated probability distribution is as follows:

State	Fair	Good	Great
Probability	0.2	0.5	0.3

The returns for each investment opportunity and each state of the economy are as follows:

	State of Economy		
Alternative	Fair	Good	Great
W	$1,000	$3,000	$6,000
X	500	4,500	6,800
Y	0	5,000	8,000
Z	− 4,000	6,000	8,500

(a) Using the decision tree approach, determine the expected return for each alternative.

(b) As a method of performing sensitivity analysis on the decision tree drawn in part (a), it could be determined how much the probabilities of the various states of the economy would have to change in order for the best alternative currently to be replaced by one of the others. For this problem, consider the two alternatives with the highest expected returns (i.e., those ranked 1 and 2 by expected returns). Assume that the probability of a "great" economy will remain constant at 0.3. What would the probability of a "fair" and a "good" economy have to be in order for alternative 2 to become alternative 1?

6. For the three-period project shown below, compute the expected value and the standard deviation for the discounted cash inflow over the project's useful life.

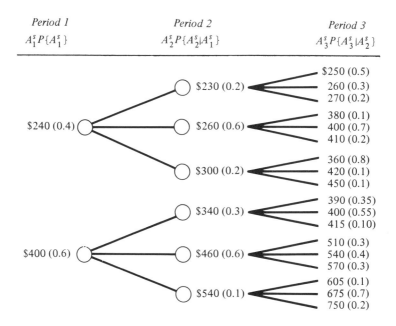

Period 1	Period 2	Period 3
$A_1^s P\{A_1^s\}$	$A_2^s P\{A_2^s|A_1^s\}$	$A_3^s P\{A_3^s|A_2^s\}$

7. For the Monte Carlo Company shown in Example 4:
   (a) Using the probability distributions shown in Example 4 and assuming independence in the cash flows over time, compute the expected NPV and the standard deviation for this distribution over the life of the project.
   (b) Assuming normality, compute the probability that the NPV will be positive as well as the probability that it will exceed $10,000.
   (c) Perform 10 simulation runs for the project shown in Example 4 and compute the mean NPV and the standard deviation of this distribution.
   (d) Assuming normality, compute the probability that the NPV will be positive as well as the probability that it will exceed $10,000, based on the results of your 10 simulation runs in part (c). Compare these results with those obtained in part (b) and comment on any differences (i.e., Why do the differences arise? Which probabilities are more reliable? etc.).

8. The Wee Producem Company is deciding whether to introduce a new product on the market. At the present time they have two decisions to make: the overall decision of whether to introduce the product with additional production costs of $15,000,000 versus dropping the project and simply suffer the loss of the $2,500,000 already invested, or to do further market research at a cost of $1,500,000 and then make the introduction decision (with the same costs as above). Wee Producem

estimates that the market research group will assign a probability of 0.7 that the product will be introduced. Because of the unusual nature of the product, only two final outcomes are possible: outcome *A* derives $40,000,000 profit while outcome *B* derives a $5,000,000 loss. The present estimated likelihood of outcome *A* is 0.6 and 0.4 for outcome *B*.

Determine the optimal strategy by using a decision tree to compare the expected returns of the different possible strategies.

IV

SPECIAL APPLICATIONS
OF CAPITAL BUDGETING

15 CAPITAL BUDGETING FOR THE MULTINATIONAL FIRM

The somewhat complicated evaluations of investment opportunities in national settings are rendered extremely complex in less familiar international environments. Capital budgeting theory does not change, but the application is bedeviled by varying institutional environments (differing governmental systems, tax laws, import and export regulations, etc.). In essence, capital budgeting in an international environment demands not only a grasp of theoretical concepts covered earlier in this text, but an intimate knowledge of local economic conditions and customs. Figure 15-1 gives an overall view of the unique variables attendant upon capital budgeting in an international setting.

In spite of the growing importance of the subject matter, the manifold number of variables and the uncertainty of their nature seems to deter model builders. This fact is very unfortunate because the rapid growth in the number of multinational corporations and the difficulty of their decision settings necessitate sophisticated tools of analysis. Monte Carlo simulation, introduced in Chapter 14 and extended in Appendix 15A, has great potential for handling the complex multinational capital investment decisions. It can incorporate the interdependence of the large number of variables in the decision process and makes it possible to visualize the dynamics of business decisions in complex settings. Furthermore, the peculiarities of international risk can be efficiently introduced through simulation into the capital investment decision area.

CAPITAL BUDGETING PROCESS

The capital budgeting objective for the multinational corporation (MNC) is the same as for a domestic firm and that is to maximize the firm's value as expressed in terms of the market price of the common shares. Therefore, for any proposed project to be attractive, firms insist that the discounted cash inflows exceed the required investment and that these inflows must exceed a specified rate of return on investment. The capital budgeting process for an MNC typically involves the following activities:

1. Identification of cash flows generated by the proposed project.
2. Identification of flows available for repatriation to the MNC.

FIGURE 15-1 Multinational Capital Budgeting Environment

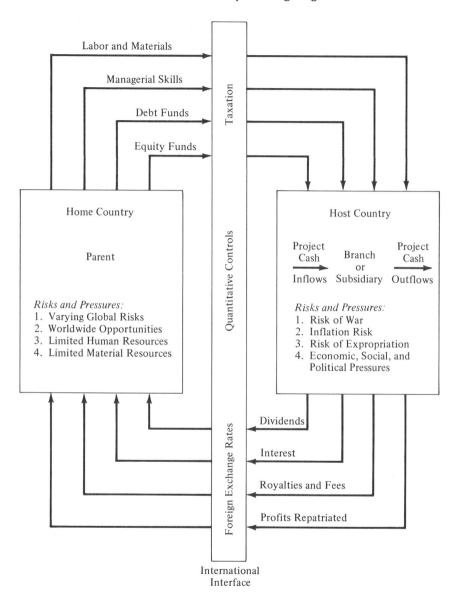

3. Conversion of cash flows by means of exchange rates.

4. Adjustments to compensate for financial risks, including sensitivity analysis.

5. Selection of a minimum rate of return.

6. Calculation of investment profitability including sensitivity analysis.

7. Acceptance or rejection of the proposed investment.

Identification of Cash Flows for Project

The MNC first concentrates its analysis on the cash flows generated by the project. A budget statement is prepared which provides estimates for the project cash inflows and cash outflows over the designated evaluation period. Generally, an investment will be analyzed over a limited period of time (10 years is typical) rather than an attempt made to forecast flows indefinitely.

The initial *cash outflows* required to purchase a subsidiary have been identified as the costs to acquire the land and fixed assets of an existing plant facility. Of course, the method of financing will have an impact on the cash outflow. Attendant with all new investments are many other startup costs that should be considered. Such costs would include selling expenses, legal expenses, initial inventories, administrative and manufacturing staffing costs, and financing costs for debt and equity. For the most part these costs can be classified as the initial working capital and organizational costs.

Furthermore, the MNC must anticipate additional investments beyond its initial commitment. In reality, original investments are usually followed by a succession of further investments, some of which may be involuntary. If a project is started within a country which provides tariff protections for fledgling industries, it may be necessary to expand operations after tariffs are removed in order to compete with foreign markets. Moreover, some countries disallow total repatriation of cash flows, thereby making reinvestment mandatory. Finally, the new venture can be set up with a large debt structure, which will require the reinvestment of profits to provide greater "financial strength."

The cash flows represent typical operating revenues and expenses. First, the MNC develops a demand forecast from such factors as historical demands, alternative sources of products, general population growth, ease of entry into the industry by competitors, and the feasibility of serving nearby markets. From this forecast the sales projections over the project period are derived.

Second, the MNC forecasts its expected expenditures for operating the subsidiary and the fees or charges that it would expect to receive from the subsidiary. These forecasts can usually be obtained from the historical data of similar ventures. Such forecasting techniques as "percent of sales" or "simple linear regressions" can be applied to the historical data to obtain reasonable estimates of the necessary expenditures.

Next, the MNC would review the tax structure of the host country. Analysis would include the income taxes, indirect taxes, and tax treaties enforced by local authorities. From these data, the estimated tax requirements can be projected.

The estimated sales, less the estimated expenses, will yield the after-tax profits from operations. These profits plus any depreciation write-offs will give the cash inflows from operations.

Identification of Cash Flows Available for Repatriation

The MNC would like to maximize the utility of the project cash throw-offs on a worldwide basis. The MNC may wish to reinvest the cash in other subsidiaries, pay dividends, pay debt obligations, or invest in new ventures. The profits from any project would have little value if the MNC could not use the cash throw-offs for these alternatives.

In essence, the MNC must determine which of the cash throw-offs it will be allowed to convert into other currencies for transfer elsewhere. The MNC must examine the existing laws pertaining to such subsidiary remittances as profits from operations, management and technical fees, royalties, loans, dividends. Moreover, a study of exchange controls in the past would be advisable to ascertain which remittances are more frequently restricted. Once the available cash flows for the MNC worldwide network have been identified, the budgeted statement for the parent may be prepared.

All anticipated remittances from the subsidiary will necessitate transactions in the foreign exchange markets. Thus, it is important that the cash flows be represented in the currencies of the two countries involved. This conversion will allow the MNC to visualize the effects of currency values and exchange rates.

Required Rates of Return and Adjustments for Risk

Before assigning a required rate of return to a particular project, it is necessary for an MNC to be certain that all risks peculiar to international activities have been defined and provided for in the total analysis. The section on international financial risks discussed the risks that might confront the MNC and offered several strategies to minimize losses. It was also mentioned that analysis of foreign tax laws and repatriation policies would assist in the proper allocation of remittances for the purpose of making funds available to the worldwide network. However, all these strategies are operational in nature and do not assist in determining the profitability of a project when evaluating the decision to invest.

A highly recommended approach for risk adjustment suggests that an MNC perform a sensitivity analysis of the factors that would influence the profitability of a project. This implies an analysis of the risks, estimating their possible changes, and applying these changes to the elements of the prepared budget data. Not only will this method serve to incorporate the variable risks, it will educate responsible persons about the inherent risks and will cause anticipation of such risks during initial project evaluation.

Some of the sensitivity adjustments could be as follows:

1. If inflation is expected in the near future, increased domestic prices could reduce domestic demands.

2. If devaluation is expected, increased foreign prices could increase domestic demands.

3. Expected inflation would increase the operating costs.

4. Expected inflation would increase asset replacement costs. If revaluation is allowed, increased depreciation write-offs would occur.

5. The new subsidiary may cause undue contraction of sales for existing subsidiaries. An estimated value for these losses could be included in the cash outflows for the project.

6. The budget statement should be scheduled over the 10-year period, showing the expected annual flows. Realistically, the project will show a series of uneven cash flows with decreasing accuracy further ahead in the 10-year projection span.

7. Conversion of the budget elements using different exchange rates is important because the many transactions involving foreign exchange are quite often subject to different duties, tariffs, or other special exchange restrictions. One single rate may not represent the estimate range adequately.

8. Imposition of previously used exchange controls, not currently in effect (but most commonly used) could be injected in the statement.

As can be readily concluded, the objective of a sensitivity analysis is to anticipate as many contingencies as possible, thereby increasing the accuracy of the project's expected returns. Feeling reasonably confident that the budgeted statement has considered all risks, the MNC may now direct its attention to the project's required rate of return.

In the case of evaluating one separate investment opportunity, it is necessary to establish a minimum rate of return which is used as a cutoff point when deciding to accept or reject the investment. The most commonly accepted minimum rate used by firms has been their cost of capital. For an MNC, this rate would represent its worldwide cost of acquiring additional funds. This rate is defined as the rate of return that must be realized to maintain the corporation's current stock price.

If an MNC perceives that greater risks are inherent with a particular investment, it may adjust for risk in a manner such as illustrated in Chapter 8. It could be perceived that the effects of inflation or exchange controls are too unpredictable, thus justifying an adjustment for risk.

Measuring the Profitability of the Investment

As intimated, the MNC is greatly concerned about its ability to recover its initial investment. This concern exists because the effects of inflation and exchange controls could ultimately restrict the repatriation of funds or greatly reduce the value of funds received. Consequently, discounted-cash-flow techniques for measuring profitability are highly recommended.

In essence, the attractiveness of any investment is based on the ability of its eventual cash inflows to exceed its required cash outflows. However, monies received in future years would be worth less in terms of purchasing power, owing to either inflation or devaluations. To measure the real value of future cash inflows, these inflows should be expressed in constant (current) values equivalent to the values of the outflows in the earlier years. If the inflows then exceed the outflows, the investment will contribute to maximizing the dollar value of the firm in present values.

It is the primary objective of discounted-cash-flow techniques to provide for the time value of money by expressing future flows in terms of present value. One final factor for imputing cash inflows has been introduced and that is to assign a terminal value to the project. It is expected that the assets of the subsidiary will have a salable value at the end of the designated period, either as an ongoing concern or through liquidation.

Acceptance of Investment

Referring to previous premises, for an investment to be acceptable, the inflows must exceed the outflows and the rate of return must not be less than the "cutoff" rate selected. If the minimum risk was assigned to the project, the firm's cost of capital would be selected for discounting. It is conceivable that an MNC would use a higher rate to compensate for the greater financial risks associated with foreign ventures. In this case the results may lead to rejection of the investment.

Furthermore, the acceptance of a proposed investment does not necessarily imply that it will be implemented. Acceptance merely includes the investment with other accepted investment opportunities. The accepted investment must now appear more attractive than the others to be fully implemented. Finally, the investment's performance will continually be reviewed after implementation. If performance is poor, abandonment procedures may be considered.

COST OF CAPITAL

Risk differences cause the cost of funds from a particular source to be higher than the sure interest rate and account for the possibility of loss and prospect of gain. It is also apparent that the type of funding chosen affects fees, flotation costs, rates of interest paid, and indirect costs, such as minimum balance deposits required. However, it is important to note that for multinational corporations the risk or degree of variability for all the preceding factors differs with the host country involved. The differences relate to inflation rates, possible changes in regulations of MNC, balance of payments, variability in labor costs, and political changes. It is for this reason that subsidiary costs of capital should be examined for the effect on the company-wide cost of capital.

The cost of borrowing is expected to vary because of business risk, financial structure, variability of earnings, company size, money-market conditions, and other variables. The cost and availability of funds in the international capital markets adds another dimension.

Effective interest rates in different national money markets vary considerably, and because, in general, bond yields are lower in the United States, a cost differential on long-term borrowing exists. This is further widened by security flotation costs also being higher outside the United States. Interest rates in underdeveloped countries are usually much higher than in developed countries because of smaller local savings; capital flight, which reduces local fund supplies; continuous inflation; and higher business risk.

A study that compares the cost of equity capital of U.S. multinational firms and their domestic counterparts looks at the possibility of higher risk for business operations abroad and the implication that the cost of capital would automatically be higher because of the entry into foreign markets.[1]

---

[1] Theodore Kohers, "The Effect of Multinational Operations on the Cost of Equity Capital: An Empirical Study," *Management International Review*, 1975.

By using a version of the dividend valuation model over 28 quarters, a sample of 110 companies from the Fortune 500 was used to evaluate cost of equity capital. The multinational firms on the list were compared to their domestic counterparts on that list using the paired-difference test to detect statistically significant differences. Seven industries were covered, including the following: nonferrous metals, fabricated metals products, electrical machinery, other machinery, petroleum refining, chemical and allied products, food products, and companies without distinction by industry. Of the seven distinct industries, only the chemical and allied products industry showed noticeably higher costs of equity capital for multinational firms. Interestingly, the oil and nonferrous metals industries have both been prone to expropriation by foreign governments. Kohers states that by making distinct differences in the capitalization rates of companies in different industries and not necessarily by domestic or MNC status, investors appear to clearly differentiate investment risks and opportunities among industries. They do not tend to unfairly discriminate against foreign operations in their appraisal of common stock investment values. From these findings it was concluded that by becoming involved in foreign business activities a company does not automatically raise its cost of capital.

The cost of short-term and medium-term funds, as mentioned earlier, now becomes a matter of operating most profitably (and prudently) while in compliance with FASB-8. Minimization of dollar investment exposure to currency devaluation leads to scheduled repatriation of dollars by dividend payments and maximum efficient utilization of local funding sources by constant comparison of short-term rates for various instruments such as overdrafts, notes, and so on. When borrowing becomes difficult as a result of the general lack of availability of funds and retention of dividends becomes necessary to augment working capital, forward hedging is an alternative to protect investments and its cost can be considered as a cost of funds. Ordinarily, forward cover against fall of currency, especially for a developing country, is expensive and considered prohibitive.

It is quite apparent from the preceding discussion in this section that risk may not be perceived as greater for a multinational firm than for a domestic company, but it definitely can take many more forms. It follows that a decision to commit capital internationally deserves careful analysis. Techniques to effectively determine the worth of a capital expenditure proposal have been the subjects of many books and papers. Brill[2] surveyed the range of techniques in practice and further presented an approach to treat subjective data that would possess certain desirable properties:

1. It would summarize relevant investment decision information in a single figure.

2. It would be useful for all types of proposals.

3. It would permit appraisal in terms of a single set of standards.

4. It would provide an easily computed index.

---

[2]Martin Brill, *An Approach to Risk Analysis in the Evaluation of Capital Ventures* (Philadelphia: Drexel Institute of Technology, 1966).

5. It would be easily understood.

6. It would be adjustable to allow for ranges of uncertainty.

The shortcoming of discounted-cash-flow calculations is described as adjusted with "not totally rational" values for risk. These values are arrived at by conventional approaches to risk analysis, which include sensitivity studies, adjustments to venture worth criteria, and the "three-level estimate" method. In sensitivity studies, the effects of unit changes in the many parameters governing the profitability of a contemplated venture are determined to establish which parameters are most significant. Management must subjectively evaluate the relevance of the variables, because the likelihood of their deviations is unknown. Adjustments to venture worth criteria to reflect levels of risk are based on the theory that risk incurred is related to the rewards expected. Results can be inconsistent, and recognition of risk in computing cash flows is more effective. In the three-level estimate approach, optimistic, pessimistic, and most likely cases are developed and intuitively assigned probabilities of occurrence. The analysis is treated as decision under risk to arrive at an expected value of investment worth for venture analysis. The subjectivity of the probability designations, in addition to the omission of the dimension of variability, leads to rejection of this approach to risk analysis for investments as well as project management.

The limitations of the techniques discussed above are better overcome by more advanced techniques that require development of distributions of return employing the methods of Monte Carlo simulation (see Appendix 15A).

To overcome the added requirement for knowledge of the distribution of each variable in the analysis, Brill[3] proposed a method utilizing reasonable estimates of the parameter distributions, thereby validly incorporating the risk dimension in venture analysis. The technique relies on the assumptions that venture analysis variables can be described by a beta distribution with ranges usually reliably obtained from experts representing a 95% confidence interval. Although still subjective, owing to the very nature of the task of prediction, the method is rational, useful, and meets the guidelines presented earlier. Major banks readily volunteer expertise and information on domestic and international banking and financial matters as part of their marketing approach to attract new customers. Such expertise, combined with a firm's knowledge of its own business, could be well applied in the simulation approach.

REPATRIATION VERSUS REINVESTMENT OF PROFITS

The decision process of whether to repatriate dividends or reinvest in the foreign subsidiary means looking beyond the original commitment and considering what is needed to protect or strengthen the original investment. This is, of course, based heavily on reassessment of market position for an extended period of time, nominally 10 years, and the related investment alternatives.[4] Consider-

[3]Ibid.
[4]David B. Zenoff and Jack Zwick, *International Financial Management* (Englewood Cliffs, N.J.: Prentice-Hall, Inc., 1969), pp. 148, 149.

ations generally include ultimate remittability of the required investment expenditures. Rather than measure returns only in terms of the local currency, inflows available to the investor are a key consideration. Inflation and money valuation forecasts play an important part in the long-range reinvestment plan. As indicated by recent moves of Japanese and German manufacturers to obtain manufacturing sites in the United States, this country holds a favored position in the struggle against inflationary effects. For this reason, U.S.-based MNCs will also lean toward expansion and improvement of domestic plants while maintaining sales and service branches overseas.

The important judgment in formulating and screening alternatives is to learn whether proposed planning will remain feasible if host-country restrictions are expected to become more stringent.

Another factor that influences the remittance decision and, therefore, the reinvestment decision of many multinational companies is taxation. Tax objectives vary and can reflect varying emphasis among companies.

Firms that are most tax-conscious will make every attempt to minimize the corporations' total tax burden and give this consideration higher priority than any others in the investment decision. This would come about by modeling the tax situation after the other project-related details and projections are evaluated.

Firms that give taxes considerable importance might give the tax burden equal weight with one or two other factors, such as the risk of leaving funds abroad or the subsidiary's requirements for funds. The latter point is considered in relation to the availability and cost of funds locally.

Some companies consider paying taxes to the United States on repatriated dividends a fact of doing business, and no effort would be made to delay or avoid this obligation. However, they do try to avoid penalty taxes for paying too high or too low a dividend as might occur in Germany.[5] A few corporations, because of the minimal amounts involved, would assign a low level of importance to any tax consideration relative to foreign dividends.

Foreign dividends exercised to suit the corporate plan regarding taxes, reinvestment, or dividends to stockholders are only one part of the total fund remittance framework. Other means include management fees, technical-service fees, royalties interest on parent loans, principal repayments on such loans, license fees, commissions on exports, and payments for merchandise obtained from the parent.[6]

Basic decisions regarding fund remittances are centralized, with the goal of maximizing corporate worldwide placement of funds. Perception of the overall needs of the entire corporate network and availability of the necessary financial data can only occur at a central office. As indicated earlier, the corporate prerogative to control and dispense funds can be affected by the policy of a host country. This is increasingly evident on all forms of fund remittance, including pricing, as active surveillance of invoices by customs agents is conducted.

[5] Ibid., p. 415.
[6] See Eiteman and Stonehill, *Multinational Business Finance*, p. 308.

SUMMARY

This chapter surveys the important area of capital budgeting for the multinational firm. The new dimensions and variables present in the international environment were outlined and discussed.

A seven-step approach was suggested to evaluate and select capital projects for the multinational firm.

The important area of the cost of capital for the multinational firm was discussed next.

Finally, repatriation vs. reinvestment of profits was addressed, since this trade-off is an important phase in the strategic planning area for the multinational firm.

The appendix that follows illustrates many of the techniques and concepts discussed in the chapter by showing a Monte Carlo simulation model for capital budgeting for the multinational firm.

APPENDIX 15A
SIMULATION-BASED MULTINATIONAL
CAPITAL BUDGETING APPROACH[7]

This appendix outlines a Monte Carlo simulation model for multinational capital budgeting. The model has been made as general as possible while not sacrificing ease of understanding and use. In order to provide adequate information and a flexible analysis, a two-stage simulation is recommended. First, each investment opportunity is evaluated in a uninational setting by the subsidiary proposing it. If it passes the first screening, it must then be analyzed from the parent's point of view. This joint evaluation is of paramount importance. Indeed, a plant built in a foreign country can be a very profitable investment in itself, but currency devaluations, tax differentials, and/or quantitive controls can make it significantly less attractive to the parent company. The proposed model handles both the case where the parent is considering a joint venture as well as a 100% participation.

Even though the model does not find the optimal set (if such a set exists and can be ascertained) of investment opportunities from the subsidiary's or parent's point of view, it does provide an operational, theoretically sound, and mathematically powerful capital project ranking methodology wherein project uncertainty as well as environmental uncertainty (including all major international variables) are incorporated into the analysis. Based on this ranking of investment proposals (consisting of empirical risk–return characteristics for several relevant evaluation criteria), both the subsidiary and parent can select the set of projects that best meets its risk–return preferences, financing availabilities, and objectives for synergy considering interactions between current

---

[7]The model presented in this appendix is based on André Fourcans and Thomas J. Hindelang, "Capital Budgeting for the Multinational Firm: A Simulation Approach," to appear in *Financial Management*.

operations and new projects. The model's two-stage simulation approach utilizing all relevant international variables is consistent with prior research in the international capital budgeting area. The model focuses well on the behavioral theory of the MNC postulated by Stonehill and Nathanson,[8] wherein they suggest an independent financial evaluation of projects by both the parent and subsidiary; further, the new model avoids the serious disadvantages the authors cite that prevail when a risk-adjusted discount rate is used to reflect political and foreign exchange uncertainties; last, the new model provides helpful information in implementing the "uncertainty absorption" program suggested by the authors, as well as arriving at an operational approach for charging each period with the cost of such a program. The model capitalizes on the strengths of the most sophisticated approach recommended by Stobaugh[9] in analyzing foreign investment climates, namely, that of risk analysis, wherein the full range of international uncertainty and variable interactions are incorporated rather than just the "optimistic," "most likely," and "pessimistic" estimates, as well as independence of variables assumed by some models.[10] Finally, the model addresses the important cultural, economic, and political aspects of the capital investment decision setting that Mauriel[11] points to as differentiating uninational from multinational operations.

Subsidiary Simulation

The subsidiary's evaluation of a given investment proposal utilizes mainly the direct project costs and revenues discussed immediately above. The analysis uses a uninational framework and considers the parent mainly as a source of funds to finance accepted projects. Furthermore, in order not to unduly complicate matters, it is assumed that the subsidiary only sells and buys inside the host country (this assumption could be relaxed, if desired).

The technical details of this stage of the simulation are presented in three illustrations. Table 15A-1 lists the relevant cash inflows and outflows for the subsidiary.

TABLE 15A-1   Subsidiary Cash Flows

Inflows	*Outflows*
Revenue from sales	Initial outlay
Salvage value	Financing costs
	Operating costs
	Host country taxes

[8]A. I. Stonehill and L. Nathanson, "Capital Budgeting and the Multinational Corporation," *California Management Review*, Summer 1968, pp. 39–54.

[9]R. B. Stobaugh, "How to Analyze Foreign Investment Climates," *Harvard Business Review*, September–October 1969, pp. 100–108.

[10]J. Chambers and S. Mullick, "Investment Decision Making in a Multinational Enterprise," *Management Accounting*, August 1971, pp. 44–59.

[11]J. J. Mauriel, "Evaluation and Control of Overseas Operations," *Management Accounting*, May 1969, pp. 35–39.

Table 15A-2 defines the variables (both exogenous and endogenous) and formulates the identities of the simulation model. Figure 15A-1 shows a flowchart of this part of the simulation.

TABLE 15A-2   Variables of the Subsidiary Simulation Model

Parameters:

SP_t = selling price per unit in year t KS = subsidiary risk-free rate
DR_t = depreciation rate for year t
MAX = total number of simulation runs to be considered

Exogenous variables:
Stochastic variables with known probability distributions:

MG_t = market growth rate for each year t
MS_t = initial market size in number of units
SM_t = share of the market for each year t
INV = initial investment required by the proposal
N = useful life of investment
FC_t = total operating fixed costs in year t
VC_t = variable operating costs per unit in year t
IC_t = interest cost associated with the project in year t
OC_t = other project related costs in year t
WC_t = working-capital needs of the project in year t
TR_t = tax rate for host country tax on project returns in year t
IR_t = rate of inflation in year t
WAR_t = probability that a war will break out in the host country during year t
$IWAR_t$ = % of loss suffered by the firm if a war occurs in year t
EX_t = probability that expropriation will take place in host country in year t
LEX_t = loss suffered by the firm if expropriation takes place in host country during year t

Endogenous variables:

$USAL_t$ = unit sales generated by the proposal in year t
REV_t = total revenue generated by the proposal in year t
TC_t = total costs associated with the project in year t
TAX_t = host country tax on taxable income generated by project in year t
$NIAT_t$ = net income after host country tax generated by project in year t
NCI_t = net cash inflow generated by project in year t
BV_t = book value of the project at the end of year t
SV_t = salvage value of the project at the end of year t
$TINF_n$ = terminal inflow if expropriation or war occurs during year n
$PAYB_m$ = payback period for the investment on the mth simulation run
NPV_m = net present value for the investment on the mth simulation run
IRR_m = discounted rate of return for the investment on the mth simulation run

Identities and operating equations:

$$BV_0 = INV$$

$$DEP_t = (DR_t)(BV_{t-1})$$

$$BV_t = BV_{t-1} - DEP_t$$

$$MS_t = (MS_{t-1})(1 + MG_{t-1}) \qquad t = 2, 3, \ldots, N$$

$$USAL_t = (MS_t)(SM_t) \qquad t = 1, 2, \ldots, N$$

$$REV_t = (SP_t)(USAL_t) \qquad t = 1\ 2, \ldots, N$$

$$TVC_t = (VC_t)(USAL_t) \qquad t = 1, 2, \ldots, N$$

$$TC_t = TVC_t + FC_t + OC_t + DEP_t \qquad t = 1, 2, \ldots, N$$

$$TAX_t = (TR_t)(REV_t - TC_t) \qquad t = 1, 2, \ldots, N$$

$$NIAT_t = REV_t - TC_t - TAX_t \qquad t = 1, 2, \ldots, N$$

$$NCI_t = NIAT_t + DEP_t - WC_t \qquad t = 1, 2, \ldots, N$$

$$SV_n = (SV_{n-1} - DEP_n)(1 + IR_n)$$

If expropriation (EX_n) occurs in year n, determine loss suffered (LEX_n), then

$$TINF_n = (1 - LEX_n)(SV_n + NCI_n)$$

If war (WAR_n) occurs in year n, determine loss suffered ($LWAR_n$), then

$$TINF_n = (1 - IWAR_n)(SV_n + NCI_n)$$

$PAYB_m$ = period is such that

$$INV - \sum_{t=1}^{i} (NCI_t + IC_t) = 0$$

$$NPV_m = \sum_{t=1}^{n} \frac{NCI_t}{(1 + KS)^t} - INV$$

IRR_m = discount rate r such that

$$\sum_{t=1}^{N} \frac{NCI_t}{(1 + r)^t} - INV = 0$$

As can be seen from Table 15A-2, the main endogenous variables which determine an investment proposal's attractiveness are the total revenue, total costs, net income after taxes, and net cash inflow each year. From these measures the payback, NPV, and IRR are computed for each simulated observation of the proposal's useful life. Empirical distributions are derived for each of these three criteria based on all simulation runs. Of course, other criteria (e.g., discounted payback, equivalent annual savings, growth in earnings per share, etc.) could be easily built into the model, depending on the needs of the individual firm.

Based on the empirical distributions of the criteria above, summary statistics (the expected value, standard deviation, measures of skewness, etc.) are computed and probability statements can be made about the likelihood that various ranges are achieved by each criterion measure. The subsidiary will then have the necessary data to rank the proposal relative to all others under consideration (which have been run through the simulation) on the basis of its

FIGURE 15A-1   Flowchart of Subsidiary Simulation

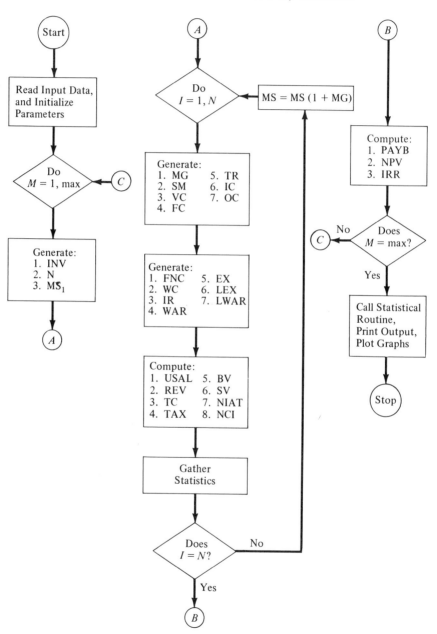

risk preferences and its evaluation of the risk–return trade-offs of the various proposals. Given this ranking of proposals, a recommendation will be made to the parent company concerning the set of proposals that the subsidiary feels should be adopted depending on availability of capital.

Two details should be mentioned about the subsidiary simulation. First, the international variables dealing with inflation risks, expropriation risks, risk of war, and taxation have been built into the subsidiary simulation. The mechanics of handling inflation are discussed below and the treatment of host-country taxation is straightforward. The occurrence of expropriation or war was obtained through a Monte Carlo determination in each year of the proposal's useful life. When it is established that either of these two events has taken place, the associated percentage loss is generated from the appropriate input distribution. This result is used to derive the terminal cash inflow of the project as a proportion of current salvage value, the yearly cash inflow, and working capital accumulated to date because of the project.

Second, the risk-free rate relevant to the subsidiary company (which will usually be different from the risk-free rate for the parent) is used in the computation of the NPV and as the relevant hurdle rate for the final comparison in the IRR method. More will be said later about the risk-free rate.

Parent-Company Simulation

The parent company takes a more global view in its evaluation of potential projects. It utilizes the empirical data relative to the project per se (i.e., project net income after taxes and net cash inflows) developed by the subsidiary simulation but also incorporates the critical international variables associated with the transfer of funds. These additional risks and uncertainties are built into the framework so that the parent can adequately assess the situation before it commits funds to a given project in a specific country. Table 15A-3 shows the cash flows from the parent's point of view.

Table 15A-4 represents the new variables and identities of importance here. Figure 15A-2 presents the flowchart of the parent's analysis.

TABLE 15A-3   Parent-Company Cash Flows

Inflows	*Outflows*
Direct savings generated by the project	Equity funds provided
Profit repatriated	Loans provided
Dividends	Labor, material, and other costs
Royalties and fees	Transportation costs
Interest and loan repayments	Taxes paid on dividends, royalties, and profit repatriated

TABLE 15A-4 Variables of the Parent-Company Simulation Model

Parameters:

DET_0 = debt funds committed to the project by the parent in year 0

EQY_0 = equity funds committed to the project by the parent in year 0

DIV_t = dividend rate as a percentage of earnings generated by the project in year t

REP_t = percent of profits repatriated in year t

KP = parent company's risk-free rate

Exogenous variables:

Stochastic variables with known probability distributions:

FER_t = foreign exchange rate in year t

ROY_t = amount of royalties and fees to be paid to the parent in year t (in terms of the subsidiary's home country currency)

SAV_t = direct savings generated by the project in year t in the parent's home country currency

LMC_t = labor, material, and other costs paid by the parent for production of the product by sub in year t in the parent's home country currency

$TRAN_t$ = transportation costs associated with importing the product in year t in the parent's home country currency

$PITR_t$ = weighted "international" tax rate on dividends, royalties, and profits repatriated

$PHTR_t$ = parent home tax rate

INT_t = interest payments made by the subsidiary to the parent (in terms of the subsidiary's home country currency)

$PRIN_t$ = principal payments made by the subsidiary to the parent in year t (in terms of the subsidiary's home country currency)

$REQY_t$ = equity funds retired by the subsidiary in year t (in terms of the subsidiary's home country currency)

Endogenous variables:

$PREV_t$ = before "international" tax total foreign revenue for the parent generated by the project in year t

PTC_t = total cost for the parent generated by project in year t

$PTAX_t$ = total paid by the parent in year t

$PITAX$ = amount of "international" tax paid by the parent

$PHTAX$ = amount of home tax paid by the parent

$PNIAT_t$ = parent's net income after all taxes

$PNCI_t$ = parent's net cash inflow in year t

$PPAYB_m$ = parent's payback for simulation run m

$PNPV_m$ = parent's net present value for simulation run m

$PIRR_m$ = parent's internal rate of return for simulation run m

Identities and operating equations:

$PREV_t = (FER_t)[(DIV_t + REP_t)(NIAT_t) + ROY_t + INT_t]$

$PTC_t = LMC_t + TRAN_t$

$PITAX_t = (PREV_t)(PITR_t)$

$$PHTAX_t = (SAV_t - PTC_t)(PHTR_t)$$
$$PTAX_t = PITAX_t + PHTAX_t$$
$$PNIAT_t = PREV_t + SAV_t - PTC_t - PTAX_t$$
$$PNCI_t = PNIAT_t + (FER_t)(PRIN_t + REQY_t)$$

$$PPAYB_m = \text{period } i \text{ such that } (DET_0 + EQY_0) - \sum_{t=0}^{i} PNCI_t = 0$$

$$PNPV_m = \sum_{t=0}^{N} \frac{PNCI_t}{(1 + KP)^t} - (DET_0 + EQY_0)$$

$$PIRR_m = \text{discount rate } r \text{ such that } \sum_{t=0}^{n} \frac{PNCI_t}{(1 + r)^t} - (DET_0 + EQY_0) = 0$$

It should be noticed from the identities and operating equations in Table 15A-4 that all cash flows which cross international boundaries are subject to foreign exchange adjustment, international taxation, and quantitative controls. In addition, the benefits to the parent company, PNIAT and PNCI, are dependent upon the direct savings in the operations, which are a result of the project as well as the dividends, profits repatriated, royalties, and interest received from the subsidiary, which are tied to the project. Both international and home country tax effects are taken into account in computing the net returns to the parent.

The same measures as before (i.e., internal rate of return, net present value, and payback) provide the criteria in the parent's evaluation of the worth of the project. Like each subsidiary, the parent can now rank all proposals on a worldwide basis using these empirical distributions and their associated statistics. The parent company's risk preferences and its evaluation of risk–return trade-offs of various proposals come into the analysis here. The parent company uses the relevant risk-free rate in the evaluation criteria.

Mechanics of the Simulation

As noted above, the simulation is designed to be flexible and complete, yet not overly demanding on the user relative to necessary data inputs. However, it was also pointed out that the more precise the input specifications are, the more exact and helpful will be the results generated by the simulation. Thus, balancing these trade-offs, the decision maker is asked to specify the exogenous variables as accurately as he can for as many years into the future as possible. It is realized, of course, that the farther into the future a user must estimate distributions, the greater is the degree of uncertainty. Offsetting this shortcoming are two countermeasures:

1. The discounting process, which weigh more distant years less significantly.

2. The fact that sensitivity analysis can be used to determine the impact of changes in the input variables on the decision criteria.

FIGURE 15A-2 Flowchart of Parent-Company Simulation

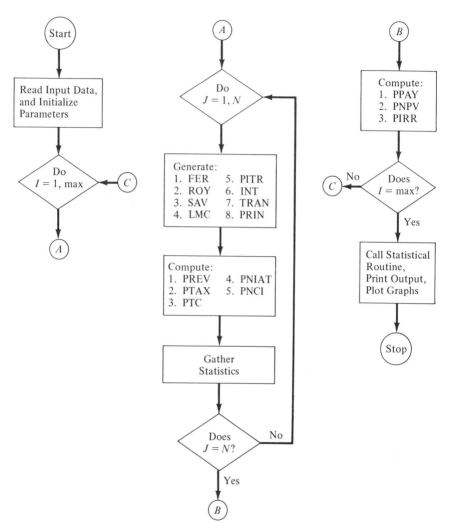

In order to make the variable estimation process as painless as possible, the user is given many alternatives to the method of specifying inputs:

1. He can provide the parameters of any well-known distribution (e.g., binomial, uniform, normal, beta, etc.).

2. He can input any discrete distribution that he feels is appropriate.

3. He can specify that the distribution is a composite of various distributions.

Inflation is dealt with in two ways. First, it can be taken into consideration in the estimation of the exogenous variables by the user specifying a different distribution for each year of the anticipated useful life of the project. Second, the distribution can be shifted to the right, every year, by the expected percent inflation. This operation can be done for selling price, variable cost, and so on. If a single distribution is specified for all periods, the inflation factor is built into the simulation and taken into consideration in the yearly revision of the distributions for the exogenous variables.

One of the important strengths of the model is the way in which it handles interdependencies among related variables. Some interrelationships can be reflected exclusively by means of an informed and careful specification of the input distribution's exogenous variables, whereas the simulation model has built in self-checks in order to adequately handle other dependencies. Examples of the former strategy would be where the user would be reminded of the fact that expected high rates of inflation in any given year must be associated with larger expected changes in foreign exchange rates for that year; further, dividend rates and percent of profits repatriated should both reflect those risks associated with a given host country—inflation risk, war and expropriation risks, taxation policies, and quantitative controls. The technique, using built-in checks, is necessitated by the fact that only after the value of an exogenous variable is generated by the simulation will the appropriate domain for a related variable be determined. For example, there is a trade-off between fixed and variable costs associated with producing a product—it is reasonable to assume that a high level of fixed costs is generally associated with a lower variable cost per unit; thus, the model restricts the feasible values of the variable-cost distribution to the lower tail whenever the value of total fixed cost generated comes from the upper tail, and vice versa. Similar relationships are built in to reflect the trade-offs between market size and market growth rate and among selling price, demand relationships, and market share.

One final important point should be mentioned. Because of the two-stage analysis of investment proposals—first by the subsidiary and then by the parent —two different risk-free rates are used. The subsidiary uses its own rate in order to determine the proposal's relative ranking, and if the project should be recommended to the parent for acquisition. In a similar vein, the parent uses the risk-free rate of its home country to determine whether funds should be committed to the product. Such an approach gives a double, somewhat independent, more stringent screening of proposals. They must survive both cutoff points in order to be adopted by the multinational firm.

It must be strongly emphasized that both the parent and subsidiary simulations use the relevant risk-free rate (rather than the cost of capital or a risk-adjusted discount rate) in computing any project's net present value. Indeed, in both stages of the simulation, the discounting operation must only reflect discounting for futurity or the time value of money and not for the specific riskiness of the project under consideration. The risk element of each investment proposal is ascertained in the simulation runs themselves. As Lewellen and Long[12] point out, to discount cash flows on each simulation run "at a rate in excess of the default-free rate" (e.g., the firm's cost of capital)

---

[12]W. G. Lewellen and M. S. Long, "Simulation vs. Single-Value Estimates in Capital Expenditure Analysis," *Decision Sciences*, Vol. 3, No. 4, October 1972, pp. 19–33.

would impose improper double adjustment for uncertainty upon the project. Thus, all that is required is to discount these empirical cash flows at the risk-free rate in order to arrive at an empirical NPV distribution which contains valuable information for both the expected return and riskiness of the project under consideration.

Validation and Analysis of the Model's Output

The following discussion is aimed at providing insight to the users of the proposed simulation model in terms of interpreting the final results and utilizing them in the capital investment decision process. Several authors have pointed to such a gap in theory and practice: Bower and Lessard[13] found in their empirical work that simulation models were not used because of "the inability to translate results into simple measures executives could reconcile with their intuition and experience and use, with other measures, to make a judgment"; Lewellen and Long[14] point to this problem by asking: "What do you do with that impressive distribution of possible outcomes once you have simulated? How should the information be digested?" Mao and Helliwell[15] found that their three sample firms had difficulty in conceptualizing and quantifying risk–return trade-offs.

The simulation methodology not only permits managers to evaluate and compare the expected performance of different potential investments, but also presents an analytical approach to determine relationships among project variables and international factors.

The main output consists in the two empirical profiles of net present value (NPV) and internal rate of return (IRR) for both the parent company and for the subsidiary. Relevant statistical measures of central tendency variability and skewness are computed for each empirical distribution.

Figure 15A-3 gives an example of the main output. Curve I represents the IRR profile for the subsidiary, whereas curve II is for the parent. As can be quickly noted in this specific case, the IRR for the parent is everywhere lower than the subsidiary's IRR. However, this need not always be the case (it would depend on the influence of foreign exchange rates, tax differentials, the relevant risk-free rates, etc.). The purpose of these two profiles is to make sure that the worthiness of the investment can be evaluated by all groups (parent's managers and possible partners in the country of the investment) with their possibly different aspirations. Therefore, an investment is considered attractive by a particular group only if the proposal meets the criteria of acceptability of that group.

How are these profiles used? As demonstrated by curve I of Figure 15A-3, there is a 98% probability that an IRR greater than or equal to 6% can be

[13]D. R. Lessard and R. S. Bower, "An Operational Approach to Risk Screening," *Journal of Finance*, May 1973, pp. 245–247.

[14]W. G. Lewellen and M. S. Long, "Reply to Comments by Bower and Lessard and Gentry," *Decision Sciences*, Vol. 4, No. 4, October 1973, pp. 575–576.

[15]J. C. T. Mao and J. F. Helliwell, "Investment Decision Under Uncertainty: Theory and Practice," *Journal of Finance*, Vol. 24, No. 2, May 1969, pp. 323–338.

FIGURE 15A-3

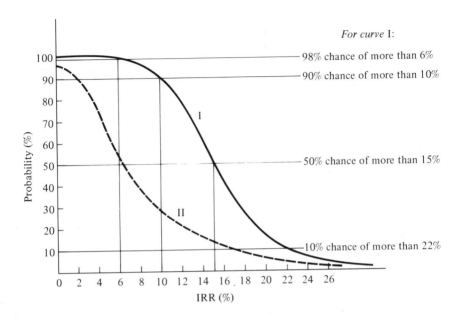

obtained, a 90% probability of the IRR exceeding 10%, a 50% probability of the IRR exceeding 15%, and a 10% probability of the IRR exceeding 22%. We know that the investment will be worthwhile (from the point of view of the subsidiary) if the IRR is at least equal to its risk-free rate. If we assume a subsidiary's risk-free rate of 10%, the chance of having an IRR $\geqslant$ 10% is 90 out of 100. The decision makers will have to decide whether they are ready to take the risk implied: 90 chances out of 100 of having a "profitable" investment, but 10 out of 100 of "losing money." The same analysis needs to be done with curve II from the point of view of the parent.

The statistics computed from the empirical distributions enable the subsidiary and the parent to evaluate risk–return trade-offs among various alternatives available. Furthermore, the analysis of the output data is rendered more sophisticated by the following elaborations. A statistical analysis subroutine using the multiple ranking criteria discussed by Kleijnen, Naylor, and Seaks[16] analyzes and determines the order of the project desirability and whether statistically significant differences exist among the ranked projects. The analysis is performed by each subsidiary and by the parent for all projects considered by the multinational firm. Such results are invaluable when the firms are faced with capital rationing and multiple, competing investment opportunities and risks.

[16] J. P. C. Kleijnen, T. H. Naylor and T. G. Seaks, "The Use of Multiple Ranking Procedures to Analyze Simulations of Management Systems," *Management Sciences*, February 1972, pp. 245–257.

In addition, because of the importance of extremes, the simulation can be rerun to evaluate the impact of all the inputs having very optimistic values and very pessimistic ones. In these cases, the simulation is constrained to pick up random values selected from the tails of the respective input distributions. Thus, each investment would have three profiles for each of the criteria. This more complete information can provide valuable insights relative to the investment's attractiveness.

A payback distribution is also given as an output of the model. This profile tells the decision maker the probable number of years required to recover the initial cash investment through cash inflows. This method of investment evaluation should only be used as a secondary criterion. However, even if the payback criterion is not a measure of profitability, it can be important for international investments. Indeed, the shorter the payback period, the smaller the risk of loss due to expropriation, war, or unfavorable foreign-exchange-rate fluctuations. Therefore, managers can consider this measure as an important aspect of the multinational investment process.

Another significant benefit from the simulation approach is that sensitivity analysis can be performed. Decision makers can change the distribution of each exogenous variable one at a time or several at a time and have a good understanding of the importance each variable has on the attractiveness of the investment. It allows an increased comprehension of the relationships among variables and their impact on the decision process. This information is extremely valuable, especially for the evaluation of the international variables, in particular for foreign exchange rates, which are difficult enough to forecast. If, for example, the final results are found to be affected very little by changes in currency values, it is clear that the uncertainty of the investment is greatly reduced. On the contrary, high sensitivity to foreign exchange rates would warn the decision maker to give special forecasting attention to this variable and to consider the addition of an annual cost for hedging against this risk (i.e., a cost for "uncertainty absorption" discussed above).

Finally, two additional aspects related to the overall model-building process deserve mention: validation of the model and variance reduction techniques. A number of the concerns and practical problems related to the use of simulation models can be overcome by means of the judicious use of these two techniques. Both Naylor[17] and Shannon[18] view the validation process as being composed of three phases: (1) establish the face validity of the model's internal structure based upon a prior knowledge, past research, and existing theory; (2) perform vigorous empirical tests of the assumptions, identities, and operating equations of the model; and (3) verify the model's ability to predict the behavior of the real system and the model's utility to decision makers. Throughout the appendix, the authors have attempted to demonstrate that

[17]T. H. Naylor, *Computer Simulation Experiments with Models of Economic Systems* (New York: John Wiley & Sons, Inc., 1971).

[18]R. E. Shannon, *System Simulation: The Art and Science* (Englewood Cliffs, N.J.: Prentice-Hall, Inc., 1975).

phase 1 of the validation process has been achieved. Extensive empirical tests of the model by the authors have also demonstrated that the proposed model has validity in the phase 2 sense. Phase 3 validity can only be established through successful implementation of the model in several multinational firms, with the demonstration that skillful application of the model leads to significantly better capital investment decisions by MNCs.

Shannon[19] and Smith[20] have good surveys of variance reduction techniques which can increase the efficiency of simulation models by increasing the precision for a fixed sample size or decreasing the sample size for a fixed degree of precision. Shannon states that these techniques do not appear to be widely used in practice and the results obtained by using the techniques can be "almost unbelievable," based on the amount of additional effort required. In establishing phase 3 validity, the authors are testing several of these techniques which are felt will help to overcome the concerns noted in footnotes 13, 14, and 15.

The model has been programmed in both the batch and the interactive modes. Of course, the latter modes are particularly conducive to sensitivity analysis and the program is written to encourage management personnel to participate with the staff experts in the process of capital investment analysis.

Conclusion and Extensions

The major emphasis of the simulation proposed in the appendix was directed at two areas:

1. The extensions of capital budgeting analysis to include both project-related and international variables relevant to the multinational firm.

2. The flexibility of a two-stage screening process, where first subsidiaries evaluate investment proposals, and then the parent company supplements the analysis by considering the project's desirability from its point of view.

The dual goals of the simulation design were to provide a robust and flexible model and to require only those information inputs that could be relatively accurately estimated. It is because of this second goal that the model does not extensively treat the interrelationships among current proposals themselves. However, an extension of the current formulation could be made by formally reflecting these portfolio effects. In addition, the model should be extended to determine the optimal set of investments on a global basis vis-à-vis a hierarchy of multiple objectives (e.g., a net income goal, a NPV goal, a growth rate in assets and market share goal, a leverage goal, a risk-posture goal, a goal concerning participation by nationals of host countries, etc.). As information systems develop great sophistication, these improvements will certainly become more feasible.

---

[19]Ibid.

[20]Dennis E. Smith, "Requirements for an 'Optimizer' for Computer Simulations," *Naval Research Logistics Quarterly*, Vol. 20, No. 1, March 1973, pp. 161–179.

1. Discuss at least four major risks that multinational firms face in their capital budgeting activities.

2. Outline a general approach to capital budgeting for the multinational firm.

3. Discuss several "operating strategies" that multinational firms can use to reduce foreign exchange risks.

4. Discuss several strategies that can be implemented to reduce the impact of inflation on the multinational firm.

5. Mention several characteristics that could point to greater risk of expropriation for the multinational firm.

6. Based on the simulation model presented in Appendix 15A, do the following things:

(a) Outline the suggested two-stage approach for capital investment evaluation by the multinational firm.

(b) For both the parent company and the subsidiary, list the major cash inflows and outflows.

(c) List the major "endogenous variables" that will be used to evaluate and rank capital projects.

(d) Discuss why both the parent company and the subsidiary will utilize their respective risk-free rates in conjunction with the simulation.

(e) Discuss how sensitivity analysis would be performed in conjunction with the simulation and why this is important.

16 LEASING

Leasing is a process whereby the owner of a particular *asset (lessor)* enters into an *agreement (lease)* with the *user (lessee)* for the latter to use the asset for a specified period of time. The lessee pays a certain amount (*lease payment*) to the lessor for the use of the asset. The leasing industry grew very slowly at the start of the twentieth century but has grown almost explosively since World War II. Leatham[1] estimates the growth rate to have been 30% yearly during the 1950s, 15% to 30% during the 1960s, and 15% during the 1970s. According to Rochwarger[2] the value of the equipment owned by the leasing industry by the end of 1975 was expected to be $100 billion, compared to $75 billion at the end of 1973. Further, he estimated that total revenues received by lessors, including manufacturers, captive leasing companies, independent leasing companies, banks, and bank holding companies increased by 20% a year from 1964 to 1974 and in 1975 would total some $30 billion. He also estimated that during the latter half of the 1970s about 20% of all equipment would be leased and that by 1980 revenues would increase to $60 billion a year.

Real estate still constitutes the largest single category of leased items, but numerous types of equipment, such as airplanes, railroad cars, ships, specialized equipment for farming, textile and oil industries, and computers, are being leased. Almost without exception any type of equipment that a business can purchase, it can also lease. Within the consumer sector leasing of durable goods, such as automobiles, washers, dryers, refrigerators, televisions, furniture, and the like, has also been increasing rapidly. The leasing industry is experiencing a dynamic growth period and is becoming increasingly important as a means of financing for business, consumers, and to some extent, government operations.

ADVANTAGES OF LEASING

From the viewpoint of the lessee, there may be many advantages to leasing versus purchasing. Naturally, a primary consideration is cost. The cost of a lease may be more or less than the cost to purchase and may differ among

[1] John T. Leatham, "No Letup in Leasing," *The Conference Board Record*, March 1974.
[2] Leonard Rochwarger, "Leased: A Proud Story To Tell," *Fortune*, November 1974.

lessees. For example, if a firm had been running at a very low profit, it might not be able to enjoy the tax benefits of investment tax credit and accelerated depreciation which are associated with the purchase of some assets. A lessor could, however, take full advantage of the tax benefits and pass them along to the lessee by means of reduced lease payments.

Aside from the financial question, many other considerations become important in deciding whether to lease or purchase. The general advantages, inherent to all leases, are described below.

1. Leases provide an alternative source of obtaining facilities and equipment for firms that have limited capital budgets. Recall from our discussion of capital rationing that we suggested a policy of indicating which proposed new projects could be leased and the expected return using a lease. Such a listing provides wide visibility with respect to alternative capital acquisition plans: some may be purchased and others leased, with the goal of selecting the most profitable combination.

2. Frequently, equipment may be leased over a longer period than would be available through conventional financing. Usually, equipment loans run for a period that is substantially shorter than the economic life of the asset, whereas leases can be obtained for nearly the total length of the asset's life. This results in spreading the cost over a longer time period.

3. Leases are quoted at fixed rates which avoid the risks associated with short/or intermediate-term financing and refinancing. Recall that many intermediate-term loans have balloon repayment features whereby the bulk of the principal is due at the end of the loan and, if the firm maintains its credit rating, forms the basis for a new loan. Such refinancing exposes the firm to added risk, as interest rates may change.

4. Leasing may conserve existing sources of credit for other uses and usually does not restrict a firm's borrowing capacity. Many loan indentures do restrict additional borrowing. Further, some firms which cannot raise the needed capital to purchase an asset due to marginal credit standings may be able to lease.

5. Leasing generally provides 100% financing, since a down payment is not required.

6. Leasing is quick and flexible as opposed to raising funds and making capital expenditures. The restrictive covenants usually found in loan indenture agreements are generally not included in lease agreements. Further, lease terms and options can be tailored to the specific need of the lessee. For example, lease payment schedules may be arranged to meet the seasonal cash flows of the lessee.

7. The total acquisition cost, including sales taxes, delivery and installation charges, and so on, may all be included in the lease payments. These front-end costs may be substantial and thereby result in heavy initial cash outflows if assets are purchased. This can be avoided through leasing.

8. Bookkeeping may be simplified since lease payments are constant over the term of the lease, and depreciation and interest records need not be maintained. Loan payments often change over the period of the loan (especially for direct reduction loans).

9. The entire lease payment is tax-deductible to the lessee. If land is involved in the lease, this is especially important, since land may not be depreciated.

10. Leasing avoids the costs of underwriting and floating new issues of stocks and bonds. Also, the public disclosure surrounding such offerings is avoided when a firm does not have to go to the capital markets to secure funds.

LEASE VERSUS PURCHASE

The preceding discussion on the merits of leasing vs. ownership must culminate in the analysis of a specific decision to lease or buy. The criterion for this decision is the same as that for all capital budgeting proposals: namely, choose the alternative that maximizes the present worth of the enterprise. As in so many other instances, however, each business firm will have its own method of applying basic principles of financial analysis. Yet there are variables common to all leasing situations, and these must be identified and measured whatever the particular framework of analysis. The key variables in lease analysis, the focus of any lease negotiation, include the following:

1. Depreciation: The tax effects of depreciation represent an advantage of ownership that is lost under leasing. Since lease analysis is carried through on a cash-flow basis, depreciation represents a tax savings, and accelerated depreciation, all things equal, tends to swing the decision in the direction of ownership by increasing cash flows in the early years.

2. Obsolescence: High rates of obsolescence (e.g., in computers and calculating equipment) increase the risks of ownership. This tends to make leasing a more attractive alternative.

3. Operating and maintenance charges: These represent an expense of ownership, although the gross charge is reduced by tax shields. If the lessor assumes these expenses as part of the lease agreement, the situation makes leasing a more attractive alternative and may reduce the overall cost of acquiring the use of the asset. This will occur if the lessor can more cheaply maintain and/or operate the asset by reason of the economies of scale.

4. Salvage or residual values: After allowance for tax effects, residual values are an advantage of ownership lost under leasing. But salvage value is a highly uncertain value. High salvage values lower the costs of ownership. The problem is to forecast salvage within a reasonable range 5 or 10 years down the road. This is not an easy assignment. On the side of the lessor, salvage value reduces the cost of leasing. Under the pressure of negotiation, the lessor may transfer some of his uncertainties to the future; that is, he might hopefully anticipate a higher residual to keep the lease payments down and win the contract.

5. Discount rate: This is perhaps one of the most controversial features in lease evaluation. It can swing the decision one way or the other. Leasing analysis uses cash flows, and these extend over several fiscal periods. The cash flows, therefore, have to be discounted for the time value of money and for risk. But the risk associated with each of the cash flows of ownership may differ significantly. There are differing degrees of risk associated with sales, operating expenses, interest charges, and residuals. By contrast, once agreed upon, lease payments are usually fixed and certain. We would, therefore, not use the same discount rate on each cash flow. How, for example, should we discount the after-tax operating costs or the tax savings of depreciation? We will discuss this problem later in the chapter.

6. *Timing of lease payments*: Since the analysis uses a discounted-cash-flow approach, the timing of the lease payments (payable annually, semiannually, quarterly, or monthly) may, in a close situation, affect the decision. Similarly, the timing of lease payments, whether they are payable in advance or at the end of a designated period, must be considered.

7. *Tax effects*: In Chapter 2 we discussed the implications of taxation on the cash flows derived from capital investments. With respect to leasing, it is important to note that lease payments are fully tax deductible by the lessee, while the lessor enjoys the advantages of depreciation. Any investment tax credits may be taken by the lessor or be passed on to the lessee. Naturally, the size of the lease payments will reflect who takes these credits. But another factor must be considered. Can a lessee fully utilize investment tax credits, accelerated depreciation, and finance changes? That is, does the firm have sufficient levels of income to make the deductions worthwhile? For example, in recent years capital-intensive industries, such as railroads, airlines, maritime shipping, steel, aluminum, and public utilities, already deferred a large portion of their taxes and stood to lose permanently the tax benefits of investment and accelerated depreciation on new projects. In like manner, oil and mining companies frequently resorted to leasing simply because depletion allowances held their effective tax rates below those of the lessor, the difference being used to reduce the lessee's net cost. These situations encouraged the use of leveraged leasing.

The question of leasing versus ownership represents a long-run financial planning decision and must be considered together with both capital budgeting and financial structure decisions. In some cases the asset to be leased or purchased will represent a mandatory investment; the project must be accepted, and the only decision is whether to acquire the asset by purchase or by lease. In such cases, lease analysis is essentially a financing decision, and we attempt to evaluate the lease against alternative ways of financing the asset. In other cases the lease arrangement itself is important in deciding whether to accept or reject a capital project. For example, some capital projects may only be available by lease; in other cases, it may not be sound financially to buy an asset, but leasing the same asset may be quite attractive. In this situation, lease proposals are incorporated in the capital budget as discrete projects, and the evaluation process should permit management to properly rank all proposed capital expenditures (including lease projects) in order of desirability.

ESTABLISHING A LEASE QUOTE

The lessor seeks to maximize present worth and will strive to negotiate a lease such that the present value of the lease payments plus the present value of the residual equals or exceeds the cost of the equipment. The lessor applies a gross discount rate to the cash flow (or quotes a lease rate) to cover the cost of capital and any additional expenses of leasing (maintenance, operating, and insurance costs, if assumed). The process of determining a lease quote by a lessor is demonstrated in Example 1.

● **EXAMPLE 1**   *Establishing a Lease Quote*[3]

A lessor may purchase equipment for $60,000. It has a 3-year life and the lease will be for 3 years. The projected salvage value is $2,000. Lessor's cost of capital is 10%, but the salvage will be discounted at 20%, owing to the higher rate of uncertainty connected to the estimate. Determine the annual lease payments, first assuming payments made at the start of each year and then at the end of each year.

Solution: First, determine the present value of the salvage using the 20% rate.

$$PV = \$2,000 \times 0.578704$$
$$= \$1,158$$

Next, determine the annual lease payments if they are made in advance. This requires finding the amount of payment which when discounted at 10% for 3 years will equal the cost of the asset less the present value of the salvage value ($60,000 − $1,158 = $58,842).

$58,842 = initial lease payment plus present value of lease payments made at start of second and third years

$58,842 = lease payment + lease payment (1.735537)

$$\text{lease payment} = \frac{\$58,842}{2.735537} = \$21,510$$

The reader should note that 1.735537 is the present value factor for 2 years at 10%. Last, determine the annual lease payment if it is made at the end of each year.

$58,842 = lease payment (2.486852)

lease payment = $23,661

The reader should note that 2.486852 is the present value factor for 3 years at 10%.   ●

Several observations should be made relating to developing a lease quote:

1. A higher expected residual value lowers the minimum acceptable rental, and vice versa.

2. The residual value is discounted at a higher rate due to the uncertainty attached to the estimate. With an asset having a longer life, this uncertainty would probably be greater.

3. If the lessee assumed the operating, maintenance, or insurance, the lessor might lower his 10% bid.

4. If the lessor had tax advantages, economies of large-scale operations, or lower financing charges, some portion might be passed to the lessee in the form of lower lease payments.

[3]Some of the material in this and following examples is adapted from: J. Clark and P. Elgers, *Analysis of Leases* (New York: AICPA Continuing Professional Education Cassette, 1975); and J.Clark, M. Clark, and P. Elgers, *Financial Management: A Capital Market Approach* (Boston: Allyn and Bacon, Inc., 1976).

5. The timing of the lease payment, whether at the beginning or end of the period, whether monthly or quarterly, affects the amount of the payment.

6. Many items are negotiable and depend on the positions of both lessor and lessee.

LEASE VERSUS PURCHASE AS A FINANCING DECISION

Like the lessor, the lessee desires to maximize present value. In our initial analysis we will make three assumptions relative to the lessee:

1. The project being considered is mandatory, so the decision is how to finance the project. The lessee needs to know which method of financing (lease or purchase) is least costly.

2. Since leasing is a form of financing comparable to indebtedness, the asset if purchased will be financed by a bank loan. The underlying reasoning states that the borrowing capacity and cost of capital to a firm will be affected in about the same way by lease or debt financing.

3. The cash flows attributable to the project (except for residual value) will be discounted at the firm's after-tax cost of debt. This assumption will be discussed in greater detail later.

For the lessee, the financial analysis of lease versus purchase is quite simple: determine the yearly cost of each, discount to present value, and make the selection based on minimizing the present value of the cash outflows. But a word of caution is necessary. We have assumed the project is mandatory and must be included as an acquisition, whether it be purchased or leased. The decision we are presently examining is therefore one of financing rather than of capital expenditure. Thus, we ignore cash inflows from operations and rather seek to minimize the present value of the outflows over the project's life. The methodology for comparison is demonstrated in Example 2.

● **EXAMPLE 2** *Lease Versus Purchase (Financing Decision)*

Assume the conditions and solutions to Example 1 and that the machine may also be purchased by the user for $60,000, financed through a 6% bank loan, and depreciated using sum-of-the-years' digits over its 3-year life. The loan would be paid back in three *equal* annual installments. The firm's cost of capital is 10%, a 20% rate is used to discount the residual value, and the tax rate is 50%. Determine the NPVs of the three alternatives: lease with start-of-year payments, lease with end-of-year payments, and purchase, assuming that the operating costs are the same whether the machine is leased or purchased.

Solution: First, consider the lease with start-of-year payments. The NPV is found as shown below, using the a 3% discount rate and 50% tax rate. The 3% represents the after-tax interest cost of the debt.

$$\text{NPV} = -\$21,510(1 - 0.5) - \$21,510(1 - 0.5)(1.913470)$$
$$= -\$10,755 - \$20,579$$
$$= -\$31,334$$

Next, consider the lease with end-of-year payments using the same 3% discount rate.

$$\text{NPV} = -\$23,661(1 - 0.5)(2.828611)$$
$$= -\$33,464$$

Last, consider the purchase. Based on a depreciable value of $58,000, the annual depreciation is as follows:

Year	Depreciation
1	$29,000
2	19,140
3	9,860
Total	$58,000

The loan schedule is the amount needed to amortize the $60,000 over a 3-year period at 6% (Appendix C, column 6):

$$\text{loan repayment} = \$60,000(0.37410981)$$
$$= \$22,447$$

The loan schedule appears in tabular form as follows:

Year	Loan Repayment	Interest	Principal	Balance
1	$22,447	$3,600	$18,847	$41,153
2	22,447	2,469	19,978	21,175
3	22,447	1,270	21,175	0
Total		$7,339	$60,000	

The loan interest payments and depreciation represent tax-deductible expenses (as would operating costs, which are not considered in this example). The yearly cash flows are determined in tabular form as follows:

Year	Principal Payment (1)	Interest Payment (2)	Depreciation (3)	Tax Shield [(2) + (3)] × (0.5) (4)	Cash Outflow (5)	PV at 3%
1	−$18,847	−$3,600	−$29,000	$16,300	−$ 6,147	−$ 5,968
2	− 19,978	− 2,469	− 19,140	10,805	− 11,642	− 10,974
3	− 21,175	− 1,270	− 9,860	5,565	− 16,880	− 15,448
					NPV	−$32,390

The present value of the outflow is −$32,390; the PV of the salvage is $1,158 (discounted at 20%), so the PV of the net cash outflow is −$31,232 if the machine is purchased.

In this case the present value of the purchase is slightly less negative than the PV of either of the two lease plans, so purchasing represents the better choice.   ●

The discount rate used in lease versus purchase analysis is a very controversial issue. How do we justify the use of the after-tax cost of debt capital as the appropriate discount rate? The choice depends upon the assessment of risk. The following considerations weigh heavily in our choice:

1. In this particular problem, the capital budgeting question has already been decided. The project is required. The expenditure is nondiscretionary. As such, the question is one of financing.

2. If the firm as a whole reasonably expects to generate sufficient taxable income from its overall operations to use all tax deductions, tax shields are to be discounted at a low rate, since they are virtually risk-free.

3. The lease would enable management to avoid uncertain (risky) operating expenses; these amounts should also be discounted at a lower rate. In fact, the idea that a lease enables a firm to avoid risk leads some authorities to suggest a discount rate even lower than the risk-free rate, but, as a practical matter, debt cost is a reasonable approximation.

4. Some lease arrangements include lease payments that are contingent on future performance or other events; other leases are readily cancellable at the option of one or the other party. These types of situations also impact the choice of a discount rate. For example, a cancellable lease may actually be less burdensome than debt, since the face amount may be an upper limit with the lessee able, if necessary, to cancel and avoid losses. Here, the after-tax cost of debt might be too high a rate of discount.

5. The salvage value proceeds are generally a very uncertain amount, and if so, we logically discount them at a higher rate than the firm's average cost of capital. The rate reflects the firm's judgment about the estimate of the amount that can probably be recovered from the asset.

In Example 2, we ignored potential differences in operating costs with leasing versus purchasing. Frequently, because of economies of scale, such operating costs may differ, depending on whether an asset is leased or purchased. If differences do exist, they must be considered as a part of the decision process. The methodology is shown in Example 3.

● *EXAMPLE 3*   Lease Versus Purchase (Financing Decision)

Assume the same conditions as Example 2 except that there is a $1,000 yearly operating cost associated with ownership but not with leasing. Consider lease payments made at the start and at the end of each year and determine the advantage of lease versus purchasing.

Solution: The solution is shown in tabular form on the facing page. Note that the figures used in column (10) for case I (after-tax lease cost) are found by multiplying the lease payment of $21,510 (determined in Example 1) by 1 minus the corporate tax rate; similarly, the figures in column (8) for case II result where $23,661 (also determined in Example 1) is multiplied by 1 minus the tax rate. Note also that when lease payments are made in advance, there is an advantage to leasing in this example, whereas if the payments are made at the end of the year, the advantage is in ownership.

Case I—Lease Payment Made in Advance

(1)	(2)	(3)	(4)	(5)	(6)	(7) [(2) + (5) + (6)]	(8) [(50% of (7)]
Loan					Operating		
Payment	Interest	Principal	Balance	Depreciation	Cost	Tax Deduction	Tax Shield
$22,447	$3,600	$18,847	$41,153	$29,000	$1,000	$33,600	$16,800
22,447	2,469	19,978	21,175	19,140	1,000	22,609	11,304
22,447	1,270	21,177	—	9,860	1,000	12,130	6,065

(9) + (6) − (8)] Ownership Cost	(10) After-Tax Lease Cost	(11) [(10) − (9)] Advantage to Ownership	(12) Discount Factor	(K_d), 3%	(13) Present Value of Own
—	$10,755	$10,755	—		$10,755.00
$ 6,647	10,755	4,108	0.970874		3,988.35
12,143	10,755	(1,388)	0.942596		(1,308.32)
17,382		(17,382)	0.915142		(15,906.99)
		2,000 salvage	0.578704	$(K_s = 20\%)$	1,157.41
				Advantage to leasing	($1,314.55)

Case II—Lease Payment Made at End of the Period

(1)	(2)	(3)	(4)	(5) [(2) + (3) + (4)]	(6) [50% of (5)]
Year	Loan Payment	Interest	Depreciation	Operating Costs	Tax Deduction	Tax Shield

Year	Loan Payment	Interest	Depreciation	Operating Costs	Tax Deduction	Tax Shield
1	$22,447	$3,600	$29,000	$1,000	$33,600	$16,800
2	22,447	2,469	19,140	1,000	22,609	11,304
3	22,447	1,270	9,860	1,000	12,130	6,065

(7) 1) + (4) − (6)] Net Ownership Cost	(8) After-Tax Lease Cost	(9) Advantage to Ownership	(10) Discount Factor (K_d), 3%	(11) Present Value of Own
$ 6,647	$11,830	$5,183	0.970874	$5,032.04
12,143	11,830	(313)	0.942596	(295.03)
17,382	11,830	(5,552)	0.915142	(5,080.86)
		2,000 salvage	0.578704 $(K_s = 20\%)$	1,157.41
			Advantage to ownership	$813.56

In Case I, since the NPV of ownership is negative, the leasing alternative represents the less costly method of financing, whereas in Case II, the reverse is true.   ●

The solution methodology demonstrated in Example 3 may be reduced to equation form by noting that the cost of the borrow and purchase alternative is the sum of loan payment for each period plus operating expenses less interest, depreciation, and operating expense tax shields, less the after-tax salvage value discounted to present value at a discount rate appropriate to the cash flows.[4] The cost of borrowing and purchasing is expressed in Equation (1):

$$\text{cost to purchase} = \sum_{t=1}^{N} \frac{P + O_t - (I_t + D_t + O_t)t_c}{(1 + K_d)^t} - \frac{S_N - (S_N - B)t_g}{(1 + K_s)^N} \tag{1}$$

where P = loan payment: interest and amortization of principal
L_t = rental payment in period t
I_t = interest payment in period t
D_t = depreciation in period t
O_t = incremental operating costs of ownership in period t
t_c = firm's tax rate on ordinary income
t_g = tax rate applicable to gains and losses on the disposal of fixed assets
S_N = expected cash value of asset in period N
B = book value of asset in period N
K_d = explicit after-tax cost of new debt capital
K_s = discount rate applied to residual value of the asset

Similarly, the cost to lease is the sum of the after-tax lease payments discounted by the after-tax cost of debt capital, as expressed in Equation (2):

$$\begin{matrix} \text{cost to lease} \\ \text{with end-of-} \\ \text{period payments} \end{matrix} = \sum_{t=1}^{N} \frac{L_t(1 - t_c)}{(1 + K_d)^t} \tag{2}$$

If lease payments were made at the start of each period, we would sum from $t = 0$ to $t = N - 1$. This would have the effect of reducing the lease payment, as was demonstrated in Examples 1 and 3.

In many instances the question of lease versus purchase is not limited to a financial decision as was the case in this section. Rather, all alternatives must be examined to ascertain whether the project is acceptable based on its merits, and then the most advantageous method of securing it determined.

LEASE VERSUS PURCHASING AS A CAPITAL BUDGETING DECISION

In our discussion of lease versus purchase as a financing decision, we indicated that the capital budgeting decision had been made (the acquisition was mandatory) and our concern lay in selecting the optimum mode for financing. Thus, we presumed conditions of certainty as to the financing and lease payment cash flows, and discounted them at the after-tax cost of debt. By

---

[4]The next section, including Equations (1) through (3), is based upon the article by R. W. Johnson and W. G. Lewellen, "Analysis of the Lease or Buy Decision," *Journal of Finance*, Vol. 27, September 1972, pp. 815–823.

contrast, *if the firm were considering the lease proposal as a distinct capital project to be ranked against all other projects, the cash flows would not be considered certain. Sales and operating costs change, tax rates and the like change frequently with business conditions, and sometimes lease payments also vary with business conditions. In this case, the financial manager would discount the separate cash flows of ownership or leasing at a rate appropriate to the level of risk.*

Moreover, it is axiomatic in capital budgeting that the return on investment be computed independently of the cost of financing. Yet in Examples 2 and 3 interest charges were explicitly included in the ownership calculations. *The reason for including interest in the calculations was the need to find the difference in the after-tax cash flows between the leasing and borrowing alternatives. The project had already been accepted, and that decision was made independently of financing.* We had to look directly to those cash flows which would affect the financing decision. By contrast, in Example 4, we view the question of purchase or lease as two distinct, independent, and mutually exclusive projects. Further, it is not necessary to make any assumption of borrowing to meet the purchase price of the asset. These modificators change the structure of the calculations in three ways:

1. It is necessary to calculate the difference between net present value of ownership and the net present value of leasing as a basis for the decision.

2. The approach follows the general rule in capital budgeting of separating the return on a project from the cost of financing: specifically, we delete the interest charges from the costs of ownership in determining net present value.

3. Allowance is made for the uncertainties of the operating cash flows, tax shields, and residuals by discounting the first two by the firm's cost of capital[5] and the latter by a rate appropriate to the risk level.

The net present value anticipated from purchase of the asset, then, is the sum of the present value of the net after-tax operating profits (revenues less operating costs) plus the discounted after-tax cash proceeds from salvage less the cost of the asset. Similarly, the net present value of the leasing project would be the present value of the revenues less the lease payments and other costs, if any, associated with leasing. In comparing the net present values of the two alternatives, the revenues are assumed to be the same in both cases, which allows their deletion from the analysis.

In practice, two steps are required. We first determine whether the project is acceptable if purchased using the methodology outlined in Chapter 6. Then we compare the net present values of ownership versus leasing using Equation (3):

$$\triangle NPV = NPV(\text{purchase}) - NPV(\text{lease})$$

$$= \sum_{t=1}^{N} \frac{t_c(D_t) - O_t(1 - t_c)}{(1 + K)^t} + \frac{S_N - (S_N - B)t_g}{(1 + K_s)^N}$$

$$- C + \sum_{t=1}^{N} \frac{L_t(1 - t_c)}{(1 + k_d)^t} \qquad (3)$$

where $\triangle NPV$ = difference between NPV(purchase) and NPV(lease)

K = firm's marginal cost of capital

---

[5]The cost of capital would be applied for projects having the same degree of risk as the firm overall. For projects of differing risk, adjustment would be made as indicated in Section II.

Excluding revenues from both NPV calculations, the net present value of ownership is the sum of depreciation tax shield, $t_c(D_t)$, less the after-tax operating costs, $O_t(1 - t_c)$, for each period discounted at the firm's cost of capital (K) plus the after-tax salvage, $S_N - (S_N - B)t_g$, discounted at some higher rate (K_s) less the cost of the equipment (C). The present value of leasing in the comparison (again excluding revenues) is the sum of after-tax rental for each period, $L_t(1 - t_c)$, discounted at the cost of debt capital (K_d). This amount is added to the present value of ownership, since it represents a negative NPV because the lease involves exclusively cash outflows. If $\triangle$NPV is positive, purchasing is perferred, while if $\triangle$NPV is negative, leasing is preferred.

The process of deciding between purchasing and leasing is demonstrated in Examples 4 and 5. In Example 4 we examine only the purchase, while in Example 5 we determine the difference in the purchase and lease costs using Equation (3) to determine which is preferable.

● **EXAMPLE 4**   *Purchase Decision*

A corporation may purchase or lease equipment costing $60,000 and having a salvage value of $2,000. If purchased, the equipment would be depreciated using sum-of-the-years' digits depreciation over its 3-year life. If leased, the lease payment would be made at year's end and the cost would be $23,661 (Solution to Example 1). In either case operating revenues would be increased by $25,000 per year and, if the equipment is *purchased*, operating costs would increase by $1,000 per year. The corporation's tax rate is 50%; its cost of capital 10%; risk-adjusted discount rate for salvage 20%; and its after-tax cost of debt 3%. Assume that investment tax credits are the same if purchased or leased and omitted for (the sake of simplicity in this example), and determine the NPV of the purchase.

Solution: The changes in corporation's income statement and cash flows are tabulated below.

Changes in Corporation's Income Statement

	Year 1	Year 2	Year 3
Revenues	$25,000	$25,000	$25,000
Operating expenses	−1,000	−1,000	−1,000
Depreciation	−29,000	−19,140	−9,860
Earnings before taxes	($5,000)	$ 4,860	$14,140
Taxes at 50%	−2,500	−2,430	−7,070
Earnings after taxes	($2,500)	$2,430	$7,070

Change in Corporation's Cash Flows

	Year 1	Year 2	Year 3
Depreciation	$29,000	$19,140	$9,860
Earnings after taxes	(2,500)	2,430	7,070
Cash flow	$26,500	$21,570	$16,930

The cash flows are shown discounted to present value below. The 10% rate is applied to the operating cash flows, while 20% is applied to the salvage value.

Time	Amount	Discount Factor		Present Value
Present	−$60,000	1.		−$60,000
1	26,500	0.909091		24,091
2	21,570	0.826446		17,826
3	16,930	0.751315		12,720
3	2,000	0.578704		1,157
			NPV	−$ 4,206

Since the NPV of the purchase is negative, the purchase is unacceptable. However, the lease may be acceptable. This determination is made using Equation (3), as demonstrated in Example 5.

● **EXAMPLE 5** *Lease Versus Purchase Comparison*

Using the information provided in Example 4, determine the $\triangle$NPV of the lease and purchase employing Equation (3).

Solution: Employing Equation (3) in a sequential manner, we have the following:

$$\sum_{t=1}^{3} \frac{t_c(D_t) - O_t(1 - t_c)}{(1 + K)^t} = (\$14,500 - \$500)(0.909091)$$

$$+ (\$9,570 - \$500)(0.826446)$$
$$+ (\$4,930 - \$500)(0.751315)$$
$$= \$12,727 + \$7,496 + \$3,328$$
$$= \$23,551$$

$$\frac{S_N - (S_N - B)t_g}{(1 + K_s)^N} = \$2,000(0.578704)$$

$$= \$1,157$$

$$C = \$60,000$$

$$\sum_{t=1}^{3} \frac{L_t(1 - t_c)}{(1 + K_d)^t} = \$11,831(0.970874) + \$11,831(0.942596)$$

$$+ \$11,831(0.915142)$$
$$= \$33,465$$

$$\triangle\text{NPV} = \$23,551 + \$1,157 - \$60,000 + \$33,465$$
$$= -\$1,827$$

The negative $\triangle$NPV means that leasing is preferable to purchasing. ●

The analysis illustrates the impact of choosing discount rates unique to the cash flows of ownership and leasing. A higher degree of risk surrounds the cash flows associated with ownership; therefore, these are discounted at the firm's cost of capital and at higher rates for salvage values. The lease cash flows, supported by contractual agreements, are discounted at the after-tax cost of debt capital.

In summary, if management has determined that it must acquire a project (i.e. it is mandatory), the essential problem is to determine the lowest cost of financing. This problem was examined in the previous section. If, however, there is no presumption, the analysis looks at two mutually independent projects: one to purchase, the other to lease. Then, these projects are evaluated with all other projects being considered using the techniques detailed in Examples 4 and 5.

The analysis is not limited to net present value; internal rate of return may be used following the same guidelines for comparison of the lease versus borrow–purchase financial decision and the discretionary lease versus purchase decision.

SUMMARY

The use of leasing has grown extensively in recent years and for many firms it offers a viable alternative to purchasing. As such, it is necessary to examine leasing as an important part of the capital budgeting decision process.

In this chapter we examined the various advantages of leasing, types of leases, and legal aspects of leasing. Then we analyzed the lease versus purchase decision, first as a financing decision when the assets involved represented mandatory expenditures, and later as a capital budgeting decision involving discretionary expenditures.

PROBLEMS

1. The Reed Manufacturing Company has a contract to produce metal parts for 5 years as a subcontractor to a large industrial firm. As it was not in a cash position to purchase the necessary metalworking equipment, it decided to lease. There were two types of equipment available: one was highly specialized, cost $80,000, and will have no salvage value at the end of 5 years. The second was highly adaptable to all kinds of metalworking uses, cost $200,000, and would have a salvage value of $75,000 at the end of 5 years. The salvage should be discounted at 10% for uncertainty.

Establish a lease quote for each machine if payments are made at the beginning and end of the year. The cost of capital is 8%.

2. The Mather Construction Company is considering purchasing or leasing a new crane whose purchase price is $75,000. The lease would run 10 years, the estimated life of the crane. If the company purchases the crane, they have projected its salvage value to be $7,500. Because of the high risk of the assigned salvage value, a 20% discount will be applied. The company's cost of borrowing is 8% and is in a 50% marginal tax bracket. The company uses straight-line depreciation.

If the company leases or buys, operating costs will be the same for the company.

The lease agreement offers two plans of 10 equal payments: (1) payment at the start of each year for $10,000 per year; (2) payment at the end of each year for $11,000 per year.

Determine the NPVs of the three alternatives: lease with start-of-the-year payments, lease with end-of-the-year payments, and purchase using 10 equal annual installments.

3. The Castaway Corporation makes disposable diapers in northeastern Pennsylvania and markets these locally. Recently, the market for Castaway Diapers has expanded so that they now need a fleet of 15 trucks for distribution purposes. The president is very traditional and believes in ownership of all equipment necessary to production and distribution: however, his finance department recommends an evaluation of leasing. Castaway will retain all drivers of the trucks regardless of the decision, and this will in no way affect the outcome of the decision.

   Castaway knows that if they purchase the trucks at $36,000 each, they can finance it through the First National Bank of Smalltown at 9% interest paid in five equal annual installments of the purchase price. They can depreciate the trucks using the SYD method. The firm's cost of capital is 12%. Salvage on the trucks is calculated on the basis of low mileage in the neighborhood of 80,000 miles, which will be $9,000 at the end of 5 years. As Castaway is uncertain as to what the mileage will actually be, they will assign the salvage a slightly higher discount rate at 15%. Maintenance on the truck will be 5 cents per mile, with an additional $606 per year for licensing fees.

   Penske Leasing has offered Castaway an operating lease for the 15 trucks at $169,594.35 if paid in arrears for their 5-year life or $162,358.50 per year if paid in advance. The terms of the lease cover all services, including tires and towing charges and licensing.

   All calculations are made on the basis of a 52-week year and 80,000 miles on the total 15 trucks. Castaway is in the 48% tax bracket.

   Determine which alternative would be the wisest choice. Show all work in tabular form. If leasing appears to be a viable alternative, explain why that is true.

4. The I-GOT-YA Company is considering purchasing a computer for $500,000. If they purchase the computer, a 7% loan must be taken out with the WE-GRAB-YOUR-MONEY Bank. Loan payments are required at the end of each year. I-GOT-YA Company uses double-declining-balance methods of depreciation with a switchover to S/L after 3 years for assets having a 5-year life. The computer is estimated to have a 5-year useful life with a salvage value of $20,000. I-GOT-YA anticipates some risk in the assigned salvage value, so a 15% discount factor is utilized in their lease vs. purchase analysis. Concurrently, the WE-LEASE-IT-ALL Company has offered to lease the same equipment to I-GOT-YA for 5 years, with the following terms and conditions:

   (1) No maintenance expense required by I-GOT-YA.
   (2) Annual rental of $117,523 if paid at the beginning of each year.
   (3) Annual rental of $130,276 if paid at the end of each year.

   If I-GOT-YA purchases the computer, they must incur an additional $1,000 of maintenance expense in addition to depreciation. The marginal tax rate for I-GOT-YA is 48%.

   (a) Calculate I-GOT-YA Company's depreciation tables for years 1–5.
   (b) Set up a loan schedule for I-GOT-YA's $500,000 loan.
   (c) Determine the advantage/disadvantage of lease vs. purchase considering rental payments at both the end and the beginning of each year.

5. Garrbadge Corporation is about to acquire a new piece of production equipment costing $100,000. The firm has the choice of borrowing the $100,000 at 10%, to be repaid in 10 annual installments of $16,273 each, or of leasing the machine for $16,500 per year, with payments at year-end. (Under the lease arrangement the firm is paying a 10% implicit interest rate; this is the rate the lessor is earning.) The machine will be used for 10 years, at the end of which time its estimated salvage value will be $10,000. If the firm leases the equipment, maintenance cost is included in the lease payment; but if it purchases the machine, it must spend an estimated $2,000 a year on maintenance. (*Note:* The decision to acquire the production equipment is not here; this decision was made previously as part of the capital budgeting process.) Determine whether the equipment should be leased or purchased if the effective income tax rate for the firm is 35%. The average after-tax cost of capital for Garrbadge Corporation is 10%.

17 CORPORATE REORGANIZATION: ACQUISITIONS AND READJUSTMENT OF FINANCIAL STRUCTURES

The acquisition of one corporation by another qualifies as a capital budgeting decision, for the project involves the alternative use of investible funds. Corporate acquisitions, accordingly, stand or fall by the same criteria applied to all discretionary capital expenditures. Consistent with the assumptions of financial management, the presumed objective of a combination is to enhance the present worth of the joint enterprise and thereby improve the wealth position of the common stockholders measured by the market value of their shares.

The elements in the articulation of an acquisition strategy to combine include the following:

1. Mode of expansion.
2. Legal forms.
3. Accounting and tax options.
4. Identifying take-over opportunities.

The measure of a successful acquisition strategy rests upon the market value of the stock. If the market value has increased, the increment in market value (postcombination) over the preacquisition values denotes the synergistic effects of the combination. The gain or loss to any one group of shareholders naturally depends upon the exchange ratios, as will be discussed in a following section. Since market values trade off risk and return, synergism results only if:

1. The combination increases earnings for the same quantity of risk.
2. The combination reduces risk while maintaining the same level of earnings.
3. Earnings and risk are both changed to improve the risk–return combination.

Equally proportionate increases in earnings and risk fo not raise market values, although the financial statements may show higher earnings per share. The combination has merely moved up the security market line.

Synergism is not easy to obtain and even more difficult to measure when achieved. The criterion assumes a linear relationship between market returns and risk (i.e., that the market is efficient). Time is also a factor. *Synergistic effects rarely appear in the fiscal period following the combination, and it may be many periods down the road before the full benefits of the combination are realized.* In the meantime, the acquiring firm may have entered upon other combinations and the national economy may have moved from one plateau to another. Under these circumstances, it becomes almost impossible to quantify precisely the synergistic effects of a single combination.

The second topic covered in this chapter has to do with adjusting the firm's financial structure. Proposals for substituting one form of security for another to readjust the firm's financial structure may also be analyzed using captial budgeting techniques. Changing the capital structure can increase the firm's present worth, and in fact some business combinations are undertaken expressly for the benefits anticipated to result from the rearrangement of the financial structure.[1] Financial readjustment projects, like other capital investment proposals, compete for available resources and are judged by the same criteria.

ACQUISITION STRATEGY

The concept of an acquisition strategy implies economic considerations, including economies of scale, market penetration, risk reduction, and the like, but at the same time also incorporates the choice of accounting methods, tax considerations, and the likelihood of antitrust involvement. All these factors must be integrated to develop a comprehensive plan for intercorporate investments, and are examined in this section.

Mode of Expansion

A firm may expand either internally or externally. Thus far in our discussion of the capital investment process, we have limited our examination to the former, so it is valuable at this juncture to enumerate the primary advantages and disadvantages of internal expansion. This will provide a benchmark for comparison as we examine external expansion.

Internal expansion enjoys the following advantages:

1. The valuation process of expansion by combination is avoided.

2. There are fewer accounting and tax problems to resolve.

3. The problem of minority stockholders does not arise.

4. Subject to some qualification, the situation may diminish the likelihood of unfavorable antitrust action.

5. The firm has the opportunity to acquire new facilities designed and located specially to meet its operational requirements, and, as a corollary, management has the opportunity to entrench the firm as a low-cost producer.

The disadvantages inherent to internal expansion also warrant close consideration:

1. The availability of funds (retained earnings or issuance of new securities) limits the scope of the expansion programs.

2. The disbursal of funds to acquire new assets may drain liquidity.

---

[1]See Wilber G. Lewellen, "A Prime Financial Rationale for the Conglomerate Merger," *The Journal of Finance*, May 1971, pp. 521–537.

3. The tempo of expansion depends upon the construction period or lead times of the assets concerned.

Alternatively, if the firm expands by combination, it will enjoy other advantages:

1. The funds available for expansion may be supplemented by the issuance of securities so that more expansion can be accomplished for the same dollar outlay and, as a corollary, to the extent the combination is financed by the exchange of securities, liquidity is conserved.

2. The firm secures additional facilities at once.

3. The acquisition may reduce the number of competitors or otherwise improve market control.

4. If the transaction meets IRS criteria, it may qualify as a tax-free exchange.

5. The combination may be the vehicle for recruiting new managerial talent.

Disadvantages associated with combination include the following:

1. The process of negotiation encompasses valuation problems, choice of accounting methodology and tax treatment, and the question of minority interests.

2. All things equal, the situation carries a higher probability of antitrust prosecution.

3. Depending upon the terms of exchange, the transaction may create a substantial tax liability for the selling corporation.

4. The acquiring firm may have to invest additional funds to integrate the facilities into its operational pattern.

5. The success of the combination depends upon the ability of management to mesh in a single operation two previously independent organizations. *The human equation in this regard presents a substantial challenge.*

Of the two approaches, internal expansion predominates, but expansion by combination is more common as the asset sizes increase.

The achievement of synergistic effects depends upon the economic substance of the combination, that is, the earnings potential and risk posture of the joint enterprise. In terms of economic substance there are five basic classes of combinations, which are described below.

1. Vertical combination. The acquiring firm expands backward toward sources of supply or forward toward market outlets. The United States Steel Corporation, for example, sought a completely integrated system from the raw-material stage to the finished product. More recent illustrations of vertical combination include the acquisition of Argo Oil Corporation by Atlantic Refining (1960) and Montgomery Ward's acquisition of the Container Corporation of America (1968). *Potentially, vertical combinations can stabilize the supply and/or demand schedules of the acquiring company, reduce inventories, facilitate production planning, and economize on working capital investment.*

2. Horizontal combination. This entails the amalgamation of competing firms at the same stage of the industrial process. Examples include the 1969 Atlantic Richfield acquisition of Sinclair Oil Corporation and McDonnell's acquisition of Douglas Aircraft Company (1967). *In addition to reducing the degree of competition, horizontal combinations offer the prospect of eliminating duplicate facilities and operation, reducing the investment in working capital, a broadened product line, and better market control.*

3. Circular combination. This strategy unites firms with distinct product lines but which share the same distribution facilities or can benefit from the same research facilities. An example of a circular combination would be a soap manufacturer acquiring a bleach manufacturer. Standard Brands and DuPont fit the type. Here again economies result from the elimination of duplicate facilities and there exists the potential for increasing demand as a result of broadening the product line.

4. Conglomerate combination. The conglomerate combines firms in different lines of endeavor. General Dynamics, for example, spans such diverse operations as aerospace manufacture, surface and subsurface marine vehicles, rubber and tire manufacture, and communications. *Among so diversified a collection of outputs, it seems difficult to envision operating economies, although risk pooling may reduce financing charges. On the other hand, the market value of the whole enterprise may increase through reducing the variance in total revenues by including firms that covary unequally with fluctuations in general business activity, by increasing capacity to leverage the capital structure, and by improving substandard earnings of the component units.*

5. Financial combination. Assuming less than perfectly correlated cash flows, the combination of two firms lowers the variability in net operating income. The improved stability in earnings should enhance the aggregate debt capacity of the combination beyond the original limits established by lending institutions for the component firms. If management takes advantage of the enlarged debt capacity, the leveraging will increase earnings per share, lower the average cost of capital, and raise the present worth of the outstanding shares.

It is easier to enumerate the theoretical advantages of different combinations than to achieve them in practice. Larger size does not invariably equate with greater efficiency. Problems of managerial effectiveness afflict all organizations, but they grow disproportionately with size. Paperwork proliferates and bureaucratic red tape discourages initiative. Moreover, the advantages of specialization can be lost with integration. Studies by the Federal Trade Commission and independent bodies suggest that the largest firms in an industry are not always the lowest-cost producers.

LEGAL FORMS OF COMBINATION

Interrelated with the economic objective of expansion is the legal form of the combination. Economic objectives influence management structure (e.g., centralized vs. decentralized management) and particular legal forms facilitate one or the other types of management structures. *Specifically, the form of combination impacts on the time required to effect the combination, the ease of financing, the degree of management control, the flexibility of the organization, the degree of permanence in the arrangement, and the tax liability of the enterprise.* The principal forms of combination—purchase of assets, mergers and consolidations, and formation of holding companies—are discussed below.

Purchase of Assets

As the term implies, the acquiring firm may purchase all or some of the seller's assets and assume all, some, or none of his liabilities. Thus, the sale of the RCA computer division to Sperry-Univac falls into the category. The procedure has several advantages:

1. The sale may not require the approval of the selling corporation's stockholders. Unless the sale changes the character of seller's business (the sale of goodwill or property forming an integral part of the business), the transaction would not require the consent of the stockholders.

2. In contrast to the merger approach described below, purchase of assets has an inherent flexibility. The acquiring corporation may purchase only those facilities pertinent to its operations and may or may not assume any liabilities. Consideration may take the form of cash, securities, or a combination thereof.

3. Tax shields may be created if the sale results in capital loss.

4. The acquiring corporation does not inherit the personnel or management problems of the selling firm.

The disadvantages associated with the purchase of assets also warrant close attention:

1. If the sale requires the consent of the shareholders, the usual problems of minority rights arise. Creditors, however, cannot object in the absence of fraud, and their liens follow the property subject to the attachment.

2. If the selling firm realizes a large gain, substantial tax liabilities may be involved.

3. Some state laws mandate the approval of the seller's stockholders when the buyer purchases the assets by issuing stock.

Merger and Consolidation

Technically speaking, in a merger, the acquiring firm assumes all the assets and liabilities of the seller and the latter is dissolved. Consolidation involves forming a new corporation which assumes the assets and liabilities of two or more selling corporations. The latter are then dissolved. The reader should bear in mind, however, that the term "merger" in *popular usage* describes all business combinations.

By way of illustration, in 1954, the Nash Corporation, renamed American Motors Corporation, acquired by *merger* the Hudson Motor Car Company. Hudson shareholders received two American Motors shares for each three Hudson shares. Nash stock exchanged share for share. In 1967, a new company, McDonnell Douglas Corporation, was formed to *consolidate* the McDonnell and Douglas corporations. Douglas shareholders received 1.75 shares of the new firm's common for each Douglas share. McDonnell shares were swapped on a one-to-one ratio.

Some advantages of the merger or consolidation include the following:

1. Taxes on intercorporate dividends may be eliminated.

2. Financial reporting is simplified by elimination of consolidated financial statements.

3. Centralization of authority is facilitated.

4. The tax expense of maintaining separate corporate entities is eliminated.

5. It may be possible to carryout a merger or consolidation as a tax-free exchange.

Disadvantages must also be considered.

1. There may be some loss of goodwill. When a small company combines with a significantly larger firm, circumstances dictate the dissolution of the smaller organization. This may result in loss of some goodwill.

2. The arrangement is inflexible. The acquiring corporation must assume all the assets and liabilities of the seller, including those of only peripheral importance.

3. Stockholders of both corporations must assent to the combination. Dissenting stockholders may demand an appraisal of their holdings and payment in cash. Dissenters may also sue to test compliance with the legal formalities stipulated by state law.

4. Negotiators must wrestle with the question of valuation, choice of accounting method, and the tax status of the selling firm's shareholders.

5. The perennial managerial problem of blending two previously distinct organizations remains. The Penn Central combination is a prime example.

Holding Company

Generally speaking, any corporation that invests in the stock of another firm constitutes a holding company. Holding companies function in all fields of business but are common to public utilities and banking, where legal restrictions set geographic limits on the establishment of new facilities. Within the study of capital investment, we are concerned with two objectives of a holding company: investment and control. Control might signify majority ownership of the outstanding shares, but often, especially if the subsidiary is a large corporation with scattered stock ownership, the investor may secure *de facto* control with relatively few shares, perhaps only 20% of the outstanding stock.

There are two functional types of holding companies: pure holding companies and holding–operating companies. The former have no operating functions. The assets consist solely of holdings in subsidiary stocks, bonds, and loans, while the chief sources of income are the dividends, interest, and fees earned from providing services to the subsidiary units. The United States Steel Corporation and American Home Products were formed *initially* with the prime purpose of acquiring stocks in operating companies. The latter represents a mixed form. General Motors, initially organized as a pure holding company, was reorganized as an operating company by converting the subsidiary corporations into GM divisions. However, the company still retains subsidiary investments in General Motors Acceptance Corporation and various foreign affiliates.

Several factors recommend the holding company:

1. It is not necessary to secure the consent of stockholders of the subsidiary corporations, and the need to pay off dissenters does not arise.

2. The parent acquires a going concern intact without loss of goodwill; if cash is paid to purchase subsidiary stock, a sum far less than the net value of the subsidiary's assets need be invested to acquire control. The parent has only to gain sufficient outstanding shares to ensure control, and where the subsidiaries have large blocks of long-term debt outstanding, this can represent a small portion of the total assets brought under control. The pyramiding of debt leverages the parent's investment.

3. The parent need not assume the liabilities of the subsidiary corporations.

4. It may make possible a combination of enterprises which legislation would not permit under a single corporate roof. By the late 1960s, virtually all the nation's larger commercial banks converted their corporate structures to holding company form to enable them to undertake such diverse functions as data processing, insurance, mutual fund sales, investment advisory services, and leasing. As banks they could not participate in these activities.

5. The holding company organizational form facilitates decentralized operations over state and international boundaries.

Several factors that detract from the holding company organization must be considered:

1. The structure may prove unstable. If the subsidiary fails to pay dividends on its preferred or misses an interest payment, the parent's investment may be lost or its control jeopardized.

2. The income tax laws work to the disadvantage of the holding company. If the holding company owns less than 80% of the subsidiary's stock, it must pay at 15% tax on dividends received from the subsidiary. This creates three tiers of taxation: the operating companies on the original income earned, the parent holding company in receipt of dividends from the operating company, and the holding company's stockholders on the dividends they receive from the parent.

3. Maintaining separate corporate entities duplicates expenses: franchise taxes, annual meetings, officers' salaries, and so on.

4. Minority interests of the subsidiary corporations can prove troublesome. The minority is there to challenge intercorporate transfers, accounting methods, investory control, or practices that appear to "exploit" the subsidiary corporations.

5. Because of historical abuses, the holding company device is regulated by the SEC under the Public Utility Holding Company Act of 1937 and the ICC under the Interstate Commerce Act.

To recapitulate, *an acquisition strategy should first define the economic substance of the combination, that is, whether the objective is to increase revenues, achieve operating economies, diversify, readjust the financial structure, or reduce the risk of ultimate failure.*[2] This will largely determine whether the combination is best accomplished by internal financing or by acquisition. It will also influence the management structure: the degree of centralization and the arrangement of line and staff functions.

---

[2]The reader will correctly observe that the statement oversimplifies the problem of motivation underlying merger activity. Mixed motives may predominate, the parties in interest having different objectives in fostering the combination. In some instances, the predominant objective may look to speculative gains from rising market prices or the issuance of new securities. The lurid details of "big killings" decorate business history books. Yet, if the combination survives, it must serve an economic purpose and indeed without some ostensible economic rationale, the stock market would probably not react positively to the announcement of the combination.

Economic substance also influences the choice of accounting methodology; that is, the accounting system should record the nature of the economic event taking place. It should record the economic substance of the transaction on a basis that permits comparison of pre- and postcombination results and facilitate the prediction of future performance. At any rate, this represents the theory. In practice, the choice of accounting methodology—purchase or pooling—has become the source of much argumentation, and the suspicion persists that some recent combinations would not have taken place except for the accounting options available. Since the choice of accounting methodology can affect earnings per share, the accounting numbers figure prominently in an acquisition strategy.

THE ACCOUNTING DECISION

Copeland and Wojdak[3] stated the essence of the accounting decision in business combinations:

> The manipulative quality of the purchase-pooling decision rule derives from the fact that acquired assets may be valued differently under the two methods. If a merger is accounted for as a purchase, acquired assets are recorded at the fair value of the consideration given by the acquiring company; however, under the pooling method they are valued at their pre-acquisition book values. . . . *The method that minimizes asset values usually maximizes profits* [italics added].

Minimizing asset values on the books reduces future charges against income. Hence, if book values exceed market values, the decision rule dictates a purchase treatment. When this condition is reversed, the pooling of interest is the appropriate treatment. But two assumptions underlie the rule: that management seeks to maximize future accounting incomes; and accounting numbers determine the market value of the common shares (i.e., the value of the combination).[4]

Empirical evidence supports the first assumption. Gagnon[5] investigated a sample of 500 mergers from New York Stock Exchange listing applications for the period 1955–1958. He found approximately 51% followed the proposed decision rule. Copeland-Wojdak[6] showed a much higher incidence of maximizing behavior in the period 1966–1967. They concluded:

> There has been a trend toward pooling since 1958 . . . and the results strongly support the hypothesis that firms record mergers by the method that maximizes reported income.

[3]Ronald M. Copeland and Joseph F. Wojdak, "Income Manipulation and the Purchase-Pooling Choice," *Journal of Accounting Research*, Autumn 1969, pp. 188–195.
[4]Ibid.
[5]Jean-Marie Gagnon, "Purchase v. Pooling-of-Interests: The Search for a Predictor," *Empirical Research in Accounting: Selected Studies*, 1969. Supplement to *Journal of Accounting Research*, pp. 187–204.
[6]Ronald M. Copeland and Joseph F. Wojdak, "Income Manipulation and the Purchase-Pooling Choice," *Journal of Accounting Research*, Autumn 1969, pp. 188–195.

A study by Anderson and Louderback[7] covered the period 1967–1974. They found about 86% of the surveyed firms followed the decision rule. Their findings seemingly lend support to an observation of Wyatt[8]:

> Accounting for a combination is commonly decided in advance of consummation of the transaction. That is, *the accounting treatment is one of the variables that must be firmed up before the final price (in terms of exchange ratios) is determined* [italics added].

The accounting methodology is an important element in the overall acquisition strategy. The characteristics of a purchase and a pooling of interests are discussed below.

Purchase

Accounting Principles Board (APB) Opinion No. 16 defines a purchase as a "business combination of two or more corporations in which an important part of the ownership interests in the acquired corporation or corporations is eliminated." The notion is one of discontinuity in voting participation, financial structure, and accountability. The characteristics of a purchase transaction follow from the definition:

1. The acquiring corporation views the transaction as an investment; that is, if the value of the consideration (cash and/or securities) exceeds the *appraised* value of the assets acquired, the excess may be recorded as goodwill. APB Opinion No. 16 requires that the portion of the excess recorded as goodwill be amortized against earnings over some reasonable period. The charge against earnings, on the other hand, while lowering accounting net income, does not qualify as a tax deduction. Other things being equal, taxable income exceeds accounting income.

2. The surviving firm records the acquired assets at their cost (i.e., current value), not the book value to the selling corporation. A new basis of accountability is established, possibly resulting in higher depreciation charges against income with consequent effects on earnings after taxes.

3. Considerations may take the form of debt securities, stock, and/or cash. Securities issued by the acquiring corporation are deemed to have been issued at current market values. Debt securities and cash are frequently used to reduce the participation of the acquired firm's shareholders in the management of the surviving corporation. As a corollary, if the surviving corporation had acquired its own voting stock (Treasury stock) in contemplation of the combination, the transaction must be recorded as a purchase.

4. The seller corporation's liabilities become the obligations of the surviving firm. However, the seller's retained earnings are not added to those of the

---

[7] John C. Anderson and Joseph G. Louderback III, "Income Manipulation and Purchase-Pooling: Some Additional Results," *Journal of Accounting Research*, Autumn 1975, pp. 338–343.
[8] Arthur R. Wyatt, "Discussion of Purchase v. Pooling-of-Interests: The Search for a Predictor," *Empirical Research in Accounting: Selected Studies*, 1967. Supplement to *Journal of Accounting Research*, pp. 187–204.

surviving firm. *Purchase accounting, in effect, capitalizes the retained earnings of the seller.* The basic notion is that one company cannot increase its retained earnings by buying another company.

As contrasted to pooling, purchasing suffers several disadvantages which can prove to be fatal impediments to a management seeking to demonstrate quickly the wisdom of the combination:

1. Given the presence of goodwill and/or a higher basis of accountability on depreciable assets, net income will be lower than if the transaction were consummated as a pooling.

2. There are negotiation problems. If the consideration includes cash, the seller may incur substantial taxable gains and demand a higher price to offset the tax bite. Or, the acquiring firm may wish the prurchase allocated to assets that may be amortized to reduce taxable income while the seller may seek to allocate the purchase price against assets that reduce his taxable gains. The objectives may be in juxtaposition.

3. The investor corporation requires earnings projections on the seller under a variety of purchase terms. This implies an understanding of the accounting methods adopted by the seller in calculating net income and an estimate of the current value of the seller's assets.

An important limitation of the purchase option should be mentioned at this point. *Under purchase, the acquiring corporation includes all of the seller's assets and liabilities in its consolidated statement, no matter when during the fiscal period the transaction was consummated. However, on the consolidated income statement, it picks up only the income of the seller applicable to the period between the transaction date and the end of the fiscal period.*

The choice between purchase or pooling depends upon the state of the economy, earning capacity of the combining firms, their financial structures, and the objectives of the ownership interests. In general, focusing only on the accounting numbers, purchase is the choice if the book value of the acquired assets exceeds their fair market value and the effective yield on the financing used is less than the return on assets for the acquired company. This situation tends to be more prevalent in a period of declining business activity. Conversely, in a period of expansion, market values tend to exceed book values and pooling may seem the attractive option.

Pooling

The APB Opinion No. 16 *describes pooling as a business combination in which the holders of substantially all the ownership interest in the constituent corporations become the owners of a single corporation that owns the assets and businesses of the constituent corporation. Continuity of voting participation and operation is the core of a pooling arrangement.* From this flow the specific features of the accounting treatment:

1. The acquisition is not viewed as an investment; rather, the two predecessor corporations combine into a single entity.

2. The original accounts (assets and liabilities) are carried over to the combined entity at book values. The transaction does not create a new basis of accountability or generate goodwill.

3. A pooling must be accomplished by an exchange of voting stock between previously independent companies. Bond and preferred stocks that alter the structure of ownership may not form part of the consideration. For the same reason, cash is ruled out along with Treasury stock acquired in comtemplation of the merger.

4. Since assets and liabilities carry over at book values, the retained earnings of the seller corporation carry over to the combination.

5. On the same premises, the minority interest is left untouched by the pooling of the majority interests.

The *stated* capital of the pooled companies may be greater or less than the total capital of the individual units. If it is greater, the excess is deducted first from the total of any other contributed capital and then from the consolidated retained earnings. If it is less, the difference is reported on the consolidated balance sheet as excess over par.

Distinct advantages can accrue to management through executing a pooling of interests:

1. The transaction may qualify as a tax-free exchange if it also meets Internal Revenue criteria.

2. The transaction does not drain liquid assets or increase the debt/equity ratio of the combination.

3. All things equal, pooling results in a higher net income due to the absence of goodwill and no change in the basis of accountability.

4. Regardless of market values, the postcombination entity bears responsibility only for the dollar amounts that existed prior to the combination. Hence, if synergism results, pooling can create "instant growth" in earnings. As a general rule, pooling is desirable if the assets of the acquired company at book are undervalued in relation to actual or potential earning power.

5. Retention of retained earnings may permit the combination to write off any deficit on the books of the acquiring firm.

6. In contrast to the purchase transaction, the combination may pick up not only the assets and liabilities of the constituents but their *full income* irrespective of the transaction date—even after the close of the fiscal year or before the auditors arrive.

Comparison of the following data highlights the advantages of pooling where the transaction could qualify as a purchase or pooling:

	Purchase	*Pooling*	*Advantage to Pooling*
Total assets	$1,010,000	$758,000	($252,000)
Net assets	932,000	680,000	(252,000)
Retained earnings	150,000	240,000	(90,000)
Expense items			
Goodwill	4,200	—	4,200
Depreciation	4,200	—	4,200
Earnings after taxes	108,600	117,000	8,400
EPS (excluding minority interest)	27.99	28.68	.69
Cash flow	124,200	120,000	4,200

Several facts warrant comment:

1. The higher asset base under the purchase results from the increase in value of fixed assets and goodwill. But the lower asset base under pooling has the potential for gains on disposal, and the larger retained earnings may allow for a higher dividend payout.

2. The difference in EPS is primarily attributable to the choice of accounting methodology (the lower earnings after taxes under purchase trace directly to the added depreciation charges and amortization of goodwill).

3. The purchase option provides better cash flow, owing to the tax shield of depreciation.

4. Whether or not the market price of the shares matches the predominant performance depends upon the P/E ratio. In this instance, the quality of the earnings—the risk posture of the combination after the merger—would principally determine whether the P/E ratio increases sufficiently to improve the wealth position of the shareholders.

The advantages to pooling are easily demonstrated in a situation where all variables are constant except for the choice of accounting method. The real world, on the other hand, shows few instances affording such simple laboratory comparisons. Instead, the relative advantage to pooling will depend upon the specific terms of the combination: the asset values, type and amounts of consideration, presence of goodwill, and so on. Earnings per share could be higher under purchase accounting depending upon the consideration mix and asset values. This simplifies the researchers' problem of assessing whether security markets ignore accounting numbers in pricing the common shares of a business combination. The accounting effects may be clouded by the presence of other variables.

In summary, pooling sees nothing of significance in the event: Assets are the same as prior to the combination and the management structure remains mostly untouched. Hence, the accounting record should leave the relationships undisturbed and the market value of the shares issued to effect the combination is of no consequence for the accounting entries. Conversely, a significant change in voting rights or the sale of substantial portion of the business suggests a purchase transaction.

Accounting Methodology and Security Prices

Combination by purchase or pooling of interests can result in significant differences in earnings per share. Do security prices reflect these differences? Will the market price of the common shares be higher if the combination is effected as a pooling rather than a purchase? Does the accounting treatment convey important information to the user of financial statements? To this point, we have assumed that managements believe in the importance of accounting numbers in shaping security prices. They are not alone. It is also widely believed by business writers that stockholders of companies using pooling make abnormal gains from higher stock prices as a direct consequence of reporting relatively higher earnings.

For example, Copeland and Wojdak[9] sampled 169 poolings and estimated that earnings were overstated by 3% to 98.15%. Lintner[10] agrees that companies which manipulate accounting numbers in mergers successfully mislead shareholders and raise the aggregate value of the combination even in a perfect securities market. Mosich[11] gives a theoretical estimate of a 60% increase in stock price of a typical merging company choosing pooling instead of purchase accounting.

On the significance of the accounting treatment for the user of financial statements, the FASB[12] surveyed analysts using financial statements in making investment and credit decisions. Most respondents expressed a greater need for appropriate disclosures about a combination rather than preference for a particular accounting method. With better disclosure, the analyst can adjust the statement amounts to reflect the economic and financial impact of the combination. Burton[13] surveyed 210 financial analysts and found them evenly split as to whether purchase or pooling presented data more meaningfully. Yet a survey of 64 financial analysts by Bullard[14] showed a marked preference for purchase accounting. In general, these and other surveys show no unanimity among users of financial statements regarding a preference for a particular accounting treatment, nor do they provide much information about why users of financial statements prefer a particular accounting treatment. Implicitly, however, the evidence points to a general conclusion; namely, analysts are alert to the effect on earnings of recording the combination as a purchase or pooling. It would seem they would allow for these effects in evaluating the combination.

Recent studies, looking at the informational content of alternative accounting methods and their effects on stock prices, seem to confirm the conclusion. These studies report that accounting manipulations not accompanied by real economic impacts (cash flows) have no statistically significant effects on stock prices. Apparently, the presence of alternative sources of information on corporate performance enables investors to look beyond the accounting numbers in assessing equity securities. Therefore, if the market is efficient, it will respond to the real economic consequences of the the combination. Kaplan and Roll, Sunder, and Ball all report that differences in accounting methodology have no statistically significant effect on security prices, and accounting data are unimportant relative to the aggregate supply of information.

---

[9]Ronald M. Copeland and Joseph F. Wojdak, "Valuation of Unrecorded Goodwill in Merger-Minded Firms," *Financial Analysts Journal*, September–October, 1969 pp. 57–62.

[10]J. Lintner, "Expectations, Mergers and Equilibrium in Purely Competitive Securities Markets," *American Economic Review*, 1971, pp. 101–111.

[11]A. N. Mosich, "Impact of Merger Accounting on Post-Merger Financial Reports," *Management Accounting*, December 1965.

[12]Financial Accounting Standards Board, *Accounting for Business Combinations and Purchased Intangibles*, August 19, 1976, pp. 36–40.

[13]John C. Burton, *Accounting for Business Combinations* (New York: Financial Executives Research Foundation, 1970).

[14]Ruth Harper Bullard, "The Effect of Accounting for Combinations on Investor Decisions,:' The University of Texas at Austin, August 1972.

But the evidence leaves much room for reasonable doubt, and so the argument will continue unabated. It will take more substantial evidence than is currently available to convince businessmen that accounting strategy has neutral effects on the market value of the combination.

Tax Options

Accounting advantages may not harmonize with preferred tax treatments. An acquisition strategy to optimize tax benefits for the acquiring corporation may result in a lower earnings per share. For example, a cash transaction treated as a *taxable exchange* and a *purchase* may generate higher tax shields and increased cash flow but carry a lower earnings per share, owing to added depreciation charges and the amortization of goodwill. To further complicate the issue, the criteria for a tax-free exchange and pooling differ. Hence, it is sometimes possible to treat the acquisition as taxable to obtain depreciation tax shields and for accounting purposes as a pooling to secure higher earnings per share.

Tax strategies conflict and the tax objectives of the buyer and seller may not coincide. Tax objectives depend upon a comparison of the purchase price for the property acquired and the seller's tax basis on the stock or other assets sold. Where purchase price is less than the tax cost, the seller will likely opt for a taxable transaction. Conversely, if the purchase price exceeds the tax cost, the seller more often seeks a tax-free transaction. The buyer, on the other hand, would aim at tax-free exchange in the first instance and a taxable exchange in the second case. Then, too, the tax position of the shareholders may differ from the tax position of their corporation so that what is good for one may not under all circumstances meet the interests of the other. The issue arises depending on whether the corporation is disposing of assets or its stockholders are selling their shares in a takeover situation.

Buyer and seller may also disagree over the allocation of the purchase price in a taxable transaction. The buyer strives to allocate the purchase price to depreciable property in order to capture the tax shields. The seller, on the other hand, seeks to allocate the purchase price to assets that qualify for capital gains or to those assets where the tax basis approximates or exceeds their purchase cost. The seller will also resist the allocations to inventories, since gains on inventory investment are taxable as ordinary income.

Finally, a tax-free exchange does not imply forgiveness, only deferral. The seller does not pay a tax at the time he or she exchanges his or her stock for shares in the acquiring corporation. Instead, the tax basis of the original shares becomes the basis of the new shares, and the seller pays a tax calculated on this basis when he *subsequently* disposes of the new shares. In short, no tax is payable at the time of the stock swap. Further, if the seller wills the shares to his or her estate, they are valued to the estate on the basis of their current worth at time of death and the entire capital gain is thus avoided. The latter arrangement at best gives the seller a vicarious satisfaction—wherever he or she may be.

IDENTIFYING TAKE-OVER OPPORTUNITIES

The articulation of an acquisition strategy (covering economic substance, accounting methodology, tax objectives, as well as the pertinent options under the security and antitrust regulations) sets the stage for the process of identifying a potential merger partner. No matter what the particular techniques employed (and each practitioner has his own angle) selection requires a forecast of future earnings and assessment of risk. There are two fundamental approaches: present value analysis and capital asset pricing. These are discussed below.

Present Value Analysis

When present value analysis is used, the earnings of the acquired firm are projected and discounted at the investor's cost of capital to obtain a theoretical market price on the shares of the investee corporation. This is compared to the actual market price to determine the net present value on the investment.

Assume that Alpha, Inc., is considering the acquisition of 100% of Delta's voting shares. Alpha's cost of capital is 10%. Delta has maintained a constant payout ratio with the current dividend at $1 per share. Earnings are expected to grow at 9% annually. Delta's shares currently sell at $52. The *theoretical price* of Delta's shares is as follows:

$$D_1 = D_0(1 + g) = \$1.00(1.09)$$

$$= \$1.09$$

$$P_0 = \frac{D_1}{K - g} = \frac{\$1.09}{0.10 - 0.09} = \$109$$

Since the theoretical price exceeds the market price (or cost of the investment) of $52, the NPV equals $57 per share. The situation, accordingly, warrants further investigation of Delta.

The NPV approach has several shortcomings. The analysis assumes that the acquired corporation will do as well after the combination as before (i.e., in the case of Delta, it will at least maintain the 9% growth rate). More important, if the acquired company is large relative to the size of the investor, the acquisition will likely change the risk–return characteristics of the surviving firm. This alters its cost of capital and upsets the calculation of NPV. Also, unless NPV is put on an expected value basis and the variance and covariances calculated, the method does not specifically assess the risk posture of the combination (i.e., the portfolio effects). Thus, the analysis at best provides only a point of departure for further investigation of a merger candidate.

EXHIBIT 17-1   Selecting a Merger Partner by CAPM

States of the Economy	P_S	R_m	R_j
Revival (S_1)	0.20	0.10	0.15
Prosperity (S_2)	0.50	0.15	0.20
Recession (S_3)	0.20	0.08	0.06
Depression (S_4)	0.10	0.06	0.03
	1.00		

Capital Asset Pricing

The NPV approach has the advantage of using concepts familiar in everyday financial practices. The Capital Asset Pricing Model (CAPM), however, enjoys theoretical superiority. Following the procedures of Chapter 10, CAPM employs the security market line or the market price of risk as the hurdle rate in identifying a potential merger partner. A required return is calculated, $E(R_j^0) = R_F + [E(R_m) - R_F](B_j)$ and compared to an expected return, $E(R_j)$, calculated independently. If the expected return exceeds the required return, $E(R_j) > E(R_j^0)$, the acquiring firm has a potential merger partner. In this case $E(R_j)$ lies above the security market line.

In Exhibit 17-1 we have assumed four possible states of the economy with related probabilities (P_S), and rates of return for the market index (R_m) and the potential merger partner (R_j). These rates of return depict the performance of the market index and the acquiring firm over the past business cycles (which are expected to hold for the future), or they may be projections of future performance allowing for deviations from past behavior. Either approach may be used. Note in Exhibit 17-1 that the required rate of return $E(R_j^0) = 16.3\%$ exceeds the expected return $E(R_j) = 14.5\%$, so j would not qualify as a desirable merger partner.

Assume a 6% risk-free rate (R_F).

Market Parameters

	P_S	R_m	$(P_S)(R_m)$	$R_m - E(R_m)$	$[R_m - E(R_m)]^2$	$[R_m - E(R_m)]^2 P_S$
S_1	0.20	0.10	0.020	-0.017	0.000289	0.0000578
S_2	0.50	0.15	0.075	$+0.033$	0.001089	0.0005445
S_3	0.20	0.08	0.016	-0.037	0.001369	0.0002738
S_4	0.10	0.06	0.006	-0.057	0.003249	0.0003249
		$E(R_m) =$	0.117		$\sigma_m^2 =$	0.001201

$$\text{Cov } R_j R_m$$

P_S	R_j	$(P_S)(R_j)$	$\dfrac{d_j}{R_j - E(R_j)}$	$\dfrac{d_m}{R_m - E(R_m)}$	$d_j d_m$	$d_j d_m P_S$
S_1 0.20	0.15	0.030	+0.005	−0.017	−0.000085	−0.000017
S_2 0.50	0.20	0.100	+0.055	+0.033	+0.001815	+0.0009075
S_3 0.20	0.06	0.012	−0.085	−0.037	+0.003145	+0.000629
S_4 0.10	0.03	0.003	−0.115	−0.027	+0.006555	+0.000655
	$E(R_j) =$	0.145			$Cov(R_j, R_m)$	= 0.002175

Then

$$B_j = \frac{\text{Cov}(R_j, R_m)}{\sigma_m^2} = \frac{0.002175}{0.001201} = 1.81$$

Therefore,

$$E(R_j^0) = R_F + [E(R_m) - R_F]B_j$$
$$= 0.06 + (0.117 - 0.06)1.81$$
$$= 0.163$$

Since the contribution of the acquired form to the combination's variance of equity rate does not affect the accept or reject decision based upon the market price of risk, diversification (the reduction of the variance) can be ignored. In the absence of synergy, $E(R_j^0) = E(R_j)$, each potential merger partner can be evaluated without reference to the firm's existing risk-return characteristics. CAPM simply assumes that the acquiring firm will always seek merger partners having estimated returns at least commensurate with their risk posture.

After identifying the merger target, the implementation of an acquisition strategy requires identification of a bargaining area: maximum and minimum exchange ratios acceptable to the shareholders of the acquiring and acquired firms. For this purpose, the model developed by Larson and Gonedes[15] offers a useful framework. This model assumes the following:

1. The objective of the combination is to enhance the market value of the common shares.

2. The shareholders will not approve of the combination unless it promises to maintain or increase their wealth position measured by the market value of their holdings.

3. The P/E ratio of the shares captures the risk–return characteristics of the merging firms. In other words, market price trades off risk and return.

4. The shares are publicly traded.

5. No synergism will eventuate in the first year of merger.

6. Bargaining is a condition of bilateral monopoly: one buyer of the shares and one seller.

[15]Kermit D. Larson and Nicholas J. Gonedes, "Business Combinations: An Exchange Ratio Determination Model," *The Accounting Review*, October 1969, pp. 720–728.

Within the bargaining area, the final exchange ratio may depend upon a balance of factors representing the strengths and weaknesses of the firms in light of the merger objectives. These include the following:

1. Liquidity. In the McConnell–Douglas merger, for example, Douglas had important contracts but had working-capital problems. McDonnell had the liquidity to rectify the deficiency, and this became an important element in effecting the combination. It is worth recalling that the primary cause of business failures in the 1970s among larger firms has been inadequate working capital.

2. Strategic assets. One firm may possess research facilities, patents, and other special assets that enhance its bargaining power.

3. Management capabilities. If one firm possesses a particularly strong management team, it may figure prominently in assessing the future prospects of the combination.

4. Tax-loss carryovers. In a tax-free exchange, tax losses carry over to the acquiring corporation, but the principal purpose of the acquisition cannot look to the tax benefits. Assuming a legitimate business objective, tax-loss carryovers are attractive where the acquiring firm has income against which deductions may be applied. In a taxable exchange, the loss remains with the selling firm and may be applied against the gain from the sale of assets.

5. Reproduction cost. In a period of sustained inflation, it may be more economical to acquire assets through combination than by new construction. The factor may motivate mergers where the acquisition of fixed assets determines the objectives of expansion.

6. Investment value. Where the merger involves combination with a newly organized firm and/or the promotion of a new process, the amount of cash actually paid into the newcomer (investment value) may influence the exchange rate.

7. Market value. Probably the most common determinant of the final exchange ratio is the relative market value of the combined firm shares. It is also the most logical element. If there exists an active market in the shares and if the market if efficient, the market will discount all that is known about the future prospects of the firms and reflect it in the market value of the shares.

8. Book values. Where conservative accounting practices have been followed, book values offer the advantage of convenience and speed in negotiation.

The reader may add other factors as earnings per share, dividend payout ratios, and so on. Suffice it to say, as the negotiations swing toward higher or lower exchange ratios, wealth is transferred from one group of shareholders to the other.

FINANCIAL STRUCTURE READJUSTMENT

A firm adds to present worth by direct investment in assets or by rearranging terms of financing. The latter may involve the following actions:

1. The substitution of one type of security for another (debt for equities or vice versa).

2. Refunding to lower interest charges on debt, to lengthen maturities, to escape onerous provisions in bond indentures, or take advantage of tax laws.

3. Repurchase, on the open market, the firm's debt or equity securities to effect savings in payouts or to effect accounting gains in the transactions.

Financial readjustment may also be part of a larger corporate strategy to assure management control or to prepare the way for expansion by acquisition. Readjustments, however, are uniquely amenable to analysis using a discounted-cash-flow approach. Refunding provides a ready illustration of DCF in evaluating readjustments of the financial structure.

Typically, refunding projects roll over debt to take advantage of declining interest rates. Moreover, for the refunding to be advantageous to the issuer, the difference between the current coupon rate and the refunding rate need not be large. The rule of thumb is 100 basis points (or a 1% rate spread) but it could be 50 or 75, depending upon the marginal tax rate of the issuer. For example, a corporation that refunds an issue by repurchasing it back at 107 does not consider 107 as its true cost. The seven points above par which the company pays is a tax-deductible interest expense. Actual after-tax cost, assuming a 48% bracket would be closer to 350 basis points.

One way to determine the break-even point on a refunding proposal is to divide the corporate by the call price. Using Indiana Bell's 9% bonds maturing in 2010, callable at 109.28, as an example, the breakeven rate (ignoring tax effects) becomes

$$\frac{\text{coupon rate}}{\text{call price}} = \frac{0.09}{1.0928} = 0.08236$$

There would be no advantage for the company in refunding unless the new interest rate were 8.236% or lower. Thus, it would require only a 0.00764 (76.4 basis points) drop in the market rate to bring the company to a break-even point on a possible refunding operation.

Refunding before maturity entails the exercise of the call privilege: an option to the issuer to redeem the outstanding bonds in whole or in part. The issue may be subject to call over its entire life (immediate call) or after lapse of a specified period. Usually, a long-term utility bond is callable after 5 years; industrial bonds generally feature 10 years of protection against call; intermediate corporate bonds may have call protection for only 3 years. In addition, some kinds are callable for any purpose; others, restricted by the indenture to enumerated purposes.

Since the call option favors the debtor at the expense of the creditor, the corporation pays for the privilege by:

1. Selling the bonds at a higher yield than would otherwise be required to dispose of the issue.

2. Granting a premium over the principal sum payable upon the exercise of the call.

3. A combination of 1 and 2. The call price is usually fixed slightly in excess of the face value, ranging from 102.5% to 110%. The exact premium depends on the life of the particular bond issue, the original offering price, and the bargaining power of the lender and the borrower.

Call prices are scaled: gradually reduced as the bonds approach maturity to enable the corporation to refund the bonds in advance of maturity without having to pay too large a premium. The schedule of call prices generally offers a certain number of basis points protection to the bondholder. For example, a 20-year, 6% bond issue offered at par might provide 15 basis points protection; that is, the call premiums are scaled so that each redemption price represents an approximate 5.85% yield to maturity. Usually, if called within the last year or 6 months before maturity, the bonds are redeemable only at par.

Refunding projects fall into two classes:

1. Pure refunding. The proceeds of the new issue cover the principal of the old issue and all expenses attending the refunding operation. No additional commitment of funds is required by the company.

2. Mixed refunding. The proceeds of the new issue do not fully cover the expenses of the project. This necessitates an additional investment by the company to float the project.

The distinction between pure and mixed refunding is important to the selection of an appropriate risk-adjusted discount rate for the project.

The discounted-cash-flow analysis of bond refunding necessitates the selection of an appropriate discount rate to determine the net present value of the transaction. The cash flows are discounted at the after-tax cost of the new debt. The reason lies in the apparent certainty or lack of variance in the cash flows. All cash flows are either fixed by provisions in the indenture or negotiation with the underwriters. Once established, the cash flows do not vary over the life of the project. From this viewpoint, refunding bears less risk than conventional capital projects and one might argue the after-tax cost of debt best describes the risk character of the cash flows.

Not all authorities would agree. To some, the risk of refunding centers on the timing of the operation. If interest rates were to decline further, the opportunity for greater gain is missed; if the project is postponed and rates rise, the present gain is lost.

Others might point to the mixed nature of the project. The firm must invest additional funds in order to refund the bond issue. Unless raised externally, the commitment of these funds dislocates the asset structure (i.e., diverts funds from other uses). Presumably, if invested in alternative projects, the funds would earn the average cost of capital or at least a return higher than the after-tax cost of debt. It might be argued, therefore, that the opportunity cost associated with this incremental investment in the refunding project constitutes the appropriate discount rate.

The cash/flow advantage to refunding measured by NPV or by the IRR may be quite substantial, as in Example 1. By contrast, the first-year accounting effects of refunding projects may result in a drop in EPS.

● **EXAMPLE 1**   *Bond Refunding*

Corporation has outstanding $20 million in debenture bonds at an 8% coupon rate. The issue has 20 years remaining to maturity. There is an unamortized discount on the issue of $500,000 and unamortized legal expenses incurred directly by the company of $200,000. The bond is presently callable at 105.

Interest rates have declined to 6% and the corporation can sell a new issue, having a 20-year maturity, with net proceeds of $19.6 million. Additional legal expenses will have to be paid in the sum of $250,000.

A 30-day overlap period will be required to cover the call on the old bonds and the issuance of the new securities. The need for an overlap lies in the possibility of last-minute delays in the registration of the new issue and final closing with the underwriting group. Corporation's effective tax rate is 50%. Determine the following:

(a) The cash outflow required for the refunding.

(b) The annual cash savings on the new issue.

(c) The net present value of the exchange and the internal rate of return.

Solution: First, consider the investment cash flow.

Call of old bonds at 105		$21,000,000
Net proceeds on sale of new bonds		19,600,000
Cash-flow deficit on exchange		$ 1,400,000
Add:		
Legal expense on new issue	$250,000	
Interest overlap—old bonds	133,333	383,333
Gross investment outlay		$ 1,783,333
Less:		
Tax savings:		
Interest overlap	$ 133,333	
Call premium	1,000,000	
Unamortized discount on		
old bonds	500,000	
Unamortized legal expenses		
on old bonds	200,000	
Total tax deductions	$1,833,333	
Tax savings (0.50)		916,666
Investment cash flow		$ 866,667

Next, consider the annual cash savings from the refunding:

Old bonds		
Interest		$1,600,000
Less		
Tax savings:		
Interest	$1,600,000	
Amortization of discount	25,000	
Amortization of legal		
expenses	10,000	
Total	$1,635,000	
Tax savings (0.50)		817,500
Net outflow		$ 782,500

New Bonds

Interest		$1,200,000
Less:		
Tax savings:		
Interest	$1,200,000	
Amortization of discount	20,000	
Amortization of legal		
expenses	12,500	
Total	$1,232,500	
Tax savings (0.50)		616,250
Net outflow on new issue		$ 583,750
Annual savings on refund		$ 198,750

An investment of $866,667 will reduce cash outflows by $198,750 for 20 years. Last, calculate the NPV and IRR:

Present value of annual savings at 3%, 20 years	$2,975,386
Less:	
Investment cash flow	866,667
Net present value	$2,108,719
Internal rate of return	22% ●

In Example 1 a positive NPV recommends acceptance of the refunding project: the present value of the interest savings over the life of the outstanding bond exceeds the cost of calling the old bond and floating the new bond.

Since the timing of the proposal is the critical factor in refunding, a single-period NPV criterion can mislead the decision maker. NPV, as calculated in Example 1, represents static analysis. It does not allow for intertemporal relationships, that is, the effect of a present decision on future decisions. In each period, management faces the option to continue the bonds outstanding or to refund; today's choice influences the next period's decision, and so on over the time horizon in debt management. Simply put, static NPV analysis ignores the option to refund repetitively and so does not link obviously related decisions into an overall program of debt management. Yet some corporations have refunded several times in periods of declining rates.

From the perspective of long-term debt management, the appropriate questions are: Given a bond issue floated in period *t*, when should it be refunded? How long should it be left outstanding? The optimum decision is the one that minimizes the cost of debt (interest, call premium, and floatation expenses) over the entire time horizon rather than in any single period. The opportunity to refund *repetitively* over time is an example of recursive optimization dealt with by dynamic programming.

The advantage of dynamic programming lies in the necessity to look beyond the desirability of the immediate benefit and take a longer perspective. The method allows the firm to decide on the optimum pattern of refunding over a finite time horizon, the maturity of any bond issued on refunding, and the cost of specific policies regarding interest and call premiums. The time horizon, of course, can be extended to any length or to an infinite horizon. Probability distributions and risk analysis may also be inserted into the calculations. The complete array of variables can be programmed for computerized models, which can be rerun under different assumed conditions for interest, call premiums, maturities, and so forth.

There remains an important caveat. Dynamic programming depends upon forecasting interest rates within reasonably close tolerances. Actually, interest-rate fluctuations should be smaller than the variances associated with the firm's operating income, yet where long time frames are involved, even small variations in interest rates may cause significant alterations in *NPV*. The efficacy of dynamic programming hinges on the sensitivity of sequence to changes in interest rates. Given precision forecasts of interest rates, dynamic programming is conceptually superior to single-period analysis. Otherwise, the problem persists.

SUMMARY

The process of corporate acquisition and change in financial structure represent capital budgeting types of problems, as they involve alternative uses for discretionary funds. The processes involved in decision making in these areas were described in this chapter. Specifically, we examined five areas relating to corporate acquisition: articulation of an acquisition strategy, identification of a merger partner, establishing a bargaining area, closing the terms of exchange, and financing the combination. Examples were provided to demonstrate the potential for synergism in combinations. The chapter concluded with a discussion of bond refinancing as a means of financial reorganization.

PROBLEMS

1. Briefly discuss the elements of the acquisition decision.
2. What are the shortcomings of a present value analysis in the acquisition decision?
3. Discuss how CAPM would be used in the acquisition decision and when it would point to an attractive merger.
4. Describe the advantages of using dynamic programming in the reorganization of the firm's financial structure.
5. A corporation has outstanding $5 million in debenture bonds at a 12% coupon rate. The issue has 10 years remaining to maturity. There is an unamortized discount on the issue of $100,000 and unamortized legal expenses incurred directly by the company of $50,000. The bond is presently callable at 106.

   Interest rates have now declined to 8% and the company can sell a new $5 million issue, 10-year maturity, with net proceeds of $4.9 million. Legal expenses will be $100,000.

The effective tax rate is 50%. A 30-day overlap period will be required to call the old issue and issue the new.

Determine the following:

(a) The cash outflow required for refunding.
(b) The annual cash savings of the new issue.
(c) The net present value of the exchange and internal rate of return.

18 PROJECT REVIEW AND CONTROL: FORECASTING AND ABANDONMENT

We have stressed the quantitative formulation of the capital budget and supporting theoretical concepts. However, the budgeting process is not an abstraction from reality; it takes place in an organization with all its attendant problems of human relations, ambitions, and political maneuvering. Some individuals may have pet projects—attachments resulting perhaps from many hard hours of detailed analysis. Others may oppose a proposal out of fear that it will shift the corporate power structure to their discomfort or holds the prospect of unemployment. The cynical quickly learn that any project can be made to look good or bad by comparing it against a sufficiently poor or strong alternative. It is for top management to monitor the process to assure that all possible alternatives have been arrayed so that a reasonably sound budget may be constructed. This chapter, closes our efforts by touching a few of the caution points in the management of the capital budget. These include the following important truths:

1. Capital budgeting necessitates forecasting.

2. Not all capital projects succeed.

3. The process of evaluating proposed capital projects must be cost-justified.

CAPITAL BUDGETING NECESSITATES FORECASTING

Capital budgeting speaks of *future revenues* and *expenses*, yet textbooks usually ignore the process of how these estimates are derived. Capital budgets are forecasts of varying duration and of greater or lesser uncertainty. But all forecasting rests upon assumptions.

In theory, an assumption is an explicit statement about the expected performance of the economy, industry, or the firm; the likelihood of disruptive events (strikes, new technology, or other unusual occurrences); and the consistency of or changes in accounting policy. Typically omitted from the assumptions stated in Exhibit 18-1 are those implicit in the choice of a forecast methodology. All forecasting techniques specify a distinctive link between

EXHIBIT 18-1 Quality of Published Assumptions: Recent U.S. Examples

1. Sales are based on the average monthly sales for the 17-month period ended September 30, 19--, and have been adjusted to reflect anticipated increases in demand as expected by the company.

2. Cost of sales . . . reflect unit cost changes in relation to increased sales volume and other factors anticipated by the company.

3. Operating expenses . . . assume no changes for inflation or otherwise during the life of the project. General operating expenses for . . . and . . . are based on assumptions of partial occupancy.

4. Cross revenues . . . are based on past trends and current charges adjusted for managerial policies contemplated for the proposed expanded facilities and anticipated price-level changes in the future.

5. Historically the . . . rates have been increased to absorb the rising costs of health-care services and accordingly have maintained a satisfactory margin of income over expenses. It is the opinion of . . . management that this trend will continue.

6. The mix of furniture to be rented has been assumed and a weighted average computed. This resulting theoretical set costs $509.40 and rents for $41.20 per month.

7. Although salaries and other costs will increase in the future, advertising costs should decrease at the assumed level of activity per store. For this reason, total expenses are assumed to remain constant.

8. Our outlook for continued rapid growth . . . is based on expansion of the boat and motorcycle trailer market, increasing market penetration, expanded geographical distribution, the introduction of new products, and, of course, the past record of the company.

9. We expect . . . to have another good year in 19--, but operating projections are less reliable than in some other . . . operations. . . . This projection is based on the expectation that a new labor agreement will be successfully negotiated . . . and that appropriate rate increases will be granted.

Source: Published annual reports of various U.S. corporations.

future revenues and various determining factors. These are *technical* assumptions that relate to the statistical model used in projecting the future.

Few companies employ a purely quantitative model to forecast revenues and expenses, but a growing number of companies make some use of quantitative projection methods. The choice of methodology is decidedly a matter of judgment and involves assumptions concerning the relevant variables and their interrelationships. Different statistical techniques, applied to the same data base, can yield different forecasts. The same technique may yield divergent results for different time spans or if other explanatory variables are included (Exhibit 18-2). Naturally, management will modify its forecasting procedures to obtain estimates with a reliability appropriate to the circumstances of the business.

Statistical models are not perfect predictors and the variance from actual sales will in part be attributable to the particular assumptions of the model. Too often these assumptions lack explicit statement; more often, they would not be understood by top management even if stated in elementary terms. The truth we seek here is that the technical assumptions combined with the effects

EXHIBIT 18-2   Some Assumptions Underlying
Forecasting Models

1. The conditions in the past which generated the observed data will persist into the future. In the concept of stationarity, the future becomes an extension of the past, and historical simulation is the standard method for validation of the model. Yet many of the changes affecting business activity spring from discontinuities and by definition are either unpredicted or unpredictable.

2. As a corollary, models generally respond to novel circumstances slowly. Rates of change are often too rapid for models to accommodate—the reaction time of the model is too slow. However, even in a stable situation, the time required to collect data, process data, and provide output to the decision maker may conflict with the time schedule of budget formulation.

3. A further corollary, if the data base is flawed—if it contains inadequate, inaccurate, or irrelevant historical information—the past may be as obscure as the future. The model cannot rise above the quality of the input data.

4. In the case of noncausal models, the variable is a function of time.

5. The evolution of the variables is completely systematic and hence predictable.

6. Except where qualified by the introduction of weights, all previous observations yield the same amount of information about the likely value of the next observation.

7. Causal models assume that the average relationship calculated between dependent and independent variable(s) will hold for the future. The task of defining these relationships is a formidable one during period of accelerated change. Models of simple static systems are easy to construct, but their naivete will likely trap the user. On the other hand, models of complex and dynamic systems require painstaking efforts and *may* improve the precision of the projections—albeit with a higher price tag for the information.

8. Unless sales and cost data are considered to be random and normally distributed, the models do not provide a statistical basis for establishing the probability of error or confidence interval estimates. In the absence of the normality presumption above, practice resorts to establishing ranges based upon past deviations between actual and projected results such that one can be reasonably certain the next period's projection will fall within the established limits. Statistically speaking, however, the assumption that future deviations will fall within the defined range is at best tenuous.

---

of leverage can convert a small variance in gross revenues into an acceptable variance in net operating revenues of the project.

Planning assumptions relate to market and production strategies as well as erratic events (e.g., outcome of litigation) and, perhaps, the intuitive adjustments of top officers. In this respect, production strategies merit special comment. The bridge that leads from project revenues to net operating revenues in a given period is distinct from the external link of revenues (or savings) to the market. Revenue projections only initiate the analysis of the project, for management has considerable latitude in responding to the market environment. It may, for example, alter the product mix, adjust production schedules, modify inventory policies, regulate discretionary expenditures, and so on. Consequently, any single projected (or most probable) revenue level can translate into a broad range of net operating cash flows.

Prime cost projections assume reliable estimates of factor prices and efficiencies in production; variable overheads may be allocated to product lines by statistical formulas and management judgment; discretionary fixed costs may actually be revised throughout the budget period; programmed fixed costs (such as supervisory salaries or financial charges) share the uncertainties of interest-rate changes and similar variations in specific price levels. Other illustrations could be introduced, but the list is sufficient to emphasize the uncertainties of projecting project earnings and stresses the variety of assumptions, environmental and internal, buttressing net cash flow estimates.

There exists a group of standard assumptions, akin to the "going concern" principle in financial accounting, which are vital to appraisal of the forecast, yet merit explicit mention only by exception. Unless alerted to the contrary, the reader of a financial forecast (or capital budget) properly assumes that the firm's accounting statements are prepared in a manner consistent with the applicable accounting principles adopted by the firm in the annual report.[1] Similarly, the composition of top corporate management, the continuing availability of normal sources of supply, reasonable stability of the tax environment, and so on, are implied unless the user is informed to the contrary.

Each forecasting and budgeting system is unique to the objective of the company. Successful forecasting commences with close collaboration among executives, other internal users of forecasted data, and systems consultants. Collaboration begins with three basic questions:

1. What is the purpose of the forecast? How is it to be used? The desired accuracy and power of the techniques chosen will largely hinge on the answers.

2. What are the staff requirements to implement the forecasting system? For example, personnel capacities vary according to the detail and accuracy required. For primarily quantitative approaches, forecasters should be competent in research techniques, in application of mathematical–statistical models, and in computer usage. On the other hand, judgmental methods call upon personnel in marketing who have long association with the industry. Best results require a blending of both types.

3. What, if any, additional facilities or services are needed to inaugurate the forecasting–budgeting space and equipment, access to computer capability, library resources, and subscriptions to external data sources?

Because information, personnel, and facilities have price tags attached, the forecast–budget system must relate to the realistic needs of the business and balance the tangible values of better information against the costs of acquiring the data. In some situations, simple techniques and few organizational shifts may well accomplish the purpose.

Viewed as an integrated system, the forecast of project cash benefits and costs represents the first step in the preparation of a comprehensive capital budget. The budget will be no better than the soundness of the forecasting techniques employed. Business forecasting, short- or long-term, is a field unto itself. However, the astute financial manager will always inquire how the budget estimates were prepared.

---

[1] Although capital budgeting is on a cash-flow basis, as we have noted, management must consider the impact of the capital budget on the firm's conventional accounting statements (see Chapters 7 and 13). A capital budget that may pass muster on an NPV or IRR basis may have severe adverse effects in the short term on the accounting statements, and this management may not choose to accept.

NOT ALL CAPITAL PROJECTS SUCCEED

The one certainty about a forecast, short- or long-term, is that it will to some degree fall wide of the mark. The project will look better or worse than anticipated. This error factor in forecasting therefore creates uncertainty and raises the question of risk. Chapter 8 spoke to the problem of measuring risk. However, the uncertainty surrounding the budget forecast also demands that management monitor the projects accepted to see if they are "on track" and where necessary face the question of abandoning the project before its expected termination date. Let's look at the abandonment alternative, for it always constitutes one of the alternatives open to management in constructing the annual capital budget. Up to now, our discussion placed the emphasis of capital budgeting on the evaluation of new potential investment opportunities.

Managing the capital budget of a corporation must be a dynamic process. Capital investments cannot be viewed as a commitment to the end. Since changes in the attractiveness of projects or even entire divisions or subsidiaries can occur from the time when they were initially considered, regular periodic reappraisals of investments must be undertaken to determine whether the value of continuing the endeavor exceeds abandoning it. Since managing the capital budget is usually a rationing problem, a company cannot afford to tie up funds in investments that are below acceptable standards. Managing the capital budget must be viewed as a continuing process of optimally allocating available funds. Thus, this process must include the reevaluation of projects already undertaken.

When investment opportunities are initially considered, key variables are identified and assumptions are made to arrive at some choice. As time passes, changes can occur that could affect these key variables. Assumptions made initially may prove incorrect, or perhaps some additional unforeseen new investment opportunities may arise. *Failure to abandon projects that are no longer desirable could be very costly. By the same reasoning, failure to abandon projects that could make funds available for substantially better investment opportunities might also be costly from an opportunity standpoint.* Therefore, the prudent financial manager must incorporate abandonment values (at various points throughout the life of the project) into the analysis for capital project evaluation and selection.

As a first approach to the abandonment problem, assume that the firm has the option to abandon the project at various points throughout its useful life. The methodology basically finds the maximum NPV of the project cash flows and the abandonment value considering all possible periods when the project can be abandoned.

In equation form, we want to determine the time period m that maximizes NPV^m:

$$NPV^m = \sum_{t=0}^{m} \frac{A_t}{(1 + k)^t} + \frac{AV_m}{(1 + k)^m} \tag{1}$$

where A_t = operating cash flow of the project in period t
k = firm's cost of capital
AV_m = abandonment value in period m
m = period when abandonment is being considered

NPV^m = net present value of the cash flows from operating the project for m periods as well as the abandonment value of the project at the end of the mth period

The use of Equation (1) is illustrated in Example 1.

● **EXAMPLE 1** *Abandonment Decision*

Consider that project Z has the following cash flows and abandonment values over its useful life:

Period	0	1	2	3	4	5
Cash Flows	−$7,500	$2,000	$2,000	$2,000	$2,000	$2,000
Abandonment Values	—	$6,200	$5,200	$4,000	$2,200	0

The firm's cost of capital is 10%. Determine the optimal time for project Z to be abandoned if it is accepted.

Solution: The analysis proceeds by preparing the following table:

Period	10% Discount Factor	Abandonment After Period: 1	2	3	4	5
1	0.909	$1,818	$1,818	$1,818	$1,818	$1,818
2	0.826		1,652	1,652	1,652	1,652
3	0.751			1,502	1,502	1,502
4	0.683				1,366	1,366
5	0.621					1,242
P.V. of operating cash flows		$1,818	$3,470	$4,972	$6,338	$7,580
P.V. of abandonment value		5,636	4,295	3,004	1,503	0
P.V. of total flows		$7,454	$7,765	$7,976	$7,841	$7,580
Investment outflow		7,500	7,500	7,500	7,500	7,500
NPV^m		($46)	$ 265	$ 476	$ 341	$ 80

As can be seen, the NPV is maximized by abandoning project Z at the end of period 3. It should also be noted that the abandonment option makes project Z considerably more attractive than if the firm had to hold the project until the end of its five-period useful life; that is, the NPV of the optimal holding period ($476 for three periods) is almost six times the NPV of the project if it is held to the end of its useful life ($80). ●

The most widely cited work in the abandonment area under conditions of changing risk posture is that due to Robichek and Van Horne,[2] wherein they

---

[2] A. A. Robichek and J. C. Van Horne, "Abandonment Value and Capital Budgeting," *Journal of Finance*, 22, No. 4, December 1967, pp. 577–590.

recommend the use of decision trees and simulation to handle abandonment values. To illustrate the use of decision trees, consider Figure 18-1, which shows the cash flows for project *A* over its 3-year useful life.[3] Notice that Figure 18-1 has the same design as the tree diagrams for single projects, which were discussed in Chapter 14. However, the presence of the abandonment option (which is shown at the bottom of the figure) necessitates that a decision-tree approach be taken to evaluate whether the project should be abandoned or not at each point in time where this option exists. Figure 18-2 shows a small part of the decision tree that would be necessary to evaluate abandoning project *A*. If the cash flow in period 1 was $1,000, in order to decide whether the project should be abandoned at the end of period 1, the entire tree in the exhibit must be folded back. We know that the value of the project if abandoned at the end of period 1 is $3,000, but we must compute the value of the decision alternative "don't abandon." This necessitates evaluation of all subsequent states of nature and decision alternatives which emanate from this branch, in order to compare the expected values of these two alternatives. The procedure then is to select the alternative at each decision node which maximizes the expected present value of future benefits. For the "abandon" alternative, the expected present value is merely the expected value of the abandonment value probability distribution; whereas for the "don't abandon" alternative, we would have to compute the present value of all future cash flows whether they be from keeping the project or abandoning it at later. This process is illustrated in Example 2.

● **EXAMPLE 2**   *Abandonment Values at End of Period 2*

For each of the cash-flow sequences shown in Figure 18-1, determine whether it would be better to abandon or retain at the end of year 2. Assume that all cash flows have already been discounted for time.

Solution: For each of the branches shown in the following decision tree, the value of not abandoning is found by summing the product of the year 3 cash flows multiplied by their respective probability of occurrence. The decision is made by comparing this value to the abandonment value of $1,900.

Period 1 Flow	Period 2 Flow	Value of Not Abandoning at End of Period 2	Decision
$1,000	$ 0	−$ 500	Abandon
1,000	500	0	Abandon
1,000	1,000	1,000	Abandon
2,000	1,000	1,000	Abandon
2,000	2,000	2,000	Don't abandon
2,000	3,000	3,000	Don't abandon
3,000	2,000	2,000	Don't abandon
3,000	3,000	3,000	Don't abandon
3,000	3,500	3,500	Don't abandon

[3]This example originally appeared in Robichek and Van Horne, ibid., pp. 579–582.

FIGURE 18-1 Expected Future Cash Flows for Project A

Period 1 Cash Flow	Period 1 Probability	Period 2 Cash Flow	Period 2 Conditional Probability	Period 3 Cash Flow	Period 3 Conditional Probability	Cash-Flow Sequence Number	Probability of Sequence (in 64ths)
$1,000	0.25	0	0.25	—$1,000	0.25	1	1/64
				— 500	0.50	2	2/64
				0	0.25	3	1/64
		$ 500	0.50	500	0.25	4	2/64
				— 0	0.50	5	4/64
				500	0.25	6	2/64
		1,000	0.25	0	0.25	7	1/64
				1,000	0.50	8	2/64
				2,000	0.25	9	1/64
2,000	0.50	1,000	0.25	0	0.25	10	2/64
				1,000	0.50	11	4/64
				2,000	0.25	12	2/64
		2,000	0.50	1,000	0.25	13	4/64
				2,000	0.50	14	8/64
				3,000	0.25	15	4/64
		3,000	0.25	2,000	0.25	16	2/64
				3,000	0.50	17	4/64
				4,000	0.25	18	2/64
3,000	0.25	2,000	0.25	1,000	0.25	19	1/64
				2,000	0.50	20	2/64
				3,000	0.25	21	1/64
		3,000	0.50	2,000	0.25	22	2/64
				3,000	0.50	23	4/64
				4,000	0.25	24	2/64
		3,500	0.25	3,000	0.25	25	1/64
				3,500	0.50	26	2/64
				4,000	0.25	27	1/64

Abandonment value at end of period:
$3,000 $1,900   0

FIGURE 18-2 Partial Decision Tree for Project A

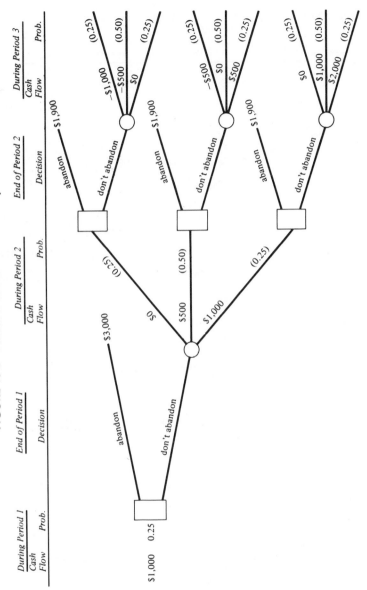

Thus, the partially folded back decision tree would appear as follows:

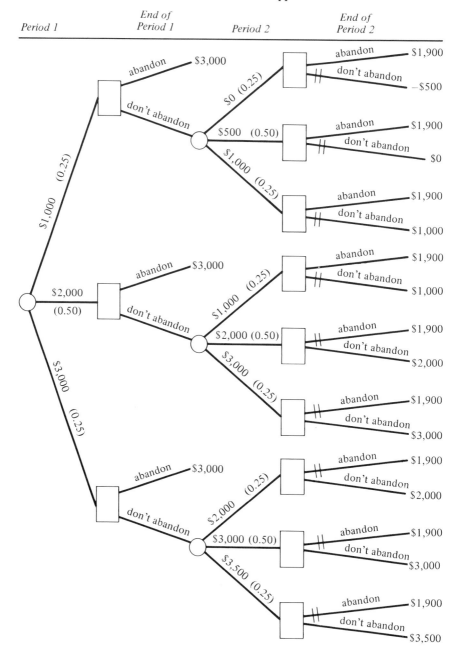

Note on page 390 that the branch of the less desirable alternative at the end of period 2 has been marked with a pair of parallel lines.   ●

Example 2 is continued below in Example 3, where we evaluate abandonment at the end of period 1. To evaluate the alternative of abandoning or not at the end of period 1, we would fold back the tree to the end of period 1. The value of not abandoning is determined by adding the value of the optimal decision at the end of period 2 (found in Example 2) to the cash flows in period 2 and then multiplying by the respective probability of occurrence and summing over all events. This is shown in Example 3.

● **EXAMPLE 3** *Abandonment Decisions at the End of Period 1*
For each of the possible cash flows of project *A* which can occur in period 1, compute the expected value of not abandoning and determine the optimal decision (abandon or not) at that point in time.

Solution: For each of the three possible cash flows in period 1, the value of not abandoning project *A* is found by multiplying column 4 by column 5 in the following table:

(1)	(2)	(3)	(4)	(5)	(6)
		Value of			*Value of Not Abandoning at the*
Period 1 Cash Flow	*Period 2 Cash Flow*	*Optimal Decision at End of Period 2*	*Sum of (2) and (3)*	*Probability of Event*	*End of Period 1*
	$ 0	$1,900	$1,900	0.25	$ 475
$1,000	500	1,900	2,400	0.50	1,200
	1,000	1,900	2,900	0.25	725
					$2,400
	$1,000	$1,900	$2,900	0.25	$ 725
2,000	2,000	2,000	4,000	0.50	2,000
	3,000	3,000	6,000	0.25	1,500
					$4,225
	$2,000	$2,000	$4,000	0.25	$1,000
3,000	3,000	3,000	6,000	0.50	3,000
	3,500	3,500	7,000	0.25	1,750
					$5,750

The decision tree folded back to the end of period 2 appears as follows:

Thus, the optimal decision at the end of period 1 would be to abandon project A if the cash flow in period 1 was $1,000; however, if the cash flow in period 1 was either $2,000 or $3,000, the optimal decision would be to continue to hold project A (i.e., to not abandon).

Summarizing the results of Examples 2 and 3 by referring back to the two decision trees drawn, we see that (1) if the period 1 cash flow was $1,000, project A should be abandoned at the end of period 1; (2) if the period 1 cash flow was $2,000, the project should be held for the second period and abandoned at the end of the second period *only* if the period 2 cash flow was $1,000 (if the period 2 cash flow is either $2,000 or $3,000, the project should be held for period 3); (3) if the period 1 cash flow is $3,000, the project should be held for its entire useful life. Following these decision rules, the firm will optimally hold or abandon project A over its life. ●

The examples demonstrated that the abandonment option increases the expected NPV of the project compared with the same project without the alternative of abandoning at various points throughout its useful life. In addition, the abandonment option also has a desirable impact on both the absolute and relative risk of the project, as well as the skewness in the distribution of the NPV values over the project's useful life. These characteristics are demonstrated in Example 4.

● **EXAMPLE 4** *Impact of Abandonment on Project Risk*

Consider project B, which has a 2-year useful life, an original cost of $400,000, and possible cash inflows (in thousands of dollars) as follows:

Period 1		Period 2		
Cash Flow	*Probability*	*Cash Flow*	*Conditional Probability*	*Cash-Flow Sequence*
$300	0.3	$250	0.30	1
		300	0.50	2
		350	0.20	3
$400	0.4	$300	0.30	4
		400	0.50	5
		500	0.20	6
$500	0.3	$400	0.30	7
		500	0.40	8
		600	0.30	9

The firm's cost of capital is 12% and the undiscounted cash flows tabulated above would lead to an expected NPV of $271,000 as follows:

Cash-Flow Sequence	*Total Present Value of Cash Flow (thousands)*	*Sequence Probability*	*Expected Value (thousands)*
1	$467	0.09	$ 42
2	507	0.15	76
3	547	0.06	33
4	596	0.12	72
5	676	0.20	135
6	756	0.08	60
7	765	0.09	69
8	845	0.12	101
9	925	0.09	$ 83
		1.00	$671

Expected present value = $671,000

Initial investment = 400,000

Expected net present value = $271,000

In addition, the calculation of the variance, semivariance, measure of skewness, and coefficient of variation for project *B* shown below uses the techniques developed in Chapters 8 and 14.

Cash-Flow Sequence	NPV of Sequence	Expected NPV	$\left(\dfrac{Sequence}{Deviation}\right)^2$	$\times$	Sequence Probability	$=$ Result
1	$ 67	$271	41,616		0.09	3,745
2	107	271	26,896		0.15	4,034
3	147	271	15,376		0.06	923
4	196	271	5,625		0.12	675
5	276	271	25		0.20	5
6	356	271	7,225		0.08	578
7	365	271	8,836		0.09	795
8	445	271	30,276		0.12	3,633
9	525	271	64,516		0.09	5,806
					1.00	20,194

$$\text{Variance} = V_B = 20,194$$
$$\text{Standard deviation} = \sigma_B = \sqrt{20,194} = \$142$$
$$\text{Semivariance} = SV_B = 9,377$$
$$\text{Measure of skewness} = V_B/2SV_B$$
$$= 1.077$$
$$\text{Coefficient of variation} = \sigma_B/E(X_B),$$
$$= 0.524$$

Now, consider that the firm has the option to abandon project B at the end of year 1 for $280,000. Compute the expected NPV, the standard deviation, variance, semivariance, measure of skewness, and coefficient of variation given the abandonment option and show that these measures dominate their counterparts given that the abandonment option did not exist.

Solution: Given the possible cash inflows in periods 1 and 2 and their associated probabilities as shown in the first table above, the expected present values of the second period's cash inflows are computed in the following table:

Cash-Flow Sequence	Cash Flow	Present[a] Value	Conditional Probability	Expected Present Value
1	$250	$199	0.3	$ 60
2	300	239	0.5	120
3	350	279	0.2	56
			Branch total	$236
4	$300	$239	0.3	$ 72
5	400	319	0.5	160
6	500	399	0.2	80
			Branch total	$312
7	$400	$319	0.3	$ 96
8	500	399	0.4	160
9	600	478	0.3	143
			Branch total	$399

Present value of salvage $(0.8929)(\$280) = \$250$

[a]PV factor = 0.7972.

If a cash inflow of $300 occurs in period 1, project B is expected to be abandoned for

$280 at the end of period 1. Cash-flow sequences 1 to 3 are reduced to one sequence with a present value of $518 (i.e., ($300 + $280)(0.8929)). In all other cases, the project is held for year 2 rather than abandoned. The following table computes the expected NPV with the abandonment option:

Cash-Flow Sequence	Total Present Value of Cash Flow	Sequence Probability	Expected Value
1–3	$518	0.3	$155
4	596	0.12	72
5	676	0.20	135
6	756	0.08	60
7	765	0.09	69
8	845	0.12	101
9	925	0.09	83
		1.00	$675

Expected present value = $675
Initial investment = 400
Expected net present value = $275

Given these calculations, we now compute the measures of risk and skewness for the abandonment option.

Cash-Flow Sequence	NPV of Sequence	Expected NPV	Sequence (Deviation)^2	×	Sequence Probability	=	Result
1–3	$118	$275	24,649		0.3		7,395
4	$196	$275	6,241		0.12		749
5	276	275	1		0.20		0
6	356	275	6,561		0.08		525
7	$365	$275	8,100		0.09		729
8	445	275	28,900		0.12		3,468
9	525	275	62,500		0.09		5,625
					1.00		18,491

Variance $= V_B$ $= 18,491$
Standard deviation $= \sigma_B = \sqrt{18,491} = \$136$
Semivariance $= SV_B = 8,144$
Measure of skewness $= V_B/2SV_B$
$= 1.135$
Coefficient of variation $= \sigma_B/E(X_B)$
$= 0.495$

Finally, the following table compares project B with and without the abandonment option, as well as the percent changes in each of the computed statistics.

Net Present Value	Without Abandonment	With Abandonment	Percent Change
Expected value	$ 271	$ 275	+1.5
Standard deviation	$ 142	$ 136	−4.2
Skewness—$V/2SV$	1.077	1.135	+5.4
Coefficient of variation	0.524	0.495	−5.5

As shown, all the measures of risk and skewness moved in a favorable direction as the abandonment option was included. Notice that the standard deviation has decreased by 4.2% and the relative size of the standard deviation to the expected return has decreased by a significant 5.5%. Further, the measure of skewness has increased 5.4%, to 1.135. Since the skewness value is greater than 1 and larger than before, the distribution is more skewed to the right than previously. A distribution more skewed to the right has a lower downside risk. Thus, the risk of *cash flows below the expected value is reduced.*   •

As can clearly be seen from Examples 2, 3, and 4, the calculations can quickly become tedious as the number of periods increase, or the number of possible cash flows each period increase, or if the abandonment value is known only by a probability distribution. Thus, Roblichek and Van Horne[4] recommended and illustrated the use of the Monte Carlo simulation under such conditions. The simulation model to handle the abandonment problem is a straightforward extension of the models discussed in Chapter 14. In addition, the interested reader is referred to the appendix in the Robichek and Van Horne article,[5] where the authors give a brief description of the simulation model they used.

Finally, Bonini[6] formulated a dynamic programming model which finds the optimal abandonment strategy under both conditions of certainty and uncertainty. The approach can also be viewed as an analytic extension of the Hillier formulation for quantifying project risk[7] where the abandonment option exists. The interested reader should consult this reference.

This section should be closed with a word of caution. Capital budgeting projects should be monitored, and it may become advantageous to terminate some. However, the abandonment decision must stand the test of maximizing shareholders' wealth. It is often extremely difficult to estimate the costs and benefits of abandoning large capital projects which may necessitate closing down or selling off a product line or division. Such changes involve disentangling accounting and tax effects, managerial reassignments, work-force dislocations, customer relations problems, community and societal impacts, and so on. Thus, the process can entail very long lead times, perhaps spanning a decade. The proper timing of abandonment and the attendant dislocations affect the ultimate decision and modify the structures of theory.

COST-JUSTIFYING CAPITAL BUDGETING

Capital budgeting must be monitored by management for yet another reason: it can be expensive in manpower, time, and facilities. The sophistication of the process naturally varies with the size of the firm and the importance of the projects under consideration. Also, the techniques we have discussed can

---

[4]Ibid., pp. 582–584.
[5]Ibid., pp. 588–589.
[6]C. P. Bonini, "Capital Investment Under Uncertainty with Abandonment Options," *Journal of Financial and Quantitative Analysis*, Vol. 12, No. 1, March 1977, pp. 39–54.
[7]F. S. Hillier, "The Derivation of Probabilistic Information for the Evaluation of Risky Investment," *Management Science*, Vol. 9, No. 3, April 1963, pp. 443–457.

be applied to a wide variety of project types: plant and equipment; lease vs. buy analysis; refunding proposals; advertising expenditures; research and development projects; and abandonment issues. So many and varied are the applications that at the outset, management must establish a cutoff point; that is, spending proposals below a certain amount will be treated as simple expenditure items. Above this amount, the budgeting process will take over.

The objective is to establish a cost-effective budgeting procedure. This is fostered by following up on projects to assure that the desired return is realized, abandoning projects that fail the test, and confirming the budgeting process to projects of a size appropriate to the analytical techniques applied. The latter, it should be noted, is not the most common sin of the U.S. financial management; rather the converse—spending large sums without appropriate analysis.

Nonetheless, one can appropriately raise the question of whether firms using the more sophisticated discounted-cash-flow methods show enhanced profitability compared to those which adhere to older rules of thumb. The evidence is uncertain on the point and the analysis difficult, owing to the presence of so many variables intruding on the firm's profitability other than the capital budgeting decision. Yet we can cite some research on the topic. George A. Christy, for example, matched earnings per share of his surveyed companies against the capital budgeting techniques employed. Christy found no significant relationship between profitability and the methodology of long-range asset management.[8]

By contrast, Suk H. Kim at the University of Detroit surveyed 114 machinery companies and related their average earnings per share to several variables: the degree of sophistication in capital budgeting, size of the firm, capital intensity, degree of risk, and debt ratio. Kim found a positive relationship between profitability and the budgeting technique when the latter is considered as a broad process involving the added variables ignored in the Christy study.[9]

SUMMARY

In this chapter we stressed the importance of financial forecasting (both short-run and long-run) in the capital budgeting decision-making process. An overview was presented of major assumptions and strategies in financial forecasting.

Next, the very important area of the review and evaluation of previously accepted capital projects was addressed. The impact of the abandonment option on the attractiveness of investment proposals was measured and illustrated by examples. Under conditions of constant risk, the optimal time to abandon a project was that period which led to a maximization of the NPV considering both the present value of project cash inflows and the present value

---

[8]George A. Christy, *Capital Budgeting: Current Practices and Their Efficiency* (Eugene, Ore.: Bureau of Economic Research, University of Oregon, 1966).
[9]"Capital Budgeting Practices in Large Corporations and Their Impact on Overall Profitability," unpublished paper.

of the abandonment value. Under conditions of changing risk, it was shown that the abandonment option increased the expected NPV, decreased both the absolute and relative risk of the project, and increased the positive skewness of the project (which reduces the downside risk of the project).

Finally, the importance of cost-effective capital project evaluation was stressed so that firms avoid committing major dollar amounts without appropriate analysis.

DISCUSSION QUESTIONS AND PROBLEMS

1. Discuss the importance of capital budgeting to a firm's overall strategic planning and the interrelationships between capital budgeting and the functional areas of finance, production, personnel, marketing, and accounting.

2. Discuss the importance of forecasting to capital budgeting and the importance of taking cognizance of the assumptions underlying forecasting models in use.

3. List at least three reasons why capital investment projects may have to be abandoned before the end of their useful lives in order to maximize shareholders' wealth.

4. The Ridgway Company is evaluating a project that could be abandoned at various points throughout its useful life. The cash flows related to the project as well as the abandonment values through time are shown below:

Period	0	1	2	3	4
Cash Flows	− $10,000	+ $4,000	+ $3,500	+ $3,000	+ $2,000
Abandonment Values		$7,000	$5,000	$3,000	$1,000

The firm's cost of capital is 12%. Compute the following:
(a) The NPV if the project is held until the end of its useful life.
(b) The optimal time to abandon the project using NPV^m shown in Equation (1).

5. The Ridgway Company is evaluating a second capital project that it feels has quite a bit more uncertainty associated with it. Namely, the firm feels that the following probabilities should be assigned to various cash flows and abandonment values (which are all considered to be independent):

		Period			
	0	1	2	3	4
Pr = 0.2	− $14,000	+ $10,000	+ $ 9,000	+ $ 8,000	+ $ 7,000
Pr = 0.5	− 20,000	+ 12,000	+ 14,000	+ 15,000	+ 16,000
Pr = 0.3	− 22,000	+ 13,000	+ 15,000	+ 17,000	+ 19,000
Abandonment Pr = 0.3		+ 10,000	+ 7,000	+ 6,000	+ 4,000
values Pr = 0.6		+ 11,000	+ 9,000	+ 7,000	+ 5,000
Pr = 0.1		+ 12,000	+ 11,000	+ 8,000	+ 6,000

The firm's cost of capital is still 12%, and this project is considered to be of average riskiness to the firm. Because of the independence between successive years' cash flows and between these flows and the abandonment values, expected values can be used to determine the NPV and the optimal time to abandon. Thus, compute the following:

(a) The expected NPV if the project is held to the end of its useful life.

(b) The optimal time to abandon the project, which is determined by maximizing the expected value of NPV^m.

6. Smith Brothers, Inc., is considering investing in a new machine to package cough drops. The machine has a potential useful life of 3 years, with a possibility of abandonment at the end of year 1 or 2. The possible cash flows, abandonment values, and their associated probabilities are as follows:

Year 1		Year 2		Year 3	
Cash Flow	Prob.	Cash Flow	Prob.	Cash Flow	Prob.
				$ 8,000	0.3
				10,000	0.3
		$ 6,000	0.2	12,000	0.4
$4,000	0.4	7,000	0.4	13,000	0.3
		8,000	0.4	15,000	0.3
				10,000	0.2
		8,000	0.2	11,000	0.4
9,000	0.6	11,000	0.6	13,000	0.4
		12,000	0.2	15,000	0.2
				16,000	0.4

At the end of year 1:		At the end of year 2:	
Value	Probability	Value	Probability
$16,000	0.2	$10,000	0.3
18,000	0.7	12,000	0.6
19,000	0.1	14,000	0.1

Smith Brothers' required rate of return for this project is 14%.

(a) Draw the complete decision tree, which represents the decision alternatives available to the firm at various points through time.

(b) For each of the possible cash flows during year 2, determine whether the project should be abandoned at the end of year 2.

(c) For each of the cash flows during year 1, determine whether the project should be abandoned at the end of year 1.

(d) Summarize your results in parts (b) and (c) concerning what the firm should do in both years for all possible cash flows that could occur (i.e., make a recommendation to Smith Brothers about whether it should hold or abandon the asset for each possible cash flow).

(e) Assuming that the project cost is $20,000, compute the expected NPV, σ_{NPV}, semivariance, measure of skewness, and coefficient of variation for the project without the abandonment option.

(f) Compute all of the measures mentioned in part (e) but this time with the abandonment option.

APPENDIX A
DETAILED BIBLIOGRAPHY

CHAPTER 1

Anderson, Leslie P., Vergil V. Miller, and Donald L. Thompson, *The Finance Function* (Scranton, Pa.: International Textbook Company, 1971).

Anthony, R. N., "The Trouble with Profit Maximization," *Harvard Business Review*, 38, (November–December 1960) 126–134.

Archer, S. H., and C. A. D'Ambrosio, *Business Finance* (New York: Macmillan Publishing Co., Inc., 1972).

Berle, A. A., Jr., and G. C. Means, *The Modern Corporation and Private Property* (New York: Macmillan Publishing Co., Inc., 1948).

Branch, Ben, "Corporate Objectives and Market Performance," *Financial Management*, 2 (Summer 1973), 24–29.

De Alessi, Louis, "Private Property and Dispersion of Ownership in Large Corporations," *Journal of Finance*, 28 (September 1973), 839–851.

Dean, J., *Capital Budgeting* (New York: Columbia University Press, 1951).

Dewing, A. S., *Financial Policy of Corporations*, 5th ed. (New York: The Ronald Press Company, 1953).

Donaldson, Gordon, "Financial Goals: Management vs. Stockholders," *Harvard Business Review*, 41 (May–June 1963), 116–129.

Elliott, J. W., "Control, Size, Growth, and Financial Performance in the Firm," *Journal of Financial and Quantitative Analysis*, 7 (January 1972), 1309–1320.

Findlay, M. Chapman, III, and G. A. Whitmore, "Beyond Shareholder Wealth Maximization," *Financial Management*, 3 (Winter 1974), 25–35.

Galbraith, J. K., *The New Industrial State* (Boston: Houghton Mifflin Company, 1967).

Greene, T. L., *Corporation Finance* (New York: G. P. Putnam's Sons, 1897).

Hibdon, J. E., *Price and Welfare Theory* (New York: McGraw-Hill Book Company, 1969).

Howard, B. B., and M. Upton, *An Introduction to Business Finance* (New York: McGraw-Hill Book Company, 1953).

Hunt, P., and C. M. Williams, *Case Problems in Finance* (Homewood, Ill.: Richard D. Irwin, Inc, 1940).

Lewellen, W. G., "Management and Ownership in the Large Firm," *Journal of Finance*, 26 (May 1969), 299–322.

Mao, J. C. T., *Quantitative Analysis of Financial Decisions* (New York: Harcourt Brace Jovanovitch 1969).

Moag, J. S., W. T. Carleton, and E. M. Lerner, "Defining the Finance Function: A Model-Systems Approach," *Journal of Finance*, 22 (December 1967), 543–556.

Moore, J. R., "The Financial Executive in the 1970s," *Financial Executive*, 35 (January 1967), 28–29, 32–34, 36.

Sauvain, H., "Comment," *Journal of Finance*, 12, 4 (December 1967), 541.

Simkowitz, Michael A., and Charles P. Jones, "A Note on the Simultaneous Nature of Finance Methodology," *Journal of Finance*, 27 (March 1972), 103–108.

Solomon, E., *The Theory of Financial Management* (New York: Columbia University Press, 1963).

Weston, J. Fred, "New Themes in Finance," *Journal of Finance*, 24 (March, 1974), 237–243.

──────, *The Scope and Methodology of Finance* (Englewood Cliffs, N. J.: Prentice-Hall, Inc., 1966).

CHAPTERS 2, 3, AND 4

Beranek, W., *Analysis for Financial Decisions* (Homewood, Ill.: Richard D. Irwin, Inc., 1963), Chap. 11.

Bierman, H., Jr., and S. Smidt, *The Capital Budgeting Decision*, 3rd ed. (New York: Macmillan Publishing Co., Inc., 1971), especially pp. 107–120.

Davidson, Sidney, and David F. Drake, "The 'Best' Tax Depreciation Method—1964," *Journal of Business*, 37 (July 1964), 258–260.

──────, and David F. Drake, "Capital Budgeting and the 'Best' Tax Depreciation Method," *Journal of Business*, 34 (October 1961), 442–452.

Dowsett, R. C., "Investment Advantages from Tax Credits and Accumulated Depreciation," *Financial Executive* (June 1966). 52 ff.

Edwards, James W., *Effects of Federal Income Taxes on Capital Budgeting* (New York: National Association of Accountants, 1969).

Findlay, M. C., III, and E. E. Williams, *An Integrated Analysis for Managerial Finance* (Englewood Cliffs, N.J.: Prentice-Hall, Inc., 1970), Chaps. 2, 7.

Flink, S. J., and D. Greenwald, *Managerial Finance* (New York: John Wiley & Sons, Inc., 1969), Chaps. 2, 8.

Grant, Eugene L., and W. Grant Ireson, *Principles of Engineering Economy* (New York: The Ronald Press Company, 1970), Chap. 17.

Hackamack, Lawrence C., *Making Equipment-Replacement Decisions* (New York: American Management Association, 1969).

Mao, J. C. T., *Quantitative Analysis of Financial Decisions* (Toronto:Macmillan Co., 1969), pp. 183 ff.

Mock, E. J., et al., *Basic Financial Management: Text, Problems and Cases* (Scranton, Pa.: International Textbook Company, 1968), Chaps. 5, 6.

Murray, Alan P., *Depreciation* (Cambridge, Mass.: International Tax Program, Harvard Law School, 1971).

Myers, J. H., "Depreciation Manipulation for Fun and Profit," *Financial Analysts Journal* (September 1969), 47–56.

Raby, William L., *The Income Tax and Business Decisions* (Englewood Cliffs, N.J.: Prentice-Hall, Inc., 1972).

Stancil, J. McN., *The Management of Working Capital* (Scranton, Pa.: Intext Educational Publishers, 1971), Chap. 7.

Van Horne, J. C., *Financial Management and Policy* (Englewood Cliffs, N.J.: Prentice-Hall, Inc., 1977), Chaps. 2, 3, and 4.

Wilkens, E. N., "Forecasting Cash Flow: Some Problems and Applications," *Management Accounting* (October 1967), 26–30.

Zimmer, R. K., and R. Gray, "Using Accelerated Depreciation in Capital Expenditure Analysis," *Management Service* (January 1969), 43–48.

CHAPTERS 5, 6, AND 7

Bauman, W. Scott, "Investment Returns and Present Values," *Financial Analysts Journal*, 25 (November–December 1969), 107–118.

Blume, Marshall E., "On the Assessment of Risk," *Journal of Finance*, 26 (March 1971), 1–10.

Bower, Richard S., and Dorothy H. Bower, "Risk and the Valuation of Common Stock," *Journal of Political Economy*, 77 (May–June 1969), 349–362.

Brigham, Eugene F., and James L. Pappas, "Duration of Growth, Changes in Growth Rates, and Corporate Share Prices," *Financial Analysts Journal*, 22 (May–June 1966), 157–162.

de Faro, Clovis, "On the Internal Rate of Return Criterion," *Engineering Economist*, 19 (April–May 1974), 165–194.

_____, "A Sufficient Condition for a Unique Nonnegative Internal Rate of Return: A Comment," *Journal of Financial and Quantitative Analysis*, 8 (September 1973), 683–684.

Doenges, R. Conrad, "The 'Reinvestment Problem' in a Practical Perspective," *Financial Management*, 1 (Spring 1972), 85–91.

Dudley, Carlton L., Jr., "A Note on Reinvestment Assumptions in Choosing Between Net Present Value and Internal Rate of Return," *Journal of Finance*, 27 (September 1972), 907–915.

Dyckman, Thomas R., and James C. Kinard, "The Discounted Cash Flow Investment Decision Model with Accounting Income Constraints," *Decision Sciences*, 4 (July 1973), 301–313.

Fama, Eugene F., "Components of Investment Performance," *Journal of Finance*, 27 (June 1972), 551–557.

_____, "Multiperiod Consumption—Investment Decisions," *American Economic Review*, 60 (March 1970), 163–174.

_____, and Merton H. Miller, *The Theory of Finance* (New York: Holt, Rinehart and Winston, Inc., 1972).

Gonedes, Nicholas J., "Information-Production and Capital Market Equilibrium," *Journal of Finance*, 30 (June 1975), 841–1864.

Gordon, Myron, *The Investment, Financing, and Valuation of the Corporation* (Homewood, Ill.: Richard D. Irwin, Inc., 1962).

Haley, Charles W., and Lawrence D. Schall, *The Theory of Financial Decisions* (New York: McGraw-Hill Book Company, 1973), Chap. 5.

Hirshleifer, J., *Investment, Interest and Capital* (Englewood Cliffs, N.J.: Prentice-Hall, Inc., 1970).

_____, "On the Theory of Optimal Investment Decision," *Journal of Political Economy*, 66 (August 1958).

Lerner, Eugene M., and Willard T. Carleton, *A Theory of Financial Analysis* (New York: Harcourt Brace Jovanovich, 1966).

_____, and A. Rappaport, "Limit DCF in Capital Budgeting," *Harvard Business Review*, 46 (September–October 1968), 133–138.

Lewellen, Wilbur G., Howard P. Lanser, and John J. McConnell, "Payback Substitutes for Discounted Cash Flow," *Financial Management*, 2 (Summer 1973), 17–23.

Lindsay, R. J., and A. W. Sametz, *Financial Management: An Analytical Approach* (Homewood, Ill.: Richard D. Irwin, Inc., 1967).

Lorie, J. H., and L. J. Savage, "Three Problems in Rationing Capital," *Journal of Business*, 28 (October 1955).

Machol, Robert E., and Eugene M. Lerner, "Risk, Ruin, and Investment Analysis," *Journal of Financial and Quantitative Analysis*, 4 (December 1969), 473–492.

Malkiel, Burton G., "Equity Yields, Growth, and the Structure of Share Prices," *American Economic Review*, 53 (December 1963), 467–494.

————, and John G. Cragg, "Expectations and the Structure of Share Prices," *American Economic Review*, 40 (September 1970), 601–617.

Mao, James C. T., "The Internal Rate of Return as a Ranking Criterion," *Engineering Economist*, 11 (Winter 1966), 1–13.

————, "A New Graphic Analysis of Fisher's Rate of Return," *Cost and Management*, 44 (November–December 1970), 24–27.

————, *Quantitative Analysis of Financial Decisions* (New York: Macmillan Publishing Co., Inc., 1969), Chaps. 6, 7.

————, "Survey of Capital Budgeting: Theory and Practice," *Journal of Finance*, 25 (May 1970), 349–360.

————, "The Valuation of Growth Stocks: The Investment Opportunities Approach," *Journal of Finance*, 21 (March 1966), 95–102.

Murdick, Robert G., and Donald D. Deming, *The Management of Capital Expenditures* (New York: McGraw-Hill Book Company, 1968).

Norstrom, Carl J., "A Sufficient Condition for a Unique Nonnegative Internal Rate of Return," *Journal of Financial and Quantitative Analysis*, 7 (June 1972), 1835–1839.

Osteryoung, Jerome, *Capital Budgeting: Long-Term Assets Selection* (Columbus, Ohio: Grid, Inc., 1974).

Pogue, Gerald A., and Kishore Lall, "Corporate Finance: An Overview," *Sloan Management Review*, 15 (Spring 1974), 19–38.

Porterfield, J. T., *Investment Decisions and Capital Costs* (Englewood Cliffs, N.J.: Prentice-Hall, Inc., 1965).

Renshaw, E., "A Note on the Arithmetic of Capital Budgeting Decisions," *Journal of Business*, 30 (July 1957).

Robichek, Alexander A., "Risk and the Value of Securities," *Journal of Financial and Quantitative Analysis*, 4 (December 1969), 513–538.

————, and Stewart C. Myers, *Optimal Financing Decisions* (Englewood Cliffs, N.J.: Prentice-Hall, Inc., 1965), Chaps. 4–6.

Schwab, Bernhard, and Peter Lusztig, "A Comparative Analysis of the Net Present Value and the Benefit-Cost Ratios as Measures of the Economic Desirability of Investments," *Journal of Finance*, 24 (June 1969), 507–516.

Shank, John K., and A. Michael Burnell, "Smooth Your Earnings Growth Rate," *Harvard Business Review*, 54 (January–February 1974), 136–141.

Solomon, Ezra, "The Arithmetic of Capital-Budgeting Decisions," *Journal of Business*, 29 (April 1956), 124–129.

————, *The Management of Corporate Capital* (New York: The Free Press, 1959).

————, *The Theory of Financial Management* (New York: Columbia University Press, 1963).

Van Horne, J. C, *Financial Management and Policy* (Englewood Cliffs, N.J.: Prentice-Hall, Inc., 1968).

Weingartner, H. Martin, "Capital Budgeting of Interrelated Projects: Survey and Synthesis," *Management Science*, 12 (March 1966), 485–516.

————, "The Excess Present Value Index—A Theoretical Basis and Critique," *Journal of Accounting Research*, 1 (Autumn 1963), 213–224.

_____, "The Generalized Rate of Return," *Journal of Financial and Quantitative Analysis*, 1 (September 1966), 1–29.

_____, *Mathematical Programming and the Analysis of Capital Budgeting Problems* (Englewood Cliffs, N.J.: Prentice-Hall, Inc., 1963).

_____, "Some New Views on the Payback Period and Capital Budgeting Decisions," *Management Science*, 15 (August 1969), 594–607.

Welter, P., "Put Policy First in DCF Analysis," *Harvard Business Review*, 48 (January–February 1970), 141–148.

Weston, F. J., and E. F. Brigham, *Managerial Finance*, 4th ed. (New York: Holt, Rinehart and Winston Inc., 1972).

Whisler, William D., "Sensitivity Analysis of Rates of Return," *Journal of Finance*, 31 (March 1976), 63–70.

Wiar, Robert C., "Economic Implications of Multiple Rates of Return in the Leveraged Lease Context," *Journal of Finance*, 28 (December 1973), 1275–1286.

CHAPTERS 8, 9, AND 10

Baesel, Jerome B., "On the Assessment of Risk: Some Further Considerations," *Journal of Finance*, 29 (December 1974), 1491–1494.

Bierman, Harold, Jr., and Warren H. Hausman, "The Resolution of Investment Uncertainty Through Time," *Management Science*, 18 (August 1972), 654–662.

_____, and Seymour Smidt, *The Capital Budgeting Decision*, Part III (New York: Macmillan Publishing Co., Inc., 1971).

Black, F., M. C. Jensen, and M. Scholes, "The Capital Asset Pricing Model: Some Empirical Tests," in M. C. Jensen, ed., *Studies in the Theory of Capital Markets* (New York: Praeger Publishers, Inc., 1972).

Bonini, Charles P., "Comment on Formulating Correlated Cash Flow Streams," *Engineering Economist*, 20 (Spring 1975), 209–214.

_____, "Evaluation of Project Risk in Capital Investments with Abandonment Options," *Research Paper 224*, Stanford Graduate School of Business, 1974.

Bower, Richard S., and Donald R. Lessard, "An Operational Approach to Risk-Screening," *Journal of Finance*, 28 (May 1973), 321–337.

Bussey, Lynn E., and G. T. Stevens, Jr., "Formulating Correlated Cash Flow Streams," *Engineering Economist*, 18 (Fall 1972), 1–30.

Buzby, Stephen L., "Extending the Applicability of Probabilistic Management Planning and Control Models," *Accounting Review*, 49 (January 1974), 42–49.

Byrne, R., A., Charnes, A. Cooper, and K. Kortanek, "Some New Approaches to Risk," *Accounting Review*, 63 (January 1968), 18–37.

Carter, E. Eugene, *Portfolio Aspects of Corporate Capital Budgeting* (Lexington, Mass.: D. C. Health & Company, 1974).

Chen, Houng-yhi, "Valuation Under Uncertainty," *Journal of Financial and Quantitative Analysis*, 2 (September 1967), 313–326.

Cohen, Kalman J., and Edwin J. Elton, "Inter-Temporal Portfolio Analysis Based upon Simulation of Joint Returns," *Management Science*, 14 (September 1967), 5–18.

Edelman, Franz, and Joel S. Greenberg, "Venture Analysis: The Assessment of Uncertainty and Risk," *Financial Executive*, 37 (August 1969), 56–62.

Elton, Edwin, and Martin J. Gruber, "Estimating the Dependence Structure of Share Prices—Inplications for Portfolio Selection," *Journal of Finance*, 28 (December 1973), 1203–1232.

————, and Martin J. Gruber, *Finance as a Dynamic Process*, (Englewood Cliffs, N.J.: Prentice-Hall, Inc., 1975), Chap. 5.

Evans, Jack, and Stephen H. Archer, "Diversification and the Reduction of Dispersion: An Empirical Analysis," *Journal of Finance*, 23 (December 1968), 761–767.

Fama, Eugene F., "Components of Investment Performance," *Journal of Finance*, 27 (June 1972), 551–567.

————, "Efficient Capital Markets: A Review of Theory and Empirical Work," *Journal of Finance*, 25 (May 1970), 333–417.

————, "Efficient Capital Markets: Restatement of the Theory," *Journal of Finance*, forthcoming.

————, "Multiperiod Consumption–Investment Decisions," *American Economic Review*, 60 (March 1970), 163–174.

————, "Risk, Return, and Equilibrium," *Journal of Political Economy*, 79 (January–February 1971), 30–55.

————, "Risk, Return, and Equilibrium: Some Clarifying Comments," *Journal of Finance*, 23 (March 1968), 29–40.

————, and James D. MacBeth, "Risk, Return, and Equilibrium: Empirical Tests," *Journal of Political Economy*, 81 (May–June 1973), 607–636.

————, and Merton H. Miller, *The Theory of Finance* (New York: Holt, Rinehart and Winston, Inc., 1972).

Francis, Jack Clark, "Intertemporal Differences in Systematic Stock Price Movements," *Journal of Financial and Quantitative Analysis*, 10 (June 1975), 205–220.

Hakansson, Nils H., "Capital Growth and the Mean-Variance Approach to Portfolio Selection," *Journal of Financial and Quantitative Analysis*, 6 (January 1971), 517–558.

Haley, Charles W., and Lawrence D. Schall, *The Theory of Financial Decisions* (New York: McGraw-Hill Book Company, 1973), Chaps. 5–7.

Hamada, Robert S., "Investment Decision with a General Equilibrium Mean-Variance Approach," *Quarterly Journal of Economics*, 85 (November 1971), 667–683.

————, "Multiperiod Capital Asset Prices in an Efficient and Perfect Market: A Valuation or Present Value Model Under Two Parameter Uncertainty," unpublished ms., University of Chicago, 1972.

————, "Portfolio Analysis, Market Equilibrium and Corporation Finance," *Journal of Finance*, 24 (March 1969), 13–32.

Harvey, R. K., and A. V. Cabot, "A Decision Theory Approach to Capital Budgeting Under Risk," *Engineering Economist*, 20 (Fall 1974), 37–49.

Hayes, Robert H., "Incorporation Risk Aversion into Risk Analysis," *Engineering Economist*, 20 (Winter 1975), 99–121.

Hillier, Frederick S., "A Basic Model for Capital Budgeting of Risky Interrelated Projects," *Engineering Economist*, 17 (October–November 1971), 1–30.

————, "The Derivation of Probabilistic Information for the Evaluation of Risky Investments," *Management Science*, 9 (April 1963), 443–457.

Hirshleifer, Jack, "Investment Decisions Under Uncertainty: Applications of the Slate-Preference Approach," *Quarterly Journal of Economics*, 80 (May 1966), 252–277.

————, *Investment, Interest and Capital* (Englewood Cliffs, N.J.: Prentice-Hall, Inc., 1970).

Jensen, Michael C., "Capital Markets: Theory and Practice," *Bell Journal of Economics and Management Science*, 3 (Autumn 1972), 357–398.

————, "Risk, the Pricing of Capital Assets, and the Evaluation of Investment Portfolios," *Journal of Business*, 42 (April 1969), 167–247.

————, *Studies in the Theory of Capital Markets* (New York: Praeger Publishers, Inc., 1972).

Johnson, K. H., and D. S. Shannon, "A Note on Diversification and the Reduction of Dispersion," *Journal of Financial Economics*, 1 (December 1974), 365–372.

Joy, O. Maurice, and Jerry O. Bradley, "A Note on Sensitivity Analysis of Rates of Return," *Journal of Finance*, 28 (December 1973), 1255–1261.

Levy, Haim, and Marshall Sarnat, "The Portfolio Analysis of Multiperiod Capital Investment Under Conditions of Risk," *Engineering Economist*, 16 (Fall 1970), 1–19.

Levy, Robert A., "On the Short Term Stationarity of Beta Coefficients," *Financial Analysts Journal*, 27 (November–December 1971), 55–62.

Lintner, John, "The Aggregation of Investors' Judgments and Preferences in Purely Competitive Security Markets," *Journal of Financial and Quantitative Analysis*, 4 (December 1969), 347–400.

———, "The Evaluation of Risk Assets and the Selection of Risky Investments in Stock Portfolios and Capital Budgets," *Review of Economics and Statistics*, 47 (February 1965), 13–37.

———, "Security Prices, Risk and Maximal Gains from Diversification," *Journal of Finance*, 20 (December 1965), 587–616.

Logue, D. E., and L. J. Merville, "Financial Policy and Market Expectations," *Financial Management* (Summer 1972), 37–44.

Markowitz, H., "Portfolio Selection," *The Journal of Finance* (March 1952), 77–91.

Martin, A. D., "Mathematical Programming of Portfolio Selections," *Management Science* (January 1955), 152–166.

Merton, Robert C., "Capital Budgeting in the Capital Asset Pricing Model," unpublished note, 1973.

———, "An Intertemporal Capital Asset Pricing Model," *Econometrica*, 45, 5 (September 1973), 867–887.

———, "Theory of Finance from the Perspective of Continuous Time," *Journal of Financial and Quantitative Analysis*, 10 (November 1975), 659–674.

Modigliani, Franco, and Gerald A. Pogue, "An Introduction to Risk and Return," *Financial Analysts Journal*, 30 (March–April 1974), 68–80, and (May–June 1974), 69–86.

Mossin, Jan, "Equilibrium in a Capital Asset Market," *Econometrica*, 34, 4 (October 1966), 768–783.

———, *Theory of Financial Markets* (Englewood Cliffs, N.J.: Prentice-Hall, Inc., 1973), Chaps. 7–8.

Myers, Stewart C., "The Application of Finance Theory to Public Utility Rate Cases," *Bell Journal of Economics and Management Science*, 3 (Spring 1972), 58–97.

———, "Procedures for Capital Budgeting Under Uncertainty," *Industrial Management Review*, 9 (Spring 1968), 1–15.

———, "A Time-State Preference Model of Security Valuation," *Journal of Financial and Quantitative Analysis*, 3 (March 1968), 1–34.

Nielsen, N. C., "The Investment Decision of the Firm Under Uncertainty and the Allocative Efficiency of Capital Markets," *Journal of Finance*, 31 (May 1976), 587–601.

Peterson, D. E., and R. B. Haydon, *A Quantitative Framework for Financial Management* (Homewood, Ill.: Richard D. Irwin, Inc., 1969), pp. 404–434.

Pettit, R. Richardson, and Randolph Westerfield, "Using the Capital Asset Pricing Model and the Market Model to Predict Security Returns," *Journal of Financial and Quantitative Analysis*, 9 (September 1974), 579–606.

Phelps, E. S., "The Accumulation of Risky Capital: A Sequential Utility Analysis," *Econometrica*, 30 (1962), 729–743.

Pogue, Gerald A., "An Extension of the Markowitz Portfolio Selection Model to Include Variable Transactions Costs, Short Sales, Leverage Policies and Taxes," *Journal of Finance*, 25 (December 1970), 1005–1027.

———, and Kishore Lall, "Corporate Finance: An Overview," *Sloan Management Review*, 15 (Spring 1974), 19–38.

Renwick, F. B., *Introduction to Investments and Finance* (New York: Macmillan Publishing Co., Inc., 1971).

Robichek, Alexander A., and Stewart C. Myers, "Conceptual Problems in the Use of Risk-Adjusted Discount Rates," *Journal of Finance*, 21 (December 1966), 727–730.

———, *Optimal Financing Decisions* (Englewood Cliffs, N.J.: Prentice-Hall, Inc., 1965), Chap. 5.

Roll, Richard, and Marcus C. Bogue, "Capital Budgeting of Risky Projects with Imperfect Markets for Physical Capital," *Journal of Finance*, 29 (May 1974), 606–612.

Rubinstein, Mark E., "A Comparative Statics Analysis of Risk Premiums," *Journal of Business*, 46 (October 1973).

——— "A Mean–Variance Synthesis of Corporate Financial Theory," *Journal of Finance*, 28 (March 1973), 167–182.

Schall, Lawrence D., "Asset Valuation, Firm Investment, and Firm Diversification," *Journal of Business*, 45 (January 1972), 11–28.

———, "Firm Financial Structure and Investment," *Journal of Financial and Quantitative Analysis*, 6 (June 1971), 925–942.

Schlaifer, R., *Probability and Statistics for Business Decisions* (New York: McGraw-Hill Book Company, 1969).

———, "A Simplified Model for Portfolio Analysis," *Management Science*, 10 (January 1963), 277–293.

Sharpe, William F., "Capital Asset Prices: A Theory of Market Equilibrium Under Conditions of Risk," *Journal of Finance*, 19 (September 1964), 425–442.

———, "Efficient Capital Markets with Risk," *Research Paper* 71, Stanford Graduate School of Business, 1972.

———, *Portfolio Analysis and Capital Markets* (New York: McGraw-Hill Book Company, 1970).

———, and Guy M. Cooper, "Risk–Return Classes of New York Stock Exchange Common Stocks," *Financial Analysts Journal*, 28 (March–April 1972), 46–54.

Stapleton, Richard C., "Portfolio Analysis, Stock Valuation and Capital Budgeting Rules for Risky Projects," *Journal of Finance*, 26 (March 1971), 95–118.

Sundem, Gary L., "Evaluating Simplified Capital Budgeting Models Using a Time-State Preference Metric," *Accounting Review*, 49 (April 1974), 306–320.

Tobin, James, "Liquidity Preference as Behavior Towards Risk," *Review of Economic Studies*, 25 (February 1958), 65–86.

Tuttle, Donald L., and Robert H. Litzenberger, "Leverage, Diversification and Capital Market Effects on a Risk-Adjusted Capital Budgeting Framework," *Journal of Finance*, 23 (June 1968), 427–443.

Van Horne, James C., "The Analysis of Uncertainty Resolution in Capital Budgeting for New Projects," *Management Science*, 15 (April 1969), 376–386.

———, "Capital-Budgeting Decisions Involving Combinations of Risky Investments," *Management Science*, 13 (October 1966), 84–92.

———, *The Function and Analysis of Capital Market Rates* (Englewood Cliffs, N.J.: Prentice-Hall, Inc., 1970).

von Neumann, J., and O. Morgenstern, *Theory of Games and Economic Behavior*, 2nd ed. (Princeton, N.J.: Princeton University Press, 1947).

Weston, J. Fred, "Investment Decisions Using the Capital Asset Pricing Model," *Financial Management*, 2 (Spring 1973), 25–33.

CHAPTER 11

Arditti, Fred D., "Risk and the Required Return on Equity," *Journal of Finance*, 22 (March 1967), 19–36.

———, and Stephen A. Tysseland, "Three Ways to Present the Marginal Cost of Capital," *Financial Management* (Summer 1973), 63–67.

Barges, Alexander, *The Effect of Capital Structure on the Cost of Capital* (Englewood Cliffs, N.J.: Prentice-Hall, Inc., 1963).

Baumol, William, and Burton G. Malkiel, "The Firm's Optimal Debt-Equity Combination and the Cost of Capital," *Quarterly Journal of Economics*, 81 (November 1967), 547–578.

Baxter, Nevins D., "Leverage, Risk of Ruin, and the Cost of Capital," *Journal of Finance*, 22 (September 1967), 395–404.

Beaver, W., P. Kettler, and M. Scholes, "The Association Between Market Determined and Accounting Determined Risk Measures," *The Accounting Review* (October 1970), 654–682.

Ben-Shahar, Haim, "The Capital Structure and the Cost of Capital: A Suggested Exposition," *Journal of Finance*, 23 (September 1968), 639–653.

———, and Abraham Ascher, "Capital Budgeting and Stock Valuation: Comment," *American Economic Review*, 57 (March 1967), 209–214.

Beranek, William, *The Effects of Leverage on the Market Value of Common Stocks* (Madison, Wis.: Bureau of Business Research and Service, University of Wisconsin, 1964).

Bodenhorn, Diran, "On the Problem of Capital Budgeting," *Journal of Finance*, 14 (December 1959), 473–492.

Boness, A. James, "A Pedagogic Note on the Cost of Capital," *Journal of Finance*, 19 (March 1964), 99–106.

Bower, Richard S., and Dorothy H. Bower, "Risk and the Valuation of Common Stock," *Journal of Political Economy*, 77 (May–June 1969), 349–362.

Brewer, D. E., and J. Michaelson, "The Cost of Capital, Corporation Finance, and the Theory of Investment: Comment," *American Economic Review*, 55 (June 1965), 516–524.

Brigham, Eugene F., and Myron J. Gordon, "Leverage, Dividend Policy, and the Cost of Capital," *Journal of Finance*, 23 (March 1968), 85–104.

Crockett, Jean, and Irwin Friend, "Capital Budgeting and Stock Valuation: Comment," *American Economic Review*, 57 (March 1967), 214–220.

Durand, David, "Costs of Debt and Equity Funds for Business: Trends and Problems of Measurement," reprinted in Ezra Solomon, ed., *The Management of Corporate Capital* (New York: The Free Press, 1959), pp. 91–116.

Gordon, Myron J., *The Cost of Capital to a Public Utility* (East Lansing, Mich.: Michigan State University, 1974).

Heins, A. James, and Case M. Sprenkle, "A Comment on the Modigliani–Miller Cost of Capital Thesis," *American Economic Review*, 59 (September 1969), 590–592.

Lerner, Eugene M., and Willard T. Carleton, "Financing Decisions of the Firm," *Journal of Finance*, 21 (May 1966), 202–214.

———, and Willard T. Carlton, "The Integration of Capital Budgeting and Stock Valuation," *American Economic Review*, 54 (September 1964), reprinted in James Van Horne, ed., *Foundations for Financial Management* (Homewood, Ill.: Richard D. Irwin, Inc., 1966), pp. 327–346; "Reply," *American Economic Review*, 57 (March 1967), 220–222.

———, and Willard T. Carlton, *A Theory of Financial Analysis* (New York: Harcourt Brace Jovanovich, 1966).

Lewellen, Wilbur G., *The Cost of Capital* (Belmont, Calif.: Wadsworth Publishing Co., Inc., 1969), Chaps. 3, 4.

Lintner, John, "Dividends, Earnings, Leverage, Stock Prices and the Supply of Capital to Corporations," *Review of Economics and Statistics*, 44 (August 1962), 243–269.

Malkiel, Burton G., *The Debt-Equity Combination of the Firm and the Cost of Capital: An Introductory Analysis* (Morristown, N.J.: General Learning Press, 1971).

———, and John G. Cragg, "Expectations and the Structure of Share Prices," *American Economic Review*, 60 (September 1970), 601–617.

Miller, M. H., and Franco Modigliani, "Cost of Capital to Electric Utility Industry," *American Economic Review*, 56 (June 1966), 333–391.

Modigliani, Franco, and M. H. Miller, "The Cost of Capital, Corporation Finance and the Theory of Investment," *American Economic Review*, 48 (June 1958), 261–297.

———, and M. H. Miller, "The Cost of Capital, Corporation Finance and the Theory of Investment: Reply," *American Economic Review*, 49 (September 1958), 655–669; "Taxes and the Cost of Capital: A Correction," ibid., 53 (June 1963), 433–443; "Reply," ibid., 55 (June 1965), 524–527; "Reply to Heins and Sprenkle," ibid., 59 (September 1969), 592–595.

Mumey, Glen A., *Theory of Financial Structure* (New York: Holt, Rinehart and Winston, Inc., 1969).

Porterfield, James T. S., *Investment Decisions and Capital Costs* (Englewood Cliffs, N.J.: Prentice-Hall, Inc., 1965).

Quirin, G. David, *The Capital Expenditure Decision* (Homewood, Ill.: Richard D. Irwin, Inc., 1967), Chaps. 5, 6.

Resek, Robert W., "Multidimensional Risk and the Modigliani–Miller Hypothesis," *Journal of Finance*, 25 (March 1970), 47–52.

Robichek, Alexander A., and Steward C. Myers, *Optimal Financing Decisions* (Englewood Cliffs, N.J.: Prentice-Hall, Inc., 1965).

Schwartz, Eli, "Theory of the Capital Structure of the Firm," *Journal of Finance*, 14 (March 1959), reprinted in James Van Horne, ed., *Foundations for Financial Management* (Homewood, Ill.: Richard D. Irwin, Inc., 1966), pp. 413–433.

———, and J. Richard Aronson, "Some Surrogate Evidence in Support of the Concept of Optimal Capital Structure," *Journal of Finance*, 22 (March 1967), 10–18.

Solomon, Ezra, "Measuring a Company's Cost of Capital," *Journal of Business*, 28 (October 1955), 240–252.

———, *The Theory of Financial Management* (New York: Columbia University Press, 1963).

Stiglitz, Joseph E., "A Re-examination of the Modigliani–Miller Theorem," *American Economic Review*, 59 (December 1969), 784–793.

Tinsley, P. A., "Capital Structure, Precautionary Balances, and Valuation of the Firm: the Problem of Financial Risk," *Journal of Financial and Quantitative Analysis*, 5 (March 1970), 33–62.

Vickers, Douglas, "The Cost of Capital and the Structure of the Firm," *Journal of Finance*, 25 (March 1970), 35–46.

Weston, J. Fred, "Investment Decisions Using the Capital Asset Pricing Model," *Financial Management* (Spring 1973), 25–33.

———, "A Test of Cost of Capital Propositions," *Southern Economic Journal*, 30 (October 1963), 105–112.

Wippern, Ronald F., "Financial Structure and the Value of the Firm," *Journal of Finance*, 21 (December 1966), 615–634.

CHAPTER 12

Beale, E. M. L., *Mathematical Programming in Practice* (Pitman, 1968).

Charnes, A., and W. W. Cooper, *Management Models and Industrial Applications of Linear Programming*, Vols. I and II (New York: John Wiley & Sons, Inc., 1961).

Dantzig, G. B., *Linear Programming Extensions* (Princeton, N.J.: Princeton University Press, 1963).

Dorfman, R., P. A. Samuelson, and R. M. Solow, *Linear Programming and Economic Analysis* (New York: McGraw-Hill Book Company, 1958).

Gale, D., *The Theory of Linear Economic Models* (New York: McGraw-Hill Book Company, 1960).

Gass, S. I., *Linear Programming: Methods and Applications*, 3rd ed. (New York: McGraw-Hill Book Company, 1969).

Karlin, S., *Mathematical Methods and Theory in Games, Programming and Economics*, Vol. I (Reading, Mass.: Addison-Wesley Publishing Co., Inc., 1959).

Koopmans, T. C., ed., *Activity Analysis of Production and Allocation, Proceeding of a Conference* (New York: John Wiley & Sons, Inc., 1951).

Kuhn, H. W., and A. W. Tucker, eds., *Linear Inequalities and Related Systems* (Princeton, N.J.: Princeton University Press, 1956).

Lasdon, L., *Optimizaton Theory for Large Systems* (New York: Macmillan Publishing Co., Inc., 1970).

Orchard–Hays, W., *Advanced Linear-Programming Computing Techniques* (New York: McGraw-Hill Book Company, 1968).

Zionts, S., *Linear and Integer Programming* (Englewood Cliffs, N.J.: Prentice-Hall, Inc., 1974).

CHAPTERS 13 AND 14

Linear and Integer Programming

Baumol, W. J., and R. E. Quandt, "Investment and Discount Rates Under Capital Rationing—A Programming Approach," *Economic Journal*, 75 (June 1965), 317–329.

Carleton, W. T., "Linear Programming and Capital Budgeting Models: A New Interpretation," *Journal of Finance* (December 1969), 825–833.

Charnes, A., W. W. Cooper, and M. H. Miller, "Application of Linear Programming to Financial Budgeting and the Costing of Funds," *Journal of Business* (January 1959), 20–46.

Elton, Edwin J., "Capital Rationing and External Discount Rates," *Journal of Finance* (June 1970), 573–584.

_____, and Martin J. Gruber, *Finance as a Dynamic Process* (Englewood Cliffs, N.J.: Prentice-Hall, Inc., 1975), Chaps. 7, 8.

Fama, Eugene E., and Merton H. Miller, *The Theory of Finance* (New York: Holt, Rinehart and Winston, Inc., 1972), Chap. 3.

Fogler, H. Russell, "Ranking Techniques and Capital Rationing," *Accounting Review*, 47 (January 1972), 134–143.

Haley, Charles W., "Taxes, the Cost of Capital and the Firm's Investment Decisions," *Journal of Finance*, 26 (September 1971), 901–918.

_____, and Lawrence D. Schall, "A Note on Investment Policy with Imperfect Capital Markets," *Journal of Finance*, 27 (March 1972), 93–96.

Lorie J. H., and L. J. Savage, "Three Problems in Rationing Capital," *Journal of Business*, 28, 4 (October 1955), 229–239.

P. Lusztig, and B. Schwab, "A Note on the Application of Linear Programming to Capital Budgeting," *Journal of Financial and Quantitative Analysis*, 3, 5 (December 1968), 427–431.

Manne A. S., "Optimal Dividend and Investment Policies for a Self-Financing Business Enterprise," *Management Science*, 15, 3 (November 1968), 119–129.

Mao, J. C. T., *Quantitative Analysis of Financial Decisions* (New York: Macmillan Publishing Co., Inc., 1969), pp. 266–280.

Martin, A. D., "Mathematical Programming of Portfolio Selections," *Management Science* (January 1955), 152–166.

Merville L. J., and L. A. Tavis, "A Generalized Model for Capital Investment," *Journal of Finance*, 28, 1 (March 1973), 109–118.

Moag, J. S., and E. M. Lerner, "Capital Budgeting Decisions Under Imperfect Market Conditions," *Journal of Finance* (June 1970), 613–621.

Myers, Stewart C., "Interactions of Corporate Financing and Investment Decisions— Implications for Capital Budgeting," *Journal of Finance*, 29 (March 1974), 1–26.

———, "A Note on Linear Programming and Capital Budgeting," *Journal of Finance*, 27 (March 1972), 89–92.

Oakford, Robert V., *Capital Budgeting* (New York: The Ronald Press Company, 1970).

Peterson, D. E., and R. B. Haydon, *A Quantitative Framework for Financial Management* (Homewood, Ill.: Richard D. Irwin, Inc., 1969), pp. 404–434.

———, and D. J. Laughhunn, "Capital Expenditure Programming and Some Alternative Approaches to Risk," *Management Science*, 17 (January 1971), 320–336.

Petty, J. William, David F. Scott, Jr., and Monroe M. Bird, "The Capital Expenditure Decision-Making Process of Large Corporations," *Engineering Economist*, 20 (Spring 1975), 159–172.

Quirin, G. David, *The Capital Expenditure Decision* (Homewood, Ill.: Richard D. Irwin, Inc., 1967).

Teichroew, Daniel, Alexander A. Robichek, and Michael Montalbano, "An Analysis of Criteria for Investment and Financing Decisions Under Certainty," *Management Science*, 12 (November 1965), 151–179.

———, Alexander A. Robichek, and Michael Montalbano, "Mathematical Analysis of Rates of Return Under Certainty," *Management Science*, 11 (January 1965), 395–403.

Weingartner, H. Martin, "Capital Budgeting of Interrelated Projects: Survey and Synthesis," *Management Science*, 12 (March 1966), 485–516.

———, "Capital Rationing: *n* Authors in Search of a Plot," *Journal of Finance*, 32 (December 1977), 1403–1431.

———, "The Excess Present Value Index—A Theoretical Basis and Critique," *Journal of Accounting Research*, 1 (Autumn 1963), 213–224.

———, "The Generalized Rate of Return," *Journal of Financial and Quantitative Analysis*, 1 (September 1966), 1–29.

———, *Mathematical Programming and the Analysis of Capital Budgeting Problems* (Englewood Cliffs, N.J.: Prentice-Hall, Inc., 1963).

Whitmore G. A., and L. R. Amey, "Capital Budgeting Under Rationing: Comments on the Lusztig and Schwab Procedure," *Journal of Financial and Quantitative Analysis*, 8, 1 (January 1973), 127–135.

Goal Programming

Charnes, A., and W. W. Cooper, *Management Models and Industrial Applications of Linear Programming*, Vols. I and II (New York: John Wiley & Sons, Inc., 1961).

Fourcans, A., and T. Hindelang, "The Incorporation of Multiple Goals in the Selection of Capital Investments," paper presented at Financial Management Association Meeting, October 1973.

Hawkins, Clark A., and Richard A. Adams, "A Goal Programming Model for Capital Budgeting," *Financial Management* (Spring 1974), 52–57.

Ignizio, James P., *Goal Programming and Extensions* (Lexington, Mass.: Lexington Books, 1977).

Ijiri, Y., *Management Goals and Accounting for Control* (Amsterdam: North-Holland Publishing Co., 1965).

Lee, Sang M., *Goal Programming for Decision Analysis* (Philadelphia: Auerbach Publishing Co., 1972).

_____, and A. J. Lerro, "Capital Budgeting for Multiple Objectives," *Financial Management* (Spring 1974), 58–66.

Monte Carlo Simulation and Decision Trees

Carter, E. E., *Portfolio Aspects of Corporate Capital Budgeting* (Lexington, Mass.: Lexington Books, 1974).

Chambers, J. C., and S. K. Mullick, "Investment Decision Making in a Multinational Enterprise," *Management Accounting* (August 1971).

Cohen, K. J., and E. J. Elton, "Intertemporal Portfolio Analysis Based on Simulation of Joint Returns", *Management Science*, 14 (September 1967), 5–18.

Fourcans, A., and T. J. Hindelang, "A Simulation Approach to Capital Budgeting for the Multinational Firm," paper presented to the 1976 Financial Management Association Conference, Montreal, Canada, October 1976.

Hertz, David B., "Investment Polices That Pay Off," *Harvard Business Review*, 46 (January–February 1968), 96–108.

_____, "Risk Analysis in Capital Investment," *Harvard Business Review*, 42 (January–February 1964), 95–106.

Hespos, Richard F., and Paul A. Strassmann, "Stochastic Decision Trees for the Analysis of Investment Decisions," *Management Science*, 11 (August 1965), 244–259.

Lewellen, Wilbur G., and Michael S. Long, "Simulation Versus Single-Value Estimates in Capital Expenditure Analysis," *Decision Sciences*, 3 (1973), 19–33.

Kryzanowski, Lawrence, Peter Lusztig, and Bernhard Schwab, "Monte Carlo Simulation and Capital Expenditure Decisions—A Case Study," *Engineering Economist*, 18 (Fall 1972), 31–48.

Magee, J. F., "How to Use Decision Trees in Capital Investment," *Harvard Business Review*, 42 (September–October 1964), 79–96.

Naylor, T. H., J. L. Balintfy, D. S. Burdick, and K. Chu, *Computer Simulation Techniques* (New York: John Wiley & Sons, Inc., 1966).

_____, and A. J. Mastai, "Investment in an Automated Warehouse: A Monte Carlo Simulation and Post-Optimality Analysis," *Proceedings of the 1971 Conference on Systems, Networks and Computers*, Mexico City, January 1971.

Philippatos, G. C., *Financial Management: Theory and Techniques* (San Francisco: Holden-Day, Inc., 1973), Chap. 21.

Robichek, Alexander A., "Interpreting the Results of Risk Analysis," *Journal of Finance*, 30 (December 1975), 1384–1386.

Salazar, R. C., and S. K. Sen, "A Simulation Model of Capital Budgeting Under Uncertainty," *Management Science*, 15 (December 1968), 161–179.

Shannon, R. E., *System Simulation: The Art and Science* (Englewood Cliffs, N.J.: Prentice-Hall, Inc., 1975).

Sundem, Gary L., "Evaluating Capital Budgeting Models in Simulated Environments," *Journal of Finance*, 30 (September 1975), 977–992.

Thuesen, G. J., "Nuclear vs. Fossil Power Plants: Evolution of Economic Evaluation Techniques," *The Engineering Economist*, 21 (Fall 1975), 21–38.

Stochastic Programming

Bernhard, Richard H., "Mathematical Programming Models for Capital Budgeting—A Survey, Generalization, and Critique," *Journal of Financial and Quantitative Analysis*, 4 (June 1969), 111–158.

Byrne, R., A. Charnes, W. W. Cooper, and K. Kortenek, "A Chance-Constrained Programming Approach to Capital Budgeting," *Journal of Financial and Quantitative Analysis*, 2 (December 1967), 339–364.

———, A. Charnes, W. W. Cooper, and K. Kortenek, "A Discrete Probability Chance Constrained Capital Budgeting Model–I and II," *Opsearch*, 6 (December 1969) 171–198, 226–261.

Charnes, A., and W. W. Cooper, "Deterministic Equivalents for Optimizing and Satisficing Under Chance Constraints," *Operations Research*, 11 (January 1963), 18–39.

Farrer, D. F., *The Investment Decision Under Uncertainty* (Engelwood Cliffs, N.J.: Prentice-Hall, Inc., 1962).

Hillier, Frederick S., "A Basic Model for Capital Budgeting of Risky Interrelated Projects," *Engineering Economist*, 20 (Fall 1974), 37–49.

———, "Chance-Constrained Programming with 0–1 or Bounded Continuous Decision Variables," *Management Science*, 14 (September 1967), 34–57.

———, "The Derivation of Probabilistic Information for the Evaluation of Risky Investments," *Management Science*, 9 (April 1963), 443–457.

———, *The Evaluation of Risky Interrelated Investments* (Amsterdam: North-Holland Publishing Co., 1969).

Lockett, A. Geoffrey, and Anthony E. Gear, "Multistage Capital Budgeting Under Uncertainty," *Journal of Financial and Quantitative Analysis*, 10 (March 1975), 21–36.

Myers, S. C., "Procedures for Capital Budgeting Under Uncertainty," *Industrial Management Review*, 9 (Spring 1968), 1–15.

Naslund, B., "A Model for Capital Budgeting Under Risk," *Journal of Business*, 39 (April 1966), 257–271.

———, and A. Whinston, "A Model of Multi-Period Investment Under Uncertainty," *Management Science*, 9 (January 1962), 184–200.

Thompson, H. E., "Mathematical Programming, the Capital Asset Pricing Model, and Capital Budgeting of Interrelated Projects," *The Journal of Finance*, 31, 1 (March 1976), 125–131.

Wilson, Robert B., "Investment Analysis Under Uncertainty," *Management Science*, 15 (August 1969), 650–664.

CHAPTER 15

Ankrom, Robert K., "Top-Level Approach to the Foreign Exchange Problem," *Harvard Business Review* (July–August 1974).

Brill, Martin, *An Approach to Risk Analysis in the Evaluation of Capital Ventures* (Philadelphia: Drexel Institute of Technology, 1966).

Carter, E. Eugene, and Rita M. Rodriguez, *International Financial Management* (Englewood Cliffs, N.J.: Prentice-Hall, Inc., 1976).

Chambers, J., S. Mullock, and D. Smith, "The Use of Simulation Models at Corning Glass Works," in A. Schrieber, ed., *Corporate Simulation Models*.

Clark, John J., Margaret T. Clark, and Peter T. Elgers, *Financial Management* (Boston: Holbrook Press, Inc., 1976).

Dunlop, J., F. Harbison, C. Kerr, and C. Meyers, *Industrialism and Industrial Man* (Cambridge, Mass.: Harvard University Press, 1960).

Einzig, P., *Foreign Exchange Crises* (New York: Macmillan Publishing Co., Inc., 1970).

Eiteman, David K., and Stonehill, Arthur I., *Multinational Business Finance* (Reading, Mass.: Addison-Wesley Publishing Co., Inc., 1973).

Feierbend, I., "Conflict, Crisis, and Collision: A Study of International Stability," *Psychology Today* (May 1968).

Friedman, W. G., and G. Kalmanoff, *Joint International Business Ventures* (New York: Columbia University Press, 1961).

Harbison, F., and C. Meyers, *Education, Manpower, and Economic Growth* (New York: McGraw-Hill Book Company, 1966).

"Hedging Against the Franc's Fall," *Business Week* (January 31, 1977), 70–72.

Hertz, D. B., "Investment Policies That Pay Off," *Harvard Business Review* (January 1968), 96–108.

————, "Risk Analysis in Capital Investment," *Harvard Business Review* (January 1964), 95–106.

Hillier, F. S., *The Evaluation of Risky Interrelated Investments* (New York: American Elsevier Publishing Co., 1969).

Kohers, Theodore, "The Effect of Multinational Operation on the Cost of Equity Capital: An Empirical Study," *Management International Review* (1975).

Lessard, D. R., and R. S. Bower, "An Operational Approach to Risk Screening," *Journal of Finance* (May 1973), 245–257.

Lewellen, W. G., and M. S. Long, "Reply to Comments by Bower & Lessard and Gentry," *Decision Sciences*, 4, 4 (October 1973), 575–576.

————, and M. S. Long, "Simulation vs. Single-Value Estimates in Capital Expenditure Analysis," *Decision Sciences*, 3, 4 (October 1972), 19–33.

Lietaer, Bernard, "Managing Risks in Foreign Exchange," *Harvard Business Review* (March 1970), 127–138.

Mao, J. C. T., and J. F. Helliwell, "Investment Decision Under Uncertainty: Theory and Practice," *Journal of Finance*, 24, 2 (May 1969), 323–338.

Mauriel, J. J. "Evaluation and Control of Overseas Operations," *Management Accounting* (May 1969), 35–39.

Naylor, T. H., *Computer Simulation Experiments with Models of Economic Systems* (New York: John Wiley & Sons, Inc., 1971).

Nemmers, and Grunewald, *Basic Managerial Finance*, pp. 360–362.

Robbins, Sidney M., and Robert B. Stobaugh, *Money in the Multinational Enterprise* (New York: Basic Books, Inc., 1973).

Rutenberg, David P., "Maneuvering Liquid Assets in a Multinational Company," *Management Science* (June 1970).

Shannon, R. E., *System Simulation: The Art & Science* (Englewood Cliffs, N.J.: Prentice-Hall, Inc., 1975).

Shapiro, Alan C., "Capital Budgeting for the Multinational Corporation," *Working Paper*, The Wharton School, University of Pennsylvania, December 1976.

————"Exchange Risk Management for the Multinational Corporation," paper presented at the 1974 Financial Management Association Convention, San Diego, Calif., October 1974.

Singer, H. W., *International Development: Growths and Change* (New York: McGraw-Hill Book Company, 1964).

Smith, Dennis E., "Requirements for an 'Optimizer' for Computer Simulations," *Naval Research Logistics Quarterly*, 20, 1 (March 1973), 161–179.

Stobaugh, R. B. "How to Analyze Foreign Investment Climates," *Harvard Business Review* (September–October 1969), 100–108.

Stonehill, Arthur D., and Leonard Nathanson, "Capital Budgeting and the Multinational Corporation," *California Management Review* (Summer 1968).

Truitt, J. F., "Expropriation of Private Foreign Investment: A Framework to Consider the Post World War II Experience of British and American Investors," unpublished D.B.A. dissertation, Indiana University, 1971.

Van Horne, J. C., *Financial Management and Policy*, 3rd ed. (Englewood Cliffs, N.J.: Prentice-Hall, Inc., 1974).

Weston, J. F., and E. F. Brigham, *Managerial Finance*, 5th ed. (Hinsdale, Ill.: The Dryden Press, 1975).

Zenoff, David B., and Jack Zwick, *International Financial Management* (Englewood Cliffs, N.J.: Prentice-Hall, Inc., 1969).

CHAPTER 16

American Institute of Certified Public Accountants, Accounting Principles Board, *Opinion 5*, "Reporting of Leases in Financial Statements of Lessee" (September 1964), and *Opinion 31*, "Disclosure of Lease Commitments by Lessees" (June 1973).

American Management Association, *Taking Stock of Leasing: A Practical Appraisal* (New York, 1965).

Anthony, R. N., and S. Schwartz, *Office Equipment, Buy or Rent?* (Boston: Management Analysis Center, Inc., 1957).

Archer, W. R. V., "Lease or Buy Decisions," *Accountant*, 162, 4964 (February 5, 1970), 193–196.

Basi, Bart A., "Tax Aspects of Leasing: Lessee's Viewpoint," *Tax Executive*, 27, 4 (July 1975), 365–378.

Batkin, A., "Leasing vs. Buying; A Guide for the Perplexed," *Financial Executive*, 41 (June 1973), 63–68.

Beechy, T. H., "The Cost of Leasing: Comment and Correction," *Accounting Review*, 45 (October 1970), 769–773.

————, "Quasi-Debt Analysis of Financial Leases," *Accounting Review*, 44 (April 1969), 375–381.

Benjamin, James J., and Robert H. Strawser, "Developments in Lease Accounting," *CPA Journal*, 46, 11 (November 1976), 33–36.

Bierman, Harold, Jr., "Accounting for Capitalized Leases: Tax Considerations," *Accounting Review*, 48, 2 (April 1973), 421–424.

Bower, R. S., "Issues in Lease Financing," *Financial Management* (Winter 1973), 25–34.

————, F. C. Herringer, and J. P. Williamson, "Lease Evaluation," *Accounting Review*, 41 (April 1966), 257–265.

Chamberlain, Douglas C., "Capitalization of Lease Obligations," *Management Accounting*, 57, 6 (December 1975), 37–38, 42.

Chasteen, Lanny G., "Implicit Factors in the Evaluation of Lease vs. Buy Alternatives," *Accounting Review*, 48, 4 (October 1973), 764–767.

Cooper, Kerry, and Robert H. Strawser, "Evaluation of Capital Investment Projects Involving Asset Leases," *Financial Management*, 4, 1 (Spring 1976), 44–49.

Davidson, Sidney, and Roman L. Weil, "Lease Capitalization and Inflation Accounting," *Financial Analysts Journal*, 31, 6 (November–December 1975), 22–29, 57.

Defliese, Philip L., "Accounting for Leases: A Broader Perspective," *Financial Executive*, 42, 7 (July 1974), 14–23.

Doenges, E. C., "The Cost of Leasing," *Engineering Economist*, 17 (Winter 1971), 31–44.

Elliott, Grover S., "Leasing of Capital Equipment," *Management Accounting*, 57, 6 (December 1975), 39–42.

Ferrara, W. L., "Capital Budgeting and Financing or Leasing Decision," *Management Accounting*, 49 (July 1968), 55–63.

_____, "Lease vs. Purchase: a Quasi-Financing Approach," *Management Accounting*, 56 (January 1974), 21–26.

_____, "Should Investment and Financing Decisions Be Separated?" *Accounting Review*, 41 (January 1966), 106–114.

Findlay, M. Chapman, III, "A Sensitivity Analysis of IRR Leasing Models," *Engineering Economist*, 20, 4 (Summer 1975), 231–241.

Gant, D. R., "A Critical Look at Lease Financing," *Controller*, 29 (June 1961), 274–277, 311–312.

_____, "Illusion in Lease Financing," *Harvard Business Review*, 37 (March–April 1959), 121–142.

Gordon, M. J., "A General Solution to the Buy or Lease Decision: A Pedogogical Note," *Journal of Finance*, 29 (March 1974), 245–250.

Griesinger, F. K., "Pros and Cons of Leasing Equipment," *Harvard Business Review*, 33 (March–April 1955), 75–89.

Hamel, H. G., *Leasing in Industry* (New York: National Industrial Conference Board, 1968).

Hawkins, D. F., and M. M. Wehle, *Accounting for Leases* (New York: Financial Executives Research Foundation, 1973).

Honig, Lawrence E., and Stephen C. Coley, "An After-Tax Equivalent Payment Approach to Conventional Lease Analysis," *Financial Management*, 4, 4 (Winter 1975), 28–35.

Jackson, J. F., Jr., *An Evaluation of Finance Leasing* (Austin, Tex.: Bureau of Business Research, University of Texas, 1967).

Johnson, R. W., and W. G. Lewellen, "Analysis of the Lease or Buy Decision," *Journal of Finance*, 27 (September 1972), 815–823.

Knutson, P. H., "Leased Equipment and Divisional Return on Capital," *N.A.A. Bulletin*, 44 (November 1962), 15–20.

Law, W. A., and M. C. Crum, *Equipment Leasing and Commercial Banks* (Chicago: Association of Reserve City Bankers, 1963).

Leasing of Industrial Equipment (Washington, D.C.: Machinery and Allied Products Institute, 1965).

MacEachron, W. D., "Leasing: A Discounted Cash-Flow Approach," *Controller*, 29 (May 1961), 213–219.

McLean, J. H., "Economic and Accounting Aspects of Lease Financing," *Financial Executive*, 31 (December 1963), 18–23.

Metz, D. H., *Leasing Standards and Procedures* (Kaukauna, Wis.: Thomas Publications, 1968).

Mitchell, G. B., "After-Tax Cost of Leasing," *Accounting Review*, 45 (April 1970), 308–314.

Nantell, Timothy, "Equivalence of Lease vs. Buy Analyses," *Financial Management*, 2, 3 (Autumn 1973), 61–65.

Parker, G. G. C., "The Lease: Use Without Ownership," *Columbia Journal of World Business*, 5 (September–October 1970), 77–82.

Reilly, F., "A Direct Cost Lease Evaluation Method," *Bank Administration* (July 1972), 22–26.

Roenfeldt, Rodney L, and James B. Henry, "Lease vs. Debt Purchase of Automobiles," *Management Accounting*, 58, 4 (October 1976), 49–54.

_____, and J. S. Osteryoung, "Analysis of Financial Leases," *Financial Management* (Spring 1973), 74–87.

Sartoris, William L., and Ronda S. Paul, "Lease Evaluation—Another Capital Budgeting Decision," *Financial Management*, 2, 2 (Summer 1973), 46–52.

Sax, F. S., "Lease or Purchase Decision—Present Value Method," *Management Accounting*, 47 (October 1965), 55–61.

Thulin, W. B., "Own or Lease: Underlying Financial Theory," *Financial Executive*, 32 (April 1964), 23–24, 28–31.

———, *Leasing of Industrial Equipment* (New York: McGraw-Hill Book Company, 1963).

Vanciel, R. F., "Lease or Borrow: New Method of Analysis," *Harvard Business Review*, 39 (September–October 1961), 122–136.

———, "Lease or Borrow: Steps in Negotiation," *Harvard Business Review*, 39 (November–December 1961), 138–159.

———, and Robert N. Anthony, "The Financial Community Looks at Leasing," *Harvard Business Review*, 37 (November–December 1959), 113–130.

Vanderwicken, P., "The Powerful Logic of the Leasing Boom," *Fortune* (November 1973).

Westbrook, David N., "Accounting for Long-Term Leases," *Cost and Management*, 48, 3 (May–June 1974), 54–58.

Weston, J. F., and R. Craig, "Understanding Lease Financing," *California Management Review*, 2 (Winter 1960), 67–75.

Wilson, C. J., "The Operating Lease and the Risk of Obsolescence," *Management Accounting*, 55 (December 1973), 41–44.

Wyman, H. E., "Financial Lease Evaluation Under Conditions of Uncertainty," *Accounting Review*, 48 (July 1973), 489–493.

Zises, A., "Lease Financing: A Reply," *Controller*, 29 (September 1961), 414–423.

CHAPTER 17

Alberts, William W., and Segall, Joel E., *The Corporate Merger* (Chicago: University of Chicago Press, 1966).

AICPA, Inc., *Accounting for Business Combinations* (Chicago: Commerce Clearing House, 1973), pp 901–942, 5321–5361.

———, *Accounting Principles Board Opinions* 16-17 (August 1970).

———, *Accounting Research Bulletin No. 48—Business Combinations* (January 1957).

AMA, *Corporate Growth Through Merger and Acquisitions* (1963).

Ansoff, H. Igor, *Acquisition Behavior of U.S. Manufacturing Firms*, 1946-65 (Nashville, Tenn.: Vanderbilt University Press, 1971).

Backman, Jules, "An Economist Looks at Accounting for Business Combinations," *Financial Analysts Journal* (July–August 1970), 39–48.

Bagley, Edward R., *Beyond the Conglomerates: The Impact of the Supercorporations on the Future Life and Business* (New York: AMACOM, 1975).

Bock, Betty, *Antitrust Issues in Conglomerate Acquisitions: Tracking a Moving Target* (New York: National Industrial Conference Board, 1969).

———, *Mergers and Markets* (New York: National Industrial Conference Board, 1969).

———, *Statistical Games and The "200 Largest" Industrials: 1954 and 1968* (New York: National Industrial Conference Board, 1970).

Briloff, Abraham J., "Dirty Pooling—How to Succeed in Business Without Really Trying," *Barron's* (July 15, 1968).

———, "Grime Shelter," *Barron's* (October 25, 1971).

———, "Much Abused Goodwill," *Barron's* (April 28, 1969).

———, *Unaccountable Accounting* (New York: Harper & Row, Inc., 1972).

———, "You Deserve a Break . . . ," *Barron's* (July 8, 1974).

Catlett, George R., and Norman O., Olson, *Accounting for Goodwill* (New York: AICPA, 1968).

Committee of Experts on Restrictive Business Practices, *Mergers and Competitive Policy: A Report* (Paris: Organization for Economic Co-operation and Development, 1974).

Conglomerate Mergers and Acquisitions (New York: St. John's Law Review Association, 1970).

Editors of Fortune, *The Conglomerate Commotion* (New York: Viking Press, Inc., 1970).

Foster, William C., "Does Pooling Present Fairly?" *CPA Journal* (December 1974), 36–41.

_____, "The Illogic of Pooling," *Financial Executive* (December 1974), 16–21.

_____, "Setting Standards for Treasury Shares," *Financial Executive* (February 1974), 48–52.

"Gimmick for All Seasons," *Forbes* (October 1, 1975), 60–62.

Gunther, Samuel P., "Lingering Pooling Problems," *The CPA Journal* (June 1973), 459–463.

Harvey, John L., and Albert Newgarden, *Management Guide to Mergers & Acquisitions* (New York: John Wiley & Sons, Inc., 1969).

Hawkins, David E., *Corporate Financial Reporting* (Homewood, Ill.: Richard D. Irwin, Inc., 1971).

Hutchinson, G. Scott, *The Business of Acquisitions and Mergers* (New York: Presidents Publishing House, 1968).

Kemp, Bernard A., *Understanding Merger Activity* (New York: New York University, 1969).

Knortz, Herbert C., "The Realities of Business Combinations," *Financial Analysts Journal* (July–August 1970), 28–32.

Laporte, Lowell, *Merger Policy in the Smaller Firm* (New York: National Industrial Conference Board, 1969).

Libby, Robert, "The Early Impact of APB Opinions No. 16 & 17, An Empirical Study," *CPA Journal* (October 1972), 839–842.

Linowes, David F., *Managing Growth Through Acquisitions* (New York: AMA, 1968).

Little, Arthur D., Inc., *Mergers and Acquisitions* (Cambridge, Mass.: 1963).

Marrow, Alfred J., David G. Powers, and Stanley E. Seashore, *Management By Participation* (New York: Harper & Row, Inc., 1967).

Mase, Myles La Grange, *Management Problems of Corporate Acquisitions* (Cambridge, Mass.: Harvard University Press, 1962).

McCarthy, George D., *Acquisitions and Mergers* (New York: The Ronald Press Company, 1963).

McCord, Jim, and Robert J. Oziel, *Conglomerates & Cogenerics* (New York: Practicing Law Institute, 1970).

Miller, Malcolm C., "Goodwill—An Aggregation Issue," *The Accounting Review* (April 1973), 286–291.

Narver, John C., *Conglomerate Mergers and Market Competition* (Berkeley, Calif.: University of California Press, 1967).

Nelson, Ralph Lowell, *Merger Movements in American Industry* (Princeton, N.J.: Princeton University Press, 1959), pp. 1895–1956.

Nicholson, John W., "Treasury Stock and Pooling of Interest," *CPA Journal* (October 1973), 913–915.

PBA Accounting Principles (New York: AICPA, 1973).

Pivar, Samuel, "Implementation of APB Opinions Nos. 16 & 17," *CPA Journal* (October 1973), 58–65.

Reid, Samuel Richardson, *Mergers, Managers, and the Economy* (New York: McGraw-Hill Book Company, 1968).

Samuels, John Malcolm, *Readings on Mergers & Takeovers* (New York: St. Martin's Press, 1972).

Sapienza, Samuel R., "Pooling Theory & Practice in Business Combinations," *Accounting Review* (April, 1962), 263–278.

Sauerhaft, Stan, *The Merger Game* (New York: T. Y. Crowell, Inc., 1971).

Seidman, J. S., "Pooling Must Go," *Barron's* (July 1 1968).

Short, Robert A., *Business Mergers* (Englewood Cliffs, N.J.: Prentice-Hall, Inc., 1967).

Steiner, Peter Otto, *Mergers: Motives Effects Policies* (Ann Arbor, Mich.: University of Michigan Press, 1976).

Strage, Mark, *Acquisition and Merger Negotiations* (New York: Presidents Publishing House, 1971).

Tearney, Michael G., "Accounting for Goodwill: A Realistic Approach," *Journal of Accountancy* (July 1973), 41–45.

Townsend, Harry, *Scale, Innovation, Merger and Monopoly* (Oxford: Pergamon Press, 1968).

Wakefield, B. Richard, "The Accounting Principles Board on the Wrong Track," *Financial Analyst Journal* (July–August 1973), 33–36.

Welcome to Our Conglomerate—You're Fired! (New York: Delacorte Press, 1971).

Winslow, John F., *Conglomerates Unlimited* (Bloomington, Ind.: Indiana University Press, 1973).

Wyatt, Arthur R., *A Critical Study of Accounting For Business Combinations* (New York: AICPA, 1963).

———, "Inequities in Accounting for Business Combinations," *Financial Executive* (December 1972), 28–35.

———, and Donald E. Kieso, *Business Combinations: Planning and Action* (Scranton, Pa.: International Textbook Company, 1969).

CHAPTER 18

Bogue, M., and R. Roll, "Capital Budgeting of Risky Projects with Imperfect Markets for Physical Capital," *Journal of Finance* (May 1974), 601–613.

Bonini, Charles P., "Capital Investment Under Uncertainty with Abandonment Options," *Journal Of Financial And Quantitative Analysis* (March 1977), 39–54.

Brennan, M. J., "An Approach to the Evaluation of Uncertain Income Streams," *Journal of Finance* (June 1973), 661–674.

Childs, Wendell M., "Management of Capital Expenditures," *Management Accounting* (January 1970), 37–40.

Dyl, Edward A., and Hugh W. Long, "Comments," *Journal of Finance* (March 1969), 88–95.

Fremgen, James M., "Capital Budgeting Practices: A Survey," *Management Accounting* (May 1973), 19–25.

Hall, Thomas W., "Post Completion Audit Procedure," *Management Accounting* (September 1975), 33–37.

Hastie, K. Larry, "One Businessman's View of Capital Budgeting," *Financial Management* (Winter 1974), 36–44.

Hicks, Carl F., Jr., and L. Lee Schmidt, Jr., "Post-Auditing the Capital Budgeting Decision," *Management Accounting* (August 1971), 24–32.

Jarrett, Jeffrey E., "An Abandonment Decision Model," *Engineering Economist* (Fall 1973), 35–46.

Joy, O. Maurice, "Abandonment Values and Abandonment Decisions: A Clarification," *Journal of Finance* (September 1976), 1225–1228.

Kemp, Patrick S., "Post-Completion Audits of Capital Investment Projects," *Management Accounting* (August 1966), 49–54.

Mao, James C. T., "Survey of Capital Budgeting: Theory and Practice," *Journal of Finance* (May 1970), 349–360.

Montgomery, John L., "Appraising Capital Expenditures," *Management Accounting* (September 1965), 3–10.

New Hauser, John J., and Jerr A. Viscione, "How Managers Feel About Advanced Capital Budgeting Methods," *Management Review* (September 1973), 16–22.

Petry, Glenn H., "Effective Use of Capital Budgeting Tools," *Business Horizons* (October 1975), 57–65.

Petty, J. William, David F. Scott, Jr., and Monroe M. Bird, "The Capital Expenditure Decision-Making Process of Large Corporations," *Engineering Economist* (Spring 1975), 159–172.

Robichek, Alexander A., and James C. Van Horne, "Abandonment Value and Capital Budgeting," *Journal of Finance* (December 1967), 577–589.

_____, and James C. Van Horne, "Reply," *Journal of Finance* (March 1969), 96–97.

Schnell, James S., and Roy S. Nicolosi, "Capital Expenditure Feedback: Project Reappraisal," *Engineering Economist*, 19 (July–August 1974), 253–261.

Schwab, B., and P. Lusztig, "A Note on Abandonment Value and Capital Budgeting," *Journal of Financial and Quantitative Analysis* (September 1970), 377–379.

Shillinglaw, Gordon, "Profit Analysis for Abandonment Decisions," in Ezra Solomon, ed., *The Management of Corporate Capital* (New York: The Free Press, 1959), pp. 269–281.

Spies, Richard R., "The Dynamies of Corporate Capital Budgeting," *Journal of Finance* (June 1974), 829–845.

Vandell, Robert F., and Paul J. Stonich, "Capital Budgeting: Theory or Results?" *Financial Executive* (August 1973), 46–56.

Vernon, Thomas H., "Capital Budgeting and the Evaluation Process," *Management Accounting* (October 1972), 19–24.

Weaver, James B., "Organizing and Maintaining a Capital Expenditure Program," *Engineering Economist* (Fall 1974), 1–35.

Weinwurm, Ernest H., "Utilization of Sophisticated Capital Budgeting Techniques in Industry," *Engineering Economist* (Summer 1974), 271–272.

APPENDIX B
COMPARATIVE
DEPRECIATION TABLES*

The following tables show the annual and cumulative depreciation for various useful lives under the straight-line, 200%-declining-balance, 150%-declining-balance, 125%-declining-balance, and sum-of-the-years-digits methods. *All amounts are expressed as percentages of the basis of the property at the time the useful life begins.*

Year	Straight-Line		200%-Declining-Balance		150%-Declining-Balance		Sum-of-Digits	
	Annual %	Cum. %	Annual %	Cum. %	Annual %	Cum. %	Annual %	Cum. %
3-Year Life								
1	33.33	33.33	66.66	66.66	50.00	50.00	50.00	50.00
2	33.33	66.66	22.22	88.88	25.00	75.00	33.33	83.33
3	33.34	100.00	7.41	96.29	12.50	87.50	16.67	100.00
4-Year Life								
1	25.00	25.00	50.00	50.00	37.50	37.50	40.00	40.00
2	25.00	50.00	25.00	75.00	23.44	60.94	30.00	70.00
3	25.00	75.00	12.50	87.50	14.65	75.59	20.00	90.00
4	25.00	100.00	6.25	93.75	9.15	84.74	10.00	100.00
5-Year Life								
1	20.00	20.00	40.00	40.00	30.00	30.00	33.33	33.33
2	20.00	40.00	24.00	64.00	21.00	51.00	26.67	60.00
3	20.00	60.00	14.40	78.40	14.70	65.70	20.00	80.00
4	20.00	80.00	8.64	87.04	10.29	75.99	13.33	93.33
5	20.00	100.00	5.18	92.22	7.20	83.19	6.67	100.00
6-Year Life								
1	16.67	16.67	33.34	33.34	25.00	25.00	28.57	28.57
2	16.67	33.34	22.22	55.56	18.75	43.75	23.81	52.38
3	16.66	50.00	14.81	70.37	14.06	57.81	19.05	71.43
4	16.67	66.67	9.87	80.24	10.55	68.36	14.29	85.72
5	16.67	83.34	6.58	86.82	7.91	76.27	9.52	95.24
6	16.66	100.00	4.39	91.21	5.93	82.20	4.76	100.00
7-Year Life								
1	14.28	14.28	28.57	28.57	21.43	21.43	25.00	25.00
2	14.28	28.56	20.41	48.98	16.83	38.26	21.43	46.43
3	14.29	42.85	14.58	63.56	13.23	51.49	17.86	64.29
4	14.29	57.14	10.41	73.97	10.40	61.89	14.29	78.58
5	14.29	71.43	7.44	81.41	8.17	70.06	10.71	89.29
6	14.29	85.72	5.31	86.72	6.42	76.48	7.14	96.43
7	14.28	100.00	3.79	90.51	5.04	81.52	3.57	100.00

*Source: *Business and Financial Tables Desk Book*, Institute for Business Planning, Englewood Cliffs. N.J. 07632, pages 181–189. Used with the permission of the publisher.

Comparative Depreciation Tables *(continued)*

Year	Straight-Line		200%-Declining-Balance		150%-Declining-Balance		125%-Declining-Balance *		Sum-of-Digits	
	Annual %	Cum. %	Annual %	Cum. %	Annual %	Cum. %	Annual %	Cum. %	Annual %	Cum. %
8-Year Life										
1	12.50	12.50	25.00	25.00	18.75	18.75			22.22	22.22
2	12.50	25.00	18.75	43.75	15.23	33.98			19.44	41.66
3	12.50	37.50	14.06	57.81	12.38	46.36			16.67	58.33
4	12.50	50.00	10.55	68.36	10.06	56.42			13.89	72.22
5	12.50	62.50	7.91	76.27	8.17	64.59			11.11	83.33
6	12.50	75.00	5.93	82.20	6.64	71.23			8.33	91.66
7	12.50	87.50	4.45	86.65	5.39	76.62			5.56	97.22
8	12.50	100.00	3.34	89.99	4.38	81.00			2.78	100.00
9-Year Life										
1	11.11	11.11	22.22	22.22	16.67	16.67			20.00	20.00
2	11.11	22.22	17.28	39.50	13.89	30.56			17.78	37.78
3	11.11	33.33	13.44	52.94	11.57	42.13			15.56	53.34
4	11.11	44.44	10.45	63.39	9.65	51.78			13.33	66.67
5	11.11	55.55	8.13	71.52	8.04	59.82			11.11	77.78
6	11.11	66.66	6.32	77.84	6.70	66.52			8.89	86.67
7	11.11	77.77	4.92	82.76	5.58	72.10			6.67	93.34
8	11.11	88.88	3.83	86.59	4.65	76.75			4.44	97.78
9	11.12	100.00	2.98	89.57	3.88	80.63			2.22	100.00
10-Year Life										
1	10.00	10.00	20.00	20.00	15.00	15.00			18.18	18.18
2	10.00	20.00	16.00	36.00	12.75	27.75			16.37	34.55
3	10.00	30.00	12.80	48.80	10.84	38.59			14.56	49.09
4	10.00	40.00	10.24	59.04	9.21	47.80			12.73	61.82
5	10.00	50.00	8.19	67.23	7.83	55.63			10.91	72.73
6	10.00	60.00	6.56	73.79	6.66	62.29			9.09	81.82
7	10.00	70.00	5.24	79.03	5.66	67.95			7.27	89.09
8	10.00	80.00	4.19	83.22	4.81	72.76			5.46	94.55
9	10.00	90.00	3.36	86.58	4.09	76.85			3.63	98.18
10	10.00	100.00	2.68	89.26	3.47	80.32			1.82	100.00
15-Year Life										
1	6.67	6.67	13.33	13.33	10.00	10.00			12.50	12.50
2	6.66	13.33	11.56	24.89	9.00	19.00			11.67	24.17
3	6.67	20.00	10.01	34.90	8.10	27.10			10.83	35.00
4	6.67	26.67	8.68	43.58	7.29	34.39			10.00	45.00
5	6.66	33.33	7.53	51.11	6.56	40.95			9.17	54.17
6	6.67	40.00	6.51	57.62	5.90	46.85			8.33	62.50
7	6.67	46.67	5.65	63.27	5.32	52.17			7.50	70.00
8	6.66	53.33	4.90	68.17	4.78	56.95			6.67	76.67
9	6.67	60.00	4.25	72.42	4.30	61.25			5.83	82.50
10	6.67	66.67	3.67	76.09	3.88	65.13			5.00	87.50
11	6.66	73.33	3.19	79.28	3.49	68.62			4.17	91.67
12	6.67	80.00	2.76	82.04	3.14	71.76			3.33	95.00
13	6.67	86.67	2.40	84.44	2.82	74.58			2.50	97.50
14	6.66	93.33	2.07	86.51	2.54	77.12			1.67	99.17
15	6.67	100.00	1.80	88.31	2.29	79.41			.83	100.00

*Available for used residential real estate acquired after 7/24/69 and having useful life of 20 years or more when acquired.

423

Comparative Depreciation Tables *(continued)*

Year	Straight-Line		200%-Declining-Balance		150%-Declining-Balance		125%-Declining-Balance		Sum-of-Digits	
	Annual %	Cum. %	Annual %	Cum. %	Annual %	Cum. %	Annual %	Cum. %	Annual %	Cum. %
					20-Year Life					
1	5.00	5.00	10.00	10.00	7.50	7.50	6.25	6.25	9.52	9.52
2	5.00	10.00	9.00	19.00	6.94	14.44	5.86	12.11	9.05	18.57
3	5.00	15.00	8.10	27.10	6.42	20.86	5.49	17.60	8.57	27.14
4	5.00	20.00	7.29	34.39	5.94	26.80	5.15	22.75	8.10	35.24
5	5.00	25.00	6.56	40.95	5.49	32.29	4.83	27.58	7.62	42.86
6	5.00	30.00	5.91	46.86	5.08	37.37	4.53	32.11	7.14	50.00
7	5.00	35.00	5.31	52.17	4.70	42.07	4.24	36.35	6.67	56.67
8	5.00	40.00	4.78	56.95	4.35	46.42	3.98	40.33	6.19	62.86
9	5.00	45.00	4.31	61.26	4.02	50.44	3.73	44.06	5.71	68.57
10	5.00	50.00	3.87	65.13	3.71	54.15	3.50	47.55	5.24	73.81
11	5.00	55.00	3.49	68.62	3.44	57.59	3.28	50.83	4.76	78.57
12	5.00	60.00	3.14	71.76	3.18	60.77	3.07	53.90	4.29	82.86
13	5.00	65.00	2.82	74.58	2.94	63.71	2.88	56.79	3.81	86.67
14	5.00	70.00	2.54	77.12	2.72	66.43	2.70	59.49	3.33	90.00
15	5.00	75.00	2.29	79.41	2.52	68.95	2.53	62.02	2.86	92.86
16	5.00	80.00	2.06	81.47	2.33	71.28	2.37	64.39	2.38	95.24
17	5.00	85.00	1.85	83.32	2.15	73.43	2.23	66.62	1.90	97.14
18	5.00	90.00	1.67	84.99	1.99	75.42	2.09	68.70	1.43	98.57
19	5.00	95.00	1.50	86.49	1.84	77.26	1.96	70.66	.95	99.52
20	5.00	100.00	1.35	87.84	1.70	78.96	1.83	72.49	.48	100.00
					25-Year Life					
1	4.00	4.00	8.00	8.00	6.00	6.00	5.00	5.00	7.69	7.69
2	4.00	8.00	7.36	15.36	5.64	11.64	4.75	9.75	7.39	15.08
3	4.00	12.00	6.77	22.13	5.30	16.94	4.51	14.26	7.07	22.15
4	4.00	16.00	6.23	28.36	4.98	21.92	4.29	18.55	6.77	28.92
5	4.00	20.00	5.73	34.09	4.68	26.60	4.07	22.62	6.47	35.39
6	4.00	24.00	5.27	39.36	4.40	31.00	3.87	26.49	6.15	41.54
7	4.00	28.00	4.86	44.22	4.14	35.14	3.68	30.17	5.85	47.39
8	4.00	32.00	4.46	48.68	3.89	39.03	3.49	33.66	5.53	52.92
9	4.00	36.00	4.10	52.78	3.66	42.69	3.32	36.98	5.23	58.15
10	4.00	40.00	3.78	56.56	3.43	46.12	3.15	40.13	4.93	63.08
11	4.00	44.00	3.48	60.04	3.23	49.35	2.99	43.12	4.61	67.69
12	4.00	48.00	3.19	63.23	3.03	52.38	2.84	45.96	4.31	72.00
13	4.00	52.00	2.94	66.17	2.86	55.24	2.70	48.67	4.00	76.00
14	4.00	56.00	2.71	68.88	2.68	57.92	2.57	51.23	3.69	79.69
15	4.00	60.00	2.49	71.37	2.52	60.44	2.44	53.67	3.39	83.08
16	4.00	64.00	2.29	73.66	2.37	62.81	2.32	55.99	3.07	86.15
17	4.00	68.00	2.11	75.77	2.23	65.04	2.20	58.19	2.77	88.92
18	4.00	72.00	1.94	77.71	2.10	67.14	2.09	60.28	2.47	91.39
19	4.00	76.00	1.78	79.49	1.97	69.11	1.99	62.26	2.15	93.54
20	4.00	80.00	1.64	81.13	1.85	70.96	1.89	64.15	1.85	95.39

Comparative Depreciation Tables *(continued)*

Year	Straight-Line		200%-Declining-Balance		150%-Declining-Balance		125%-Declining-Balance		Sum-of-Digits	
	Annual %	Cum. %	Annual %	Cum. %	Annual %	Cum. %	Annual %	Cum. %	Annual %	Cum. %
				25-Year Life *(continued)*						
21	4.00	84.00	1.51	82.64	1.74	72.70	1.79	65.94	1.53	96.92
22	4.00	88.00	1.39	84.03	1.64	74.34	1.70	67.65	1.23	98.15
23	4.00	92.00	1.28	85.31	1.54	75.88	1.62	69.26	.93	99.08
24	4.00	96.00	1.17	86.48	1.45	77.33	1.54	70.80	.61	99.69
25	4.00	100.00	1.08	87.56	1.36	78.69	1.46	72.26	.31	100.00
				30-Year Life						
1	3.33	3.33	6.67	6.67	5.00	5.00	4.16	4.16	6.45	6.45
2	3.34	6.67	6.22	12.89	4.75	9.75	3.99	8.16	6.24	12.69
3	3.33	10.00	5.81	18.70	4.51	14.26	3.83	11.99	6.02	18.71
4	3.33	13.33	5.42	24.12	4.29	18.55	3.67	15.65	5.81	24.52
5	3.34	16.67	5.06	29.18	4.07	22.62	3.51	19.17	5.59	30.11
6	3.33	20.00	4.72	33.90	3.87	26.49	3.37	22.54	5.37	35.48
7	3.33	23.33	4.40	38.30	3.68	30.17	3.23	25.76	5.17	40.65
8	3.34	26.67	4.12	42.42	3.49	33.66	3.09	28.86	4.94	45.59
9	3.33	30.00	3.84	46.26	3.32	36.98	2.96	31.82	4.73	50.32
10	3.33	33.33	3.58	49.84	3.15	40.13	2.84	34.66	4.52	54.84
11	3.34	36.67	3.34	53.18	2.99	43.12	2.72	37.38	4.30	59.14
12	3.33	40.00	3.12	56.30	2.84	45.96	2.61	39.99	4.09	63.23
13	3.33	43.33	2.92	59.22	2.70	48.66	2.50	42.49	3.87	67.10
14	3.34	46.67	2.72	61.94	2.57	51.23	2.40	44.89	3.65	70.75
15	3.33	50.00	2.53	64.47	2.44	53.67	2.30	47.19	3.44	74.19
16	3.33	53.33	2.37	66.84	2.32	55.99	2.20	49.39	3.23	77.42
17	3.34	56.67	2.21	69.05	2.20	58.19	2.11	51.50	3.01	80.43
18	3.33	60.00	2.07	71.12	2.09	60.28	2.02	53.52	2.80	83.23
19	3.33	63.33	1.92	73.04	1.99	62.27	1.94	55.45	2.58	85.81
20	3.34	66.67	1.80	74.84	1.89	64.16	1.86	57.31	2.36	88.17
21	3.33	70.00	1.68	76.52	1.80	65.96	1.78	59.09	2.15	90.32
22	3.33	73.33	1.56	78.08	1.70	67.66	1.70	60.79	1.94	92.26
23	3.34	76.67	1.46	79.54	1.62	69.28	1.63	62.43	1.72	93.98
24	3.33	80.00	1.37	80.91	1.54	70.82	1.57	63.99	1.61	95.49
25	3.33	83.33	1.27	82.18	1.46	72.28	1.50	65.49	1.29	96.78
26	3.34	86.67	1.19	83.37	1.39	73.67	1.44	66.93	1.07	97.85
27	3.33	90.00	1.11	84.48	1.32	74.99	1.38	68.31	.86	98.71
28	3.33	93.33	1.03	85.51	1.25	76.24	1.32	69.63	.65	99.36
29	3.34	96.67	.97	86.48	1.19	77.43	1.27	70.89	.43	99.79
30	3.33	100.00	.90	87.38	1.13	78.56	1.21	72.11	.21	100.00
				33-1/3 Year Life						
1	3.00	3.00	6.00	6.00	4.50	4.50	3.75	3.75	5.82	5.82
2	3.00	6.00	5.64	11.64	4.30	8.80	3.61	7.36	5.65	11.47
3	3.00	9.00	5.30	16.94	4.10	12.90	3.47	10.83	5.47	16.95
4	3.00	12.00	4.98	21.93	3.92	16.82	3.34	14.18	5.30	22.25
5	3.00	15.00	4.68	26.61	3.74	20.56	3.22	17.40	5.17	27.37

Comparative Depreciation Tables (continued)

Year	Straight-Line Annual %	Straight-Line Cum. %	200%-Declining-Balance Annual %	200%-Declining-Balance Cum. %	150%-Declining-Balance Annual %	150%-Declining-Balance Cum. %	125%-Declining-Balance Annual %	125%-Declining-Balance Cum. %	Sum-of-Digits Annual %	Sum-of-Digits Cum. %
				33-1/3 Year Life (continued)						
6	3.00	18.00	4.40	31.00	3.57	24.14	3.10	20.49	4.95	32.32
7	3.00	21.00	4.14	35.15	3.41	27.55	2.98	23.47	4.76	37.10
8	3.00	24.00	3.89	39.03	3.16	30.81	2.87	26.34	4.60	41.70
9	3.00	27.00	3.66	42.70	3.11	33.93	2.76	29.11	4.43	46.13
10	3.00	30.00	3.44	46.14	2.97	36.90	2.66	31.77	4.25	50.38
11	3.00	33.00	3.23	49.37	2.84	39.74	2.56	34.32	4.08	54.46
12	3.00	36.00	3.04	52.41	2.71	42.45	2.46	36.79	3.90	58.36
13	3.00	39.00	2.86	55.26	2.59	45.04	2.37	39.16	3.73	62.10
14	3.00	42.00	2.68	57.95	2.47	47.51	2.28	41.44	3.55	65.64
15	3.00	45.00	2.52	60.47	2.36	49.88	2.20	43.63	3.38	69.02
16	3.00	48.00	2.37	62.84	2.26	52.13	2.11	45.75	3.20	72.22
17	3.00	51.00	2.23	65.07	2.15	54.29	2.03	47.78	3.03	75.25
18	3.00	54.00	2.10	67.17	2.06	56.34	1.95	49.74	2.85	78.10
19	3.00	57.00	1.97	69.14	1.96	58.31	1.88	51.63	2.68	80.78
20	3.00	60.00	1.85	71.00	1.88	60.18	1.81	53.44	2.50	83.28
21	3.00	63.00	1.74	72.73	1.79	61.97	1.75	55.19	2.33	85.61
22	3.00	66.00	1.64	74.37	1.71	63.69	1.68	56.87	2.15	87.77
23	3.00	69.00	1.54	75.90	1.63	65.32	1.62	58.48	1.98	89.75
24	3.00	72.00	1.45	77.35	1.56	66.88	1.56	60.04	1.81	91.56
25	3.00	75.00	1.36	78.71	1.49	68.37	1.50	61.54	1.63	93.19
26	3.00	78.00	1.28	79.99	1.42	69.79	1.44	62.98	1.46	94.64
27	3.00	81.00	1.20	81.19	1.36	71.15	1.39	64.37	1.28	95.92
28	3.00	84.00	1.13	82.32	1.30	72.45	1.34	65.71	1.11	97.03
29	3.00	87.00	1.06	83.38	1.24	73.69	1.29	66.99	.93	97.96
30	3.00	90.00	1.00	84.37	1.18	74.88	1.24	68.23	.76	98.72
31	3.00	93.00	.94	85.31	1.13	76.01	1.19	69.42	.58	99.30
32	3.00	96.00	.88	86.19	1.08	77.09	1.15	70.57	.41	99.71
33	3.00	99.00	.93	87.02	1.03	78.12	1.10	71.67	.23	99.94
33⅓	1.00	100.00	.26	87.28	.33	78.45	.35	71.95	.06	100.00
				35-Year Life						
1	2.86	2.86	5.71	5.71	4.29	4.29	3.57	3.57	5.56	5.56
2	2.86	5.72	5.38	11.09	4.10	8.39	3.44	7.02	5.40	10.96
3	2.85	8.57	5.07	16.16	3.93	12.32	3.32	10.34	5.24	16.20
4	2.86	11.43	4.78	20.94	3.76	16.08	3.20	13.54	5.08	21.28
5	2.86	14.29	4.51	25.45	3.60	19.68	3.09	16.63	4.92	26.20
6	2.85	17.14	4.25	29.70	3.44	23.12	2.98	19.60	4.76	30.96
7	2.86	20.00	4.01	33.71	3.29	26.41	2.87	22.48	4.60	35.56
8	2.86	22.86	3.78	37.49	3.15	29.56	2.77	25.24	4.44	40.00
9	2.85	25.71	3.56	41.05	3.02	32.58	2.67	27.91	4.29	44.29
10	2.86	28.57	3.36	44.41	2.89	35.47	2.57	30.49	4.13	48.42

Comparative Depreciation Tables *(continued)*

Year	Straight-Line		200%-Declining-Balance		150%-Declining-Balance		125%-Declining-Balance		Sum-of-Digits	
	Annual %	Cum. %	Annual %	Cum. %	Annual %	Cum. %	Annual %	Cum. %	Annual %	Cum. %

35-Year Life *(continued)*

Year	Annual %	Cum. %	Annual %	Cum. %	Annual %	Cum. %	Annual %	Cum. %	Annual %	Cum. %
11	2.86	31.43	3.17	47.58	2.77	38.24	2.48	32.97	3.97	52.39
12	2.85	34.28	2.99	50.57	2.65	40.89	2.39	35.36	3.81	56.20
13	2.86	37.14	2.82	53.39	2.53	43.42	2.31	37.67	3.65	59.85
14	2.86	40.00	2.66	56.05	2.42	45.84	2.23	39.90	3.49	63.34
15	2.85	42.85	2.51	58.56	2.32	48.16	2.15	42.05	3.33	66.67
16	2.86	45.71	2.37	60.93	2.22	50.38	2.07	44.12	3.18	69.85
17	2.86	48.57	2.23	63.16	2.13	52.51	2.00	46.11	3.02	72.87
18	2.85	51.42	2.10	65.26	2.03	54.54	1.92	48.04	2.86	75.73
19	2.86	54.28	1.98	67.24	1.95	56.49	1.86	49.89	2.70	78.43
20	2.86	57.14	1.87	69.11	1.86	58.35	1.79	51.68	2.54	80.97
21	2.86	60.00	1.76	70.87	1.79	60.14	1.73	53.41	2.38	83.35
22	2.86	62.86	1.66	72.53	1.71	61.85	1.66	55.07	2.22	85.57
23	2.86	65.72	1.57	74.10	1.64	63.49	1.60	56.68	2.06	87.63
24	2.85	68.57	1.48	75.58	1.56	65.05	1.55	58.22	1.90	89.53
25	2.86	71.43	1.40	76.98	1.50	66.55	1.49	59.72	1.75	91.28
26	2.86	74.29	1.32	78.30	1.43	67.98	1.44	61.15	1.59	92.87
27	2.85	77.14	1.24	79.54	1.37	69.35	1.39	62.54	1.43	94.30
28	2.86	80.00	1.17	80.71	1.31	70.66	1.34	63.88	1.27	95.57
29	2.86	82.86	1.10	81.81	1.26	71.92	1.29	65.17	1.11	96.68
30	2.85	85.71	1.04	82.85	1.20	73.12	1.24	66.41	.95	97.63
31	2.86	88.57	.98	83.83	1.15	74.27	1.20	67.61	.79	98.42
32	2.86	91.43	.92	84.75	1.10	75.37	1.16	68.77	.63	99.05
33	2.85	94.28	.87	85.62	1.06	76.43	1.12	69.88	.47	99.52
34	2.86	97.14	.82	86.44	1.01	77.44	1.08	70.96	.32	99.84
35	2.86	100.00	.77	87.21	.97	78.41	1.04	72.00	.16	100.00

40-Year Life

Year	Annual %	Cum. %	Annual %	Cum. %	Annual %	Cum. %	Annual %	Cum. %	Annual %	Cum. %
1	2.50	2.50	5.00	5.00	3.75	3.75	3.13	3.13	4.88	4.88
2	2.50	5.00	4.75	9.75	3.61	7.36	3.03	6.15	4.75	9.63
3	2.50	7.50	4.51	14.26	3.47	10.83	2.93	9.09	4.64	14.27
4	2.50	10.00	4.29	18.55	3.34	14.17	2.84	11.93	4.51	18.78
5	2.50	12.50	4.07	22.62	3.22	17.39	2.75	14.68	4.39	23.17
6	2.50	15.00	3.87	26.49	3.10	20.49	2.67	17.34	4.27	27.44
7	2.50	17.50	3.68	30.17	2.98	23.47	2.58	19.93	4.14	31.58
8	2.50	20.00	3.49	33.66	2.87	26.34	2.50	22.43	4.03	35.61
9	2.50	22.50	3.32	36.98	2.76	29.10	2.42	24.85	3.90	39.51
10	2.50	25.00	3.15	40.13	2.66	31.76	2.35	27.20	3.78	43.29
11	2.50	27.50	2.99	43.12	2.56	34.32	2.27	29.48	3.66	46.95
12	2.50	30.00	2.84	45.96	2.46	36.78	2.20	31.68	3.54	50.49
13	2.50	32.50	2.71	48.67	2.37	39.15	2.13	33.82	3.41	53.90
14	2.50	35.00	2.56	51.23	2.28	41.43	2.07	35.88	3.29	57.19
15	2.50	37.50	2.44	53.67	2.20	43.63	2.00	37.89	3.18	60.37

Comparative Depreciation Tables (continued)

Year	Straight-Line Annual %	Cum. %	200%-Declining-Balance Annual %	Cum. %	150%-Declining-Balance Annual %	Cum. %	125%-Declining-Balance Annual %	Cum. %	Sum-of-Digits Annual %	Cum. %
				40-Year Life (continued)						
16	2.50	40.00	2.32	55.99	2.11	45.74	1.94	39.83	3.04	63.41
17	2.50	42.50	2.20	58.19	2.03	47.77	1.88	41.71	2.93	66.34
18	2.50	45.00	2.09	60.28	1.96	49.73	1.82	43.53	2.81	69.15
19	2.50	47.50	1.99	62.27	1.88	51.61	1.76	45.30	2.68	71.83
20	2.50	50.00	1.88	64.15	1.81	53.42	1.71	47.01	2.56	74.39
21	2.50	52.50	1.79	65.94	1.75	55.17	1.66	48.66	2.44	76.83
22	2.50	55.00	1.71	67.65	1.68	56.85	1.60	50.27	2.32	79.15
23	2.50	57.50	1.62	69.27	1.62	58.47	1.55	51.82	2.19	81.34
24	2.50	60.00	1.53	70.80	1.56	60.03	1.51	53.33	2.07	83.41
25	2.50	62.50	1.46	72.26	1.50	61.53	1.46	54.78	1.94	85.37
26	2.50	65.00	1.39	73.65	1.44	62.97	1.41	56.20	1.82	87.19
27	2.50	67.50	1.32	74.97	1.39	64.36	1.37	57.57	1.71	88.90
28	2.50	70.00	1.25	76.22	1.34	65.70	1.33	58.89	1.59	90.49
29	2.50	72.50	1.19	77.41	1.29	66.99	1.28	60.18	1.46	91.95
30	2.50	75.00	1.13	78.54	1.24	68.23	1.24	61.42	1.34	93.29
31	2.50	77.50	1.07	79.61	1.19	69.42	1.21	62.63	1.22	94.51
32	2.50	80.00	1.02	80.63	1.15	70.57	1.17	63.79	1.10	95.61
33	2.50	82.50	.97	81.60	1.10	71.67	1.13	64.93	.98	96.58
34	2.50	85.00	.92	85.52	1.06	72.73	1.10	66.02	.86	97.44
35	2.50	87.50	.87	83.39	1.02	73.75	1.06	67.08	.73	98.17
36	2.50	90.00	.83	84.22	.98	74.73	1.03	68.11	.61	98.78
37	2.50	92.50	.79	85.01	.95	75.68	1.00	69.11	.49	99.27
38	2.50	95.00	.75	85.76	.91	76.59	.97	70.07	.36	99.63
39	2.50	97.50	.71	86.47	.88	77.47	.94	71.01	.25	99.88
40	2.50	100.00	.68	87.15	.85	78.32	.91	71.92	.12	100.00
					45-Year Life					
1	2.22	2.22	4.44	4.44	3.33	3.33	2.78	2.78	4.35	4.35
2	2.22	4.44	4.24	8.68	3.22	6.55	2.70	5.48	4.25	8.60
3	2.22	6.66	4.05	12.73	3.12	9.67	2.63	8.10	4.15	12.75
4	2.23	8.89	3.87	16.60	3.01	12.68	2.55	10.66	4.06	16.81
5	2.22	11.11	3.70	20.30	2.91	15.59	2.48	13.14	3.96	20.77
6	2.22	13.33	3.54	23.84	2.81	18.40	2.41	15.55	3.86	24.63
7	2.22	15.55	3.38	27.22	2.72	21.12	2.35	17.90	3.77	28.40
8	2.23	17.78	3.23	30.45	2.63	23.75	2.28	20.18	3.67	32.07
9	2.22	20.00	3.09	33.54	2.54	26.29	2.22	22.40	3.57	35.64
10	2.22	22.22	2.95	36.49	2.46	28.75	2.16	24.55	3.48	39.12
11	2.22	24.44	2.82	39.31	2.38	31.13	2.10	26.65	3.38	42.50
12	2.23	26.67	2.69	42.00	2.30	33.43	2.04	28.68	3.28	45.78
13	2.22	28.89	2.57	44.57	2.22	35.65	1.98	30.67	3.19	48.97
14	2.22	31.11	2.46	47.03	2.15	37.80	1.93	32.59	3.09	52.06
15	2.22	33.33	2.35	49.38	2.07	39.87	1.87	34.46	3.00	55.06

Comparative Depreciation Tables *(continued)*

Year	Straight-Line		200%-Declining-Balance		150%-Declining-Balance		125%-Declining-Balance		Sum-of-Digits	
	Annual %	Cum. %	Annual %	Cum. %	Annual %	Cum. %	Annual %	Cum. %	Annual %	Cum. %
				45-Year Life *(continued)*						
16	2.23	35.56	2.25	51.63	2.00	41.87	1.82	36.28	2.90	57.96
17	2.22	37.78	2.15	53.78	1.94	43.81	1.77	38.05	2.80	60.76
18	2.22	40.00	2.05	55.83	1.87	45.68	1.72	39.77	2.70	63.46
19	2.22	42.22	1.96	57.79	1.81	47.49	1.67	41.45	2.61	66.07
20	2.23	44.45	1.87	59.66	1.75	49.24	1.63	43.07	2.51	68.58
21	2.22	46.67	1.79	61.45	1.69	50.93	1.58	44.66	2.42	71.00
22	2.22	48.89	1.71	63.16	1.64	52.57	1.54	46.19	2.32	73.32
23	2.22	51.11	1.63	64.79	1.58	54.15	1.49	47.69	2.22	75.54
24	2.23	53.34	1.56	66.35	1.53	55.68	1.45	49.14	2.13	77.67
25	2.22	55.56	1.49	67.84	1.48	57.16	1.41	50.55	2.03	79.70
26	2.22	57.78	1.42	69.26	1.43	58.59	1.37	51.93	1.93	81.63
27	2.22	60.00	1.36	70.62	1.38	59.97	1.34	53.26	1.84	83.47
28	2.23	62.23	1.30	71.92	1.33	61.30	1.30	54.56	1.74	85.21
29	2.22	64.45	1.24	73.16	1.29	62.59	1.26	55.82	1.64	86.85
30	2.22	66.67	1.18	74.34	1.25	63.84	1.23	57.05	1.55	88.40
31	2.22	68.89	1.13	75.47	1.21	65.05	1.19	58.24	1.45	89.85
32	2.23	71.12	1.08	76.55	1.17	66.22	1.16	59.40	1.35	91.20
33	2.22	73.34	1.03	77.58	1.13	67.35	1.13	60.53	1.26	92.46
34	2.22	75.56	.98	78.56	1.09	68.44	1.10	61.63	1.16	93.62
35	2.22	77.78	.94	79.50	1.05	69.49	1.07	62.69	1.06	94.68
36	2.22	80.00	.90	80.40	1.02	70.51	1.04	63.73	.97	95.65
37	2.23	82.23	.86	81.26	.98	71.49	1.01	64.74	.87	96.52
38	2.22	84.45	.82	82.08	.95	72.44	.98	65.72	.77	97.29
39	2.22	86.67	.78	82.86	.92	73.36	.95	66.67	.68	97.97
40	2.22	88.89	.75	83.61	.89	74.25	.93	67.59	.58	98.55
41	2.23	91.12	.72	84.33	.86	75.11	.90	68.49	.48	99.03
42	2.22	93.34	.69	85.02	.83	75.94	.88	69.37	.39	99.42
43	2.22	95.56	.66	85.68	.80	76.74	.85	70.22	.29	99.71
44	2.22	97.78	.63	86.31	.78	77.52	.83	71.05	.19	99.90
45	2.22	100.00	.60	86.91	.75	78.27	.80	71.85	.10	100.00
					50-Year Life					
1	2.00	2.00	4.00	4.00	3.00	3.00	2.50	2.50	3.92	3.92
2	2.00	4.00	3.84	7.84	2.91	5.91	2.44	4.94	3.85	7.77
3	2.00	6.00	3.69	11.53	2.82	8.73	2.38	7.31	3.76	11.53
4	2.00	8.00	3.54	15.07	2.74	11.47	2.32	9.63	3.69	15.22
5	2.00	10.00	3.39	18.46	2.66	14.13	2.26	11.89	3.60	18.82
6	2.00	12.00	3.26	21.72	2.58	16.71	2.20	14.09	3.53	22.35
7	2.00	14.00	3.14	24.86	2.50	19.21	2.15	16.24	3.45	25.80
8	2.00	16.00	3.00	27.86	2.42	21.63	2.09	18.33	3.38	29.18
9	2.00	18.00	2.89	30.75	2.35	23.98	2.04	20.38	3.29	32.47
10	2.00	20.00	2.77	33.52	2.28	26.26	1.99	22.37	3.22	35.69

Comparative Depreciation Tables *(continued)*

Year	Straight-Line		200%-Declining-Balance		150%-Declining-Balance		125%-Declining-Balance		Sum-of-Digits	
	Annual %	Cum. %	Annual %	Cum. %	Annual %	Cum. %	Annual %	Cum. %	Annual %	Cum. %
				50-Year Life *(continued)*						
11	2.00	22.00	2.66	36.18	2.21	28.47	1.94	24.31	3.15	38.82
12	2.00	24.00	2.55	38.73	2.15	30.62	1.89	26.20	3.06	41.88
13	2.00	26.00	2.45	41.18	2.08	32.70	1.84	28.05	2.98	44.86
14	2.00	28.00	2.35	43.53	2.02	34.72	1.80	29.84	2.91	47.77
15	2.00	30.00	2.26	45.79	1.96	36.68	1.75	31.60	2.82	50.59
16	2.00	32.00	2.17	47.96	1.90	38.58	1.71	33.31	2.74	53.33
17	2.00	34.00	2.08	50.04	1.84	40.42	1.67	34.98	2.67	56.00
18	2.00	36.00	2.00	52.04	1.79	42.21	1.63	36.60	2.59	58.59
19	2.00	38.00	1.92	53.96	1.73	43.94	1.58	38.19	2.51	61.10
20	2.00	40.00	1.84	55.80	1.68	45.62	1.55	39.73	2.43	63.53
21	2.00	42.00	1.77	57.57	1.63	47.25	1.51	41.24	2.35	65.88
22	2.00	44.00	1.70	59.27	1.58	48.83	1.47	42.71	2.28	68.16
23	2.00	46.00	1.62	60.89	1.53	50.36	1.43	44.14	2.19	70.35
24	2.00	48.00	1.57	62.46	1.49	51.85	1.40	45.54	2.12	72.47
25	2.00	50.00	1.50	63.96	1.44	53.29	1.36	46.90	2.04	74.51
26	2.00	52.00	1.44	65.40	1.40	54.69	1.33	48.23	1.96	76.47
27	2.00	54.00	1.39	66.79	1.36	56.05	1.29	49.52	1.87	78.35
28	2.00	56.00	1.33	68.12	1.32	57.37	1.26	50.78	1.81	80.16
29	2.00	58.00	1.27	69.39	1.28	58.64	1.23	52.01	1.72	81.88
30	2.00	60.00	1.22	70.61	1.24	59.89	1.20	53.21	1.65	83.53
31	2.00	62.00	1.18	71.79	1.20	61.09	1.17	54.38	1.57	85.10
32	2.00	64.00	1.13	72.92	1.17	62.26	1.14	55.52	1.49	86.59
33	2.00	66.00	1.08	74.00	1.13	63.39	1.11	56.63	1.41	88.00
34	2.00	68.00	1.04	75.04	1.10	64.49	1.08	57.72	1.33	89.33
35	2.00	70.00	1.00	76.04	1.07	65.56	1.06	58.78	1.26	90.59
36	2.00	72.00	.96	77.00	1.03	66.59	1.03	59.81	1.18	91.77
37	2.00	74.00	.92	77.92	1.00	67.59	1.00	60.81	1.09	92.86
38	2.00	76.00	.88	78.80	.97	68.56	.98	61.79	1.02	93.88
39	2.00	78.00	.85	79.65	.94	69.50	.96	62.75	.94	94.82
40	2.00	80.00	.81	80.46	.92	70.42	.93	63.68	.87	95.69
41	2.00	82.00	.78	81.24	.89	71.31	.91	64.58	.78	96.47
42	2.00	84.00	.75	81.99	.86	72.17	.89	65.47	.71	97.18
43	2.00	86.00	.72	82.71	.84	73.01	.86	66.33	.62	97.80
44	2.00	88.00	.69	83.40	.81	73.82	.84	67.18	.55	98.35
45	2.00	90.00	.67	84.07	.79	74.61	.82	68.00	.47	98.82
46	2.00	92.00	.64	84.71	.76	75.37	.80	68.80	.40	99.22
47	2.00	94.00	.61	85.32	.74	76.11	.78	69.58	.31	99.53
48	2.00	96.00	.59	85.90	.72	76.83	.76	70.34	.24	99.77
49	2.00	98.00	.57	86.47	.70	77.53	.74	71.08	.15	99.92
50	2.00	100.00	.54	87.01	.67	78.20	.72	71.80	.08	100.00

APPENDIX C
COMPOUND INTEREST AND ANNUITY TABLES*

COMPOUND INTEREST AND ANNUITY TABLE

**1.00 %
ANNUAL**

	Amount Of 1	Amount Of 1 Per Period	Sinking Fund Payment	Present Worth Of 1	Present Worth Of 1 Per Period	Periodic Payment To Amortize 1	Constant Annual Percent	Total Interest	Annual Add-on Rate	
	What a single $1 deposit grows to in the future. The deposit is made at the beginning of the first period.	What a series of $1 deposits grow to in the future. A deposit is made at the end of each period.	The amount to be deposited at the end of each period that grows to $1 in the future.	What $1 to be paid in the future is worth today. Value today of a single payment tomorrow.	What $1 to be paid at the end of each period is worth today. Value today of a series of payments tomorrow.	The mortgage payment to amortize a loan of $1. An annuity certain, payable at the end of each period, worth $1 today.	The annual payment, including interest and principal, to amortize a loan of $100.	The total interest paid over the term on a loan of $1. The loan is amortized by regular periodic payments.	The average annual interest rate on a loan that is completely amortized by regular periodic payments.	
	$S=(1+i)^n$	$S_{\overline{n}}=\dfrac{(1+i)^n-1}{i}$	$\dfrac{1}{S_{\overline{n}}}=\dfrac{i}{(1+i)^n-1}$	$V^n=\dfrac{1}{(1+i)^n}$	$A_{\overline{n}}=\dfrac{1-V^n}{i}$	$\dfrac{1}{A_{\overline{n}}}=\dfrac{i}{1-V^n}$				

YR										YR
1	1.010000	1.000000	1.00000000	0.990099	0.990099	1.01000000	101.00	0.010000	1.00	1
2	1.020100	2.010000	0.49751244	0.980296	1.970395	0.50751244	50.76	0.015025	0.75	2
3	1.030301	3.030100	0.33002211	0.970590	2.940985	0.34002211	34.01	0.020066	0.67	3
4	1.040604	4.060401	0.24628109	0.960980	3.901966	0.25628109	25.63	0.025124	0.63	4
5	1.051010	5.101005	0.19603980	0.951466	4.853431	0.20603980	20.61	0.030199	0.60	5
6	1.061520	6.152015	0.16254837	0.942045	5.795476	0.17254837	17.26	0.035290	0.59	6
7	1.072135	7.213535	0.13862828	0.932718	6.728195	0.14862828	14.87	0.040398	0.58	7
8	1.082857	8.285671	0.12069029	0.923483	7.651678	0.13069029	13.07	0.045522	0.57	8
9	1.093685	9.368527	0.10674036	0.914340	8.566018	0.11674036	11.68	0.050663	0.56	9
10	1.104622	10.462213	0.09558208	0.905287	9.471305	0.10558208	10.56	0.055821	0.56	10
11	1.115668	11.566835	0.08645408	0.896324	10.367628	0.09645408	9.65	0.060995	0.55	11
12	1.126825	12.682503	0.07884879	0.887449	11.255077	0.08884879	8.89	0.066185	0.55	12
13	1.138093	13.809328	0.07241482	0.878663	12.133740	0.08241482	8.25	0.071393	0.55	13
14	1.149474	14.947421	0.06690117	0.869963	13.003703	0.07690117	7.70	0.076616	0.55	14
15	1.160969	16.096896	0.06212378	0.861349	13.865053	0.07212378	7.22	0.081857	0.55	15
16	1.172579	17.257864	0.05794460	0.852821	14.717874	0.06794460	6.80	0.087114	0.54	16
17	1.184304	18.430443	0.05425806	0.844377	15.562251	0.06425806	6.43	0.092387	0.54	17
18	1.196147	19.614748	0.05098205	0.836017	16.398269	0.06098205	6.10	0.097677	0.54	18
19	1.208109	20.810895	0.04805115	0.827740	17.226008	0.05805115	5.81	0.102983	0.54	19
20	1.220190	22.019004	0.04541531	0.819544	18.045553	0.05541531	5.55	0.108306	0.54	20
21	1.232392	23.239194	0.04303075	0.811430	18.856983	0.05303075	5.31	0.113646	0.54	21
22	1.244716	24.471586	0.04086372	0.803396	19.660379	0.05086372	5.09	0.119002	0.54	22
23	1.257163	25.716302	0.03888584	0.795442	20.455821	0.04888584	4.89	0.124374	0.54	23
24	1.269735	26.973465	0.03707347	0.787566	21.243387	0.04707347	4.71	0.129763	0.54	24
25	1.282432	28.243200	0.03540675	0.779768	22.023156	0.04540675	4.55	0.135169	0.54	25
26	1.295256	29.525631	0.03386888	0.772048	22.795204	0.04386888	4.39	0.140591	0.54	26
27	1.308209	30.820888	0.03244553	0.764404	23.559608	0.04244553	4.25	0.146029	0.54	27
28	1.321291	32.129097	0.03112444	0.756836	24.316443	0.04112444	4.12	0.151484	0.54	28
29	1.334504	33.450388	0.02989502	0.749342	25.065785	0.03989502	3.99	0.156956	0.54	29
30	1.347849	34.784892	0.02874811	0.741923	25.807708	0.03874811	3.88	0.162443	0.54	30
31	1.361327	36.132740	0.02767573	0.734577	26.542285	0.03767573	3.77	0.167948	0.54	31
32	1.374941	37.494068	0.02667089	0.727304	27.269589	0.03667089	3.67	0.173468	0.54	32
33	1.388690	38.869009	0.02572744	0.720103	27.989693	0.03572744	3.58	0.179005	0.54	33
34	1.402577	40.257699	0.02483997	0.712973	28.702666	0.03483997	3.49	0.184559	0.54	34
35	1.416603	41.660276	0.02400368	0.705914	29.408580	0.03400368	3.41	0.190129	0.54	35
36	1.430769	43.076878	0.02321431	0.698925	30.107505	0.03321431	3.33	0.195715	0.54	36
37	1.445036	44.507647	0.02246805	0.692005	30.799510	0.03246805	3.25	0.201318	0.54	37
38	1.459527	45.952724	0.02176150	0.685153	31.484663	0.03176150	3.18	0.206937	0.54	38
39	1.474123	47.412251	0.02109046	0.678337	32.163003	0.03109046	3.11	0.212572	0.55	39
40	1.488864	48.886373	0.02045560	0.671653	32.834686	0.03045560	3.05	0.218224	0.55	40
41	1.503752	50.375237	0.01985102	0.665003	33.499689	0.02985102	2.99	0.223892	0.55	41
42	1.518790	51.878989	0.01927563	0.658419	34.158108	0.02927563	2.93	0.229576	0.55	42
43	1.533978	53.397779	0.01872737	0.651900	34.810008	0.02872737	2.88	0.235277	0.55	43
44	1.549318	54.931757	0.01820461	0.645445	35.455454	0.02820461	2.83	0.240994	0.55	44
45	1.564811	56.481075	0.01770505	0.639055	36.094508	0.02770505	2.78	0.246727	0.55	45
46	1.580459	58.045885	0.01722775	0.632728	36.727236	0.02722775	2.73	0.252476	0.55	46
47	1.596263	59.626344	0.01677111	0.626463	37.353699	0.02677111	2.68	0.258242	0.55	47
48	1.612226	61.222608	0.01633384	0.620260	37.973959	0.02633384	2.64	0.264024	0.55	48
49	1.628348	62.834834	0.01591474	0.614119	38.588079	0.02591474	2.60	0.269822	0.55	49
50	1.644632	64.463182	0.01551273	0.608039	39.196118	0.02551273	2.56	0.275637	0.55	50

*Source: *Thorndike Encyclopedia of Banking and Financial Tables*, Warren, Gorham and Lamont, Inc., New York, pp. 6–352 through 6–373. Used with permission.

Compound Interest and Annuity Tables *(continued)*

COMPOUND INTEREST AND ANNUITY TABLE

2.00 %
ANNUAL

		Amount Of 1	Amount Of 1 Per Period	Sinking Fund Payment	Present Worth Of 1	Present Worth Of 1 Per Period	Periodic Payment To Amortize 1	Constant Annual Percent	Total Interest	Annual Add-on Rate	
		What a single $1 deposit grows to in the future. The deposit is made at the beginning of the first period.	What a series of $1 deposits grow to in the future. A deposit is made at the end of each period.	The amount to be deposited at the end of each period that grows to $1 in the future.	What $1 to be paid in the future is worth today. Value today of a single payment tomorrow.	What $1 to be paid at the end of each period is worth today. Value today of a series of payments tomorrow.	The mortgage payment to amortize a loan of $1. An annuity certain, payable at the end of each period, worth $1 today.	The annual payment, including interest and principal, to amortize completely a loan of $100.	The total interest paid over the term on a loan of $1. The loan is amortized by regular periodic payments.	The average interest rate on a loan that is completely amortized by regular periodic payments.	
		$S=(1+i)^n$	$S_{\overline{n}}=\dfrac{(1+i)^n-1}{i}$	$\dfrac{1}{S_{\overline{n}}}=\dfrac{i}{(1+i)^n-1}$	$V^n=\dfrac{1}{(1+i)^n}$	$A_{\overline{n}}=\dfrac{1-V^n}{i}$	$\dfrac{1}{A_{\overline{n}}}=\dfrac{i}{1-V^n}$				
YR											YR
1	1	1.020000	1.000000	1.00000000	0.980392	0.980392	1.02000000	102.00	0.020000	2.00	1
2	2	1.040400	2.020000	0.49504950	0.961169	1.941561	0.51504950	51.51	0.030099	1.50	2
3	3	1.061208	3.060400	0.32675467	0.942322	2.883883	0.34675467	34.68	0.040264	1.34	3
4	4	1.082432	4.121608	0.24262375	0.923845	3.807729	0.26262375	26.27	0.050495	1.26	4
5	5	1.104081	5.204040	0.19215839	0.905731	4.713460	0.21215839	21.22	0.060792	1.22	5
6	6	1.126162	6.308121	0.15852581	0.887971	5.601431	0.17852581	17.86	0.071155	1.19	6
7	7	1.148686	7.434283	0.13451196	0.870560	6.471991	0.15451196	15.46	0.081584	1.17	7
8	8	1.171659	8.582969	0.11650980	0.853490	7.325481	0.13650980	13.66	0.092078	1.15	8
9	9	1.195093	9.754628	0.10251544	0.836755	8.162237	0.12251544	12.26	0.102639	1.14	9
10	10	1.218994	10.949721	0.09132653	0.820348	8.982585	0.11132653	11.14	0.113265	1.13	10
11	11	1.243374	12.168715	0.08217794	0.804263	9.786848	0.10217794	10.22	0.123957	1.13	11
12	12	1.268242	13.412090	0.07455960	0.788493	10.575341	0.09455960	9.46	0.134715	1.12	12
13	13	1.293607	14.680332	0.06811835	0.773033	11.348374	0.08811835	8.82	0.145539	1.12	13
14	14	1.319479	15.973938	0.06260197	0.757875	12.106249	0.08260197	8.27	0.156428	1.12	14
15	15	1.345868	17.293417	0.05782547	0.743015	12.849264	0.07782547	7.79	0.167382	1.12	15
16	16	1.372786	18.639285	0.05365013	0.728446	13.577709	0.07365013	7.37	0.178402	1.12	16
17	17	1.400241	20.012071	0.04996984	0.714163	14.291872	0.06996984	7.00	0.189487	1.11	17
18	18	1.428246	21.412312	0.04670210	0.700159	14.992031	0.06670210	6.68	0.200638	1.11	18
19	19	1.456811	22.840559	0.04378177	0.686431	15.678462	0.06378177	6.38	0.211854	1.12	19
20	20	1.485947	24.297370	0.04115672	0.672971	16.351433	0.06115672	6.12	0.223134	1.12	20
21	21	1.515666	25.783317	0.03878477	0.659776	17.011209	0.05878477	5.88	0.234480	1.12	21
22	22	1.545980	27.298984	0.03663140	0.646839	17.658048	0.05663140	5.67	0.245891	1.12	22
23	23	1.576899	28.844963	0.03466810	0.634156	18.292204	0.05466810	5.47	0.257366	1.12	23
24	24	1.608437	30.421862	0.03287110	0.621721	18.913926	0.05287110	5.29	0.268906	1.12	24
25	25	1.640606	32.030300	0.03122044	0.609531	19.523456	0.05122044	5.13	0.280511	1.12	25
26	26	1.673641	33.670906	0.02969923	0.597579	20.121036	0.04969923	4.97	0.292180	1.12	26
27	27	1.706886	35.344324	0.02829309	0.585862	20.706898	0.04829309	4.83	0.303913	1.13	27
28	28	1.741024	37.051210	0.02698967	0.574375	21.281272	0.04698967	4.70	0.315711	1.13	28
29	29	1.775845	38.792235	0.02577836	0.563112	21.844385	0.04577836	4.58	0.327572	1.13	29
30	30	1.811362	40.568079	0.02464992	0.552071	22.396456	0.04464992	4.47	0.339498	1.13	30
31	31	1.847589	42.379441	0.02359635	0.541246	22.937702	0.04359635	4.36	0.351487	1.13	31
32	32	1.884541	44.227030	0.02261061	0.530633	23.468335	0.04261061	4.27	0.363539	1.14	32
33	33	1.922231	46.111570	0.02168653	0.520229	23.988564	0.04168653	4.17	0.375656	1.14	33
34	34	1.960676	48.033802	0.02081867	0.510028	24.498592	0.04081867	4.09	0.387835	1.14	34
35	35	1.999890	49.994478	0.02000221	0.500028	24.998619	0.04000221	4.01	0.400077	1.14	35
36	36	2.039887	51.994367	0.01923285	0.490223	25.488842	0.03923285	3.93	0.412383	1.15	36
37	37	2.080685	54.034255	0.01850678	0.480611	25.969453	0.03850678	3.86	0.424751	1.15	37
38	38	2.122299	56.114940	0.01782057	0.471187	26.440641	0.03782057	3.79	0.437182	1.15	38
39	39	2.164745	58.237238	0.01717114	0.461948	26.902589	0.03717114	3.72	0.449675	1.15	39
40	40	2.208040	60.401983	0.01655575	0.452890	27.355479	0.03655575	3.66	0.462230	1.16	40
41	41	2.252200	62.610023	0.01597188	0.444010	27.799489	0.03597188	3.60	0.474847	1.16	41
42	42	2.297244	64.862223	0.01541729	0.435304	28.234794	0.03541729	3.55	0.487526	1.16	42
43	43	2.343189	67.159468	0.01488993	0.426769	28.661562	0.03488993	3.49	0.500267	1.16	43
44	44	2.390053	69.502657	0.01438794	0.418401	29.079963	0.03438794	3.44	0.513069	1.17	44
45	45	2.437854	71.892710	0.01390962	0.410197	29.490160	0.03390962	3.40	0.525933	1.17	45
46	46	2.486611	74.330564	0.01345342	0.402154	29.892314	0.03345342	3.35	0.538857	1.17	46
47	47	2.536344	76.817176	0.01301792	0.394268	30.286582	0.03301792	3.31	0.551842	1.17	47
48	48	2.587070	79.353519	0.01260184	0.386538	30.673120	0.03260184	3.27	0.564888	1.18	48
49	49	2.638812	81.940590	0.01220396	0.378958	31.052078	0.03220396	3.23	0.577994	1.18	49
50	50	2.691588	84.579401	0.01182321	0.371528	31.423606	0.03182321	3.19	0.591160	1.18	50

Compound Interest and Annuity Tables *(continued)*

OMPOUND INTEREST AND ANNUITY TABLE

3.00 %
ANNUAL

	Amount Of 1	Amount Of 1 Per Period	Sinking Fund Payment	Present Worth Of 1	Present Worth Of 1 Per Period	Periodic Payment To Amortize 1	Constant Annual Percent	Total Interest	Annual Add-on Rate	
	What a single $1 deposit grows to in the future. The deposit is made at the beginning of the first period.	What a series of $1 deposits grow to in the future. A deposit is made at the end of each period.	The amount to be deposited at the end of each period that grows to $1 in the future.	What $1 to be paid in the future is worth today. Value today of a single payment tomorrow.	What $1 to be paid each period is worth today. Value today of a series of payments tomorrow.	The mortgage payment to amortize a loan of $1. An annuity certain, payable at the end of each period, worth $1 today.	The annual payment, including interest and principal, to amortize completely a loan of $100.	The total interest paid over the term of $1. The loan is amortized by regular periodic payments.	The average annual interest rate on a loan that is completely amortized by regular periodic payments.	
	$S=(1+i)^n$	$S_{\overline{n}}=\dfrac{(1+i)^n-1}{i}$	$\dfrac{1}{S_{\overline{n}}}=\dfrac{i}{(1+i)^n-1}$	$V^n=\dfrac{1}{(1+i)^n}$	$A_{\overline{n}}=\dfrac{1-V^n}{i}$	$\dfrac{1}{A_{\overline{n}}}=\dfrac{i}{1-V^n}$				YR
1	1.030000	1.000000	1.00000000	0.970874	0.970874	1.03000000	103.00	0.030000	3.00	1
2	1.060900	2.030000	0.49261084	0.942596	1.913470	0.52261084	52.27	0.045222	2.26	2
3	1.092727	3.090900	0.32353036	0.915142	2.828611	0.35353036	35.36	0.060591	2.02	3
4	1.125509	4.183627	0.23902705	0.888487	3.717098	0.26902705	26.91	0.076108	1.90	4
5	1.159274	5.309136	0.18835457	0.862609	4.579707	0.21835457	21.84	0.091773	1.84	5
6	1.194052	6.468410	0.15459750	0.837484	5.417191	0.18459750	18.46	0.107585	1.79	6
7	1.229874	7.662462	0.13050635	0.813092	6.230283	0.16050635	16.06	0.123544	1.76	7
8	1.266770	8.892336	0.11245639	0.789409	7.019692	0.14245639	14.25	0.139651	1.75	8
9	1.304773	10.159106	0.09843386	0.766417	7.786109	0.12843386	12.85	0.155905	1.73	9
10	1.343916	11.463879	0.08723051	0.744094	8.530203	0.11723051	11.73	0.172305	1.72	10
11	1.384234	12.807796	0.07807745	0.722421	9.252624	0.10807745	10.81	0.188852	1.72	11
12	1.425761	14.192030	0.07046209	0.701380	9.954004	0.10046209	10.05	0.205545	1.71	12
13	1.468534	15.617790	0.06402954	0.680951	10.634955	0.09402954	9.41	0.222384	1.71	13
14	1.512590	17.086324	0.05852634	0.661118	11.296073	0.08852634	8.86	0.239369	1.71	14
15	1.557967	18.598914	0.05376658	0.641862	11.937935	0.08376658	8.38	0.256499	1.71	15
16	1.604706	20.156881	0.04961085	0.623167	12.561102	0.07961085	7.97	0.273774	1.71	16
17	1.652848	21.761588	0.04595253	0.605016	13.166118	0.07595253	7.60	0.291193	1.71	17
18	1.702433	23.414435	0.04270870	0.587335	13.753513	0.07270870	7.28	0.308757	1.72	18
19	1.753506	25.116868	0.03981388	0.570286	14.323799	0.06981388	6.99	0.326464	1.72	19
20	1.806111	26.870374	0.03721571	0.553676	14.877453	0.06721571	6.73	0.344314	1.72	20
21	1.860295	28.676486	0.03487178	0.537549	15.415024	0.06487178	6.49	0.362307	1.73	21
22	1.916103	30.536780	0.03274739	0.521893	15.936917	0.06274739	6.28	0.380443	1.73	22
23	1.973587	32.452884	0.03081390	0.506692	16.443608	0.06081390	6.09	0.398720	1.73	23
24	2.032794	34.426470	0.02904742	0.491934	16.935542	0.05904742	5.91	0.417138	1.74	24
25	2.093778	36.459264	0.02742787	0.477606	17.413148	0.05742787	5.75	0.435697	1.74	25
26	2.156591	38.553042	0.02593829	0.463695	17.876842	0.05593829	5.60	0.454396	1.75	26
27	2.221289	40.709634	0.02456421	0.450189	18.327031	0.05456421	5.46	0.473204	1.75	27
28	2.287928	42.930923	0.02329323	0.437077	18.764108	0.05329323	5.33	0.492211	1.76	28
29	2.356566	45.218850	0.02211467	0.424346	19.188455	0.05211467	5.22	0.511325	1.76	29
30	2.427262	47.575416	0.02101926	0.411987	19.600441	0.05101926	5.11	0.530578	1.77	30
31	2.500080	50.002678	0.01999893	0.399987	20.000428	0.04999893	5.00	0.549967	1.77	31
32	2.575083	52.502759	0.01904662	0.388337	20.388766	0.04904662	4.91	0.569492	1.78	32
33	2.652335	55.077841	0.01815612	0.377026	20.765792	0.04815612	4.82	0.589152	1.79	33
34	2.731905	57.730177	0.01732196	0.366045	21.131837	0.04732196	4.74	0.608947	1.79	34
35	2.813862	60.462082	0.01653920	0.355383	21.487220	0.04653920	4.66	0.628875	1.80	35
36	2.898278	63.275944	0.01580379	0.345032	21.832252	0.04580379	4.59	0.648937	1.80	36
37	2.985227	66.174223	0.01511162	0.334983	22.167235	0.04511162	4.52	0.669130	1.81	37
38	3.074783	69.159449	0.01445934	0.325226	22.492462	0.04445934	4.45	0.689455	1.81	38
39	3.167027	72.234233	0.01384385	0.315754	22.808215	0.04384385	4.39	0.709910	1.82	39
40	3.262038	75.401260	0.01326238	0.306557	23.114772	0.04326238	4.33	0.730495	1.83	40
41	3.359899	78.663298	0.01271241	0.297628	23.412400	0.04271241	4.28	0.751209	1.83	41
42	3.460696	82.023196	0.01219167	0.288959	23.701359	0.04219167	4.22	0.772050	1.84	42
43	3.564517	85.483892	0.01169811	0.280543	23.981902	0.04169811	4.17	0.793019	1.84	43
44	3.671452	89.048409	0.01122985	0.272372	24.254274	0.04122985	4.13	0.814113	1.85	44
45	3.781596	92.719861	0.01078518	0.264439	24.518713	0.04078518	4.08	0.835333	1.86	45
46	3.895044	96.501457	0.01036254	0.256737	24.775449	0.04036254	4.04	0.856677	1.86	46
47	4.011895	100.396501	0.00996051	0.249259	25.024708	0.03996051	4.00	0.878144	1.87	47
48	4.132252	104.408396	0.00957777	0.241999	25.266707	0.03957777	3.96	0.899733	1.87	48
49	4.256219	108.540648	0.00921314	0.234950	25.501657	0.03921314	3.93	0.921444	1.88	49
50	4.383906	112.796867	0.00886549	0.228107	25.729764	0.03886549	3.89	0.943275	1.89	50

Compound Interest and Annuity Tables *(continued)*

COMPOUND INTEREST AND ANNUITY TABLE

4.00 %
ANNUAL

		Amount Of 1	Amount Of 1 Per Period	Sinking Fund Payment	Present Worth Of 1	Present Worth Of 1 Per Period	Periodic Payment To Amortize 1	Constant Annual Percent	Total Interest	Annual Add-on Rate	
		What a single $1 deposit grows to in the future. The deposit is made at the beginning of the first period.	What a series of $1 deposits grow to in the future. A deposit is made at the end of each period.	The amount to be deposited at the end of each period grows to $1 in the future.	What $1 to be paid in the future is worth today.	What $1 to be paid at the end of each period is worth today.	The mortgage payment to amortize a loan of $1. An annuity certain, payable at the end of each period, worth $1 today.	The annual payment, including interest and principal, to amortize completely a loan of $100.	The total interest paid over the term of $1. The loan is amortized by regular periodic payments.	The average annual interest rate on a loan that is completely amortized by regular periodic payments.	
YR		$S=(1+i)^n$	$S_{\overline{n}}=\dfrac{(1+i)^n-1}{i}$	$\dfrac{1}{S_{\overline{n}}}=\dfrac{i}{(1+i)^n-1}$	$V^n=\dfrac{1}{(1+i)^n}$	$A_{\overline{n}}=\dfrac{1-V^n}{i}$	$\dfrac{1}{A_{\overline{n}}}=\dfrac{i}{1-V^n}$				YR
1	1	1.040000	1.000000	1.00000000	0.961538	0.961538	1.04000000	104.00	0.040000	4.00	1
2	2	1.081600	2.040000	0.49019608	0.924556	1.886095	0.53019608	53.02	0.060392	3.02	2
3	3	1.124864	3.121600	0.32034854	0.888996	2.775091	0.36034854	36.04	0.081046	2.70	3
4	4	1.169859	4.246464	0.23549005	0.854804	3.629895	0.27549005	27.55	0.101960	2.55	4
5	5	1.216653	5.416323	0.18462711	0.821927	4.451822	0.22462711	22.47	0.123136	2.46	5
6	6	1.265319	6.632975	0.15076190	0.790315	5.242137	0.19076190	19.08	0.144571	2.41	6
7	7	1.315932	7.898294	0.12660961	0.759918	6.002055	0.16660961	16.67	0.166267	2.38	7
8	8	1.368569	9.214226	0.10852783	0.730690	6.732745	0.14852783	14.86	0.188223	2.35	8
9	9	1.423312	10.582795	0.09449299	0.702587	7.435332	0.13449299	13.45	0.210437	2.34	9
10	10	1.480244	12.006107	0.08329094	0.675564	8.110896	0.12329094	12.33	0.232909	2.33	10
11	11	1.539454	13.486351	0.07414904	0.649581	8.760477	0.11414904	11.42	0.255639	2.32	11
12	12	1.601032	15.025805	0.06655217	0.624597	9.385074	0.10655217	10.66	0.278626	2.32	12
13	13	1.665074	16.626838	0.06014373	0.600574	9.985648	0.10014373	10.02	0.301868	2.32	13
14	14	1.731676	18.291911	0.05466897	0.577475	10.563123	0.09466897	9.47	0.325366	2.32	14
15	15	1.800944	20.023588	0.04994110	0.555265	11.118387	0.08994110	9.00	0.349117	2.33	15
16	16	1.872981	21.824531	0.04582000	0.533908	11.652296	0.08582000	8.59	0.373120	2.33	16
17	17	1.947900	23.697512	0.04219852	0.513373	12.165669	0.08219852	8.22	0.397375	2.34	17
18	18	2.025817	25.645413	0.03899333	0.493628	12.659297	0.07899333	7.90	0.421880	2.34	18
19	19	2.106849	27.671229	0.03613862	0.474642	13.133939	0.07613862	7.62	0.446634	2.35	19
20	20	2.191123	29.778079	0.03358175	0.456387	13.590326	0.07358175	7.36	0.471635	2.36	20
21	21	2.278768	31.969202	0.03128011	0.438834	14.029160	0.07128011	7.13	0.496882	2.37	21
22	22	2.369919	34.247970	0.02919881	0.421955	14.451115	0.06919881	6.92	0.522374	2.37	22
23	23	2.464716	36.617889	0.02730906	0.405726	14.856842	0.06730906	6.74	0.548108	2.38	23
24	24	2.563304	39.082604	0.02558683	0.390121	15.246963	0.06558683	6.56	0.574084	2.39	24
25	25	2.665836	41.645908	0.02401196	0.375117	15.622080	0.06401196	6.41	0.600299	2.40	25
26	26	2.772470	44.311745	0.02256738	0.360689	15.982769	0.06256738	6.26	0.626752	2.41	26
27	27	2.883369	47.084214	0.02123854	0.346817	16.329586	0.06123854	6.13	0.653441	2.42	27
28	28	2.998703	49.967583	0.02001298	0.333477	16.663063	0.06001298	6.01	0.680363	2.43	28
29	29	3.118651	52.966286	0.01887993	0.320651	16.983715	0.05887993	5.89	0.707518	2.44	29
30	30	3.243398	56.084938	0.01783010	0.308319	17.292033	0.05783010	5.79	0.734903	2.45	30
31	31	3.373133	59.328335	0.01685535	0.296460	17.588494	0.05685535	5.69	0.762516	2.46	31
32	32	3.508059	62.701469	0.01594859	0.285058	17.873551	0.05594859	5.60	0.790355	2.47	32
33	33	3.648381	66.209527	0.01510357	0.274094	18.147646	0.05510357	5.52	0.818418	2.48	33
34	34	3.794316	69.857909	0.01431147	0.263552	18.411198	0.05431477	5.44	0.846702	2.49	34
35	35	3.946089	73.652225	0.01357732	0.253415	18.664613	0.05357732	5.36	0.875206	2.50	35
36	36	4.103933	77.598314	0.01288688	0.243669	18.908282	0.05288688	5.29	0.903928	2.51	36
37	37	4.268090	81.702246	0.01223957	0.234297	19.142579	0.05223957	5.23	0.932864	2.52	37
38	38	4.438813	85.970336	0.01163192	0.225285	19.367864	0.05163192	5.17	0.962013	2.53	38
39	39	4.616366	90.409150	0.01106083	0.216621	19.584485	0.05106083	5.11	0.991372	2.54	39
40	40	4.801021	95.025516	0.01052349	0.208289	19.792774	0.05052349	5.06	1.020940	2.55	40
41	41	4.993061	99.826536	0.01001738	0.200278	19.993052	0.05001738	5.01	1.050712	2.56	41
42	42	5.192784	104.819598	0.00954020	0.192575	20.185627	0.04954020	4.96	1.080688	2.57	42
43	43	5.400495	110.012382	0.00908989	0.185168	20.370795	0.04908989	4.91	1.110865	2.58	43
44	44	5.616515	115.412877	0.00866464	0.178046	20.548841	0.04866454	4.87	1.141240	2.59	44
45	45	5.841176	121.029392	0.00826246	0.171198	20.720040	0.04826246	4.83	1.171811	2.60	45
46	46	6.074823	126.870568	0.00788205	0.164614	20.884654	0.04788205	4.79	1.202574	2.61	46
47	47	6.317816	132.945390	0.00752189	0.158283	21.042936	0.04752189	4.76	1.233529	2.62	47
48	48	6.570528	139.263206	0.00718065	0.152195	21.195131	0.04718065	4.72	1.264671	2.63	48
49	49	6.833349	145.833734	0.00685712	0.146341	21.341472	0.04685712	4.69	1.295999	2.64	49
50	50	7.106683	152.667084	0.00655020	0.140713	21.482185	0.04655020	4.66	1.327510	2.66	50

Compound Interest and Annuity Tables *(continued)*

5.00 %
ANNUAL

	Amount Of 1	Amount Of 1 Per Period	Sinking Fund Payment	Present Worth Of 1	Present Worth Of 1 Per Period	Periodic Payment To Amortize 1	Constant Annual Percent	Total Interest	Annual Add-on Rate	
	What a single $1 deposit grows to in the future. The deposit is made at the beginning of the first period.	What a series of $1 deposits grow to in the future. A deposit is made at the end of each period.	The amount to be deposited at the end of each period that grows to $1 in the future.	What $1 to be paid in the future is worth today. Value today of a single payment tomorrow.	What $1 to be paid at the end of each period is worth today. Value today of a series of payments tomorrow.	The mortgage payment to amortize a loan of $1. An annuity certain, payable at the end of each period, worth $1 today.	The annual payment, including interest and principal, to amortize completely a loan of $100.	The total interest paid over the term of $1. The loan is amortized by regular periodic payments.	The average annual interest rate on a loan that : completely amortized by regular periodic payments.	
	$S=(1+i)^n$	$S_{\overline{n}}=\dfrac{(1+i)^n-1}{i}$	$\dfrac{1}{S_{\overline{n}}}=\dfrac{i}{(1+i)^n-1}$	$V^n=\dfrac{1}{(1+i)^n}$	$A_{\overline{n}}=\dfrac{1-V^n}{i}$	$\dfrac{1}{A_{\overline{n}}}=\dfrac{i}{1-V^n}$				
										YR
1	1.050000	1.000000	1.00000000	0.952381	0.952381	1.05000000	105.00	0.050000	5.00	1
2	1.102500	2.050000	0.48780488	0.907029	1.859410	0.53780488	53.79	0.075610	3.78	2
3	1.157625	3.152500	0.31720856	0.863838	2.723248	0.36720856	36.73	0.101626	3.39	3
4	1.215506	4.310125	0.23201183	0.822702	3.545951	0.28201183	28.21	0.128047	3.20	4
5	1.276282	5.525631	0.18097480	0.783526	4.329477	0.23097480	23.10	0.154874	3.10	5
6	1.340096	6.801913	0.14701747	0.746215	5.075692	0.19701747	19.71	0.182105	3.04	6
7	1.407100	8.142008	0.12281982	0.710681	5.786373	0.17281982	17.29	0.209739	3.00	7
8	1.477455	9.549109	0.10472181	0.676839	6.463213	0.15472181	15.48	0.237775	2.97	8
9	1.551328	11.026564	0.09069008	0.644609	7.107822	0.14069008	14.07	0.266211	2.96	9
10	1.628895	12.577893	0.07950457	0.613913	7.721735	0.12950457	12.96	0.295046	2.95	10
11	1.710339	14.206787	0.07038889	0.584679	8.306414	0.12038889	12.04	0.324278	2.95	11
12	1.795856	15.917127	0.06282541	0.556837	8.863252	0.11282541	11.29	0.353905	2.95	12
13	1.885649	17.712983	0.05645577	0.530321	9.393573	0.10645577	10.65	0.383925	2.95	13
14	1.979932	19.598632	0.05102397	0.505068	9.898641	0.10102397	10.11	0.414336	2.96	14
15	2.078928	21.578564	0.04634229	0.481017	10.379658	0.09634229	9.64	0.445134	2.97	15
16	2.182875	23.657492	0.04226991	0.458112	10.837770	0.09226991	9.23	0.476319	2.98	16
17	2.292018	25.840366	C.03869914	0.436297	11.274066	0.08869914	8.87	0.507885	2.99	17
18	2.406619	28.132385	0.03554622	0.415521	11.689587	0.08554622	8.56	0.539832	3.00	18
19	2.526950	30.539004	0.03274501	0.395734	12.085321	0.08274501	8.28	0.572155	3.01	19
20	2.653298	33.065954	0.03024259	0.376889	12.462210	0.08024259	8.03	0.604852	3.02	20
21	2.785963	35.719252	0.02799611	0.358942	12.821153	0.07799611	7.80	0.637918	3.04	21
22	2.925261	38.505214	0.02597051	0.341850	13.163003	0.07597051	7.60	0.671351	3.05	22
23	3.071524	41.430475	0.02413682	0.325571	13.488574	0.07413682	7.42	0.705147	3.07	23
24	3.225100	44.501999	0.02247090	0.310068	13.798642	0.07247090	7.25	0.739302	3.08	24
25	3.386355	47.727099	0.02095246	0.295303	14.093945	0.07095246	7.10	0.773811	3.10	25
26	3.555673	51.113454	0.01956432	0.281241	14.375185	0.06956432	6.96	0.808672	3.11	26
27	3.733456	54.669126	0.01829186	0.267848	14.643034	0.06829186	6.83	0.843880	3.13	27
28	3.920129	58.402583	0.01712253	0.255094	14.898127	0.06712253	6.72	0.879431	3.14	28
29	4.116136	62.322712	0.01604551	0.242946	15.141074	0.06604551	6.61	0.915320	3.16	29
30	4.321942	66.438848	0.01505144	0.231377	15.372451	0.06505144	6.51	0.951543	3.17	30
31	4.538039	70.760790	0.01413212	0.220359	15.592811	0.06413212	6.42	0.988096	3.19	31
32	4.764941	75.298829	0.01328042	0.209866	15.802677	0.06328042	6.33	1.024973	3.20	32
33	5.003189	80.063771	0.01249004	0.199873	16.002549	0.06249004	6.25	1.062171	3.22	33
34	5.253348	85.066959	0.01175545	0.190355	16.192904	0.06175545	6.18	1.099685	3.23	34
35	5.516015	90.320307	0.01107171	0.181290	16.374194	0.06107171	6.11	1.137510	3.25	35
36	5.791816	95.836323	0.01043446	0.172657	16.546852	0.06043446	6.05	1.175640	3.27	36
37	6.081407	101.628139	0.00983979	0.164436	16.711287	0.05983979	5.99	1.214072	3.28	37
38	6.385477	107.709546	0.00928423	0.156605	16.867893	0.05928423	5.93	1.252801	3.30	38
39	6.704751	114.095023	0.00876462	0.149148	17.017041	0.05876462	5.88	1.291820	3.31	39
40	7.039989	120.799774	0.00827816	0.142046	17.159086	0.05827816	5.83	1.331126	3.33	40
41	7.391988	127.839763	0.00782229	0.135282	17.294368	0.05782229	5.79	1.370714	3.34	41
42	7.761588	135.231751	0.00739471	0.128840	17.423208	0.05739471	5.74	1.410578	3.36	42
43	8.149667	142.993339	0.00699333	0.122704	17.545912	0.05699333	5.70	1.450713	3.37	43
44	8.557150	151.143006	0.00661625	0.116861	17.662773	0.05661625	5.67	1.491115	3.39	44
45	8.985008	159.700156	0.00626615	0.111297	17.774070	0.05626173	5.63	1.531778	3.40	45
46	9.434258	168.685164	0.00592820	0.105997	17.880066	0.05592820	5.60	1.572697	3.42	46
47	9.905971	178.119422	0.00561421	0.100949	17.981016	0.05561421	5.57	1.613868	3.43	47
48	10.401270	188.025393	0.00531843	0.096142	18.077158	0.05531843	5.54	1.655285	3.45	48
49	10.921333	198.426663	0.00503965	0.091564	18.168722	0.05503965	5.51	1.696943	3.46	49
50	11.467400	209.347996	0.00477674	0.087204	18.255925	0.05477674	5.48	1.738837	3.48	50

Compound Interest and Annuity Tables *(continued)*

COMPOUND INTEREST AND ANNUITY TABLE

6.00 %

ANNUAL

		Amount Of 1	Amount Of 1 Per Period	Sinking Fund Payment	Present Worth Of 1	Present Worth Of 1 Per Period	Periodic Payment To Amortize 1	Constant Annual Percent	Total Interest	Annual Add-on Rate
		What a single $1 deposit grows to in the future. The deposit is made at the beginning of the first period.	What a series of $1 deposits grow to in the future. A deposit is made at the end of each period.	The amount to be deposited at the end of each period that grows to $1 in the future.	What $1 to be paid in the future is worth today. Value today of a single payment tomorrow.	What $1 to be paid at the end of each period is worth today. Value today of a series of payments tomorrow.	The mortgage payment to amortize a loan of $1. An annuity, certain, payable at the end of each period, worth $1 today.	The annual payment, including interest and principal, to amortize completely a loan of $100.	The total interest paid over the term of $1. The loan is amortized by regular periodic payments.	The average annual interest rate on a loan that is completely amortized by regular periodic payments.
		$S=(1+i)^n$	$S_{\overline{n}|}=\dfrac{(1+i)^n-1}{i}$	$\dfrac{1}{S_{\overline{n}|}}=\dfrac{i}{(1+i)^n-1}$	$V^n=\dfrac{1}{(1+i)^n}$	$A_{\overline{n}|}=\dfrac{1-V^n}{i}$	$\dfrac{1}{A_{\overline{n}|}}=\dfrac{i}{1-V^n}$			
YR										YR
1	1	1.060000	1.000000	1.00000000	0.943396	0.943396	1.06000000	106.00	0.060000	6.00
2	2	1.123600	2.060000	0.48543689	0.889996	1.833393	0.54543689	54.55	0.090874	4.54
3	3	1.191016	3.183600	0.31410981	0.839619	2.673012	0.37410981	37.42	0.122329	4.08
4	4	1.262477	4.374616	0.22859149	0.792094	3.465106	0.28859149	28.86	0.154366	3.86
5	5	1.338226	5.637093	0.17739640	0.747258	4.212364	0.23739640	23.74	0.186982	3.74
6	6	1.418519	6.975319	0.14336263	0.704961	4.917324	0.20336263	20.34	0.220176	3.67
7	7	1.503630	8.393838	0.11913502	0.665057	5.582381	0.17913502	17.92	0.253945	3.63
8	8	1.593848	9.897468	0.10103594	0.627412	6.209794	0.16103594	16.11	0.288288	3.60
9	9	1.689479	11.491316	0.08702224	0.591898	6.801692	0.14702224	14.71	0.323200	3.59
10	10	1.790848	13.180795	0.07586796	0.558395	7.360087	0.13586796	13.59	0.358680	3.59
11	11	1.898299	14.971643	0.06679294	0.526788	7.886875	0.12679294	12.68	0.394722	3.59
12	12	2.012196	16.869941	0.05927703	0.496969	8.383844	0.11927703	11.93	0.431324	3.59
13	13	2.132928	18.882138	0.05296011	0.468839	8.852683	0.11296011	11.30	0.468481	3.60
14	14	2.260904	21.015066	0.04758491	0.442301	9.294984	0.10758491	10.76	0.506189	3.62
15	15	2.396558	23.275970	0.04296276	0.417265	9.712449	0.10296276	10.30	0.544441	3.63
16	16	2.540352	25.672528	0.03895214	0.393646	10.105895	0.09895214	9.90	0.583234	3.65
17	17	2.692773	28.212880	0.03544480	0.371364	10.477260	0.09544480	9.55	0.622562	3.66
18	18	2.854339	30.905653	0.03235654	0.350344	10.827603	0.09235654	9.24	0.662418	3.68
19	19	3.025600	33.759992	0.02962086	0.330513	11.158116	0.08962086	8.97	0.702796	3.70
20	20	3.207135	36.785591	0.02718456	0.311805	11.469921	0.08718456	8.72	0.743691	3.72
21	21	3.399564	39.992727	0.02500455	0.294155	11.764077	0.08500455	8.51	0.785095	3.74
22	22	3.603537	43.392290	0.02304557	0.277505	12.041582	0.08304557	8.31	0.827003	3.76
23	23	3.819750	46.995828	0.02127848	0.261797	12.303379	0.08127848	8.13	0.869405	3.78
24	24	4.048935	50.815577	0.01967900	0.246979	12.550358	0.07967900	7.97	0.912296	3.80
25	25	4.291871	54.864512	0.01822672	0.232999	12.783356	0.07822672	7.83	0.955668	3.82
26	26	4.549383	59.156383	0.01690435	0.219810	13.003166	0.07690435	7.70	0.999513	3.84
27	27	4.822346	63.705766	0.01569717	0.207368	13.210534	0.07569717	7.57	1.043823	3.87
28	28	5.111687	68.528112	0.01459255	0.195630	13.406164	0.07459255	7.46	1.088591	3.89
29	29	5.418388	73.639798	0.01357961	0.184557	13.590721	0.07357961	7.36	1.133809	3.91
30	30	5.743491	79.058186	0.01264991	0.174110	13.764831	0.07264891	7.27	1.179467	3.93
31	31	6.088101	84.801677	0.01179222	0.164255	13.929086	0.07179222	7.18	1.225559	3.95
32	32	6.453387	90.889778	0.01100224	0.154957	14.084043	0.07100224	7.11	1.272075	3.98
33	33	6.840590	97.343165	0.01027293	0.146186	14.230230	0.07027293	7.03	1.319007	4.00
34	34	7.251025	104.183755	0.00959843	0.137912	14.368141	0.06959843	6.96	1.366346	4.02
35	35	7.686087	111.434780	0.00897386	0.130105	14.498246	0.06897386	6.90	1.414085	4.04
36	36	8.147252	119.120867	0.00839483	0.122741	14.620987	0.06839483	6.84	1.462214	4.06
37	37	8.636087	127.268119	0.00785743	0.115793	14.736780	0.06785743	6.79	1.510725	4.08
38	38	9.154252	135.904206	0.00735812	0.109239	14.846019	0.06735812	6.74	1.559609	4.10
39	39	9.703507	145.058458	0.00689377	0.103056	14.949075	0.06689377	6.69	1.608857	4.13
40	40	10.285718	154.761966	0.00646154	0.097222	15.046207	0.06646154	6.65	1.658461	4.15
41	41	10.902861	165.047684	0.00605886	0.091719	15.138016	0.06605886	6.61	1.708413	4.17
42	42	11.557033	175.950545	0.00568342	0.086527	15.224543	0.06568342	6.57	1.758703	4.19
43	43	12.250455	187.507577	0.00533312	0.081630	15.306173	0.06533312	6.54	1.809324	4.21
44	44	12.985482	199.758032	0.00500606	0.077009	15.383182	0.06500606	6.51	1.860266	4.23
45	45	13.764611	212.743514	0.00470050	0.072650	15.455832	0.06470050	6.48	1.911522	4.25
46	46	14.590487	226.508125	0.00441485	0.068538	15.524370	0.06441485	6.45	1.963083	4.27
47	47	15.465917	241.098612	0.00414768	0.064658	15.589028	0.06414768	6.42	2.014941	4.29
48	48	16.393872	256.564529	0.00389765	0.060998	15.650027	0.06389765	6.39	2.067087	4.31
49	49	17.377504	272.958401	0.00366356	0.057546	15.707572	0.06366356	6.37	2.119515	4.33
50	50	18.420154	290.335905	0.00344429	0.054288	15.761861	0.06344429	6.35	2.172214	4.34

Compound Interest and Annuity Tables *(continued)*

COMPOUND INTEREST AND ANNUITY TABLE

7.00 % ANNUAL

		Amount Of 1	Amount Of 1 Per Period	Sinking Fund Payment	Present Worth Of 1	Present Worth Of 1 Per Period	Periodic Payment To Amortize 1	Constant Annual Percent	Total Interest	Annual Add-on Rate		
		What a single $1 deposit grows to in the future. The deposit is made at the beginning of the first period.	What a series of $1 deposits grow to in the future. A deposit is made at the end of each period.	The amount to be deposited at the end of each period that grows to $1 in the future.	What $1 to be paid in the future is worth today. Value today of a single payment tomorrow.	What $1 to be paid at the end of each period is worth today. Value today of a series of payments tomorrow.	The mortgage payment to amortize a loan of $1. An annuity certain, payable at the end of each period, worth $1 today.	The annual payment, including interest and principal, to amortize completely a loan of $100.	The total interest paid over the term of $1. The loan is amortized by regular periodic payments.	The average annual interest rate that is completely amortized by regular periodic payments.		
		$S=(1+i)^n$	$S_{\overline{n}|}=\dfrac{(1+i)^n-1}{i}$	$\dfrac{1}{S_{\overline{n}|}}=\dfrac{i}{(1+i)^n-1}$	$V^n=\dfrac{1}{(1+i)^n}$	$A_{\overline{n}|}=\dfrac{1-V^n}{i}$	$\dfrac{1}{A_{\overline{n}|}}=\dfrac{i}{1-V^n}$					
YR												**YR**
1	1	1.070000	1.000000	1.00000000	0.934579	0.934579	1.07000000	107.00	0.070000	7.00	1
2	2	1.144900	2.070000	0.48309179	0.873439	1.808018	0.55309179	55.31	0.106184	5.31	2
3	3	1.225043	3.214900	0.31105167	0.816298	2.624316	0.38105167	38.11	0.143155	4.77	3
4	4	1.310796	4.439943	0.22522812	0.762895	3.387211	0.29522812	29.53	0.180912	4.52	4
5	5	1.402552	5.750739	0.17389069	0.712986	4.100197	0.24389069	24.39	0.219453	4.39	5
6	6	1.500730	7.153291	0.13979580	0.666342	4.766540	0.20979580	20.98	0.258775	4.31	6
7	7	1.605781	8.654021	0.11555322	0.622750	5.389289	0.18555322	18.56	0.298873	4.27	7
8	8	1.718186	10.259803	0.09746776	0.582009	5.971299	0.16746776	16.75	0.339742	4.25	8
9	9	1.838459	11.977989	0.08348647	0.543934	6.515232	0.15348647	15.35	0.381378	4.24	9
10	10	1.967151	13.816448	0.07237750	0.508349	7.023582	0.14237750	14.24	0.423775	4.24	10
11	11	2.104852	15.783599	0.06335690	0.475093	7.498674	0.13335690	13.34	0.466926	4.24	11
12	12	2.252192	17.888451	0.05590199	0.444012	7.942686	0.12590199	12.60	0.510824	4.26	12
13	13	2.409845	20.140643	0.04965085	0.414964	8.357651	0.11965085	11.97	0.555461	4.27	13
14	14	2.578534	22.550488	0.04434494	0.387817	8.745468	0.11434494	11.44	0.600829	4.29	14
15	15	2.759032	25.129022	0.03979462	0.362446	9.107914	0.10979462	10.98	0.646919	4.31	15
16	16	2.952164	27.888054	0.03585765	0.338735	9.446649	0.10585765	10.59	0.693722	4.34	16
17	17	3.158815	30.840217	0.03242519	0.316574	9.763223	0.10242519	10.25	0.741228	4.36	17
18	18	3.379932	33.999033	0.02941260	0.295864	10.059087	0.09941260	9.95	0.789427	4.39	18
19	19	3.616528	37.378965	0.02675301	0.276508	10.335595	0.09675301	9.68	0.838307	4.41	19
20	20	3.869684	40.995492	0.02439293	0.258419	10.594014	0.09439293	9.44	0.887859	4.44	20
21	21	4.140562	44.865177	0.02228900	0.241513	10.835527	0.09228900	9.23	0.938069	4.47	21
22	22	4.430402	49.005739	0.02040577	0.225713	11.061240	0.09040577	9.05	0.988927	4.50	22
23	23	4.740530	53.436141	0.01871393	0.210947	11.272187	0.08871393	8.88	1.040420	4.52	23
24	24	5.072367	58.176671	0.01718902	0.197147	11.469334	0.08718902	8.72	1.092536	4.55	24
25	25	5.427433	63.249038	0.01581052	0.184249	11.653583	0.08581052	8.59	1.145263	4.58	25
26	26	5.807353	68.676470	0.01456103	0.172195	11.825779	0.08456103	8.46	1.198587	4.61	26
27	27	6.213868	74.483823	0.01342573	0.160930	11.986709	0.08342573	8.35	1.252495	4.64	27
28	28	6.648838	80.697691	0.01239193	0.150402	12.137111	0.08239193	8.24	1.306974	4.67	28
29	29	7.114257	87.346529	0.01144865	0.140563	12.277674	0.08144865	8.15	1.362011	4.70	29
30	30	7.612255	94.460786	0.01058640	0.131367	12.409041	0.08058640	8.06	1.417592	4.73	30
31	31	8.145113	102.073041	0.00979691	0.122773	12.531814	0.07979691	7.98	1.473704	4.75	31
32	32	8.715271	110.218154	0.00907292	0.114741	12.646555	0.07907292	7.91	1.530333	4.78	32
33	33	9.325340	118.933425	0.00840807	0.107235	12.753790	0.07840807	7.85	1.587466	4.81	33
34	34	9.978114	128.258765	0.00779674	0.100219	12.854009	0.07779674	7.78	1.645089	4.84	34
35	35	10.676581	138.236878	0.00723396	0.093663	12.947672	0.07723396	7.73	1.703189	4.87	35
36	36	11.423942	148.913460	0.00671531	0.087535	13.035208	0.07671531	7.68	1.761751	4.89	36
37	37	12.223618	160.337402	0.00623685	0.081809	13.117017	0.07623685	7.63	1.820763	4.92	37
38	38	13.079271	172.561020	0.00579505	0.076457	13.193473	0.07579505	7.58	1.880212	4.95	38
39	39	13.994820	185.640292	0.00538676	0.071455	13.264928	0.07538676	7.54	1.940084	4.97	39
40	40	14.974458	199.635112	0.00500914	0.066780	13.331709	0.07500914	7.51	2.000366	5.00	40
41	41	16.022063	214.609570	0.00465962	0.062412	13.394120	0.07465962	7.47	2.061045	5.03	41
42	42	17.144257	230.632240	0.00433591	0.058329	13.452449	0.07433591	7.44	2.122108	5.05	42
43	43	18.344355	247.776496	0.00403590	0.054513	13.506962	0.07403590	7.41	2.183543	5.08	43
44	44	19.628460	266.120851	0.00375769	0.050946	13.557908	0.07375769	7.38	2.245338	5.10	44
45	45	21.002452	285.749311	0.00349957	0.047613	13.605522	0.07349957	7.35	2.307481	5.13	45
46	46	22.472424	306.751763	0.00325996	0.044499	13.650020	0.07325996	7.33	2.369958	5.15	46
47	47	24.045707	329.224386	0.00303744	0.041587	13.691608	0.07303744	7.31	2.432760	5.18	47
48	48	25.728907	353.270093	0.00283070	0.038867	13.730474	0.07283070	7.29	2.495873	5.20	48
49	49	27.529930	378.999000	0.00263853	0.036324	13.766799	0.07263853	7.27	2.559288	5.22	49
50	50	29.457025	406.528929	0.00245985	0.033948	13.800746	0.07245985	7.25	2.622992	5.25	50

Compound Interest and Annuity Tables *(continued)*

COMPOUND INTEREST AND ANNUITY TABLE

**8.00 %
ANNUAL**

		Amount Of 1	Amount Of 1 Per Period	Sinking Fund Payment	Present Worth Of 1	Present Worth Of 1 Per Period	Periodic Payment To Amortize 1	Constant Annual Percent	Total Interest	Annual Add-on Rate		
		What a single $1 deposit grows to in the future. The deposit is made at the beginning of the first period.	What a series of $1 deposits grow to in the future. A deposit is made at the end of each period.	The amount to be deposited at the end of each period that grows to $1 in the future.	What $1 is worth today. Value today of a single payment tomorrow.	What $1 to be paid at the end of each period is worth today. Value today of a series of payments tomorrow.	The mortgage payment to amortize a loan of $1. An annuity certain, payable at the end of each period, worth $1 today.	The annual payment, including interest and principal, to amortize a loan completely with regular periodic payments.	The total interest paid over the term of $1. The loan is amortized by regular periodic payments.	The average annual interest rate on a loan that is completely amortized by periodic payments.		
		$S=(1+i)^n$	$S_{\overline{n}}=\dfrac{(1+i)^n-1}{i}$	$\dfrac{1}{S_{\overline{n}}}=\dfrac{i}{(1+i)^n-1}$	$V^n=\dfrac{1}{(1+i)^n}$	$A_{\overline{n}}=\dfrac{1-V^n}{i}$	$\dfrac{1}{A_{\overline{n}}}=\dfrac{i}{1-V^n}$					
YR												**YR**
1	1	1.080000	1.000000	1.00000000	0.925926	0.925926	1.08000000	108.00	0.080000	8.00	1
2	2	1.166400	2.080000	0.48076923	0.857339	1.783265	0.56076923	56.08	0.121538	6.08	2
3	3	1.259712	3.246400	0.30803351	0.793832	2.577097	0.38803351	38.81	0.164101	5.47	3
4	4	1.360489	4.506112	0.22192080	0.735030	3.312127	0.30192080	30.20	0.207683	5.19	4
5	5	1.469328	5.866601	0.17045645	0.680583	3.992710	0.25045645	25.05	0.252282	5.05	5
6	6	1.586874	7.335929	0.13631539	0.630170	4.622880	0.21631539	21.64	0.297892	4.96	6
7	7	1.713824	8.922803	0.11207240	0.583490	5.206370	0.19207240	19.21	0.344507	4.92	7
8	8	1.850930	10.636628	0.09401476	0.540269	5.746639	0.17401476	17.41	0.392118	4.90	8
9	9	1.999005	12.487558	0.08007971	0.500249	6.246888	0.16007971	16.01	0.440717	4.90	9
10	10	2.158925	14.486562	0.06902949	0.463193	6.710081	0.14902949	14.91	0.490295	4.90	10
11	11	2.331639	16.645487	0.06007634	0.428883	7.138964	0.14007634	14.01	0.540840	4.92	11
12	12	2.518170	18.977126	0.05269502	0.397114	7.536078	0.13269502	13.27	0.592340	4.94	12
13	13	2.719624	21.495297	0.04652181	0.367698	7.903776	0.12652181	12.66	0.644783	4.96	13
14	14	2.937194	24.214920	0.04129685	0.340461	8.244237	0.12129685	12.13	0.698156	4.99	14
15	15	3.172169	27.152114	0.03682954	0.315242	8.559479	0.11682954	11.69	0.752443	5.02	15
16	16	3.425943	30.324283	0.03297687	0.291890	8.851369	0.11297687	11.30	0.807630	5.05	16
17	17	3.700018	33.750226	0.02962943	0.270269	9.121638	0.10962943	10.97	0.863700	5.08	17
18	18	3.996019	37.450244	0.02670210	0.250249	9.371887	0.10670210	10.68	0.920638	5.11	18
19	19	4.315701	41.446263	0.02412763	0.231712	9.603599	0.10412763	10.42	0.978425	5.15	19
20	20	4.660957	45.761964	0.02185221	0.214548	9.818147	0.10185221	10.19	1.037044	5.19	20
21	21	5.033834	50.422921	0.01983225	0.198656	10.016803	0.09983225	9.99	1.096477	5.22	21
22	22	5.436540	55.456755	0.01803207	0.183941	10.200744	0.09803207	9.81	1.156706	5.26	22
23	23	5.871464	60.893296	0.01642217	0.170315	10.371059	0.09642217	9.65	1.217710	5.29	23
24	24	6.341181	66.764759	0.01497796	0.157699	10.528758	0.09497796	9.50	1.279471	5.33	24
25	25	6.848475	73.105940	0.01367878	0.146018	10.674776	0.09367878	9.37	1.341969	5.37	25
26	26	7.396353	79.954415	0.01250713	0.135202	10.809978	0.09250713	9.26	1.405185	5.40	26
27	27	7.988061	87.350768	0.01144810	0.125187	10.935165	0.09144810	9.15	1.469099	5.44	27
28	28	8.627106	95.338830	0.01048891	0.115914	11.051078	0.09048891	9.05	1.533689	5.48	28
29	29	9.317275	103.965936	0.00961854	0.107328	11.158406	0.08961854	8.97	1.598938	5.51	29
30	30	10.062657	113.283211	0.00882743	0.099377	11.257783	0.08882743	8.89	1.664823	5.55	30
31	31	10.867669	123.345868	0.00810728	0.092016	11.349799	0.08810728	8.82	1.731326	5.58	31
32	32	11.737080	134.213537	0.00745081	0.085200	11.434999	0.08745081	8.75	1.798426	5.62	32
33	33	12.676050	145.950620	0.00685163	0.078889	11.513888	0.08685163	8.69	1.866104	5.65	33
34	34	13.690134	158.626670	0.00630411	0.073045	11.586934	0.08630411	8.64	1.934340	5.69	34
35	35	14.785344	172.316804	0.00580326	0.067635	11.654568	0.08580326	8.59	2.003114	5.72	35
36	36	15.968172	187.102148	0.00534467	0.062625	11.717193	0.08534467	8.54	2.072408	5.76	36
37	37	17.245626	203.070320	0.00492440	0.057986	11.775179	0.08492440	8.50	2.142203	5.79	37
38	38	18.625276	220.315945	0.00453894	0.053690	11.828869	0.08453894	8.46	2.212480	5.82	38
39	39	20.115296	238.941221	0.00418513	0.049713	11.878582	0.08418513	8.42	2.283220	5.85	39
40	40	21.724521	259.056519	0.00386016	0.046031	11.924613	0.08386016	8.39	2.354406	5.89	40
41	41	23.462483	280.781040	0.00356149	0.042621	11.967235	0.08356149	8.36	2.426021	5.92	41
42	42	25.339482	304.243523	0.00328684	0.039464	12.006699	0.08328684	8.33	2.498047	5.95	42
43	43	27.366640	329.583005	0.00303414	0.036541	12.043240	0.08303414	8.31	2.570468	5.98	43
44	44	29.555972	356.949646	0.00280152	0.033834	12.077074	0.08280152	8.29	2.643267	6.01	44
45	45	31.920449	386.505617	0.00258728	0.031328	12.108402	0.08258728	8.26	2.716428	6.04	45
46	46	34.474085	418.426067	0.00238991	0.029007	12.137409	0.08238991	8.24	2.789936	6.07	46
47	47	37.232012	452.900152	0.00220799	0.026859	12.164267	0.08220799	8.21	2.863776	6.09	47
48	48	40.210573	490.132164	0.00204027	0.024869	12.189136	0.08204027	8.21	2.937933	6.12	48
49	49	43.427419	530.342737	0.00188557	0.023027	12.212163	0.08188557	8.19	3.012393	6.15	49
50	50	46.901613	573.770156	0.00174286	0.021321	12.233485	0.08174286	8.18	3.087143	6.17	50

Compound Interest and Annuity Tables *(continued)*

COMPOUND INTEREST AND ANNUITY TABLE

9.00 %
ANNUAL

		Amount Of 1	Amount Of 1 Per Period	Sinking Fund Payment	Present Worth Of 1	Present Worth Of 1 Per Period	Periodic Payment To Amortize 1	Constant Annual Percent	Total Interest	Annual Add-on Rate	
		What a single $1 deposit grows to in the future. The deposit is made at the beginning of the first period.	What a series of $1 deposits grow to in the future. A deposit is made at the end of each period.	The amount to be deposited at the end of each period that grows to $1 in the future.	What $1 to be paid in the future is worth today. Value today of a single payment tomorrow.	What $1 to be paid at the end of each period is worth today. Value today of a series of payments tomorrow.	The mortgage payment to amortize a loan of $1. An annuity certain, payable at the end of each period, worth $1 today.	The annual payment, including interest and principal, to amortize a loan of $100.	The total interest paid over the term of $1. The loan is amortized by regular periodic payments.	The average annual interest rate on a loan that is completely amortized by regular periodic payments.	
		$S=(1+i)^n$	$S_{\overline{n}}=\dfrac{(1+i)^n-1}{i}$	$\dfrac{1}{S_{\overline{n}}}=\dfrac{i}{(1+i)^n-1}$	$V^n=\dfrac{1}{(1+i)^n}$	$A_{\overline{n}}=\dfrac{1-V^n}{i}$	$\dfrac{1}{A_{\overline{n}}}=\dfrac{i}{1-V^n}$				
YR											**YR**
1	1	1.090000	1.000000	1.00000000	0.917431	0.917431	1.09000000	109.00	0.090000	9.00	1
2	2	1.188100	2.090000	0.47846890	0.841680	1.759111	0.56846890	56.85	0.136938	6.85	2
3	3	1.295029	3.278100	0.30505476	0.772183	2.531295	0.39505476	39.51	0.185164	6.17	3
4	4	1.411582	4.573129	0.21866866	0.708425	3.239720	0.30866866	30.87	0.234675	5.87	4
5	5	1.538624	5.984711	0.16709246	0.649931	3.889651	0.25709246	25.71	0.285462	5.71	5
6	6	1.677100	7.523335	0.13291978	0.596267	4.485919	0.22291978	22.30	0.337519	5.63	6
7	7	1.828039	9.200435	0.10869052	0.547034	5.032953	0.19869052	19.87	0.390834	5.58	7
8	8	1.992563	11.028474	0.09067438	0.501866	5.534819	0.18067438	18.07	0.445395	5.57	8
9	9	2.171893	13.021036	0.07679880	0.460428	5.995247	0.16679880	16.68	0.501189	5.57	9
10	10	2.367364	15.192930	0.06582009	0.422411	6.417658	0.15582009	15.59	0.558201	5.58	10
11	11	2.580426	17.560293	0.05694666	0.387533	6.805191	0.14694666	14.70	0.616413	5.60	11
12	12	2.812665	20.140720	0.04965066	0.355535	7.160725	0.13965066	13.97	0.675808	5.63	12
13	13	3.065805	22.953385	0.04356656	0.326179	7.486904	0.13356656	13.36	0.736365	5.66	13
14	14	3.341727	26.019160	0.03843417	0.299246	7.786150	0.12843417	12.85	0.798064	5.70	14
15	15	3.642482	29.360916	0.03405888	0.274538	8.060688	0.12405888	12.41	0.860883	5.74	15
16	16	3.970306	33.003399	0.03029991	0.251870	8.312558	0.12029991	12.03	0.924799	5.78	16
17	17	4.327633	36.973705	0.02704625	0.231073	8.543631	0.11704625	11.71	0.989786	5.82	17
18	18	4.717120	41.301338	0.02421229	0.211994	8.755625	0.11421229	11.43	1.055821	5.87	18
19	19	5.141661	46.018458	0.02173041	0.194490	8.950115	0.11173041	11.18	1.122878	5.91	19
20	20	5.604411	51.160120	0.01954648	0.178431	9.128546	0.10954648	10.96	1.190930	5.95	20
21	21	6.108808	56.764530	0.01761663	0.163698	9.292244	0.10761663	10.77	1.259949	6.00	21
22	22	6.658600	62.873338	0.01590499	0.150182	9.442425	0.10590499	10.60	1.329910	6.05	22
23	23	7.257874	69.531939	0.01438188	0.137781	9.580207	0.10438188	10.44	1.400783	6.09	23
24	24	7.911610	76.789813	0.01302256	0.126405	9.706612	0.10302256	10.31	1.472541	6.14	24
25	25	8.623081	84.700896	0.01180625	0.115968	9.822580	0.10180625	10.19	1.545156	6.18	25
26	26	9.399158	93.323977	0.01071536	0.106393	9.928972	0.10071536	10.08	1.618599	6.23	26
27	27	10.245082	102.723135	0.00973941	0.097608	10.026580	0.09973941	9.98	1.692842	6.27	27
28	28	11.167140	112.968217	0.00885205	0.089548	10.116128	0.09885205	9.89	1.767857	6.31	28
29	29	12.172182	124.135356	0.00805572	0.082155	10.198283	0.09805572	9.81	1.843616	6.36	29
30	30	13.267678	136.307539	0.00733635	0.075371	10.273654	0.09733635	9.74	1.920091	6.40	30
31	31	14.461770	149.575217	0.00668560	0.069148	10.342802	0.09668560	9.67	1.997254	6.44	31
32	32	15.763329	164.036987	0.00609619	0.063438	10.406240	0.09609619	9.61	2.075078	6.48	32
33	33	17.182028	179.800315	0.00556173	0.058200	10.464441	0.09556173	9.56	2.153537	6.53	33
34	34	18.728411	196.982344	0.00507660	0.053395	10.517835	0.09507660	9.51	2.232604	6.57	34
35	35	20.413968	215.710755	0.00463584	0.048986	10.566821	0.09463584	9.47	2.312254	6.61	35
36	36	22.251225	236.124723	0.00423505	0.044941	10.611763	0.09423505	9.43	2.392462	6.65	36
37	37	24.253835	258.375948	0.00387033	0.041231	10.652993	0.09387033	9.39	2.473202	6.68	37
38	38	26.436680	282.629783	0.00353820	0.037826	10.690820	0.09353820	9.36	2.554452	6.72	38
39	39	28.815982	309.066463	0.00323555	0.034703	10.725523	0.09323555	9.33	2.636186	6.76	39
40	40	31.409420	337.882445	0.00295961	0.031838	10.757360	0.09295961	9.30	2.718384	6.80	40
41	41	34.236268	369.291865	0.00270789	0.029209	10.786569	0.09270789	9.28	2.801023	6.83	41
42	42	37.317532	403.528133	0.00247814	0.026797	10.813366	0.09247814	9.25	2.884082	6.87	42
43	43	40.676110	440.845665	0.00226837	0.024584	10.837950	0.09226837	9.23	2.967540	6.90	43
44	44	44.336660	481.521775	0.00207675	0.022555	10.860505	0.09207675	9.21	3.051377	6.93	44
45	45	48.327286	525.858734	0.00190165	0.020692	10.881197	0.09190165	9.20	3.135574	6.97	45
46	46	52.676742	574.186021	0.00174160	0.018984	10.900181	0.09174160	9.18	3.220113	7.00	46
47	47	57.417649	626.862762	0.00159525	0.017416	10.917597	0.09159525	9.16	3.304977	7.03	47
48	48	62.585237	684.280411	0.00146139	0.015978	10.933575	0.09146139	9.15	3.390147	7.06	48
49	49	68.217908	746.865648	0.00133893	0.014659	10.948234	0.09133893	9.14	3.475608	7.09	49
50	50	74.357520	815.083556	0.00122687	0.013449	10.961683	0.09122687	9.13	3.561343	7.12	50

Compound Interest and Annuity Tables *(continued)*

COMPOUND INTEREST AND ANNUITY TABLE

10.00 %
ANNUAL

		Amount Of 1	Amount Of 1 Per Period	Sinking Fund Payment	Present Worth Of 1	Present Worth Of 1 Per Period	Periodic Payment To Amortize 1	Constant Annual Percent	Total Interest	Annual Add-on Rate		
		What a single $1 deposit grows to in the future. The deposit is made at the beginning of the first period.	What a series of $1 deposits grow to in the future. A deposit is made at the end of each period.	The amount to be deposited at the end of each period that grows to $1 in the future.	What $1 to be paid in the future is worth today. Value today of a single payment tomorrow.	What $1 to be paid at the end of each period is worth today. Value today of a series of payments tomorrow.	The mortgage payment to amortize a loan of $1. An annuity certain, payable at the end of each period, worth $1 today.	The annual payment, including interest and principal, to amortize completely a loan of $100.	The total interest paid over the term on a loan of $1. The loan is amortized by regular periodic payments.	The average annual interest rate on a loan that is completely amortized by regular periodic payments.		
		$S=(1+i)^n$	$S_{\overline{n}}=\dfrac{(1+i)^n-1}{i}$	$\dfrac{1}{S_{\overline{n}}}=\dfrac{i}{(1+i)^n-1}$	$V^n=\dfrac{1}{(1+i)^n}$	$A_{\overline{n}}=\dfrac{1-V^n}{i}$	$\dfrac{1}{A_{\overline{n}}}=\dfrac{i}{1-V^n}$					
YR											YR	
1	1	1.100000	1.000000	1.00000000	0.909091	0.909091	1.10000000	110.00	0.100000	10.00	1	
2	2	1.210000	2.100000	0.47619048	0.826446	1.735537	0.57619048	57.62	0.152381	7.62	2	
3	3	1.331000	3.310000	0.30211480	0.751315	2.486852	0.40211480	40.22	0.206344	6.88	3	
4	4	1.464100	4.641000	0.21547080	0.683013	3.169865	0.31547080	31.55	0.261883	6.55	4	
5	5	1.610510	6.105100	0.16379748	0.620921	3.790787	0.26379748	26.38	0.318987	6.38	5	
6	6	1.771561	7.715610	0.12960738	0.564474	4.355261	0.22960738	22.97	0.377644	6.29	6	
7	7	1.948717	9.487171	0.10540550	0.513158	4.868419	0.20540550	20.55	0.437838	6.25	7	
8	8	2.143589	11.435888	0.08744402	0.466507	5.334926	0.18744402	18.75	0.499552	6.24	8	
9	9	2.357948	13.579477	0.07364054	0.424098	5.759024	0.17364054	17.37	0.562765	6.25	9	
10	10	2.593742	15.937425	0.06274539	0.385543	6.144567	0.16274539	16.28	0.627454	6.27	10	
11	11	2.853117	18.531167	0.05396314	0.350494	6.495061	0.15396314	15.40	0.693595	6.31	11	
12	12	3.138428	21.384284	0.04676332	0.318631	6.813692	0.14676332	14.68	0.761160	6.34	12	
13	13	3.452271	24.522712	0.04077852	0.289664	7.103356	0.14077852	14.08	0.830121	6.39	13	
14	14	3.797498	27.974983	0.03574622	0.263331	7.366687	0.13574622	13.58	0.900447	6.43	14	
15	15	4.177248	31.772482	0.03147378	0.239392	7.606080	0.13147378	13.15	0.972107	6.48	15	
16	16	4.594973	35.949730	0.02781662	0.217629	7.823709	0.12781662	12.79	1.045066	6.53	16	
17	17	5.054470	40.544703	0.02466413	0.197845	8.021553	0.12466413	12.47	1.119290	6.58	17	
18	18	5.559917	45.599173	0.02193022	0.179859	8.201412	0.12193022	12.20	1.194744	6.64	18	
19	19	6.115909	51.159090	0.01954687	0.163508	8.364920	0.11954687	11.96	1.271390	6.69	19	
20	20	6.727500	57.274999	0.01745962	0.148644	8.513564	0.11745962	11.75	1.349192	6.75	20	
21	21	7.400250	64.002499	0.01562439	0.135131	8.648694	0.11562439	11.57	1.428112	6.80	21	
22	22	8.140275	71.402749	0.01400506	0.122846	8.771540	0.11400506	11.41	1.508111	6.86	22	
23	23	8.954302	79.543024	0.01257181	0.111678	8.883218	0.11257181	11.26	1.589152	6.91	23	
24	24	9.849733	88.497327	0.01129978	0.101526	8.984744	0.11129978	11.13	1.671195	6.96	24	
25	25	10.834706	98.347059	0.01016807	0.092296	9.077040	0.11016807	11.02	1.754202	7.02	25	
26	26	11.918177	109.181765	0.00915904	0.083905	9.160945	0.10915904	10.92	1.838135	7.07	26	
27	27	13.109994	121.099942	0.00825764	0.076278	9.237223	0.10825764	10.83	1.922956	7.12	27	
28	28	14.420994	134.209936	0.00745101	0.069343	9.306567	0.10745101	10.75	2.008628	7.17	28	
29	29	15.863093	148.630930	0.00672807	0.063039	9.369606	0.10672807	10.68	2.095114	7.22	29	
30	30	17.449402	164.494023	0.00607925	0.057309	9.426914	0.10607925	10.61	2.182377	7.27	30	
31	31	19.194342	181.943425	0.00549621	0.052099	9.479013	0.10549621	10.55	2.270383	7.32	31	
32	32	21.113777	201.137767	0.00497172	0.047362	9.526376	0.10497172	10.50	2.359095	7.37	32	
33	33	23.225154	222.251544	0.00449941	0.043057	9.569432	0.10449941	10.45	2.448480	7.42	33	
34	34	25.547670	245.476699	0.00407371	0.039143	9.608575	0.10407371	10.41	2.538506	7.47	34	
35	35	28.102437	271.024368	0.00368971	0.035584	9.644159	0.10368971	10.37	2.629140	7.51	35	
36	36	30.912681	299.126805	0.00334306	0.032349	9.676508	0.10334306	10.34	2.720350	7.56	36	
37	37	34.003949	330.039486	0.00302994	0.029408	9.705917	0.10302994	10.31	2.812108	7.60	37	
38	38	37.404343	364.043434	0.00274692	0.026735	9.732651	0.10274692	10.28	2.904383	7.64	38	
39	39	41.144778	401.447778	0.00249098	0.024304	9.756956	0.10249098	10.25	2.997148	7.68	39	
40	40	45.259256	442.592556	0.00225941	0.022095	9.779051	0.10225941	10.23	3.090377	7.73	40	
41	41	49.785181	487.851811	0.00204980	0.020086	9.799137	0.10204980	10.21	3.184042	7.77	41	
42	42	54.763699	537.636992	0.00185999	0.018260	9.817397	0.10185999	10.19	3.278120	7.81	42	
43	43	60.240069	592.400692	0.00168805	0.016600	9.833998	0.10168805	10.17	3.372586	7.84	43	
44	44	66.264076	652.640761	0.00153224	0.015091	9.849089	0.10153224	10.16	3.467418	7.88	44	
45	45	72.890484	718.904837	0.00139100	0.013719	9.862808	0.10139100	10.14	3.562595	7.92	45	
46	46	80.179532	791.795321	0.00126295	0.012472	9.875280	0.10126295	10.13	3.658096	7.95	46	
47	47	88.197485	871.974853	0.00114682	0.011338	9.886618	0.10114682	10.12	3.753901	7.99	47	
48	48	97.017234	960.172338	0.00104148	0.010307	9.896926	0.10104148	10.11	3.849991	8.02	48	
49	49	106.718957	1057.189572	0.00094590	0.009370	9.906296	0.10094590	10.10	3.946349	8.05	49	
50	50	117.390853	1163.908529	0.00085917	0.008519	9.914814	0.10085917	10.09	4.042959	8.09	50	

Compound Interest and Annuity Tables *(continued)*

COMPOUND INTEREST AND ANNUITY TABLE

11.00 %
ANNUAL

		Amount Of 1	Amount Of 1 Per Period	Sinking Fund Payment	Present Worth Of 1	Present Worth Of 1 Per Period	Periodic Payment To Amortize 1	Constant Annual Percent	Total Interest	Annual Add-on Rate		
		What a single $1 deposit grows to in the future. The deposit is made at the beginning of the first period.	What a series of $1 deposits grow to in the future. A deposit is made at the end of each period.	The amount to be deposited at the end of each period that grows to $1 in the future.	What $1 to be paid in the future is worth today. Value today of a single payment tomorrow.	What $1 to be paid at the end of each period is worth today. Value today of a series of payments tomorrow.	The mortgage payment to amortize a loan of $1. An annuity certain, payable at the end of each period, worth $1 today.	The annual payment, including interest and principal, to amortize completely a loan of $100.	The total interest paid over the term on a loan of $1. The loan is amortized by regular periodic payments.	The average annual interest rate on a loan that is completely amortized by regular periodic payments.		
		$S=(1+i)^n$	$S\overline{n}=\dfrac{(1+i)^n-1}{i}$	$\dfrac{1}{S\overline{n}}=\dfrac{i}{(1+i)^n-1}$	$V^n=\dfrac{1}{(1+i)^n}$	$A\overline{n}=\dfrac{1-V^n}{i}$	$\dfrac{1}{A\overline{n}}=\dfrac{i}{1-V^n}$					
YR												YR
1	1	1.110000	1.000000	1.00000000	0.900901	0.900901	1.11000000	111.00	0.110000	11.00	1
2	2	1.232100	2.110000	0.47393365	0.811622	1.712523	0.58393365	58.40	0.167867	8.39	2
3	3	1.367631	3.342100	0.29921307	0.731191	2.443715	0.40921307	40.93	0.227639	7.59	3
4	4	1.518070	4.709731	0.21232635	0.658731	3.102446	0.32232635	32.24	0.289305	7.23	4
5	5	1.685058	6.227801	0.16057031	0.593451	3.695897	0.27057031	27.06	0.352852	7.06	5
6	6	1.870415	7.912860	0.12637656	0.534641	4.230538	0.23637656	23.64	0.418259	6.97	6
7	7	2.076160	9.783274	0.10221527	0.481658	4.712196	0.21221527	21.23	0.485507	6.94	7
8	8	2.304538	11.859434	0.08432105	0.433926	5.146123	0.19432105	19.44	0.554568	6.93	8
9	9	2.558037	14.163972	0.07060166	0.390925	5.537048	0.18060166	18.07	0.625415	6.95	9
10	10	2.839421	16.722009	0.05980143	0.352184	5.889232	0.16980143	16.99	0.698014	6.98	10
11	11	3.151757	19.561430	0.05112101	0.317283	6.206515	0.16112101	16.12	0.772331	7.02	11
12	12	3.498451	22.713187	0.04402729	0.285841	6.492356	0.15402729	15.41	0.848327	7.07	12
13	13	3.883280	26.211638	0.03815099	0.257514	6.749870	0.14815099	14.82	0.925963	7.12	13
14	14	4.310441	30.094918	0.03322820	0.231995	6.981865	0.14322820	14.33	1.005195	7.18	14
15	15	4.784589	34.405359	0.02906524	0.209004	7.190870	0.13906524	13.91	1.085979	7.24	15
16	16	5.310894	39.189948	0.02551675	0.188292	7.379162	0.13551675	13.56	1.168268	7.30	16
17	17	5.895093	44.500843	0.02247148	0.169633	7.548794	0.13247148	13.25	1.252015	7.36	17
18	18	6.543553	50.395936	0.01984287	0.152822	7.701617	0.12984287	12.99	1.337172	7.43	18
19	19	7.263344	56.939488	0.01756250	0.137678	7.839294	0.12756250	12.76	1.423688	7.49	19
20	20	8.062312	64.202832	0.01557564	0.124034	7.963328	0.12557564	12.56	1.511513	7.56	20
21	21	8.949166	72.265144	0.01383793	0.111742	8.075070	0.12383793	12.39	1.600597	7.62	21
22	22	9.933574	81.214309	0.01231310	0.100669	8.175739	0.12231310	12.24	1.690888	7.69	22
23	23	11.026267	91.147884	0.01097118	0.090693	8.266432	0.12097118	12.10	1.782337	7.75	23
24	24	12.239157	102.174151	0.00978721	0.081705	8.348137	0.11978721	11.98	1.874893	7.81	24
25	25	13.585464	114.413307	0.00874024	0.073608	8.421745	0.11874024	11.88	1.968506	7.87	25
26	26	15.079865	127.998771	0.00781258	0.066314	8.488058	0.11781258	11.79	2.063127	7.94	26
27	27	16.738650	143.078636	0.00699816	0.059742	8.547800	0.11699816	11.70	2.158707	8.00	27
28	28	18.579901	159.817286	0.00625715	0.053822	8.601622	0.11625715	11.63	2.255200	8.05	28
29	29	20.623691	178.397187	0.00560547	0.048488	8.650110	0.11560547	11.57	2.352559	8.11	29
30	30	22.892297	199.020878	0.00502460	0.043683	8.693793	0.11502460	11.51	2.450738	8.17	30
31	31	25.410449	221.913174	0.00450627	0.039354	8.733146	0.11450627	11.46	2.549694	8.22	31
32	32	28.205599	247.323624	0.00404329	0.035454	8.768600	0.11404329	11.41	2.649385	8.28	32
33	33	31.308214	275.529222	0.00362938	0.031940	8.800541	0.11362938	11.37	2.749770	8.33	33
34	34	34.752118	306.837437	0.00325905	0.028775	8.829316	0.11325905	11.33	2.850808	8.38	34
35	35	38.574851	341.589555	0.00292749	0.025924	8.855240	0.11292749	11.30	2.952462	8.44	35
36	36	42.818085	380.164406	0.00263044	0.023355	8.878594	0.11263044	11.27	3.054696	8.49	36
37	37	47.528074	422.982490	0.00236416	0.021040	8.899635	0.11236416	11.24	3.157474	8.53	37
38	38	52.756162	470.510564	0.00212535	0.018955	8.918590	0.11212535	11.22	3.260763	8.58	38
39	39	58.559340	523.266726	0.00191107	0.017077	8.935666	0.11191107	11.20	3.364532	8.63	39
40	40	65.000867	581.826064	0.00171873	0.015384	8.951051	0.11171873	11.18	3.468749	8.67	40
41	41	72.150963	646.826934	0.00154601	0.013860	8.964911	0.11154601	11.16	3.573386	8.72	41
42	42	80.087569	718.977896	0.00139086	0.012486	8.977397	0.11139086	11.14	3.678416	8.76	42
43	43	88.897201	799.065465	0.00125146	0.011249	8.988646	0.11125146	11.13	3.783813	8.80	43
44	44	98.675893	887.962666	0.00112617	0.010134	8.998780	0.11112617	11.12	3.889552	8.84	44
45	45	109.530242	986.638559	0.00101354	0.009130	9.007910	0.11101354	11.11	3.995609	8.88	45
46	46	121.578568	1096.168801	0.00091227	0.008225	9.016135	0.11091227	11.10	4.101964	8.92	46
47	47	134.952211	1217.747369	0.00082119	0.007410	9.023545	0.11082119	11.09	4.208596	8.95	47
48	48	149.796954	1352.699580	0.00073926	0.006676	9.030221	0.11073926	11.08	4.315485	8.99	48
49	49	166.274619	1502.496533	0.00066556	0.006014	9.036235	0.11066556	11.07	4.422612	9.03	49
50	50	184.564827	1668.771152	0.00059924	0.005418	9.041653	0.11059924	11.06	4.529962	9.06	50

441

Compound Interest and Annuity Tables *(continued)*

COMPOUND INTEREST AND ANNUITY TABLE

12.00 %
ANNUAL

	Amount Of 1 Per Period	Amount Of 1	Sinking Fund Payment	Present Worth Of 1	Present Worth Of 1 Per Period	Periodic Payment To Amortize 1	Constant Annual Percent	Total Interest	Annual Add-on Rate
	What a single $1 deposit grows to in the future. The deposit is made at the beginning of the first period.	What a series of $1 deposits grow to in the future. A deposit is made at the end of each period.	The amount to be deposited at the end of each period that grows to $1 in the future.	What $1 to be paid in the future is worth today. Value today of a single payment tomorrow.	What $1 to be paid at the end of each period is worth today. Value today of a series of payments tomorrow.	The mortgage payment to amortize a loan of $1. An annuity certain, payable at the end of each period, worth $1 today.	The annual payment, including interest and principal, to amortize completely a loan of $100.	The total interest paid over the term of $1. The loan is completely amortized by regular periodic payments.	The average annual interest rate on a loan that is amortized by regular periodic payments.
	$S=(1+i)^n$	$S_{\overline{n}|}=\dfrac{(1+i)^n-1}{i}$	$\dfrac{1}{S_{\overline{n}|}}=\dfrac{i}{(1+i)^n-1}$	$V^n=\dfrac{1}{(1+i)^n}$	$A_{\overline{n}|}=\dfrac{1-V^n}{i}$	$\dfrac{1}{A_{\overline{n}|}}=\dfrac{i}{1-V^n}$			

YR										YR
1	1	1.120000	1.000000	1.00000000	0.892857	0.892857	1.12000000	112.00	0.120000	12.00	1
2	2	1.254400	2.120000	0.47169811	0.797194	1.690051	0.59169811	59.17	0.183396	9.17	2
3	3	1.404928	3.374400	0.29634898	0.711780	2.401831	0.41634898	41.64	0.249047	8.30	3
4	4	1.573519	4.779328	0.20923444	0.635518	3.037349	0.32923444	32.93	0.316938	7.92	4
5	5	1.762342	6.352847	0.15740973	0.567427	3.604776	0.27740973	27.75	0.387049	7.74	5
6	6	1.973823	8.115189	0.12322572	0.506631	4.111407	0.24322572	24.33	0.459354	7.66	6
7	7	2.210681	10.089012	0.09911774	0.452349	4.563757	0.21911774	21.92	0.533824	7.63	7
8	8	2.475963	12.299693	0.08130284	0.403883	4.967640	0.20130284	20.14	0.610423	7.63	8
9	9	2.773079	14.775656	0.06767889	0.360610	5.328250	0.18767889	18.77	0.689110	7.66	9
10	10	3.105848	17.548735	0.05698416	0.321973	5.650223	0.17698416	17.70	0.769842	7.70	10
11	11	3.478550	20.654583	0.04841540	0.287476	5.937699	0.16841540	16.85	0.852569	7.75	11
12	12	3.895976	24.133133	0.04143681	0.256675	6.194374	0.16143681	16.15	0.937242	7.81	12
13	13	4.363493	28.029109	0.03567720	0.229174	6.423548	0.15567720	15.57	1.023804	7.88	13
14	14	4.887112	32.392602	0.03087125	0.204620	6.628168	0.15087125	15.09	1.112197	7.94	14
15	15	5.473566	37.279715	0.02682424	0.182696	6.810864	0.14682424	14.69	1.202364	8.02	15
16	16	6.130394	42.753280	0.02339002	0.163122	6.973986	0.14339002	14.34	1.294240	8.09	16
17	17	6.866041	48.883674	0.02045673	0.145644	7.11963u	0.14045673	14.05	1.387764	8.16	17
18	18	7.689966	55.749715	0.01793731	0.130040	7.249670	0.13793731	13.80	1.482872	8.24	18
19	19	8.612762	63.439681	0.01576300	0.116107	7.365777	0.13576300	13.58	1.579497	8.31	19
20	20	9.646293	72.052442	0.01387878	0.103667	7.469444	0.13387878	13.39	1.677576	8.39	20
21	21	10.803848	81.698736	0.01224009	0.092560	7.562003	0.13224009	13.23	1.777042	8.46	21
22	22	12.100310	92.502584	0.01081051	0.082643	7.644646	0.13081051	13.09	1.877831	8.54	22
23	23	13.552347	104.602894	0.00955996	0.073788	7.718434	0.12955996	12.96	1.979879	8.61	23
24	24	15.178629	118.155241	0.00846344	0.065882	7.784316	0.12846344	12.85	2.083123	8.68	24
25	25	17.000064	133.333870	0.00749997	0.058823	7.843139	0.12749997	12.75	2.187499	8.75	25
26	26	19.040072	150.333934	0.00665186	0.052521	7.895660	0.12665186	12.67	2.292948	8.82	26
27	27	21.324881	169.374007	0.00590409	0.046894	7.942554	0.12590409	12.60	2.399411	8.89	27
28	28	23.883866	190.698887	0.00524387	0.041869	7.984423	0.12524387	12.53	2.506828	8.95	28
29	29	26.749930	214.582754	0.00466021	0.037383	8.021806	0.12466021	12.47	2.615146	9.02	29
30	30	29.959922	241.332684	0.00414366	0.033378	8.055184	0.12414366	12.42	2.724310	9.08	30
31	31	33.555113	271.292606	0.00368606	0.029802	8.084986	0.12368606	12.37	2.834268	9.14	31
32	32	37.581726	304.847719	0.00328033	0.026609	8.111594	0.12328033	12.33	2.944970	9.20	32
33	33	42.091533	342.429446	0.00292031	0.023758	8.135352	0.12292031	12.30	3.056370	9.26	33
34	34	47.142517	384.520979	0.00260064	0.021212	8.156564	0.12260064	12.27	3.168422	9.32	34
35	35	52.799620	431.663496	0.00231662	0.018940	8.175504	0.12231662	12.24	3.281082	9.37	35
36	36	59.135574	484.463116	0.00206414	0.016910	8.192414	0.12206414	12.21	3.394309	9.43	36
37	37	66.231843	543.598690	0.00183939	0.015098	8.207513	0.12183959	12.19	3.508065	9.48	37
38	38	74.179664	609.830533	0.00163980	0.013481	8.220993	0.12163980	12.17	3.622312	9.53	38
39	39	83.081224	684.010197	0.00146197	0.012036	8.233030	0.12146197	12.15	3.737017	9.58	39
40	40	93.050970	767.091420	0.00130363	0.010747	8.243777	0.12130363	12.14	3.852145	9.63	40
41	41	104.217087	860.142391	0.00116260	0.009595	8.253372	0.12116260	12.12	3.967667	9.68	41
42	42	116.723137	964.359478	0.00103696	0.008567	8.261939	0.12103696	12.11	4.083552	9.72	42
43	43	130.729914	1081.082615	0.00092500	0.007649	8.269589	0.12092500	12.10	4.199775	9.77	43
44	44	146.417503	1211.812529	0.00082521	0.006830	8.276418	0.12082521	12.09	4.316309	9.81	44
45	45	163.987604	1358.230032	0.00073625	0.006098	8.282516	0.12073625	12.08	4.433131	9.85	45
46	46	183.666116	1522.217636	0.00065694	0.005445	8.287961	0.12065694	12.07	4.550219	9.89	46
47	47	205.706050	1705.883752	0.00058621	0.004861	8.292822	0.12058621	12.06	4.667552	9.93	47
48	48	230.390776	1911.589803	0.00052312	0.004340	8.297163	0.12052312	12.06	4.785110	9.97	48
49	49	258.037669	2141.980579	0.00046686	0.003875	8.301038	0.12046686	12.05	4.902876	10.01	49
50	50	289.002190	2400.018249	0.00041666	0.003460	8.304498	0.12041666	12.05	5.020833	10.04	50

Compound Interest and Annuity Tables *(continued)*

		Amount Of 1	Amount Of 1 Per Period	Sinking Fund Payment	Present Worth Of 1	Present Worth Of 1 Per Period	Periodic Payment To Amortize 1	Constant Annual Percent	Total Interest	Annual Add-on Rate		
		What a single $1 deposit grows to in the future. The deposit is made at the beginning of the first period.	What a series of $1 deposits grow to in the future. A deposit is made at the end of each period.	The amount to be deposited at the end of each period that grows to $1 in the future.	What $1 to be paid in the future is worth today. Value today of a single payment tomorrow.	What $1 to be paid at the end of each period is worth today. Value today of a series of payments tomorrow.	The mortgage payment to amortize a loan of $1. An annuity certain, payable at the end of each period, worth $1 today.	The annual payment, including interest and principal, to amortize completely a loan of $100.	The total interest paid over the term on a loan of $1. The loan is amortized by regular periodic payments.	The average annual interest rate on a loan that is completely amortized by regular periodic payments.		
		$S=(1+i)^n$	$S\overline{n}=\dfrac{(1+i)^n-1}{i}$	$\dfrac{1}{S\overline{n}}=\dfrac{i}{(1+i)^n-1}$	$V^n=\dfrac{1}{(1+i)^n}$	$A\overline{n}=\dfrac{1-V^n}{i}$	$\dfrac{1}{A\overline{n}}=\dfrac{i}{1-V^n}$					
YR											YR	
1	1	1.130000	1.000000	1.00000000	0.884956	0.884956	1.13000000	113.00	0.130000	13.00	1	
2	2	1.276900	2.130000	0.46948357	0.783147	1.668102	0.59948357	59.95	0.198967	9.95	2	
3	3	1.442897	3.406900	0.29352197	0.693050	2.361153	0.42352197	42.36	0.270566	9.02	3	
4	4	1.630474	4.849797	0.20619420	0.613319	2.974471	0.33619420	33.62	0.344777	8.62	4	
5	5	1.842435	6.480271	0.15431454	0.542760	3.517231	0.28431454	28.44	0.421573	8.43	5	
6	6	2.081952	8.322706	0.12015323	0.480319	3.997550	0.25015323	25.02	0.500919	8.35	6	
7	7	2.352605	10.404658	0.09611080	0.425061	4.422610	0.22611080	22.62	0.582776	8.33	7	
8	8	2.658444	12.757263	0.07838672	0.376160	4.798770	0.20838672	20.84	0.667094	8.34	8	
9	9	3.004042	15.415707	0.06486890	0.332885	5.131655	0.19486890	19.49	0.753820	8.38	9	
10	10	3.394567	18.419749	0.05428956	0.294588	5.426243	0.18428956	18.43	0.842896	8.43	10	
11	11	3.835861	21.814317	0.04584145	0.260698	5.686941	0.17584145	17.59	0.934256	8.49	11	
12	12	4.334523	25.650178	0.03898608	0.230706	5.917647	0.16898608	16.90	1.027833	8.57	12	
13	13	4.898011	29.984701	0.03335034	0.204165	6.121812	0.16335034	16.34	1.123554	8.64	13	
14	14	5.534753	34.882712	0.02866750	0.180677	6.302488	0.15866750	15.87	1.221345	8.72	14	
15	15	6.254270	40.417464	0.02474178	0.159891	6.462379	0.15474178	15.48	1.321127	8.81	15	
16	16	7.067326	46.671735	0.02142624	0.141496	6.603875	0.15142624	15.15	1.422820	8.89	16	
17	17	7.986078	53.739060	0.01860844	0.125218	6.729093	0.14860844	14.87	1.526343	8.98	17	
18	18	9.024268	61.725138	0.01620085	0.110812	6.839905	0.14620085	14.63	1.631615	9.06	18	
19	19	10.197423	70.749406	0.01413439	0.098064	6.937969	0.14413439	14.42	1.738553	9.15	19	
20	20	11.523088	80.946829	0.01235379	0.086782	7.024752	0.14235379	14.24	1.847076	9.24	20	
21	21	13.021089	92.469917	0.01081433	0.076798	7.101550	0.14081433	14.09	1.957101	9.32	21	
22	22	14.713831	105.491006	0.00947948	0.067963	7.169513	0.13947948	13.95	2.068549	9.40	22	
23	23	16.626629	120.204837	0.00831913	0.060144	7.229658	0.13831913	13.84	2.181340	9.48	23	
24	24	18.788091	136.831465	0.00730826	0.053225	7.282883	0.13730826	13.74	2.295398	9.56	24	
25	25	21.230542	155.619556	0.00642593	0.047102	7.329985	0.13642593	13.65	2.410648	9.64	25	
26	26	23.990513	176.850098	0.00565451	0.041683	7.371668	0.13565451	13.57	2.527017	9.72	26	
27	27	27.109279	200.840611	0.00497907	0.036888	7.408556	0.13497907	13.50	2.644435	9.79	27	
28	28	30.633486	227.949890	0.00438693	0.032644	7.441200	0.13438693	13.44	2.762834	9.87	28	
29	29	34.615839	258.583376	0.00386742	0.028889	7.470088	0.13386742	13.39	2.882150	9.94	29	
30	30	39.115898	293.199215	0.00341065	0.025565	7.495653	0.13341065	13.35	3.002320	10.01	30	
31	31	44.200965	332.315113	0.00300919	0.022624	7.518277	0.13300919	13.31	3.123285	10.08	31	
32	32	49.947090	376.516078	0.00265553	0.020021	7.538299	0.13265553	13.27	3.244990	10.14	32	
33	33	56.440212	426.463168	0.00234487	0.017718	7.556016	0.13234487	13.24	3.367381	10.20	33	
34	34	63.777439	482.903380	0.00207081	0.015680	7.571696	0.13207081	13.21	3.490407	10.27	34	
35	35	72.068506	546.680819	0.00182922	0.013876	7.585572	0.13182922	13.19	3.614023	10.33	35	
36	36	81.437412	618.749325	0.00161616	0.012279	7.597851	0.13161616	13.17	3.738182	10.38	36	
37	37	92.024276	700.186738	0.00142819	0.010867	7.608718	0.13142819	13.15	3.862843	10.44	37	
38	38	103.987432	792.211014	0.00126229	0.009617	7.618334	0.13126229	13.13	3.987967	10.49	38	
39	39	117.505798	896.198445	0.00111582	0.008510	7.626844	0.13111582	13.12	4.113517	10.55	39	
40	40	132.781552	1013.704243	0.00098648	0.007531	7.634376	0.13098648	13.10	4.239459	10.60	40	
41	41	150.043153	1146.485795	0.00087223	0.006665	7.641040	0.13087223	13.09	4.365761	10.65	41	
42	42	169.548763	1296.528948	0.00077129	0.005898	7.646938	0.13077129	13.08	4.492394	10.70	42	
43	43	191.590103	1466.077712	0.00068209	0.005219	7.652158	0.13068209	13.07	4.619330	10.74	43	
44	44	216.496816	1657.667814	0.00060326	0.004619	7.656777	0.13060326	13.06	4.746543	10.79	44	
45	45	244.641402	1874.164630	0.00053357	0.004088	7.660864	0.13053357	13.06	4.874011	10.83	45	
46	46	276.444784	2118.806032	0.00047196	0.003617	7.664482	0.13047196	13.05	5.001710	10.87	46	
47	47	312.382606	2395.250816	0.00041749	0.003201	7.667683	0.13041749	13.05	5.129622	10.91	47	
48	48	352.992345	2707.633422	0.00036933	0.002833	7.670516	0.13036933	13.04	5.257728	10.95	48	
49	49	398.881350	3060.625767	0.00032673	0.002507	7.673023	0.13032673	13.03	5.386010	10.99	49	
50	50	450.735925	3459.507117	0.00028906	0.002219	7.675242	0.13028906	13.03	5.514453	11.03	50	

COMPOUND INTEREST AND ANNUITY TABLE

14.00 % ANNUAL

	Amount Of 1	Amount Of 1 Per Period	Sinking Fund Payment	Present Worth Of 1	Present Worth Of 1 Per Period	Periodic Payment To Amortize 1	Constant Annual Percent	Total Interest	Annual Add-on Rate
	What a single $1 deposit grows to in the future. The deposit is made at the beginning of the first period.	What a series of $1 deposits grow to in the future. A deposit is made at the end of each period.	The amount to be deposited at the end of each period that grows to $1 in the future.	What $1 to be paid in the future is worth today.	What $1 to be paid at the end of each period is worth today. Value today of a series of payments tomorrow.	The mortgage payment to amortize a loan of $1. An annuity certain, payable at the end of each period, worth $1 today.	The annual payment, including interest and principal, to amortize completely a loan of $100.	The total interest paid over the term on a loan of $1. The loan is completely amortized by regular periodic payments.	The average annual interest rate on a loan that is completely amortized by regular periodic payments.
	$S=(1+i)^n$	$S_{\overline{n}}=\dfrac{(1+i)^n-1}{i}$	$\dfrac{1}{S_{\overline{n}}}=\dfrac{i}{(1+i)^n-1}$	$V^n=\dfrac{1}{(1+i)^n}$	$A_{\overline{n}}=\dfrac{1-V^n}{i}$	$\dfrac{1}{A_{\overline{n}}}=\dfrac{i}{1-V^n}$			

YR										YR
1	1.140000	1.000000	1.00000000	0.877193	0.877193	1.14000000	114.00	0.140000	14.00	1
2	1.299600	2.140000	0.46728972	0.769468	1.646661	0.60728972	60.73	0.214579	10.73	2
3	1.481544	3.439600	0.29073148	0.674972	2.321632	0.43073148	43.08	0.292194	9.74	3
4	1.688960	4.921144	0.20320478	0.592080	2.913712	0.34320478	34.33	0.372819	9.32	4
5	1.925415	6.610104	0.15128355	0.519369	3.433081	0.29128355	29.13	0.456418	9.13	5
6	2.194973	8.535519	0.11715750	0.455587	3.888668	0.25715750	25.72	0.542945	9.05	6
7	2.502269	10.730491	0.09319238	0.399637	4.288305	0.23319238	23.32	0.632347	9.03	7
8	2.852586	13.232760	0.07557002	0.350559	4.638864	0.21557002	21.56	0.724560	9.06	8
9	3.251949	16.085347	0.06216838	0.307508	4.946372	0.20216838	20.22	0.819515	9.11	9
10	3.707221	19.337295	0.05171354	0.269744	5.216116	0.19171354	19.18	0.917135	9.17	10
11	4.226232	23.044516	0.04339427	0.236617	5.452733	0.18339427	18.34	1.017337	9.25	11
12	4.817905	27.270749	0.03666933	0.207559	5.660292	0.17666933	17.67	1.120032	9.33	12
13	5.492411	32.088654	0.03116366	0.182069	5.842362	0.17116366	17.12	1.225128	9.42	13
14	6.261349	37.581065	0.02660914	0.159710	6.002072	0.16660914	16.67	1.332528	9.52	14
15	7.137938	43.842414	0.02280896	0.140096	6.142168	0.16280896	16.29	1.442134	9.61	15
16	8.137249	50.980352	0.01961540	0.122892	6.265060	0.15961540	15.97	1.553846	9.71	16
17	9.276464	59.117601	0.01691544	0.107800	6.372859	0.15691544	15.70	1.667562	9.81	17
18	10.575169	68.394066	0.01462115	0.094561	6.467420	0.15462115	15.47	1.783181	9.91	18
19	12.055693	78.969235	0.01266316	0.082948	6.550369	0.15266316	15.27	1.900600	10.00	19
20	13.743490	91.024928	0.01098600	0.072762	6.623131	0.15098600	15.10	2.019720	10.10	20
21	15.667578	104.768418	0.00954486	0.063826	6.686957	0.14954486	14.96	2.140442	10.19	21
22	17.861039	120.435996	0.00830317	0.055988	6.742944	0.14830317	14.84	2.262670	10.28	22
23	20.361585	138.297035	0.00723081	0.049112	6.792056	0.14723081	14.73	2.386309	10.38	23
24	23.212207	158.658620	0.00630284	0.043081	6.835137	0.14630284	14.64	2.511268	10.46	24
25	26.461916	181.870827	0.00549841	0.037790	6.872927	0.14549841	14.55	2.637460	10.55	25
26	30.166584	208.332743	0.00480001	0.033149	6.906077	0.14480001	14.49	2.764800	10.63	26
27	34.389906	238.499327	0.00419288	0.029078	6.935155	0.14419288	14.42	2.893208	10.72	27
28	39.204493	272.889233	0.00366449	0.025507	6.960662	0.14366449	14.37	3.022606	10.80	28
29	44.693122	312.093725	0.00320417	0.022375	6.983037	0.14320417	14.33	3.152921	10.87	29
30	50.950159	356.786847	0.00280279	0.019627	7.002664	0.14280279	14.29	3.284084	10.95	30
31	58.083181	407.737006	0.00245256	0.017217	7.019881	0.14245256	14.25	3.416029	11.02	31
32	66.214826	465.820186	0.00214675	0.015102	7.034983	0.14214675	14.22	3.548696	11.09	32
33	75.484902	532.035012	0.00187958	0.013248	7.048231	0.14187958	14.19	3.682026	11.16	33
34	86.052788	607.519914	0.00164604	0.011621	7.059852	0.14164604	14.17	3.815965	11.22	34
35	98.100178	693.572702	0.00144181	0.010194	7.070045	0.14144181	14.15	3.950463	11.29	35
36	111.834203	791.672881	0.00126315	0.008942	7.078987	0.14126315	14.13	4.085473	11.35	36
37	127.490992	903.507084	0.00110680	0.007844	7.086831	0.14110680	14.12	4.220592	11.41	37
38	145.339731	1030.998076	0.00096993	0.006880	7.093711	0.14096993	14.10	4.356857	11.47	38
39	165.687293	1176.337806	0.00085010	0.006035	7.099747	0.14085010	14.09	4.493154	11.52	39
40	188.883514	1342.025099	0.00074514	0.005294	7.105041	0.14074514	14.08	4.629806	11.57	40
41	215.327206	1530.908613	0.00065321	0.004644	7.109685	0.14065321	14.07	4.766781	11.63	41
42	245.473015	1746.235819	0.00057266	0.004074	7.113759	0.14057266	14.06	4.904052	11.68	42
43	279.839237	1991.708833	0.00050208	0.003573	7.117332	0.14050208	14.06	5.041590	11.72	43
44	319.016730	2271.548070	0.00044023	0.003135	7.120467	0.14044023	14.05	5.179370	11.77	44
45	363.679072	2590.564800	0.00038602	0.002750	7.123217	0.14038602	14.04	5.317371	11.82	45
46	414.594142	2954.243872	0.00033850	0.002412	7.125629	0.14033850	14.04	5.455571	11.86	46
47	472.637322	3368.838014	0.00029684	0.002116	7.127744	0.14029684	14.03	5.593951	11.90	47
48	538.806547	3841.475336	0.00026032	0.001856	7.129600	0.14026032	14.03	5.732495	11.94	48
49	614.239464	4380.281883	0.00022830	0.001628	7.131228	0.14022830	14.03	5.871186	11.98	49
50	700.232988	4994.521346	0.00020022	0.001428	7.132656	0.14020022	14.03	6.010011	12.02	50

Compound Interest and Annuity Tables *(continued)*

COMPOUND INTEREST AND ANNUITY TABLE

15.00 %
ANNUAL

		Amount Of 1	Amount Of 1 Per Period	Sinking Fund Payment	Present Worth Of 1	Present Worth Of 1 Per Period	Periodic Payment To Amortize 1	Constant Annual Percent	Total Interest	Annual Add-on Rate		
		What a single $1 deposit grows to in the future. The deposit is made at the beginning of the first period.	What a series of $1 deposits grow to in the future. A deposit is made at the end of each period.	The amount to be deposited at the end of each period that grows to $1 in the future.	What $1 to be paid in the future is worth today. Value today of a single payment tomorrow.	What $1 to be paid at the end of each period is worth today. Value today of a series of payments tomorrow.	The mortgage payment to amortize a loan of $1. An annuity certain, payable at the end of each period, worth $1 today.	The annual payment, including interest and principal, to amortize completely a loan of $100.	The total interest paid over the term on a loan of $1. The loan is amortized by regular periodic payments.	The average annual interest rate on a loan that is completely amortized by regular periodic payments.		
		$S=(1+i)^n$	$S_{\overline{n}} = \dfrac{(1+i)^n-1}{i}$	$\dfrac{1}{S_{\overline{n}}} = \dfrac{i}{(1+i)^n-1}$	$V^n = \dfrac{1}{(1+i)^n}$	$A_{\overline{n}} = \dfrac{1-V^n}{i}$	$\dfrac{1}{A_{\overline{n}}} = \dfrac{i}{1-V^n}$					
YR												**YR**
1	1	1.150000	1.000000	1.00000000	0.869565	0.869565	1.15000000	115.00	0.150000	15.00	1
2	2	1.322500	2.150000	0.46511628	0.756144	1.625709	0.61511628	61.52	0.230233	11.51	2
3	3	1.520875	3.472500	0.28797696	0.657516	2.283225	0.43797696	43.80	0.313931	10.46	3
4	4	1.749006	4.993375	0.20026535	0.571753	2.854978	0.35026535	35.03	0.401061	10.03	4
5	5	2.011357	6.742381	0.14831555	0.497177	3.352155	0.29831555	29.84	0.491578	9.83	5
6	6	2.313061	8.753738	0.11423691	0.432328	3.784483	0.26423691	26.43	0.585421	9.76	6
7	7	2.660020	11.066799	0.09036036	0.375937	4.160420	0.24036036	24.04	0.682523	9.75	7
8	8	3.059023	13.726819	0.07285009	0.326902	4.487322	0.22285009	22.29	0.782801	9.79	8
9	9	3.517876	16.785842	0.05957402	0.284262	4.771584	0.20957402	20.96	0.886166	9.85	9
10	10	4.045558	20.303718	0.04925206	0.247185	5.018769	0.19925206	19.93	0.992521	9.93	10
11	11	4.652391	24.349276	0.04106898	0.214943	5.233712	0.19106898	19.11	1.101759	10.02	11
12	12	5.350250	29.001667	0.03448078	0.186907	5.420619	0.18448078	18.45	1.213769	10.11	12
13	13	6.152788	34.351917	0.02911046	0.162528	5.583147	0.17911046	17.92	1.328436	10.22	13
14	14	7.075706	40.504705	0.02468849	0.141329	5.724476	0.17468849	17.47	1.445639	10.33	14
15	15	8.137062	47.580411	0.02101705	0.122894	5.847370	0.17101705	17.11	1.565256	10.44	15
16	16	9.357621	55.717472	0.01794769	0.106865	5.954235	0.16794769	16.80	1.687163	10.54	16
17	17	10.761264	65.075093	0.01536686	0.092926	6.047161	0.16536686	16.54	1.811237	10.65	17
18	18	12.375454	75.836357	0.01318629	0.080805	6.127966	0.16318629	16.32	1.937353	10.76	18
19	19	14.231772	88.211811	0.01133635	0.070265	6.198231	0.16133635	16.14	2.065391	10.87	19
20	20	16.366537	102.443583	0.00976147	0.061100	6.259331	0.15976147	15.98	2.195229	10.98	20
21	21	18.821518	118.810120	0.00841475	0.053131	6.312462	0.15841679	15.85	2.326753	11.08	21
22	22	21.644746	137.631638	0.00726577	0.046201	6.358663	0.15726577	15.73	2.459847	11.18	22
23	23	24.891458	159.276384	0.00627839	0.040174	6.398837	0.15627839	15.63	2.594403	11.28	23
24	24	28.625176	184.167841	0.00542983	0.034934	6.433771	0.15542983	15.55	2.730316	11.38	24
25	25	32.918953	212.793017	0.00469940	0.030378	6.464149	0.15469940	15.47	2.867485	11.47	25
26	26	37.856796	245.711970	0.00406981	0.026415	6.490564	0.15406981	15.41	3.005815	11.56	26
27	27	43.535315	283.568766	0.00352648	0.022970	6.513534	0.15352648	15.36	3.145215	11.65	27
28	28	50.065612	327.104080	0.00305713	0.019974	6.533508	0.15305713	15.31	3.285600	11.73	28
29	29	57.575454	377.169693	0.00265133	0.017369	6.550877	0.15265133	15.27	3.426888	11.82	29
30	30	66.211772	434.745146	0.00230020	0.015103	6.565980	0.15230020	15.24	3.569006	11.90	30
31	31	76.143538	500.956918	0.00199618	0.013133	6.579113	0.15199618	15.20	3.711882	11.97	31
32	32	87.565068	577.100456	0.00173280	0.011420	6.590533	0.15173280	15.18	3.855450	12.05	32
33	33	100.699829	664.665524	0.00150452	0.009931	6.600463	0.15150452	15.16	3.999649	12.12	33
34	34	115.804803	765.365353	0.00130657	0.008635	6.609099	0.15130657	15.14	4.144423	12.19	34
35	35	133.175523	881.170156	0.00113485	0.007509	6.616607	0.15113485	15.12	4.289720	12.26	35
36	36	153.151852	1014.345680	0.00098586	0.006529	6.623137	0.15098586	15.10	4.435491	12.32	36
37	37	176.124630	1167.497532	0.00085653	0.005678	6.628815	0.15085653	15.09	4.581692	12.38	37
38	38	202.543324	1343.622161	0.00074426	0.004937	6.633752	0.15074426	15.08	4.728282	12.44	38
39	39	232.924823	1546.165485	0.00064676	0.004293	6.638045	0.15064676	15.07	4.875224	12.50	39
40	40	267.863546	1779.090308	0.00056209	0.003733	6.641778	0.15056209	15.06	5.022483	12.56	40
41	41	308.043078	2046.953854	0.00048853	0.003246	6.645025	0.15048853	15.05	5.170030	12.61	41
42	42	354.249540	2354.996933	0.00042463	0.002823	6.647848	0.15042463	15.05	5.317834	12.66	42
43	43	407.386971	2709.246473	0.00036911	0.002455	6.650302	0.15036911	15.04	5.465872	12.71	43
44	44	468.495017	3116.633443	0.00032086	0.002134	6.652437	0.15032086	15.04	5.614118	12.76	44
45	45	538.769269	3585.128460	0.00027893	0.001856	6.654293	0.15027893	15.03	5.762552	12.81	45
46	46	619.584659	4123.897729	0.00024249	0.001614	6.655907	0.15024249	15.03	5.911154	12.85	46
47	47	712.522358	4743.482388	0.00021082	0.001403	6.657310	0.15021082	15.03	6.059908	12.89	47
48	48	819.400712	5456.004744	0.00018328	0.001220	6.658531	0.15018328	15.02	6.208798	12.93	48
49	49	942.310819	6275.405458	0.00015935	0.001061	6.659592	0.15015935	15.02	6.357808	12.98	49
50	50	1083.657442	7217.716277	0.00013855	0.000923	6.660515	0.15013855	15.02	6.506927	13.01	50

Compound Interest and Annuity Tables *(continued)*

COMPOUND INTEREST AND ANNUITY TABLE

16.00 %
ANNUAL

YR	YR	Amount Of 1	Amount Of 1 Per Period	Sinking Fund Payment	Present Worth Of 1	Present Worth Of 1 Per Period	Periodic Payment To Amortize 1	Constant Annual Percent	Total Interest	Annual Add-on Rate	YR
		What a single $1 deposit grows to in the future. The deposit is made at the beginning of the first period.	What a series of $1 deposits grow to in the future. A deposit is made at the end of each period.	The amount to be deposited at the end of each period that grows to $1 in the future.	What $1 to be paid in the future is worth today.	What $1 to be paid at the end of each period is worth today.	The mortgage payment to amortize a loan of $1. An annuity certain, payable at the end of each period, worth $1 today.	The annual payment, including interest and principal, to amortize completely a loan of $100.	The total interest paid over the term of $1. The loan is amortized by regular periodic payments.	The average interest rate annual on a loan that is completely amortized by regular periodic payments.	
		$S=(1+i)^n$	$S_{\overline{n}}=\dfrac{(1+i)^n-1}{i}$	$\dfrac{1}{S_{\overline{n}}}=\dfrac{i}{(1+i)^n-1}$	$V^n=\dfrac{1}{(1+i)^n}$	$A_{\overline{n}}=\dfrac{1-V^n}{i}$	$\dfrac{1}{A_{\overline{n}}}=\dfrac{i}{1-V^n}$				
1	1	1.160000	1.000000	1.00000000	0.862069	0.862069	1.16000000	116.00	0.160000	16.00	1
2	2	1.345600	2.160000	0.46296296	0.743163	1.605232	0.62296296	62.30	0.245926	12.30	2
3	3	1.560896	3.505600	0.28525787	0.640658	2.245890	0.44525787	44.53	0.335774	11.19	3
4	4	1.810639	5.066496	0.19737507	0.552291	2.798181	0.35737507	35.74	0.429500	10.74	4
5	5	2.100342	6.877135	0.14540938	0.476113	3.274294	0.30540938	30.55	0.527047	10.54	5
6	6	2.436396	8.977477	0.11138987	0.410442	3.684736	0.27138987	27.14	0.628339	10.47	6
7	7	2.826220	11.413873	0.08761268	0.353830	4.038565	0.24761268	24.77	0.733289	10.48	7
8	8	3.278415	14.240093	0.07022426	0.305025	4.343591	0.23022426	23.03	0.841794	10.52	8
9	9	3.802961	17.518508	0.05708249	0.262953	4.606544	0.21708249	21.71	0.953742	10.60	9
10	10	4.411435	21.321469	0.04690108	0.226684	4.833227	0.20690108	20.70	1.069011	10.69	10
11	11	5.117265	25.732904	0.03886075	0.195417	5.028644	0.19886075	19.89	1.187468	10.80	11
12	12	5.936027	30.850169	0.03241473	0.168463	5.197107	0.19241473	19.25	1.308977	10.91	12
13	13	6.885791	36.786196	0.02718411	0.145227	5.342334	0.18718411	18.72	1.433393	11.03	13
14	14	7.987518	43.671987	0.02289797	0.125195	5.467529	0.18289797	18.29	1.560572	11.15	14
15	15	9.265521	51.659505	0.01935752	0.107927	5.575456	0.17935752	17.94	1.690363	11.27	15

17.00 %
ANNUAL

YR	YR	Amount Of 1	Amount Of 1 Per Period	Sinking Fund	Present Worth Of 1	Present Worth Per Period	Periodic Payment	Constant Annual Percent	Total Interest	Annual Add-on Rate	YR
1	1	1.170000	1.000000	1.00000000	0.854701	0.854701	1.17000000	117.00	0.170000	17.00	1
2	2	1.368900	2.170000	0.46082949	0.730514	1.585214	0.63082949	63.09	0.261659	13.08	2
3	3	1.601613	3.538900	0.28257368	0.624371	2.209585	0.45257368	45.26	0.357721	11.92	3
4	4	1.873887	5.140513	0.19453311	0.533650	2.743235	0.36453311	36.46	0.458132	11.45	4
5	5	2.192448	7.014400	0.14256386	0.456111	3.199346	0.31256386	31.26	0.562819	11.26	5
6	6	2.565164	9.206848	0.10861480	0.389839	3.589185	0.27861480	27.87	0.671689	11.19	6
7	7	3.001242	11.772012	0.08494724	0.333195	3.922380	0.25494724	25.50	0.784631	11.21	7
8	8	3.511453	14.773255	0.06768989	0.284782	4.207163	0.23768989	23.77	0.901519	11.27	8
9	9	4.108400	18.284708	0.05469051	0.243404	4.450566	0.22469051	22.47	1.022215	11.36	9
10	10	4.806828	22.393108	0.04465660	0.208037	4.658604	0.21465660	21.47	1.146566	11.47	10
11	11	5.623989	27.199937	0.03676479	0.177810	4.836413	0.20676479	20.68	1.274413	11.59	11
12	12	6.580067	32.823926	0.03046558	0.151974	4.988387	0.20046558	20.05	1.405587	11.71	12
13	13	7.698679	39.403993	0.02537814	0.129892	5.118280	0.19537814	19.54	1.539916	11.85	13
14	14	9.007454	47.102672	0.02123022	0.111019	5.229299	0.19123022	19.13	1.677223	11.98	14
15	15	10.538721	56.110126	0.01782209	0.094888	5.324187	0.18782209	18.79	1.817331	12.12	15

Compound Interest and Annuity Tables *(continued)*

18.00 % ANNUAL

		Amount Of 1	Amount Of 1 Per Period	Sinking Fund Payment	Present Worth Of 1	Present Worth Of 1 Per Period	Periodic Payment To Amortize 1	Constant Annual Percent	Total Interest	Annual Add-on Rate	
		What a single $1 deposit grows to in the future. The deposit is made at the beginning of the first period.	What a series of $1 deposits grow to in the future. A deposit is made at the end of each period.	The amount to be deposited at the end of each period that grows to $1 in the future.	What $1 to be paid in the future is worth today. Value today of a single payment tomorrow.	What $1 to be paid at the end of each period is worth today. Value today of a series of payments tomorrow.	The mortgage payment to amortize a loan of $1. An annuity certain, payable at the end of each period, worth $1 today.	The annual payment, including interest and principal, to amortize completely a loan of $100.	The total interest paid over the term of $1. The loan is amortized by regular periodic payments.	The average annual interest rate on a loan that is completely amortized by regular periodic payments.	
		$S = (1+i)^n$	$S_{\overline{n}} = \dfrac{(1+i)^n - 1}{i}$	$\dfrac{1}{S_{\overline{n}}} = \dfrac{i}{(1+i)^n - 1}$	$V^n = \dfrac{1}{(1+i)^n}$	$A_{\overline{n}} = \dfrac{1 - V^n}{i}$	$\dfrac{1}{A_{\overline{n}}} = \dfrac{i}{1 - V^n}$				
YR											**YR**
1	1	1.180000	1.000000	1.00000000	0.847458	0.847458	1.18000000	118.00	0.180000	18.00	1
2	2	1.392400	2.180000	0.45871560	0.718184	1.565642	0.63871560	63.88	0.277431	13.87	2
3	3	1.643032	3.572400	0.27992386	0.608631	2.174273	0.45992386	46.00	0.379772	12.66	3
4	4	1.938778	5.215432	0.19173867	0.515789	2.690062	0.37173867	37.18	0.486955	12.17	4
5	5	2.287758	7.154210	0.13977784	0.437109	3.127171	0.31977784	31.98	0.598889	11.98	5
6	6	2.699554	9.441968	0.10591013	0.370432	3.497603	0.28591013	28.60	0.715461	11.92	6
7	7	3.185474	12.141522	0.08236200	0.313925	3.811528	0.26236200	26.24	0.836534	11.95	7
8	8	3.758859	15.326996	0.06524436	0.266038	4.077566	0.24524436	24.53	0.961955	12.02	8
9	9	4.435454	19.085855	0.05239482	0.225456	4.303022	0.23239482	23.24	1.091553	12.13	9
10	10	5.233836	23.521309	0.04251464	0.191064	4.494086	0.22251464	22.26	1.225146	12.25	10
11	11	6.175926	28.755144	0.03477639	0.161919	4.656005	0.21477639	21.48	1.362540	12.39	11
12	12	7.287593	34.931070	0.02862781	0.137220	4.793225	0.20862781	20.87	1.503534	12.53	12
13	13	8.599359	42.218663	0.02368621	0.116288	4.909513	0.20368621	20.37	1.647921	12.68	13
14	14	10.147244	50.818022	0.01967806	0.098549	5.008062	0.19967806	19.97	1.795493	12.82	14
15	15	11.973748	60.965266	0.01640278	0.083516	5.091578	0.19640278	19.65	1.946042	12.97	15

19.00 % ANNUAL

YR											**YR**
1	1	1.190000	1.000000	1.00000000	0.840336	0.840336	1.19000000	119.00	0.190000	19.00	1
2	2	1.416100	2.190000	0.45662100	0.706165	1.546501	0.64662100	64.67	0.293242	14.66	2
3	3	1.685159	3.606100	0.27730789	0.593416	2.139917	0.46730789	46.74	0.401924	13.40	3
4	4	2.005339	5.291259	0.18899094	0.498669	2.638586	0.37899094	37.90	0.515964	12.90	4
5	5	2.386354	7.296598	0.13705017	0.419049	3.057635	0.32705017	32.71	0.635251	12.71	5
6	6	2.839761	9.682952	0.10327429	0.352142	3.409777	0.29327429	29.33	0.759646	12.66	6
7	7	3.379315	12.522713	0.07985490	0.295918	3.705695	0.26985490	26.99	0.888984	12.70	7
8	8	4.021385	15.902028	0.06288506	0.248671	3.954366	0.25288506	25.29	1.023080	12.79	8
9	9	4.785449	19.923413	0.05019220	0.208967	4.163332	0.24019220	24.02	1.161730	12.91	9
10	10	5.694684	24.708862	0.04047131	0.175602	4.338935	0.23047131	23.05	1.304713	13.05	10
11	11	6.776674	30.403546	0.03289090	0.147565	4.486500	0.22289090	22.29	1.451800	13.20	11
12	12	8.064242	37.180220	0.02689602	0.124004	4.610504	0.21689602	21.69	1.602752	13.36	12
13	13	9.596448	45.244461	0.02210215	0.104205	4.714709	0.21210215	21.22	1.757328	13.52	13
14	14	11.419773	54.840909	0.01823456	0.087567	4.802277	0.20823456	20.83	1.915284	13.68	14
15	15	13.589530	66.260682	0.01509191	0.073586	4.875863	0.20509191	20.51	2.076379	13.84	15

Compound Interest and Annuity Tables *(continued)*

COMPOUND INTEREST AND ANNUITY TABLE

20.00 %
ANNUAL

		Amount Of 1	Amount Of 1 Per Period	Sinking Fund Payment	Present Worth Of 1	Present Worth Of 1 Per Period	Periodic Payment To Amortize 1	Constant Annual Percent	Total Interest	Annual Add-on Rate		
		What a single $1 deposit grows to in the future. The deposit is made at the beginning of the first period.	What a series of $1 deposits grow to in the future. A deposit is made at the end of each period.	The amount to be deposited at the end of each period that grows to $1 in the future.	What $1 to be paid in the future is worth today. Value today of a single payment tomorrow.	What $1 to be paid at the end of each period is worth today. Value today of a series of payments tomorrow.	The mortgage payment to amortize a loan of $1. An annuity certain, payable at the end of each period, worth $1 today.	The annual payment, including interest and principal, to amortize completely a loan of $100.	The total interest paid over the term of $1. The loan is amortized by regular periodic payments.	The average annual interest rate on a loan that is completely amortized by regular periodic payments.		
		$S=(1+i)^n$	$S_{\overline{n}}=\dfrac{(1+i)^n-1}{i}$	$\dfrac{1}{S_{\overline{n}}}=\dfrac{i}{(1+i)^n-1}$	$V^n=\dfrac{1}{(1+i)^n}$	$A_{\overline{n}}=\dfrac{1-V^n}{i}$	$\dfrac{1}{A_{\overline{n}}}=\dfrac{i}{1-V^n}$					
YR												YR
1	1	1.200000	1.000000	1.00000000	0.833333	0.833333	1.20000000	120.00	0.200000	20.00	1
2	2	1.440000	2.200000	0.45454545	0.694444	1.527778	0.65454545	65.46	0.309091	15.45	2
3	3	1.728000	3.640000	0.27472527	0.578704	2.106481	0.47472527	47.48	0.424176	14.14	3
4	4	2.073600	5.368000	0.18628912	0.482253	2.588735	0.38628912	38.63	0.545156	13.63	4
5	5	2.488320	7.441600	0.13437970	0.401878	2.990612	0.33437970	33.44	0.671899	13.44	5
6	6	2.985984	9.929920	0.10070575	0.334898	3.325510	0.30070575	30.08	0.804234	13.40	6
7	7	3.583181	12.915904	0.07742393	0.279082	3.604592	0.27742393	27.75	0.941967	13.46	7
8	8	4.299817	16.499085	0.06060942	0.232568	3.837160	0.26060942	26.07	1.084875	13.56	8
9	9	5.159780	20.798902	0.04807946	0.193807	4.030967	0.24807946	24.81	1.232715	13.70	9
10	10	6.191736	25.958682	0.03852276	0.161506	4.192472	0.23852276	23.86	1.385228	13.85	10
11	11	7.430084	32.150419	0.03110379	0.134588	4.327060	0.23110379	23.12	1.542142	14.02	11
12	12	8.916100	39.580502	0.02526496	0.112157	4.439217	0.22526496	22.53	1.703180	14.19	12
13	13	10.699321	48.496603	0.02062000	0.093464	4.532681	0.22062000	22.07	1.868060	14.37	13
14	14	12.839185	59.195923	0.01689306	0.077887	4.610567	0.21689306	21.69	2.036503	14.55	14
15	15	15.407022	72.035108	0.01388212	0.064905	4.675473	0.21388212	21.39	2.208232	14.72	15

21.00 %
ANNUAL

YR											YR
1	1	1.210000	1.000000	1.00000000	0.826446	0.826446	1.21000000	121.00	0.210000	21.00	1
2	2	1.464100	2.210000	0.45248869	0.683013	1.509460	0.66248869	66.25	0.324977	16.25	2
3	3	1.771561	3.674100	0.27217550	0.564474	2.073934	0.48217550	48.22	0.446526	14.88	3
4	4	2.143589	5.445661	0.18363244	0.466507	2.540441	0.39363244	39.37	0.574530	14.36	4
5	5	2.593742	7.589250	0.13176533	0.385543	2.925984	0.34176533	34.18	0.708827	14.18	5
6	6	3.138428	10.182992	0.09820296	0.318631	3.244615	0.30820296	30.83	0.849218	14.15	6
7	7	3.797498	13.321421	0.07506707	0.263331	3.507946	0.28506707	28.51	0.995469	14.22	7
8	8	4.594973	17.118919	0.05841490	0.217629	3.725576	0.26841490	26.85	1.147319	14.34	8
9	9	5.559917	21.713892	0.04605347	0.179859	3.905434	0.25605347	25.61	1.304481	14.49	9
10	10	6.727500	27.273809	0.03666521	0.148644	4.054078	0.24666521	24.67	1.466652	14.67	10
11	11	8.140275	34.001309	0.02941063	0.122846	4.176924	0.23941063	23.95	1.633517	14.85	11
12	12	9.849733	42.141584	0.02372953	0.101526	4.278450	0.23372953	23.38	1.804754	15.04	12
13	13	11.918717	51.991317	0.01923398	0.083905	4.362355	0.22923398	22.93	1.980042	15.23	13
14	14	14.420994	63.909493	0.01564713	0.069343	4.431698	0.22564713	22.57	2.159060	15.42	14
15	15	17.449402	78.330487	0.01276642	0.057309	4.489007	0.22276642	22.28	2.341496	15.61	15

Compound Interest and Annuity Tables *(continued)*

COMPOUND INTEREST AND ANNUITY TABLE

Amount Of 1	Amount Of 1 Per Period	Sinking Fund Payment	Present Worth Of 1	Present Worth Of 1 Per Period	Periodic Payment To Amortize 1	Constant Annual Percent	Total Interest	Annual Add-on Rate
What a single $1 deposit grows to in the future. The deposit is made at the beginning of the first period.	What a series of $1 deposits grow to in the future. A deposit is made at the end of each period.	The amount to be deposited at the end of each period that grows to $1 in the future.	What $1 to be paid in the future is worth today. Value today of a single payment tomorrow.	What $1 to be paid at the end of each period is worth today. Value today of a series of payments tomorrow.	The mortgage payment including interest and principal, to amortize certain, payable at the end of each period, worth $1 today.	The annual payment, including interest and principal, of $1. The loan is amortized completely a loan of $100.	The total interest paid over the term on a loan of $1. The loan is amortized by regular periodic payments.	The average annual interest rate on a loan that is completely amortized by regular periodic payments.
$S = (1+i)^n$	$S_{\overline{n}\|} = \dfrac{(1+i)^n - 1}{i}$	$\dfrac{1}{S_{\overline{n}\|}} = \dfrac{i}{(1+i)^n - 1}$	$V^n = \dfrac{1}{(1+i)^n}$	$A_{\overline{n}\|} = \dfrac{1 - V^n}{i}$	$\dfrac{1}{A_{\overline{n}\|}} = \dfrac{i}{1 - V^n}$			

YR

YR											YR
1	1	1.220000	1.000000	1.00000000	0.819672	0.819672	1.22000000	122.00	0.220000	22.00	1
2	2	1.488400	2.220000	0.45045045	0.671862	1.491535	0.67045045	67.05	0.340901	17.05	2
3	3	1.815848	3.708400	0.26965807	0.550707	2.042241	0.48965807	48.97	0.468974	15.63	3
4	4	2.215335	5.524248	0.18102011	0.451399	2.493641	0.40102011	40.11	0.604080	15.10	4
5	5	2.702708	7.739583	0.12920593	0.369999	2.863640	0.34920593	34.93	0.746030	14.92	5
6	6	3.297304	10.442291	0.09576648	0.303278	3.166918	0.31576443	31.58	0.894587	14.91	6
7	7	4.022711	13.739595	0.07278235	0.248589	3.415506	0.29278235	29.28	1.049476	14.99	7
8	8	4.907707	17.762306	0.05629900	0.203761	3.619268	0.27629900	27.63	1.210392	15.13	8
9	9	5.987403	22.670013	0.04411114	0.167017	3.786285	0.26411114	26.42	1.377000	15.30	9
10	10	7.304631	28.657416	0.03489498	0.136899	3.923184	0.25489498	25.49	1.548950	15.49	10
11	11	8.911650	35.962047	0.02780709	0.112213	4.035397	0.24780709	24.79	1.725878	15.69	11
12	12	10.872213	44.873697	0.02228477	0.091978	4.127375	0.24228477	24.23	1.907417	15.90	12
13	13	13.264100	55.745911	0.01793854	0.075391	4.202766	0.23793854	23.80	2.093201	16.10	13
14	14	16.182202	69.010011	0.01449065	0.061796	4.264562	0.23449065	23.45	2.282869	16.31	14
15	15	19.742287	85.192213	0.01173816	0.050653	4.315215	0.23173816	23.18	2.476072	16.51	15

YR											YR
1	1	1.230000	1.000000	1.00000000	0.813008	0.813008	1.23000000	123.00	0.230000	23.00	1
2	2	1.512900	2.230000	0.44843049	0.660982	1.473990	0.67843049	67.85	0.356861	17.84	2
3	3	1.860867	3.742900	0.26711251	0.537384	2.011374	0.49711251	49.72	0.491518	16.38	3
4	4	2.288866	5.603767	0.17845139	0.436897	2.448272	0.40845139	40.85	0.633806	15.85	4
5	5	2.815306	7.892633	0.12670042	0.355201	2.803473	0.35670042	35.68	0.783502	15.67	5
6	6	3.462826	10.707939	0.09338865	0.288781	3.092254	0.32338865	32.34	0.940332	15.67	6
7	7	4.259276	14.170765	0.07056782	0.234782	3.327036	0.30056782	30.06	1.103975	15.77	7
8	8	5.238909	18.430041	0.05425924	0.190879	3.517916	0.28425924	28.43	1.274074	15.93	8
9	9	6.443859	23.668950	0.04224944	0.155187	3.673102	0.27224944	27.23	1.450245	16.11	9
10	10	7.925946	30.112809	0.03320846	0.126168	3.799270	0.26320846	26.33	1.632085	16.32	10
11	11	9.748914	38.038755	0.02628898	0.102576	3.901846	0.25628898	25.63	1.819179	16.54	11
12	12	11.991164	47.787669	0.02092590	0.083395	3.985240	0.25092590	25.10	2.011111	16.76	12
13	13	14.749132	59.778833	0.01672833	0.067801	4.053041	0.24672833	24.68	2.207468	16.98	13
14	14	18.141432	74.527964	0.01341778	0.055122	4.108163	0.24341778	24.35	2.407849	17.20	14
15	15	22.313961	92.669396	0.01079105	0.044815	4.152978	0.24079105	24.08	2.611866	17.41	15

Compound Interest and Annuity Tables *(continued)*

COMPOUND INTEREST AND ANNUITY TABLE

24.00 % ANNUAL

		Amount Of 1	Amount Of 1 Per Period	Sinking Fund Payment	Present Worth Of 1	Present Worth Of 1 Per Period	Periodic Payment To Amortize 1	Constant Annual Percent	Total Interest	Annual Add-on Rate		
		What a single $1 deposit grows to in the future. The deposit is made at the beginning of the first period.	What a series of $1 deposits grow to in the future. A deposit is made at the end of each period.	The amount to be deposited at the end of each period that grows to $1 in the future.	What $1 to be paid in the future is worth today. Value today of a single payment tomorrow.	What $1 to be paid in the future each period is worth today. Value today of a series of payments tomorrow.	The mortgage payment to amortize a loan of $1. An annuity certain, payable at the end of each period, worth $1 today.	The annual payment, including interest and principal, to amortize a loan of $100.	The total interest paid over the term on a loan of $1. The loan is amortized by regular periodic payments.	The average interest rate annual on a loan that is completely amortized by regular periodic payments.		
		$S=(1+i)^n$	$S_{\overline{n}}=\dfrac{(1+i)^n-1}{i}$	$\dfrac{1}{S_{\overline{n}}}=\dfrac{i}{(1+i)^n-1}$	$V^n=\dfrac{1}{(1+i)^n}$	$A_{\overline{n}}=\dfrac{1-V^n}{i}$	$\dfrac{1}{A_{\overline{n}}}=\dfrac{i}{1-V^n}$					
YR												YR
1	1	1.240000	1.000000	1.00000000	0.806452	0.806452	1.24000000	124.00	0.240000	24.00	1
2	2	1.537600	2.240000	0.44642857	0.650364	1.456816	0.68642857	68.65	0.372857	18.64	2
3	3	1.906624	3.777600	0.26471834	0.524487	1.981303	0.50471834	50.48	0.514155	17.14	3
4	4	2.364214	5.684224	0.17592551	0.422974	2.404277	0.41592551	41.60	0.663702	16.59	4
5	5	2.931625	8.048438	0.12424771	0.341108	2.745384	0.36424771	36.43	0.821239	16.42	5
6	6	3.635215	10.980063	0.09107416	0.275087	3.020471	0.33107416	33.11	0.986445	16.44	6
7	7	4.507667	14.615278	0.06842155	0.221844	3.242316	0.30842155	30.85	1.158951	16.56	7
8	8	5.589507	19.122945	0.05229320	0.178907	3.421222	0.29229320	29.23	1.338346	16.73	8
9	9	6.930988	24.712451	0.04046543	0.144280	3.565502	0.28046543	28.05	1.524189	16.94	9
10	10	8.594426	31.643440	0.03160213	0.116354	3.681856	0.27160213	27.17	1.716021	17.16	10
11	11	10.657088	40.237865	0.02485221	0.093834	3.775691	0.26485221	26.49	1.913374	17.39	11
12	12	13.214789	50.894953	0.01964831	0.075673	3.851363	0.25964831	25.97	2.115780	17.63	12
13	13	16.386338	64.109741	0.01559825	0.061026	3.912390	0.25559825	25.56	2.322777	17.87	13
14	14	20.319059	80.496079	0.01242297	0.049215	3.961605	0.25242297	25.25	2.533922	18.10	14
15	15	25.195633	100.815138	0.00991915	0.039689	4.001294	0.24991915	25.00	2.748787	18.33	15

25.00 % ANNUAL

YR											YR
1	1	1.250000	1.000000	1.00000000	0.800000	0.800000	1.25000000	125.00	0.250000	25.00	1
2	2	1.562500	2.250000	0.44444444	0.640000	1.440000	0.69444444	69.45	0.388889	19.44	2
3	3	1.953125	3.812500	0.26229508	0.512000	1.952000	0.51229508	51.23	0.536885	17.90	3
4	4	2.441406	5.765625	0.17344173	0.409600	2.361600	0.42344173	42.35	0.693767	17.34	4
5	5	3.051758	8.207031	0.12184674	0.327680	2.689280	0.37184674	37.19	0.859234	17.18	5
6	6	3.814697	11.258789	0.08881950	0.262144	2.951424	0.33881950	33.89	1.032917	17.22	6
7	7	4.768372	15.073486	0.06634165	0.209715	3.161139	0.31634165	31.64	1.214392	17.35	7
8	8	5.960464	19.841858	0.05039851	0.167772	3.328911	0.30039851	30.04	1.403188	17.54	8
9	9	7.450581	25.802322	0.03875620	0.134218	3.463129	0.28875620	28.88	1.598806	17.76	9
10	10	9.313226	33.252903	0.03007256	0.107374	3.570503	0.28007256	28.01	1.800726	18.01	10
11	11	11.641532	42.566129	0.02349286	0.085899	3.656403	0.27349286	27.35	2.008421	18.26	11
12	12	14.551745	54.207661	0.01844758	0.068719	3.725122	0.26844758	26.85	2.221371	18.51	12
13	13	18.189894	68.759576	0.01454343	0.054976	3.780098	0.26454343	26.46	2.439065	18.76	13
14	14	22.737368	86.949470	0.01150093	0.043980	3.824078	0.26150093	26.16	2.661013	19.01	14
15	15	28.421709	109.686838	0.00911686	0.035184	3.859263	0.25911686	25.92	2.886753	19.25	15

Compound Interest and Annuity Tables *(continued)*

COMPOUND INTEREST AND ANNUITY TABLE

	Amount Of 1	Amount Of 1 Per Period	Sinking Fund Payment	Present Worth Of 1	Present Worth Of 1 Per Period	Periodic Payment To Amortize 1	Constant Annual Percent	Total Interest	Annual Add-on Rate
	What a single $1 deposit grows to in the future. The deposit is made at the beginning of the first period.	What a series of $1 deposits grow to in the future. A deposit is made at the end of each period.	The amount to be deposited at the end of each period that grows to $1 in the future.	What $1 to be paid in the future is worth today. Value today of a single payment tomorrow.	What $1 to be paid at the end of each period is worth today. Value today of a series of payments tomorrow.	The mortgage payment to amortize a loan of $1. An annuity certain, payable at the end of each period, worth $1 today.	The annual payment, including interest and principal, to amortize completely a loan of $100.	The total interest paid over the term on a loan of $1. The loan is amortized by regular periodic payments.	The average annual interest rate on a loan that is completely amortized by regular periodic payments.
	$S=(1+i)^n$	$S_{\overline{n}|}=\frac{(1+i)^n-1}{i}$	$\frac{1}{S_{\overline{n}|}}=\frac{i}{(1+i)^n-1}$	$V^n=\frac{1}{(1+i)^n}$		$A_{\overline{n}|}=\frac{1-V^n}{i}$	$\frac{1}{A_{\overline{n}|}}=\frac{i}{1-V^n}$		

YR											YR
1	1	1.300000	1.000000	1.00000000	0.769231	0.769231	1.30000000	130.00	0.300000	30.00	1
2	2	1.690000	2.300000	0.43478261	0.591716	1.360947	0.73478261	73.48	0.469565	23.48	2
3	3	2.197000	3.990000	0.25062657	0.455166	1.816113	0.55062657	55.07	0.651880	21.73	3
4	4	2.856100	6.187000	0.16162922	0.350128	2.166241	0.46162922	46.17	0.846517	21.16	4
5	5	3.712930	9.043100	0.11058155	0.269329	2.435570	0.41058155	41.06	1.052908	21.06	5
6	6	4.826809	12.756030	0.07839430	0.207176	2.642746	0.37839430	37.84	1.270366	21.17	6
7	7	6.274852	17.582839	0.05687364	0.159366	2.802112	0.35687364	35.69	1.498115	21.40	7
8	8	8.157307	23.857691	0.04191521	0.122589	2.924702	0.34191521	34.20	1.735322	21.69	8
9	9	10.604499	32.014998	0.03123536	0.094300	3.019001	0.33123536	33.13	1.981118	22.01	9
10	10	13.785849	42.619497	0.02346344	0.072538	3.091539	0.32346344	32.35	2.234634	22.35	10
11	11	17.921604	56.405346	0.01772882	0.055799	3.147338	0.31772882	31.78	2.495017	22.68	11
12	12	23.298085	74.326950	0.01345407	0.042922	3.190260	0.31345407	31.35	2.761449	23.01	12
13	13	30.287511	97.625036	0.01024327	0.033017	3.223277	0.31024327	31.03	3.033163	23.33	13
14	14	39.373764	127.912546	0.00781784	0.025398	3.248675	0.30781784	30.79	3.309450	23.64	14
15	15	51.185893	167.286310	0.00597778	0.019537	3.268211	0.30597778	30.60	3.589667	23.93	15

YR											YR
1	1	1.350000	1.000000	1.00000000	0.740741	0.740741	1.35000000	135.00	0.350000	35.00	1
2	2	1.822500	2.350000	0.42553191	0.548697	1.289438	0.77553191	77.56	0.551064	27.55	2
3	3	2.460375	4.172500	0.23966447	0.406442	1.695880	0.58966447	58.97	0.768993	25.63	3
4	4	3.321506	6.632875	0.15076419	0.301068	1.996948	0.50076419	50.08	1.003057	25.08	4
5	5	4.484033	9.954381	0.10045828	0.223014	2.219961	0.45045828	45.05	1.252291	25.05	5
6	6	6.053445	14.438415	0.06925968	0.165195	2.385157	0.41925968	41.93	1.515558	25.26	6
7	7	8.172151	20.491860	0.04879987	0.122367	2.507523	0.39879987	39.88	1.791599	25.59	7
8	8	11.032404	28.664011	0.03488695	0.090642	2.598165	0.38488695	38.49	2.079096	25.99	8
9	9	14.893745	39.696415	0.02519119	0.067142	2.665308	0.37519119	37.52	2.376721	26.41	9
10	10	20.106556	54.590160	0.01831832	0.049735	2.715043	0.36831832	36.84	2.683183	26.83	10
11	11	27.143850	74.696715	0.01338747	0.036841	2.751884	0.36338747	36.34	2.997262	27.25	11
12	12	36.644198	101.840566	0.00981927	0.027289	2.779173	0.35981927	35.99	3.317831	27.65	12
13	13	49.469667	138.484764	0.00722101	0.020214	2.799387	0.35722101	35.73	3.643873	28.03	13
14	14	66.784051	187.954431	0.00532044	0.014974	2.814361	0.35532044	35.54	3.974486	28.39	14
15	15	90.158469	254.738482	0.00392559	0.011092	2.825453	0.35392559	35.40	4.308884	28.73	15

COMPOUND INTEREST AND ANNUITY TABLE

40.00 %
ANNUAL

	Amount Of 1	Amount Of 1 Per Period	Sinking Fund Payment	Present Worth Of 1	Present Worth Of 1 Per Period	Periodic Payment To Amortize 1	Constant Annual Percent	Total Interest	Annual Add-on Rate
	What a single $1 deposit grows to in the future. The deposit is made at the beginning of the first period.	What a series of $1 deposits grow to in the future. A deposit is made at the end of each period.	The amount to be deposited at the end of each period that grows to $1 in the future.	What $1 to be paid in the future is worth today. Value today of a single payment tomorrow.	What $1 to be paid at the end of each period is worth today. Value today of a series of payments tomorrow.	The mortgage payment to amortize a loan of $1. An annuity certain, payable at the end of each period, worth $1 today.	The annual payment, including interest and principal, to amortize completely a loan of $100.	The total interest paid over the term on a loan of $1. The loan is amortized by regular periodic payments.	The average annual interest rate on a loan that is completely amortized by regular periodic payments.
	$S=(1+i)^n$	$S_{\overline{n}}=\dfrac{(1+i)^n-1}{i}$	$\dfrac{1}{S_{\overline{n}}}=\dfrac{i}{(1+i)^n-1}$	$V^n=\dfrac{1}{(1+i)^n}$	$A_{\overline{n}}=\dfrac{1-V^n}{i}$	$\dfrac{1}{A_{\overline{n}}}=\dfrac{i}{1-V^n}$			

YR											YR
1	1	1.400000	1.000000	1.00000000	0.714286	0.714286	1.40000000	140.00	0.400000	40.00	1
2	2	1.960000	2.400000	0.41666667	0.510204	1.224490	0.81666667	81.67	0.633333	31.67	2
3	3	2.744000	4.360000	0.22935780	0.364431	1.588921	0.62935780	62.94	0.888073	29.60	3
4	4	3.841600	7.104000	0.14076577	0.260308	1.849229	0.54076577	54.08	1.163063	29.08	4
5	5	5.378240	10.945600	0.09136091	0.185934	2.035164	0.49136091	49.14	1.456805	29.14	5
6	6	7.529536	16.323840	0.06126010	0.132810	2.167974	0.46126010	46.13	1.767561	29.46	6
7	7	10.541350	23.853376	0.04192279	0.094865	2.262839	0.44192279	44.20	2.093460	29.91	7
8	8	14.757891	34.394726	0.02907422	0.067760	2.330599	0.42907422	42.91	2.432594	30.41	8
9	9	20.661047	49.152617	0.02034480	0.048400	2.378999	0.42034480	42.04	2.783103	30.92	9
10	10	28.925465	69.813664	0.01432384	0.034572	2.413571	0.41432384	41.44	3.143238	31.43	10
11	11	40.495652	98.739129	0.01012770	0.024694	2.438265	0.41012770	41.02	3.511405	31.92	11
12	12	56.693912	139.234781	0.00718211	0.017639	2.455904	0.40718211	40.72	3.886185	32.38	12
13	13	79.371477	195.928693	0.00510390	0.012599	2.468503	0.40510390	40.52	4.266351	32.82	13
14	14	111.120068	275.300171	0.00363240	0.008999	2.477502	0.40363240	40.37	4.650854	33.22	14
15	15	155.568096	386.420239	0.00258786	0.006428	2.483930	0.40258786	40.26	5.038818	33.59	15

APPENDIX D
TABLE OF THE NORMAL DISTRIBUTION

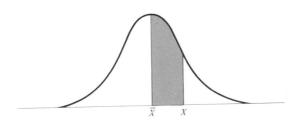

The table of areas of the normal curve between $\overline{X}$ and X for Z values is computed as follows:

$$Z = \frac{X - \overline{X}}{\sigma}$$

z	.00	.01	.02	.03	.04	.05	.06	.07	.08	.09
0.0	.0000	.0041	.0080	.0120	.0160	.0199	.0239	.0279	.0319	.0359
0.1	.0398	.0438	.0478	.0517	.0557	.0596	.0636	.0675	.0714	.0753
0.2	.0793	.0832	.0871	.0910	.0948	.0987	.1026	.1064	.1103	.1141
0.3	.1179	.1217	.1255	.1293	.1331	.1368	.1406	.1443	.1480	.1517
0.4	.1554	.1591	.1628	.1664	.1700	.1736	.1772	.1808	.1844	.1879
0.5	.1915	.1950	.1985	.2019	.2054	.2088	.2123	.2157	.2190	.2224
0.6	.2257	.2291	.2324	.2357	.2389	.2422	.2454	.2486	.2517	.2549
0.7	.2580	.2611	.2642	.2673	.2704	.2734	.2764	.2794	.2823	.2852
0.8	.2881	.2910	.2939	.2967	.2995	.3023	.3051	.3078	.3106	.3133
0.9	.3159	.3186	.3212	.3238	.3264	.3289	.3315	.3340	.3365	.3389
1.0	.3413	.3438	.3461	.3485	.3508	.3531	.3554	.3577	.3599	.3621
1.1	.3643	.3665	.3686	.3708	.3729	.3749	.3770	.3790	.3810	.3830
1.2	.3849	.3869	.3888	.3907	.3925	.3944	.3962	.3980	.3997	.4015
1.3	.4032	.4049	.4066	.4082	.4099	.4115	.4131	.4147	.4162	.4177
1.4	.4192	.4207	.4222	.4236	.4251	.4265	.4279	.4292	.4306	.4319
1.5	.4332	.4345	.4357	.4370	.4382	.4394	.4406	.4418	.4429	.4441
1.6	.4452	.4463	.4474	.4484	.4495	.4505	.4515	.4525	.4535	.4545
1.7	.4554	.4564	.4573	.4582	.4591	.4599	.4608	.4616	.4625	.4633
1.8	.4641	.4649	.4656	.4664	.4671	.4678	.4686	.4693	.4699	.4706
1.9	.4713	.4719	.4726	.4732	.4738	.4744	.4750	.4756	.4761	.4767
2.0	.4772	.4778	.4783	.4788	.4793	.4798	.4803	.4808	.4812	.4817
2.1	.4821	.4826	.4830	.4834	.4838	.4842	.4846	.4850	.4854	.4857
2.2	.4861	.4864	.4868	.4871	.4875	.4878	.4881	.4884	.4887	.4890
2.3	.4893	.4896	.4898	.4901	.4904	.4906	.4909	.4911	.4913	.4916
2.4	.4918	.4920	.4922	.4925	.4927	.4929	.4931	.4932	.4934	.4936
2.5	.4938	.4940	.4941	.4943	.4945	.4946	.4948	.4949	.4951	.4952
2.6	.4953	.4955	.4956	.4957	.4959	.4960	.4961	.4962	.4963	.4964
2.7	.4965	.4966	.4967	.4968	.4969	.4970	.4971	.4972	.4973	.4974
2.8	.4974	.4975	.4976	.4977	.4977	.4978	.4979	.4979	.4980	.4981
2.9	.4981	.4982	.4982	.4983	.4984	.4984	.4985	.4985	.4986	.4986
3.0	.4987	.4987	.4987	.4988	.4988	.4989	.4989	.4989	.4990	.4990

APPENDIX E

ANSWERS TO SELECTED PROBLEMS

Chapter 2

1. $400,000 \times 0.271 = \$108,400$

3. Recapture $= \$18,667 \times 0.48 = \$8,960$

$$\text{Net tax} = \$6,294 \begin{cases} \$8,960 & \text{Tax} \\ \$3,000 & \text{Tax on long-term capital gain} \\ \$\ 834 & \text{Recapture of ITC} \\ \$6,500 & \text{Less ITC on new} \end{cases}$$

5. ITC $= (\$700,000 - \$100,000) \times 2/3 \times 0.10 = \$40,000$; therefore, no tax liability and \$29,500 of ITC for carry-back and carry-forward.

7. (a) Tax $= \$17,700$; (b) 1231 loss $= \$15,000$;
   (c) recapture of ITC $= \$1,667$, ITC on new $= \$7,500$, taxable income $= \$47,500$; therefore, tax at 20% $= \$9,950$

$$\begin{array}{rl} = \$9,950 & \text{Tax} \\ + 1,667 & \text{Recapture ITC} \\ - 7,500 & \text{ITC on new} \\ \hline \$4,117 & \text{tax liability} \end{array}$$

9. (a) Cumulative depreciation $= \$976,950$, book value $= \$523,050$, no capital gain; (b) recapture of depreciation $= \$226,950$; (c) tax $= \$108,936$

11. Tax refunds: $4,000 $6,100 $1,000
                     1973   1974   1975

Chapter 3

1. (a) \$18,000;[1] (b) Old cash flow $= \$6,160$, new cash flow $= \$9,200$
   (c)

Year	Old	New	Difference
0	—	$-\$18,000$	$-\$18,000$
1–10	\$6,160	9,200	$+3,040$

1. Based on keeping old truck less than 5 years.

3. (c)

Year	Old	New	Difference
0	—	−$18,000	−$18,000
1–5	+$6,640	+ 9,200	+ 2,560
6–10	+ 4,680	+ 9,200	+ 4,520

5. (c)

Year	Old	New	Difference
0	—	−$22,000	−$22,000
1–5	+$6,640	+ 9,200	+ 2,560
5	− 10,000		+ 10,000
6–10	+ 6,160	+ 9,200	+ 3,040

7. Total cost = $3,775,000 + working cap. = $50,000 + Tax on sale of old = $153,600 − Sale of old = $720,000 − ITC on new = 377,500 ⇒ Net cash outflow = $2,881,100

9. Cash flows in thousands: year 1 = $84.55, year 2 = $75.10, year 3 = $72.40, year 4 = $76.10, year 5 = $83.97

Chapter 4

1. $109,658.91 × 0.10296276 = $11,290.78

3. $1,490.39

4. $4,952.70

5. $14,200

7. $53.10

9. $206,723/year for last 5 years

13. $742,857

Chapter 5

1. 4.54 years

3. Project A = 3 years, B = 4 years, C = $3\frac{3}{4}$ years

5. 12 years approx.

7. Project A = 6.7 years, B = 6.2 years; therefore select Project B.

Chapter 6

1. NPV_A = $1,009.16, NPV_B = $2,326.29, PI_A = 1.05, PI_B = 1.08

3. NPV = − $6,142, IRR = 6.28%

5. IRR = 18.125%

7. EAC_{new} = $4,703,487, EAC_{old} = $5.447,401

Chapter 7

5. (a) $NPV_A = \$4,005$, $NPV_B = \$3,343$, $IRR_A = 19\%$, $IRR_B = 22\%$
  (b) Obviously, Project A is preferred.
7. (a) $NPV_A = \$4,841$, $NPV_B = \$4,950$, $IRR_A = 27\%$, $IRR_B = 18.5\%$;
  (b) $NPV_A^* = \$8,645$, $NPV_B^* = \$6,723$, $IRR_A^* = 19\%$, $IRR_B^* = 17\%$. EKG is clearly
  superior at a 15% reinvestment rate.
9. $NPV_O = \$9,791$, $NPV_P = \$54,074$, $NPV_Q = \$121,742$
13. Machine $A = \$1,374.89$, machine $B = \$1,187.06$

Chapter 8

1. (a) $\bar{R}_A = 4,000$; $\bar{R}_B = 4,000$; (b) $MAD_A = 400$, $MAD_B = 800$; (d) $\sigma_A = 548$; $\sigma_B = 1095$
3. $\alpha = 0.939$
5. $\overline{CE} = \$6,352$
7. $\overline{RAR}_A = \$265$, $\overline{RAR}_B = -\$6,275$
9. $\overline{RAR} = -\$5,127$, $\overline{CE} = \$263$
11. (a) $\overline{CE}_A = 8.6$; $\overline{CE}_B = 8.48$;
  (b) independent $\sigma_A = 7.54$, $\sigma_B = 7.98$

Chapter 9

1. $\sigma_A = \$16,426.46$, $\sigma_B = \$66,394.65$, $Cov_{AB} = \$89,735,217.46$
2. $\sigma_{12}^2 = 0.19$, $\sigma_{13}^2 = 2.82$, $\sigma_{14}^2 = 0.94$, $\sigma_{23}^2 = 1.324$, $\sigma_{24}^2 = 3.4406$, $\sigma_{34}^2 = 0.94$
3. $\bar{R}_X = 200$, $\bar{R}_Y = 175$, $\sigma_X^2 = 2,000$, $\sigma_Y^2 = 6,875$, $\sigma_P^2 = 2,218.75$
7. Portfolio 2 is optimal: $L = 0.1413$

Chapter 10

1. $\alpha = 0.047$, $\beta = 0.5$
3. (a) 0.0001; (b) 0.00017; (c) 0.000025; (d) 0.0001933
5. $\pm 2.37\%$
6. (a) $E(R_P) = 0.10088$; (b) 0.884; (c) 0.0111
9. $B_1 = 0.24$; $B_2 = 1.62$; $B_3 = 0.56$

Chapter 11

1. After tax 4.186%
3. $K_i = 0.0485$, $_nK_p = 0.0513$, $_nk_e = 0.1096$, marginal C of C = 8.02%
5. $E(R_1) = 0.115$, $B_1 = 3.154$, $E(R_2) = 0.037$, $B_2 = 1.426$, $E(R_3) = 0.07$, $B_3 = 0.4776$
  0.4776

Chapter 12

1. 133.3 units product X; 500 units product Y;
$3,649.99 profit

4.

Value	X	Y
Δ^+	$1.875	∞
Δ^-	$3.00	$2.50

7. (a) 250 acres corn; 625 acres wheat; no soybeans
(b) $32,500

8.

	S_1	S_2	S_3
Δ^+	$6,667	$ 333.33	∞
Δ^-	4,000	1,000.00	125

11. $X_1 = 500$; $X_2 = 450$; $S_3 = 50$; profit $= \$33,000$

Chapter 13

4. (b)

	Manpower	Management	Machine Hours	Budget Yr 1	Budget Yr 2	Budget Yr 3
Δ^+	∞	1.38	∞	1.25	∞	∞
Δ^-	11.76	0.71	24.65	3.0	5.0	7.35

6. (c)

	Budget Constraint Yr 1	Yr 2	Yr 3
Δ^+	90	∞	17.51
Δ^-	60	10	140.35

Chapter 14
3. See Figures 14-1 and 14-2 as well as Example 3 in Chapter 14.

5. (a) $\bar{A}_w = \$3,500$; $\bar{A}_x = \$4,390$; $\bar{A}_y = \$4,900$; $\bar{A}_z = \$4,750$

7. (a) $\overline{\text{NPV}} = \$21,970$; $\sigma_{\text{NPV}} = \$69,000,000$

Chapter 16
1. First equipment $-$ payments at beginning $= \$18,552.33$
First equipment $-$ payments at end $= \$20,036.52$

3. Payment in arrears − advantage to ownership = $39,048
Payment in advance − advantage to ownership = $107,108.
5. Advantage to lease = $5,744

Chapter 17

5. Gross investment outlay = $300,000; annual savings on refund = $102,500; NPV = $329,821.50

Chapter 18

4. Optimal time to abandon is at the end of year 3 with an NPV of $631.
6. (e) Standard deviation = $4,173; skewness = 1.005; coefficient of variation = 3.07; $\overline{NPV}$ = $1,358

AUTHOR INDEX[1]

---

[1]This index includes authors who have been referred to directly in the text. The page(s) noted correspond to chapter footnotes or source lines. A complete bibliography by chapters is included as Appendix A.

SUBJECT INDEX